JANE SUMMERS
MICHAEL GARDINER
CHARLES W. LAMB
JOSEPH F. HAIR
CARL McDANIEL

ESSENTIALS OF MARKETING

2ND EDITION

THOMSON

Australia · Canada · Mexico · Singapore · Spain · United Kingdom · United States

Level 7, 80 Dorcas Street
South Melbourne, Victoria
Australia 3205

Email: highereducation@thomsonlearning.com.au
Website: www.thomsonlearning.com.au

First published in 2001 by South-Western College Publishing as *Essentials of Marketing*, by Charles W. Lamb, Joseph F. Hair and Carl McDaniel. Authorised adaptation of the original by South-Western College Publishing, Cincinnati, Ohio.

First edition published in 2003
This edition published 2005
10 9 8 7 6 5 4 3 2 1
10 09 08 07 06 05

Copyright © 2005 Nelson Australia Pty Limited.

COPYRIGHT

Reproduction and Communication for educational purposes
The Australian *Copyright Act 1968* (the Act) allows a maximum of one chapter or 10% of the pages of this work, whichever is the greater, to be reproduced and/or communicated by any educational institution for its educational purposes provided that the educational institution (or the body that administers it) has given a remuneration notice to Copyright Agency Limited (CAL) under the Act.

For details of the CAL licence for educational institutions contact:

Copyright Agency Limited
Level 19, 157 Liverpool Street
Sydney NSW 2000
Telephone: (02) 9394 7600
Facsimile: (02) 9394 7601
E-mail: info@copyright.com.au

Reproduction and Communication for other purposes
Except as permitted under the Act (for example a fair dealing for the purposes of study, research, criticism or review) no part of this book may be reproduced, stored in a retrieval system, communicated or transmitted in any form or by any means without prior written permission. All enquiries should be made to the publisher at the address above.

Copyright owners may take legal action against a person who infringes on their copyright through unauthorised copying. Enquiries should be directed to the publisher.

National Library of Australia
Cataloguing-in-Publication data

Essentials of marketing.

   2nd ed.
   Includes index.
   ISBN 0 17 012267 0.

   1. Marketing - Textbooks. I. Summers, Jane, 1962- .

   658.8

Editor: Roz Edmond
Project editor: Kate McGregor
Publishing manager: Michael Tully
Indexer: Russell Brooks
Text designer: Jo Groud
Cover designer: Olga Lavecchia
Cover photography: Wendy Lees
Photo researcher: Cardinal Syntax/Diane Cardinal
Typeset in Res Publica Regular, 10.5/13 points by Jo Groud
Production controller: Jodie Van Teylingen
Printed in China by China Translation & Printing Services Ltd

This title is published under the imprint of Thomson.
Nelson Australia Pty Limited ACN 058 280 149 (incorporated in Victoria) trading as Thomson Learning Australia.

The URLs contained in this publication were checked for currency during the production process. Note, however, that the publisher cannot vouch for the ongoing currency of URLs.

Brief Contents

Part one: The marketing experience — 1
- 1: An overview of marketing — 4
- 2: Consumer decision-making — 24
- 3: Business decision-making — 66

Part two: Customer information — 103
- 4: Segmenting and targeting markets — 108
- 5: Decision support systems and marketing research — 142

Part three: Managing the marketing elements: Product and distribution decisions — 181
- 6: Product and service concepts — 184
- 7: Developing and managing products — 218
- 8: Marketing channels and logistics decisions — 246

Part four: Managing the marketing elements: Integrated marketing communication and pricing decisions — 303
- 9: Integrated marketing communication (IMC) — 306
- 10: Promotions mix — 344
- 11: Pricing concepts — 388

Part five: The world of marketing — 433
- 12: Global marketing — 438
- 13: Marketing strategy — 470

Contents

Preface	xii
Resources guide	xiii
Acknowledgements	xvii
About the authors	xviii

Part one: The marketing experience — 1

1: An overview of marketing — 4

What is marketing?	6	Marketing offers outstanding career opportunities	15
Marketing exchange	7	Marketing is important to you	15
Marketing orientations	8	Looking ahead	15
Sales and marketing orientations	9	The marketing process	16
Customer value	9	Connect it	18
Customer satisfaction	11	Summary	18
Building relationships	11	Define it	19
Why study marketing?	13	Review it	19
Marketing plays an important role in society	14	Discuss it	20
Marketing is important to businesses	14	Watch it	21
		Click it	22
		Answer key	23

2: Consumer decision-making — 24

The importance of understanding consumer behaviour	26	External influences on consumer buying decisions	38
The consumer decision-making process	27	Social influences on consumer buying decisions	45
Need recognition	28	Internal influences on consumer buying decisions	48
Information search	30	Psychological influences on consumer buying decisions	52
Evaluation of alternatives and purchase	32	Connect it	57
Post-purchase behaviour	33	Summary	57
Types of consumer buying decisions and involvement	34	Define it	59
Factors determining the level of consumer involvement	36	Review it	59
		Apply it	60
Marketing implications of involvement	37	Try it	61
Factors influencing consumer buying decisions	38	Watch it	62
		Click it	63
		Answer key	64

3: Business decision-making — 66

What is business-to-business marketing?	68	Location of buyers	71
Business versus consumer markets	69	Distribution structure	71
Demand	69	Nature of buying	72
Purchase volume	71	Nature of buying influence	72
Number of customers	71	Type of negotiations	72
		Use of reciprocity	73

Use of leasing	73	**Types of business products**	**82**
Primary promotional method	73	Major equipment	82
Business buying behaviour	**73**	Accessory equipment	83
Buying centres	73	Raw materials	83
Implications of buying centres for the marketing manager	74	Component parts	84
		Processed materials	84
Evaluative criteria	75	Supplies	84
Buying situations	76	Business services	85
Purchasing ethics	77	**Connect it**	**85**
Customer service	77	**Summary**	**85**
Relationship marketing and strategic alliances	**78**	**Define it**	**86**
		Review it	**86**
Major categories of business customers	**81**	**Apply it**	**87**
		Try it	**88**
Producers	81	**Watch it**	**89**
Resellers	81	**Click it**	**90**
Governments	81	**Answer key**	**91**
Institutions	82		

Part two: Customer information — 103

4: Segmenting and targeting markets — 108

Market segmentation	**110**	Designing, implementing and maintaining appropriate marketing mixes	129
The importance of market segmentation	**112**		
Steps in segmenting a market	**113**	**Global issues in market segmentation and marketing**	**133**
Selecting a market or product category for study	113	**Connect it**	**133**
		Summary	**134**
Choosing a basis or bases for segmenting consumer markets	113	**Define it**	**135**
		Review it	**135**
Choosing a basis or bases for segmenting business markets	121	**Apply it**	**137**
		Try it	**137**
Selecting segmentation descriptors	122	**Watch it**	**138**
		Click it	**139**
Profiling and analysing segments	124	**Answer key**	**139**
Selecting target markets	125		

5: Decision support systems and marketing research — 142

Marketing decision support systems	**144**	When should marketing research be conducted?	167
The role of marketing research	**145**		
Management uses of marketing research	146	**Connect it**	**167**
		Summary	**167**
Steps in a marketing research project	**148**	**Define it**	**168**
		Review it	**168**
Problem definition	148	**Apply it**	**170**
Research design	150	**Try it**	**171**
Sampling	162	**Watch it**	**172**
Data collection and analysis	163	**Click it**	**174**
Recommendations	164	**Answer key**	**174**
Scanner-based research	**165**		

Part three: Managing the marketing elements: Product and distribution decisions — 181

6: Product and service concepts — 184

What is a product? 186	The importance of services 204
Types of products 187	**How services differ from goods** 205
Convenience products 188	Intangibility 205
Shopping products 189	Inseparability 205
Speciality products 190	Heterogeneity 206
Unsought products 190	Perishability 206
Product items, lines and mixes 191	**Services marketing in manufacturing** 206
Adjustments to product items, lines and mixes 193	**Packaging** 207
Product line contraction 194	Packaging functions 208
Branding 195	Labelling 210
Benefits of branding 195	Universal product codes 210
Branding strategies 199	**Connect it** 211
Generic products versus branded products 199	**Summary** 211
Manufacturers' brands versus private brands 201	**Define it** 212
Individual brands versus family brands 201	**Review it** 212
Co-branding 201	**Apply it** 214
Trademarks 202	**Try it** 214
	Watch it 215
	Click it 216
	Answer key 217

7: Developing and managing products — 218

The importance of new products 221	Implications for marketing management 235
Categories of new products 221	**The spread of new products** 236
The new-product development process 222	Diffusion of innovation 236
New-product strategy 223	Product characteristics and the rate of adoption 237
Idea generation 223	Marketing implications of the adoption process 239
Idea screening 226	**Connect it** 240
Business analysis 227	**Summary** 240
Development 227	**Define it** 241
Test marketing 229	**Review it** 241
Commercialisation 231	**Apply it** 242
Product life cycles 232	**Try it** 243
Introductory stage 233	**Watch it** 243
Growth stage 234	**Click it** 245
Maturity stage 234	**Answer key** 245
Decline stage 235	

8: Marketing channels and logistics decisions — 246

Marketing channels 249	**Channel intermediaries and their functions** 251
Providing specialisation and division of labour 249	Types of channel intermediaries 251
Overcoming discrepancies 249	Channel functions performed by intermediaries 252
Providing contact efficiency 250	

Channel structures	**254**	Transportation	279
Channels for consumer products	255	**Trends in logistics**	**280**
Channels for business-to-business		Automation	280
and industrial products	256	Outsourcing logistics functions	280
Alternative channel arrangements	256	**Channel and distribution decisions**	**282**
Channel strategy decisions	**258**	The role of retailing	282
Factors affecting channel choice	258	**Classification of retail operations**	**282**
Levels of distribution intensity	261	Ownership	282
Channel relationships	**262**	Level of service	283
Channel power, control		Product assortment	283
and leadership	262	Price	284
Channel conflict	263	**Main types of retail operations**	**285**
Channel partnering	265	Retail outlets	285
Logistics decisions and supply		Non-store retailing	286
chain management	**266**	**Channels and distribution**	
The evolution of integrated logistics		**decisions – services**	**286**
and supply chain management	268	**Channels and distribution**	
Benefits of supply chain		**decisions – electronic**	**288**
management	269	Electronic retailing	288
Balancing logistics service and cost	**271**	**Connect it**	**289**
Integrated functions		**Summary**	**289**
of the supply chain	**272**	**Define it**	**293**
Sourcing and procurement	273	**Review it**	**293**
Production scheduling	274	**Apply it**	**294**
Order processing	275	**Try it**	**296**
Stock control	276	**Watch it**	**296**
Warehousing and materials		**Click it**	**298**
handling	278	**Answer key**	**299**

Part four: Managing the marketing elements: Integrated marketing communication and pricing decisions   303

9: Integrated marketing communication (IMC)   306

The role of promotion		AIDA and the promotional mix	322
in the marketing mix	**308**	**Factors affecting**	
Personal selling	309	**the promotional mix**	**323**
The promotional mix	**310**	Nature of the product	323
Direct marketing	310	Stage in the product life cycle	324
Advertising	310	Target market characteristics	325
Sales promotion	311	Type of buying decision	325
Public relations	312	Available funds	326
Integrated marketing		Push and pull strategies	326
communications	312	**Personal selling**	**328**
Marketing communication	**314**	Relationship selling	329
The communication process		**Direct marketing**	**332**
and the promotional mix	318	Electronic retailing	335
The goals and tasks of promotion	**319**	**Connect it**	**336**
Persuading	320	**Summary**	**336**
Reminding	320	**Define it**	**338**
Promotional goals		**Review it**	**338**
and the AIDA concept	**320**	**Apply it**	**339**

x CONTENTS

Try it	340
Watch it	341
Click it	342
Answer key	343

10: Promotions mix — 344

Effects of advertising	**346**
Advertising and market share	347
Advertising and the consumer	348
Advertising and brand loyalty	348
Advertising and product attributes	348
Main types of advertising	**349**
Institutional advertising	350
Product advertising	351
Steps in creating an advertising campaign	**353**
Determine campaign objectives	354
Make creative decisions	354
Making media decisions	**359**
Media type	359
Media selection considerations	364
Media scheduling	366
Evaluating the ad campaign	367
Sales promotion	**367**
The objectives of sales promotion	368
Tools for consumer sales promotion	369
Tools for trade sales promotion	373
Public relations	**375**
Major public relations tools	376
Managing unfavourable publicity	379
Connect it	**380**
Summary	**380**
Define it	**382**
Review it	**382**
Apply it	**383**
Try it	**384**
Watch it	**385**
Click it	**387**
Answer key	**387**

11: Pricing concepts — 388

The importance of price	**390**
What is price?	390
The importance of price to marketing managers	391
Pricing objectives	**392**
Profit-oriented pricing objectives	392
Sales-oriented pricing objectives	393
Status quo pricing objectives	394
The demand determinant of price	**394**
The nature of demand	394
Elasticity of demand	394
The cost determinant of price	**397**
Mark-up pricing	398
Profit maximisation pricing	399
Break-even pricing	400
Other determinants of price	**401**
Stages in the product life cycle	401
The competition	402
Distribution strategy	403
The impact of the electronic environment	404
Promotion strategy	407
Demands of large customers	407
The relationship of price to quality	408
How to set a price on a product	**409**
Establish pricing goals	409
Estimate demand, costs and profits	410
Choose a price strategy	410
The legality and ethics of price strategy	**413**
Predatory pricing	414
Tactics for fine-tuning the base price	**414**
Discounts, allowances, rebates and value pricing	414
Value-based pricing	415
Geographic pricing	415
Special pricing tactics	416
Connect it	**419**
Summary	**419**
Define it	**421**
Review it	**421**
Apply it	**422**
Try it	**423**
Watch it	**424**
Click it	**425**
Answer key	**426**

Part five: The world of marketing — 433

12: Global marketing — 438

Benefits of global marketing 440
- Importance of global marketing 441

External environment facing global marketers 442
- Culture 442
- Economic and technological development 445
- Political structure 446
- Demographic makeup 450
- Natural resources 450

The global marketing mix 451
- Product and promotion 451
- Pricing 456
- Distribution 456
- Channels and distribution decisions – global markets 457

Impact of the electronic environment 462
Connect it 463
Summary 463
Define it 464
Review it 464
Try it 465
Apply it 466
Watch it 466
Click it 468
Answer key 468

13: Marketing strategy — 470

An organisational overview of strategy 472

Marketing orientations 474
- Production orientation (focusing on manufacturing efficiency) 474
- Sales orientation (focusing on selling existing products) 474
- Marketing orientation (focusing on customer needs and wants) 475
- Relationship marketing orientation (focusing on relationships with existing suppliers and customers) 476

The nature of strategic planning 476
Marketing strategy and plans 477
Developing and implementing a marketing plan 479
- Defining the organisational mission and objectives 480
- Performing a situation analysis 481

The external marketing environment 481
Understanding the external environment 481
- Environmental management 482

Sociocultural environment 483
- Baby boomers: demanding change 483
- Generation X: savvy and cynical 485
- Generation Y: born to shop 486
- Generation Z: the silent generation 487
- Marketing-oriented values 487
- Growth of component lifestyles 487
- The changing character of families 488

Economic environment
- Rising incomes 489
- Inflation 489
- Recession 489

Technological environment 490
Political and legal environment 490
- Federal legislation 492
- Regulatory agencies 492

Competitive environment 493
- Industry 493
- Competition 494
- Competitors 494

Describing target markets 494
- Establishing components of the marketing mix for each target market 495
- Implementation and control processes 497

Social and ethical behaviour 498
- Morality and business ethics 499
- Ethical business decision-making 500
- Ethical guidelines 500

Corporate social responsibility 501
Connect it 501
Summary 502
Define it 505
Review it 505
Click it 506
Answer key 506

Glossary 512
Endnotes 522
Index 530

Preface

After teaching introductory marketing for more than 20 years, we saw the need for a text that simplified and made relevant the principles and concepts of marketing for students. The American text *Essentials of Marketing*, by Lamb, Hair and McDaniel, provided the framework for such a text, one that was exciting, colourful and theoretically solid and could be easily read and understood by a range of different levels of students. This Australasian edition of that text contains additional Australasian content, examples, cases and websites. We also expanded some of the theoretical content in areas where we felt that traditional marketing texts have long been deficient.

In addition, we have presented the material in a consumer-oriented manner, so that students are better able to relate the material to their own experiences in the marketplace. Our 'build-up' approach begins by posing the question 'What is marketing?' to students; it then moves to a consumer-oriented examination of marketing, from both the individual and organisational consumer perspectives. The various elements of marketing are then examined in an applied manner. Once students have understood these concepts, they are more able to extend their knowledge and thinking to embrace the planning and strategy elements of a marketing course. Our experience has shown that, often, students don't grasp the full implications of the content of these areas early in an introductory marketing course, which is why the marketing strategy chapter is at the conclusion of the text. The website includes marketing plan worksheets which guide students through the key milestones of preparing a marketing plan.

We believe that the use of fresh, relevant and timely examples, cases and activities to reinforce the principles and concepts has produced a lively and interesting text that students will be motivated to read. By focusing only on the *essential* elements of marketing theory, we have produced a text that will be ideal for many different levels of marketing courses as it omits the unnecessary and wordy academic content often found in introductory marketing texts.

This text will enable students to understand and apply the principles of marketing; better still, they will enjoy reading it! Marketing instructors will find that the text and supplementary materials cover all the relevant introductory marketing theory, in a concise and well-structured format, with a wealth of additional resources such as video and written case studies, Web-based and team activities, entrepreneurial cases, PowerPoint slides, Instructor's Manual and Examview test bank. Finally, the consumer focus of the text has also made it a relevant resource that even marketing practitioners will embrace.

RESOURCES GUIDE   xiii

FOR THE STUDENT

As you read this text you will find a wealth of features in every chapter and part to help you understand and enjoy your studies of the principles of marketing.

Learning objectives are listed at the start of each chapter to give you a clear sense of what the chapter will cover.

When *key terms* are used in the text for the first time, they are defined in the text and bolded for easy identification. A full list of key terms is also available in the glossary which can be found at the back of the book.

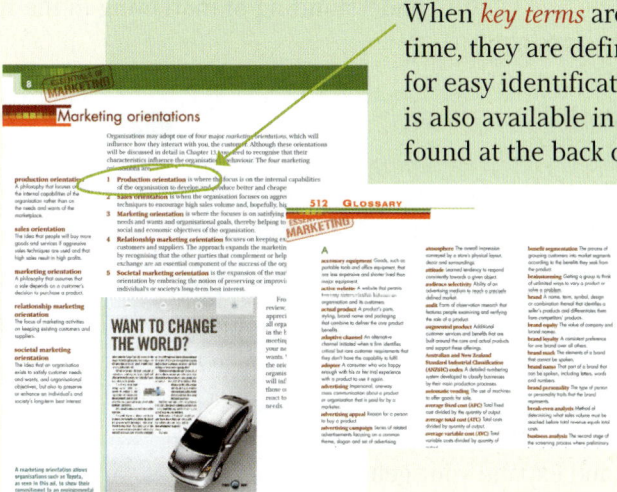

Sometimes product's claim to be safer than an existing product raises ethic issues as the Ethics in marketing box indicates.

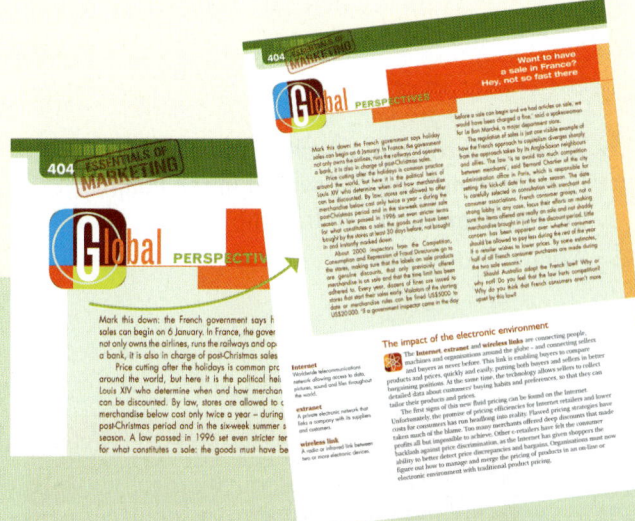

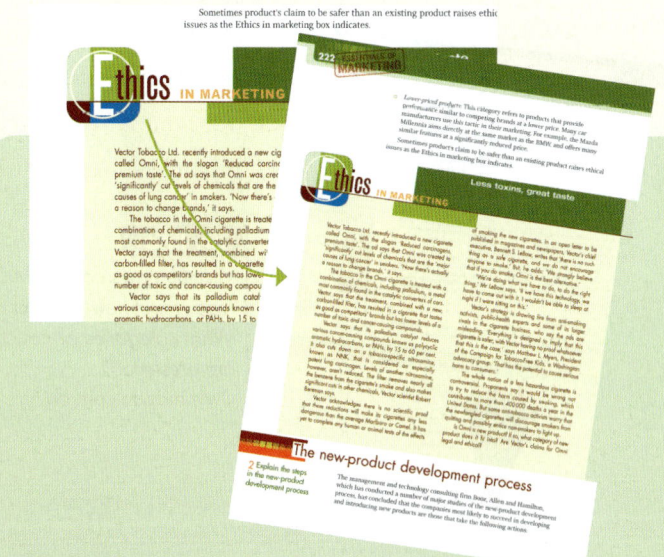

Global perspectives sections put marketing in an international context, using overseas examples to complement the local content of the text.

Each chapter has an *Ethics in marketing* section, ensuring that ethics remain a central part of your study of marketing.

xiv RESOURCES GUIDE

Throughout the text, *Entrepreneurial insights* sections provide important tips and illustrate successful marketing campaigns, to give you a greater understanding of marketing in the real world.

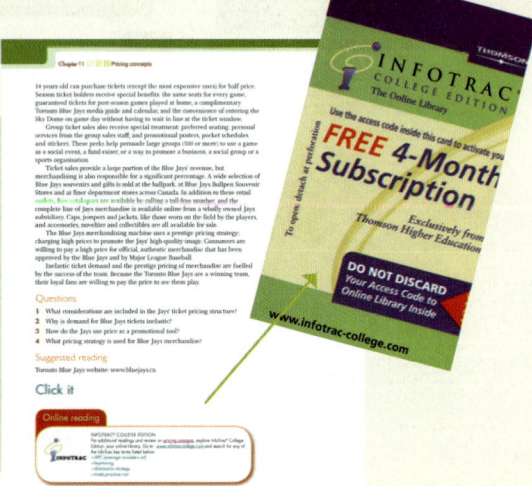

Infotrac ® search terms are available in the *Click it* section at the end of each chapter. Included with this text is a passcode that gives you a FREE four-month subscription to InfoTrac College Edition. This online library will provide you with access to full-text articles from thousands of scholarly and popular periodicals. Don't restrict yourself to the search terms provided throughout the book, think of your own search terms and expand your general marketing knowledge.

Weblinks throughout each chapter assist you in researching topics covered in the chapter, including questions to link the website with what you've learned.

A *Marketing Plan* template is included on the website. Use the information provided in the text and the questions and guidelines provided on the web to help you build your own marketing plan.

RESOURCES GUIDE

At the end of each chapter you'll find several learning tools to help you to not only review the chapter and key concepts but to help you extend your learning.

The *Connect it* section gives a brief account of the material covered in the chapter and explains why it is relevant.

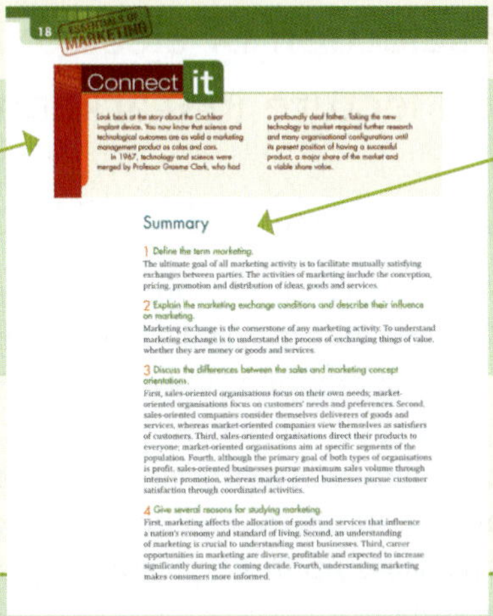

The end of chapter *Summary* addresses each learning objective listed at the start of the chapter, giving you a snapshot of the chapter's content.

Define it lists all of the key terms used in the chapter, with page references to where the term was explained.

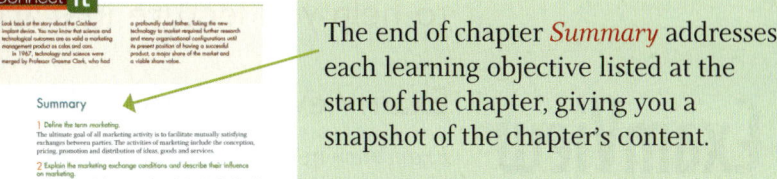

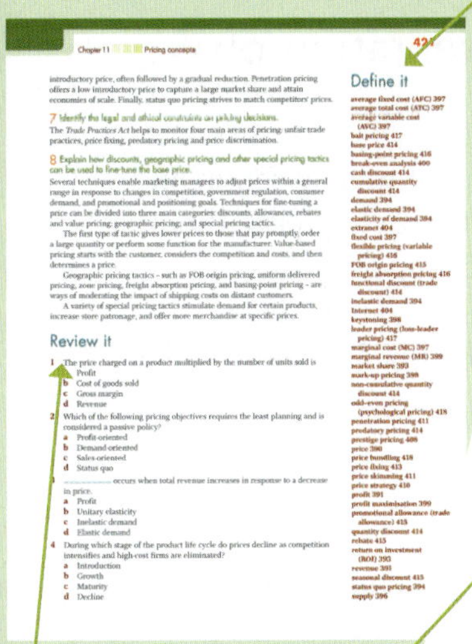

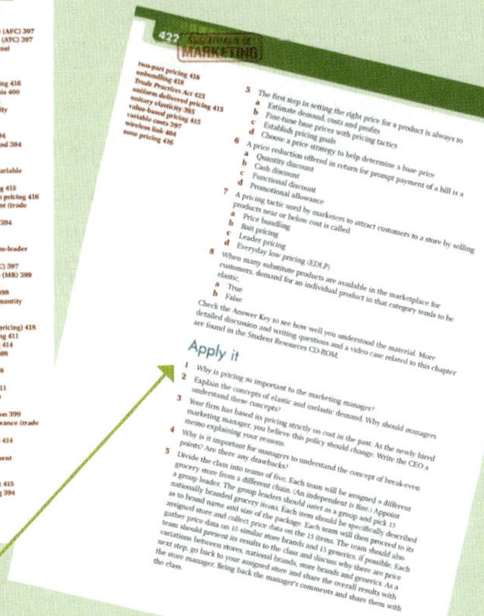

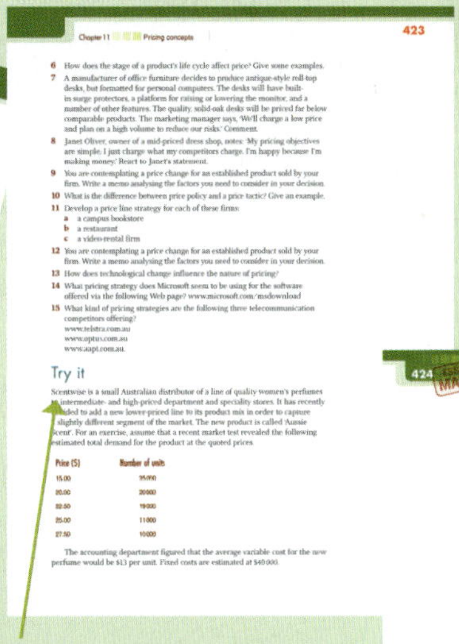

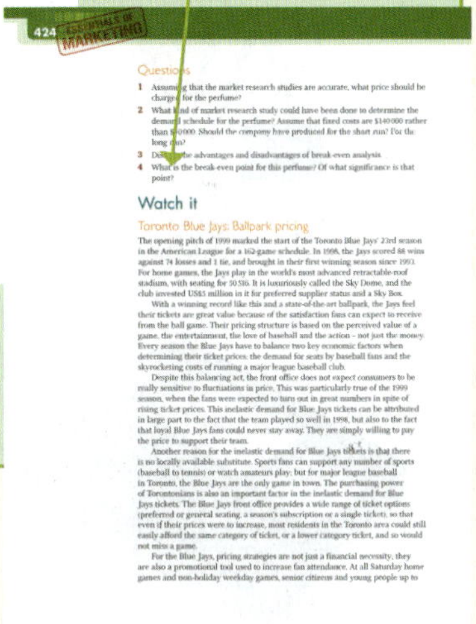

Review it multiple-choice questions and *Apply it* short-answer questions test your learning.

The *Try it* section presents a brief case study with review questions.

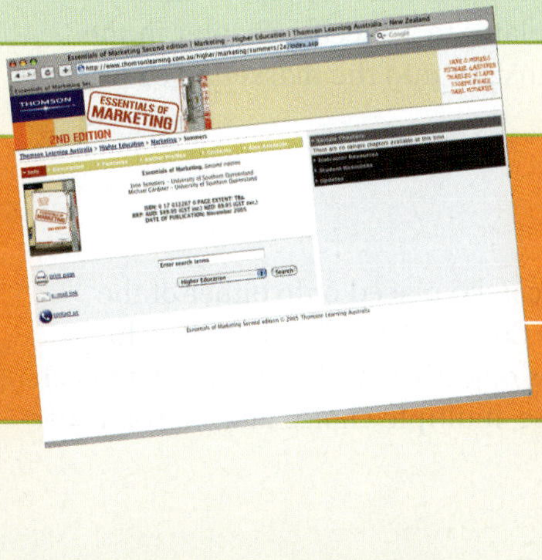

A video case study is outlined in the *Watch it* section, including review questions.

For updates and news relating to *Essentials of Marketing*, please go to the companion website.

www.thomsonlearning.com.au/higher/marketing/summers/2e

RESOURCES GUIDE

FOR THE INSTRUCTOR

Thomson Learning is pleased to provide you with an extensive selection of electronic and online supplements to help you lecture in marketing.

ExamView Testbank CD ROM

ExamView helps you create, customise and deliver tests in minutes for both print and online. The Quick Test Wizard and Online Test Wizard guide you step by step through the test-creation process. The program also allows you to see the test you are creating on the screen exactly as it will print or display online. With ExamView's complete word-processing capabilities, you can add an unlimited number of new questions to the bank, edit existing questions and build tests of up to 250 questions using up to 12 question types. You can now export the files into Blackboard or WebCT.

Instructor's Manual and PowerPoint Presentation on CD-ROM

The Instructor's Manual provides you with a wealth of content to help set up and administer a marketing subject. It includes learning objectives, chapter outlines, key points, figures from the text, adjunct teaching and warm-up activities as well as solutions to problems in the text. Also included on the CD-ROMs are PowerPoint presentations to accompany Essentials of Marketing. Use these slides to reinforce key marketing principles.

Artwork CD-ROM

The Artwork CD-Rom includes digital files of graphs, tables, pictures and flow charts from the text that can be used in a variety of media. Use them in WebCT or Blackboard, PowerPoint presentations or copy them onto overheads.

Videos

The video series contains video case studies featuring some of today's most innovative marketing companies. Each case relates to a specific chapter in the text and will give your students a real-world insight into the marketing concepts they are learning.

Blackboard and WebCT

Thomson has developed unique content that can be placed onto either of the above course management systems through a Course Cartridge that's free to adopters. This is original content that includes objectives and summaries for each topic, practices tests that include true and false, multiple choice and short-answer questions.

ACKNOWLEDGEMENTS xvii

A comprehensive text such as this could not have been developed without the generous input of many people. We wish to thank the original authors of the American text, Charles W. Lamb, Joseph F. Hair and Carl McDaniel, for allowing us to use their excellent text as a template for this edition. We must also acknowledge the Australian publishers, Thomson Learning, who have made this text possible. Their many hours of behind-the-scenes input, editorial comment and assistance have been invaluable. Specifically, we thank Michael Tully, Roz Edmond and Kate McGregor, who have helped us directly.

The authors would also like to thank the many Australian and New Zealand academics who have reviewed various chapters of the text and provided us with valuable and welcome feedback and suggestions. This extensive review process has certainly helped to ensure the rigour and relevance of this text for the Australasian marketplace.

The members of the department of marketing at the University of Southern Queensland also deserve a mention for their collegiate and professional support and for providing much-needed ideas and inspiration during times of despair.

Acknowledgements

The authors and publisher would like to gratefully credit or acknowledge the following:

Photographs

AAP Image, pp.225, 42; Advertising Archive, pp.366, 396; Australian Consumers' Association, p.30; Avis, p.132;BMW, p.378; Bulmer Australia Ltd, p.208; Cardinal Syntax, © Diane Cardinal, p.443; Cooee Picture Library, p.80; Copper Leife / Craig Forsythe, pp.287, 126, 372; Corbis © Kelley Mooney, p.70/ © Kevin Wilton, p.76/ © R.W. Jones, p.157/ © Jim Cummins p.417/ © LWA-Dean Tardif, p.484; Department of Information Systems, University of Melbourne, p.160; Digital Vision, p.83;Fairfax Photos, © Jim Rice, p.266/ © Viki Lascaris, p.286; Getty Images, pp.313, 326, 485; Image Addict, pp. 165, 408; JNCO Jeans, p.47; NewsPix, pp.6,.192, 254, 316; Nissan Motor Co. (Australia) Pty. Ltd., p.311; Osh Kosh B'Gosh, p.127; PhotoDisc / Getty Images p. 111/ © Tim Boyle, p.189; Photolibrary.com p.14; Qantas Airways Ltd, p.12;SABA © Andrew Brookes, p.449; Smart Lease, p 78; Target, p.390; The Advertising Archives, p.310; The Picture Desk, p. 10; TNT Australia, p.281; Toyota Motor Corporation Australia, p.8.

Text

Reprinted with permission from American Demographics, pp. 47, 49,444; Austar, p.365; Reprinted with permission from John Burnett, p.318; Reproduced by permission of Council of Supply Chain Management Professionals, p.270; iLounge, p.238; Reprinted from Industrial Marketing Management, Donald M. Jackson and Michael F. D'Amico, 'Products and Markets Served by Distributors and Agents', February 1989, pp. 27-33, with permission from Elsevier P.252; David Frederick Ross. 'Competing Through Supply Chain Management: Creating Market-Winning Strategies Through Supply Chain Partnerships.' (New York: Chapman & Hall 1998) with permission from Springer, p.265; Don E. Schultz, William A. Robinson and Lisa A. Petrison, Sales Promotion Essentials, 2nd edn. Reprinted by permission of NTC Publishing Group, United States, p.368; Reproduced by permission of Unilever Australia, p. 130.

Every attempt has been made to trace and acknowledge copyright holders. Where the attempt has been unsuccessful, the publisher welcomes information that would redress the situation.

About the Authors

Dr Jane Summers is the head of the marketing and tourism department in the Faculty of Business at the University of Southern Queensland. She has spent many years as a marketing practitioner and, more recently, as an academic. Her teaching and research interests are in the areas of consumer behaviour, e-marketing and sport marketing. She teaches and supervises a number of research students at undergraduate and postgraduate levels.

Michael Gardiner has been teaching for the past 10 years at several Queensland universities. Prior to that, he worked in the private and public sectors for 10 years as a marketing consultant, researcher and analyst. Michael is the Queensland chair for the Market Research Society of Australia (MRSA) and councillor for the Queensland branch of the Australian Marketing Institute (AMI). He has also been recognised with the Certified Practising Marketing (CPM) qualification from the AMI, and with the Qualified Professional Market Researcher (QPMR) qualification from the MRSA.

Charles W. Lamb, Jr is the M.J. Neeley Professor of Marketing, M.J. Neeley School of Business, Texas Christian University. He served as chair of the department of marketing from 1982 to 1988 and again from 1997 to the present. He is currently serving as chairman of the board of governors of the Academy of Marketing Science.

Joseph F. Hair, Jr is Alvin C. Copeland Endowed Chair of Franchising and Director, Entrepreneurship Institute, Louisiana State University. Previously, he held the Phil B. Hardin Chair of Marketing at the University of Mississippi. He has taught graduate and undergraduate marketing and marketing research courses.

Carl McDaniel is a professor of marketing at the University of Texas – Arlington, where he has been chairman of the marketing department since 1976. He has been an instructor for more than 20 years and is the recipient of several awards for outstanding teaching. He has also been a district sales manager for South-western Bell Telephone Company. Currently, he serves as a board member of the North Texas Higher Education Authority.

THE MARKETING EXPERIENCE

What is marketing, and how does it relate to you – the customer?

PART ONE

An overview of marketing	Chapter 1
Consumer decision-making	Chapter 2
Business decision-making	Chapter 3

Cross-functional connections

The six million dollar man is alive and well with the bionic ear

Professor Graeme Clark is head of the Department of Otolaryngology at the University of Melbourne, which is based at the Royal Victorian Eye and Ear Hospital. Professor Clark was responsible for the invention and development of the Cochlear implant device and is in charge of the active program undertaken at the hospital.

Background

Interest in artificially stimulating the auditory nerve was first sparked by the Italian physicist Count Alessandro Volta in the 18th century. Volta was also the first person to develop the electric battery.

Since Volta's time, researchers have carried out work on effects of electrically stimulating the cochlea and auditory nerve. These basic studies indicate that the best chance of enabling a profoundly deaf patient to understand speech is by multiple-electrode stimulation of the auditory nerve fibres. To do this requires implanting a receiver–stimulator device. It wasn't until the integrated circuit was developed that the implanting of a receiver–stimulator device in a patient became a real possibility.

Development of the bionic ear

In 1967, Professor Clark began researching implantable hearing devices. Having grown up in a home with a deaf father, Professor Clark was determined to improve the quality of life for those who could not hear. Eleven years later, in 1978, a 48-year-old male who had lost his hearing following a head injury 18 months previously was implanted with a 10-channel integrated circuit device the size of a 20-cent piece. The surgery went well and the recipient could hear his wife speaking to him. Subsequent implants led Professor Clark to believe the cochlear implant could be improved upon and made available to a larger group of people through commercial development.

In 1979, Nucleus, a group of companies that manufactured highly developed medical equipment, became interested in the commercial potential of Professor Clark's work. In 1981, with the University of Melbourne and the Australian government, Nucleus set out to develop a commercially viable cochlear implant and to carry out a worldwide clinical trial.

In 1983, Cochlear was established as a corporate entity to continue its commercial operations. Cochlear further developed the prototype based on the University of Melbourne research, and engineered a more advanced 22-channel implant and the WSP (wearable speech processor). The design philosophy was to make a flexible cochlear implant with sophisticated sound processing in the externally worn speech processor. This allowed the recipient to take advantage of improvements in technology without surgically replacing their implanted device.

In 1988, Cochlear became a wholly owned subsidiary of Pacific Dunlop. In 1995, Pacific Dunlop sold it, and it became a successfully floated, publicly listed company on the Australian Stock Exchange.

Since that time, Cochlear's constant growth is a tribute to its innovative technology, dedicated employees and the desire of thousands of individuals to hear. Today, Cochlear is a world leader in cochlear ear implants, with more than

Part one

30 000 Nucleus recipients worldwide and a global network of support and care in more than 50 countries.

This effort has had two major outcomes over and above the development of hearing for the profoundly deaf. First is the further development of the share market. While the technology sector took centre stage for many investors during the late 1990s and into 2000, health care was receiving some attention from observant investors who watched the sector climb, particularly in the field of biotechnology. While many health-care companies have great growth prospects, they cannot match Cochlear, which has been a top 10 holding for some time. Cochlear shares have risen a huge 1400 per cent since 1995, when it was unshackled from beleaguered conglomerate Pacific Dunlop and listed in its own right. It returned 37.8 per cent of profits to shareholders in 2000, which represented the fifth year of 20 per cent-plus growth.

As well as its impeccable share market performance, there is also for investors a feel-good factor, given Cochlear's ethical, life-enhancing products. Some analysts believe that the launch of Cochlear's advanced speech processor, the *ESPrit G*, in December 2001 could see even better times ahead.

The second outcome has been the advancement of marketing in the development of the organisation and its product. In particular, Cochlear has now snatched 65 per cent of the market, a rare feat for an Australian company. In 2001, the company started beefing up its marketing drive. The steady release of new and improved products provides new revenue streams and allows it to generate new interest.[1]

Questions for discussion

1 Identify the key components that allowed the bionic ear to be developed for the market.

2 This product is seen as having a service and a good component. Is it servicing one person with each implant or many? Is this a consumer market-type product or a social product? Why do you say that?

An overview of marketing

CHAPTER ONE

LEARNING OBJECTIVES

After studying this chapter, you should be able to

1. Define the term *marketing*
2. Explain the marketing exchange conditions and their influence on marketing
3. Discuss the differences between the sales and marketing concept orientations
4. Give several reasons for studying marketing
5. Describe the marketing process

For organisations to avoid being surprised by shifts in consumer and business behaviour, they must understand their customers. This understanding goes far beyond the reviewing of customer or business satisfaction. It means appreciating customers' unstated and unmet needs and knowing their businesses or lifestyles in ways that extend beyond their use of current products.

Mambo is an Australian surf and streetwear company. It was founded in 1984 by Dare Jennings, whose dream of an international design and fashion empire was born out of the simple belief that almost any idiot could make a few dollars by sticking a picture on the back of a T-shirt and selling it.

Launched with a nice pair of boardshorts and a professionally printed range of fashionably oversized T-shirts, Mambo has evolved from a raucous and sardonic curiosity into an international lifestyle company with 15 stores around the world, a UK licensee, and a constantly growing team of agents and distributors throughout Europe, Scandinavia, Asia, New Zealand and South America.

Mambo on-line

How does Mambo use its home page to connect with its market? What aspects of the home page suggest to you that this is a youth-oriented organisation?
www.mambo.com.au

Their catalogue has grown along with their reputation: what was a small but flamboyant collection of essential lifestyle accessories has grown to a huge collection of quintessential leisure requisites, available in all the usual sizes and fashionable colours: Mambo 'Loud shirts', T-shirts, Mambo Menswear, Goddess (for women), Kid Mambo, swimwear, Mambo 'Sunnies' (eyewear), surfboards, caps, bags, wallets, watches, jewellery, ceramics, posters, postcards, books and CDs.

They also 'mount regular exhibitions of original *Mambo* art, give creative and/or financial support to worthy individuals and culturally significant events, worship strange gods, square dance in round houses, covet our neighbour's ox, and generally go where no man has bothered to go before'.[2]

Why do you think Mambo has been so successful in meeting the needs of young adults? This issue is explored in this chapter.

Mambo Clothing artist Reg Mombassa with T-shirt art.

What is marketing?

1 Define the term *marketing*

What does the term *marketing* mean to you? Many people think it means the same as personal selling. Others think marketing is the same as personal selling and advertising. Still others believe that marketing has something to do with making products available in stores, arranging displays and maintaining inventories of products for future sales. Actually, marketing includes all these activities and more.

Marketing has two facets. First, it can be considered a philosophy, an attitude, a perspective or a management orientation that stresses customer satisfaction. (These views will be discussed in more detail later in the book.)

Second, marketing can also be seen as a process used to apply the philosophy, attitude, perspective or management orientation. The Australian and American marketing associations' definition encompasses both perspectives. It suggests that **marketing** is 'the process of planning and executing the conception, pricing, promotion, and distribution of ideas, goods, and services to create exchanges that satisfy individual and organizational goals'.[3]

Marketing is a social science, meaning that things are not always clear-cut as in a pure study like chemistry. It is a relatively new area of business study and is likely to change and be modified as academics and practitioners understand more about marketing.

The remainder of the chapter will consider some key concepts: marketing exchange, marketing orientation, and the concepts of customer value and satisfaction.

marketing
The process of planning and executing the conception, pricing, promotion and distribution of ideas, goods and services to create exchanges that satisfy individual and organisational goals.

Marketing exchange

Exchange is a key function of marketing. The concept of exchange is quite simple. It means that you must give up something of value to get something of value you would rather have. Normally we think of money as the medium of exchange. That is, we 'give up' money (representing something of value) to 'get' the goods and services that are of equal or more value to us as buyers. Exchange does not always require money, though. Two people may barter or trade such items as lunches, computer games, time, effort, or behaviours and ways of thinking. For example, if a politician asks you to vote for him/her, they are asking you to give up your vote in exchange for their promises. Anti-smoking and anti-drinking campaigns ask you to give up certain behaviours in exchange for a healthier and more socially responsible lifestyle.

For exchange to take place, five conditions need to occur:
1. There must be at least two parties (that is, people or groups of people/organisations).
2. Each party must have something of value that the other party also wants.
3. Each party must be able to communicate with the other party and deliver the goods or services sought by the other party.
4. Each party must be free to accept or reject the other's offer.
5. Each party must want to deal with the other party.[4]

Exchange won't always take place even if all these conditions exist. They are, however, needed for exchange to be possible. For example, you may place an advertisement in your local newspaper to sell your car. Several people may call you to ask about the car, some may test-drive it, and one or more may even make you an offer. As you can see, all five exchange conditions exist, but unless you reach an agreement with a buyer and actually sell the car, an exchange won't take place.

Now that you have a basic understanding of marketing exchange, it is important to understand how an organisation's marketing orientations will influence the way they deal with you as a customer.

2 Explain the marketing exchange conditions and their influence on marketing

exchange
The idea that people give up something to receive something they would rather have.

How does AMI Online target its resources to managers and to students?
www.ami.org.au

Marketing orientations

Organisations may adopt one of four major *marketing orientations*, which will influence how they interact with you, the customer. Although these orientations will be discussed in detail in Chapter 13, you need to recognise that their characteristics influence the organisation's behaviour. The four marketing orientations are:

1. **Production orientation** is where the focus is on the internal capabilities of the organisation to develop and produce better and cheaper products.
2. **Sales orientation** is when the organisation focuses on aggressive sales techniques to encourage high sales volume and, hopefully, high profits.
3. **Marketing orientation** is where the focuses is on satisfying customers' needs and wants and organisational goals, thereby helping to develop the social and economic objectives of the organisation.
4. **Relationship marketing orientation** focuses on keeping existing customers and suppliers. The approach expands the marketing orientation by recognising that the other parties that complement or help facilitate the exchange are an essential component of the success of the organisation.
5. **Societal marketing orientation** is the expansion of the marketing orientation by embracing the notion of preserving or improving an individual's or society's long-term best interest.

From this brief review, you should appreciate that not all organisations are in the business of meeting and satisfying your needs and wants. What's more, the orientation that organisations adopt will influence how those organisations react to you and your needs.

production orientation
A philosophy that focuses on the internal capabilities of the organisation rather than on the needs and wants of the marketplace.

sales orientation
The idea that people will buy more goods and services if aggressive sales techniques are used and that high sales result in high profits.

marketing orientation
A philosophy that assumes that a sale depends on a customer's decision to purchase a product.

relationship marketing orientation
The focus of marketing activities on keeping existing customers and suppliers.

societal marketing orientation
The idea that an organisation exists to satisfy customer needs and wants, and organisational objectives, but also to preserve or enhance an individual's and society's long-term best interest.

A marketing orientation allows organisations such as Toyota, as seen in this ad, to show their commitment to an environmental philosophy on automotive development.

Sales and marketing orientations

The sales and marketing orientations are the most commonly adopted orientations by organisations. Personnel in sales-oriented organisations tend to be 'inward-looking', focusing on selling what the organisation makes rather than presenting what the market wants. Many of the historic sources of competitive advantage – technology, innovation and economies of scale – allowed companies to focus their efforts internally and prosper. Today, however, many successful organisations derive their **competitive advantage** from an external, market-oriented focus. A marketing orientation has helped companies such as Dell Computer and Hewlett-Packard outperform their competitors.[5] Today, key issues in developing competitive advantage include creating customer value, maintaining customer satisfaction and building long-term relationships.

3 Discuss the differences between the sales and marketing concept orientations

competitive advantage
The idea that a product can solve a set of customer problems better than any competitor's product.

Customer value

Customer value is the ratio of benefits to the thing that must be forgone to obtain those benefits. As the Global perspectives box in this section illustrates, the customer determines the value of both the benefits and the sacrifices.

customer value
The ratio of benefits to the sacrifice necessary to obtain those benefits.

The customer, not the seller, defines value

Global PERSPECTIVES

Accessing and being competitive in the Asian markets is the goal of many small and medium-sized enterprises in Australia and New Zealand. However, like many new ventures, being successful in a new country requires the organisation to understand the economic, cultural and legal restrictions on the way organisations behave and market their products in this international environment. While many companies look successful in the short term, many fail in the longer term to be successful in their own right.

Consider a small organisation that offers a market research service so that pedestrian, vehicle and electronic traffic are measured for a particular traffic flow. It has been very successful in Australia over the past five years and is looking to expand into the Asian markets of Malaysia, India and Thailand. At the outset, the organisation approached each market in the same way that it approached the Australian market. However, it soon became apparent that the international markets were different from the Australian market. The customers needed their services, but wanted different or augmented elements to this product. It is these augmented products, such as the relationship between the provider and the buyer, and the way in which funds are transferred, that make the product in these three countries different from each other and from the domestic market.

Ultimately, it is the customer who determines the attributes of any product, as well as the value to be placed on the attributes an organisation provides for a particular product. In this case, the Australian organisation initially failed to recognise the unique differences of each country, based on their relationship and the way in which they transferred funds on completing each transaction. On becoming aware of these issues, the organisation modified its relationship and the product offering for each country to meet the needs of its customers so that they could value the product offering provided by the organisation.

Explain how the Australian service provider organisation enhanced customer value in the Asian countries.

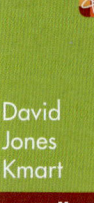

David Jones Kmart

on-line

Has David Jones identified its customers? Based on the organisation of its web page, how would you describe David Jones' marketing management orientation? Compare this web page with the Kmart web page. How do these two competitors present their image to the marketplace?

www.davidjones.com.au
www.kmart.com.au

The car industry also illustrates the importance of creating customer value. To penetrate the fiercely competitive luxury car market, Lexus adopted a customer-driven approach, with emphasis on service. Lexus stresses product quality with a standard of zero defects in manufacturing. The service-quality goal is to treat each customer as one would treat a guest in one's home, to pursue the perfect person-to-person relationship and to strive to improve continually. This pursuit has enabled Lexus to establish a clear quality image and to capture a significant share of the luxury car market.

Customer value is not simply a matter of high quality. A high-quality product that is available only at a high price won't be perceived as good value, nor will bare-bones services or low-quality goods selling for a low price. Instead, customers value goods and services of the quality they expect and that are sold at prices they are willing to pay. Value can be used to sell a $170 600 Lexus LS430 as well as a $10 Eagle Boys pizza.

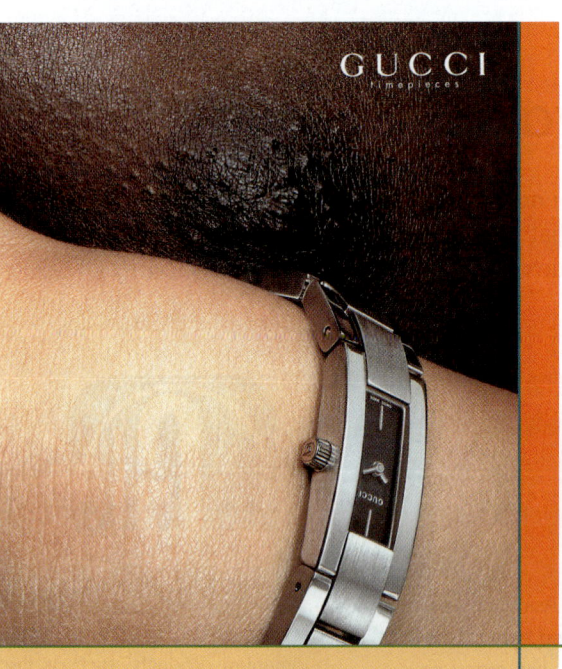

Creating customer value is the linchpin to successful marketing, but because value is determined by the customer's perception alone, it can be difficult to quantify. Do you think this Gucci watch ad captures the quality image that the luxury watch manufacturer wants to convey?

Marketers interested in customer value focus on the following:

1. *They offer products that perform.* This is the bare minimum requirement. Consumers have lost patience with shoddy merchandise.
2. *They give consumers more than they expect.* Soon after Toyota launched Lexus, the company had to order a recall. The weekend before the recall, dealers telephoned all the Lexus owners, personally arranging to pick up the cars and offering replacement vehicles.
3. *They avoid unrealistic pricing.* Consumers couldn't understand why Kellogg's cereals commanded a premium over other brands, so Kellogg's market share fell five per cent in the late 1980s.
4. *They give the buyer facts.* Today's sophisticated consumer wants informative advertising and knowledgeable salespeople.
5. *They offer organisation-wide commitment in service and after-sales support.* People fly Virgin Blue, a low-fare carrier, because the airline believes that flying should be affordable. It is committed to providing true value for money.

It doesn't provide a lot of fancy add-ons, such as frequent flyer programs, tickets and 'free' meals, but it does offer friendly and reliable service, consistently. The airline's employees are energetic, enthusiastic and talented. They were chosen because they are passionate about working for Virgin Blue and are confident that they will have the most dynamic, friendly, customer-service-focused team in the sky.[6]

Customer satisfaction

Customer satisfaction is the feeling that a product has met or exceeded your (the customer's) expectations. Keeping current customers satisfied is just as important as attracting new ones and a lot less expensive. Organisations that have a reputation for delivering high levels of customer satisfaction do things differently from their competitors. Top management is obsessed with customer satisfaction, and employees throughout the organisation understand the link between their job and satisfied customers. The culture of the organisation is to focus on delighting customers rather than on selling products.

Officeworks, the office supplies retailer, offers great prices on its paper, pens, fax machines and other office supplies, but its main strategy is to grow by providing customers with the best solutions to their problems. Their approach is to provide solutions to their office, printing and stationery needs.

Building relationships

Relationship marketing is the name of a strategy that entails forging long-term partnerships with customers. Companies build relationships with customers by offering value and providing customer satisfaction. Companies benefit from repeat sales and referrals that lead to increases in sales, market share and profits. Costs fall because serving existing customers is less expensive than attracting new ones. Keeping a customer costs about a quarter of what it costs to attract a new customer; and the probability of retaining a customer is over 60 per cent, whereas the probability of landing a new customer is less than 30 per cent.[7]

The Internet is an effective tool for generating relationships with customers because of its ability to interact with the customer. With the Internet, companies can use email for fast customer service, discussion groups for building a sense of community, and database tracking of buying habits for customising products.[8]

Customers also benefit from stable relationships with suppliers. Business buyers have found that partnerships with their suppliers are essential to producing high-quality products while cutting costs.[9] Customers remain loyal to organisations that provide them with greater value and satisfaction than they expect from competing organisations. This value and satisfaction can come in a variety of forms ranging from financial benefits to a sense of well-being or confidence in a supplier, and structural bonds.[10]

Reward programs are an example of financial incentives to customers in exchange for their continuing patronage. For example, in frequent flyer programs members who fly a certain number of kilometres or fly a specified number of times earn a free flight or some other award such as free accommodation.

---

customer satisfaction
The feeling that a product has met or exceeded the customer's expectations.

Do you think Officeworks is after the one-off sale, or is it focused on developing long-term customer satisfaction?
www.officeworks.com.au

relationship marketing
A strategy that entails forging long-term partnerships with customers and is based on the marketing orientation.

How does Ezibuy show the company's commitment to its customers?
www.ezibuy.com.au/content/index.php?rnd=1097111395

Reward programs encourage customers to become loyal to specific organisations or brands and reward them for this behaviour.

Frequent flyer programs encourage customers to become loyal to specific airlines and reward them for their continuing patronage.

Ethics IN MARKETING

Smoking rates

National surveys of children's smoking habits have been conducted since 1984. The smoking rates of children aged between 12 and 17 have been tracked every three years since 1984. The findings show that between 1984 and 1990, the prevalence of smoking among 12- to 15-year-olds decreased and smoking also decreased for 16- and 17-year-olds between 1984 and 1987. However, a different trend emerged in 1990 and 1993. It was found that there were more male smokers in 1993 than in 1990 across all age groups. Equally, it was found that there was an increase in female smokers across all age groups in 1990 and that remained static in 1993. It was also identified that smoking prevalence was higher among girls and boys in all categories except for the very youngest age groups sampled.[11]

In January 2001, Philip Morris, a cigarette manufacturer in Australia, launched two new products. These products were not new brands, lower levels of nicotine or different-tasting cigarettes; they were product enhancements such as the slow-burning cigarette and the no-smoke cigarette. These two products were launched as community enhancements of a product that would benefit society as a whole. The slow-burning cigarette was presented as the cigarette that would restrict the starting of bushfires by smokers who carelessly disposed of their butts. The second product, the no- or little-smoke cigarette, is a device that catches the smoke from the cigarette while it is burning. It does not capture the smoke from the smoker while exhaling.

What do you think of these two new products?

A sense of well-being occurs when a customer establishes an ongoing relationship with a provider such as a physician, a bank, a hairdresser or an accountant. The social bonding that takes place between provider and customer involves personalisation and customisation of the relationship. Organisations can develop these bonds by referring to customers by name and providing continuity of service through the same representative. Most successful relationship marketing strategies depend on customer-oriented personnel, effective training programs, employees with authority to make decisions and solve problems, and teamwork. The Entrepreneurial insights box in this section offers several relationship tips for small local organisations to use in competing with large national or international marketers.

David versus Goliath

The scenario is familiar: the big, heartless megastore moves in just outside town, offering everything under the sun and trampling local corner stores in the process. How can local retailers save their stores?

A recent study produced the following seven tips:

1. Work with other local retailers to offer a complete merchandise selection. Consumers complained they couldn't find everything they needed on 'Main Street', so they had to travel to shop.
2. Build strong customer relationships. Local retailers should think back to the days when sales assistants knew the name of every customer who walked in the door and try to build that kind of personal bond to offer a benefit that the large, impersonal store can't provide.
3. Get involved with local events and government. Local retailers should identify strongly and overtly with the communities they serve. This might include sponsoring local sports teams, breakfasts with industry and government leaders, and helping local schools to raise funds.
4. Update merchandise more frequently. If local retailers improve their selection, they can convince consumers the best products can be found close to home. They can even charge higher prices because consumers will be willing to pay them for the convenience.
5. Train your sales force so they understand their importance in delivering customer satisfaction.
6. Conduct formal customer research. Distribute customer satisfaction cards in stores with questions regarding service, merchandise selection and store appearance. This may help spot problems before they drive customers away.
7. On the other hand, don't be afraid to send customers away. Use the *Miracle on 34th Street* approach if your business does not carry an item requested by a customer: suggesting another local store will build trust and keep customers shopping in town.[12]

Why study marketing?

4 Give several reasons for studying marketing

Now that you have been introduced to the meaning of the term *marketing* and to how marketing's elements are put into effect by organisations, you may be asking, 'What's in it for me?' or 'Why should I study marketing?' These are good questions. Whether you are majoring in a business field other than marketing (for example, accounting, finance or management information systems) or a non-business field (for example, journalism, nursing, economics or agriculture), there are several important reasons to study marketing: marketing plays an important role in society, marketing is important to the success of businesses, marketing offers outstanding career opportunities, and marketing affects your life every day as a consumer.

Not-for-profit organisations use marketing tools such as this ad to raise funds and help support medical research by the organisations for the benefit of the community at large.

How might you use the census to analyse a specific market segment?
www.abs.gov.au

Marketing plays an important role in society

The Australian Bureau of Statistics predicts that the Australian population will reach 21.5 million by 2010. Think about how many transactions are needed each day to feed, clothe and shelter a population of this size. The number is huge. And yet, it all works quite well, partly because the well-developed economic systems in the country are efficiently distributing the output of farms and factories. In relation to food purchases alone, marketing makes food available when we want it, in the desired quantities, at accessible locations, and in sanitary and convenient packages and forms (such as instant and frozen foods).

Marketing is important to businesses

The basic objectives of most organisations are survival, profits (cost minimisation) and growth. Marketing contributes directly to achieving these objectives. Marketing includes the following activities, which are vital to business organisations: assessing the wants and satisfactions of present and potential customers, designing and managing product offerings, determining prices and pricing policies, developing distribution strategies, and communicating with present and potential customers.

All businesspeople, regardless of specialisation or area of responsibility, need to be familiar with the terminology and fundamentals of accounting, finance, management and marketing. People in all business areas need to be able to communicate with specialists in other areas. Furthermore, marketing is not just a job done by people in a marketing department. Marketing is a part of the job of everyone in the organisation. As David Packard, the co-founder of Hewlett-Packard, said: 'Marketing is too important to be left (just) to the marketing department.'[13] Therefore, a basic understanding of marketing is important to all businesspeople.

Marketing offers outstanding career opportunities

The majority of careers in Australia and New Zealand are in marketing, owing to the service sectors of these countries being so strong. Marketing offers great career opportunities in such areas as professional selling, marketing research, advertising, public relations, services, retail buying, distribution management, product management, product development, wholesaling and information technology. The Australian Marketing Institute, Public Relations Institute of Australia and the Australian Market and Social Research Society publish brochures and books that provide extensive information about career opportunities in marketing. Marketing career opportunities also exist in a variety of non-business organisations, including hospitals, museums, universities, the armed forces, and various government and social service agencies.

As the world marketplace becomes more challenging, organisations of all sizes are going to have to become better at marketing and better marketers. Surveys show that small business makes up over 80 per cent of all jobs in Australia and New Zealand. Regardless of your title or job activity, you will need to be able to market your products to the world. Employees with marketing skills will be highly regarded. The Entrepreneurial insights box in this chapter offers several tips for those who might be interested in owning and operating their own business franchise.

Marketing is important to you

Marketing plays a major role in your everyday life. You take part in the marketing process every day as a consumer of goods and services. About half of every dollar you spend pays for marketing costs, such as marketing research, product development, packaging, transportation, storage, advertising and sales expenses. By developing a better understanding of marketing, you will become a better informed and more discriminating consumer. You will better understand the buying process and be able to negotiate better with sellers. Moreover, you will be better prepared to demand satisfaction when the products you buy don't meet the standards promised by the manufacturer, service provider or the marketer.

Looking ahead

This book is divided into 13 chapters organised into five parts. The chapters are written from your perspective. Each chapter starts with a brief list of learning objectives followed by a short story about a marketing situation faced by an organisation. After each of these opening vignettes, thought-provoking questions link the story to the subject addressed in the chapter. Your instructor may wish to begin chapter discussions by asking members of your class to share their views about the questions.

5 Describe the marketing process

The marketing process

Earlier, marketing was defined as the process of planning and executing the conception, pricing, promotion and distribution of ideas, goods and services to create exchanges that satisfy individual and organisational objectives. While this all sounds very complicated, it makes more sense when you can understand the overall process of marketing. The marketing process adopted by an organisation includes the following activities:

1. Finding out what benefits people want the organisation to deliver and the wants they wish the organisation to satisfy (market opportunity analysis; Chapters 2, 3 and 5)
2. Developing a marketing strategy to satisfy the desires of selected target markets by: deciding exactly which wants, and whose wants, the organisation will try to satisfy (target market strategy; Chapter 4); setting marketing objectives; and developing appropriate marketing activities (the marketing mix strategies; Chapters 6 to 11)
3. Gathering, analysing and interpreting information about the environment (environmental scanning; Chapter 13)
4. Understanding the organisation's mission and the role that marketing plays in fulfilling this vision (Chapter 13)
5. Implementing the strategy (Chapter 13)
6. Periodically evaluating marketing efforts and making changes if needed (Chapter 13)
7. Chapter 12 looks specifically at the areas of international and global marketing.

As we can see in Exhibit 1.1, most of marketing theory's emphasis is placed on the organisation. However, when you study marketing your base for understanding is couched in your own experiences. We all like to buy things.

In this first part of the book, we look at your understanding and experience of marketing. Then, in Part 2, we will look at the way organisations go about gathering information about you and the market, and how they break the market down into smaller groups of customers they can serve. In Parts 3 and 4, you will see how organisations use marketing theory to develop their strategy to serve your needs while maintaining their own objectives. Part 5 adds the final component to the understanding of marketing, which is that marketing cannot be conducted in isolation; it needs a general understanding of the business and cultural environment within which it operates.

In addition to the structure of the book, you will find that examples of global marketing are highlighted in most chapters. This should help you to understand that marketing takes place all over the world, between buyers and sellers from across the street, and between those across the world in different countries. These and other global marketing examples throughout the book, marked with the icon shown above, are intended to help you develop a global perspective on marketing.

Marketing ethics is another important topic selected for special treatment throughout the book. Chapters include highlighted stories about firms or industries that have faced ethical dilemmas or have engaged in practices that some consider unethical. Questions are posed to focus your thinking on the key ethical issues raised in each story.

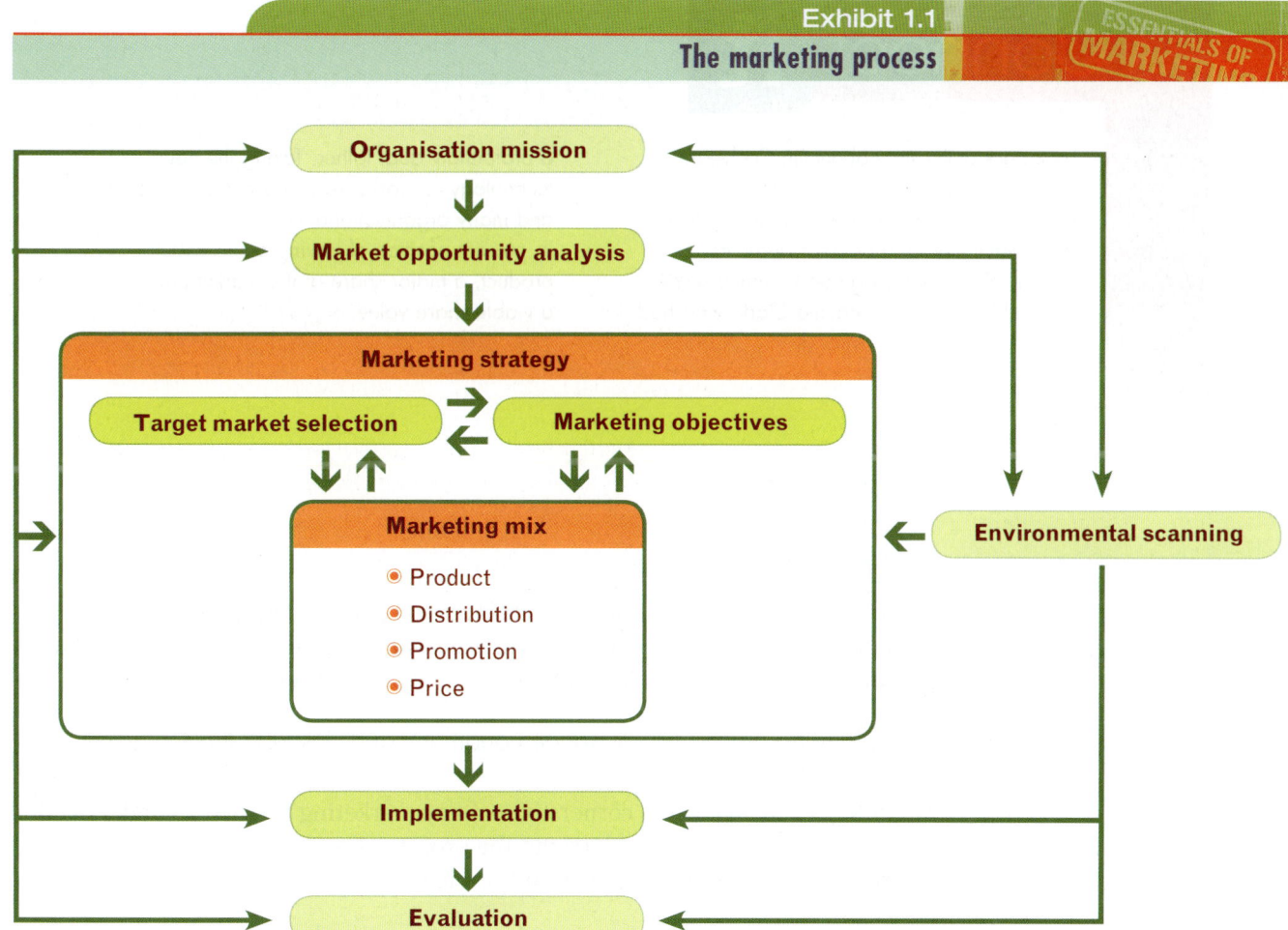

Exhibit 1.1 The marketing process

The application of marketing using electronic and mobile devices is a further topic selected for special treatment throughout the book. Chapters include highlighted examples and practices of electronic marketing used by organisation. Some questions are posed to focus your thinking.

Delivering superior customer value is a key to marketing success in an increasingly competitive environment. Examples of creating or delivering superior customer value are integrated throughout the text.

Entrepreneurial insights are highlighted with special boxes. Every chapter also includes an application case related to small business. This material, which you will find on the Student Resources CD-ROM, illustrates how entrepreneurs and small businesses can use the principles and concepts discussed in the book. Also included in those supplementary resources are video cases.

End-of-chapter materials include a final comment on the chapter-opening vignette (Connect it), a summary of the major topics examined, a list of the key terms introduced in the chapter, a review quiz and answer key, and discussion and writing questions (which include Internet and team activities).

The on-line icon is placed throughout the text to identify examples relating to technology. All these features are intended to help you develop a more thorough understanding of marketing and to enjoy the learning process.

Connect it

Look back at the story about the Cochlear implant device. You now know that science and technological outcomes are as valid a marketing management product as colas and cars.

In 1967, technology and science were merged by Professor Graeme Clark, who had a profoundly deaf father. Taking the new technology to market required further research and many organisational configurations until its present position of having a successful product, a major share of the market and a viable share value.

Summary

1 Define the term *marketing*.

The ultimate goal of all marketing activity is to facilitate mutually satisfying exchanges between parties. The activities of marketing include the conception, pricing, promotion and distribution of ideas, goods and services.

2 Explain the marketing exchange conditions and describe their influence on marketing.

Marketing exchange is the cornerstone of any marketing activity. To understand marketing exchange is to understand the process of exchanging things of value, whether they are money or goods and services.

3 Discuss the differences between the sales and marketing concept orientations.

First, sales-oriented organisations focus on their own needs; market-oriented organisations focus on customers' needs and preferences. Second, sales-oriented companies consider themselves deliverers of goods and services, whereas market-oriented companies view themselves as satisfiers of customers. Third, sales-oriented organisations direct their products to everyone; market-oriented organisations aim at specific segments of the population. Fourth, although the primary goal of both types of organisations is profit, sales-oriented businesses pursue maximum sales volume through intensive promotion, whereas market-oriented businesses pursue customer satisfaction through coordinated activities.

4 Give several reasons for studying marketing.

First, marketing affects the allocation of goods and services that influence a nation's economy and standard of living. Second, an understanding of marketing is crucial to understanding most businesses. Third, career opportunities in marketing are diverse, profitable and expected to increase significantly during the coming decade. Fourth, understanding marketing makes consumers more informed.

Review it

1 _____ is the process of planning and executing the conception, pricing, promotion and distribution of ideas, goods and services to create exchanges that satisfy individual and organisational goals.
   a   Change
   b   Marketing
   c   Selling
   d   Organisational focus

2 The marketing management orientation in which the organisation's focus is on its own internal capabilities, rather than on the desires of the marketplace, is called a
   a   Production orientation
   b   Sales orientation
   c   Marketing orientation
   d   Relationship marketing orientation

3 A sales orientation
   a   Helps organisations to understand the needs and wants of the marketplace
   b   Focuses on customer wants and needs so that the organisation can distinguish its products from competitors' offerings
   c   Is based on the idea that people will buy more goods and services if aggressive sales techniques are used
   d   Proves that companies can convince people to buy goods and services that they neither want nor need

4 A manager states to the organisation's shareholders: 'We are in the business of maximising perceived value for our customers.' What marketing management orientation is this organisation practising?
   a   A production orientation
   b   A sales orientation
   c   A marketing orientation
   d   A relationship marketing orientation

5 Which of the following marketing management orientations is described by phrases such as 'inter-functional coordination', 'delivery of superior value' and 'competitor intelligence'?
   a   A production orientation
   b   A sales orientation
   c   A marketing orientation
   d   A relationship marketing orientation

6 Customer value is
   a   The ratio of benefits to the sacrifice needed to obtain those benefits
   b   The outcome of most transactions for organisations using a sales orientation
   c   The number of items sold that are of high quality and high cost
   d   The outcome of most transactions for organisations using a production orientation

Define it

competitive advantage 9
customer satisfaction 11
customer value 9
exchange 7
marketing 6
marketing orientation 8
production orientation 8
relationship marketing 11
relationship marketing orientation 8
sales orientation 8
societal marketing orientation 8

7 The key issues facing a manager whose organisation is practising a _____ are creating customer value, maintaining customer satisfaction and building long-term relationships.
   a production orientation
   b sales orientation
   c simple trade orientation
   d marketing orientation

8 Many _____ oriented organisations consider individuals' and societies' best interests in the long term. Select the right answer.
   a relationship marketing
   b sales
   c societal marketing
   d marketing

9 In a sales orientation, the customer, not the seller, defines value.
   a True
   b False

10 The study of marketing is important in that it is something that affects almost everyone's life every day.
   a True
   b False

Check the Answer Key to see how well you understood the material. More detailed discussion and writing questions and a video case related to this chapter are found in the Student Resources CD-ROM.

Discuss it

1 Your company's CEO has decided to restructure the organisation and become more market-oriented. She is going to announce the changes at an upcoming meeting. She has asked you to prepare a short speech outlining the general reasons for the new company orientation.

2 Donald E. Petersen, past chairman of the board of Ford Motor Company in the United States, remarked, 'If we aren't customer driven, our cars won't be either.' Explain how this statement impacts on your understanding of marketing.

3 A friend of yours agrees with the adage, 'People don't know what they want – they only want what they know.' Write a letter to your friend expressing the extent to which you think marketers shape consumer wants.

4 Your local supermarket's slogan is 'It's your store.' However, when you asked one of the stock people to help you find a bag of chips, he told you it wasn't his job and that you should look a little harder. On your way out, you noticed a sign with an address for complaints. Draft a letter explaining why the supermarket's slogan will never be credible unless their employees carry it out.

5 Write a letter to a friend or family member explaining why you think that a marketing course will help you and your career in fields other than marketing.

6 Form a group of three or four members. Suppose you and your colleagues all work for an up-and-coming gourmet coffee company that has several stores, mostly in large cities across Australia and New Zealand. Your team has been assigned the task of assessing whether the company should begin marketing on the Internet. Each member has been assigned to visit three or four Internet sites for ideas. Some possibilities are:

Peninsular Surf at www.surfshop.com.au
2cherries at www.2cherries.com.au/
Subway at www.subway.com/sub1/student_ed
Kia at www.kia.com.au

7   Use your imagination and look up others. As you can see, many companies are easy to find, as long as you can spell their names. Typically, you would use the following:
www.companyname.com

8   Has Internet marketing helped the companies whose sites you visited? If so, how? What factors should your company consider before committing to Internet activity? Prepare a three- to five-minute presentation to give to your class.

9   What is the AMI? What does it do? How do its services benefit marketers? www.ami.com.au

Watch it

Lord of the Boards

Burton Snowboards, the industry leader, is the brainchild of Jake Burton, an avid snowboard rider. Jake's recipe for success is simple: 'We always focused on the sport and everything else took care of itself.' Burton practically invented the sport in 1977 when he first made crude snowboards in a workshop in Vermont, in the United States. By 1978, he had hit upon a successful formula (horizontally laminated wood) and made 300 boards with a US$88 price tag. The next decade saw Jake spending time and money lobbying ski areas to open their slopes to snowboarders. Now they are free to ride just about everywhere. Competitors noted that while they pegged snowboarding as a regional sport, Jake kept his eye on the big picture. He always had a vision. Campaigning tirelessly for snowboarding at resorts led to the creation of the US Open snowboard competition. By 1994, the *Wall Street Journal* spotted the trend and called snowboarding the fastest-growing sport. And then, the ultimate: snowboarding made its debut in the 1998 Winter Olympics in Nagano, Japan.

Jake didn't let the Olympics go to his head. He kept his company on a clear course of product development, R&D and lots of riding. The company provides a free season pass to Stowe ski area in Vermont and private lessons for newbies (new riders), so excuses for not riding are hard to find. The sport draws mainly the under-30 crowd, with 88 per cent 12 to 24 years old, 83 per cent male and 17 per cent female. The Newbie snowboarding guide gives the basics on the Burton website, starting with the idea that equipment and clothing can make or break the ride. First comes the choice of ride (Freestyle, Freeride or Carving), then three riding options. Next is the choice of board – produced in different lengths with different graphics. Boots and bindings are picked next, followed by clothing with the right fit. An on-snow demonstration is considered a must, so Burton posts its travel schedule on the Internet and offers free, local demonstrations and a chance to try on boots, bindings and the whole setup on the snow. Burton also suggests taking a lesson for maximum fun and safety.

Staying close to the customer is a company hallmark. Burton Snowboards builds on a group of people to get feedback to improve both the company and the sport. Talking to pro riders, sales reps, designers, testers and Internet users helps the company to find out what the riders want. For example, when the company needs new ideas for graphics, designers fly all over the world, sit face-to-face and look at what has been developed. The idea is to provide snowboard equipment to all people. To do this, Burton keeps on adding to its product line. Snowboarding performance may be gender blind, but fit is not. That is why Burton manufactures gender-specific clothing and boots that are completely different for men and women in fit but are matched in performance. Years of refining the cut of women's clothing have yielded a line of fully featured gear that really works for snowboarding. Women are the fastest-growing segment of riders, and while there are no specific women's boards or bindings, Burton works with their team riders to create board dimensions, flexes and bindings that work well for smaller, lighter riders. Burton plans to offer functional gear for women, men and riders of all sizes, abilities and styles. And as more and more kids aged six to 14 get into riding, Burton is stepping up and delivering products that meet the demands of these mini-snowboarders. Sometimes kids ride first and the parents follow suit. In the process, snowboarding becomes a family passion.

The Burton strategy has paid off. Annual sales figures are now estimated at well over US$150 million, and the company has 500 employees in Vermont and around the world. As the sport of snowboarding matures, many people in the snowboarding community are using the sport to make valuable social contributions that enrich lives. In 1994, Jake Burton started the Chill Program to share snowboarding with poor and at-risk kids. While it is true that heavy industry competition is out there, innovation and love of the sport still make Jake Burton Lord of the Boards.

Questions

1. Describe the exchange process at Burton.
2. How has Jake Burton's entrepreneurial philosophy made his company successful?
3. Does Burton use a sales orientation or a marketing orientation? Explain.
4. How does Burton Snowboards achieve customer satisfaction?

Suggested reading

Reade Bailey, 'Jake Burton, King of the Hill', *Ski*, February 1998, pp. 60–7.

Eric Blehm, 'The Day of the Locusts', *GQ*, December 1997, pp. 186–7.

Burton Snowboards 1998 Press Kit.

Burton Snowboards website: www.burton.com.

Click it

Online reading

INFOTRAC® COLLEGE EDITION
For additional readings and review on an overview of marketing, explore InfoTrac® College Edition, your online library. Go to: www.infotrac-college.com and search for any of the InfoTrac key terms listed below:
- societal marketing
- relationship marketing
- marketing exchange
- customer value

Chapter 1 An overview of marketing

Answer key

1. *Answer*: b, pp. 6–7 *Rationale*: This is the definition of marketing as given by the American Marketing Association.
2. *Answer*: a, p. 8 *Rationale*: In production orientation, the organisation's management assesses its resources and abilities rather than the needs of the marketplace.
3. *Answer*: c, p. 8 *Rationale*: The fundamental problem with the sales orientation is the lack of understanding of the needs and wants of the marketplace.
4. *Answer*: c, p. 8 *Rationale*: Remember what business the organisation is in when practising the marketing concept – that is, satisfaction of customer needs and wants.
5. *Answer*: c, p. 8 *Rationale*: Organisations that adopt the marketing orientation focus on making the customer satisfied through delivering value. This goal is often achieved by carefully examining the internal and external environment facing the organisation.
6. *Answer*: a, p. 8 *Rationale*: A marketing orientation is based on the premise of customer value; offering benefits to the customer that are superior to those of competing goods or services.
7. *Answer*: d, p. 8 *Rationale*: Notice that these issues are 'outward looking', which is a key attribute distinguishing a marketing orientation from a sales orientation.
8. *Answer*: c, p. 8 *Rationale*: Societal marketing is where organisations satisfy customers needs and wants; organisational objectives; and maintain or enhance individual and society's long-term best interests.
9. *Answer*: b, p. 9 *Rationale*: This situation is true in a marketing orientation, not a sales orientation.
10. *Answer*: a, p. 15 *Rationale*: About half of every dollar spent on goods and services goes towards marketing costs, such as marketing research, distribution and promotion.

Consumer decision-making

CHAPTER TWO

LEARNING OBJECTIVES

After studying this chapter, you should be able to

1. Explain why marketing managers should understand consumer behaviour
2. Analyse the components of the consumer decision-making process
3. Explain the consumer's post-purchase evaluation process
4. Identify the types of consumer buying decisions and explain how they relate to consumer involvement
5. Identify and understand cultural factors that affect consumer buying decisions
6. Identify and understand social factors that affect consumer buying decisions
7. Identify and understand individual factors that affect consumer buying decisions
8. Identify and understand the psychological factors that affect consumer buying decisions

Marketers have always been interested in how consumers spend their money. How they spend defines who they are. Cash-register receipts combined with interviews of consumers have produced spending data that reveal an evolving national portrait of consumption trends: concrete evidence of changing buying patterns, as well as shifts in consumers' beliefs and attitudes.

One trend that is showing considerable growth globally is the increasingly strong social conscience being shown by consumers both as individuals and as corporations. The latest figures from the US show that approximately 25 per cent of the adult population is beginning to make value-based choices in more and more product categories (Co-Op America 2004). Even non-traditional consumption areas of investment and banking are seeing the impact of socially conscious consumers. So what are these consumers seeking from their interactions?

Socially conscious consumers consider the origins of their purchases, preferring those that are organic, or that are made from ingredients that have come from developing countries where ethical trading relations have been

Journal of Research for Consumers on-line

Have a look at this interesting site. Not only does it provide informative and educational articles for academics and ordinary consumers about consumption issues, but it also provides links and information relating to social conscience issues for consumers. After browsing some of the information on this site (like the story about coffee) do you think you now might change your behaviour as a consumer?
www.jrconsumers.com/

Australian Ethical Investments on-line

The growing number of consumers with a social conscience has also created opportunities for investment organisations that offer a guaranteed investment portfolio. Have a look at his organisation and see how they have positioned themselves. Would you invest with them?
www.austethical.com.au/Home
www.jrconsumers.com/

established. They also want investment options that are certified as ethical and considerate of worldwide social issues. Even choice of clothing brands is considered by this segment who have been known to boycott or avoid certain brands because of the manufacturer's record on social issues such as the environment or working conditions.

So who are these people and how strong is this movement? Current research suggests that this market segment worldwide is growing (Couglan 2003), and that they definitely do have specific characteristics. While as a general group they represent a wide range of other socio-demographic segments in society, they do have in common the following: (1) they are more likely to be women (60 per cent); (2) they are likely to be older (over 35); (3) they are in the medium income range for western societies; (4) they are upper-middle class; (5) they are information junkies; (6) they are avid readers and radio listeners; (7) they are careful consumers; (8) they have a cognitive style (they think and question); (9) they see their home as a retreat or nest; (10) they have a desire for authentic and experiential purchases. Thus, key products that best reflect these values and are most attractive to this group occur in the areas of arts and culture, wellness health care, eco-travel, education, natural body care products and socially responsible businesses (Co-Op America 2004).

Even corporate consumers (those organisations who buy and sell products and services to other organisations) are influenced by this growing consumer trend. Companies that buy and use cocoa and coffee products are increasingly being pressured by their end-user consumers to make sure that they are dealing with fair trading groups that have been established to protect the rights and profits of small independent farmers producing these commodities in poor developing countries.

So why is this important for prospective marketing students to know? Well, to be effective marketers, you need to understand who your customers are and what makes them tick and what they get excited about (hopefully your product or service). So, as with this particular segment of the market, to be able to capitalise on market trends like this you need to understanding your customers better and know how they think. So let's look at this topic further.

Source: Adapted from Couglan, S. 2003, 'Consumers show moral support', *The Guardian*, December 13; and Co-Op, Co-Op America, 2004, 'Forty-Four Million Americans can't be wrong'.

The importance of understanding consumer behaviour

1 Explain why marketing managers should understand consumer behaviour

Consumers' product and service preferences are constantly changing. In order to address this constant state of flux and to create a proper marketing mix for a well-defined market, marketing managers must have a thorough knowledge of consumer behaviour. **Consumer behaviour** describes how you, the consumer, make purchase decisions and how you use and dispose of the purchased goods or services. The study of consumer behaviour also includes the analysis of factors that influence purchase decisions and product use.

Understanding how you, as a consumer, make purchase decisions can help marketing managers in several ways. For example, if a marketer of new cars knows, through research, that fuel consumption is the most important attribute to its potential customers when choosing a new car, then the company may consider this factor in their car designs in order to satisfy this need.

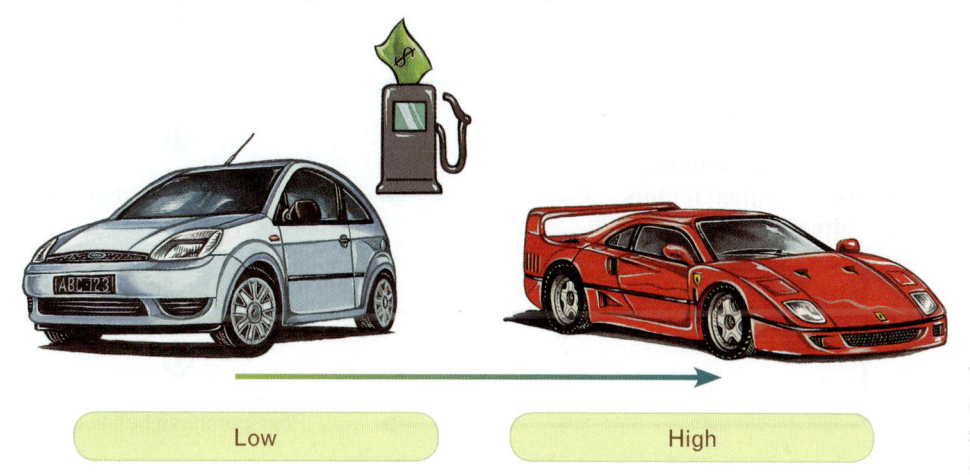

Level of importance of decision: Low → High

consumer behaviour
Processes a consumer uses to make purchase decisions, as well as to use and dispose of purchased goods and services; also includes factors that influence purchase decisions and the use of products.

The consumer decision-making continuum takes into account that some decisions are routine (such as buying petrol) and others are complex (such as buying a car).

However, if the marketer knows that this particular attribute does not produce a comparative advantage in the company's particular brand of car (in other words, there are other brands with better fuel consumption), and further, that this is not a feature that can be changed easily, then they may attempt to use different promotional techniques to influence customers' decision-making processes and encourage them to consider other features. For example, the manufacturer can advertise the car's maintenance-free features and sporty European styling, or perhaps its incredible safety options and internal spaciousness, while downplaying fuel consumption, in the hope that customers will see these features as being more important than fuel consumption.

The consumer decision-making process

When buying products, you, the consumer, generally follow a **consumer decision-making process**, shown in Exhibit 2.1. This process consists of five stages: (1) need recognition, (2) information search, (3) evaluation of alternatives, (4) purchase, and (5) post-purchase behaviour. These five steps represent a general process, which moves you from recognition of a product or service need to the final evaluation of a purchase.

This process is often used as a guide for studying how consumers make decisions. It is important to note that this guide does not assume that decisions will proceed in order through all of the steps of the process. In fact, the process can be exited at any time and a purchase may not even be made. Explanations as to why progression through these steps varies are offered at the end of this chapter, in the section on the types of consumer buying decisions. Before we address this issue, we will describe each step in the process in greater detail.

2 Analyse the components of the consumer decision-making process

consumer decision-making process
Step-by-step process used by consumers when buying goods or services.

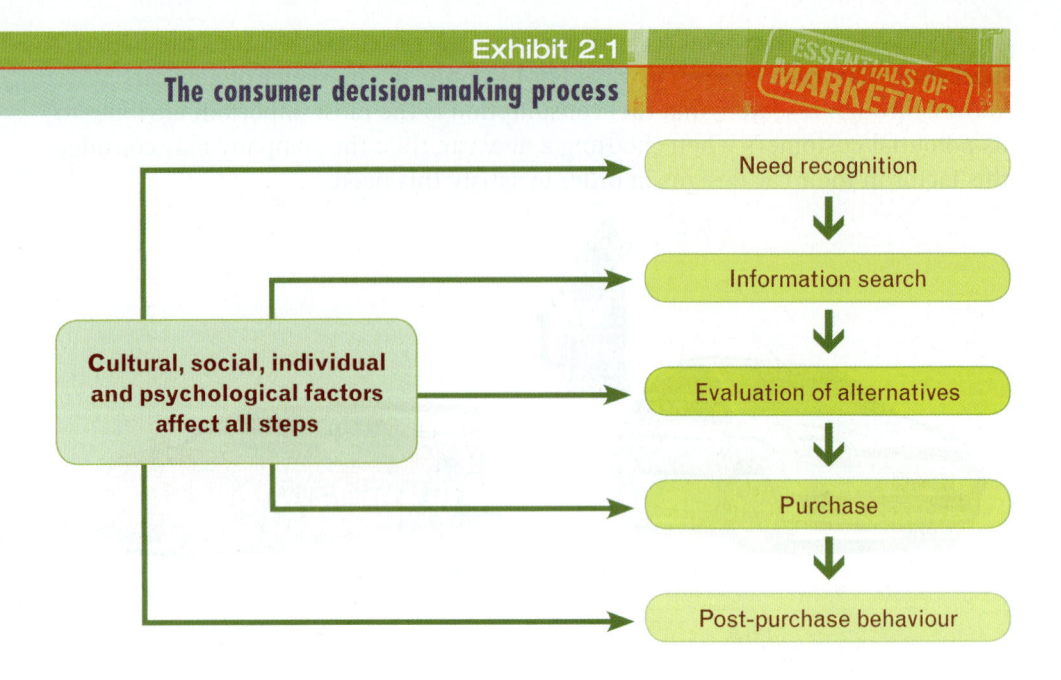

Exhibit 2.1
The consumer decision-making process

Cultural, social, individual and psychological factors affect all steps

- Need recognition
- Information search
- Evaluation of alternatives
- Purchase
- Post-purchase behaviour

Need recognition

The first stage in the consumer decision-making process is need recognition. **Need recognition** occurs when a consumer is faced with an imbalance between actual and desired states. For example, do you often feel thirsty after strenuous exercise? Has a television commercial for a new sporty style of car ever made you wish you could buy it? Do you ever get tempted to try Pantene shampoo just to see if your hair will really look as shiny as those women in the ads?

Need recognition is triggered when people are exposed to either an internal or an external **stimulus**. Hunger, desire and thirst are *internal stimuli*; the colour of a car, the design of a package, a brand name mentioned by a friend, an advertisement on television, or perfume worn by a stranger are considered *external stimuli*.

A marketing manager's objective is to get you (the consumer) to recognise an imbalance between your present state (actual state) and your future preferred state (desired state). They can do this on a simple level by understanding basic human drives and behaviour patterns. For example, if you have just finished playing a game of sport or perhaps a session at the gym or other form of strenuous exercise and you are thirsty, you may be encouraged to think about selecting a particular brand of sports drink to quench your thirst. This action could be based on an ad you saw where people in a similar situation also had a sports drink and felt refreshed:

- Actual state – tired and thirsty after exercise
- Desired state – feeling refreshed and vital
- Solution – drink a particular brand of sports drink.

On a more complex level, marketers can also attempt to stimulate perceived differences between a customer's actual and desired states and, in turn, stimulate customer demand, by stimulating a desire for products or services (or for features in existing products and services) that are not based on pure necessity. These desires are known as wants. A **want** exists when someone has an unfulfilled need and has determined that a particular good or service will satisfy it.

need recognition
Occurs when a consumer is faced with an imbalance between actual and desired states.

stimulus
Any unit of input affecting one or more of the five senses: sight, smell, taste, touch or hearing.

want
Recognition of an unfulfilled need and a product that will satisfy it.

Young children might want toys, video games and cricket equipment. Teenagers may want CDs, fashionable clothes and pizza. A want can be for a specific product or brand, or it can be for a certain attribute or feature of a product. For example, older consumers want goods and services that offer convenience, comfort and security. Remote-control appliances, home deliveries, speaker phones and motorised carts are all designed for comfort and convenience. Likewise, a transmitter that can signal an ambulance or the police if the person wearing it has an emergency, offers security for older consumers.

Need recognition is an imbalance between a consumer's actual state (tired and thirsty) and their ideal state (refreshed and vital).

Consumers recognise unfulfilled wants in various ways. The two most common occur when a current product isn't performing adequately or when people are about to run out of something that is generally kept on hand. Consumers may also recognise unfulfilled wants if they hear about or see a product whose features make it appear superior to the one they are currently using. Such wants are usually created by advertising and other promotional activities. For example, a young teenager may develop a strong desire for the new Sony PlayStation after seeing it on display in a store or advertised on television, or hearing about its features from a friend (non-marketing source).

Marketers selling their products in global markets must carefully observe the needs and wants of consumers in various regions. The Australian wine industry is a good example of this. Australian wine now outsells French wine in key markets like Britain and the US, because it is better adapted to consumer's tastes and partly because it is good value for money (Fuller 2004). So how did this happen, and how has the Australian wine industry managed to capture large slices of the European, Japanese and US wine-drinking markets in the space of just a few years?[1]

Part of the answer lies in understanding consumer behaviour. No one is claiming that Australia has the world's best or biggest wine industry, but it is an industry that listens to its consumers. Not only does Australian wine compare very favourably with its European counterparts in terms of taste and technical specifications, but Australian wine producers have concentrated on demystifying wine in an attempt to increase market share. Australian wine has names that the English-speaking market can pronounce, they have simple and attractive labels and, most importantly, they produce consistent styles of wine that people want to drink – liquid food, if you must.[2] The Australian wine industry is not attached to tradition, history or emotion; it is therefore likely to be immune to changes, which is not the case with the more established and older European wineries. The importance of staying in touch with your markets and understanding and then delivering on their changing needs and wants is critical, even if those

Information search

After recognising a need or want, consumers search for information about the various alternatives available to satisfy it. An information search can occur internally, externally or using a combination of both. **Internal information search** is the process of recalling information stored in the memory. This stored information stems largely from previous experience with a product. For example, if while shopping you encounter a brand of cake mix that you tried some time ago, by searching your memory, you can probably remember whether it tasted good and was easy to prepare.

internal information search
Process of recalling information stored in the memory.

Non-marketing-controlled information sources include personal experience, personal sources and public sources such as consumer reports like *Choice* magazine, produced by the Australian Consumers Association.

In contrast, an **external information search** seeks information from the outside environment. This external information can be from one of two sources: non-marketing-controlled and marketing-controlled. A **non-marketing-controlled information source** is one not associated with marketers promoting a product. A friend, for example, might recommend a Compaq laptop because he or she bought one and likes it. Non-marketing-controlled information sources include personal experience (trying or observing a new product), personal sources (family, friends, acquaintances and co-workers) and public sources, such as consumer reports and other rating organisations (such as *Choice* magazine). For example, in a recent study of consumer behaviour in relation to purchase of over-the-counter (OTC) medications, it was determined that most consumers rely heavily on the recommendations of doctors and pharmacists and more than half of those interviewed began using a medication on the advice of a pharmacist.[3] In this example, customers perceive doctors and pharmacists to be a non-biased, reliable source of information about OTC medications. However, in reality, pharmaceutical companies spend a lot of time and money cultivating these experts in an attempt to encourage them to support their particular brands.

external information search
Process of seeking information in the outside environment.

non-marketing-controlled information source
Product information source that is not associated with advertising or promotion.

Non-marketing-controlled information is often a key resource for consumers facing even the smallest of buying decisions. *Choice* magazine is a highly recognised publication produced by the Australian Consumers Association which performs extensive tests on a wide variety of consumer goods and services (www.choice.com.au).

A **marketing-controlled information source**, on the other hand, is biased towards a specific brand because it originates from marketers promoting that brand. Marketing-controlled information sources include mass-media advertising (radio, newspaper, television and magazine advertising), sales promotion (contests, displays, premiums and so forth), salespeople, product labels and packaging. Many consumers are wary about the information they receive from marketing-controlled sources, arguing that most marketing campaigns stress the positive attributes of the particular brand they promote and that they don't mention the brand's failings. These sentiments tend to be strongest among better-educated and higher-income consumers. For example, in relation to the OTC study mentioned earlier, only 13 per cent of those surveyed indicated that advertising was important in their decision to purchase OTC medications.

> **marketing-controlled information source**
> Product information source that originates with marketers promoting the product.

The extent to which an individual conducts an external search depends on the perceived risk of purchasing the product, which in turn is influenced by knowledge about the product or service being considered, prior experience with the type of purchase, the consumer's level of confidence in their decision-making ability and the level of interest in the product or service. Generally, the greater the perceived risk of the purchase, the greater the search by the consumer for alternative brands. For example, assume a consumer wants to buy a new car. The decision is a relatively risky one, mainly because of the cost involved and also because this is usually a purchase that would not be made regularly and therefore the consumer is likely to be inexperienced in the purchase process. Finally, a consumer who begins to search for information about cars in order to make a purchase is likely to be highly interested in the purchase. The level of confidence in their ability to make a good decision about a car purchase without support from others (friends, family or experts) will also be low. In addition, many of us know little about the mechanics of cars, so we feel apprehensive about any information that we may receive that deals with engine performance or other technical details.

In this case, the consumer would be motivated to search for information about different models, different features, fuel consumption, durability, passenger capacity and so forth. They may also decide to gather more information about models and brands of car than they may need, because the trouble and time expended in finding this information is less expensive than the cost of buying the wrong car. In this type of purchase, they are also more likely to combine internal and external search and would probably include a lot of non-marketer-controlled information sources in their searching (advice from friends, family and so forth).

By contrast, a consumer is less likely to expend great effort in searching for the right kind of bath soap. If they make the wrong selection, the cost is minimal and they will have an opportunity to make another selection in a short period of time. It is a decision process that they have experience in (make regularly) and they are confident in their ability to evaluate the options available because the level of technical information is minimal.

There are, therefore, four major factors that influence a consumer's level of perceived risk and that will, in turn, affect their information search behaviour:

consumer knowledge, confidence in their decision-making ability, product experience and the level of interest in the outcome (see Exhibit 2.2). Consumers who perceive higher risk with a purchase expend more effort in an external information search and consult a greater number of different types of information sources than do those who perceive lower levels of risk.

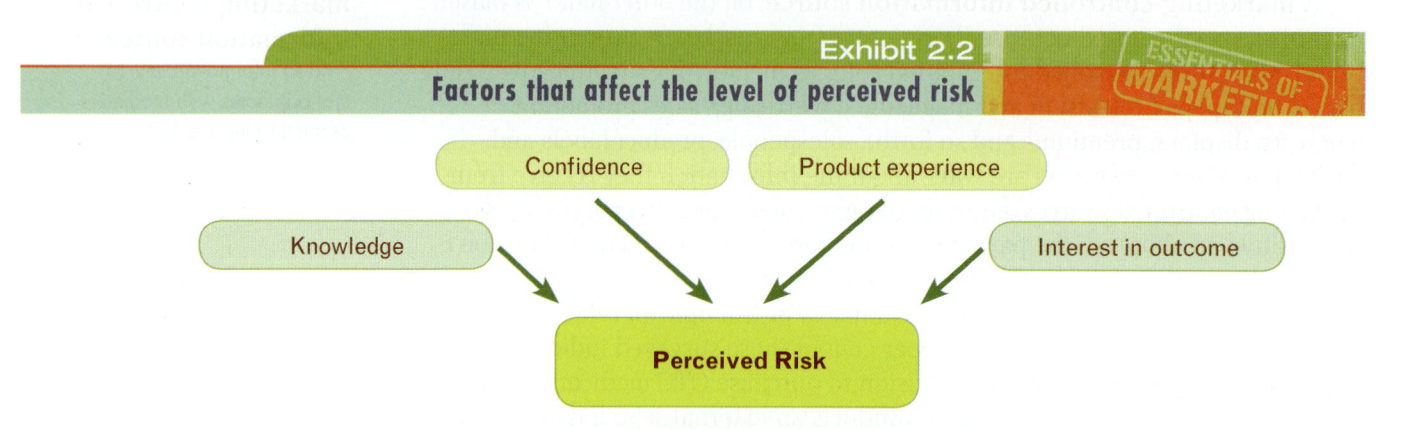

Exhibit 2.2
Factors that affect the level of perceived risk

Knowledge, Confidence, Product experience, Interest in outcome → Perceived Risk

A consumer's information search should yield a group of brands, called the buyer's **evoked set** (or **consideration set**), which are the most preferred options. From the evoked set, the options will be further evaluated and a choice finally made. Consumers don't consider all the brands available to them in a product category, but they do seriously consider a much smaller sub-set of brands. For example, there are dozens of brands of shampoo and close to 200 types of car available in Australia and New Zealand, yet most consumers seriously contemplate only about four shampoos and no more than five brands of car when faced with a purchase decision. It is a challenge, and the ultimate responsibility, for marketers to ensure that their brands are, at worst, in the consideration set for consumers and, at best, in the evoked set: brands that are not in these groups are not even considered in the evaluation stage by consumers.

evoked set (consideration set)
Group of brands, resulting from an information search, from which a buyer can choose.

Evaluation of alternatives and purchase

After gathering information and constructing an evoked set of products, the consumer can now make a decision. They will use the information stored in their memory and information obtained from outside sources to develop a set of criteria by which they judge the options available. One way to begin narrowing the number of choices in the evoked set is to pick a product attribute and then examine all products in the set to see which ones don't have that attribute. For example, assume that John is thinking about buying a new CD player. He is interested in it having a remote control and the ability to hold several discs at one time (product attributes), so he excludes all CD players without these features. Marketers attempt to attract customers by communicating the attributes their brand possesses and excels at.

Another way to narrow the number of choices is to use 'cut-offs'. These are minimum or maximum levels of an attribute that an option must have to be considered further. Suppose John still must choose from a wide array of remote control, multi-disc CD players. He then considers another product attribute, such as price. Given the amount of money he has saved, John decides he cannot spend more than $200. Therefore, he can exclude all CD players priced above $200. A final way to narrow the choices is to rank the attributes under consideration in order of importance and evaluate the products based on how well they perform on the most important attributes. To reach a final decision, John would pick the most important attributes, such as a remote control or ability to hold several discs at a time, weigh the merits of each brand, and then evaluate alternative players on those criteria.

If new brands are added to an evoked set, the consumer's evaluation of the existing brands in that set changes. As a result, certain brands in the original set may become more desirable. For example, suppose John sees two CD players, one priced at $100 and one at $150. At the time, he may judge the $150 player as too expensive and choose not to purchase it. However, if he then adds to his list of alternatives (evoked set) another CD player that is priced at $250, he may come to judge the $150 one as less expensive and therefore decide to purchase it.

The goal of the marketing manager is to determine which attributes are most important in influencing a consumer's choice. Several factors may collectively affect a consumer's evaluation of products. A single attribute, such as price, may not adequately explain how consumers form their evoked set.[4] Moreover, attributes thought to be important to the marketer may not be very important to the consumer. For example, one study found that car warranty coverage was the least important factor in a consumer's purchase of a car, yet many car manufacturers still stress this attribute in their marketing communications.[5]

A brand name can also have a significant impact on a consumer's ultimate choice. Consumers use brand names either consciously or subconsciously to help them simplify their decision-making processes. A brand is an intangible element of a product or service, and is defined by consumers' impressions of the people who use it, as well as by their own experience. There are more than 6000 brand names listed in Australia, so you can well imagine the competition these brands face to ensure that they attract their chosen customers, and then maintain that relevance and attraction.[6] A brand is a manufacturer's promise of what they can achieve for us. Consumers may come to trust certain brands based on their experiences with them.

Following the evaluation of alternatives, consumers then decide which product to buy, where to buy it and how to pay for it, or they might decide not to buy a product at all. If the decision to make a purchase is made, then the next step in the process is an evaluation of the product after the purchase.

Post-purchase behaviour

When buying products, consumers expect certain outcomes from the purchase. How well these expectations are met determines whether they are satisfied or dissatisfied with the purchase. Consider this example: a person buys a used car with somewhat low expectations about the car's actual performance. Surprisingly, the car turns out to be one of the best cars they have ever owned. Thus, the buyer's satisfaction is high because their fairly low expectations were exceeded. On the other hand, a consumer who buys a brand-new car would expect it to perform especially well. But if the car turns out to be a 'lemon' (poor performer), they will be very dissatisfied because their high expectations have not been met. Price often creates high expectations. One study found that higher monthly pay TV bills were associated with greater expectations for cable service. Over time, pay TV subscribers tended to drop the premium-priced channels because their high expectations were not being met.[7] Smart marketers have learned that it is often better to under-promote a product and then over-deliver so as to help increase the chances of their customers feeling satisfied.

3 Explain the consumer's post-purchase evaluation process

cognitive dissonance
Inner tension that a consumer experiences after recognising an inconsistency between behaviour and values or opinions.

For the marketing manager, an important element in the consumer's post-purchase evaluation is to reduce any lingering doubts that the decision was sound. When people recognise inconsistency between their values or opinions and their behaviour, they feel an inner tension called **cognitive dissonance**. For example, suppose you were to spend half your monthly salary on a new high-tech stereo system. If you stopped to think how much you have spent, you would probably feel some level of dissonance. Dissonance occurs because the person knows the purchased product has some disadvantages as well as some advantages. In the case of the stereo, the disadvantage of cost battles the advantage of technological superiority. Consumers ask themselves, 'Did I make the right decision?' Consumers can be satisfied with their product performance and still feel dissonance. You might love your new stereo, and it may have fantastic sound. But you still feel concerned about its cost and whether you should have bought it.

Consumers reduce dissonance by justifying their decision. They might seek new information that reinforces positive ideas about the purchase, avoid information that contradicts their decision, or reverse the original decision by returning the product. People who have just bought a new car often read more advertisements for the car they have just bought than for other cars in order to reduce dissonance. In some instances, people deliberately seek contrary information in order to refute it and reduce dissonance. Dissatisfied customers sometimes rely on word of mouth – letting friends and family know they are displeased, all in an effort to reduce their levels of cognitive dissonance.

Marketing managers can help to reduce dissonance through effective communication. For example, a customer-service manager may slip a note inside the package congratulating the buyer on making a wise decision. Post-purchase letters sent by manufacturers and dissonance-reducing statements in instruction booklets may help customers to feel at ease with their purchase. Advertising that displays the product's superiority over competing brands or offering product guarantees can also help to relieve the possible dissonance of someone who has already bought the product. The car dealers Infiniti, for example, recently offered refunds to new-car buyers within three days of their purchase if they decided they were dissatisfied. Dealers also offered a price protection plan: if prices went down on a new Infiniti, anyone who paid more than the lower price in the previous 30 days was entitled to a refund of the difference.[8]

Types of consumer buying decisions and involvement

4 Identify the types of consumer buying decisions and explain how they relate to consumer involvement

involvement
Amount of time and effort a buyer invests in the search, evaluation and decision processes of consumer behaviour.

All consumer buying decisions fall along a continuum with three broad categories: routine response behaviour, limited decision-making and extensive decision-making (see Exhibit 2.3). Products and services in these three categories can best be described in terms of five factors: (1) level of consumer involvement; (2) length of time to make a decision; (3) cost of the good or service; (4) degree of information search; and (5) the number of alternatives considered. The level of consumer involvement is perhaps the most significant determinant in classifying buying decisions. **Involvement** is the amount of time and effort a potential buyer invests in the search, evaluation and decision processes of consumer behaviour.

Exhibit 2.3
Continuum of consumer buying decisions

	Routine	Limited	Extensive
Involvement	low	low to moderate	high
Time	short	short to moderate	long
Cost	low	low to moderate	high
Information search	internal only	mostly internal	internal and external
Number of alternatives	one	few	many

Frequently purchased, low-cost goods and services are generally associated with **routine response behaviour** (or **habitual buying behaviour**). These goods and services can also be called low-involvement products because you would normally spend little time on searching for information about these products and little time on the actual decision before making the purchase. Usually, buyers are familiar with several different brands in the product category but stick with one brand. Consumers engaged in routine response behaviour normally don't experience problem recognition until they are exposed to advertising or see the product displayed on a store shelf, or are faced with an out-of-stock situation. Your parents, for example, would not have stood at the cereal shelf in the grocery store for 20 minutes thinking about which brand of cereal to buy for you when you were a child. Instead, they would most likely have walked by the shelf, found the family's usual brand and put it into the trolley.

Goods and services that are purchased regularly and that are not considered expensive can also be associated with **limited decision-making**. In this type of decision-making, there are low levels of involvement (although higher than in routine decisions) because consumers do expend moderate effort in searching for information or in considering various alternatives.

Suppose your family's usual brand of cereal, Kellogg's Rice Bubbles, is unavailable in the supermarket. Completely out of cereal at home, your parent must now select another brand. Before making a final selection, he or she may pull from the shelf several brands similar to Kellogg's Rice Bubbles, such as Rice Crispies and Rice Puffs, to compare their nutritional value and kilojoules and to decide whether the family would like the new cereal.

Consumers practise **extensive decision-making** when buying an unfamiliar, expensive product or an infrequently bought item. This process is the most complex type of consumer buying decision and is associated with high involvement on the part of the consumer.

This process resembles the model outlined in Exhibit 2.1. These consumers want to make the right decision, so they want to know as much as they can about the product category and available brands. People usually experience cognitive dissonance only when buying high-involvement products. Buyers use several criteria for evaluating their options and spend much time seeking information. Buying a home or a car, for example, requires extensive decision-making.

The type of decision-making that consumers use to purchase a product does not necessarily remain constant. For example, if a routinely purchased product no longer satisfies, consumers may practise limited or extensive decision-making to switch to another brand. And people who first use extensive decision-making may

---

routine response behaviour (habitual buying behaviour)
Type of decision-making exhibited by consumers buying frequently purchased, low-cost goods and services; requires little search and decision time.

limited decision-making
Type of decision-making that requires a moderate amount of time for gathering information and deliberating about an unfamiliar brand in a familiar product category.

extensive decision-making
Most complex type of consumer decision-making, used when buying an unfamiliar, expensive product or an infrequently bought item; requires use of several criteria for evaluating options and much time for seeking information.

then use limited or routine decision-making for future purchases. For example, a new mother may first extensively evaluate several brands of disposable nappies before selecting one. Subsequent purchases of nappies will then become routine.

Factors determining the level of consumer involvement

The level of involvement in the purchase depends on five factors: previous experience, interest, perceived risk, situation and social visibility.

Previous experience

When you have had previous experience with a product or service, the level of involvement typically decreases. After repeated product trials, you learn to make quick choices. Because you are familiar with the product and know whether it will satisfy your needs, you become less involved in the purchase. For example, if you had certain pollen allergies you would typically buy the sinus medicine that has relieved your symptoms in the past.

Interest

Involvement is directly related to consumer interests, as in cars, music, movies, bicycling or electronics. Naturally, these areas of interest vary from one individual to another, and as the level of interest increases the level of involvement also increases. Although some people have little interest in nursing homes, a person with elderly parents in poor health may be very interested.

Perceived risk of negative consequences

As the perceived risk of purchasing a product increases, so does the level of involvement. The types of risks that concern consumers include financial risk, social risk and psychological risk. Financial risk is exposure to loss of wealth or purchasing power. Because high risk is associated with high-priced purchases, consumers tend to become extremely involved. Therefore, price and involvement are usually directly related: as price increases, so does the level of involvement. For example, someone who is thinking of buying a home will normally spend much time and effort in finding the right one. Consumers take social risks when they buy products that can affect other people's social opinions of them (for example, driving an old, beaten-up car or wearing unstylish clothes). Buyers undergo psychological risk if they feel that making the wrong decision might cause some concern or anxiety. For example, should a working parent hire a babysitter or enrol the child in a day-care centre?

Situation

The circumstances of a purchase may temporarily transform a low-involvement decision into a high-involvement one. High involvement comes into play when the consumer perceives risk in a specific situation. For example, an individual might routinely buy low-priced brands of spirits and wine. However, when the boss visits, the consumer might make a high-involvement decision and buy more prestigious brands.

Social visibility

Involvement also increases as the social visibility of a product increases. Social visibility includes clothing (especially designer labels), jewellery, cars, furniture, and even our homes or the suburbs we live in. All these items make a statement about the purchaser and, therefore, carry a social risk.

Marketing implications of involvement

Marketing strategy varies depending on the level of involvement associated with the product. For high-involvement product purchases, marketing managers have several responsibilities. First, promotion to the target market should be extensive and informative. A good ad gives consumers the information they need for making the purchase decision, as well as specifying the benefits and unique advantages of owning the product. For example, manufacturers of high-tech computers and peripheral equipment such as scanners, printers and modems run lengthy ads that detail technical information about such attributes as performance, resolution and speed.

For low-involvement product purchases, consumers may not recognise their wants until they are in the store. Therefore, in-store promotion is an important tool when promoting low-involvement products. Marketing managers have to focus on package design so that the product will be eye-catching and easily recognised on the shelf. Examples of products that take this approach are Campbell's soups, Omo detergent, Cracker Barrel cheese and Heinz tomato sauce. In-store displays also stimulate sales of low-involvement products. A good display can explain the product's purpose and prompt recognition of a want. Displays of health and beauty-aid items in supermarkets have been known to increase sales many times above normal. Coupons, cents-off deals and two-for-one offers also effectively promote low-involvement items.

Super Cheap Auto aims high

Entrepreneurial INSIGHTS

Named the national entrepreneur in the retail, consumer and industrial products for 2004, Super Cheap Auto is a true Australian success story. Being able to walk that divide between Super Cheap Auto's customer base and the 'big end of town' is one of the secrets behind the automotive parts and accessories retailer's huge growth in a highly competitive category. When Bob Thorn joined Super Cheap Auto (SCA) in 1993, it boasted eight Queensland stores. In November 2003, SCA opened nine Australasian stores — in one day. The amazing growth of the corporate-owned chain — 27 per cent compound over the past decade — stands as testament to Thorn's exceptional entrepreneurial and management skills (matched by his racing skills; Thorn placed fifth in Bathurst in 1998). SCA's listing on the Australian Stock Exchange earlier this year further highlights his grand vision for the business.

Thorn puts the success, among other things, down to the strength of team culture within the organisation and an understanding of their customers and the market opportunities. Customers have really taken to the Super Cheap Auto shopping difference and have relished the increase in product variety. Super Cheap Auto is the DIY customer's paradise. The SCA website states that their products relate to the car, the garage, the trailer, the boat and the yard — covering everything from automotive parts and accessories, handyman items, tools and equipment to 4x4 and marine — and that they are dedicated to the needs and expectations of our ever expanding customer base. To this end, in 2004 SCA introduced a new range of products specifically aimed at the growing market of women who enjoyed the chance to add their own personal style to their cars. 'We have expanded our range to provide more choice for women who are looking to "dress up" their car and give it a signature look,' Bob Thorn, managing director said. 'The range provides women with the opportunity to personalise the interior of their vehicle, and give it that woman's touch with a bit of flair and colour added to the interior.'[9]

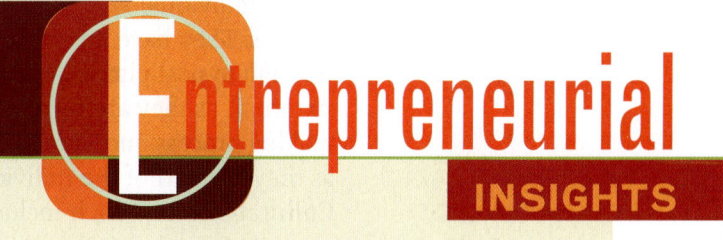

Super Cheap Auto on-line

Can you identify any recent marketing strategies that Super Cheap Auto appears to be using? What impact do you think the Internet will have on Super Cheap's market penetration? www.supercheapauto.com

Linking a product to a higher-involvement issue is another tactic that marketing managers can use to increase the sales of a low-involvement product. For example, many food products are no longer just nutritious but also low in fat or cholesterol. Although packaged food may normally be a low-involvement product, reference to health issues raises the involvement level. Rolled oats have been around for hundreds of years. To take advantage of today's interest in health and low-fat foods, Uncle Tobys is using health appeals in its advertising, claiming that soluble fibre from porridge, as part of a low-fat, low-cholesterol diet, may reduce the risk of heart disease. Many entrepreneurs have managed to spot market opportunities in advance of their competitors and thus have been able to create an almost unbeatable niche for their products. See the Entrepreneurial insights box for the story of Super Cheap Auto – an Australian success story in terms of understanding customer's needs and innovative marketing strategies.

Factors influencing consumer buying decisions

The consumer decision-making process does not occur in a vacuum. Cultural, social, individual and psychological factors strongly influence the decision process. They have an effect from the time a consumer perceives a stimulus through to post-purchase behaviour. Cultural and social factors are defined as 'external', as they are factors that are 'outside' the individual and the decision-making process. Individual and psychological factors are defined as 'internal', as they are part of the individual and are 'inside' the decision-making process. Cultural factors, which include culture and values, subculture and social class, exert the broadest influence over consumer decision-making. Social factors sum up the social interactions between a consumer and influential groups of people, such as reference groups, opinion leaders and family members. Individual factors, which include gender, age, family life-cycle stage, personality, self-concept and lifestyle, are unique to each individual and play a major role in the types of products and services consumers want. Psychological factors determine how consumers perceive and interact with their environments and influence the ultimate decisions they make. These factors include perception, motivation, learning, beliefs and attitudes. Exhibit 2.4 summarises these influences.

External influences on consumer buying decisions

The first group of factors that influence consumer decision-making are external factors. These factors exert the broadest and deepest influence over consumer behaviour and decision-making. Marketers must understand the way culture and its accompanying values, as well as a person's subcultures and social class, influence their buying behaviour.

Exhibit 2.4
Factors that affect the consumer decision-making process

Cultural factors
- Culture and values
- Subculture
- Social class

Social Factors
- Reference groups
- Opinion leaders
- Family

Individual factors
- Gender
- Age and family life-cycle stage
- Personality, self-concept and lifestyle

Psychological factors
- Perception
- Motivation
- Learning Beliefs and attitudes

→ Consumer decision-making process → Buy/don't buy

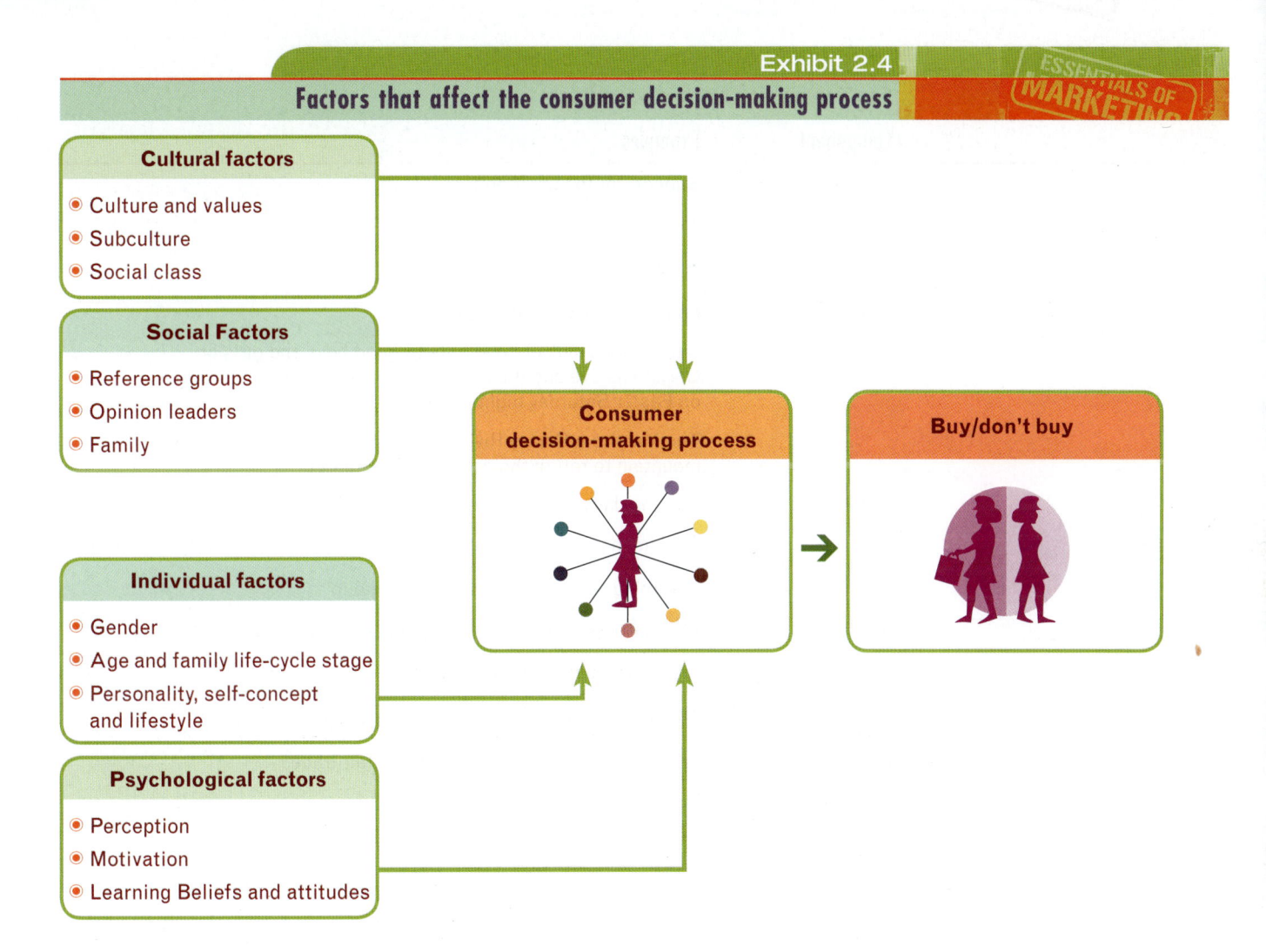

Culture and values

Culture is the essential character of a society that distinguishes it from other cultural groups. The underlying elements of every culture are the values, language, myths, customs, rituals and laws that shape the behaviour of the culture, as well as the artefacts, or products, of that behaviour as they are transmitted from one generation to the next. Exhibit 2.5 lists some of the defining components of Australian culture.

Culture is pervasive. Cultural values and influences are the ocean in which individuals swim, and of which most are completely unaware. What people eat, how they dress, what they think and feel, and what languages they speak are all dimensions of culture. Culture encompasses all the things consumers do without conscious choice because their culture's values, customs and rituals are ingrained in their daily habits.

Culture is functional. Human interaction creates values and prescribes acceptable behaviour for each culture. By establishing common expectations, culture gives order to society. Sometimes these expectations are coded into laws. For example, drivers in our culture must stop at a red light. At other times these expectations are taken for granted. For example, hospitals are open 24 hours, while traditionally banks are open only during weekday office hours.

5 Identify and understand the cultural factors that affect consumer buying decisions

culture
Set of values, norms, attitudes and other meaningful symbols that shape human behaviour and the artefacts, or products, of that behaviour as they are transmitted from one generation to the next.

Exhibit 2.5
Components of Australian culture

Component	Examples
Values	Support for the underdog
	Tall poppy syndrome
	A 'fair go'
Language	English is the official language.
Myths	Santa Claus delivers presents to good boys and girls on Christmas Eve and the Easter Bunny delivers chocolate eggs on Easter Saturday night.
	The Man from Snowy River galloped down an impenetrable mountain to return the colt from Old Regret.
Customs	Bathing daily
	Shaking hands when greeting new people
	Returning a shout when drinking at a pub
Rituals	Playing cricket in the back yard at Christmas time
	Christmas lunch with the family
	The man always cooks the meat at a barbecue.
Laws	The *Trade Practices Act* provides for fair trade.
Material artefacts	Diamond engagement rings
	The boxing kangaroo and 'Fatso' the fat-arse wombat

value
Enduring belief that a specific mode of conduct is personally or socially preferable to another mode of conduct.

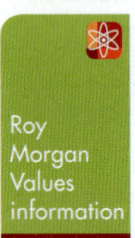

Roy Morgan Values information on-line
Go to the Roy Morgan Values Segments site and see what the latest research says about the core values of Australian society. Which group do you fit into and why do you think so?
www.roymorgan.com.au/products/values
Take the on-line VALS personality test to see where you fit in.
www.future.sri.com/VALS/presurvey.shtml

Culture is learned. Individuals are not born knowing the values and norms of their society. Instead, they learn what is acceptable from family, teachers and friends. As members of our society, children learn to shake hands when they greet someone, to drive on the left-hand side of the road and to call cooked chicken a 'chook'.

Culture is dynamic. It adapts to changing needs and an evolving environment. The rapid growth of technology in the last hundred years has accelerated the rate of cultural change. TV has changed entertainment patterns and family communication and has heightened public awareness of political and other news events. Automation has increased the amount of leisure time we have and, in some ways, has changed the traditional work ethic. Cultural norms will continue to evolve because of our need for social patterns that solve problems.

The most defining element of a culture is its **values** – the enduring beliefs shared by a society that a specific mode of conduct is personally or socially preferable to another mode of conduct. People's value systems have a major effect on their consumer behaviour.

Consumers with similar value systems tend to react alike to prices and other marketing-related inducements. Values also correspond to consumption patterns. People who want to protect the environment try to buy only products that won't harm it. Values can also influence consumers' TV viewing habits or the magazines they read. For example, people who strongly object to violence avoid crime shows and those who oppose pornography don't buy *Penthouse* or *Playboy*, nor do they watch *Sex and the City*. The Roy Morgan Australian Values Segments, or those that are central to the Australian way of life, are presented in Exhibit 2.6.

Exhibit 2.6
The Roy Morgan Australian Values Segments™

Young Optimism	This group comprises students and young professionals who are career-oriented – they are ambitious, are progressive thinkers, and tend to be active people who participate in sports, travel, music and socialising activities.
Socially Aware	Australians in this socio-economic group are early adopters and influencers who are socially active, community-minded and progressive. They need a lot of information before making a purchase decision.
Something Better	Competitive and ambitious, they seek the better things in life, often extending their budget by using credit cards to display images of their success. They seek more power, improved status and security.
Visible Achievement	Career- and success-motivated people who work for stimulation and financial reward. Family-focused, this value segment seeks quality and value for money.
Look at Me	Younger, unsophisticated and active people, who are highly conscious of image and fashion. Self-centred and peer-driven, they spend 100 per cent of what they earn.
Conventional Family	Younger families whose lives centre around marriage and raising a family. They strive to build homes and to improve their family's standard of living. They enjoy spending time with friends and family.
Traditional Family	Australia's largest group aged 50-plus, with grown-up families and contented home lives. They enjoy spending time with grandchildren, are financially secure and want community respect.
Real Conservatism	Mature people who hold conservative social, moral and ethical values and like a safe, ordered and predictable society. They are asset-rich, income-poor.
A Fairer Deal	This group contains unskilled and semi-skilled workers aged less than 35 years. They tend to be blue-collar people with financial insecurity, which creates a pessimistic view of life.
Basic Needs	Older, mainly retired people, who hold conservative moral, social and religious values and look for security and control of their lives. Their reduced expectations of life are in line with their reduced income.

Source: Neal, Quester and Hawkins, *Consumer Behaviour: Implications for Marketing Strategy*, 3rd edn (Sydney: McGraw-Hill Irwin, 2002), p. 325.

The personal values of target consumers have important implications for marketing managers. When marketers understand the core values that underlie the attitudes that shape the buying patterns of Australia's consumers and how these values were moulded by experiences, they can then target their message more effectively. For example, the personal value systems of matures, baby boomers, generation Xers and generation Ys are all quite different. The key to understanding matures, or people born before 1945, is recognising the impact of the Depression and the Second World War on their lives. Facing these two immense challenges shaped a generation characterised by discipline, self-denial, financial and social conservatism, and a sense of obligation. Baby boomers, those people born in the bountiful postwar period between 1945 and 1964, believe they are entitled to the wealth and opportunity that seemed endless in their youth. Generation Xers, or baby busters, are very accepting of diversity and individuality. They are also a very entrepreneurial-driven generation, ready to tackle life's challenges for themselves rather than as part of a crowd.[10]

Values represent what is important in people's lives. Therefore, marketers watch carefully for shifts in consumers' values over time. For example, the increase in the value of 'doing it yourself' (DIY) in the Australian culture has seen the upsurge in these types of television programs and associated magazines such as *Better Homes and Gardens*, *Live This* and so on. This trend has even influenced

Better Homes and Gardens on-line

Have a look at this site and see the evidence of the DIY values popular in Australia at the present time. Now look at the Great Outdoors site. Are there any similarities? What do you think the next popular value change might be with Australian consumers?
www.bhg.com.au/aptrix/bhg.nsf/Content/Home+Page
www.greatoutdoors.i7.com.au

Australian's love of travel and leisure, with DIY travel shows such as *The Great Outdoors* and *Getaway* showing viewers how to organise and make the most of their overseas and domestic travel.

Understanding culture differences

Underlying core values can vary across cultures. For example, Asian cultures place high emphasis on social harmony, Americans on an individual's rights and responsibilities, and Australians on fair reward for fair effort. In a survey of Asian and American business executives, it was noted that Asian businesspeople place hard work, respect for learning and honesty high among their values. American businesspeople, by contrast, ranked freedom of expression as their most highly rated value – an issue that did not even rate with the Asians in the sample.[11] Other areas where cultural differences can impact marketing decisions are relationships with colour, language differences and differences in perception of time and space.

As more companies expand their operations globally, the need to understand the cultures of foreign countries becomes more important. Marketers should become familiar with the culture and adapt to it. What's fashionable in Boston could be a flop in Mumbai, or even in Sydney, if marketers are not sensitive to the nuances of the local culture. Read about the experiences several companies have had in adapting their products to foreign cultures in the Global perspectives box.

Pokemon has emerged as a subcultural phenomenon with children all over the world. They have their own language and a range of behaviours that also result from membership of the group.

Global PERSPECTIVES

The pace of life and use of time around the world

How consumers view and use time varies greatly across cultures. These measures relate to the deeply rooted values that each culture shares.

Several researchers have been studying the tempo of life in other cultures as well as how people spend their time. Robert Levine, professor of psychology at California State University, Fresno, in the United States, has been studying the tempo of life in other cultures for over a decade. John Robinson, a sociology professor from the University of Maryland at College Park, has been involved in the Americans' Use of Time Project since its beginnings in 1965. Here is what these two researchers have found on how Americans and other cultures view and use time.

From his research, Levine developed three measures of the pace of life: (1) walking speed – the speed with which pedestrians in downtown areas walk a distance of 60 feet (approximately 20 metres); (2) work speed – how quickly postal clerks complete a standard request to purchase a stamp; and (3) accuracy of public clocks. Data were collected in at least one large city in each of 31 nations around the world to measure each country's pace of life.

Japan and Western European countries scored fastest overall, with Switzerland achieving the distinction of first place. Bank clocks in Switzerland, for example, were off by an average of only 19 seconds. Following Switzerland were Ireland, Germany, Japan, Italy, England, Sweden, Austria and the Netherlands. The United States, represented in the survey by New York City, scored a respectable sixth place on walking speed, but ranked twenty-third on postal times and twentieth on clock accuracy, for an overall rank of sixteenth place.

There were few surprises at the slow end of the list, where the last eight ranks were occupied by non-industrialised countries from Africa, Asia, the Middle East and Latin America. Slowness in countries such as Brazil, Indonesia and Mexico, all of which fell to the bottom of the pace-of-life scale, seeps into the fabric of daily life. Brazilians not only expect a casual approach to time, but also seem to have abandoned any semblance of fidelity to the clock. When asked how long they would wait for a late arriver to show up at a nephew's birthday party, for example, Brazilians said they would hold on for an average of 129 minutes – over two hours! Few Brazilians wear watches, and the watches they do wear are often inaccurate.

How people spend their time also varies from culture to culture. For example, time-use specialists often refer to France, Germany and other Western European countries as 'eating and sleeping cultures' because Europeans spend much more time than Americans or Asians on these two activities. Europeans also work fewer hours per week and enjoy more vacation time, up to six weeks' mandatory vacation in some European countries. In Sweden, vacation time goes as high as eight weeks of the year. In contrast, people in Japan and the United States spend more time working and take fewer vacations than their European counterparts. Workers in Japan, for example, put in an annual average of 202 hours more than workers in the United States and 511 hours more than workers in Germany. In a study comparing people living in the Netherlands to people in California, the Dutch spend much less time than Californians do working, travelling, shopping and watching television. Instead, the Dutch spend their time on entertainment and social activities, education, childcare, sports, hobbies and housework.

How Americans spend their time also varies among ethnic subcultures. Over the decades that John Robinson has been studying how Americans use time, he has found distinct differences in how African-American, Asian, Hispanic and non-Hispanic white subcultures in the United States spend their time. This phenomenon reflects in part on their value systems. African-Americans, for example, tend to spend more time on religious activities, spending almost twice as much time going to church as whites do. Whites spend the most time on housework, Asians spend the most time on education, and Hispanics spend the most time on childcare.

All cultures have something to learn from others' conceptions of time. Without fully understanding a cultural context, marketers are likely to misinterpret its people's motives. The result, inevitably, is conflict. Marketers who use sales personnel to sell in other countries where the pace of life and the use of time vary greatly must consider the customs of each culture. For example, marketers from a relatively fast-paced culture such as the United States can blunder badly when selling to slower-paced Mexican neighbours.

Marketers can adjust to another culture's sense of time by learning to translate appointment times. For example, is it appropriate to arrive a little late or is punctuality important? In Mexico it is understood that you should arrive late when invited to a social function. Additionally, marketers should understand the line between work time and social time. Recall that in the United States, the typical ratio of time spent on-task and time spent socialising on the job is about 80:20. But in countries such as India and Nepal, the balance is closer to 50:50.

One of the hardest aspects of time for people of fast cultures to assimilate is the move from 'clock time' to 'event time'. Clock time uses the hour on the clock to schedule activities, and event time allows activities to transpire according to their own spontaneous schedule. A move from clock time to event time, however, requires a complete shift of consciousness and entails the suspension of industrialised society's golden rule: 'Time is money.' Middle Eastern people, for example, resist fixed schedules, viewing them as rude and insulting. Americans, Japanese and Europeans, on the other hand, are very tied to clock time in their daily life.[12]

subculture
Homogeneous group of people who share elements of the overall culture as well as unique elements of their own group.

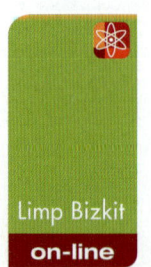

Limp Bizkit on-line

What kind of marketing program could you design to attract the subculture of Limp Bizkit followers? Visit their website to see how marketers are currently doing this. What other elements of the site could help you to design a successful program?
www.limpbizkit.com

social class
Group of people in a society who are considered nearly equal in status or community esteem, who regularly socialise among themselves, both formally and informally, and who share behavioural norms.

Subculture

A culture can be divided into subcultures on the basis of demographic characteristics, geographic regions, political beliefs, religious beliefs, national and ethnic background, religious beliefs and political beliefs. A **subculture** is a homogeneous group of people who share elements of the overall culture, as well as cultural elements unique to their own group. Within subcultures, people's attitudes, values and purchase decisions are even more similar than they are within the broader culture. Subcultural differences may result in considerable variation within a culture in what, how, when and where people buy goods and services.

Identifying subcultures can be a difficult task for a marketing manager. If they can be identified, marketers can design products and services to meet the needs and wants of these specific market segments.

Social class

Australia, like other societies, does have a **social class** system. A social class is a group of people who are considered nearly equal in status or community esteem, who regularly socialise among themselves both formally and informally, and who share behavioural norms.

A number of techniques have been used to measure social class, and a number of criteria have been used to define it. The majority of Australians today define themselves as middle class, regardless of their actual income or educational attainment. This phenomenon is most likely due to the fact that working-class Australians tend to aspire to the middle-class lifestyle, while some of those who do achieve affluence may downwardly aspire to respectable middle-class status as a matter of principle.[13] Attaining goals and achieving status and prestige are important to middle-class consumers. People falling into the middle class live in the gap between the haves and the have-nots. They aspire to the lifestyle of the more affluent, but are constrained by the economic realities and cautious attitudes they share with the working class.

Marketers are interested in social class for two main reasons. First, social class often indicates which medium to use for advertising. Suppose an insurance company seeks to sell its policies to middle-class families. It might advertise during the local evening news, because middle-class families tend to watch more television than other classes do. If the company wants to sell more policies to upscale individuals, it might place a print ad in business publications such as *The Australian* or *Business Review Weekly*, which are read by more educated and affluent people.

Second, social class may also tell marketers where certain types of consumers shop. Wealthy, upper-class shoppers tend to frequent expensive stores, places where members of the other classes might feel uncomfortable. Marketers also know that middle-class consumers regularly visit shopping centres. Therefore, marketers with products to sell to the middle class may decide to distribute their merchandise through shopping centres.

Broad social class categories are becoming less useful to marketers as indicators of purchase behaviour. One of the reasons seems to be the fragmentation of Australian society into distinct subgroups, each with unique tastes and desires. Recent economic trends have also added to the disintegration of broad class structures. Many thousands of the jobs that provided for a comfortable middle-class lifestyle have simply vanished, along with long-term income security. As a result, subgroups have formed within the vast middle class, each defined by different opportunities, expectations and outlooks.

Social influences on consumer buying decisions

Most consumers, you included, are likely to seek out others' opinions when making significant buying decisions in an attempt to reduce the search and evaluation effort, as well as any uncertainty that may be involved in the decision process. This is also true for decisions where the levels of perceived risk are high. Consumers may also seek out the opinions of others for guidance on new goods or services, products with image-related attributes or because attribute information is lacking or uninformative.[14] Specifically, consumers interact socially with reference groups, opinion leaders and family members to obtain product information and decision approval.

6 Identify and understand the social factors that affect consumer buying decisions

Reference groups

All the formal and informal groups that influence the buying behaviour of an individual are that person's **reference groups**. Consumers may use products or brands to identify with or become a member of a group. They learn from observing how members of their reference groups consume, and they use the same criteria to make their own consumer decisions. Reference groups can be categorised very broadly as either direct or indirect (see Exhibit 2.7).

reference group
Group in society that influences an individual's purchasing behaviour.

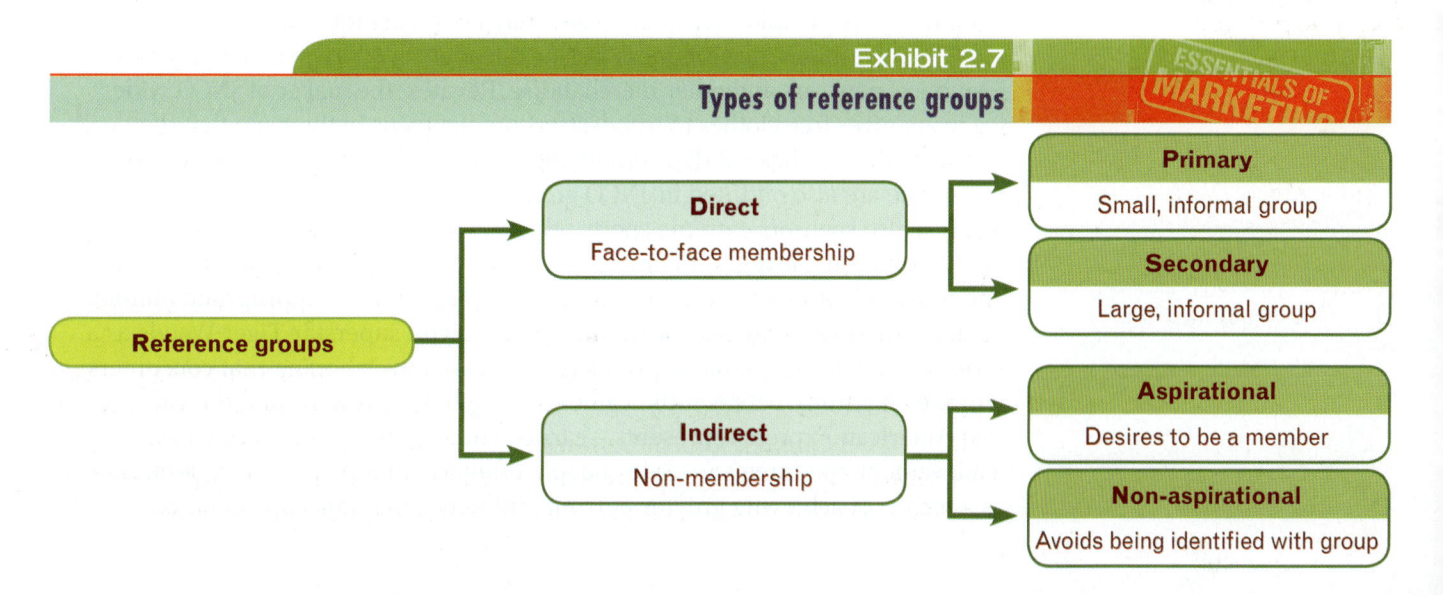

Exhibit 2.7 Types of reference groups

Reference groups
- Direct — Face-to-face membership
  - Primary — Small, informal group
  - Secondary — Large, informal group
- Indirect — Non-membership
  - Aspirational — Desires to be a member
  - Non-aspirational — Avoids being identified with group

The activities, values and goals of reference groups directly influence consumer behaviour. For marketers, reference groups have three important implications: (1) they serve as information sources and influence perceptions; (2) they affect an individual's aspiration levels; and (3) their norms either constrain or stimulate consumer behaviour. For example, over 40 per cent of people seek the advice of family and friends when shopping for doctors, lawyers or car mechanics. Individuals also are likely to seek others' advice in selecting a restaurant for a special occasion or deciding which movie to see.[15]

In Japan, companies have long relied on the nation's high school girls to give them advice during product testing. Fads that catch on among teenage girls often become big trends throughout the country and among Japanese consumers in general. Food manufacturers frequently recruit Tokyo schoolgirls to sample potato chip recipes or chocolate bars. Television networks survey high school girls to fine-tune story lines for higher ratings on prime-time shows. Other companies pay girls to keep diaries of what they buy. Warner-Lambert hired high school girls in 1995 to help choose a new gum flavour. After extensive chewing and comparing, the girls settled on a flavour that became Trickle, now Japan's best-selling bubble gum.[16]

Opinion leaders

Reference groups frequently include individuals known as group leaders or **opinion leaders**, those who influence others. Obviously, it is important for marketing managers to persuade such people to purchase their goods or services. Many goods and services that are integral parts of our lives today got their initial boost from these influential opinion leaders. For example, opinion leaders well ahead of the general public embraced VCRs, and they were also among the first to turn sport-utility vehicles and four-wheel-drives into the 'family vehicle' of the new millennium.

Opinion leaders are often the first to try new goods and services out of pure curiosity. They are typically activists in their communities, on the job and in the marketplace. Furthermore, opinion leaders tend to be self-indulgent, making them more likely to explore unproven but intriguing goods and services. This combination of curiosity, activism and self-indulgence makes opinion leaders trendsetters in the consumer marketplace. Exhibit 2.8 lists some products and services about which people often seek the advice of an opinion leader before purchasing.

Opinion leadership is a casual, face-to-face phenomenon and usually very inconspicuous, so locating opinion leaders can be a challenge. Thus, marketers often try to create opinion leaders. They may use young television 'soap' stars to model new fashions, or prominent business leaders or sportspeople to promote insurance, new cars and other merchandise. Revatex, the maker of JNCO wide-leg jeans, gives free clothes to trendsetters among teens in the hope that they will influence the purchase of their brand. Big name bands and music people in the rave scene are also outfitted in JNCO gear to extend the popularity of the clothing. Revatex also sponsors extreme-sports athletes who are also favoured by this crowd.

On a national level, companies sometimes use movie stars, sports figures and other celebrities to promote products, hoping they are appropriate opinion leaders. American Express, for example, signed golf superstar Tiger Woods as a spokesperson for its financial products. The company is hoping that consumers will see an affinity between the values that Woods represents and the values that American Express represents – earned success, discipline, hard work, achievement and integrity.[17] Sales people often ask to use opinion leaders' names as a means of achieving greater personal influence in a sales presentation

opinion leader
Individual who influences the opinions of others.

Chapter 2 Consumer decision-making

Exhibit 2.8
Words of wisdom: Opinion leaders' consumer clout extends far beyond their own purchases

Average number of people to whom opinion leaders recommended products* in the past year and millions of recommendations made since 1995

	Average number of recommendations	Millions of recommendations made
Restaurant	5.0	70
Vacation destination	5.1	44
TV show	4.9	45
Car	4.1	29
Retail store	4.7	29
Clothing	4.5	24
Consumer electronics	4.5	16
Office equipment	5.8	12
Shares, mutual fund, CD etc.	3.4	12

*Among those who recommended the product at all

Source: Roper Starch Worldwide, Inc., New York, NY. Adapted from 'Maximizing the Market with Influentials', *American Demographics*, July 1995, p. 42.

The makers of JNCO jeans give free clothing to people who they believe will be opinion leaders: DJs, band members from new, hip rock groups, and so on. Can you identify the opinion leaders in your social group? Name some products or services that they seem to promote.

socialisation process
How cultural values and norms are passed down to children.

Family

The family is the most important social institution for many consumers, strongly influencing values, attitudes, self-concept and buying behaviour. For example, a family that strongly values good health will have a grocery list distinctly different from that of a family that views every dinner as a gourmet event. Moreover, the family is responsible for the **socialisation process**, the passing down of cultural values and norms to children. Children learn by observing their parents' consumption patterns, and so they will tend to shop in a similar pattern.

Decision-making roles among family members tend to vary significantly, depending on the type of item purchased. Family members assume a variety of roles in the purchase process. *Initiators* are the ones who suggest or initiate the purchase process. The initiator can be any member of the family. For example, your sister might initiate the product search by asking for a new bicycle as a birthday present. *Influencers* are those members of the family whose opinions are valued. In our example, Mum might function as a price-range watchdog, an influencer whose main role is to veto or approve price ranges. Your brother may give his opinion on certain makes of bicycles. The *decision-maker* is the member of the family who actually makes the decision to buy or not to buy. For example, Dad may choose the final brand and model of bicycle to buy after seeking further information from your sister about cosmetic features such as colour and imposing additional criteria of his own, such as durability and safety. The *purchaser* (probably Dad or Mum) is the one who actually exchanges money for the product. Finally, the *consumer* is the actual user – your sister, in the case of the bicycle.

Children today can have great influence over their parents' purchase decisions. In many families, with both parents working and pushed for time, children may be encouraged to participate. In addition, children in single-parent households become more involved in family decision-making at an earlier age than children in two-parent households. Children are especially influential in decisions about food, as shown in Exhibit 2.9. Children often help to decide where the family goes for fast food, and many children influence the choice of a full-service restaurant. Children have input into the kinds of food the family eats at home as well, and influence the specific brands their parents buy. Finally, children influence purchase decisions for toys, clothes, holidays, recreation and cars, even though they are usually not the actual purchasers of such items. Marketers are aware of the consumer power of children: it is estimated in the United States that children aged 12 and under spend approximately US$24 billion a year and influence another US$300 billion in household spending; the Australian pre-teen market (21 per cent of the Australian population) is just as influential.[18]

7 Identify and understand the individual factors that affect consumer buying decisions

Internal influences on consumer buying decisions

A person's buying decision is also influenced by personal characteristics that are unique to each individual, such as gender, age and stage in the family life cycle, and personality, self-concept and lifestyle. Some individual characteristics are generally stable over the course of one's life. Most people don't change their gender, and the act of changing personality or lifestyle requires a reorientation of one's life. In the case of age and life-cycle stage, these changes occur gradually over time.

Exhibit 2.9
Children's influence on household purchases

Aggregate spending in millions of dollars influenced by children aged four to 12 on selected items, and per child spending, 1997

	Aggregate spending	Per-child spending
Food and beverages	$110 320	$3131
Entertainment	$25 620	$727
Automobiles	$17 740	$503
Apparel	$17 540	$498
Electronics	$6400	$182
Health and beauty	$3500	$101

Source: From James U. McNeal, 'Tapping the Three Kids' Markets', *American Demographics*, April 1998. © 1998 PRIMEDIA Intertec, Stamford, CT. Reprinted with permission.

Gender

Physiological differences between men and women result in different needs for items such as health and beauty products. Just as important are the distinct cultural, social and economic roles played by men and women and the effects that these have on their decision-making processes. Women, for example, look for different features when purchasing a car than do men. Since women in most Western countries assume the majority of child-rearing activities – shuttling the children to and from school, play dates and sport, for example – they often look for vehicles that are large and versatile enough for these activities. As a result, minivan manufacturers have implemented strategies to accommodate female drivers, such as resizing door handles and controls for women's smaller hands, and repositioning seats and pedals.

Men and women also shop differently. Studies show that men and women share similar motivations in terms of where to shop – that is, seeking reasonable prices, merchandise quality and a friendly, low-pressure environment – but they don't necessarily feel the same about shopping in general. Most women enjoy shopping; their male counterparts claim to dislike the experience and shop only out of necessity. Further, men desire simple shopping experiences, stores with less variety, and convenience. Stores that are easy to shop in, that are near home or the office, or that have knowledgeable staff appeal more to men than to women.[19]

Age and family life-cycle stage

The age and family life-cycle stage of a consumer can have a significant impact on consumer behaviour. The age of the consumer generally determines what products they will be interested in purchasing. Consumer tastes in food, clothing, cars, furniture and recreation are often age-related; for example, the favourite magazines for pre-teens aged eight to 12 include *Smash Hits*, *Nickelodeon* and *Barbie*. But as these consumers become teenagers their tastes in magazines diverge in favour of sports titles for boys and fashion/lifestyle titles for girls.

Related to a person's age is their place in the family life cycle. The family life cycle is an orderly series of stages through which consumers' attitudes and behavioural tendencies evolve through maturity, experience, and changing income and status. Marketers often define their target markets in terms of family life cycle, such as 'young singles', 'young married with children' and 'middle-aged married without children'. For example, young singles spend more than average on alcoholic beverages, education and entertainment. New parents typically increase their spending on health care, clothing, housing and food, and decrease their spending on alcohol, education and transportation. Households with older children spend more on food, entertainment, personal care products and education, as well as cars and petrol. After their children leave home, spending by older couples on vehicles, women's clothing, health care and long-distance calls typically increases. For example, families with children aged six to 17 years are the biggest ready-to-eat cereal consumers, spending 75 per cent more than the average family. In contrast, young singles under age 35 spend 54 per cent less than expected on ready-to-eat cereals.[20]

Marketers should also be aware of the non-traditional life-cycle paths that affect consumption behaviour, such as divorced parents, lifelong singles and childless couples. Since the 1950s, the influx of women into the labour force has transformed family structure so much that in 1997 only 17 per cent of American households conformed to the traditional model of a wage-earning dad, a stay-at-home mum and one or more children.[21] Further, according to the Australian Bureau of Statistics, single-father families in which a single father has custody of his children are growing at an annual rate of 10 per cent. The shift towards custodial fathers is part of a broader societal change that has put more women on the career track and given men more options at home.[22]

Personality, self-concept and lifestyle

Each consumer has a unique personality. **Personality** is a broad concept that can be thought of as a way of organising and grouping the consistencies of an individual's reactions to situations. Thus, personality combines psychological makeup and environmental forces. It includes people's underlying dispositions, especially their most dominant characteristics. Some marketers believe that personality influences the types and brands of products purchased. For example, the type of car, clothes or jewellery a consumer buys may reflect one or more personality traits. Personality traits such as those listed in Exhibit 2.10 may be used to describe a consumer's personality.

personality
Way of organising and grouping the consistencies of an individual's reactions to situations.

Exhibit 2.10
Some common personality traits

- Adaptability
- Need for affiliation
- Aggressiveness
- Need for achievement
- Ascendancy
- Autonomy
- Dominance
- Deference
- Defensiveness
- Emotionalism
- Orderliness
- Sociability
- Stability
- Self-confidence

Self-concept, or self-perception, is how consumers perceive themselves. Self-concept includes attitudes, perceptions, beliefs and self-evaluations. Although self-concept may change, the change is often gradual. Through self-concept, people develop an identity, which in turn provides for consistent and coherent behaviour.

Self-concept combines the **ideal self-image** (the way you like to be) and the **real self-image** (how you actually perceive yourself). Generally, we try to raise our real self-image towards our ideal (or at least narrow the gap). Consumers seldom buy products that jeopardise their self-image. For example, someone who sees herself as a trendsetter usually buys clothing that reflects this image.

Human behaviour depends largely on self-concept. Because consumers seek to protect their identity as individuals, the products they buy, the stores they patronise and the credit cards they carry support their self-image. Men and women's fragrances, for example, tend to reflect the self-images of their wearers. Chanel's Egoïste is for the man who has everything and knows it. Likewise, Elizabeth Taylor's White Diamonds perfume is 'the fragrance dreams are made of' for all those women who strive for legendary beauty.[23] Cosmetics company L'Oreal's slogan for their product is 'Because I'm Worth It!' It is aimed at women who want to indulge their sense of self-worth and their self-image.

An important component of self-concept is *body image*, the perception of the attractiveness of one's own physical features. For example, individuals who have plastic surgery often experience significant improvements in their overall body image and self-concept. Moreover, a person's perception of body image can be a stronger reason for weight loss than either good health or other social factors.[24] Sales of at-home hair colour to ageing baby boomers have substantially increased as more middle-aged men and women colour their hair in order to 'age gracefully'. Johnson and Johnson launched a skin cream, Nivea, which fights the 'appearance of wrinkles', targeted at the ageing baby boomer generation and L'Oreal has an entire product range titled 'age defying skin care'. Likewise, health clubs, exercise equipment manufacturers and diet plans target consumers who want to improve their self-concept by exercising and losing weight.

Personality and self-concept are reflected in lifestyle. A **lifestyle** is a mode of living, as identified by a person's activities, interests and opinions (AIO). *Psychographics* is the analytical technique used to examine consumer lifestyles and to categorise consumers. Unlike personality characteristics, which are hard to describe and measure, lifestyle characteristics are useful in segmenting and targeting consumers. Many industries now use psychographics to better understand their market segments. For example, the car industry has a psychographic segmentation scheme for classifying car buyers into one of six groups according to their attitudes towards cars and the driving experience. At the two extremes are 'gearheads', true car enthusiasts who enjoy driving and working on their cars themselves, and 'negatives', who view cars as a necessary evil that they would just as soon do without. Lifestyle segmentation can be used in many different applications for many different product categories, even down to the selection of colour schemes for cafes and sporting centres. Psychographics and lifestyle segmentation schemes are discussed in more detail in Chapter 4.

self-concept
How a consumer perceives himself, or herself, in terms of attitudes, perceptions, beliefs and self-evaluations.

ideal self-image
The way an individual would like to be.

real self-image
The way an individual actually perceives himself or herself.

lifestyle
Mode of living as identified by a person's activities, interests and opinions.

8 Identify and understand the psychological factors that affect consumer buying decisions

Psychological influences on consumer buying decisions

An individual's buying decisions are further influenced by psychological factors: perception, motivation, learning, and beliefs and attitudes. These factors are what consumers use to interact with their world. They are the tools consumers use to recognise their feelings, gather and analyse information, formulate thoughts and opinions, and take action. Unlike the other three influences on consumer behaviour, psychological influences can be affected by a person's environment because they are applied on specific occasions.[25] For example, you will perceive different stimuli and process these stimuli in different ways depending on whether you are sitting in class concentrating on the instructor, sitting outside class talking to friends or sitting in your home watching television.

Perception

The world is full of stimuli. A stimulus is any unit of input affecting the five senses: sight, smell, taste, touch and hearing. The process by which we select, organise and interpret these stimuli into a meaningful and coherent picture is called **perception**. In essence, perception is how we see the world around us and how we recognise that we have a consumption problem.

People cannot perceive every stimulus in their environment. Therefore, they use **selective exposure** to decide which stimuli to notice and which to ignore. A typical consumer is exposed to over 150 advertising messages a day but notices only between 11 and 20. The familiarity of an object, contrast, movement, intensity (such as increased volume) and smell are cues that influence perception. Consumers use these cues to identify and define products and brands. The shape of a product's packaging, such as Coca-Cola's signature contour bottle, for example, can influence perception. Colour is another cue and it plays a key role in consumers' perceptions. For example, several years ago, bleach was added to many laundry detergents to improve their performance; however, many consumers didn't believe the claims of improvement because the product looked the same. One manufacturer, Procter and Gamble, added blue beads to their normally white detergent. While the blue beads didn't actually have anything to do with the product's performance, consumers could 'see' the difference and the detergent became very successful because consumers perceived a difference from other detergents.

What consumers perceive may also depend on the stimuli's vividness or shock value. Graphic warnings of the hazards associated with a product's use are perceived more readily and remembered more accurately than less vivid warnings or warnings that are written in text. 'Sexier' ads excel at attracting the attention of younger consumers. Companies such as Calvin Klein and Guess use sensuous ads to 'cut through the clutter' of competing ads and other stimuli to capture the attention of the target audience. Similarly, Benetton ads use shock value to cut through the clutter by portraying topical social issues, from racism to homosexuality.

Which stimuli will be perceived often depends on the individual. People can be exposed to the same stimuli under identical conditions but perceive them very differently. For example, two people viewing a TV commercial may have different interpretations of the advertising message. One person may be thoroughly engrossed by the message and become highly motivated to buy the product. Thirty seconds after the ad ends, the second person may not be able to recall the content of the message or even the product advertised.

perception
Process by which people select, organise and interpret stimuli into a meaningful and coherent picture.

selective exposure
Process whereby a consumer notices certain stimuli and ignores other stimuli.

Marketing implications of perception

Marketers must recognise the importance of cues, or signals, in consumers' perception of products. Marketing managers first identify the important attributes, such as price or quality, that the targeted consumers want in a product and then design signals to communicate these attributes. For example, consumers will pay more for chocolate bars wrapped in expensive-looking foil packages. But shiny labels on wine bottles signify less expensive wines; dull labels indicate more expensive wines. Companies often find that more expensive products sell better because consumers perceive them to be of a higher quality – this is often the case in relation to wine, where more expensive wines often sell better than the cheaper ones. Marketers also often use product warranties as a signal to consumers that the product is of higher quality than competing products. Consumers who perceive these warranties as highly credible perceive the product to be of higher quality.

Of course, brand names send signals to consumers. Brand names such as 'Close-Up' toothpaste, 'Eveready' batteries and 'Soft-touch' moisturising soap identify important product qualities. Names chosen for search engines and websites on the Internet, such as Yahoo!, Excite and Jumbo!, are intended to convey excitement and intensity. Companies might even change their names to send messages to consumers. Today's power utility companies, faced with the looming prospect of fierce competition in the wake of deregulation, are increasingly changing their names to project a bright new image to customers. The traditional, stodgy 'South East Queensland Electricity Board' style of power utility names that consumers have often learned to dislike have given way to names such as Energex and CINergy.

Marketing managers who intend to do business in global markets should be aware of how foreign consumers perceive their products.

For example, in Japan, product labels are often written in English or French, even though they may not translate into anything meaningful. But many Japanese associate foreign words on product labels with the exotic, the expensive and with high quality. Marketers have often been suspected of sending advertising messages subconsciously to consumers in what is known as subliminal perception. The controversy began in 1957 when a researcher claimed to have increased popcorn and Coca-Cola sales at a movie theatre after flashing 'Eat popcorn' and 'Drink Coca-Cola' on the screen every five seconds for 1/300th of a second, although the audience did not consciously recognise the messages. Almost immediately consumer protection groups became concerned that advertisers were brainwashing consumers and this practice was made illegal in California and Canada. Although the researcher later admitted to making up the data and scientists have been unable to replicate the study since, consumers are still wary of hidden messages that advertisers may be sending.

Motivation

By studying motivation, marketers can analyse the major forces influencing consumers to buy or not buy products. When you buy a product, you usually do so to fulfil some kind of need. These needs become motives when aroused sufficiently. For example, suppose this morning you were so hungry before class that you needed to eat something. In response to that need, you stopped at McDonald's for an Egg McMuffin. In other words, you were motivated by hunger to stop at McDonald's. **Motives** are the driving forces that cause a person to take action to satisfy specific needs.

motive
Driving force that causes a person to take action to satisfy specific needs.

Maslow's hierarchy of needs
Method of classifying human needs and motivations into five categories in ascending order of importance: physiological, safety, social, esteem and self-actualisation.

Why are people driven by particular needs at particular times? One popular theory is **Maslow's hierarchy of needs**, shown in Exhibit 2.11, which arranges needs in ascending order of importance from physiological needs, through to safety, social and esteem needs, to self-actualisation. As a person fulfils one need, a higher-level need becomes more important.

The most basic human needs are *physiological* – that is, needs for food, water and shelter. Because they are essential to survival, these needs must be satisfied first. Ads showing a juicy hamburger or a runner gulping down Gatorade after a marathon exemplify the use of appeals to satisfy physiological needs.

Exhibit 2.11
Maslow's heirarchy of needs

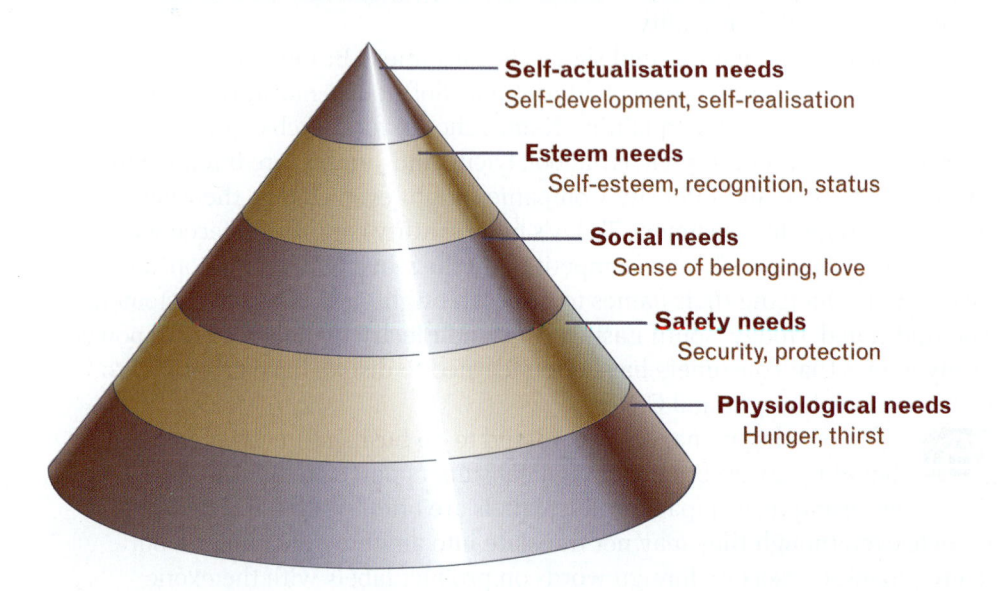

- **Self-actualisation needs**
  Self-development, self-realisation
- **Esteem needs**
  Self-esteem, recognition, status
- **Social needs**
  Sense of belonging, love
- **Safety needs**
  Security, protection
- **Physiological needs**
  Hunger, thirst

Safety needs include security and freedom from pain and discomfort. Marketers often exploit consumers' fears and anxieties about safety to sell their products. For example, many of today's vacuum cleaner manufacturers are trying to capitalise on consumers' fears about indoor air pollution and anxieties over allergies. The companies claim that advanced filters in their latest models can trap microscopic contaminants that can jeopardise people's health. One ad from US vacuum maker Miele Appliances warns of the 'deadly world of lung-damaging particles' that older vacuums can't trap. Replacing your vacuum, the ad says, 'is a lot easier than replacing your lungs'. The ad even carries the symbol of the American Lung Association. The Ethics in marketing box discusses how marketers often play on social needs rather than fear to sell their products.

Learning

learning
Process that creates changes in behaviour, immediate or expected, through experience and practice.

Almost all consumer behaviour results from **learning**, which is the process that creates changes in behaviour through experience and practice. It is not possible to observe learning directly, but we can infer when it has occurred by a person's actions. For example, suppose you see an advertisement for a new and improved cold medicine. If you go to the chemist's that day and buy that remedy, we infer that you have learned something about the cold medicine.

Learning generally occurs on two levels, either through learning by doing something (experiential learning) or learning by thinking and working something out (cognitive learning). Assume, for example, that you are standing at a soft-drink vending machine and notice a new diet flavour with an artificial sweetener. But someone has told you that diet drinks leave an aftertaste, so you choose a different drink. You have learned that you would not like this new diet drink without ever trying it.

Social needs as a marketing tool

Ethics in Marketing

After physiological and safety needs have been fulfilled, social needs – especially love and a sense of belonging – become the focus. Love includes acceptance by one's peers as well as sex and romantic love. Marketing managers probably appeal more to this need than to any other. Ads for clothes, cosmetics and holiday packages suggest that buying the product can bring love. The need to belong is also a favourite of marketers. Nike promotes its Air Jordan athletic shoes, for example, as not just plain, old sneakers; they're part of a fashion statement, part of an athletic statement. Lace them up, and the wearer looks cool and plays cool – just like Michael Jordan, the shoe's spokesperson and namesake.[26]

Love is acceptance without regard to one's contribution; esteem is acceptance based on one's contribution to the group. **Self-esteem** needs include self-respect and a sense of accomplishment. Esteem needs also include prestige, fame and recognition of one's accomplishments. Mont Blanc pens, Mercedes-Benz automobiles and David Jones stores all appeal to esteem needs. Asian consumers, in particular, are strongly motivated by status and prestige. Asian individuals are always conscious of their place in a group, institution or society as a whole. The importance of gaining social recognition turns Asians into probably the most image-conscious consumers in the world. Status-conscious Asians won't hesitate to spend freely on premium brands, such as BMW, Mercedes-Benz, and the best Scotch whisky and French cognac.[27] This may explain why jewellery sales at Tiffany's in Japan continue to rise, even in the face of one of Japan's worst economic recessions.[28]

The highest level of human need, according to Maslow, is self-actualisation. It refers to finding self-fulfilment and self-expression, reaching the point in life at which 'people are what they feel they should be'. Maslow believed that few people ever attain this level. Even so, advertisements may focus on this type of need. For example, American Express ads convey the message that acquiring its card is one of the highest attainments in life. Likewise, the Australian Defence Force slogan urges young people to join to get 'the edge!' with their chosen careers and to experience 'unreal' opportunities in the process.

Even children must satisfy more than just the basic physiological and safety needs. Mattel's Barbie doll, for example, fulfils a fundamental need that all girls share by playing out what it might be like in the grown-up world. Through Barbie, girls dream of achievement, glamour, romance, adventure and nurturing. These dreams touch on many timeless needs, ranging from pride and success to belonging and love. Mattel zeros in on these core needs and addresses them with different Barbie products. Over the years, Barbie has been a teacher, a fashion model, a girlfriend, a dentist, an astronaut, a sister and a veterinarian, to name a few.[29]

self-esteem
The opinion one holds of oneself.

Reinforcement and repetition boost learning. Reinforcement can be positive or negative. If you see a store selling frozen yoghurt (stimulus), buy it (response) and find the yoghurt to be quite refreshing (reward), your behaviour has been positively reinforced. On the other hand, if you buy a new flavour of yoghurt and it doesn't taste good (negative reinforcement), you won't buy that flavour of yoghurt again. Without positive or negative reinforcement, a person won't be motivated to repeat the behaviour pattern or to avoid it. Thus, if a new brand evokes neutral feelings, some marketing activity, such as a price change or an increase in promotion, may be required to induce further consumption. Learning theory is helpful in reminding marketers that concrete and timely actions are what reinforce desired consumer behaviour.

Repetition is a key strategy in promotional campaigns because it can lead to increased learning. Qantas uses repetitious jingles in its advertising so that consumers will learn that 'Qantas is an Australian airline', because 'We still call Australia home!' Generally, to heighten learning, advertising messages should be spread over time rather than clustered at one time.

Beliefs and attitudes

belief
Organised pattern of knowledge that an individual holds as true about his or her world.

Beliefs and attitudes are closely linked to values. A **belief** is an organised pattern of knowledge that an individual holds as true about his or her world. A consumer may believe that Sony's camcorder makes the best home videos, tolerates hard use and is reasonably priced. These beliefs may be based on knowledge, faith or hearsay. Consumers tend to develop a set of beliefs about a product's attributes and then, through these beliefs, form a *brand image* – a set of beliefs about a particular brand. In turn, the brand image shapes consumers' attitudes towards the product.

attitude
Learned tendency to respond consistently towards a given object.

Attitudes tend to be more enduring and complex than beliefs, because they consist of clusters of interrelated beliefs. An **attitude** is a learned tendency to respond consistently towards a given object, such as a brand. Attitudes also encompass an individual's value system, which represents personal standards of good and bad, right and wrong, and so forth; therefore, attitudes tend to be more enduring and complex than beliefs.

For an example of the nature of attitudes, consider the differing attitudes of consumers around the world towards the habit of purchasing on credit. Australians have long been enthusiastic about charging goods and services and are willing to pay high interest rates for the privilege of postponing payment. But to many European consumers, doing what amounts to taking out a loan – even a small one – to pay for anything seems absurd. Germans, especially, are reluctant to buy on credit. Italy has a sophisticated credit and banking system well suited to handling credit cards, but Italians prefer to carry cash, often huge wads of it. Most Japanese consumers have credit cards, but card purchases amount to less than 1 per cent of all consumer transactions. The Japanese have long looked down on credit purchases but acquire cards to use while travelling abroad.[30]

If a good or service is meeting its profit goals, positive attitudes towards the product merely need to be reinforced. However, if the brand is not succeeding, the marketing manager must strive to change the target consumers' attitudes towards it. Changes in attitude tend to grow out of an individual's attempt to reconcile long-held values with a constant stream of new information. This change can be accomplished in three ways: (1) changing beliefs about the brand's attributes; (2) changing the relative importance of these beliefs; and (3) adding new beliefs.

Changing beliefs about a service can be more difficult, because service attributes are intangible. Convincing consumers to switch hairstylists or lawyers or to go to a shopping centre dental clinic can be much more difficult than getting them to change brands of razor blades. Image, which is also largely intangible, significantly determines service patronage. What is a 'better doctor'? How do consumers become convinced that they will get better dental care in a shopping centre than through a family dentist? Service marketing is explored in detail in Chapter 6.

Companies attempting to market their goods internationally may need to help consumers add new beliefs about a product in general. Many hygiene practices common in most Western countries, for example, are unheard of in some other countries. In rural India, most Indians have never handled such products as a toothbrush or a tube of toothpaste. For generations, they have used charcoal powder and indigenous plants to cleanse their mouths. To educate Indians on the benefits of toothpaste, Colgate-Palmolive sends marketers to rural villages on market day equipped with half-hour infomercials featuring Colgate toothpaste. A story of a couple on their wedding night sends Colgate's message: 'Colgate is good for your breath, teeth and love life.' The infomercial wraps up with a dentist explaining that the traditional oral-hygiene methods, such as charcoal powder, are ineffective. Free samples are passed out while a Colgate marketer demonstrates how to use the Colgate toothpaste and toothbrush.

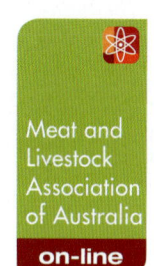

Meat and Livestock Association of Australia
on-line

How is the MLA trying to change the perception of red meat as a poor food for health and instead encourage consumers to consider it as an important part of a balanced diet? Visit its website and determine if its information successfully counters this perception.
www.mla.com.au

Connect it

Returning to the discussion that opened the chapter, you should now be able to see how cultural, social, individual and psychological factors affect the consumer decision-making process. Both individual and business consumers are becoming more socially aware and demanding more socially conscious operations and production practices from their suppliers, and they are prepared to pay for the privilege. Consumer behaviour is a fascinating and often intricate process whether you study it at the individual consumer level or at the organisational level. An appreciation of consumer behaviour and the factors that influence it will help you to identify target markets and design effective marketing strategies.

Summary

1 Explain why marketing managers should understand consumer behaviour.
Consumer behaviour describes how consumers make purchase decisions and how they use and dispose of the products they buy. An understanding of consumer behaviour reduces marketing managers' uncertainty when they are defining a target market and designing a marketing mix.

2 Analyse the components of the consumer decision-making process.
The consumer decision-making process begins with need recognition, when stimuli trigger awareness of an unfulfilled want. If additional information is required to

make a purchase decision, the consumer may engage in an internal or external information search. The consumer then evaluates the additional information and establishes purchase guidelines. Finally, a purchase decision is made.

3 Explain the consumer's post-purchase evaluation process.

Consumer post-purchase evaluation is influenced by pre-purchase expectations, the pre-purchase information search and the consumer's general level of self-confidence. Cognitive dissonance is the inner tension that a consumer experiences after recognising a purchased product's disadvantages. When a purchase creates cognitive dissonance, consumers tend to react by seeking positive reinforcement for the purchase decision, avoiding negative information about the purchase decision or revoking the purchase decision by returning the product.

4 Identify the types of consumer buying decisions and explain how they relate to consumer involvement.

Consumer decision-making falls into three broad categories. First, consumers exhibit routine response behaviour for frequently purchased, low-cost items that require very little decision effort; routine response behaviour is typically characterised by brand loyalty. Second, consumers engage in limited decision-making for occasional purchases or for unfamiliar brands in familiar product categories. Third, consumers practise extensive decision-making when making unfamiliar, expensive or infrequent purchases. High-involvement decisions usually include an extensive information search and a thorough evaluation of alternatives. In contrast, low-involvement decisions are characterised by brand loyalty and a lack of personal identification with the product. The main factors affecting the level of consumer involvement are price, interest, perceived risk of negative consequences, situation and social visibility.

5 Identify and understand the external factors that affect consumer buying decisions.

There are a number of external factors that impact consumer buying decisions and these include: culture, the impact of reference groups, opinion leaders and family. Culture is the essential character of a society that distinguishes it from other cultural groups. The underlying elements of every culture are the values, language, myths, customs, rituals, laws and the artefacts or products that are transmitted from one generation to the next. The most defining element of a culture is its values – the enduring beliefs shared by a society that a specific mode of conduct is personally or socially preferable to another mode of conduct.

Consumers seek out others' opinions for guidance on new products or services and products with image-related attributes, or because attribute information is lacking or uninformative. Consumers may use products or brands to identify with or become a member of a reference group. Opinion leaders are members of reference groups who influence others' purchase decisions. Family members also influence purchase decisions; children tend to shop in patterns similar to those of their parents.

6 Identify and understand the individual factors that affect consumer buying decisions.

Individual factors that affect consumer-buying decisions include: gender; age and family life-cycle stage; and personality, self-concept and lifestyle. Beyond obvious physiological differences, men and women differ in their social and economic roles that affect consumer buying decisions. How old a consumer is generally indicates what products they may be interested in purchasing. Marketers often define their target markets in terms of consumers' life-cycle stage, following changes in consumers' attitudes and behavioural tendencies as they mature. Finally, certain products and brands reflect consumers' personality, self-concept and lifestyle.

7 Identify and understand the psychological factors that affect consumer buying decisions.

Psychological factors include perception, motivation, learning, values, beliefs and attitudes. These factors allow consumers to interact with the world around them, recognise their feelings, gather and analyse information, formulate thoughts and opinions, and take action. Perception allows consumers to recognise their consumption problems. Motivation is what drives consumers to take action to satisfy specific consumption needs. Almost all consumer behaviour results from learning, which is the process that creates changes in behaviour through experience. Consumers with similar beliefs and attitudes tend to react alike to marketing-related inducements.

Review it

1. The first stage of consumer decision-making when consumers are faced with an imbalance between desired and actual states is
   a. Need recognition
   b. Information search
   c. Evaluation of alternatives
   d. Purchase

2. Information that a consumer receives that is biased towards a particular product is usually
   a. Internal information
   b. Internal stimuli
   c. Non-marketing-controlled information
   d. Marketing-controlled information

3. A consumer's information search yields a group of brands that are the consumer's most preferred alternatives. This group is called:
   a. The consumer wants
   b. The evoked set
   c. The external stimuli
   d. The set of possible alternatives

4. Frequently purchased, low-cost goods and services are usually associated with _____ consumer decision-making.
   a. Constant
   b. Routine
   c. Limited
   d. Extensive

5. Which of the following is *not* a factor that determines the level of consumer involvement when making a purchase decision?
   a. Interest
   b. Perceived risk
   c. Price
   d. Social visibility

Define it

attitude 56
belief 56
cognitive dissonance 34
consumer behaviour 27
consumer decision-making process 27
culture 39
evoked set (consideration set) 32
extensive decision-making 35
external information search 30
ideal self-image 51
internal information search 30
involvement 34
learning 54
lifestyle 51
limited decision-making 35
marketing-controlled information source 31
Maslow's hierarchy of needs 54
motive 53
need recognition 28
non-marketing-controlled information source 30
opinion leader 46
perception 52
personality 50
real self-image 51
reference group 45
routine response behaviour (habitual buying behaviour) 35
selective exposure 52
self-concept 51
self-esteem 55
social class 44
socialisation process 48
stimulus 28
subculture 44
value 40
want 28

6 The most defining element of a culture is its
   a Values
   b Traditions
   c Beliefs
   d Religion

7 Attitudes, motivation and learning influence consumer decision-making. These factors are best classified as
   a Cultural
   b Social
   c Individual
   d Psychological

8 Since consumers cannot perceive every stimulus in their environment, they often use selective _____ to decide which stimuli to notice and which to ignore.
   a Exposure
   b Distortion
   c Retention
   d Attention

9 To get a consumer to buy a firm's good or service, it must often change the consumer's attitude towards it. Which of the following is not one of the three ways in which this attitude change can be accomplished?
   a Changing learning processes
   b Changing beliefs about product attributes
   c Changing the importance of beliefs
   d Adding new beliefs

10 Conceptual learning, which changes the consumer's marketplace behaviour, is accomplished through direct product experience.
   a True
   b False

Check the Answer Key to see how well you understood the material. More detailed discussion and writing questions and a video case related to this chapter are found in the Student Resources CD-ROM.

Apply it

1 Describe the three categories of consumer decision-making behaviour. Name typical products for which each type of consumer behaviour is used.

2 The type of decision-making a consumer uses for a product does not necessarily remain constant. Why? Support your answer with an example from your own experience.

3 How do beliefs and attitudes influence consumer behaviour? How can negative attitudes towards a product be changed? How can marketers alter beliefs about a product? Give some examples of how marketers have changed negative attitudes about a product or added or altered beliefs about a product.

4 Recall an occasion when you experienced cognitive dissonance about a purchase. In a letter to a friend, describe the event and explain what you did about it.

5 Family members play many different roles in the buying process: initiator, influencer, decision-maker, purchaser and consumer. In your family, name who might play each of these roles in the purchase of a personal computer system, Froot Loops breakfast cereal, Calvin Klein Obsession cologne for men and dinner at McDonald's.

6   You are a new marketing manager for a firm that produces a line of athletic shoes to be targeted to the skateboard subculture. For your boss, write a memo listing some product attributes that might appeal to this subculture and recommend some marketing strategies. (Maybe visit the World Industries website for some guidance: www.worldind.com.)

7   Assume you are involved in the following consumer decision situations: (a) renting a video to watch with your roommates; (b) choosing a fast-food restaurant to go to with a new friend; (c) buying a popular music compact disc; and (d) buying jeans to wear to class. List the factors that would influence your decision in each situation and explain your responses.

8   Visit the Toyota website at www.toyota.com.au. Does Toyota provide much assistance to people looking to buy a car? Look at some other dealer sites and see if they have ways of assisting consumers with their decision-making process. Develop a hypothetical evoked set of three of four models of Toyota and discuss what sorts of evaluative criteria you would use to make a choice. Compare your results with others in the class and discuss why there are differences.

Try it

Deli Depot is a new franchise opportunity offering cold and hot sandwiches, soup, chilli con carne, fresh and frozen yoghurt, cakes and biscuits. It is positioned to compete with Subway and similar sandwich restaurants. Its unique advantages include special sauces on sandwiches, supplementary menu items such as soup and cakes, and quick delivery within specified zones.

The franchise package offered to franchisees includes information on the factors that typically influence consumers' selection of casual eating places.

These selection factors, in order from most important to least important, include food taste, food variety, value for money, restaurant reputation, friendliness of employees and convenience of location.

Robert Powell and a group of investors purchased the right to all franchise locations in the Brisbane metropolitan area. His group estimates that five units can be opened successfully in the first year and that a total of 30 can be opened in the first five years. Because this is a new franchise, potential customers must first be made aware of Deli Depot and then convinced to try it. Over the long run, a loyal customer base must be established to make each Deli Depot a success.

Questions

1   Are Deli Depot's unique advantages strong enough to attract customers from Subway and other sandwich competitors? Why or why not?

2   Are all the important customer selection factors for sandwich restaurants included in the list? Do you agree with the importance rankings? Explain your answers.

3   How can Robert and his group make potential customers aware of the new Deli Depot locations and menu selections?

4 How can Robert and his group convince individuals who try Deli Depot to become regular customers?

Watch it

Vermont Teddy Bear Co.: Workin' hard for the honey

In the tradition of Teddy Roosevelt and the 1902 'Great American Teddy Bear', the Vermont Teddy Bear brand carries on a rich heritage based on the best American values of compassion, generosity, friendship and a zesty sense of whimsy and fun. Founded in 1981, The Vermont Teddy Bear Co. Inc. is a designer, manufacturer and marketer of teddy bears and related products that appeal to customers' core values. Because the Vermont Teddy Bear Co. believes that people's value systems have a great effect on what they buy, it has designed bears around popular American themes. Americans admire hard work, entrepreneurship, achievement and success, so the company has a line of occupational bears. There's Businessman Bear, Doctor Bear, Webster the Computer Bear and Teacher Bear. Americans also value youth and health, hence the appeal for Fitness Bear. And in that sports-crazed country, official NFL Bears score big points.

The backbone of the Vermont Teddy Bear Co. is the patented and trademarked Bear-Gram. Bear-Grams are personalised teddy bears that are delivered directly to the recipient for special occasions such as birthdays, anniversaries, weddings and new births, as well as Valentine's Day, Christmas and Mother's Day. Sales are heavily seasonal. The key to the company's sales approach is the concept that buying decisions are based on individual differences. That's why the teddy bears are so highly customised. The company realises that men and women shop differently, and their cultural, social and economic roles affect their buying decisions.

It has therefore identified its customer profile as being primarily the urban professional male who waits until the last minute to buy a gift but who still wants something special. With individual differences in mind, the company created bears to fit different ages – Grandmother Bear, Baby Bears and Classic Birthday Bears. Different lifestyles – Golf Bears, Cowboy and Cowgirl Bears. Different life-cycle stages – Bride and Groom Bears, Pregnancy Bears, Anniversary Bears. Different personality traits – Cheerleader Bear. These irresistible furry creatures come in a variety of sizes with different coloured fur dressed in nearly 100 different personalised outfits.

Throughout the 1980s, the company wholesaled teddy bears to speciality stores and retailed them through its own outlets. Then in 1990, it introduced radio advertising for the Bear-Gram, positioning it as a novel gift for Valentine's Day and offering listeners a toll-free number to call to order from sales reps, known as Bear Counsellors. This test proved so successful that the concept was expanded to other major radio markets. Now, advertising for Valentine's Day has grown to 105 radio stations in 11 different markets, as well as on one syndicated network. Radio ads are frequently tagged with a reference to the company website, which in turn provides visual support for the radio advertising. This advertising works well for impulse buyers who hear the radio spot and make the decision to buy.

It is not surprising that annual sales peak at Valentine's Day because the strongest and most endearing message of the teddy bears is the message of love. Even the company catalogue is titled 'Red Hot ... Catalogue of Love'. Strong psychological influences affect consumer buying decisions, and teddy bears satisfy the important social needs of love and a sense of belonging. Whether it's the Sweetheart Bear or Cupid Bear, these romantic classics deliver the perfect bear hug. Family tours of the teddy bear factory and store in Shelburne, Vermont, drew over 129 000 visitors in 1997. And to make the factory visit more entertaining and draw additional traffic, the company implemented the Make-A-Friend-For-Life bear assembly area, where visitors can participate in the creation of their own teddy bear. Customers are not only buying a customised and personalised product, but they are also emotionally investing themselves in its design.

Unlike flowers, which only last for a short time, a Vermont Teddy Bear is steadfast and comes with a lifetime guarantee. Designed, cut and sewn by hand, each bear can be a future heirloom, and if it becomes injured, it can be sent to the Teddy Bear Hospital to be repaired at no charge. All Vermont Teddy Bears arrive at their destinations smiling in a fun gift box with sweets and a personalised message.

This complete understanding of its customers and what motivates their buying decisions has paid off. Total company revenues for 1997 reached US$16 489 000, showing that these bears are workin' hard for the honey.

Questions

1. Describe the cultural effects on the consumer buying decision for a teddy bear. See Exhibit 2.4.
2. Describe the individual factors that affect the consumer buying decision for a teddy bear. See Exhibit 2.4.
3. Describe the psychological factors that affect the consumer buying decision for a teddy bear. See Exhibit 2.4.
4. Describe the level of involvement for purchasing a teddy bear. See Exhibit 2.3.

Suggested reading

Vermont Teddy Bear Co. catalogue website: www.vtbear.com.

© 2003 Nelson Australia Pty Limited

Click it

Online reading

INFOTRAC® COLLEGE EDITION
For additional readings and review on consumer decision-making, explore InfoTrac® College Edition, your online library. Go to: www.infotrac-college.com and search for any of the InfoTrac key terms listed below:
- post-purchase behaviour
- consumer culture and values
- cognitive dissonance
- evoked set

Answer key

1. *Answer*: a, p. 28 *Rationale*: Need recognition is the first stage of consumer decision-making and is triggered when the consumer is exposed to either an internal or external stimulus.

2. *Answer*: d, p. 31 *Rationale*: Marketing-controlled information sources provide information on specific products through advertising, sales promotion and personal salespeople.

3. *Answer*: b, p. 32 *Rationale*: Sometimes known as the consideration set, the evoked set represents the group of products, within a particular category, that the buyer will further evaluate and make a choice from.

4. *Answer*: b, p. 35 *Rationale*: These types of goods and services are also commonly called low-involvement products because consumers spend little time on search and decision-making prior to purchase.

5. *Answer*: c, pp. 35–6 *Rationale*: While concern with price can be an element of perceived risk (financial risk), it is not automatically a factor that influences consumer involvement.

6. *Answer*: a, p. 40 *Rationale*: Values are those enduring beliefs shared by a society that specify modes of conduct that are preferable over others.

7. *Answer*: d, p. 38 *Rationale*: These factors are what consumers use to interact with their world, recognise feelings, and gather and analyse information.

8. *Answer*: a, p. 52 *Rationale*: Selective exposure means that consumers will use certain cues such as packaging or brand names to identify what information about products they should process further and what should be ignored.

9. *Answer*: a, pp. 56–7 *Rationale*: Changes in attitude can only be accomplished by a change in the way in which the individual attempts to reconcile old values with new information. This is done by changing beliefs about the product's attributes, changing the importance of certain beliefs or adding new consumer beliefs.

10. *Answer*: b, p. 54 *Rationale*: There are two types of learning: experiential and conceptual. Experiential learning occurs when a specific product experience changes the consumer's behaviour.

Business decision-making

CHAPTER THREE

LEARNING OBJECTIVES

After studying this chapter, you should be able to

1. Describe the unique aspects of business-to-business buying behaviour
2. Explain the differences between business and consumer markets
3. Discuss the unique aspects of business-to-business buying behaviour
4. Discuss the role of relationship marketing in business-to-business marketing
5. Identify the four main categories of business market customers
6. Describe the seven types of business goods and services

The success of many corporations today is directly related not only to their relationships with customers but also to the number and quality of their business relationships with other companies and to an understanding of the forces that impact their business. Many organisations are struggling to differentiate their products and services in an environment where customers are increasingly looking to reduce margins and to drive value down to the most common denominator – price. These pressures, coupled with advances in technology and pressures on organisational buyers to make quality decisions, have resulted in an increasing degree of commoditisation in many industries. Companies are always seeking competitive advantage through differentiation and through increasing uniqueness of their offerings, but if you don't understand your customers needs and their ability to recognise and appreciate your uniqueness then this is not a good approach.

Office Max on-line

Click on the website for the Office Max and see how they communicate the value they can offer business customers. Do you think they are competing on price or some other area of competitive advantage?
www.officemax.com.au

In order for organisations to make gains against the downward spiral of commoditisation, customers have to be able to comprehend, calculate or measure the value you are adding to the product offering. If they can't do this, they will ignore the features that they believe they don't need and look for factors that they can judge to assist in their decision-making (like functionality and ultimately price). Further, business marketers need to understand that their customers have additional pressures on them by their own organisations to make quality and efficient buying decisions. They tend to consider the unique value of your offering in light of how it impacts their job responsibility and performance as well as the performance of their organisation. Many organisational buyers prefer to build closer relationships with fewer vendors and as such more players are often included in the buying process located at higher levels in the organisation. This means that organisational marketers need to manage the complexity of communicating the value of their product from multiple perspectives and to each individual considering their particular job responsibility and self-interest. Gone are the days of locating the one, 'decision-maker' and using the same approach to communicate the unique value offer is destined for failure.

Therefore it is just as important in an organisational marketing setting to view the world through your customer's eyes and to see the problems and pressures they face. Business environments are competitive and technological advances are rapidly altering both industries and markets. If organisations are to resist the move to mass commoditisation and retain their competitive advantage then they need to understand and to assist their customers with the problems they face.

Adapted from Thull, J. 2004, *Driving Forces of Commoditization*, Business Marketing Association, 21 Feb 2005.

What is business-to-business marketing?

1 Describe the unique aspects of business-to-business buying behaviour

business-to-business marketing
The marketing of goods and services to individuals and organisations for purposes other than personal consumption.

Business-to-business marketing is the marketing of goods and services to individuals and organisations for purposes other than personal consumption. The sale of an overhead projector to your university or TAFE college is an example of business-to-business marketing. Business products include those that are used to manufacture other products, become parts of other products, aid the normal operations of an organisation, or are acquired for resale without any substantial change in form. The key characteristic distinguishing business goods and services from consumer goods and services is intended use, not physical characteristics. A product that is purchased for personal or family consumption or as a gift is a consumer product. If that same product, such as a computer or a mobile phone, is bought for use in a business, it is a business product. The emergence of the Internet has made business markets more competitive than ever before. With the Internet, every business in the world is potentially a local competitor. Many business marketers now realise that the Internet is a valuable tool for expanding markets and better serving customers.

Business versus consumer markets

The basic philosophy and practice of marketing is the same whether the customer is a business organisation or a consumer. Business markets, however, have characteristics different from consumer markets. Exhibit 3.1 summarises the main differences between business and consumer markets. These can be categorised as demand factors, purchase volume, number of customers, location of buyers, distribution structure, nature of buying, nature of buying influence, the type of negotiations, use of reciprocity, use of leasing, and primary promotional method. Each of these will be discussed in turn.

2 Explain the differences between business and consumer markets

Demand

Consumer demand for products is quite different from demand in the business market. Unlike consumer demand, business demand is derived, inelastic, joint and fluctuating. These terms will now be discussed in more detail.

Derived demand

The demand for business products is often termed **derived demand** because organisations buy products to be used in producing consumer products. In other words, the demand for these products is derived from the demand for consumer products. For example, two-thirds of the components that the Chrysler Corporation uses in manufacturing cars for the US market come from outside sources. This includes 60 000 different items purchased from 1140 suppliers.[1]

Because demand is derived, business marketers must carefully monitor demand patterns and changing preferences in final consumer markets, even though their customers are not in those markets. Moreover, business marketers must carefully monitor their customers' forecasts, because derived demand is based on expectations of future demand for those customers' products.

Some business marketers not only monitor final consumer demand and customer forecasts but also try to influence final consumer demand. They do this for several reasons, sometimes in an attempt to smooth out consumer demand cycles and at other times in an attempt to influence the total demand for their products.

Aluminium producers use television and magazine advertisements to point out the convenience and recycling opportunities that aluminium offers to consumers, who can choose to purchase soft drinks in either aluminium or plastic containers.

derived demand
The demand for business products.

Dell Computer on-line

What special offers and systems does Dell Computer provide for its business clients? What industry sectors do you think it is trying to service? Go to the Dell Computer website and have a look.
www.dell.com.au

Inelastic demand

The demand for many business products is inelastic with regard to price. *Inelastic demand* means that an increase or decrease in the price of the product won't significantly affect demand for the product.

The price of a product used in the production of or as part of a final product is often a minor portion of the final product's total price. Therefore, demand for the final consumer product is not affected. If the price of automotive paint or engine parts rose significantly, say 200 per cent in one year, do you think the number of new cars sold that year would be affected? Probably not.

Exhibit 3.1
Major characteristics of business markets compared to consumer markets

Characteristic	Business market	Consumer market
Demand	Organisational	Individual
Purchase volume	Larger	Smaller
Number of customers	Fewer	Many
Location of buyers	Geographically concentrated	Dispersed
Distribution structure	More direct	More indirect
Nature of buying	More professional	More personal
Nature of buying influence	Multiple	Single
Type of negotiations	More complex	Simpler
Use of reciprocity	Yes	No
Use of leasing	Greater	Lesser
Primary promotional method	Personal selling	Advertising

Joint demand

Joint demand occurs when two or more items are used together in a final product. For example, a decline in the availability of memory chips will slow production of computers, which will in turn reduce the demand for disk drives. Many business products, such as axe heads and axe handles, exemplify joint demand.

joint demand
The demand for two or more items used together in a final product.

Recent marketing campaigns highlight the convenience and recycling benefits of aluminium cans and products. By also mentioning the positive environmental impact of using aluminium, producers hope to influence consumer demand.

Fluctuating demand

The demand for business products – particularly new plant and equipment – tends to be more unstable than the demand for consumer products. A small increase or decrease in consumer demand can produce a much larger change in demand for the facilities and equipment needed to make the consumer product. Economists refer to this phenomenon as the **multiplier effect** (or **accelerator principle**).

Cummins Engine Company, a producer of heavy-duty diesel engines, uses sophisticated surface grinders to make parts. Suppose Cummins is using 20 surface grinders. Each machine lasts about 10 years. Purchases have been timed so that two machines will wear out and be replaced annually. If the demand for engine parts does not change, two grinders will be bought this year. If the demand for parts declines slightly, only 18 grinders may be needed and Cummins won't replace the worn ones. However, suppose in the next year demand returns to previous levels plus a little more. To meet the new level of demand, Cummins will need to replace the two machines that wore out in the first year, the two that wore out in the second year, plus one or more additional machines. The multiplier effect works this way in many industries, producing highly fluctuating demand for business products.

> **multiplier effect (accelerator principle)**
> Phenomenon in which a small increase or decrease in consumer demand can produce a much larger change in demand for the facilities and equipment needed to make the consumer product.

Purchase volume

Business customers buy in much larger quantities than consumers. Just think how large an order Kellogg typically places for the wheat bran and sultanas used to manufacture Sultana Bran. Imagine the number of tyres that Ford or Holden buys at one time. The Ford Motor Company during 2000 had vehicle sales in Australia of 125 000. This means 625 000 tyres were used (including the spare) to fit the cars.

Number of customers

Business marketers usually have far fewer customers than consumer marketers. The advantage is that it is a lot easier to identify prospective buyers, monitor current customers' needs and levels of satisfaction, and personally attend to existing customers. The main disadvantage is that each customer becomes crucial – especially for those manufacturers that have only one customer, as may be the case for businesses that have the government as their customer.

Location of buyers

Business customers tend to be much more geographically concentrated than consumers. For example, more than half the nation's business buyers are located in the major capital cities in Australia, and yet there are many firms, located in Victoria, that manufacture car products.

Distribution structure

Many consumer products pass through a distribution system that includes the producer, one or more wholesalers and a retailer. However, because of many of the characteristics already mentioned, such as small customer numbers that are geographically concentrated, channels of distribution are typically shorter in business marketing. Direct channels, where manufacturers market directly to business customers, are much more common.

Many businesses that market directly to users are discovering that new media, such as CD-ROMs and the World Wide Web, offer great potential for reaching new and existing customers domestically and around the world, while reducing costs to both buyers and sellers.[2]

Nature of buying

Unlike consumers, most business buyers usually approach purchasing rather formally. Businesses use professionally trained purchasing agents or buyers who usually get to know the items and the sellers well. These relationships are important to both the suppliers and the buyers. Strong relationships generally mean purchasers will be loyal to a particular supplier and the supplier will have the opportunity to really understand and deliver on the customer's needs.

Nature of buying influence

Typically, more people are involved in a single business purchase decision than in a consumer purchase. Experts from fields as varied as quality control, marketing and finance, as well as professional buyers and users, may be grouped in a buying centre (discussed later in this chapter).

Type of negotiations

Consumers are used to negotiating price on cars and real estate. In most cases, however, consumers expect sellers to set the price and other conditions of sale, such as time of delivery and credit terms. In contrast, negotiating is common in business marketing. Buyers and sellers negotiate product specifications, delivery dates, payment terms and other pricing matters. Sometimes these negotiations occur during many meetings over several months. Final contracts are often very long and detailed.

Businesses commonly lease expensive equipment such as cars because it reduces the capital outflow, allows them to acquire the latest model, gives them better services and gains them tax advantages.

Use of reciprocity

Business purchasers often choose to buy from their own customers, a practice known as **reciprocity**. For example, General Motors (GM) buys engines for use in its cars and trucks from Borg Warner, which, in turn, buys many of the cars and trucks it needs from GM. This practice is neither unethical nor illegal unless one party coerces the other. Reciprocity is generally considered a reasonable business practice. If all possible suppliers sell a similar product for about the same price, doesn't it make sense to buy from those firms that buy from you? The marketing challenge for other companies is to overcome the competitive advantage gained by a reciprocated supplier. This can be done through emphasising other values and benefits the organisation may offer.

> **reciprocity**
> A practice where business purchasers choose to buy from their own customers.

Use of leasing

Consumers normally buy products rather than lease them. However, businesses commonly lease expensive equipment such as computers, construction equipment and vehicles, and cars. Leasing allows firms to reduce capital outflow, acquire a seller's latest products, receive better services and gain tax advantages.

The lessor, the firm providing the product, may be either the manufacturer or an independent firm. The benefits to the lessor include greater total revenue from leasing compared to selling and an opportunity to do business with customers who cannot afford to buy.

Primary promotional method

Business marketers emphasise personal selling in their promotion efforts, especially for expensive items, custom-designed products, large-volume purchases and situations requiring negotiations. The sale of many business products requires a great deal of personal contact. Personal selling is discussed in more detail in Chapter 10.

Business buying behaviour

As you probably have already concluded, business buyers behave differently from consumers. Understanding how purchase decisions are made in organisations is the first step in developing a business-to-business selling strategy. Five important aspects of business buying behaviour are buying centres, evaluative criteria, buying situations, purchasing ethics and customer service.

> **3** Discuss the unique aspects of business-to-business buying behaviour

Buying centres

A **buying centre** includes all those persons in an organisation who become involved in the purchase decision. Membership and influence vary from company to company. For example, in engineering-dominated firms such as Bell Helicopter, the buying centre may consist almost entirely of engineers. In marketing-oriented firms such as Toyota and IBM, marketing and engineering have almost equal authority. In consumer goods firms such as Unilever, product managers and other marketing decision-makers may dominate the buying centre. In a small manufacturing company, almost everyone may be a member.

> **buying centre**
> A group including all those persons who become involved in the purchase decision.

The number of people involved in a buying centre varies with the complexity and importance of a purchase decision. The composition of the buying group will usually change from one purchase to another and sometimes even during various stages of the buying process. To make matters more complicated, buying centres don't appear on formal organisation charts. Noting the change in buying centre membership over time, an IBM executive remarked, 'I started out (in the 1980s) selling to the corner office [CEO], then we got moved to the CFO, and then to the data processing manager, and finally to the data centre manager.'[3]

For example, even though a formal committee may have been set up to choose a new computer system for a company, it is only part of the buying centre. Other people, such as the managing director, often play informal yet powerful roles. In a lengthy decision-making process, such as finding a new computer system, some members may drop out of the buying centre when they can no longer play a useful role. Others whose talents are needed then become part of the centre. No formal announcement of 'who is in' and 'who is out' is ever made.

Roles in the buying centre

As in family purchasing decisions, several people may play a role in the business purchase process:

- *Initiator*: the person who first suggests making a purchase.
- *Influencers/evaluators*: people who influence the buying decision. They often help to define specifications and provide information for evaluating options. Technical personnel are especially important as influencers.
- *Gatekeepers*: group members who regulate the flow of information. Frequently, the purchasing agent views the gatekeeping role as a source of their power. A secretary may also act as a gatekeeper by determining which vendors get an appointment with a buyer.
- *Decider*: the person who has the formal or informal power to choose or approve the selection of the supplier or brand. In complex situations, it is often difficult to determine who makes the final decision.
- *Purchaser*: the person who actually negotiates the purchase. It could be anyone from the managing director of the company to the purchasing agent, depending on the importance of the decision.
- *Users*: members of the organisation who will actually use the product. Users often initiate the buying process and help to define product specifications. An example illustrating these basic roles is shown in Exhibit 3.2.

Implications of buying centres for the marketing manager

Successful vendors realise the importance of identifying who is in the decision-making unit, each member's relative influence in the buying decision and each member's evaluative criteria. Successful selling strategies often focus on determining the most important buying influences and tailoring sales presentations to the evaluative criteria most important to these buying-centre members.

For example, Loctite Corporation, the manufacturer of Super Glue and industrial adhesives and sealants, found that engineers were the most important influencers and deciders in adhesive and sealant purchase decisions. As a result, Loctite focused its marketing efforts on production and maintenance engineers.

Exhibit 3.2
Buying centre roles for computer purchases

Role	Illustration
Initiator	Managing director proposes to replace company's computer network.
Influencers/evaluators	Company accountant and computing section manager have an important say about which system and vendor the company will deal with.
Gatekeepers	Various department heads for purchasing and data processing analyse the company's needs and recommend likely matches with potential vendors.
Decider	The head of the purchasing centre, or possibly the chief accountant, with advice from others, selects the vendor the company will deal with and the system it will buy.
Purchaser	The purchasing department negotiates the terms of sale.
Users	All divisional and departmental employees use the computers.

Evaluative criteria

Business buyers evaluate products and suppliers against three important criteria: quality, service and price – in that order.

Quality

Quality refers to technical suitability. A superior tool can do a better job in the production process, and superior packaging can increase dealer and consumer acceptance of a brand. Evaluation of quality also applies to the salesperson and the salesperson's firm. Business buyers want to deal with reputable salespeople and companies that are financially responsible. Quality improvement should be part of every organisation's marketing strategy.

Service

Almost as much as they want satisfactory products, business buyers want satisfactory service. A purchase offers several opportunities for service. Suppose a vendor is selling heavy equipment. Pre-purchase service could include a survey of the buyer's needs. After thorough analysis of the survey findings, the vendor could prepare a report and recommendations in the form of a purchasing proposal. If a purchase results, post-purchase service might consist of installing the equipment and training those who will be using it. Other after-sale services may also include maintenance and repairs. Another service that business buyers seek is dependability of supply. They must be able to count on delivery of what was ordered when it is scheduled to be delivered. Buyers also welcome services that help them to sell their finished products. Services of this sort are especially appropriate when the seller's product is an identifiable part of the buyer's end product.

Price

Business buyers want to buy at low prices – at the lowest prices, under most circumstances. However, a buyer who pressures a supplier to cut prices to a point where the supplier loses money on the sale almost forces shortcuts on quality. The buyer also may, in effect, force the supplier to quit selling to him or her. Then a new source of supply will have to be found.

Many international business buyers use similar evaluative criteria. One study of South African buyers of high-tech laboratory instruments found that they use the following evaluative criteria, in descending order: technical service, perceived product reliability, after-sales support, supplier's reputation, ease of maintenance, ease of operation, price, confidence in the sales representative and product flexibility.[4]

Businesses require satisfactory after-sales service. This may mean installing the equipment of training employees in its use.

Buying situations

Often business firms, especially manufacturers, must decide whether to make something or buy it from an outside supplier. The decision is essentially one of economics. Can an item of similar quality be bought at a lower price elsewhere? If not, is manufacturing it in-house the best use of limited company resources? For example, Briggs & Stratton, a major manufacturer of four-cylinder engines, might be able to save $150 000 annually on outside purchases by spending $500 000 on the equipment needed to produce gas throttles internally. Yet Briggs & Stratton could also use that $500 000 to upgrade its carburettor assembly line, which would save $225 000 annually. If a firm does decide to buy a product instead of making it, the purchase will be a new buy, a modified rebuy or a straight rebuy.

New buy

new buy
A situation requiring the purchase of a product for the first time.

A **new buy** is a situation requiring the purchase of a product for the first time. For example, suppose a law firm decides to replace word-processing machinery with microcomputers. This situation represents the greatest opportunity for new vendors. No long-term relationship has been established for this product, specifications may be somewhat fluid, and buyers are generally more open to new vendors.

If the new item is a raw material or a critical component part, the buyer cannot afford to run out of supply. The seller must be able to convince the buyer that the seller's firm can consistently deliver a high-quality product on time.

Modified rebuy

A **modified rebuy** is normally less critical and less time-consuming than a new buy. In a modified-rebuy situation, the purchaser wants some change in the original good or service. It may be a new colour, greater strength in a component part, more respondents in a marketing research study or additional services in a cleaning contract.

Because buyer and seller are familiar with each other and credibility has been established, the two parties can concentrate on the specifics of the modification. But in some cases, modified rebuys are open to outside bidders. The purchaser uses this strategy to ensure that the new terms are competitive. An example would be a law firm deciding to buy more powerful computers. The firm may open the bidding to all interested suppliers, even though they have made purchases from one particular firm for some time. This practice allows them to examine the price/quality offerings of several suppliers.

> **modified rebuy**
> Situation where the purchaser wants some change in the original good or service.

Straight rebuy

Vendors prefer a **straight rebuy** situation. The purchaser is not looking for new information or other suppliers. An order is placed and the product is provided as in previous orders. Usually a straight rebuy is routine because the terms of the purchase have been agreed to in earlier negotiations. An example would be the law firm purchasing printer cartridges from the same supplier on a regular basis.

One common instrument used in straight rebuy situations is the purchasing contract. Purchasing contracts are used with products that are bought often and in high volume. In essence, the purchasing contract makes the buyer's decision-making routine and promises the salesperson a sure sale. The advantage to the buyer is a quick, confident decision and, to the salesperson, reduced or eliminated competition.

Suppliers must remember not to take straight rebuy relationships for granted. Retaining existing customers is much easier than attracting new ones.

> **straight rebuy**
> Buying situation in which the purchaser reorders the same goods or services without looking for new information or investigating other suppliers.

Purchasing ethics

The ethics of business buyer and seller relationships are often scrutinised and sometimes criticised by superiors, associates, other prospective suppliers, the general public and the news media. Managers of organisations need to consider what will be acceptable and proper behaviour and a clear message about the integrity and values of that organisation. The Ethics in marketing box discusses some of these issues.

Customer service

Business marketers are increasingly recognising the benefits of developing a formal system to monitor customer opinions and perceptions of the quality of customer service. Companies such as McDonald's, Coles Myer and GMH build their strategies not only around products but also around a few highly developed service skills. Many firms are finding new ways to enhance customer service through technology. Business marketers are leading the way in the adoption of new media technologies such as on-line services, CD-ROMs and the World Wide Web. Federal Express Corporation, for example, began a service on the Web in November 1994 that gave customers a direct window into FedEx's package-tracking database (www.fedex.com.au). FedEx is now saving about US$2 million per year and improving customer service by replacing humans with a website.[5]

Ethics IN MARKETING

The benefits of integrity

To build integrity in an organisation, the top management must clearly define the company's core values. Values statements that deal with issues of integrity and ethics go way beyond feel-good statements in vision and mission statements of organisations. Instead they reflect what the organisation is, what it stands for, the types of behaviours that are accepted and the company's core identity. There are many cases where maintaining standards high in ethics and integrity can cost organisations money, time and possibly customers. Take the example of a company importing goods to Australia from another country. The goods are being held overseas in customs and it has been made known that the payment of a bribe (common practice in the country of origin) would release the goods.

Does the Australian executive pay the bribe, meet the budget targets and get the products to market, or take a moral perspective, have the goods held indefinitely in customs and possibly miss the market opportunity? Similarly, what if setting high standards of integrity, and ensuring that your practices and employees abide by the law, increases costs of operations to the point where the competitive position of the organisation is compromised? So how do managers deal with these sorts of dilemmas? Well, interestingly, there is a definite increase in the number of consumers and organisations who only want to deal with those companies that publish and abide by a strong and clear policy of integrity and ethics and these behaviours are being translated into the corporate image and brand. So while taking the easy option can be attractive, those organisations that operate with integrity are also now beginning to benefit.

Adapted from: Hooijberg, R. 2005, 'How to ensure integrity', *Chief Executive*, January/February, Vol 205.

Relationship marketing and strategic alliances

4 Discuss the role of relationship marketing in business-to-business marketing

As Chapter 1 explained, relationship marketing is the strategy that entails seeking and establishing ongoing partnerships with customers. Relationship marketing is redefining the fundamental roles of business buyers and sellers. Suppliers are making major adjustments in their thinking, management styles and methods of responding to purchasers' standards and operational requirements. A satisfied customer is one of the best sources of business. When the customer knows that the supplier can meet expectations and deliver on what the supplier has promised, trust is created; and trust is the foundation of most successful relationship marketing efforts.[6] According to Louis V. Gerstner, Jr, chairman and chief executive of IBM in the United States, the most basic notion of how to succeed in business is talking to customers, learning their needs and figuring out how to satisfy them.[7]

A **strategic alliance**, sometimes called a **strategic partnership**, is a cooperative agreement between business firms. Strategic alliances can take the form of licensing or distribution agreements, joint ventures, research and development consortia, and partnerships. They may be between manufacturers, manufacturers and customers, manufacturers and suppliers, and manufacturers

strategic alliance (strategic partnership)
A cooperative agreement between business firms.

and channel intermediaries. Many of you would be familiar with the strategic alliances used by many international airlines now, where groups of airlines transfer benefits and facilities to each others customers. In this form of manufacturing strategic alliance, all partners benefit from an enlarged customer base without the added cost of infrastructure (building airport lounges around the world) and without the added marketing costs.

The Global perspectives box below provides an example of a strategic alliance between BHP and a smaller mineral exploration company, Exco.

BHP and Exco (the big and the small)

Global PERSPECTIVES

In 1997, BHP began a commercial arrangement with a purpose-built company, Exco, for mineral exploration. BHP and Exco have formed a strategic alliance, which aims to aggressively pursue agreed exploration opportunities. These opportunities are generated from BHP's database and its previous exploration programs.

When a suitable exploration site is uncovered, BHP and Exco agree that the area is to be subject to the rights of the strategic alliance agreement. Subsequently, Exco has the rights to explore the area for a specified time, provided that minimum expenditure guidelines are met. If Exco's exploration uncovers a resource with an in-ground value of less than $2 billion, Exco has the right to apply for the mining lease for the area. Where a resource is uncovered with an in-ground value equal to or greater than $2 billion, BHP is then entitled to the resource.

The main reason for BHP initiating such an alliance is that its exploration activities are focused on large tonnage, high-grade ore bodies. Consequently, many target areas are uncovered that don't meet BHP's criteria, but have high potential for economic mineralisation. Exco's role within the alliance is therefore to complement BHP's exploration style by applying different models and exploration methods.[8]

The trend towards forming strategic alliances is accelerating rapidly. The consulting firm Booz, Allen & Hamilton reports that some 32 000 alliances were formed around the world between 1995 and 1998, and 75 per cent of them were international alliances.[9] Some industry analysts don't necessarily agree that this trend towards strategic alliances is always a good thing. According to *Global Futures Bulletin*, the annual revenue of the world's 500 largest corporations is US$10 trillion, about twice the size of the gross domestic product of the United States. Further, in several industries such as computers, software and media, more than 40 per cent of the world market is controlled by fewer than five companies. This concentration of power in the hands of a few companies is seen as problematic for regulatory authorities and for smaller businesses.[10] In spite of these concerns, strategic alliances offer companies the opportunity to lower their costs and to expand their market opportunities by capitalising on other countries' and companies' strengths. For example, in Japan, IBM has a strategic alliance with Ricoh to distribute low-end computers and another with Fuji Bank to market financial systems. IBM has similar links with other Japanese firms. Ford and Mazda have collaborated on at least 10 different car models.

Xerox on-line

What can you find out about Xerox's partnerships from its website?
www.xerox.com

Many companies have realised that strategic partnerships are more than just important – they are critical. Xerox management, for example, has decided that in order to maintain its leadership position in the reprographics industry, the company must 'include suppliers as part of the Xerox family'. This strategy often means reducing the number of suppliers, treating those that remain as allies, sharing strategic information freely, and drawing on supplier expertise in developing new products that can meet the quality, cost and delivery standards of the marketplace.

In a Volkswagen truck assembly plant in Brazil, seven different suppliers make components in the plant using their own equipment. These supplier workers then fasten the components to a chassis moving down an assembly line through the various suppliers' spaces.[11]

Business marketers form strategic alliances to add value to what they do well by partnering with others who have complementary expertise to achieve the following:[12]

- Access to markets or to technology
- Economies of scale that might be gained by combining manufacturing, R&D or marketing activities
- Faster entry of new products to markets
- Sharing of risk.

Some alliances are extremely successful and some are dismal failures. Exhibit 3.3 identifies six hints for making an alliance successful.

Exhibit 3.3

Hints for making strategic alliances successful

- Trust one another (alliances break down when one partner becomes greedy).
- Share a common interest in meeting customer needs.
- Bring different skills to the market.
- Share gains (and have a built-in system for ongoing change).
- Understand which party will have direct contact with the customer.
- Understand that success and profitability are tied to customer satisfaction.

Source: From 'Alliance Highlights', *Fortune*, Best Practices Symposium, 30 March 1998. Reprinted by permission.

The producer segment of the business market includes manufacturing, such as this vehicle production line, as well as construction, finance, transportation, real estate and others.

Major categories of business customers

The business market consists of four main categories of customers: producers, resellers, governments and institutions.

5 Identify the four main categories of business market customers

Producers

The producer segment of the business market includes profit-oriented individuals and organisations that use purchased goods and services to produce other products, to incorporate into other products, or to facilitate the daily operations of the organisation. Examples of producers include construction, manufacturing, transportation, finance, real estate and food service firms. Some of these firms are small and others are among the world's largest businesses.

Individual producers often buy large quantities of goods and services. Companies such as General Motors spend more than US$70 billion annually on business products such as steel, metal components and tyres. Companies such as General Electric, Dupont and IBM spend over US$60 million daily for business goods and services.[13]

Resellers

The reseller market includes retail and wholesale businesses that buy finished goods and resell them for a profit. A retailer sells mainly to final consumers; wholesalers sell mostly to retailers and other organisational customers. There are approximately 70 000 retailers and 38 500 wholesalers operating in Australia. Consumer product firms such as Unilever, Kraft General Foods and Coca-Cola sell directly to large retailers and retail chains and through wholesalers to smaller retail units. Retailing and wholesaling are explored in detail in Chapter 8.

Business product distributors are wholesalers that buy business products and resell them to business customers. They often carry thousands of items in stock and employ sales forces to call on business customers. Businesses that wish to buy 1000 pencils or 100 kilograms of fertiliser typically purchase these items from local distributors rather than directly from manufacturers such as Crayola or Incitec.

Governments

A third major segment of the business market is government. Government organisations include thousands of federal, state and local buying units. Contracts for government purchases are often put out for tender. Interested vendors submit bids (usually sealed) to provide specified products during a particular time. Usually the lowest bidder is awarded the contract, and when the lowest bidder is not awarded the contract, strong evidence must be presented to justify the decision. Grounds for rejecting the lowest bid include lack of experience, inadequate financing or poor past performance. Bidding allows all potential suppliers an equal chance at winning government contracts and helps to ensure that public funds are spent wisely.

Federal government

Name just about any good or service and it is likely that someone in the federal government uses it. The federal government is one of the largest customers of Australian businesses.

Although much of the federal government's buying is centralised, no single federal agency contracts for all the government's requirements, and no single buyer in any agency purchases all that the agency needs. We can view the federal government as a combination of several large companies with overlapping responsibilities and thousands of small independent units.

One popular source of information about government procurement can be found on the federal government website at www.fed.gov.au in the business section. It contains information on how to tender and what tenders are currently available, as well as on the standards that are required for government purchasing.

State government

Selling to states can be less frustrating for both small and large vendors than selling to the federal government. As in the case of federal government buying, state governments send their buying requirements to tender. Information on how to tender and what tenders are currently available can also be found on the various state government websites, such as www.qld.gov.au and www.nsw.gov.au. State buying agencies include school districts, highway departments, government-operated hospitals and housing agencies.

Institutions

The fourth major segment of the business market is institutions that seek to achieve goals other than the standard business goals of profit, market share and return on investment. This segment includes schools, hospitals, TAFE colleges and universities, churches, labour unions, civic clubs, foundations and other non-profit organisations.

Types of business products

6 Describe the seven types of business goods and services

Business products generally fall into one of the following seven categories, depending on their use: major equipment, accessory equipment, raw materials, component parts, processed materials, supplies and business services.

Major equipment

major equipment
Capital goods such as large or expensive machines, mainframe computers, blast furnaces, generators, aeroplanes and buildings.

Major equipment includes such capital goods as large or expensive machines, mainframe computers, blast furnaces, generators, aeroplanes and buildings. (These items are also commonly called **installations**.) Major equipment is depreciated over time rather than charged as an expense in the year it is purchased; in addition, it is often custom-designed for each customer. Personal selling is an important part of the marketing strategy for major equipment because distribution channels are almost always direct from the producer to the business user.

Accessory equipment

Accessory equipment is generally less expensive and shorter lived than major equipment. Examples include portable drills, power tools, microcomputers and fax machines. Accessory equipment is often charged as an expense in the year it is bought rather than depreciated over its useful life. In contrast to major equipment, accessories are more often standardised and are usually bought by more customers. These customers tend to be widely dispersed. For example, all types of businesses buy microcomputers.

Local industrial distributors (wholesalers) play an important role in the marketing of accessory equipment because business buyers often purchase accessories from them. Regardless of where accessories are bought, advertising is a more vital promotional tool for accessory equipment than for major equipment.

accessory equipment
Goods, such as portable tools and office equipment, that are less expensive and shorter lived than major equipment.

Raw materials

Raw materials are unprocessed extractive or agricultural products – for example, mineral ore, timber, wheat, corn, fruits, vegetables and fish. Raw materials become part of finished products. Extensive users, such as steel or timber mills and food canners, generally buy huge quantities of raw materials. Because there are often a large number of relatively small sellers of raw materials, none can greatly influence price or supply. Thus, the market tends to set the price of raw materials, and individual producers have little pricing flexibility. Promotion is almost always via personal selling, and distribution channels are usually direct from producer to business user.

raw materials
Unprocessed extractive or agricultural products such as mineral ore, timber, wheat, corn, fruits, vegetables or fish.

Raw materials such as logs become part of finished products and are generally purchased in huge quantities.

Component parts

Component parts are either finished items ready for assembly or products that need very little processing before becoming part of some other product. Examples include spark plugs, tyres and motors for cars. A special feature of component parts is that they often retain their identity after becoming part of the final product. For example, tyres are clearly recognisable as part of a car. Moreover, because component parts often wear out, they may need to be replaced several times during the life of the final product. Thus, there are two important markets for many component parts: the original equipment manufacturer (OEM) market and the replacement market.

Many of the business features listed in Exhibit 3.1 characterise the OEM market. The difference between unit costs and selling prices in the OEM market is often small, but profits can be substantial because of volume buying.

The replacement market is composed of organisations and individuals buying component parts to replace worn-out parts. Because components often retain their identity in final products, users may choose to replace a component part with the same brand used by the manufacturer – for example, the same brand of car tyres or battery. The replacement market operates differently from the OEM market, however. Whether replacement buyers are organisations or individuals, they tend to demonstrate the characteristics of consumer markets that were shown in Exhibit 3.1. Consider, for example, a car replacement part. Purchase volume is usually small and there are many customers, geographically dispersed, who typically buy from car dealers or parts stores. Negotiations don't occur, and neither reciprocity nor leasing is usually an issue.

Manufacturers of component parts often direct their advertising towards replacement buyers. Cooper Tire & Rubber, for example, makes and markets component parts – car and truck tyres – for the replacement market only. Ford and other car makers compete with independent firms in the market for replacement car parts.

Processed materials

Processed materials are used directly in manufacturing other products. Unlike raw materials, they have had some processing. Examples include sheet metal, chemicals, speciality steel, timber, corn syrup and plastics. Unlike component parts, processed materials don't retain their identity in final products.

Most processed materials are marketed to OEMs or to distributors servicing the OEM market. Processed materials are generally supplied according to customer specifications or some industry standard, as is the case with steel and timber. Price and service are important factors in choosing a vendor.

Supplies

Supplies are consumable items that don't become part of the final product – for example, detergents, paper towels, pencils and paper. Supplies are normally standardised items that purchasing agents routinely buy. Supplies typically have relatively short lives and are inexpensive compared to other business goods. Because supplies generally fall into one of three categories – maintenance, repair or operating supplies – this category is often referred to as MRO items.

---

component parts
Either finished items ready for assembly or products that need very little processing before becoming part of some other product.

processed materials
Products used directly in manufacturing other products.

supplies
Consumable items that don't become part of the final product.

Competition in the MRO market is intense. Bic and PaperMate, for example, compete intensely for business purchases of inexpensive ballpoint pens.

Business services

Business services are expense items that don't become part of a final product. Businesses often retain outside providers to perform advertising, legal, management consulting, marketing research, maintenance, cleaning and other services. Hiring an outside provider makes sense when it costs less than hiring or assigning an employee to perform the task and when an outside provider is needed for particular expertise.

> **business services**
> Expense items that don't become part of a final product.

Connect it

Look back at the story about how business marketers need to understand their customers and the complex issues that they deal with when making buying decisions. Successful business marketers attempt to consider the buying process from their customer's perspective and to present solutions to their buying problems that will add value to the products they are attempting to sell. To ignore the customer is to take for granted their needs and increase the risk of commoditisation of the product offering. Global businesses also need to be aware of the ethics of aligning with others and doing business in other parts of the world that may have different values. Regardless of the type of business market, marketers need to consider the totality of their actions and the impact they will have on both their customers and their industry.

Summary

1 Discuss the unique aspects of business-to-business buying behaviour.
Business buying behaviour is distinguished by five fundamental characteristics. First, buying is normally undertaken by a buying centre consisting of many people who range widely in authority level. Second, business buyers typically evaluate alternative products and suppliers based on quality, service and price in that order. Third, business buying falls into three general categories: new buys, modified rebuys and straight rebuys. Fourth, the ethics of business buyers and sellers are often scrutinised. Fifth, customer service before, during and after the sale plays a big role in business purchase decisions.

2 Explain the main differences between business and consumer markets.
In business markets, demand is derived, price-inelastic, joint and fluctuating. Purchase volume is much larger than in consumer markets, customers are fewer in number and more geographically concentrated, and distribution channels are more direct. Buying is approached more formally using professional purchasing agents, more people are involved in the buying process, negotiation is more complex, and reciprocity and leasing are more common. And, finally, selling strategy in business markets normally focuses on personal contact rather than on advertising.

Define it

accessory equipment 83
business services 85
business-to-business marketing 68
buying centre 73
component parts 84
derived demand 69
joint demand 70
major equipment 82
modified rebuy 77
multiplier effect (accelerator principle) 71
new buy 76
processed materials 84
raw materials 83
reciprocity 73
straight rebuy 77
strategic alliance (strategic partnership) 78
supplies 84

3 Discuss the role of relationship marketing and strategic alliances in business-to-business marketing.

Relationship marketing entails seeking and establishing long-term alliances or partnerships with customers. A strategic alliance is a cooperative agreement between business firms. Firms form alliances to enhance what they do well by partnering with others who have complementary skills.

4 Identify the four main categories of business market customers.

Producer markets consist of for-profit organisations and individuals who buy products to use in producing other products, as components of other products or in facilitating business operations. Reseller markets consist of wholesalers and retailers that buy finished products to resell for profit. Government markets include federal, state and local governments that buy goods and services to support their own operations and serve the needs of citizens. Institutional markets consist of very diverse non-profit institutions whose main goals don't include profit.

5 Describe the seven types of business goods and services.

Major equipment includes capital goods, such as heavy machinery. Accessory equipment is typically less expensive and shorter lived than major equipment. Raw materials are extractive or agricultural products that have not been processed. Component parts are finished or near-finished items to be used as parts of other products. Processed materials are used to manufacture other products. Supplies are consumable and not used as part of a final product. Business services are intangible products that many companies use in their operations.

Review it

1. Business products are those that
   a. Are used to manufacture other products
   b. Become part of another product
   c. Aid the normal operations of an organisation
   d. Are all of the above

2. The Internet has
   a. Made business markets less competitive
   b. Made business markets more competitive
   c. Had little impact on the level of competitiveness in business markets
   d. Not significantly impacted the business marketplace

3. If you market goods to producers, you must also research sales trends in related consumer markets because demand for your products is
   a. Relational
   b. Elastic
   c. Derived
   d. Institutional

4. Which element of promotion is used most frequently with business products such as major equipment, accessory equipment or component parts?
   a. Personal selling
   b. Sales promotion
   c. Public relations
   d. Advertising

5 In a buying centre, the gatekeeper
   a First suggests making a purchase
   b Influences the buying decision
   c Regulates the flow of information
   d Has the power to approve the selection of brand

6 In which criteria order do business buyers evaluate products?
   a Quality, service, price
   b Price, service, quality
   c Service, price, quality
   d Price, quality, service

7 Business firms make three types of buying decisions which align with the decision-making continuum used by individual consumers. These decisions types are
   a New buy, rebuy and modified buy
   b New buy, modified buy and full rebuy
   c New buy, modified buy and straight rebuy
   d New buy, rebuy and straight rebuy

8 _____ marketing is the strategy that entails seeking and establishing ongoing partnerships with customers.
   a Relationship
   b Business
   c Consumer
   d Administered

9 The four major categories or segments of the business market are
   a Schools, hospitals, factories and warehouses
   b Producers, consumers, retailers and wholesalers
   c Producers, resellers, governments and institutions
   d Institutions, agriculture, retailers and wholesalers

10 There are seven types of business products. Component parts are
    a Unprocessed extractive or agricultural products
    b Goods such as portable tools and office equipment
    c Products that need very little processing before being used
    d Products used directly in manufacturing other products

Check the Answer Key to see how well you understood the material. More detailed discussion and writing questions and a video case related to this chapter are found in the Student Resources CD-ROM.

Apply it

1 How might derived demand affect the manufacturing of a car?
2 Why is relationship or personal selling the best way to promote in business marketing?
3 A colleague of yours has sent you an email seeking your advice as he attempts to sell a new voice-mail system to a local business. Send him a return email describing the various people who might influence the customer's buying decision. Be sure to include suggestions for dealing with the needs of each of these individuals.

4 Intel Corporation supplies microprocessors to Compaq for use in their computers. Describe the buying situation in this relationship, keeping in mind the rapid development of technology in this industry.

5 In small groups, brainstorm examples of companies whose products fall into the different business categories. (Avoid examples already listed in the chapter.) Compile a list of 10 specific business products including at least one in each category. Then match up with another group. Have each group take turns naming a product and have the other group identify its appropriate category. Try to resolve all discrepancies by discussion.

6 Some identified products might appropriately fit into more than one category.

7 The Department of Employment, Workplace Relations and Small Business (www.dewrsb.gov.au) publishes a website that gives hints, tips and websites it considers most useful to small businesses. Visit one or more of these sites and then write a memo to a colleague who is considering starting a new business. Describe why he or she should visit this website.

8 What business publications, search facilities, sources and services does the following website offer? www.news.ninemsn.com.au/smallbusiness/default.asp

9 Compare the above website to the Australian Bureau of Statistics site. How do they compare for ease of use and information value for small business? www.abs.gov.au

10 How could you use the following website to help plan a business trip to Sydney? Name three articles featured in the latest version of this site that relate specifically to business-to-business marketing activity. www.buscentre.com.au

Try it

Dan White is an independent video producer whose biggest client is the Queensland Department of Primary Industries (QDPI). Although this account is big enough to support the entire business, Dan has developed other lines of business to eliminate the risks involved with having only one customer. Dan has also landed a sizeable account through a high school friend who is the manager of Good Hands Insurance. This also happens to be the company that underwrites Dan's life insurance. Additionally, Dan is hired to work on various projects for large production companies. Dan generated this business through long-term relationships built by working on projects for the QDPI. As Dan prepares his business plan for the upcoming year, he is contemplating several strategic changes. Because of the increasing speed at which the video industry is evolving, Dan has observed two important trends. First, he is finding it increasingly difficult to own the latest video equipment that his customers are demanding. Second, Dan's clients are not able to keep up with the recent developments in the industry and would be willing to pay more for his expertise. Dan is looking into a lease for new equipment and is contemplating an increase in his prices.

Questions

1 What ANZSIC code would you assign to Dan's business?
2 Is Dan's choice to use Good Hands Insurance ethical? Why or why not?
3 How can Dan use the inelasticity of demand to his advantage?
4 Would you advise Dan to lease or buy the new equipment? Why?

Watch it

Burke, Inc.: Business-to-business alliances

As one of the premier international business research and consulting firms Burke, Inc. provides services to other businesses to help them grow and remain competitive in the marketplace. The successful Cincinnati-based firm has offices and affiliates throughout the United States plus an international division, with headquarters in London, which operates in 11 European countries and Japan. To offer solutions to businesses, Burke has four divisions: Burke Marketing Research, Burke Customer Satisfaction Associates, Burke Strategic Consulting Group and The Training and Development Centre.

Burke, Inc. owes its success to the number and quality of its business relationships. Today's business environment is so complex that companies can no longer operate independently to fulfil their needs, and strategic alliances offer viable solutions. Burke brings more than 65 years of industry experience to each business alliance and has joined with companies in a wide variety of industries – agriculture, communications, financial services, entertainment, publishing, travel, insurance, communications and health care.

According to Burke's business philosophy, a strategic alliance is particularly strong when both partners bring expertise and different skills to the table. These complementary assets might include access to markets or to technology, economies of scale gained by combining research and development or marketing activities, and sharing of risk. Recently, Burke teamed up with a publisher to produce a national consumer guide to non-prescription drugs. The publisher and author lacked the experience and sophisticated tools needed to gather immediate and accurate information from pharmacists, so they asked Burke Marketing Research to join them. Together, the writer, publisher and researchers produced a very thorough national consumer's guide. Burke was able to provide the timely information that its partner needed to gain a competitive advantage. Strategic alliances can be particularly beneficial when companies face stiff competition in the marketplace.

Yet Burke does not take a 'biscuit cutter' approach that gives different partners solutions cut from the same mould. Rather, working in teams, researchers customise methods for a specific industry and product or service category. Burke's strong belief in teamwork and specialised service influences every alliance and ultimately strengthens its relationships with its partners. Everyone at Burke understands that business clients operate in different marketing environments and have different business objectives, so each business client works with an account team to see that objectives are met efficiently, economically and on time. The team analyses each client's business needs and focuses Burke's broad resources on specific requirements.

Recently, the Burke Strategic Consulting Group formed a partnership with Armstrong Laing, a computer software company, to provide consulting support for businesses that purchase Armstrong Laing's management software. Burke will use the software to assist clients in understanding their true costs and in pinpointing the link between long-term strategies and day-to-day decisions. 'This partnership allows us to provide innovative solutions to clients who want better financial results through cost management programs,' said Diane Salamon, vice president of Burke, Inc. At the same time, Armstrong Laing describes the partnership as a marriage of management expertise and cutting-edge software that will help customers attain leadership positions in their industries. Teaming up with an outside provider of business services made sense for Armstrong Laing because the company did not have management consulting expertise in-house. And like most business-to-business marketers, Armstrong Laing was selling its products in very large quantities to established organisations such as American Express and Blue Cross/Blue Shield and wanted to offer its clients a comprehensive approach of the highest quality. Still another element of Burke's alliances is relationship marketing – that is, seeking and establishing *ongoing* partnerships. For example, one client was a multinational restaurant company that wished to define its strengths and determine the effect of a change in advertising. To provide this information, Burke built a model to show how market share might be affected by different advertising and made predictions based on this model. But the relationship did not end there. Burke continued to set clear priorities for future communication and operating strategies. This long-term relationship allowed the restaurant company to get maximum ROI (return on image) for its advertising dollars. Long-term relationships like this build trust among partners, especially when they share a common interest in meeting customer needs. In Burke's opinion, far greater customer satisfaction can be achieved through a strategic business alliance.

Questions

1. Why is Burke, Inc. considered a business marketer?
2. Review Exhibit 3.3. Does Burke follow the tips for making strategic alliances successful?
3. How did Burke's strategic business alliance with Armstrong Laing create a competitive advantage in the marketplace?
4. How does Burke use the principles of relationship marketing?

Suggested reading

Burke Marketing Research Press Kit, Burke, Inc. website: www.burke.com.

Press Releases: Burke Marketing Research.

Conducts Survey for National Consumer Guide; Burke Strategic Consulting Group, Armstrong Laing Form Partnership.

© 2003 Nelson Australia Pty Limited

Click it

Online reading

INFOTRAC® COLLEGE EDITION

For additional readings and review on business decision-making, explore InfoTrac® College Edition, your online library. Go to: www.infotrac-college.com and search for any of the InfoTrac key terms listed below:
- business-to-business marketing
- purchase volume
- buying centres
- strategic marketing alliance

Answer key

1. *Answer*: d, p. 68 *Rationale*: The key characteristic distinguishing business products from consumer products is intended use, not any physical characteristics.

2. *Answer*: b, p. 68 *Rationale*: The emergence of the Internet has made business markets more competitive than ever because now every business in the world has the potential to become a local competitor.

3. *Answer*: c, p. 69 *Rationale*: The demand for business products is called derived demand because organisations buy products to be used in producing products for consumers. Because demand is derived, business marketers must carefully monitor demand patterns and changing preferences in final consumer markets, even though their direct customers are not in those markets.

4. *Answer*: a, p. 72 *Rationale*: Personal selling is often relied on to promote these products, in part, because they are often sold directly to the buyer from the producer without using any intermediaries in the distribution channel.

5. *Answer*: c, p. 74 *Rationale*: Gatekeepers are often secretaries or administrative assistants to purchasing agents who control access to the buyer and information to and from that person.

6. *Answer*: a, p. 75 *Rationale*: Although business buyers will shop for price and service, quality is usually the most important attribute they use in selection of a supplier.

7. *Answer*: c, p. 76-7 *Rationale*: Firms must decide whether to make their component parts or to purchase them from an outside supplier. The degree of complexity and difficulty of this decision will depend on how often the firm has had to make the decision in the past and their level of experience with the purchase.

8. *Answer*: a, p. 78 *Rationale*: Relationships are a key term in marketing today. Marketers are learning that the best source of new business is from an existing relationship with a satisfied customer.

9. *Answer*: c, p. 81 *Rationale*: Although these are the major categories of the business market, there are many different types of buyers under each category. For example, the reseller market includes all forms of distributors, wholesalers and retailers who resell products for a profit.

10. *Answer*: c, p. 84 *Rationale*: Component parts retain their identity after becoming part of their final product and need very little processing to be used.

Cross-functional connections
SOLUTIONS

Questions

1 Identify the key components that allowed the bionic ear to be developed for the market.

With any new product, there need to be key triggers that help to develop the new idea. For the bionic ear, the first step was the research carried out in the 19th century which identified how the ear works. Second was the development of the electronic stimulus of the auditory nerves. Third was the development of the electronic device necessary to activate the nerves. Fourth was the possible miniaturisation of the electronics by the integrated circuit. Fifth was the desire by Professor Clark to develop a hearing device that would aid the profoundly deaf, such as his father. The final trigger was the knowledge and desire to take a product into the commercial arena and the marketing effort to develop such a strategy.

2 This product is seen as having both a service and a good component. Is it servicing one person with each implant or many? Is this a consumer market-type product or a social product? Why do you say that?

To address this question, it is necessary to consider the three dimensions of a product. The core dimension of the bionic ear is to help the profoundly deaf to hear. The actual dimension is the cochlear implant and the associated equipment to activate the ear successfully, and the augmented elements are the additional services, warranties and guarantees, information, and so on.

Thus, this product has both good and service components. As such, the product offering to the patient is the ability to hear, along with the ancillary components. However, the product could be seen as a pure service to the immediate family and the community, as the product allows a deaf person to hear in our audio world. Any product that helps the profoundly deaf, the blind, or the like, to develop their skills in the community will always be seen as a service to the community and, as such, will be promoted by using social marketing efforts. However, for the recipient it is seen as a good and a service that gives an added dimension to their lives.

Marketing miscues
Yakult

The Japanese-based company Yakult has spent more than three years trying to persuade Australians to buy Yakult, a drink that maintains the balance of bacteria in the intestinal tract. The product is made by fermenting skim milk, sugar, water and an acid-resistant strain of bacteria that can reach the small intestine without being destroyed by stomach acids. The main benefits of the product are that it provides a balanced digestive system.

In spite of this benefit, it has proved difficult to persuade Australian consumers that the murky-white drink sold under an unusual name has any advantages to offer. This product is what is known as a 'functional food' – a product that is modified to offer a therapeutic benefit. While functional food is a big product category in other countries, in Australia it has been slow to develop. Yoghurts that contain various bacteria have emerged in recent years and now account for almost 50 per cent of yoghurt sales; however, Yakult is the first big functional food brand in Australia.

Part One Closing
Marketing Miscues

In spite of the large investment made by the company to establish the product – more than $10 million in marketing and more than $20 million in factories and other physical aspects – the company does not expect to make a profit for several years. The initial marketing efforts have also been adjusted following the acknowledgement that they were not consumer-friendly and did not adequately explain what the product was or why people should drink it. There has also been little consistency in the advertising messages and brand image, with the company using two different advertising agencies in less than four years.

The new advertising for Yakult aims to educate consumers about the product benefits as well as product use – when and how to use the product. The results are beginning to show with sales now estimated at 50 million bottles per year.

However, it looks like Yakult won't enjoy all of the gains its experiences and learning about Australian consumers has brought. As in many other industries, one company spends years establishing the new product category, with rivals sneering about the foolishness of such a strategy. They spend millions of dollars educating consumers about the benefits of the product and then, just as sales and acceptance start to build, those rivals who said it would fail, rush into the category with me-too products. So, in Australia, we are now seeing the introduction of more health milk drinks, the most notable of which is Vaalia by QUF. (*Vaalia* is Finnish for 'well-being'.) Yakult now has a major competitor. QUF has recently spent more than $4 million promoting the Vaalia range of yoghurts and fruit smoothies.

They use a 'good taste' platform, whereas Yakult still uses the 'good for you' benefits. It will be interesting to see who wins the battle for the hearts and minds of consumers. Current research shows that consumers in the functional-food category are less concerned with taste and more concerned with health related benefits, so Vaalia's advertising – which currently does not mention health benefits – may also need to be adjusted if it wants to capture this segment of the market.

© 2003 Nelson Australia Pty Limited

Questions

1. Using the consumer behaviour model in Chapter 2, explain what variables in the model Yakult may use to influence more people to buy their product.

2. Do you think that these companies have understood their consumers? Explain your answer.

3. Marketing is about much more than just advertising and promotion. What other marketing-related issues does this case raise for companies trying to develop new opportunities?

4. Have you ever tried these products? As a potential consumer, what advice could you give to both Yakult and QUF to make their marketing efforts more viable?

Source: Adapted from N. Shoebridge, 'Good-guy Bacteria Start to Multiply', *Business Review Weekly*, 27 October 1997.

PART ONE CLOSING

CRITICAL THINKING

Critical thinking

A wave of success

Action sportswear – surfing, skiing, street and adventure sportswear – has an annual turnover of approximately $20 billion. In this market in Australia, the surfwear industry (including apparel 50 per cent, footwear 15 per cent, surfboards and other equipment 35 per cent) has a $1 billion annual turnover. These products are aimed at people aged 12–30 and it seems that young kids and even older people want to wear these brands and they are fiercely brand loyal. This category includes brands such as Billabong, Mambo, Globe, Quicksilver, Rip Curl and Mooks.

In spite of the incredible growth of these companies and their loyal market following, they are wary of flooding the market with too much product. Most of these companies own their own stores; where there are no company stores, retailers have to make submissions to be allowed to stock the brands. These submissions are very detailed and need to include such information as location, product range, background of the retailer and the presence of competitor brands in the area. The evaluation process for a retail submission can take as long as two years, so carefully do these companies control their distribution and protect their brands, and they are wary of avoiding a mass-market approach. For example, Billabong had 600 stores 10 years ago and now has only 650 stores.

These big surfwear companies will only stock their products in surf shops and youth-oriented clothing chains, avoiding department stores and discounters.

This exclusivity in distribution has been accepted by the target market who are prepared to pay premium prices for the articles they purchase in these speciality stores. Billabong is known to be almost 'paranoid' about its brand, going to great lengths to ensure that it stays faithful to its surfing origins and is not placed on myriad different product categories. For example, a recent move by the company to launch a range of footwear and sunglasses was abandoned as it was determined that these types of products would hurt its surf–ski brand image. Instead, the company has embraced the strategy of expansion through brand acquisition rather than brand extension.

One of the principal factors driving the success of the surf, ski and skate brands is the expansion of brands aimed at women. In the past, these brands were squarely aimed at men, with only about 30 per cent of the floor space in retail outlets allocated to women's products. Now most surf outlets have at least 60 per cent allocated to women's wear, which has dramatically lifted their sales.

In relation to promotion, most of these surfwear companies have restricted their marketing efforts to the surf industry, avoiding mass-market campaigns. Billabong, Rip Curl and Quicksilver restrict their communications to surfing magazines and they are heavy sponsors of surfing events and individual athletes. Those products with a skate and streetware range use similar methods (but with a skating focus) and also use music DJs and extreme sporting contests to advertise their products. Given that many of these companies are now worth billions of dollars, this humble approach to their markets is interesting. Indeed, most of these companies are quick to emphasise to their customers that they haven't changed much in the last 30 years and that they are all still fundamentally surfers (albeit wealthy ones), just with a lot more accountants working for them.

© 2003 Nelson Australia Pty Limited

PART ONE CLOSING
CRITICAL THINKING

Questions

1. Chapter 1 discusses various marketing orientations. Identify which orientation you think these surfwear companies are using and justify why you have nominated the particular orientation.

2. Do you think that these companies have understood their consumers? Explain your answer.

3. Selection of the outlets seems to be very important to the surfwear companies. This can be considered in terms of distribution strategy (discussed in Chapter 8), but it is also in response to the consumer behaviour of the targeted markets. What consumer behaviour elements do you think influence the selection of an outlet location of retailer? Explain your answer.

4. Given the surfwear companies' recognition of the age and locality of their customers, is it ethical or moral for them to charge such premium prices to children as young as 12?

5. Why do you think it is important for the companies to present themselves as not changing their original philosophy and as still being active members of the surf culture?

Sources: Adapted from J. Stensholt, 'Strategy: Sportswear Goes Sky-high', *Business Review Weekly*, 6 July 2001; and S. Lloyd, 'A Wave of Success', *Business Review Weekly*, 29 November 2001.

© 2003 Nelson Australia Pty Limited

PART ONE CLOSING
Marketing plan

Outline of a marketing plan

Developing a marketing plan is one of the key tools used by marketers to ensure that their marketing strategy for a particular product has a greater level of success. A marketing plan has many sections. Throughout this text – in particular at the end of each of the five parts – you will be asked to complete portions of the marketing plan according to the sections or topics that have been covered in that part. Don't be concerned about how the plan will come together until you have completed the five parts. In fact, the marketing plan won't look like a marketing plan until it is completed at the end of Part 5. We have provided you with questions and worksheets on the website to assist your progression. Go there after you have completed the 'Activities' section on p. 101 below.

To commence your experience in developing a marketing plan, you need to select a product from an organisation from which you can gain information. This information can be primary data (that is, gathered through your contacts and experience with this organisation) or secondary data (that is, obtained from places such as libraries, trade journals and government agencies).

An example of a product may be a pizza from the Pizza Hut organisation.

MARKETING PLAN

I Business mission
- What is the mission of the organisation? What business is it in? How well is its mission understood throughout the organisation? In what business does the organisation wish to be, five years from now?
- Does the organisation define its business in terms of benefits its customers want, rather than in terms of goods and services?

II Objectives
- Can the organisation's mission statement be translated into operational terms regarding the organisation's objectives?
- What are the stated objectives of the organisation? Are they formally written down? Do they lead logically to clearly stated marketing objectives? Are objectives based on sales, profits or customers?
- Are the organisation's marketing objectives stated in hierarchical order? Are they specific so that progress towards achievement can be measured?
- Are the objectives reasonable in light of the organisation's resources? Are the objectives ambiguous? Do the objectives specify a time frame?
- Is the organisation's main goal to maximise customer satisfaction or to get as many customers as possible?

III Situation analysis (SWOT analysis)
- Is there a strategic window that must be taken into account?
- Have one or more differential advantages been identified in the SWOT analysis?
- Are these advantages sustainable against the competition?

PART ONE CLOSING
MARKETING PLAN

A. Internal strengths and weaknesses
- What is the history of the organisation, including sales, profits and organisational philosophies?
- What is the nature of the organisation and its current situation?
- What resources does the organisation have (financial, human, time, experience, assets, skills)?
- What policies inhibit the achievement of the organisation's objectives with respect to organisation, resource allocation, operations, hiring, training, and so on?

B. External opportunities and threats
- **Social:** What main social and lifestyle trends will have an impact on the organisation? What action has the organisation been taking in response to these trends?
- **Demographic:** What impact will forecasted trends in the size, age, profile and distribution of population have on the organisation? How will the changing nature of the family, the increase in the proportion of women in the workforce, and changes in the ethnic composition of the population affect the organisation? What action has the organisation taken in response to these developments and trends? Has the organisation re-evaluated its traditional products and expanded the range of specialised offerings to respond to these changes?
- **Economic:** What main trends in taxation and income sources will have an impact on the organisation? What action has the organisation taken in response to these trends?
- **Political, legal and financial:** What laws are now being proposed at international, federal, state and local levels that could affect marketing strategy and tactics? What recent changes in regulations and court decisions affect the organisation? What political changes at each government level are taking place? What action has the organisation taken in response to these legal and political changes?
- **Competition:** Which organisations are competing with the organisation directly by offering a similar product? Which organisations are competing with the organisation indirectly by securing its prime prospects' time, money, energy or commitment? What new competitive trends seem likely to emerge? How effective is the competition? What benefits do competitors offer that the organisation does not? Is it appropriate for the organisation to compete?
- **Technological:** What main technological changes are occurring that affect the organisation?
- **Ecological:** What is the outlook for the cost and availability of natural resources and energy needed by the organisation? Are the organisation's products, services and operations environmentally friendly?

IV Marketing strategy

A. Target market strategy
- Are the members of each market homogeneous or heterogeneous with respect to geographic, sociodemographic and behavioural characteristics?
- What are the size, growth rate, and national and regional trends in each of the organisation's market segments?
- Is the size of each market segment sufficiently large or important to warrant a unique marketing mix?

PART ONE CLOSING
MARKETING PLAN

- Are market segments measurable and accessible to distribution and communication efforts?
- Which are the high- or low-opportunity segments?
- What are the evolving needs and satisfactions being sought by target markets?
- What benefits does the organisation offer to each segment? How do these benefits compare with benefits offered by competitors?
- Is the organisation positioning itself with a unique product? Is the product needed?
- How much of the organisation's business is repeat versus new business? What percentage of the public can be classified as non-users, light users and heavy users?
- How do current target markets rate the organisation and its competitors with respect to reputation, quality and price? What is the organisation's image with the specific market segments it seeks to serve?
- Does the organisation try to direct its products only to specific groups of people or to everybody?
- Who buys the organisation's products? How does a potential customer find out about the organisation? When and how does a person become a customer?
- What are the main reasons given by potential customers for not buying the organisation's products?
- How do customers find out about and decide to purchase the product? When and where?
- Should the organisation seek to expand, contract or change the emphasis of its selected target markets? If so, in which target markets, and how vigorously?
- Could the organisation more usefully withdraw from some areas in which there are alternative suppliers and use its resources to serve new, unserved customer groups?
- What publics other than target markets (financial, media, government, citizen, local, general and internal) represent opportunities or problems for the organisation?

B. Marketing mix

- Does the organisation seek to achieve its objectives chiefly though coordinated use of marketing activities (product, distribution, promotion and pricing) or only though intensive promotion?
- Are the objectives and roles of each element of the marketing mix clearly specified?

1 Product

- What are the main product/service offerings of the organisation? Do they complement each other, or is there unnecessary duplication?
- What are the features and benefits of each product offering?
- Where is the organisation and each major product in its life cycle?
- What are the pressures among various target markets to increase or decrease the range and quality of products?
- What are the main weaknesses in each product area? What are the main complaints? What goes wrong most often?
- Is the product name easy to pronounce? Spell? Recall?
- Is it descriptive, and does it communicate the benefits the product offers? Does the name distinguish the organisation or product from all others?
- What warranties are offered with the product? Are there other ways to guarantee customer satisfaction?
- Does the product offer good customer value?
- How is customer service handled?
- How is service quality assessed?

PART ONE CLOSING
MARKETING PLAN

2 Place/distribution
- Should the organisation try to deliver its offerings directly to customers, or can it better deliver selected offerings by involving other organisations? What channel(s) should be used in distributing product offerings?
- What physical distribution facilities should be used? Where should they be located? What should be their main characteristics?
- Are members of the target market willing and able to travel some distance to buy the product?
- How good is access to facilities? Can access be improved? Which facilities need priority attention in these areas?
- How are facility locations chosen? Is the site accessible to the target markets? Is it visible to the target markets?
- What is the location and atmosphere of retail establishments? Do these retailers satisfy customers?
- When are products made available to users (season of year, day of week, time of day)? Are these times most appropriate?

3 Promotion
- How does a typical customer find out about the organisation's products?
- Does the message the organisation delivers gain the attention of the intended target audience? Does it address the wants and needs of the target market, and does it suggest benefits or a means for satisfying these wants? Is the message appropriately positioned?
- Does the promotion effort effectively inform, persuade, educate and remind customers about the organisation's products?
- Does the organisation establish budgets and measure effectiveness of promotional efforts?

a. Advertising
- Which media are currently being used? Has the organisation chosen the type of media that will best reach its target markets? Are the types of media used the most cost-effective, and do they contribute positively to the organisation's image?
- Are the dates and times the ads will appear the most appropriate? Has the organisation prepared several versions of its advertisements?
- Does the organisation use an outside advertising agency? What functions does the ad agency perform for the organisation?
- What system is used to handle consumer enquiries resulting from advertising and promotions? What follow-up is done?

b. Public relations
- Is there a well-conceived public relations and publicity program? Does the program include a means of responding to bad publicity?
- How is public relations normally handled by the organisation? By whom? Have those responsible nurtured working relationships with media outlets?
- Is the organisation using all available public relations avenues? Is an effort made to understand each of the publicity outlets' needs and to provide each with story types that will appeal to its audience in readily usable forms?
- What does the annual report say about the organisation and its products? Who is being effectively reached by this vehicle? Does the benefit of publication justify the cost?

c. Personal selling
- How much of a typical salesperson's time is spent soliciting new customers as compared to serving existing customers?

Part one closing
Marketing plan

- How is it determined which prospect will be called on and by whom? How is the frequency of contacts determined?
- How is the sales team compensated? Are there incentives for encouraging more business?
- How is the sales team organised and managed?
- Has the sales team prepared an approach tailored to each prospect?
- Has the organisation matched sales personnel with the target market characteristics?
- Is there appropriate follow-up to the initial personal selling effort? Are customers made to feel appreciated?
- Can database or direct marketing be used to replace or supplement the sales team?

d. Sales promotion
- What is the specific purpose of each sales promotion activity? Why is it offered? What does it try to achieve?
- What categories of sales promotion are being used? Is sales promotion directed to the trade, the final consumer, or both?
- Is the effort directed at all the organisation's key publics or restricted to only potential customers?

4 Price
- What levels of pricing and specific prices should be used?
- What mechanisms does the organisation have to ensure that the prices charged are acceptable to customers?
- How price-sensitive are customers?
- If a price change is put into effect, how will the number of customers change? Will total revenue increase or decrease?
- Which method is used for establishing a price: going rate, demand-oriented or cost-based?
- What discounts are offered, and with what rationale?
- Has the organisation considered the psychological dimensions of price?
- Have price increases kept pace with cost increases, inflation or competitive levels?
- How are price promotions used?
- Do interested prospects have opportunities to sample products at an introductory price?
- What methods of payment are accepted? Is it in the organisation's best interest to use these various payment methods?

V Implementation, evaluation and control
- Is the marketing organisation structured appropriately to implement the marketing plan?
- What specific activities must take place? Who is responsible for these activities?
- What is the implementation timetable?
- What other marketing research is necessary?
- What will the financial impact be of this plan on a one-year projected income statement? How does projected income compare with expected revenue if the plan is not implemented?
- What are the performance standards?
- What monitoring procedures (audits) will take place and when?
- Does it seem as though the organisation is trying to do too much or not enough?
- Are the core marketing strategies for achieving objectives sound? Are the objectives being met, and are the objectives appropriate?
- Are enough resources (or too many resources) allocated to accomplish the marketing objectives?

Part one closing
Activities

Activities

Part 1 discusses the marketing experience that you have been exposed to most of your life. It considers your experiences with organisations and the products they offer to the market, in order to satisfy your needs and wants. It also recognises that the determination and selection of a product to satisfy your needs and wants, and the needs and wants of organisations, are influenced by environmental and social factors.

The marketing plan process isn't easy and does take time. In addressing the questions in this first part and the remaining four parts, you will build up a marketing plan for the organisation for your selected product.

At this stage in your study of marketing, you should be able to describe the current situation of the organisation and discuss the product offering's marketing mix. You should be able to do the following:

- Describe the target markets used by the organisation.
- List the main products offered by the organisation.
- Indicate the features and benefits of the product offering.
- Describe how the typical customer finds out about the product.
- Indicate how price-sensitive the customers are.
- Define the product at the industry level.
- Define the product at a category level.
- Identify the direct and indirect competitors to the selected product.
- Describe the types of people who buy the product.
- Describe the decision process customers go through in determining to purchase your selected product.

Go now to the website and add your answers to the appropriate worksheet.

CUSTOMER INFORMATION
How organisations gather and use information about their customers

PART TWO

Segmenting and targeting markets	Chapter 4
Decision support systems and marketing research	Chapter 5

Cross-functional connections

Information gathering a way to make better decisions

Understanding customers and other stakeholders is at the heart of the information-gathering process. Whether it is determining individual buying behaviour, sharpening the company's target-marketing skills or understanding competitive actions, market research is the key to attaining organisation-wide success. The traditional perception of market research is that it is 'owned' by the marketing department or marketing manager and that the information is not relevant to the business. However, many companies have come to realise that the market belongs to the entire company, making it everyone's responsibility to understand the marketplace and use that information to make better decisions.

Dulux has concentrated extensively on improving the focus and direction of the company. The company's strategy involves better market research processes and the giving out of that information to all parts of the organisation. The ultimate goal is to utilise such information to move new and improved products into the marketplace much more quickly.

Historically marketing information and its use has been seen as 'touchy-feely' data when compared to the quantitative, 'hard' data utilised by other functional areas such as engineers and accountants and company boards. It is important that these people are educated to understand that marketing data can be as valid in decision-making as the financial bottom line when making company-wide decisions.

Apart from the need for a general cross-functional sharing of data, there are four main areas in which marketing's information-gathering and dissemination processes need to be formally integrated with its functional counterparts:

- Benchmarking studies
- Customer visits
- Customer satisfaction studies
- Forecasting.

Benchmarking is the process of comparing a firm's performance in various activities against a competitor's performance in the same activities. Some benchmarking studies also incorporate information from non-competing companies. Hotelier organisations in Ireland might benchmark its practices against a world-class food distributor because both companies are involved in serving food to customers. A benchmarking study may focus on cross-company comparisons of purchasing processes, inventory management, product development cycles, hiring practices, payroll processes and order fulfilment. Gathering information on a firm's competitors during a benchmarking study clearly falls within the expertise of the marketing personnel and involves an extensive amount of secondary research.

Additionally, the type of information collected during a benchmarking study crosses functional boundaries. Thus, it is imperative that market researchers understand the functional-level processes in all business areas. These market

Part Two

researchers will be communicating with managers in manufacturing (for inventory management and order fulfilment activities), research and development (for product development cycles), human resources (for hiring practices) and finance/accounting (for payroll processes). The market researcher needs input from all functional areas to collect the information that will allow his or her organisation to understand best practices.

However, no organisation can be good at all things, so it is important that external secondary data is collected across a number of organisations to determine where the organisation fits within the industry sector. Finally benchmarking requires that the organisation constantly seeks better solutions and practices.

Customers input into development and improvement of goods and services helps organisations reach higher levels of success. Many companies now benefit by sending members of the product development team for customer visits. It is not unusual to hear about research and development engineers making site visits in order to better understand customers' needs or to watch how a finished product is used in the business process. When customer visits first became popular, engineers were accompanied by marketing people to the customer site. Companies felt that engineers were too focused on functional needs and would not be able to interact personally with the customer.

Companies and engineers have begun to realise that engineering is no longer a functional area that works internally, and engineers alone are now completing site visits. Intuit Corp., in the United States, uses customer site visits in the ongoing development and refinement of the company's software products. It is not unusual for software developers to visit small-business owners at their home offices to observe the company's software products in use. The software developers watch the customer's movements when using the computer program. The goal is to gain a better understanding of the way users 'think' regarding logical next moves in the program and to incorporate these moves in later versions of the product or in new products.

Additionally, Kodak attempts to gain a better understanding of how customers use its products by sending manufacturing employees to visit professional users. Kodak depends on accurate marketplace information in understanding the customers' buying processes and the actual usage of Kodak products. Customer satisfaction is driven by issues related to the firm's operational functions (inventory management, capital budgeting) and its operational capabilities (technology, procedures), as well as its product mix. Therefore, a valid customer satisfaction study should gather information that can be shared with manufacturing (regarding satisfaction with speed of delivery), research and development (regarding satisfaction with product quality),

Cross-functional connections

human resources (regarding satisfaction with complaint handling) and finance/accounting (regarding satisfaction with credit policies). All of these functional areas need to have input into the design of such studies. Retailers have long included personnel as one element of their marketing mix. The Myer and David Jones department stores have found that their personnel are critical in maintaining customer satisfaction.

Forecasting crosses the boundaries of multiple business functions. For example, marketing may offer a discount on a particular price. The impact of this price discount is felt simultaneously in many functional areas. A key functional partner in a price discount is manufacturing. The production plan will have to accommodate the expected increase in product sales and the commonly below-average product sales immediately after the discount period. Although it is easy for marketers to change price, manufacturers' plans cannot be changed overnight. The impact of a price change may be felt in the company's production schedule, the level of finished goods inventory and the availability of raw materials. Unfortunately, marketing's ability to make price changes quickly has been the cause of much conflict between marketing and manufacturing. Much of a firm's financial planning is driven by the company's sales forecast. Marketing has historically had a reputation for being too optimistic in its projections. Thus, financial planners have been known to take the sales forecast with 'a grain of salt', and planning has often evolved around a lower-than-predicted level of sales. Marketing, then, looks at financial planners as too conservative and as basing their plans on internal data that are not driven by the marketplace.

Marketplace information is a key driver in all decisions made by a company. Therefore, it is imperative that all functional areas participate in the gathering and dissemination of information. Navistar International Transportation Corp., in the United States, has attempted to bring its customer-oriented marketing research to the forefront in its production processes. Navistar has been an innovator in linking marketplace information to the shop floor, allowing manufacturing to customise products quickly and efficiently to meet specific customer demands. Using electronic data interchange (EDI), the company has been able to integrate its marketing research results into its production processes. This strategy has enabled it to adopt a true customer focus, while simultaneously cutting costs. Success in today's global environment depends on all functional areas understanding the firm's customers and competitors. Thorough analysis of marketplace opportunities requires an interactive process between marketing and other business functions.

Part two

Questions for discussion

1. Why do you think market research is perceived as being 'owned' by the marketing department?

2. Where should market research be formally integrated across functional departments?

3. What data differences exist across functions?

CHAPTER FOUR
Segmenting and targeting markets

LEARNING OBJECTIVES

After studying this chapter, you should be able to

1 Describe the characteristics of markets and market segments
2 Explain the importance of market segmentation
3 List the steps involved in segmenting markets
4 Describe the bases commonly used to segment consumer markets
5 Describe the bases for segmenting business markets
6 Discuss the criteria for successful market segmentation
7 Discuss alternative strategies for selecting target markets
8 Explain how and why organisations implement positioning strategies and how product differentiation plays a role
9 Discuss global market segmentation and targeting issues

The following article discusses the growing number of fresh fruit juice outlets opening in Australia.

Forget the whirr of the coffee machine – the sound of juice extractors can now be heard in retail strips, ritzy shopping centres, airports and gyms around the world. It is a sound that is catching on in Australia, as the juice and smoothie bar concept is heralded by some retailers and investors as the next big thing in food retailing and franchising.

The juice and smoothie store has become a retail phenomenon in the United States. There are more than 2000 juice bars in the United States, with the chains Jamba Juice, Smoothie King, Juice It Up and Juice Stop dominating the market.

The PepsiCo-owned Jamba Juice started 10 years ago with one store in California. It now has 300 stores in 17 states. Selling wheatgrass shots, smoothies, juice combinations, hangover cures and drinks with names such as Get A Life, juice bars are a long way from hippie health food stores. Retailers have moved well away from that concept to a slicker, sophisticated urban niche where the juice bar experience is all about feeling good and getting a lift. At Doctor Juice in North Sydney, perky staff wear white pharmacy coats in the 'hospital clean' store,

Jamba Juice on-line

What segments do you think need to be considered? Of the three target market strategies, which do you think should be adopted if this is a newly emerging market?
www.jambajuice.com

where they prepare fresh juices with names such as First Aid (mango, banana and orange), the bestseller Get A Life (banana, pineapple and spirulina – protein-rich algae) and Sick Puppy (coconut, orange and banana). Eighteen months after it opened, Doctor Juice serves about 300 juices a day (with prices from $4) to customers who the owner of Doctor Juice, Gary Pogson, says range from 'suits' to Hare Krishnas.

Late last year, Pogson opened a $100 000 store in the international arrivals hall at Sydney Airport. He plans other stores in Sydney this year. 'I want to create a brand,' he says. 'No one has yet created an Australian juice-bar brand.'

Brian Ansell, director of Melbourne's jBar, says: 'We want to be the Starbucks of the juice world.' Ansell has opened two jBar juice bars during the past six months and has plans for five more in the next six months, with a possibility of selling jBar franchises. The jBar stores offer every imaginable combination of juice, smoothie and ice treat in a space-age realm of splash-proof, silent blenders, ice contraptions and trays of sprouted wheatgrass.

Australian juice bars are a long way from market saturation; there are growing number of juice bars in the cities' central business districts and in large shopping centres. Using names that include Sejuice, Boost, Zupajuice, the life juice co. and Fresh, they are all variations on the US juice and smoothie bar model.

Feeling Fruity can regularly sell over 1000 smoothies and juices in the entertainment section of Melbourne's Chadstone shopping centre. A director of Feeling Fruity, Jason Kartmell, has a background in the fruit trade and opened his first juice bar in Melbourne 12 years ago as a way of 'getting rid of fruit' from his city fruit stall. He opened the first Feeling Fruity store, selling juices, fresh fruit salads and yoghurts, in the food hall of the David Jones store in Melbourne in 1994. There are now 16 Feeling Fruity stores, and Kartmell has franchised the business in the expansion to Sydney and Brisbane.

Kartmell says he has had a lot of interest in the Feeling Fruity concept from potential franchisees. Pogson of Doctor Juice says he gets franchise inquiries every day. He says he will stick to shopping centres because he believes that strip shopping areas cannot bring enough clients.

Kartmell is happy that the competition is hotting up: 'The more juice bars, the better. We need to get to the point where people get up in the morning and pop out to get their juice for the day.'[1]

The issues raised in this article will be explored further in this chapter.

Market segmentation

1 Describe the characteristics of markets and market segments

The term *market* means different things to different people. You are familiar with terms such as supermarket, stock market, labour market, fish market and flea market. All these types of markets share several characteristics. First, they are composed of people like you (consumer markets) or organisations (business markets). Second, you and organisations have needs and wants that can be satisfied with particular product groups. For example, you may have a need to listen to recorded music. This need can be satisfied with a number of products, including MP3 players, minidisc players, CDs, vinyl records, cassette tapes, digital audio tapes and so on. All of these products grouped together are products

Chapter 4 Segmenting and targeting markets

that can satisfy a need. Third, you and organisations have the ability to buy the products you seek. Fourth, you and organisations are willing to exchange your resources, usually money or credit, for desired products. Therefore, we can say that a **market** is (1) people or organisations with (2) needs or wants that they have (3) the ability and (4) the willingness to buy. A group of people or an organisation that lacks any one of these characteristics is not a market. Note how similar the characteristics of a market are to the exchange process discussed in Chapter 1.

A **market segment** is a subgroup of people or organisations within a market, which share one or more characteristics that cause them to have similar product needs. At one extreme, we can define every person and every organisation in the world as a market segment because each is unique. This has recently been termed mass micro-marketing. At the other extreme, we can define the entire consumer market as one large market segment and the business market as another large segment, which is commonly called mass marketing.

market
People or organisations with needs or wants and the ability and willingness to buy.

market segment
A subgroup of people or organisations sharing one or more characteristics that cause them to have similar product needs.

Exhibit 4.1
Concept of market segmentation

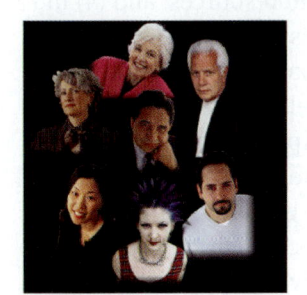

No market segmentation

Fully segmented market

Market segmentation by gender: M, F

Market segmentation by age group: 1, 2, 3

Market segmentation by gender and age group

From a marketing perspective, market segments can be described as somewhere between the two extremes. The process of dividing a market into meaningful, relatively similar, viable and identifiable segments or groups is called **market segmentation**. The purpose of market segmentation is to enable the marketer to tailor marketing mixes (see Parts 3 and 4) to meet the needs of one or more specific segments.

Exhibit 4.1 illustrates the concept of market segmentation. Each box represents a market consisting of seven persons. This market might vary from one homogeneous market of seven people to a market consisting of seven individual segments.

market segmentation
The process of dividing a market into meaningful, relatively similar and identifiable segments or groups.

The importance of market segmentation

2 Explain the importance of market segmentation

Until the 1960s, few organisations practised market segmentation. When they did, it was more likely a haphazard effort than a formal marketing strategy.

On 29 November 1948, Holden produced its first successfully mass-produced Australian car. It was a six-cylinder, four-door, six-seater sedan. The only thing different between the first and last car to roll off the plant that year was the colour. The mid-1950s saw the first variation in the production line with the development of the station wagon. Today Holden make 16 different models for the Australian market based on diverse consumer preferences for different uses, sizes, needs and street appeal.

Market segmentation plays a key role in the marketing strategy of almost all successful organisations and is a powerful marketing tool for several reasons: (1) nearly all markets include groups of people or organisations with different product needs and preferences; (2) market segmentation helps marketers to define customer needs and wants more precisely; (3) because market segments differ in size and potential, segmentation helps decision-makers to define marketing objectives more accurately and to better allocate resources; and (4) in turn, performance can be better evaluated when objectives are more precise.

The jeans industry in Australia was going through small changes in the late 1960s. In 1970, Just Jeans opened their first store in the belief that a jeans store was a fad and would only last a few years. However, by April 1971, jeans were being considered as acceptable dress for all occasions. The larger department stores held only basic stock and just a few sizes. With the growing demand for jeans, and Just Jeans' ability to provide fractional sizes, which meant jeans that fit, the store flourished and many more stores were opened. During the late 1970s and early 1980s, the jeans went through many alterations and changes, including flared, cuffed, adorned, printed on, ripped, stretched, frayed, stone washed, acid washed and distressed, to better meet customer needs. Subsequently, Levi's in the United States decided to go back to basics and jeans in Australia followed the fashion. This change was seen as consistent with the younger generation of the time's need for simple and basic items, and jean sales once again soared. In 2000, Just Jeans Group Limited announced an increase in net profit after tax for the half-year to 29 July of $2.15 million, up 133 per cent from the previous year. Sales for the half-year were $167.7 million, up 5.5 per cent on the previous year.

Just Jeans' ability to keep a focus on the changing needs of various market segments and to continually meet the needs of the ageing youth market has allowed it to take a shop concept of the late 1960s and develop it into a viable business in the 2000s.

Marketers need to be aware not only of basic demographic information, but also of the characteristics of buyers and potential buyers, and of the needs being satisfied by the product. For example, three couples on the same income and in the same age group who live in the same suburb may be three very different groups of people in terms of market segments, requiring different marketing strategies and styles of marketing communication.[2] Some researchers in this area have said that segmentation is part process, part art. If the process is well understood, then the marketer has more opportunity to focus on the art.

Chapter 4 — Segmenting and targeting markets

Steps in segmenting a market

The purpose of market segmentation, in both consumer and business markets, is to identify marketing opportunities. Exhibit 4.2 traces the steps in segmenting a market. Note that steps 5 and 6 are actually marketing activities that follow market segmentation (steps 1 to 4).

3 List the steps involved in segmenting markets

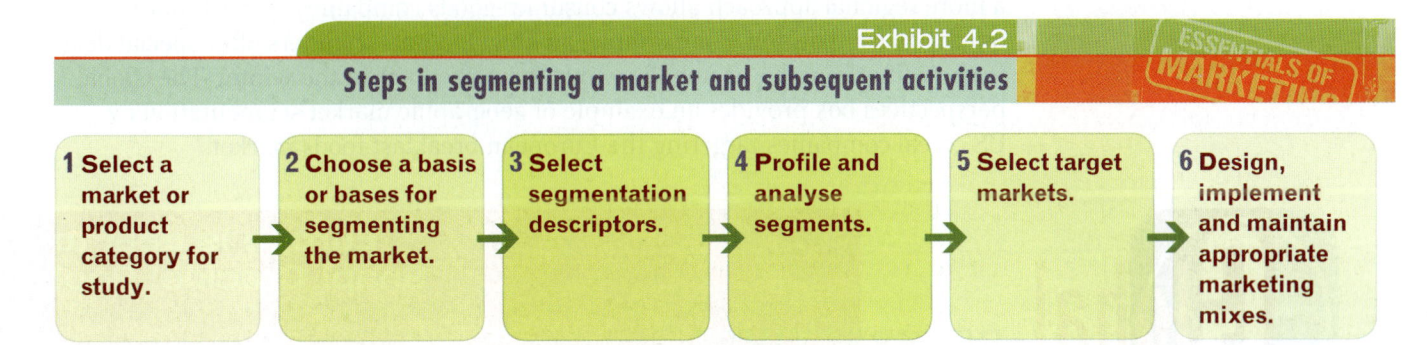

Exhibit 4.2 Steps in segmenting a market and subsequent activities

1. Select a market or product category for study. → 2. Choose a basis or bases for segmenting the market. → 3. Select segmentation descriptors. → 4. Profile and analyse segments. → 5. Select target markets. → 6. Design, implement and maintain appropriate marketing mixes.

Selecting a market or product category for study

The first step is to define the overall market or product category to be studied. It may be a market in which the organisation already competes, a new but related market or product category, or a totally new one. For instance, Carlton United Breweries (CUB) closely examined the beer market before introducing citrus- and herb-flavoured beers for the Australian connoisseur market. www.matildabay.com.au/

Choosing a basis or bases for segmenting consumer markets

This step requires managerial insight, creativity and market knowledge. There are no scientific procedures for selecting segmentation variables. Marketers use **segmentation bases**, or variables, which are characteristics of individuals, groups or organisations, to divide a total market into segments. The choice of segmentation bases is crucial because an inappropriate segmentation strategy may lead to lost sales and missed profit opportunities. The key is to identify bases that will produce substantial, measurable and accessible segments that exhibit different response patterns to marketing mixes.

The ultimate goal of this process is to describe a number of segments that cover the market. One example of this can be seen with Exhibit 4.7 which shows variables from the various bases used to define the snack food market.

A detailed description of the bases and their segment descriptor will now be discussed.

Geographic base

Geographic segmentation refers to segmenting markets using geographic variables such as region of the country or world, market size, market density or climate. Market density means the number of people within a unit of land, such as a census tract. Climate is commonly used for geographic segmentation because of its dramatic impact on people's needs and purchasing behaviour. For example,

Carlton United Breweries on-line

What beer markets is CUB in, and what markets do you think it could enter in the future? Should it develop the wine market or beer market further?
www.fosters.com.au/corporate/companies/cub/cub.asp

segmentation bases (variables)
Characteristics of individuals, groups or organisations.

geographic segmentation
Segmenting markets by region of the country or world, market size, market density or climate.

4 Describe the bases commonly used to segment consumer markets

air-conditioning, evaporative air coolers and heating systems are products with varying appeal, depending on climate and geographic location.

Consumer goods organisations take a regional approach to marketing for four reasons. First, many organisations need to find new ways to generate sales because of sluggish and intensely competitive markets. Second, computerised checkout counters with scanners enable retailers to assess accurately which brands sell best in their region. Third, many packaged-goods manufacturers are introducing new regional brands intended to appeal to local preferences. Fourth, a more regional approach allows consumer-goods companies to react more quickly to competition. For example, awning and patio builders offer special deals in the winter months, as nobody wants these products in the winter. The Global perspectives box provides an example of geographic market segmentation by US cereal companies targeting the European breakfast-foods market.

Global Perspectives

Europe is deaf to Snap! Crackle! Pop!

Cereal companies view European countries such as Italy as an opportunity for growth at a time when the US cereal market is in decline. However, after years of aggressive marketing campaigns and health-awareness programs in Italy, promoting the benefits of cereal, most Italians continue to eat breakfast Italian style: espresso or cappuccino and biscotti dipped into the coffee. American cereals like corn flakes have been available in Italy since the 1950s. But until this decade they were considered a niche product and relegated to the nation's pharmacies and health-food stores. Some progress has been made, as a growing number of Italian parents are now giving their children cereal for breakfast.

In the early 1990s when US companies started encountering problems at home, they began looking at markets abroad. Kellogg, for example, started investing heavily in Europe, entering Italy full steam and opening manufacturing plants in Latvia and Denmark. For an American cereal company, Europe offered distinct advantages, including higher prices and profit margins, cheaper television time and fewer competitors. But Kellogg's timing was unfortunate. The fall of European trade restrictions as the European Union moved towards the single market made so many plants unnecessary, especially when the number of people eating cereal was not multiplying so rapidly.

As they look for a turnaround, the cereal companies are trying to take advantage of some cultural shifts. The traditional long European lunch is giving way to the American habit of grabbing a quick bite, making a bigger breakfast essential. Also, large US-style supermarkets with wide aisles are taking over from smaller retail stores, which are less inclined to switch to new, untried products.

At one modern Milanese supermarket, cereals occupy a prominent shelf position – the boxes are stacked on top of the fruit counter, and beneath them are multipacks of milk cartons. One mother in the store who is loading up on Kellogg's Corn Flakes and All-Bran says she buys the cereal for her kids – they see commercials on television and tell her what to buy.

Cereal ads in Italy feature hazy sunrises, fields of rain and wholesome-looking families. They also emphasise the American nature of the product; one Kellogg's Corn Flakes ad uses a series of child Elvis impersonators and begins 'the best things always come from America'. Several newer ads have a more Italian look. For example, one ad shows an Italian farm family eating breakfast outside their old stone house while their child is talking on a mobile phone – an essential element of modern Italian life.

Kellogg now dominates Italy's cereal market with an estimated 61 per cent market share but has come under attack from store brands launched by domestic retail chains. Furthermore, US cereal makers face new competition from an Italian food manufacturer, Banila SpA, which recently introduced a pressed cereal breakfast bar. Called Armonie, it is marketed as a nutritious breakfast food ideal for dipping in milk or coffee, just like biscotti. Ads for Armonie show a young woman flinging open the windows to let the sun shine in and then dipping the cereal bars in milk.[3]

Could cereal companies more effectively segment the Italian cereal market? What segments might be promising? How should they position their products?

Demographic base

Marketers often segment markets based on demographic information because it is widely available and often related to consumers' buying and consuming behaviour. Some common bases of **demographic segmentation** are age, gender, income, ethnic background and family life cycle. The discussion here provides some important information about the main demographic segments.

Age segmentation

Children influence a great deal of family consumption. In the United States, combining allowance, earnings and gifts, children 14 years old and younger spend an estimated US$20 billion per year and influence how another US$200 billion is spent.[4] Attracting children is a popular strategy for many companies because they hope to instil brand loyalty early. Finding that having to pester Mum to take them to get their film processed inhibited kids from taking photographs, Kodak introduced a camera set that includes a single-use camera packaged with an envelope to mail the film back to Kodak for developing.[5]

Gender segmentation

Marketers of products such as clothing, cosmetics, personal care items, magazines, jewellery and footwear commonly segment markets by gender. For example, 95 per cent of users of Sports Zone, an American website that offers a constant flow of sports news generated by ESPN (www.msn.espn.go.com/main.html), are men.[6] However, brands that have traditionally been marketed to men, such as Gillette razors and Rogaine baldness remedy, are increasing their efforts to attract women.[7] Even the National Rugby League has launched an aggressive effort to retain and add to its female fans. 'Women's' products such as cosmetics, household products and furniture are also being marketed to men.

Income segmentation

Income is a popular demographic variable for segmenting markets because income level influences consumers' discretionary income, which in turn influences their wants and determines their buying power. Many markets are segmented by income, including the markets for housing, clothing, cars and food. For example, value retailers such as the discount chain Crazy Clark's are drawing low- and fixed-income customers with easy access, small stores and rock-bottom pricing. David Jones, on the other hand, has moved away from the rural and middle-income markets by targeting higher-income consumers in upscale areas.

Family life-cycle segmentation

The demographic factors of gender, age and income often don't sufficiently explain why consumer buying behaviour varies. Frequently, differences in consumption patterns among people of the same age and gender result from their being in different stages of the family life cycle. The **family life cycle (FLC)** is a series of stages determined by a combination of age, marital status and the presence or absence of children.

Exhibit 4.3 illustrates traditional and contemporary FLC patterns and shows how families' needs, incomes, resources and expenditures differ at each stage. The horizontal flow shows the traditional family life cycle. The lower part of the exhibit gives some of the characteristics and purchase patterns of families in each stage of the traditional life cycle. The exhibit also acknowledges that about half of all first marriages end in divorce. When young marrieds move into the young divorced stage, their consumption patterns often revert to those of the young single stage of the cycle. About four out of five divorced persons remarry by middle age and re-enter the traditional life cycle, as indicated by the 'recycled flow' in the exhibit.

---

demographic segmentation
Segmenting markets by age, gender, income, ethnic background and family life cycle.

family life cycle (FLC)
A series of stages determined by a combination of age, marital status and the presence or absence of children.

Exhibit 4.3
Family life cycle

→ Usual flow
→ Recycled flow
▢ Traditional flow

Flow chart stages:
- Young single
- Young married without children
- Young divorced without children
- Young married with children
- Young divorced with children
- Middle-aged married with children
- Middle-aged divorced with children
- Middle-aged married without dependent children
- Middle-aged divorced without dependent children
- Middle-aged married without children
- Middle-aged divorced without children
- Older married
- Older unmarried

Young single
- Few financial burdens
- Fashion opinion leaders
- Recreation-oriented
- Buy: basic kitchen equipment, basic furniture, cars, equipment for mating game, holidays

Young married without children / Defacto couples
- Better off financially than they will be in near future
- Highest purchase rate and highest average purchase of durables
- Buy: cars, refrigerators, stoves, sensible and durable furniture, holidays

Young married with children
- Home purchasing at peak
- Liquid assets low
- Dissatisfied with financial position and amount of money saved
- Interested in new products
- Like advertised products
- Buy: washing machines, dryers, televisions, baby food, chest rubs, cough medicine, vitamins, dolls, wagons, bicycles, skates

Middle-aged married with children
- Financial position better
- More wives work
- Some children get jobs
- Hard to influence with advertising
- High average purchase of durables
- Buy: new and more tasteful furniture, car travel, unnecessary appliances, boats, dental services, magazines

Middle-aged married without children / Middle-aged single
- Home ownership at peak
- Most satisfied with financial position and money saved
- Interested in travel, recreation, self-education
- Make gifts and contributions
- Not interested in new products
- Buy: holidays, luxuries, home improvements

Older married
- Drastic cut in income
- Stay home
- Buy: medical appliances, medical care, products that aid health, sleep and digestion

Older unmarried
- Drastic cut in income
- Special need for attention, affection and security
- Buy: same medical and product needs as other retired group

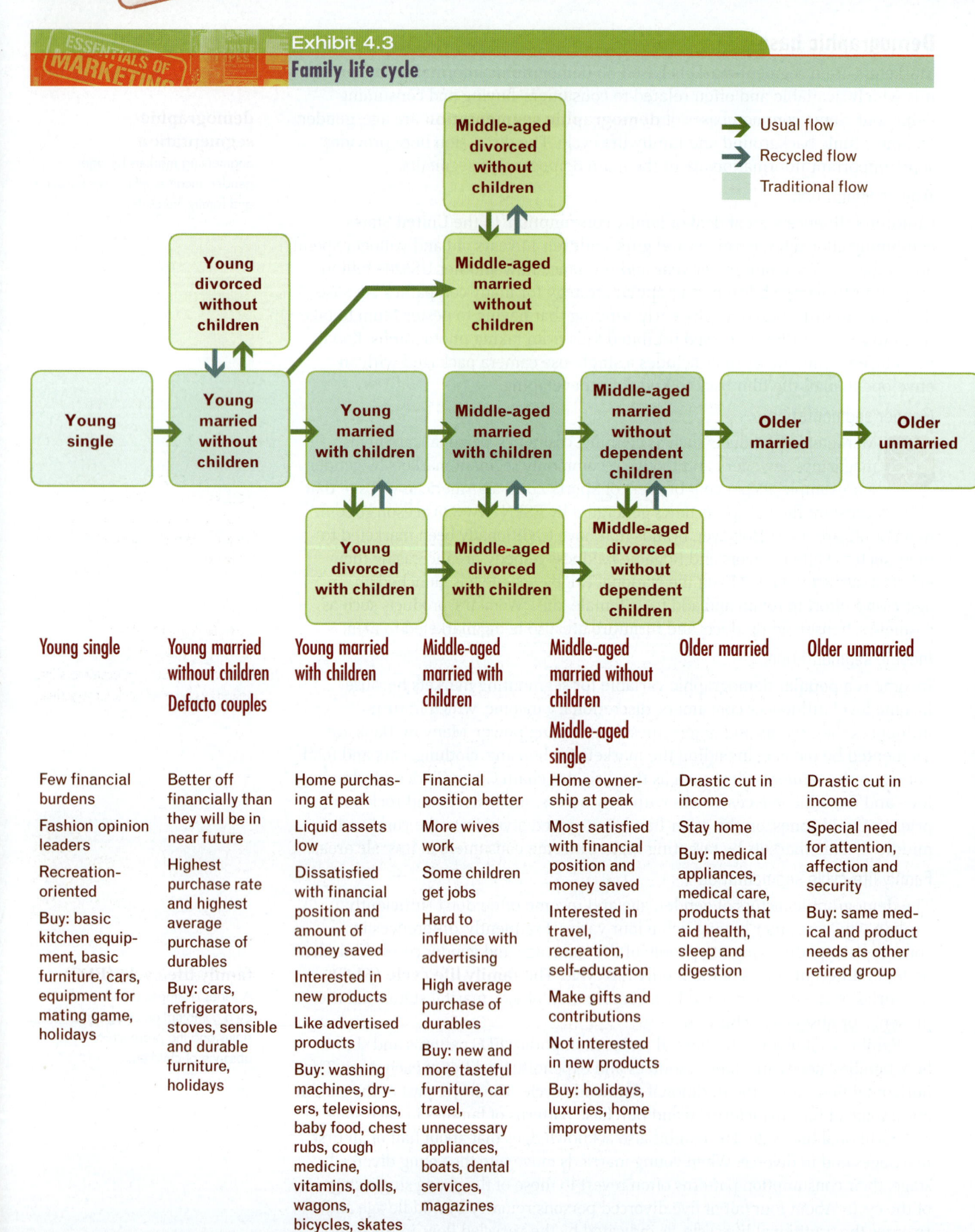

Psychographic base

Age, gender, income, family life-cycle stage and other demographic variables are usually helpful in developing segmentation strategies, but often they don't paint the entire or best picture. Demographics provide the skeleton, but psychographics add meat to the bones. **Psychographic segmentation** is market segmentation based on the following variables:

- *Personality*: Personality reflects a person's traits, attitudes and habits. Porsche dealers understand the demographics of the Porsche owner as a 40-something male, tertiary educated and earning over $80 000 per year. However, research discovered five personality types within this general demographic category that more effectively segmented Porsche buyers. Exhibit 4.4 describes the five segments.[8]
- *Motives*: Marketers of baby products and life insurance appeal to consumers' emotional motives – namely, to care for their loved ones. Using appeals to economy, reliability and dependability, carmakers such as Subaru and Suzuki target customers with rational motives. Carmakers such as Mercedes-Benz and Jaguar appeal to customers with status-related motives.
- *Lifestyles*: Lifestyle segmentation divides people into groups according to the way they spend their time, the importance of the things around them, their beliefs, and socio-economic characteristics such as income and education. For example, Harley-Davidson divides its customers into seven lifestyle segments, from 'cocky misfits' who are most likely to be arrogant troublemakers, to 'laid-back camper types' committed to cycling and nature, to 'classy capitalists' who have wealth and privilege.[9]
- *Geodemographics*: **Geodemographic segmentation** clusters potential customers into neighbourhood lifestyle categories. It combines geographic, demographic and lifestyle segmentations. Geodemographic segmentation helps marketers to develop marketing programs tailored to prospective buyers who live in small geographic regions, such as neighbourhoods, or who have very specific lifestyle and demographic characteristics. While this approach is successful in some countries due to class structures, it is not as successful in Australia and New Zealand.

psychographic segmentation
Market segmentation on the basis of personality, motives, lifestyles and geodemographics.

Candy Net on-line

For what life-cycle stage does this web page cater? Is this realistic in the Australian and New Zealand community?
www.candy.net.au

geodemographic segmentation
Segmenting potential customers into neighbourhood lifestyle categories.

Exhibit 4.4 Taxonomy of Porsche buyers

Type	% of all owners	Description
Top guns	27%	Driven, ambitious types. Power and control matter. They expect to be noticed.
Elitists	24%	Old-money blue bloods. A car is just a car, no matter how expensive. It is not an extension of personality.
Proud patrons	23%	Ownership is an end in itself. Their car is a trophy earned for hard work, and who cares if anyone sees them in it?
Bon vivants	17%	Worldly jet setters and thrill seekers. Their car heightens the excitement in their already passionate lives.
Fantasists	9%	A timid person who aspires to greatness. Their car is an escape. Not only are they uninterested in impressing others with it, but they also feel a little guilty about owning one.

Psychographic variables can be used individually to segment markets or can be combined with other variables to provide a detailed description of market segments. One well-known combination approach, offered by SRI International, is called VALS 2 (version 2 of SRI's Values and Lifestyles program). The Australian equivalent is known as Roy Morgan's Values Segments.

As Exhibit 4.5 shows, the segments in Roy Morgan's Values Segments are classified on two dimensions: (1) vertically by their life satisfaction, quality expectation and individualism; and (2) horizontally by price expectation, attractiveness to innovation and perceived progressiveness.

Exhibit 4.5
The Roy Morgan mind set

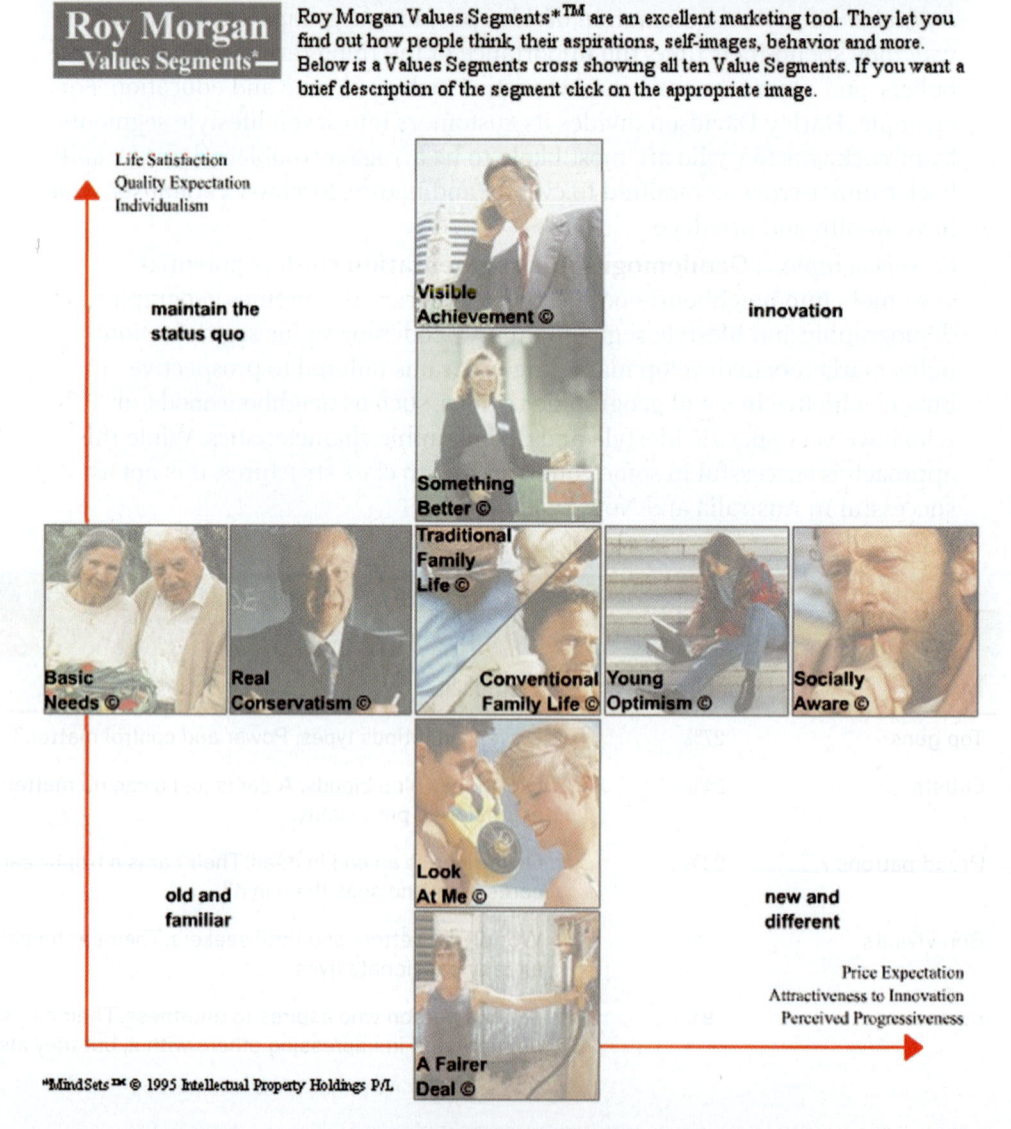

Roy Morgan Values Segments®™ are an excellent marketing tool. They let you find out how people think, their aspirations, self-images, behavior and more. Below is a Values Segments cross showing all ten Value Segments. If you want a brief description of the segment click on the appropriate image.

Life Satisfaction
Quality Expectation
Individualism

maintain the status quo

innovation

- Visible Achievement©
- Something Better©
- Traditional Family Life©
- Basic Needs©
- Real Conservatism©
- Conventional Family Life©
- Young Optimism©
- Socially Aware©
- Look At Me©
- A Fairer Deal©

old and familiar

new and different

Price Expectation
Attractiveness to Innovation
Perceived Progressiveness

"MindSets"™ © 1995 Intellectual Property Holdings P/L

Source: Roy Morgan Research: Roy Morgan Values Segments™: www.roymorgan.com.au/products/values/index-print.html.

Exhibit 4.6 describes the nine psychographic segments identified by Roy Morgan. Using only the two key dimensions – life satisfaction/quality expectation/individualism and price expectation/attractiveness to innovation/perceived progressiveness – nine groups of adult consumers who have distinctive attitudes, behaviour patterns and decision-making styles are identified.

Exhibit 4.6
The Roy Morgan Values Segments™

Visible Achievement: Successful, highly individualistic, realistic and very practical people who are confident in their own abilities and position. They place great emphasis on family life and retain traditional values about home, work and society. As consumers they look for quality and value for money.

Something Better: Competitive, individualistic and ambitious people who are seeking more out of their life. They are concerned about image, are conscious of social status, and as consumers will purchase to demonstrate their success to others.

Basic Need: Mature, happy people content with what they have. They have a strong attachment to traditional institutions such as community and church, and enjoy a wisdom that comes with grey hair.

Real Conservatism: Hold very conservative social, moral and ethical values, and are cautious about new things and ideas. They believe strongly in the established order of things and have a great interest in their own local community. As consumers they are attracted to value, quality and older, established brands.

Traditional Family Life: Mature, family-focused people who believe strongly in security, reliability and providing better opportunities for their family. They are resistant to change and value the traditional family role and structure.

Young Optimism: Young, innovative, impulsive and enthusiastic people who are interested in technology and world affairs. They are eager to learn, so are heavy readers of newspapers and magazines. Often financially disorganised, they are avid consumers who regularly live on credit.

Socially Aware: People who are community-minded and socially active. They are thinkers, can be idealistic, and are attracted to things that are new and innovative. Due to their thirst for knowledge, they are heavy consumers of newspapers and magazines.

Look At Me: Rebellious, socially active and very conscious of conforming to their peer group. They are short-term thinkers who often consider themselves invincible. Money is important but is essentially a means to an end.

A Fairer Deal: Pessimistic, cynical and hostile people who believe life treats them unfairly. Money is more important than job satisfaction. They tend to be heavy consumers of radio and television, often using them as methods for escaping from their world.

Source: Roy Morgan Research: Roy Morgan Values Segments™: www.roymorgan.com.au/products/values/index-print.html.

Benefit base

Benefit segmentation is the process of grouping customers into market segments according to the benefits they seek from the product. Most types of market segmentation are based on the assumption that this variable and customers' needs are related. Benefit segmentation is different because it groups potential customers based on their needs or wants rather than some other characteristic, such as age or gender. The snack-food market, for example, can be divided into six benefit segments, as shown in Exhibit 4.7.

Demographic information associated with people seeking certain benefits should not be used alone to develop customer profiles. It is far better to integrate psychographic, behavioural, geographic and/or geodemographic information

benefit segmentation
The process of grouping customers into market segments according to the benefits they seek from the product.

Usage-rate base

Usage-rate segmentation divides a market by the amount of product bought or consumed. Categories vary with the product, but they are likely to include some combination of the following: former users, potential users, first-time users, light or irregular users, medium users and heavy users. Segmenting by usage rate enables marketers to focus their efforts on heavy users or to develop multiple marketing mixes aimed at different segments. Because heavy users often account for a sizeable portion of all product sales, some marketers focus on the heavy-user segment.

The **80/20 principle** holds that 20 per cent of all customers generate 80 per cent of the demand. Even though the validity of this principle is now being challenged in the literature, it does suggest that a small proportion of customers account for a large proportion of a business's trade.

In a variant of usage-rate segmentation, some companies try to attract non-users. For example, using a suburban letterbox drop, Pizza Hut delivered direct-mail packages to local residents, which included a 10 per cent discount coupon on collecting a pizza.

Clearly from this example in Exhibit 4.7 we can see that the snack food market can be divided into 36 segments. At this time we have conclude step two of the segmentation process for consumer markets. However, choosing the bases for segmenting business markets is slightly different and this will be discussed next before considering the third step of the segmenting process.

usage-rate segmentation
Dividing a market by the amount of product bought or consumed.

80/20 principle
Principle that holds that 20 per cent of all customers generate 80 per cent of the demand.

Sanitarium on-line
How does Sanitarium, maker of healthy food products, use benefit segmentation on its website? What other types of segmentation are evident on the site?
www.sanitarium.com.au

Exhibit 4.7
Lifestyle segmentation of the snack-food market

	Nutritional snackers	Weight watchers	Guilty snackers	Party snackers	Indiscriminate snackers	Economical snackers
% of snackers	22%	14%	9%	15%	15%	18%
Lifestyle characteristics	Self-assured, controlled	Outdoor types, influential, venturesome.	Highly anxious, isolated	Sociable	Hedonistic	Self-assured, price-oriented.
Benefits sought	Nutritious without artificial ingredients, natural	Low in kilojoules, quick energy	Low in kilojoules, good tasting	Good to serve guests, served with pride, go well with beverages	Good tasting, satisfies hunger	Low in price, best value
Consumption level of snacks	Light	Light	Heavy	Average	Heavy	Average
Type of snacks usually eaten	Fruits, vegetables, cheese	Yoghurt, vegetables	Yoghurt, biscuits, crackers. confectionary	Nuts, potato chips, crackers pretzels	Confectionary, ice cream, biscuits, potato chips, pretzels, popcorn	No specific products
Demographics	Better educated, have younger children	Younger, single	Younger or older, female, lower socio economic status	Middle-aged, non-urban	Teenager	Have large family, better educated

Choosing a basis or bases for segmenting business markets

The business market consists of four broad segments: producers, resellers, institutions and government. (For a detailed discussion of the characteristics of these segments, see Chapter 3.) Whether marketers focus on only one or on all four of the segments to be discussed, they are likely to find diversity among potential customers. Thus, further market segmentation offers just as many benefits to business marketers as it does to consumer product marketers. Business market segmentation variables can be classified into two main categories: macrosegmentation variables and microsegmentation variables.

5 Describe the bases for segmenting business markets

Macrosegmentation

Macrosegmentation variables are used to divide business markets into segments according to the following general characteristics:

1. *Geographic location*: The demand for some business products varies considerably from one region to another. Some markets tend to be regional because buyers prefer to purchase from local suppliers, and distant suppliers often have difficulty competing in terms of price and service. Therefore, organisations that sell to geographically concentrated industries benefit by locating operations close to the market.
2. *Customer type*: Segmenting by customer type allows business marketers to tailor their marketing mixes to the unique needs of particular types of organisations or industries. Many companies are finding this form of segmentation to be quite effective.
3. *Customer size*: Volume of purchase (heavy, moderate and light) is a commonly used business-to-business segmentation basis. Another is the buying organisation's size, which may affect its purchasing procedures, the types and quantities of products it needs, and its responses to different marketing mixes. Banks frequently offer different services, lines of credit and overall attention to commercial customers based on their size and/or liquidity.
4. *Product use*: Many products, especially raw materials such as steel, timber and petroleum, have diverse applications. How customers use a product may influence the amount they buy, their buying criteria and their selection of vendors. For example, a producer of springs may have customers that use the product in applications as diverse as making machine tools, bicycles, surgical devices, office equipment, telephones and missile systems.

macrosegmentation
Method of dividing business markets into segments based on general characteristics such as geographic location, customer type, customer size and product use.

Microsegmentation

Macrosegmentation often produces market segments that are too diverse for targeted marketing strategies. Thus, marketers often find it useful to divide macrosegments based on such variables as customer size or product use into smaller microsegments. **Microsegmentation** is the process of dividing business markets into segments based on the characteristics of decision-making units within a macrosegment. Microsegmentation enables the marketer to clearly identify market segments and more precisely define target markets. These are some of the typical microsegmentation variables:[10]

microsegmentation
The process of dividing business markets into segments based on the characteristics of decision-making units within a macrosegment.

1. *Key purchasing criteria*: Marketers can segment some business markets by ranking purchasing criteria such as product quality, prompt and reliable delivery, supplier reputation, technical support and price. For example, Atlas

satisficers
Contact familiar suppliers and place the order with the first to satisfy product and delivery requirements.

optimisers
Type of business customer that considers numerous suppliers, both familiar and unfamiliar, solicits bids and studies all proposals carefully before selecting one.

Corporation in the United States developed a commanding position in the industrial door market by providing customised products in just four weeks, which is much faster than the industry average of 12 to 15 weeks. Atlas's primary market is companies with an immediate need for customised doors.

2 *Purchasing strategies*: The purchasing strategies of buying organisations can shape microsegments. Two purchasing profiles that have been identified are satisficers and optimisers. **Satisficers** contact familiar suppliers and place the order with the first to satisfy product and delivery requirements. **Optimisers** consider numerous suppliers (both familiar and unfamiliar), solicit bids and study all proposals carefully before selecting one. Recognising satisficers and optimisers is quite easy. A few key questions during a sales call, such as 'Why do you buy product X from vendor A?', usually produce answers that identify purchaser profiles.

3 *Importance of purchase*: Classifying business customers according to the significance they attach to the purchase of a product is especially appropriate when customers use the product differently. This approach is also appropriate when the purchase is considered routine by some customers but very important by others. For example, a small entrepreneur would consider a laser printer a major capital purchase, but a large office would find it a normal expense.

4 *Personal characteristics*: The personal characteristics of purchase decision-makers (their demographic characteristics, decision style, tolerance for risk, confidence level, job responsibilities, and so on) influence their buying behaviour and thus offer a viable basis for segmenting some business markets. IBM computer buyers, for example, are sometimes characterised as being more risk averse than buyers of less expensive clones that perform essentially the same functions. In advertising, therefore, IBM stresses its reputation for high quality and reliability.

Selecting segmentation descriptors

6 Discuss the criteria for successful market segmentation

After choosing one or more bases, the marketer must select the segmentation descriptors. Descriptors identify the specific segmentation variables to use. For example, if a company selects demographics as a basis of segmentation, it may use age, occupation and income as descriptors. A company that selects usage segmentation needs to decide whether to go after heavy users, non-users or light users.

Markets can be segmented using a single variable, such as age group, or several variables, such as age group, gender and education. Although it is less precise, single-variable segmentation has the advantage of being simpler and easier to use than multiple-variable segmentation. The disadvantages of multiple-variable segmentation are that it is often harder to use than single-variable segmentation; usable secondary data are less likely to be available; and as the number of segmentation bases increases, the size of individual segments decreases. Nevertheless, the current trend is towards using more rather than fewer variables to segment most markets. Multiple-variable segmentation is clearly more precise than single-variable segmentation.

Consumer goods marketers commonly use one or more of the following characteristics to segment markets: geography, demographics, psychographics, benefits sought and usage rate.

Building children's databases on the Net

Ethics IN MARKETING

Mr Jelly Belly is awfully sweet to kids on-line. The rotund mascot at sweets maker Herman Goelitz, Inc.'s World Wide Web site offers visitors free samples of jelly beans – so long as they spill the beans about their name, address, gender, age and where they shop. Only in the fine-print disclaimer does Mr Jelly Belly reveal what might be done with this personal data: ' ... anything you disclose to us is ours. So we can do anything we want with the stuff you post. We can reproduce it, disclose it, transmit it, publish it, broadcast it, and post it someplace else.'

As millions of kids go on-line, marketers are in hot pursuit. Eager to reach an enthusiastic audience more open to pitches than the typical adult buried in junk mail, companies often entertain people on-line with games and contests. But to play, these sites frequently require children to fill out questionnaires about themselves and their families and friends – valuable data to be sorted and stored in marketing databases.

'It's a huge problem. It's deceptive and fraudulent,' says Marc Rotenberg, director of the Electronic Privacy Information Center, an on-line privacy-rights group. 'Kids don't know how their personal information is being used.' He adds that typical on-line questionnaires are 'much more detailed than the traditional cereal-box promotion.'

Marketers, however, have been gathering information about kids for decades, dating back to the first decoder ring and proof of purchase. Some experts question whether a raft of new legislation is the right answer, rather than simply extended current rules on fraudulent and deceptive practices to the on-line market.

Companies are chomping at the bit for details from on-line surfers, no matter how young. At Microsoft Corp.'s Kids pages, signing the guest book means offering up the name, email address, whether the user is a boy or a girl, and the home address. Kids are encouraged to answer questions about what they like to do on-line but are also asked, ' ... can a Microsoft representative contact you?' If so, 'Please include your telephone number including area code.'[12]

Isn't what Herman Goelitz, Inc. is doing with Mr Jelly Belly just an extension of compiling a mailing list of who ordered decoder rings in the old days? Defend your answer. Do you agree with Marc Rotenberg or think that everyone should simply lighten up? Do you think new legislation is needed to address the building of Jelly Belly-type databases? Why or why not?

A relatively new and somewhat controversial development in marketing to children entails building children's databases on the Internet. The Ethics in marketing box in this chapter explains the practice and controversy.

Changing population profiles

Other age segments are also appealing targets for marketers. In Australia, there were approximately 4 million people born between 1980 and 1994, termed Generation Y, and 2.7 million born between 1961 and 1981.[11] Termed Generation Xers, these consumers are usually computer-literate, making them a large and viable market for the Internet and Internet service providers.

Generation Xers are likely to have school-age children at home and to outspend all other age groups on food at home, housing, clothing and alcohol. Those baby boomers (1946 to 1960) spend more than any other group on food away from home, transportation, entertainment, education, personal insurance and pensions.[13] Research has shown that, as the baby boomers move into this age bracket, they are willing to try new brands. In fact, consumers in this age group don't like to be stereotypically portrayed as 'old'.

Seniors (aged 65 and over) are especially attracted to companies that build relationships by taking the time to get to know them and their preferences. For example, older customers say they prefer catalogue shopping to retail outlets because of dissatisfaction with customer service at retail stores. In comparison, a mailing done to target Medicare supplement prospects that included Valentine cards to seniors received a very positive response.[14]

Profiling and analysing segments

The profile should include the segments' size, expected growth, purchase frequency, current brand usage, brand loyalty, and long-term sales and profit potential. This information can then be used to rank potential market segments by profit opportunity, risk, consistency with organisational mission and objectives, and other factors important to the organisation.

Marketers segment markets for three important reasons. First, segmentation enables marketers to identify groups of customers with similar needs and to analyse the characteristics and buying behaviour of these groups. Second, segmentation provides marketers with information to help them design marketing mixes specifically matched with the characteristics and desires of one or more segments. Third, segmentation is consistent with the marketing concept of satisfying customer wants and needs while meeting the organisation's objectives.

To be useful, a segmentation scheme must produce segments that meet four basic criteria:

- *Substantiality*: A segment must be large enough to warrant developing and maintaining a special marketing mix. This criterion does not necessarily mean that a segment must have many potential customers. Marketers of custom-designed homes and business buildings, commercial aircraft and large computer systems typically develop marketing programs tailored to each potential customer's needs. In most cases, however, a market segment needs many potential customers to make commercial sense.
- *Identifiability and measurability*: Segments must be identifiable and their size measurable. Data about the population within geographic boundaries, the number of people in various age categories, and other social and demographic characteristics are often easy to get, and they provide concrete measures of segment size. Suppose that a social service agency wants to identify segments by their readiness to participate in a drug and alcohol program or in prenatal care. Unless the agency can measure how many people are willing, indifferent or unwilling to participate, it will have trouble gauging whether there are enough people to justify setting up the service.
- *Accessibility*: The organisation must be able to reach members of targeted segments with customised marketing mixes. Some market segments are hard to reach – for example, senior citizens (especially those with reading or hearing disabilities), individuals who don't speak English and the illiterate.
- *Responsiveness*: As explained earlier, markets can be segmented using any criteria that seem logical. However, unless one market segment responds to a marketing mix differently from other segments, that segment need not be treated separately. For instance, if all customers are equally price-conscious about a product, there is no need to offer high-, medium- and low-priced versions to different segments.

Selecting target markets

Selecting target markets is not a part but a natural outcome of the segmentation process. It is a major decision that influences and often directly determines the organisation's marketing mix. So far, this chapter has focused on the market segmentation process, which is only the first step in deciding whom to approach about buying a product. The next task is to choose one or more target markets. A **target market** is a group of people or organisations for which an organisation designs, implements and maintains a marketing mix intended to meet the needs of that group, resulting in mutually satisfying exchanges. The three general strategies for selecting target markets – undifferentiated, concentrated and multi-segment targeting – are shown in Exhibit 4.8, which illustrates the advantages and disadvantages of each targeting strategy.

7 Discuss alternative strategies for selecting target markets

target market
A group of people or organisations for which an organisation designs, implements and maintains a marketing mix intended to meet the needs of that group, resulting in mutually satisfying exchanges.

Exhibit 4.8 Advantages and disadvantages of target marketing strategies

Targeting strategy	Advantages	Disadvantages	Patterns
Undifferentiated targeting	⊙ Potential savings on production/marketing costs	⊙ Unimaginative product offerings ⊙ Company more susceptible to competition	⊙ Undifferentiated strategy
Concentrated targeting	⊙ Concentration of resources ⊙ Can better meet the needs of a narrowly defined segment ⊙ Allows some small firms to better compete with larger firms ⊙ Strong positioning	⊙ Segments too small, or changing ⊙ Large competitors may more effectively market to niche segment	⊙ Concentrated strategy
Multi-segment targeting	⊙ Greater financial success ⊙ Economies of scale in production/marketing	⊙ High costs ⊙ Cannibalisation	⊙ Multi-segment strategy

Undifferentiated targeting

An organisation using an **undifferentiated targeting strategy** essentially adopts a mass-market philosophy, viewing the market as one big market with no individual segments. The organisation uses one marketing mix for the entire market. An organisation that adopts an undifferentiated targeting strategy assumes that individual customers have similar needs that can be met with a common marketing mix.

The first organisation in an industry sometimes uses an undifferentiated targeting strategy. With no competition, the organisation may not need to tailor marketing mixes to the preferences of market segments. Henry Ford's famous quote about the Model T is a classic example of an undifferentiated targeting strategy: 'They can have their car in any colour they want, as long as it's black.' At one time, Coca-Cola used this strategy with a single product and a single size of its familiar green bottle. Marketers of commodity products, such as flour and sugar, are also likely to use an undifferentiated targeting strategy.

undifferentiated targeting strategy
Marketing approach that views the market as one big market with no individual segments and thus requires a single marketing mix.

The Ford Model T is a classic example of undifferentiated targeting. Could you argue that by producing a single product for all markets, Henry Ford was positioning his car as a commodity? Why or why not?

One advantage of undifferentiated marketing is the potential for saving on production and marketing. Because only one item is produced, the organisation should be able to achieve economies of mass production. Also, marketing costs may be lower when there is only one product to promote and a single channel of distribution. Too often, however, an undifferentiated strategy emerges by default rather than by design, reflecting a failure to consider the advantages of a segmented approach. The result is often sterile, unimaginative product offerings that have little appeal to anyone.

Another problem associated with undifferentiated targeting is that it makes the company more susceptible to competitive inroads. Coca-Cola forfeited its position as the leading seller of cola drinks in supermarkets to Pepsi-Cola in the late 1950s, when Pepsi began offering several sizes of containers.

You might think an organisation producing a standard product such as toilet paper would adopt an undifferentiated strategy. However, this market has industrial segments and consumer segments. Industrial buyers want an economical, single-ply product sold in boxes of a hundred rolls. The consumer market demands a more versatile product in smaller quantities. Within the consumer market, the product is differentiated as coloured or white, with designer print or no print, cushioned or non-cushioned, and economy priced or luxury priced. Fort Howard Corporation, the market share leader in the United States in industrial toilet paper, does not even sell to the consumer market.

Concentrated targeting

With a **concentrated targeting strategy**, an organisation selects a market **niche** (one segment of a market) for targeting its marketing efforts. Because the organisation is appealing to a single segment, it can concentrate on understanding the needs, motives and satisfactions of that segment's members and on developing and maintaining a highly specialised marketing mix. Some organisations find that concentrating resources and meeting the needs of a narrowly defined market segment is more profitable than spreading resources over several different segments.

For example, many travel agencies, facing tougher competition, are trying to stand apart from one another by appealing to niche groups. Singles Travel Connections, in Adelaide, targets single travellers of both sexes, while Valentine Travel (in Victoria) and Posh Trips (in New South Wales) cater only for women travellers.[15]

Small organisations often adopt a concentrated targeting strategy to compete effectively with much larger organisations. Niche markets often provide opportunities for the entrepreneur, as illustrated in the Entrepreneurial insights box.

Some organisations, on the other hand, use a concentrated strategy to establish a strong position in a desirable market segment. Porsche, for instance, targets an upscale automobile market through 'class appeal, not mass appeal'.

Concentrated targeting violates the old adage, 'Don't put all your eggs in one basket.' If the chosen segment is too small or if it shrinks because of environmental changes, the organisation may suffer negative consequences. For example, OshKosh B'Gosh, a highly successful organisation selling children's wear in the 1980s, was so successful it could not sell clothes to anyone else. Attempts at marketing older children's clothing, women's casual clothes and maternity wear were all abandoned. Now, recognising it is in the children's-wear business, the company is expanding into products such as children's shoes, eyewear and plush toys.[17]

OshKosh B'Gosh, Inc. was so successful with its children's wear that it could not sell to anyone else. Faced with a concentrated market, the company is expanding into children's shoes, eyewear and plush toys.

concentrated targeting strategy
A strategy used to select one segment of a market or targeting marketing efforts.

niche
One segment of a market.

Singles Travel Connections
Posh Trips
on-line
How do these companies try to stand apart from the competition by targeting special groups?
www.singlestravel.com.au
www.poshtrips.com.au

OshKosh B'Gosh
on-line
What targeting strategies are now adopted by OshKosh B'Gosh? Does this strategy allow it to venture into new markets?
www.oshkoshbgosh.com

Entrepreneurial Insights

Businesses gain a foothold through niche marketing

The estimated annual turnover for the franchise industry in Australia exceeds $30 billion and is growing rapidly. In the United States, franchise operations account for more than 50 per cent of all US retail sales. According to analysts, niche marketing is the biggest source of this success, enabling small retailers to compete with big retailers such as Coles Myer.

Analysts say the key to a successful retail franchise is to identify and exploit a specialist product that satisfies consumer needs. A number of companies are doing this. For example, Battery World stocks a large range of batteries in categories ranging from phone batteries to hearing aid and specialist custom-built batteries. Battery World expects to maintain its excellent growth by focusing on the niche area of batteries and by providing high levels of customer service through their battery customisation strategies.

Another example is Just Cuts, which aims to bridge the gap between the old barber's shop and the conventional salon. Their objective is to provide customers with a quality hairstyle in the minimum time, with no appointments, pre-set prices and a written guarantee to ensure high standards. This franchise began in 1990 in New South Wales, when its founder, Denis McFadden, decided to do something completely different. The idea consisted of a 'No appointment $6 Style Cut', available for the period of an Advance Australia promotion in Sydney. The response to this offer was outstanding and the idea of Just Cuts was born. Here was the perfect opportunity to give the public what they felt was of great benefit to them: a convenient, quality style cut at an affordable price. At present, there are 130 Just Cuts salons throughout Australia and New Zealand, with plans for further expansion in both countries for 2002.

Tried and tested retail concepts are frequently being franchised with an emphasis on extraordinary service to distinguish them from more traditional stores. Dymocks book stores are a good example of this approach. By 1980, Dymocks, though still the doyen of Sydney bookstores, was looking and feeling a little shopworn. It would have been very easy for the grand old store to slide into a gradual decline. It was this which decided John Pemberton Curlewis Forsyth, William Dymock's great-grandnephew, to take over the company in 1981, selling his own successful printing and publishing business to do so. He wished to preserve the company's 19th-century character, charm and tradition, but he also realised that it would be impossible to live in the past. He investigated book retailing methods in the United Kingdom, the United States, Europe and Japan and returned ready to implement retailing concepts that were unheard of in Australia, and only recently introduced overseas. The historic old store in George Street was completely revamped internally without destroying its old charm. Specially designed gondolas and displays were built, colour-corrected lighting was introduced, and the most sophisticated computerised customer enquiry service for books in the English-speaking world was designed and installed. Additionally, Dymocks established a telephone ordering facility to cater for those customers who are unable to visit the stores to purchase books. Dymocks had entered the 21st century without discarding more than a century of tradition and it was at this time that it also moved into franchising. Dymocks now has 96 franchise outlets in Australia, New Zealand, Hong Kong and Singapore.

Mark Siebert, president of a Chicago-based franchising consulting firm, emphasises the tremendous amount of potential in sticking with a well-defined niche. 'We're seeing more and more specialisation,' he says. 'If you try to be too much, you're going to have a hard time. By focusing, you're going to be successful.'[16]

Multi-segment targeting

multi-segment targeting strategy
A strategy that chooses two or more well-defined market segments and develops a distinct marketing mix for each.

An organisation that chooses to serve two or more well-defined market segments and develops a distinct marketing mix for each has a **multi-segment targeting strategy**. Sometimes organisations use different promotional appeals, rather than completely different marketing mixes, as the basis for a multi-segment strategy. Beer marketers such as Carlton United Breweries advertise and promote special events targeted towards different market segments. The beverages and containers, however, don't differ for those market segments.

Multi-segment targeting offers many potential benefits to organisations, including greater sales volume, higher profits, larger market share and economies of scale in manufacturing and marketing. Yet it may also involve greater product design, production, promotion, inventory, marketing research and management costs. Before deciding to use this strategy, organisations should compare the benefits and costs of multi-segment targeting to those of undifferentiated and concentrated targeting.

Another potential cost of multi-segment targeting is **cannibalisation**, which occurs when sales of a new product cut into sales of an organisation's existing products. For example, pharmaceutical organisations have been introducing new over-the-counter antacids that block the production of stomach acids, rather than treat heartburn with traditional antacids that work by neutralising stomach acids. However, these organisations are aware that the new heartburn drugs are likely to cannibalise their traditional antacid products.

cannibalisation
Situation that occurs when sales of a new product cut into sales of a firm's existing products.

Designing, implementing and maintaining appropriate marketing mixes

The marketing mix is usually described in terms of product, distribution, promotion and pricing strategies intended to bring about mutually satisfying exchange relationships with target markets. Chapters 6 to 13 explore these topics in detail.

8 Explain how and why organisations implement positioning strategies and how product differentiation plays a role

Positioning

The term **positioning** refers to developing a specific marketing mix to influence potential customers' overall perception of a brand, product line or organisation in general. (**Position** is the place a product, brand or group of products occupies in consumers' minds relative to competing offerings.) Consumer goods marketers are particularly concerned with positioning. Campbell Brothers markets many different laundry detergents, each with a unique position, as illustrated in Exhibit 4.9.

Positioning assumes that consumers compare products based on important features. Marketing efforts that emphasise irrelevant features are therefore likely to misfire. For example, Schweppes Clear, a clear cola, failed because consumers perceived the 'clear' positioning as more of a marketing gimmick than a benefit.

Effective positioning requires assessing the positions occupied by competing products, determining the important dimensions underlying these positions, and choosing a position in the market where the organisation's marketing efforts will have the greatest impact.

Product differentiation is a positioning strategy that many organisations use to distinguish their products from those of competitors. The distinctions can be either real or perceived. Tandem Computer designed machines with two central processing units and two memories for computer systems that can never afford to be down or lose their databases (for example, an airline reservation system). In this case, Tandem used product differentiation to create a product with very real advantages for the target market. However, many everyday products, such as bleaches, aspirin, unleaded petrol and some soaps, are differentiated by such trivial means as brand names, packaging, colour, smell or 'secret' additives. The marketer attempts to convince consumers that a particular brand is distinctive and that they should demand it over competing brands.

Some organisations, instead of using product differentiation, position their products as being similar to competing products or brands. Artificial sweeteners advertised as tasting like sugar or margarine tasting like butter are two examples.

positioning
Developing a specific marketing mix to influence potential customers' overall perception of a brand, product line or organisation in general.

position
The place a product, brand or groups of products occupies in consumers' minds relative to competing offerings.

product differentiation
A positioning strategy that some firms use to distinguish their products from those of competitors.

Exhibit 4.9
Brands of laundry detergent

I have a question about...

- **OMO High Performance** (Australia only)
- **Persil High Performance** (New Zealand only)
- **Omomatic** (Australia only)
- **Low Suds Persil High Performance** (New Zealand only)
- **Cold Water Surf**
- **Drive**
- **Softly**
- **Lux Flakes**
- **Velvet**
- **Sunlight**
- **Comfort**
- **Huggie** (New Zealand only)

I need info on..
- Caring for my clothes
- Caring for my feather doona or duvet
- Enzymes in detergents
- My septic tank
- Removing stains from my clothes
- Stain Removal Methods
- Washing my clothes

Source: www.consumerlink.unilever.com/laundry.

Exhibit 4.10
Perceptual maps and positioning strategies for General Motors passenger cars

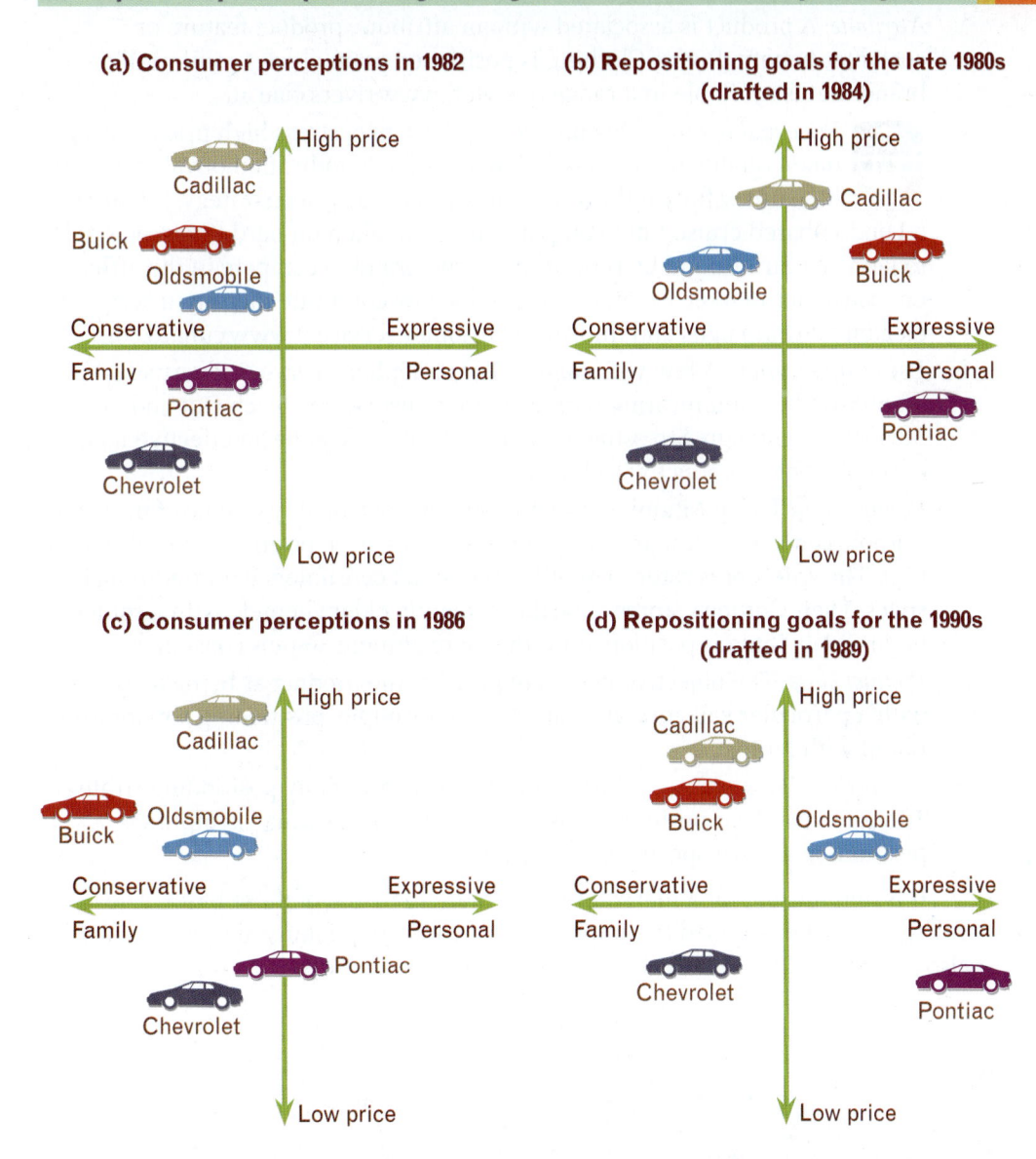

(a) Consumer perceptions in 1982

(b) Repositioning goals for the late 1980s (drafted in 1984)

(c) Consumer perceptions in 1986

(d) Repositioning goals for the 1990s (drafted in 1989)

Perceptual mapping

Perceptual mapping is a means of displaying or graphing, in two or more dimensions, the location of products, brands or groups of products in customers' minds. For example, the perceptual map in Exhibit 4.10 is the result of a 1982 study in the United States by General Motors of consumers' perceptions of the five GM car divisions: Buick, Cadillac, Chevrolet, Oldsmobile and Pontiac. Consumer perceptions are plotted on two axes. The horizontal axis ranges from conservative and family-oriented at one extreme to expressive and personal at the other. The vertical axis is used to rate price perceptions, and it ranges from high to low. Note that in 1982 the various GM divisions were not perceived as especially distinctive. Consumers did not clearly distinguish one brand from another, especially on the conservative/family versus expressive/personal dimension.

perceptual mapping
A means of displaying or graphing, in two or more dimensions, the location of products, brands or groups of products in customers' minds.

Positioning bases

Organisations use a variety of bases for positioning, including the following:[18]

- *Attribute*: A product is associated with an attribute, product feature or customer benefit. Rivers Clothing is positioned as an always comfortable brand that is available in a range of styles. www.rivers.com.au

- *Price and quality*: This positioning base may stress high price as a signal of quality or emphasise low price as an indication of value. Kmart has successfully followed the low-price and value strategy. Cunard's, a London-based cruise-liner company that had fallen on hard times, was able to launch a turnaround by repositioning the brand to compete in the affluent consumer market. Changes included a new corporate identity, a series of elegant ad campaigns and improved customer service.[19] www.cunard.com

- *Use or application*: A few years ago, Telstra telephone service advertising emphasised communicating with loved ones using the 'Reach Out and Touch Someone' campaign. Stressing uses or applications can be an effective means of positioning a product with buyers.

- *Product user*: This positioning base focuses on a personality or type of user. Zale Corporation has several jewellery store concepts, each positioned to a different user. The Zale stores cater to middle-of-the-road consumers with traditional styles. Their Gordon's stores appeal to a slightly older clientele with a contemporary look. Guild is positioned for the more affluent 50-plus consumer.[20]

- *Product class*: The objective here is to position the product as being associated with a particular category of products – for example, positioning a margarine brand with butter.

- *Competitor*: Positioning against competitors is part of any positioning strategy. The Avis rental car positioning as number one in Australia exemplifies positioning against specific competitors.

It is not unusual for a marketer to use more than one of these bases. The Telstra campaign stressed the importance of contacting family and friends but also emphasised the relatively low cost of long-distance calls.

Avis positions itself as the market leader, while others attempt to attract a different market by offering different services and automotive packages.

Repositioning

Sometimes products or companies are repositioned in order to sustain growth in slow markets or to correct positioning mistakes. **Repositioning** is changing consumers' perceptions of a brand in relation to competing brands.

New imported cars to Australia have a tariff. Over the last ten years this tariff has been reduced from 20 per cent to 10 per cent. One car company decided to pass on the higher prices in Australia by positioning the car at the premium end of the market. With the latest reduction in tariff in 2005 being a reduction of 5 per cent, the car company is now positioning their cars as premium product at an affordable price.

repositioning
Changing consumers' perceptions of a brand in relation to competing brands.

Global issues in market segmentation and marketing

Chapter 2 discussed the trend towards global market standardisation, which enables organisations such as Coca-Cola, Colgate-Palmolive, McDonald's and Nike to market similar products using similar marketing strategies in many different countries. This chapter discussed the trend towards targeting smaller, more precisely defined markets.

9 Discuss global market segmentation and targeting issues

The tasks involved in segmenting markets, selecting target markets, and designing, implementing and maintaining appropriate marketing mixes are the same whether the marketer has a local perspective or a global vision. The main difference is the segmentation variables commonly used. Countries are commonly grouped using such variables as per capita gross domestic product, geography, religion, culture or political system.

Some organisations have tried to group countries or customer segments around the world using lifestyle or psychographic variables. So-called Asian yuppies in places such as Singapore, Hong Kong, Japan and South Korea have substantial spending power and exhibit purchase and consumption behaviour similar to that of their better-known counterparts in the United States. In this case, organisations may be able to use a global market standardisation approach.

Connect it

In the article on juice bars at the beginning of this chapter, we looked at the process of market segmentation that refers to the process of dividing a market into meaningful, relatively similar, and identifiable segments or groups. Targeting is selecting one or more market segments for which an organisation designs, implements and maintains distinctive marketing mixes.

In this relatively new market, different organisations are segmenting the same market in many different ways, due to their identification of different traits on which they have segmented the market. In so doing, these organisations have eked out different market targets and adopted appropriate marketing mixes to match these markets. Thus, it is clear that there is no one way of segmenting a market or identifying a particular target market. The successful practice of market segmentation and selection depends upon the identification of appropriate market variables that will allow for successful segmentation.

Summary

1 Describe the characteristics of markets and market segments.
A market is composed of individuals or organisations with the ability and willingness to make purchases to fulfil their needs or wants. A market segment is a group of individuals or organisations with similar product needs because of one or more common characteristics.

2 Explain the importance of market segmentation.
Before the 1960s, few businesses targeted specific market segments. Today, segmentation is a crucial marketing strategy for nearly all successful organisations. Market segmentation enables marketers to tailor marketing mixes to meet the needs of particular population segments. Segmentation helps marketers to identify consumer needs and preferences, areas of declining demand and new marketing opportunities.

3 List the steps involved in segmenting markets.
Six steps are involved when segmenting markets: (1) Selecting a market or product category for study; (2) choosing a basis or bases for segmenting the market; (3) selecting segmentation descriptors; (4) profiling and analysing segments; (5) selecting target markets; and (6) designing, implementing and maintaining appropriate marketing mixes.

4 Describe the bases commonly used to segment consumer markets.
There are five commonly used bases for segmenting consumer markets. Geographic segmentation is based on region, size, density and climate characteristics. Demographic segmentation consists of age, gender, income level, ethnicity and family life-cycle characteristics. Psychographic segmentation includes personality, motives and lifestyle characteristics. Benefits sought are a type of segmentation that identifies customers according to the benefits they seek in a product. Finally, usage segmentation divides a market by the amount of product purchased or consumed.

5 Describe the bases for segmenting business markets.
Business markets can be segmented on two bases. First, macrosegmentation divides markets according to general characteristics, such as location and customer type. Second, microsegmentation focuses on the decision-making units within macrosegments.

6 Discuss the criteria for successful market segmentation.
Successful market segmentation depends on four basic criteria. First, a market segment must be substantial; it must have enough potential customers to be worthwhile. Second, a market segment must be identifiable and measurable. Third, members of a market segment must be accessible to marketing efforts. Fourth, a market segment must respond to particular marketing efforts in a way that distinguishes it from other segments.

Chapter 4 Segmenting and targeting markets

7 Discuss alternative strategies for selecting target markets.
Marketers select target markets using three different strategies: undifferentiated targeting, concentrated targeting and multi-segment targeting. An undifferentiated targeting strategy assumes that all members of a market have similar needs that can be met with a single marketing mix. A concentrated targeting strategy focuses all marketing efforts on a single market segment. Multi-segment targeting is a strategy that uses two or more marketing mixes to target two or more market segments.

8 Explain how and why organisations implement positioning strategies and how product differentiation plays a role.
Positioning is used to influence consumer perceptions of a particular brand, product line or organisation in relation to competitors. The term *position* refers to the place that the offering occupies in consumers' minds. To establish a unique position, many organisations use product differentiation, emphasising the real or perceived differences between competing offerings. Products may be differentiated based on attribute, price and quality, use or application, product user, product class or competitor.

9 Discuss global market segmentation and targeting issues.
The key tasks in market segmentation, targeting and positioning are the same regardless of whether the target market is local, regional, national or multinational. The main differences are the variables used by marketers in analysing markets and assessing opportunities and the resources needed to implement strategies.

Review it

1 The process of dividing a market into meaningful, relatively similar and identifiable groups is called
   a   Product positioning
   b   Market segmentation
   c   Product differentiation
   d   Market penetration

2 Why is market segmentation a key to successful marketing strategy?
   a   Many groups of customers have different needs and preferences.
   b   It helps to define customer needs and wants more precisely.
   c   It helps more accurately to define marketing objectives and allocate resources.
   d   All of the above are reasons that segmentation is important to marketing strategy.

3 Which of the following are important criteria for successful market segmentation?
   a   Product differentiation, concentrated targeting and perceptual mapping
   b   A clearly defined target market, highly educated marketers and experienced management teams
   c   Substantiality, measurability, accessibility and responsiveness
   d   Product positioning, product development and product differentiation

Define it

benefit segmentation 119
cannibalisation 129
concentrated targeting strategy 127
demographic segmentation 115
family life cycle (FLC) 115
geodemographic segmentation 117
geographic segmentation 113
macrosegmentation 121
market 111
market segment 111
market segmentation 111
microsegmentation 121
multi-segment targeting strategy 128
niche 127
optimisers 122
perceptual mapping 131
position 129
positioning 129
product differentiation 129
psychographic segmentation 117
repositioning 133
satisficers 122
segmentation bases (variables) 113
target market 125
undifferentiated targeting strategy 125
usage-rate segmentation 120
80/20 principle 120

4 Variables such as age, gender and income represent common variables of _____ segmentation.
   a   Demographic
   b   Geographic
   c   Psychographic
   d   Behavioural

5 Variables such as personality, motives and lifestyles represent common variables of _____ segmentation.
   a   Demographic
   b   Geographic
   c   Psychographic
   d   Behavioural

6 Macrosegmentation of businesses divides business markets according to which of the following general characteristics?
   a   Geographic location
   b   Customer type
   c   Product use
   d   All of the above

7 Once an organisation selects a market or product category for study, what is the next step in the market segmentation process?
   a   Selecting segmentation descriptors
   b   Profiling market segments
   c   Designing appropriate marketing mixes for each segment
   d   Choosing the variables for segmenting the market

8 Which of the following does *not* describe undifferentiated targeting?
   a   Undifferentiated targeting views the market as one big market with no individual segments.
   b   Undifferentiated targeting is a strategy for the first organisation to enter an industry.
   c   Undifferentiated targeting selects a specific niche within which to market.
   d   Undifferentiated targeting can save companies money on production and marketing.

9 Repositioning is
   a   A positioning strategy companies use to distinguish their products from those of their competitors
   b   Dividing a market by the amount of product bought or sold
   c   Changing consumers' perceptions of a brand in relation to competing brands
   d   Grouping customers into market segments according to the benefits they seek from the product

10 Positioning is a means of displaying or graphing, in two or more dimensions, the locations of products, brands or groups of producers in customers' minds.
   a   True
   b   False

Check the Answer Key to see how well you understood the material. More detailed discussion and writing questions and a video case related to this chapter are found in the Student Resources CD-ROM.

Apply it

1. Describe market segmentation in terms of the historical evolution of marketing.
2. Choose magazine ads for five different products. For each ad, write a description of the demographic characteristics of the targeted market.
3. Form a team with two other students. Select a product category and brand that are familiar to your team. Using Exhibit 4.8, prepare a market segmentation report and describe a targeting plan.
4. Explain concentrated (niche) targeting. Describe a company not mentioned in the chapter that uses a concentrated targeting strategy.
5. Form a team with two or three other students. Create an idea for a new product. Describe the segment (or segments) you are going to target with the product and develop a positioning strategy for the product.
6. Choose a product category (e.g. blue jeans) and identify at least three different brands and their respective positioning strategies. How is each position communicated to the target audience?
7. Create a perceptual map for the different brands of one of the following products: diet and regular colas, Holden cars, fast-food hamburger restaurants, or a product of your choice.
8. Investigate how Virgin Blue uses its website to cater to its market segments. www.virginblue.com.au
9. How are visitors to the following website segmented when seeking relevant job openings? Try this search engine and report your results. www.seek.com.au
10. Write a letter to your bank manager suggesting ideas for increasing the bank's profits and enhancing customer service by improving segmentation and targeting strategies. Make your suggestions specific.

Try it

Judy Brown has always loved working with animals. She has experience in pet grooming, boarding and in-home pet sitting. Judy wants to open a full-service business utilising her skills that is uniquely positioned in relation to the traditional pet grooming/boarding businesses that operate in the town where she lives. Customers who use these current pet services deliver their pets to the organisations and later pick them up. Most are open between 9 a.m. and 6 p.m. from Monday to Friday.

Judy lives in a medium-sized city that is close to a major airport. Many high-tech industries are located in or near her city, so many people are employed in managerial and information technology positions, and they frequently travel as part of their jobs. A lot of families have pets, so Judy thinks there is a market for pet-related services, despite the current competition.

Questions

1. How should Judy segment the market for pet services?
2. What targeting strategy should Judy use to start her business? Should this strategy change as her business prospers and grows?
3. How should Judy position her pet services business against her competition?

Watch it

Labelle Management: Something for everyone

Sizzling burgers, shakes and fries, pizza or a thick steak. What's your pleasure? Labelle Management, which owns and operates 31 restaurants and hotels, has them all. With headquarters in Mt Pleasant, Michigan, in the United States, Labelle has been in the restaurant business since 1948. When McDonald's came to town in the 1970s, Labelle's owners faced stiff competition and decided to add franchises to their holdings.

They now own six restaurants located on the main street in town. The key to Labelle's success is its use of benefit segmentation. It groups its customers into market segments according to the benefits they seek from the various restaurant formats.

Customers are mainly targeted according to needs and wants. Although Labelle's restaurants compete with one another for customers, they can all coexist because the same people want different benefits at different times.

How does this concept work? Mt Pleasant is a university town, home to Central Michigan University, an undergraduate campus with 17 000 students who choose different restaurants on different occasions. Late at night after studying, the students crave pizza delivered to their dorm, so they call Pixies. This original Labelle, 1950s-style, drive-in restaurant offers fast food at low prices, plus rock'n'roll and lots of nostalgia. Labelle works with sororities, fraternities, athletic groups and clubs on campus for special events. Students, however, aren't the only ones who are in a hurry. Pixies is the perfect dinner stop for mums on the go, driving the kids to soccer games, piano lessons or swimming. For those not interested in fast food but still interested in low prices, Labelle has other options. Ponderosa Steak House is a no-frills franchise offering very good value. For those who are really hungry – students or workers – there are big, juicy steaks, big helpings of potatoes, veggies and desserts. Customers get a lot of food for the money, and Ponderosa is a natural for groups. The atmosphere is simple, and service is mainly buffetstyle. Labelle's Big Boy Restaurants appeal to families, blue-collar workers and seniors because of the moderate prices (US$3 to US$8) for the famous double-decker hamburgers, sandwiches, salads and dinners. Students also turn out in droves for the US$4.99 all-you-can-eat breakfast buffet. Big Boy has been around for a long time, and customers can always count on getting the same good food at the same price. The familiar menu and friendly service account for the high customer loyalty at Big Boy, where managers are selected for their ability to get along with customers of all ages.

On the weekends, students, families and friends in Mt Pleasant like to relax and have fun, so ethnic food can be a nice change of pace from everyday meals. The family-priced Italian bistro, Italian Oven, features pasta, salads and pizza cooked in wood-burning ovens. What makes Italian Oven even more attractive is that it offers entertainment in the form of wandering singers, musicians and magicians.

It's hard to beat the old Irish pub atmosphere of Bennigan's. Out for a beer, the 20-somethings like to hang out at this upbeat, upscale bar and grill, although the average tab is at least US$10 per person. Part of creating a fun dining experience is creating a daring menu, and new items with trendy names and spicy tastes are standard fare at Bennigan's. Customers expect a high level of service at this Labelle restaurant, which means orders taken promptly and tasty food. College students, businesspeople and the ladies' lunch crowd like to come to Bennigan's, so the managers and staff have to be attentive, laid-back and fun in order to meet the needs of such a diverse customer base.

Although Labelle Management casts its nets to attract a wide variety of customers, it adds perks for frequent patrons. Based on the adage that 20 per cent of all customers generate 80 per cent of demand, Labelle Management tries hard to keep its steady customers happy so they will come back more often. Because 25 per cent of Bennigan's sales come from the bar, Bennigan's offers a beer card; those who drink 100 or more imported beers get their names on the plaque over the bar. And those who eat six of Pixies' famous Coney Dogs or eight Bitty Burgers have their names written on the wall of fame. Labelle Management knows Mt Pleasant backwards and forwards and works overtime through diversified restaurant concepts to give community members what they want.

Questions

1. How does Labelle Management use benefit segmentation to target various market segments?
2. Describe the benefits provided by each restaurant format.
3. How does Labelle Management use usage-rate segmentation?
4. Explain how service is a benefit that varies with restaurant format.

Suggested reading

Labelle Management website: www.labellemgt.com

Video by Learnet Inc.

© 2003 Nelson Australia Pty Limited

Click it

Online reading

INFOTRAC® COLLEGE EDITION
For additional readings and review on segmenting and targeting markets, explore InfoTrac® College Edition, your online library. Go to: www.infotrac-college.com and search for any of the InfoTrac key terms listed below:
- marketing taxonomy
- benefit segmentation
- multi-segment targeting

Answer key

1. *Answer*: b, p. 111 *Rationale*: The idea of market segmentation is to enable marketers to tailor marketing mixes to better meet the needs of specific groups of customers.
2. *Answer*: d, p. 112 *Rationale*: Segmentation is important for all of these reasons because they are consistent with the marketing concept: satisfying customer needs while meeting organisational objectives.

3. *Answer*: c, p. 124 *Rationale*: Segments that can meet these four criteria are useful to marketers because they ensure that an organisation can effectively market to members of the segment.

4. *Answer*: a, p. 115 *Rationale*: Demographic segmentation uses characteristics of customers that are easily measured, such as age, income, gender, ethnic background and family life cycle.

5. *Answer*: c, p. 117 *Rationale*: Psychographic segmentation uses characteristics of customers, in addition to traditional demographic variables, that help to add a further understanding of their marketplace behaviour.

6. *Answer*: d, p. 121 *Rationale*: These three sets of variables, as well as customer size, are all used as macro-segmentation variables in the segmentation of business markets.

7. *Answer*: d, p. 124 *Rationale*: Once the organisation defines the overall market or product category to be studied, it must select the segmentation bases or variables. Remember: these bases must meet the four basic criteria discussed in the chapter.

8. *Answer*: c, p. 125 *Rationale*: An organisation using an undifferentiated targeting strategy adopts a mass-market philosophy, viewing the market as one big market with no individual segments.

9. *Answer*: c, p. 133 *Rationale*: Sometimes goods, services or organisations need to be repositioned in order to sustain growth in slow markets or to correct past positioning errors.

10. *Answer*: b, p. 133 *Rationale*: The term *positioning* refers to the development of a specific marketing mix to influence potential customers' overall perception of a brand relative to competitive offerings.

Decision support systems and marketing research

CHAPTER FIVE

Learning Objectives

After studying this chapter, you should be able to

1. Explain the concept and purpose of a marketing decision support system
2. Define marketing research and explain its importance to marketing decision-making
3. Describe the steps involved in conducting a marketing research project
4. Discuss the growing importance of scanner-based research
5. Explain when marketing research should and should not be conducted

Consider the following report from a market researcher on the profile of US female executives' use of the Internet.

NetSmart discovered that there are no cohesive subgroups of the female on-line population; women have overlapping, multifaceted responsibilities and interests. They are overwhelmed with multiple demands and their focus is based on the current priority rather than on a single-minded pursuit. As an executive and investor, she goes on-line for convenience and success.

Almost two-thirds of women on-line work full-time (64 per cent), and make computers and the Internet a part of the way they work, play, interact and shop. Instead of picking up a phone, women log on-line, with email their preferred means of communication.

Perceived benefits

- Eighty-eight per cent feel the Internet saves them time.
- Eighty-six per cent value the convenience.
- Seventy-one per cent say it lets them bank and shop after retail hours.

NetSmart on-line

Want to know more about women on the Web? Read the Executive Summary at www.netsmart-research.com/main-sum.html

Role of the Internet as an important business tool

These executives use the Internet to:

- Send or respond to email
- Do business research on-line
- Communicate with other employees
- Work from home (25 per cent).

Along with career and family responsibilities, women have personal needs and interests, from finance to fitness to fashion. They go on-line to stay on top of current events, get stock tips and, of course, find out about the latest fashion trends. There are actually two aspects to this personal on-line usage: 'escape from stress' and 'self-indulgence'.[1]

This type of marketing research can help companies better understand women who use the Web. Managers can better target specific women's markets. They can also build websites that are more effective. What are the various techniques for conducting marketing research? Should managers always do marketing research before they make a decision? How does marketing research relate to decision support systems?

This chapter discusses ways that organisations can gather information about the customer so that they can ensure better marketing decisions are made.

Marketing decision support systems

1 Explain the concept and purpose of a marketing decision support system

Accurate and timely information is the lifeblood of marketing decision-making. Good information can help to maximise an organisation's sales and efficiently use the organisation's scarce resources. To prepare and adjust marketing plans, managers need a system for gathering everyday information about developments in the marketing environment – that is, for gathering **marketing intelligence**. The system most commonly used these days for gathering marketing intelligence is called a marketing decision support system.

A marketing **decision support system (DSS)** is an interactive, flexible, computerised information system that enables managers to obtain and manipulate information as they are making decisions. A DSS gives managers access to useful data from their own desks.

The characteristics of a true DSS system include:

- *Interactivity*: Managers can simply click buttons on their computers to access the information they want and in the form they want instantaneously.
- *Flexibility*: A DSS allows the data to be arranged in many different format and can be very detailed or summarised. It can be as simple or complex as the user requires, matching information to the problem at hand. For example, the CEO can see highly aggregated figures, and the marketing analyst can view very detailed breakdowns.
- *Discovery orientation*: Managers can probe for trends, isolate problems and ask 'what if' questions.
- *Accessibility*: A DSS is easy to learn and use by managers who are not skilled with computers. Novice users should be able to choose a standard, or default, method of using the system. They can bypass optional features so they can work with the basic system right away while gradually learning to apply its advanced features.

marketing intelligence
Everyday information about developments in the marketing environment that managers use to prepare and adjust marketing plans.

decision support system (DSS)
An interactive, flexible, computerised information system that enables managers to obtain and manipulate information as they are making decisions.

Jayne Smith, new products manager for the You Good Thing organisation, provides a hypothetical example showing how DSS can be used. To evaluate sales of a recently introduced product, Jayne can 'call up' sales by the week, then by the month, breaking them down by, say, customer segments. As she works at her desktop computer, her enquiries can go in several directions, depending on the decision at hand. If her train of thought raises questions about monthly sales last quarter compared to forecasts, she can use her DSS to analyse problems immediately. Jayne might see that her new product's sales were significantly below forecast. Were her forecasts too optimistic? She compares other products' sales to her forecasts and finds that the targets were very accurate. Was something wrong with the product? Is her sales department getting insufficient leads, or is it not putting leads to good use? Thinking a minute about how to examine that question, she checks ratios of leads converted to sales product by product. The results disturb her. Only five per cent of the new product's leads generated orders, compared to the organisation's 12 per cent all-product average. Why? Jayne guesses that the sales team is not supporting the new product vigorously enough. Quantitative information from the DSS could perhaps provide more evidence to back that suspicion. But already having enough quantitative knowledge to satisfy herself, the new product manager acts on her intuition and experience and decides to have a chat with her sales manager.

Perhaps the fastest-growing use of DSS is for **database marketing**, which is the creation of a large computerised file of customers' and potential customers' profiles and purchase patterns. It is usually the key tool for successful micromarketing, which relies on very specific information about a market. However, each DSS requires information to be loaded in the first place. In the next section we consider the marketing research process as one approach for collecting and interpreting information which can be integrated into the DSS.

Nokia on-line

When Nokia asks you to join the club, is it doing disguised marketing research or gathering information for the DSS?
www.club.nokia.com.au/ login/ join_club_nokia/default.asp

database marketing
The creation of a large computerised file of customers' and potential customers' profiles and purchase patterns.

The role of marketing research

Marketing research is the process of planning, collecting and analysing data relevant to a marketing decision. The results of this analysis are then communicated to management. Marketing research plays a key role in the marketing system. It provides decision-makers with data on the effectiveness of the current marketing mix and insights for necessary changes. Furthermore, marketing research is a main data source for both management information systems and DSS.

Marketing research has three roles: descriptive, diagnostic and predictive. Its *descriptive* role includes gathering and presenting factual statements. For example, what is the historic sales trend in the industry? What are consumers' attitudes towards a product and its advertising? Its *diagnostic* role includes explaining data. For example, what was the impact on sales of a change in the design of the package? Its *predictive* function is to address 'what if' questions. For example, how can the researcher use the descriptive and diagnostic research to predict the results of a planned marketing decision?

2 Define marketing research and explain its importance to marketing decision-making

marketing research
The process of planning, collecting and analysing data relevant to a marketing decision.

Management uses of marketing research

Marketing research can help managers in several ways:

- It improves the quality of decision-making.
- It helps managers to trace problems.
- It helps managers to focus on the importance of keeping customers.
- It assists managers in better understanding the marketplace, and alerts them to marketplace trends.
- It helps managers to gauge the perceived value of their goods and services as well as the level of customer satisfaction.

Improving the quality of decision-making

Managers can sharpen their decision-making by using marketing research to explore the desirability of various marketing alternatives. For example, Eagle Boys Pizza recently decided to stop competing on price and coupons, as this form of competition inevitably leads to small margins. Marketing research indicated that many Australians support the 'Buy Australian' policy. The organisation conducted their own research and found consumers of the delivered pizza market were influenced by price, coupons and toppings. However, the research also found that a portion of these customers (market segment) were interested in buying from an organisation that was wholly Australian owned and operated. On this basis, Eagle Boys Pizza changed their pricing policy to a fair price that delivered an exceptional Australian pizza.

Tracing problems

Another way managers use marketing research is to find out why a plan backfires. Was the initial decision incorrect? Did an unforeseen change in the external environment cause the plan to fail? How can the same mistake be avoided in the future?

In the United States, Keebler introduced Sweet Spots, a shortbread biscuit with a huge chocolate drop on it. It has had acceptable sales and is still on the market, but only after using marketing research to overcome several problems. Soon after the biscuit's introduction, Keebler increased the box size from 100 grams at US$2.29 to 150 grams at US$3.19. Demand immediately fell. Market research showed that Sweet Spots were now considered more of a luxury than an everyday item. Keebler lowered the price and went back to the 100 grams box. Even though Sweet Spots originally was aimed at upscale adult females, the organisation also tried to appeal to children. In subsequent research, Keebler found that the package graphics appealed to the buyer of confectionery but not to children.[2]

Focusing on the importance of keeping existing customers

A complex link exists between your customer satisfaction and your customer loyalty to an organisation. Long-term relationships don't just happen but are grounded in the delivery of service and value by the organisation. Keeping you as a customer pays big dividends for organisations as it aids in repeat sales and referrals by you to friends, which in turn increases revenues and grows market share. Costs fall because organisations spend less money and energy attempting to replace defectors. Steady customers are easy to serve because they understand the process and make fewer demands on employees' time. Increased customer retention also drives job satisfaction and pride, which leads to higher employee retention. In turn, the knowledge employees acquire, as they stay longer, increases productivity. A Bain & Company study estimates that a decrease in the customer defection rate of 5 per cent can boost profits by 25–95 per cent.[3]

The ability to retain customers is based on an intimate understanding of their needs. This knowledge comes primarily from marketing research. For example, British Airways recast its first-class transatlantic service based on detailed marketing research. Most airlines stress top-of-the-line service in their transatlantic first-class cabins. British Air research found that most first-class passengers simply wanted to sleep. British Air now gives premium flyers the option of dinner on the ground, before takeoff, in the first-class lounge. Once on board, they can slip into British Air pyjamas, put their heads on comfortable pillows, slip under blankets and enjoy an interruption-free flight. On arrival, first-class passengers can have breakfast, use comfortable dressing rooms and showers, and even have their clothes pressed before they set off for business. These changes in British Air's first-class service were driven strictly by marketing research.[4]

Understanding the ever-changing marketplace

Marketing research also helps managers to understand what is going on in the marketplace and to take advantage of opportunities. Historically, marketing research has been practised for as long as marketing has existed. The early Phoenicians carried out market demand studies as they traded in the various ports along the shores of the Mediterranean Sea. Marco Polo's diary indicates he was performing a marketing research function as he travelled to China. There is even evidence that the Spanish systematically conducted market surveys as they explored the New World, and there are examples of marketing research conducted during the Renaissance. Today, a pizza marketing manager might consider offering coupons with the introduction of a new pizza topping. The coupon would be used as a promotional tool to complement television advertising. The question arises as to who should receive the coupons. The sales promotion would be more effective if coupons were to be mailed to those households most likely to redeem them. Previous experience with home-delivered pizza coupon redemptions suggests that heavy users of home-delivered pizza are most likely to redeem the coupons. The next logical question for the marketing manager would be, 'Are there any identifiable demographic characteristics common to heavy coupon users but not to light users?' Market research revealed that the only statistically significant difference is young adults living with other young adults, families with teenagers, and university students. The marketing manager would then specify this characteristic when developing the mailbox drop for the new pizza coupons.

Understanding the marketplace is not limited to industrialised countries. It is important for managers all over the world to understand the ever-changing marketplace and their customers – see the Global perspectives box.

Gauging value and measuring satisfaction

Finally, marketing research allows managers to identify customers' perceptions about their goods and services, rather than relying on their own feelings about how the product is working in the market. It is often the case that managers are surprised or enlightened when they discover that their customers' attitudes differ from their own about product benefits or even product uses. Customer satisfaction and expectations can also be determined through marketing research. Linked to measures of satisfaction are concepts such as customer loyalty and repeat purchase intention, which can also be measured through marketing research and have been shown to be linked to business success.

Global PERSPECTIVES

Marketing research examines demand for a prawn-flavoured potato chip

Janjaree Thanma flips through a fat folder of market research, thinking about a prawn-flavoured potato chip. Janjaree, who directs marketing for Frito-Lay chips in Bangkok, Thailand, has found that prawn is the favourite flavour of Thais – based on marketing research. But that doesn't necessarily put it in the chips. The Thais said they thought an American snack with a native flavour such as tom yam, or prawn, is inappropriate – much as Frito-Lay people in China, after similar tests, ruled out the most popular flavour, dog.

Thais may 'perceive a good snack as a Western snack', Thanma says. After testing 500 flavours, her management team eschewed tom yam for now and stayed with American flavours such as barbecue.

Such painstaking research helps Frito-Lay's blitz of the market in Thailand. In 1995, the PepsiCo, Inc. unit bought out its Thai partner, took over a production plant, hired 1500 farmers to grow potatoes according to its strict criteria, and unleashed a market campaign featuring television ads and a brigade of 'promoter girls' who greeted shoppers in stores. Frito-Lay's sales in Thailand tripled in the first 12 months after the takeover and are forecast at 70 million bags a year.[5]

Do you think that marketing research can be effectively used in most countries of the world? What might be different about conducting marketing research abroad versus in Australia or New Zealand?

Steps in a marketing research project

3 Describe the steps involved in conducting a marketing research project

Virtually all organisations engage in some marketing research because it offers decision-makers many benefits. Some companies spend millions on marketing research; others, particularly smaller organisations, conduct informal, limited-scale research studies. For example, when a hair stylist moved to the Queensland Gold Coast he wanted to establish a chain of 10 salons in the region within 10 years. The first step in the conquest of the region was to identify a niche market that would appreciate a different level of service. Once the research was completed, the first salon was opened, followed by three other regional salons within 18 months due to the high demand.

Whether a research project costs $200 or $2 million, the same general process should be followed. The marketing research process is a scientific approach to decision-making that maximises the chance of getting accurate and meaningful results. Exhibit 5.1 traces the steps: (1) defining the marketing problem; (2) planning the research design; (3) sampling; (4) collecting and analysing the data; and (5) reporting and recommending.

Problem definition

The research process begins with the recognition of a marketing problem or opportunity. As changes occur in the organisation's external environment, marketing managers are faced with the questions, 'Should we change the existing marketing mix?' and, if so, 'How?' Marketing research may be used to evaluate product, promotion, distribution or pricing alternatives. In addition, it is used to find and evaluate new market opportunities. For example, there has

Exhibit 5.1
The marketing research process

Marketing information system (MIS)
- Internal records
- Marketing intelligence
- Marketing research

- Recommendation
- Problem definition

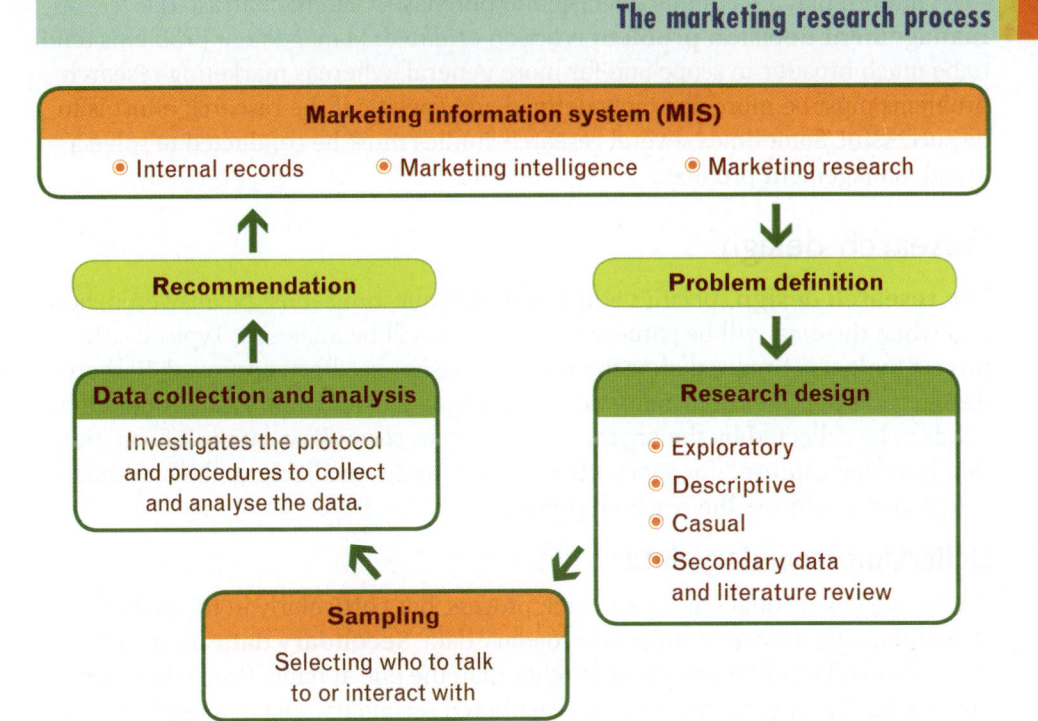

- **Data collection and analysis**: Investigates the protocol and procedures to collect and analyse the data.

- **Research design**
  - Exploratory
  - Descriptive
  - Casual
  - Secondary data and literature review

- **Sampling**: Selecting who to talk to or interact with

been an increase in the number of potential retirees as the baby boomers reach retirement age. As they have aged, this group of people have been wealthier, more independent and more demanding of product variations than their parents' generation.

For savvy marketers, such statistics represent opportunities. Marketing research can home in on these and clarify where the best opportunities lie. Different styles of retirement accommodation and health facilities are developing. Greater diversity in travel and leisure opportunities is being programmed in response to new demands. Sometimes research can lead to unexpected results requiring creative uses of the marketing mix. Car manufacturers have identified that children have a major influence on the type of car purchased in the family household. Originally, the selection of a car was thought to be a male decision. Later it was identified that while the male looked at the engine, performance and technical detail, the female of the household tended to look for style, colour and interior qualities. The most recent research has identified that children influence the type of car, depending on current trends, be it the selection of a sedan, four-wheel drive or commuter vehicle. In addition, marketing research has discovered that parents often let their children play a tie-breaking role in deciding what car to purchase.

The experiences of car manufacturers illustrate an important point about problem/opportunity definition. The **marketing research problem** is information-oriented. It involves determining what information is needed and how that information can best be obtained efficiently and effectively. The **marketing research objective**, then, is to provide insightful decision-making information. This requires specific pieces of information needed to answer the marketing research problem. Managers must combine this information with their own experience and other information to make a sound decision.

marketing research problem
Determining what information is needed and how that information can be obtained efficiently and effectively.

marketing research objective
Specific information needed to solve a marketing research problem; the objective should provide insightful decision-making information.

management decision problem
Broad-based problem that requires marketing research in order for managers to take proper action.

research design
Specifies which research questions must be answered, how and when the data will be gathered, and how the data will be analysed.

secondary data
Data previously collected for any purpose other than the one at hand.

In our example, the marketing research objective was to determine what role children play in a family's decision to purchase a car. In contrast, the **management decision problem** is action-oriented. Management problems tend to be much broader in scope and far more general, whereas marketing research problems must be more narrowly defined and specific if the research effort is to be successful. Sometimes several research studies must be conducted to solve a broad management problem.

Research design

The **research design** specifies which research questions must be answered, how and when the data will be gathered, and how it will be analysed. Typically, the project budget is finalised after the research design has been approved. Research design looks at issues of primary or secondary data use. Primary data is data that needs to be collected by the organisation whereas secondary data is information that has been captured for some other purpose and is available to the marketing researcher to address the research problem.

Collecting secondary data

A valuable tool throughout the research process, but particularly in the problem/opportunity identification stage, is secondary data. **Secondary data** are data previously collected for any purpose other than the one at hand. People both inside and outside the organisation may have gathered secondary data to meet their needs. Exhibit 5.2 describes traditional sources of secondary data. Most research efforts rely at least partly on secondary data, which can usually be obtained quickly and inexpensively. The problem is locating relevant secondary data.

Secondary data save time and money if they help to solve the researcher's problem. Even if the problem is not solved, secondary data have other advantages. They can aid in formulating the problem statement and suggest research methods and other types of data needed for solving the problem. In addition, secondary data can pinpoint the kinds of people to approach and their locations and serve as a basis of comparison with other data. The disadvantages of secondary data stem mainly from a mismatch between the researcher's unique problem and the purpose for which the secondary data were originally gathered, which are typically different. For example, a major consumer products manufacturer wanted to determine the market potential for a fireplace log made of coal rather than compressed wood by-products. The researcher found plenty of secondary data about total wood consumed as fuel, quantities consumed in each state, and types of wood burned. Secondary data were also available about consumer attitudes and purchase patterns of wood by-product fireplace logs. The wealth of secondary data provided the researcher with many insights into the artificial log market. Yet nowhere was there any information that would tell the organisation whether consumers would buy artificial logs made of coal.

The quality of secondary data may also pose a problem. Often secondary data sources don't give detailed information that would enable a researcher to assess their quality or relevance. Whenever possible, a researcher needs to address these important questions: Who gathered the data? Why were the data obtained? What methodology was used? How were classifications (such as heavy users versus light users) developed and defined? When was the information gathered?

Exhibit 5.2
Traditional sources of secondary data

Source	Description and examples
Internal information	
• Sales • Costs • Distribution reports • Miscellaneous	• Information that an organisation collects for other purposes in the normal course of business. It can include financial data, seasonal data, complaints about or appreciation of product offerings, and even the management information system that has manipulated the data in a new way.
External information	
• Government agencies	• External information is information that has been gathered for other reasons and, as such, may not be totally relevant to the research task at hand. • It can include government reports, statistical data from the departments and specific data collected by the Australian Bureau of Statistic or Statistics New Zealand for the census.
• Libraries	• Libraries are the repository of articles, journals, newspapers and books that can be stored in hard copy, microfiche and on-line via home networks and Internet access to other networks.
• Commercial vendors	• These organisations collect, analyse and interpret the findings from the data. They can be longitudinal studies over many years to monitor trends, or one-off studies of a particular phenomenon. • www.acnielsen.com.au • www.roymorgan.com/pressreleases/2002/im30.html
• Trade associations	• Trade associations and professional bodies often release information relating to trends that affect their industry.
• Other sources	• Grocers Industry Guide • Wool Industry Guide • Corporations such as Coles Myer

Secondary information from the Internet

Gathering secondary data, although necessary in almost any research project, has traditionally been a tedious job. The researcher often had to write to government agencies, trade associations or other secondary data providers and then wait days or weeks for a reply that might never come. Often, one or more trips to the library were required and the researcher might find that needed reports were on loan or missing. The rapid development of the Internet promises to eliminate the drudgery associated with the collection of secondary data but adds the problem of persons placing inappropriate or incorrect data on the Internet.

Discussion boards and newsgroups

A primary means of communicating with other professionals and special interest groups on the Internet is through discussion boards and newsgroups. These are good sources of secondary data. With an Internet connection and newsreader software, you can visit any newsgroup supported by your service provider. If your service provider does not offer newsgroups or does not carry the group in which you are interested, you can find one of the publicly available newsgroup servers that do carry the group in which you are interested.

Internet
Worldwide telecommunications network allowing access to data, pictures, sound and files throughout the world.

World Wide Web (Web)
Component of the Internet designed to simplify text and images.

Databases on CD-ROM

A number of companies offer database packages on CD-ROM for personal computers. Users can also import data on subscribers, readership or advertisers, and display them as reports and maps, or export data into other standard software packages, such as spreadsheets, word-processing and graphics applications.

The Australian Bureau of Statistics has also made 1991 and 1996 census data available on CD-ROM for use on PCs. Information available includes 1300 categories of population, education, marital status, number of children in the home, home value or monthly rent, and income data. The ABS also offers MapInfo files, which provide a digital street map of the whole of Australia. They include mapping files that identify the locations of streets, highways, railroads, pipelines, power lines and airports. Boundary files identify local government, municipalities, census tracts, census block groups, statistical districts, rivers and lakes.

Good secondary data can help researchers to conduct a thorough situation analysis. With that information, researchers can list their unanswered questions and rank them. Researchers must then decide the exact information required to answer the questions.

Gathering primary data

Sometimes research questions can be answered by gathering more secondary data; otherwise, primary data may be needed. **Primary data**, or information collected for the first time, can be used for solving the particular problem under investigation. The main advantage of primary data is that they will answer a specific research question that secondary data cannot answer. For example, suppose Eagle Boys Pizza developed two new recipes for two-minute delivery. Which one will consumers like better? Secondary data won't help to answer this question. Instead, targeted consumers must try each recipe and evaluate the tastes, textures and appearances of each pizza. Moreover, primary data are current and researchers know the source. Sometimes researchers gather the data themselves rather than outsourcing the projects. Researchers also specify the methodology of the research. Secrecy can be maintained because the information is proprietary. In contrast, secondary data are available to all interested parties for relatively small fees.

Gathering primary data is expensive; costs can range from a few thousand dollars for a limited survey to several million for a nationwide study. For example, a nationwide, 15-minute telephone interview with 1000 adult males can cost $50 000 for everything, including a data analysis and report. Because primary data gathering is so expensive, organisations commonly cut back on the number of interviews to save money. Larger companies that conduct many research projects use another cost-saving technique. They piggyback studies, or gather data on two different projects using one questionnaire. The drawback is that answering questions about, say, dog food and gourmet coffee may be confusing to respondents. Piggybacking, also known as an omnibus, requires a longer interview (sometimes half an hour or longer), which tires respondents. The quality of the answers typically declines, with people giving curt replies and thinking, 'When will this end?' A lengthy interview also makes people less likely to participate in other research surveys.[6]

However, the disadvantages of primary data gathering are usually offset by the advantages. It is often the only way of solving a research problem. And with a variety of techniques available for research – including surveys, in-depth interviews, observations and experiments – primary research can address almost any marketing question.

primary data
Information collected for the first time. Can be used for solving the particular problem under investigation.

Chapter 5 ■ ■ ■ Decision support systems and marketing research

Exhibit 5.3
Characteristics of various types of survey research

Characteristic	In-home personal interviews	Mall intercept interviews	Telephone interviews from interviewer's home	Central-location telephone interviews	Self-administered and one-off mail surveys	Mail panel surveys	Computer disk by mail	Internet interviews	Focus groups
Cost	High	Moderate	Moderate to low	Moderate	Low	Moderate	Moderate	Moderate to low	Low
Time span	Moderate	Moderate	Fast	Fast	Slow	Relatively slow	Relatively slow	Moderate	Fast
Use of interview probes	Yes	Yes	Yes	Yes	No	Yes	No	Yes, if interactive	Yes
Ability to show concepts to respondent	Yes (also taste tests)	Yes (also taste tests)	No	No	Yes	Yes	Yes	Yes	Yes
Management control over interview	Low	Moderate	Low	High	n/a	n/a	n/a	High if interview used	High
General data quality	High	Moderate	Moderate to low	High to moderate	Moderate to low	Moderate	High to moderate	High to moderate	Moderate
Ability to collect large amounts of data	High	Moderate	Moderate to low	Moderate to low	Low to moderate	Moderate	High	High	Moderate
Ability to handle complex questionnaires	High	Moderate	Moderate	High if computer assisted	Low	Low	High	High	Low

Survey research (usually descriptive)

The most popular technique for gathering primary data is **survey research**, in which a researcher interacts with people to obtain facts, opinions and attitudes. Exhibit 5.3 summarises the characteristics of the most popular forms of survey research.

In-home personal interviews Although in-home personal interviews often provide high-quality information, they tend to be very expensive because of the interviewers' travel time and transport costs. Therefore, market researchers tend to conduct fewer in-home personal interviews today than they did in the past.

Nevertheless, this form of survey research has some important advantages. The respondent is interviewed at home, in a natural setting where many consumption decisions are actually made. Also, the interviewer can get the respondent to interact with items such as package designs, or conduct taste or product use tests. An interviewer can also probe when necessary – a technique used to clarify a person's response. For example, an interviewer might ask,

survey research
The most popular technique for gathering primary data in which a researcher interacts with people to obtain facts, opinions and attitudes.

'What did you like best about the salad dressing you just tried?' The respondent might reply, 'The taste.' This answer doesn't provide a lot of information, so the interviewer could probe by saying, 'Can you tell me a little bit more about the taste?' The respondent then elaborates: 'Yes, it's not too sweet, it has the right amount of pepper, and I love that hint of garlic.'

Mall intercept interviews The **mall intercept interview** is conducted in the common areas of shopping malls or in a market research office within the mall. It is the economy version of the door-to-door interview with personal contact between interviewer and respondent, minus the interviewer's travel time and transport costs. To conduct this type of interview, the research organisation rents office space in the mall or pays a significant daily fee. One drawback is that it is hard to get a representative sample of the population.

mall intercept interview
Survey research method that involves interviewing people in the common areas of shopping malls.

Mall intercept interviews must be brief. Only the shortest ones are conducted while respondents are standing. Usually researchers invite respondents to their office for interviews, which are still rarely over 15 minutes long. The researchers often show respondents concepts for new products or a test commercial, or have them taste a new food product. The overall quality of mall intercept interviews is about the same as telephone interviews (see below).

Marketing researchers are applying new technology in mall interviewing. The first technique is **computer-assisted personal interviewing**. The researcher conducts in-person interviews, reads questions to the respondent from a computer screen, and directly keys the respondent's answers into the computer. A second approach is **computer-assisted self-interviewing**. A mall interviewer intercepts and directs willing respondents to nearby computers. Each respondent reads questions on the computer screen and directly keys his or her answers into the computer. The third use of technology is fully automated self-interviewing. Respondents are guided by interviewers or independently approach a centrally located computer station or kiosk, read questions on the screen and directly key their answers into the computer.

computer-assisted personal interviewing
Interviewing method in which the interviewer reads the questions from a computer screen and enters the respondent's data directly into the computer.

computer-assisted self-interviewing
Interviewing method in which a mall interviewer intercepts and directs willing respondents to nearby computers where the respondent reads questions on the computer screen and directly keys his or her answers into the computer.

Telephone interviews Compared to the personal interview, the telephone interview costs less and may provide the best sample of any survey procedure. Most telephone interviewing is conducted from a specially designed phone room called a **central-location telephone (CLT) facility**. A phone room has many phone lines, individual interviewing stations, sometimes monitoring equipment, headsets, and permits the research organisation to interview people nationwide from a single location.

central-location telephone (CLT) facility
A specially designed phone room used to conduct telephone interviewing.

Many CLT facilities offer computer-assisted interviewing (CATI). The interviewer reads the questions from a computer screen and enters the respondent's data directly into the computer. The researcher can stop the survey at any point and immediately print out the survey results. Thus, a researcher can get a sense of the project as it unfolds and fine-tune the research design if necessary. An on-line interviewing system can also save time and money because data entry occurs as the response is recorded, rather than as a separate process after the interview.

Mail surveys Mail surveys have several benefits: relatively low cost, elimination of interviewer's bias, centralised control, and actual or promised anonymity for respondents (which may draw more candid responses). Some researchers feel that mail questionnaires give the respondent a chance to reply more thoughtfully and to check records, talk to family members, and so forth. Yet mail questionnaires usually produce low response rates.

Low response rates pose a problem because certain elements of the population tend to respond more than others. The resulting sample may therefore not represent the surveyed population. For example, the sample may have too many retired people and too few working people. In this instance, answers to a question about attitudes towards Centrelink might indicate a much more favourable overall view of the system than is actually the case. Another serious problem with mail surveys is that no one probes respondents to clarify or elaborate on their answers.

Mail panels offer an alternative to the one-off mail survey. A mail panel consists of a sample of households recruited to participate by mail for a given period. Panel members often receive gifts in return for their participation. Essentially, the panel is a sample used several times. In contrast to one-off mail surveys, the response rates from mail panels are high. Rates of 70 per cent (of those who agree to participate) are not uncommon. A more recent addition to this process is the replacement of the mail medium with a telephone call.

Computer disk by mail The **computer disk by mail survey** medium has all the advantages and disadvantages of a typical mail survey. An additional advantage is that a disk survey can incorporate skip patterns into the survey. For example, a question might ask, 'Do you own a cat?' If your answer is 'no', then you would skip all questions related to cat ownership. A disk survey will perform this function automatically. A disk survey can also use respondent-generated words in questions throughout the survey. It can easily display a variety of graphics and directly relate them to questions. Finally, a disk survey eliminates the need to encode data from paper surveys. The primary disadvantage is that the respondent must have access to, and be willing to use, a computer. This survey system has tended to be replaced by the Internet as the communication medium.

Internet surveys The popularity of Internet surveys surged in the late 1990s. Reasons for this trend include the greater speed of response, reduced printing costs, all the advantages of the computer disk and the ability to show video. Another benefit of using the Internet for market research is the ability to reach large numbers of people. It is hard to imagine another medium that can provide so much potential while remaining economically feasible. The Internet is an international arena where many barriers to communication have been erased.

Despite the advantages of Internet surveys there are still many drawbacks, the largest being the unrepresentativeness of the population as a whole. Users of the Internet tend to be educated, technically oriented and relatively young. Over time, this will change as the Internet integrates with media such as digital media. Currently, there are some populations, such as computer products purchasers and home users, business and professional users of Internet services, who are ideal for Internet surveys.

A second problem is security on the Internet. Users today are understandably worried about privacy issues. A third problem occurs when an **unrestricted Internet sample** is set up on the Internet. In such a sample, anyone who desires can complete the questionnaire any number of times. The results are therefore skewed by repeat voting, which makes the result invalid. A simple solution to repeat respondents is to lock respondents out of the site after they have filled out the questionnaire.

computer disk by mail survey
Like a typical mail survey, only the respondents receive and answer questions on a disk.

integrated interviewing
A new interviewing method in which a respondent is interviewed on the Internet.

unrestricted Internet sample
Anyone with a computer and modem can fill out the questionnaire.

screened Internet sample
Internet sample with quotas based on desired sample characteristics.

Screened and recruited Internet samples[7] These are two other types of Internet samples. **Screened Internet samples** adjust for the unrepresentativeness of the self-selected respondents by imposing quotas based on some desired sample characteristics. These are often demographic characteristics such as gender, income or geographic region, or product-related criteria such as past purchase behaviour, job responsibilities or current product use. The applications for screened samples are generally similar to those for unrestricted samples. Screened sample questionnaires typically use a branching or skip pattern for asking screening questions to determine whether or not the full questionnaire should be presented to a respondent. Some Web survey systems can make immediate market segment calculations that assign a respondent to a particular segment based on screening questions, then select the appropriate questionnaire to match the respondent's segment.

Alternatively, some Internet research providers maintain a 'panel house' that recruits respondents who fill out a preliminary classification questionnaire. This information is used to classify respondents into demographic segments. Clients specify the desired segments, and the respondents who match the desired demographics are permitted to fill out the questionnaires of all clients who specify that segment.

recruited Internet sample
Respondents are pre-recruited. After qualifying to participate, they are sent a questionnaire by email or directed to a secure website to fill out a questionnaire.

Recruited Internet samples are used for targeted populations in surveys that require more control over the makeup of the sample. Respondents are recruited by telephone, mail, email or in person. After qualification, they are sent the questionnaire by email or are directed to a website that contains a link to the questionnaire. At websites, passwords are normally used to restrict access to the questionnaire to the recruited sample members. Since the makeup of the sample is known, completions can be monitored, and follow-up messages can be sent to those who don't complete the questionnaire, in order to improve the participation rate.

Recruited samples are ideal in applications that already have a database from which to recruit the sample. For example, a good application would be a survey that used a customer database to recruit respondents for a purchaser satisfaction study.

Entrepreneurial Insights

The Internet is a great tool for entrepreneurs who want to conduct marketing research

The Internet is the 'great equaliser' for small business owners wishing to conduct marketing research. Secondary research, for example, is at your fingertips simply through the use of a search engine. Do you want to know what people are saying about your industry and products? Go to a chat room.

Survey research was often too expensive for small businesses to hire a marketing research organisation. Even without using a research organisation, hiring and training interviewers was expensive and many entrepreneurs simply didn't have the knowledge of how to conduct a survey.

On-line surveys offer a whole new approach for small businesses to inexpensively conduct survey research. Current versions of Microsoft Internet Explorer and Netscape Navigator fully support transparent interactivity for on-line surveys. This development allows the entrepreneur to create a much more sophisticated survey than is possible through mail surveys. For example, complicated skip patterns can be built into on-line surveys. A simple skip pattern would be, 'Do you own a dog?' If the answer is 'no', all of the questions pertaining to dog ownership would be skipped.

What are several pitfalls that the entrepreneur should guard against when conducting on-line surveys? When should owners of small businesses rely on the expertise of the marketing research organisation?

Focus groups   A **focus group** is a type of personal interviewing. Often recruited by random telephone screening, eight people with certain desired characteristics form a focus group. These qualified consumers are usually offered an incentive (typically $30 to $50) to participate in a group discussion. The meeting place (sometimes resembling a living room, sometimes featuring a conference table) has audio, video and perhaps Internet recording equipment. It also likely has a viewing room with a one-way mirror so that clients (manufacturers or retailers) may watch the session. During the session, a moderator, hired by the research organisation, leads the group discussion.

Focus groups are much more than question-and-answer interviews. The distinction is made between 'group dynamics' and 'group interviewing'. The interaction provided in **group dynamics** is essential to the success of focus-group research; this interaction is the reason for conducting group rather than individual research. One of the essential assumptions of group-session usage is the idea that a response from one person may become a stimulus for another, thereby generating an interplay of responses that may yield more than if the same number of people had contributed independently.

Focus groups are occasionally used to brainstorm new product ideas or to screen concepts for new products. A baking soda manufacturer asked consumers how they used their product. To their amazement, the uses were far greater than just for baking and led to new promotional campaigns and markets.

By using the Internet, clients can now view, live, their focus groups around the country. The researcher can get a full-group view, or a close-up, zoom or pan shot of the participants. The researcher can also communicate directly with the moderator using an ear receiver.

focus group
Seven to 10 people who participate in a group discussion led by a moderator.

group dynamics
Group interaction essential to the success of focus group research. Through the use of focus groups, manufacturers can discover many new uses for their products.

Through the use of focus groups, manufacturers can discover many new uses for their products.

The newest development in qualitative research is the on-line focus groups where special links are created and people can respond either by typing their responses or by using products such as Netmeeting. A number of organisations are currently offering this new means of conducting focus groups. Advantages of this new use of medium include cost effectiveness, broader geographic speed and accessibility. Disadvantages include the inability to allow respondents to develop rapport and to monitor body language to check for honesty and candidness of responses from the focus group members.

Questionnaire design

All forms of survey research require a questionnaire. Questionnaires ensure that all respondents will be asked the same series of questions. Questionnaires include three basic types of questions: open-ended, closed-ended and scaled-response (see Exhibit 5.4). An **open-ended question** encourages an answer phrased in the respondent's own words. Researchers get a rich array of information based on the respondent's frame of reference. In contrast, a **closed-ended question** asks the respondent to make a selection from a limited list of responses. Traditionally, marketing researchers separate the two-choice question (called *dichotomous*) from the many-item type (often called *multiple choice*). A **scaled-response question** is a closed-ended question designed to measure the intensity of a respondent's answer.

Closed-ended and scaled-response questions are easier to tabulate than open-ended questions because response choices are fixed. On the other hand, if the researcher is not careful in designing the closed-ended question, an important choice might be omitted. For example, suppose this question were asked on a food study: 'What do you normally add to a sandwich, besides meat, that you have prepared at home?'

Avocado	1
Cheese	2
Lettuce	3
Mayonnaise	4
Olives (black/green)	5
Onions (red/white)	6
Capsicum (red/green)	7
Sour cream	8

The list seems complete, doesn't it? However, consider the following responses: 'I usually add tomato'; 'I cut up a mixture of lettuce and spinach'; 'I'm a vegetarian; I don't use meat at all. My sandwich is filled only with cheese'. How would you code these replies? As you can see, the question needs an 'other' category.

A good question must also be asked clearly and concisely, and ambiguous language must be avoided. Consider, for example, this question: 'Do you live within 10 minutes of here?' The answer depends on the mode of transportation (maybe the person walks), driving speed, perceived time and other factors. Instead, respondents should see a map with certain areas highlighted and be asked whether they live within one of those areas.

Clarity also implies using reasonable terminology. A questionnaire is not a vocabulary test. Jargon should be avoided, and language should be geared to the target audience. A question such as 'What is the level of efficacy of your preponderant dishwasher powder?' would probably be greeted by a lot of blank stares. It would be much simpler to say, 'Are you (1) very satisfied, (2) somewhat satisfied, or (3) not satisfied with your current brand of dishwasher powder?'

---

open-ended question
Interview question that encourages an answer phrased in the respondent's own words.

closed-ended question
Interview question that asks the respondent to make a selection from a limited list of responses.

scaled-response question
A closed-ended question designed to measure the intensity of a respondent's answer.

Exhibit 5.4
Types of questions found on questionnaires for national market research

Open-ended questions	Closed-ended questions	Scaled-response question
1 What advantages, if any, do you think ordering from a mail-order catalogue offers compared to shopping at a local retail outlet? (*Probe*: What else?)	**Dichotomous** 1 Did you heat the product before serving it? Yes .... 1 No 2	Do you agree with the statement: Bank fees for saving accounts are too high. (*Tick one*) _____ Strongly disagree _____ Disagree _____ Neither aggress nor disagree _____ Agree _____ Strongly agree
2 Why do you have one or more of your rugs or carpets professionally cleaned rather than you or someone else in the household cleaning them?	2 The federal government doesn't care what people like me think. Agree .... 1 Disagree 2	
3 What is there about the colour of the eye shadow that makes you like it the best?	**Multiple choice** 1 I'd like you to think back to the last footwear of any kind that you bought. I'll read you a list of descriptions and would like for you to tell me which category they fall into. (*Read list and tick proper category*.) Dress and/or formal .... 1 Casual .... 2 Canvas/trainer/gym shoes .... 3 Specialised athletic shoes .... 4 Boots .... 5 2 In the last three months, have you used Noxzema skin cream ... (*Tick all that apply*.) As a facial wash .... 1 For moisturising the skin .... 2 For treating blemishes .... 3 For cleansing the skin .... 4 For treating dry skin .... 5 For softening skin .... 6 For sunburn .... 7 For making the facial skin smooth 8	

Stating the survey's purpose at the beginning of the interview also improves clarity. The respondents should understand the study's intentions and the interviewer's expectations. Sometimes, of course, to get an unbiased response, the interviewer must initially disguise the true purpose of the study. If an interviewer says, 'We're conducting an image study for National Australia Bank' and then proceeds to ask a series of questions about the bank, chances are the responses will be biased. Many times respondents will try to provide answers that they believe are 'correct' or that the interviewer wants to hear.

Finally, to ensure clarity, the interviewer should avoid asking two questions in one – for example, 'How did you like the taste of the base and the topping from an Eagle Boys pizza?' This should be divided into two questions, one concerning taste of the base and the other the taste of the topping.

A question should not only be clear but also unbiased. A question such as 'Have you purchased any quality Black & Decker tools in the past six months?' biases respondents to think of the topic in a certain way (in this case, to link quality and Black & Decker tools). Questions can also be leading: 'Weren't you pleased with the good service you received last night at the Holiday Inn?' (The respondent is all but instructed to say 'yes'.) These examples are obvious; unfortunately, bias is usually more subtle. Even an interviewer's clothing or gestures can create bias.

Observation research

In contrast to survey research, **observation research** does not rely on direct interaction with people. The three types of observation research are people watching people, people watching an activity, and machines watching people. There are two types of *people watching people* research:

1. *Mystery shoppers*: Researchers posing as customers observe the quality of service offered by retailers. Market research organisations send researchers to an organisation to evaluate their salespeople's courtesy, knowledge and helpfulness. This information then goes back to the organisation and is used to refine the training and delivery processes for the researched organisation.

2. *One-way mirror observations*: At the Fisher-Price Play Laboratory in the United States, children are invited to spend 12 sessions playing with toys. Toy designers watch through one-way mirrors to see how children react to Fisher-Price's and other makers' toys. Fisher-Price, for example, had difficulty designing a toy lawn mower that children would play with. A designer, observing behind the mirror, noticed the children's fascination with soap bubbles. He then created a lawn mower that spewed soap bubbles. It sold over a million units in the first year.

> **observation research**
> Research method that relies on three types of observation: people watching people, people watching activity, and machines watching people.

Organisations use the IDEA-Lab at the University of Melbourne to observe people using new or adapted technology.

One form of observation research that features people watching an activity is known as an **audit**, the examination and verification of the sale of a product. Audits generally fall into two categories: retail audits, which measure sales to final consumers, and wholesale audits, which determine the amount of product moved from warehouses to retailers. Wholesalers and retailers allow auditors into their stores and stockrooms to examine the organisation's sales and order records in order to verify product flows. In turn, the retailers and wholesalers receive cash compensation and basic reports about their operations from the audit organisations.

For machines watching people, observation equipment falls into two categories:

- *Traffic counters*: The most popular form of machine-based observation research relies on machines that measure the flow of vehicles over a stretch of roadway. Outdoor advertisers rely on traffic counts to determine the number of exposures per day to a billboard. Retailers use the information to decide where to place a store. Convenience stores, for example, require a moderately high traffic volume to be profitable. This type of observation equipment can be electronic or mechanical.
- *Passive people meter*: Soon a camera-like device will be available to measure the size of television audiences. The passive system, packaged to resemble a VCR and placed on top of the TV, is programmed to recognise faces and record electronically when specific members of a family watch TV. It notes when viewers leave the room and even when they avert their eyes from the screen. Strangers are listed as visitors. Passive people meters are necessary because advertisers are demanding more proof of viewership and the television networks are under pressure to show that advertising is reaching its intended targets. (Ratings are used to help set prices for commercial time.)

All observation techniques offer at least two advantages over survey research. First, bias from the interviewing process is eliminated. Second, observation doesn't rely on the respondent's willingness to provide data.

Conversely, observation techniques also have two important disadvantages. First, subjective information is limited because motivations, attitudes and feelings are not measured. Second, data collection costs may run high unless the observed behaviour patterns occur frequently, briefly or somewhat predictably.

Experiments (causal design)

An **experiment** is another design a researcher can use to gather primary data. The researcher alters one or more variables – price, package design, shelf space, advertising theme, advertising expenditures – while observing the effects of those alterations on another variable (usually sales). The best experiments are those in which all factors are held constant except the ones being manipulated. The researcher can then observe that changes in sales, for example, result from changes in the amount of money spent on advertising.

Holding all other factors constant in the external environment is a monumental and costly, if not impossible, task. Such factors as competitors' actions, the weather and economic conditions are beyond the researcher's control. Yet market researchers have ways to account for the ever-changing external environment. Mars, the confectionery company, was losing sales to other confectionery companies. Traditional surveys showed that the shrinking chocolate bar was not perceived as good value. Mars wondered whether a bigger bar sold at the same price would increase sales enough to offset the

audit
Form of observation research that features people examining and verifying the sale of a product.

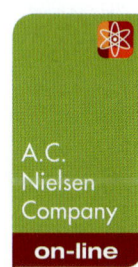

A.C. Nielsen Company
on-line
How does A.C. Nielsen's 40 000-household Consumer Panel provide insights into consumer purchase behaviour? What Internet resources are available through this site?
www.acnielsen.com.au

experiment
Method a researcher uses to gather primary data.

higher ingredient costs. The organisation designed an experiment in which the marketing mix stayed the same in different markets but the size of the bar varied. The substantial increase in sales of the bigger bar quickly proved that the additional revenue would more than cover the additional costs. Mars increased the bar size – and its market share and profits.

Sampling

Once the researchers decide how they will collect primary data, their next step is to select the sampling procedures they will use. An organisation can seldom take a census of all possible users of a new product, nor can they all be interviewed. Therefore, an organisation must select a sample of the group to be interviewed. A **sample** is a sub-set of a larger population.

Several questions must be answered before a sampling plan is chosen. First, the population, or **universe**, of interest must be defined. The sample will be drawn from this group. It should include all the people whose opinions, behaviour, preferences, attitudes, and so on are of interest to the marketer. For example, in a study whose purpose is to determine the market for a new canned dog food, the universe might be defined to include all current buyers of canned dog food.

After the universe has been defined, the next question is whether the sample must be representative of the population. If the answer is 'yes', a probability sample is needed. Otherwise, a non-probability sample might be considered.

Probability samples

A **probability sample** is one in which every element in the population has a known statistical likelihood of being selected. Its most desirable feature is that scientific rules can be used to ensure that the sample represents the population.

One type of probability sample is a random sample. A **random sample** must be arranged in such a way that every element of the population has an equal chance of being selected as part of the sample. For example, suppose a university is interested in getting a cross-section of student opinions on a proposed sports complex to be built using student union fees. If the university can acquire an up-to-date list of all the enrolled students, it can draw a random sample by using random numbers from a table (found in most statistics books) to select students from the list. Common forms of probability and non-probability samples are shown in Exhibit 5.5.

Non-probability samples

Any sample in which little or no attempt is made to get a representative cross-section of the population can be considered a **non-probability sample**. A common form of a non-probability sample is the **convenience sample**, based on using respondents who are convenient or readily accessible to the researcher – for example, employees, friends or relatives.

Non-probability samples are acceptable as long as the researcher understands their non-representative nature. Because of their lower cost, non-probability samples are the basis of much marketing research.

Types of errors

Whenever a sample is used in marketing research, two major types of error occur: measurement error and sampling error. **Measurement error** occurs when there is a difference between the information desired by the researcher and the information provided by the measurement process. For example, people may tell an interviewer that they purchase XXXX beer when they don't. Measurement error generally tends to be larger than sampling error.

---

sample
A sub-set of a population.

universe
The population from which a sample will be drawn.

probability sample
A sample in which every element in the population has a known statistical likelihood of being selected.

random sample
Sample arranged in such a way that every element of the population has an equal chance of being selected as part of the sample.

non-probability sample
Any sample in which little or no attempt is made to get a representative cross-section of the population.

convenience sample
A form of non-probability sample using respondents who are convenient or readily accessible to the researcher – for example, employees, friends or relatives.

measurement error
Error that occurs when there is a difference between the information desired by the researcher and the information provided by the measurement process.

Exhibit 5.5
Types of samples

	Probability samples
Simple random sample	Every member of the population has a known and equal chance of selection.
Stratified sample	Population is divided into mutually exclusive groups (such as gender or age), then random samples are drawn from *each* group.
Cluster sample	Population is divided into mutually exclusive groups (such as geographic areas), then a random sample of clusters is selected. The researcher then collects data from all the elements in the selected clusters or from a probability sample of elements within each selected cluster.
Systematic sample	A list of the population is obtained – e.g. all persons with a cheque account at XYZ Bank – and a *skip interval* is obtained. The skip interval is obtained by dividing the sample size by the population size. If the sample size is 100 and the bank has 1000 customers, then the skip interval is 10. The beginning number is randomly chosen within the skip interval. If the beginning number is 8, then the skip pattern would be 8, 18, 28 …
	Non-probability samples
Convenience sample	The researcher selects the easiest population members from whom to obtain information.
Judgement sample	The researcher's selection criteria are based on personal judgement that the elements (persons) chosen will likely give accurate information.
Quota sample	The researcher finds a prescribed number of people in several categories; e.g. owners of large dogs versus owners of small dogs. Respondents are not selected on probability sampling criteria.
Snowball sample	The selection of additional respondents is made on the basis of referrals from the initial respondents. This is used when a desired type of respondent is hard to find; e.g. persons who have taken round-the-world cruises in the last three years. This technique employs the old adage 'Birds of a feather flock together'.

Sampling error occurs when a sample somehow does not represent the target population. Sampling error can be one of several types. Non-response error occurs when the sample actually interviewed differs from the sample drawn. This error happens because the people originally selected to be interviewed either refused to cooperate or were inaccessible. For example, people who feel embarrassed about their drinking habits may refuse to talk about them.

sampling error
Error that occurs when a sample somehow does not represent the target population.

Data collection and analysis

Marketing research field service organisations collect most primary data. A **field service organisation** specialises in interviewing respondents on a subcontracted basis. Many have offices throughout the country. A typical marketing research study involves data collection in several cities, requiring the marketer to work with a comparable number of field service organisations. To ensure uniformity among all subcontractors, detailed field instructions should be developed for every job. Nothing should be open to chance; no interpretations of procedures should be left to subcontractors.

Besides conducting interviews, field service organisations provide focus group facilities, mall intercept locations, test product storage and kitchen facilities to prepare test-food products. They also conduct retail audits (counting the amount of a product sold off retail shelves). After an in-home interview is completed, field service supervisors validate the survey by recontacting about 15 per cent of the respondents. The supervisors verify that certain responses were recorded properly and that the people were actually interviewed.

field service organisation
Organisation that specialises in interviewing respondents on a subcontracted basis.

Analysing the data

After collecting the data, the marketing researcher proceeds to the next step in the research process: data analysis. The purpose of this analysis is to interpret and draw conclusions from the mass of collected data. The marketing researcher tries to organise and analyse those data by using one or more techniques common to marketing research: one-way frequency counts, cross-tabulations and more sophisticated statistical analysis. Of these three techniques, one-way frequency counts are the simplest. One-way frequency tables record the responses to a question. For example, the answers to the question 'What brand of microwave popcorn do you buy most often?' would provide a one-way frequency distribution. One-way frequency tables are always done in data analysis, at least as a first step, because they provide the researcher with a general picture of the study's results.

A **cross-tabulation**, or 'cross-tab', lets the analyst look at the responses to one question in relation to the responses to one or more other questions. For example, what is the association between gender and the brand of microwave popcorn bought most frequently? Hypothetical answers to this question are shown in Exhibit 5.6. Although the Uncle Tobys brand was popular with both males and females, it was more popular with females. Compared with women, men strongly preferred Pop Rite, whereas women were more likely than men to buy Weight Watchers popcorn.

Researchers can use many other more powerful and sophisticated statistical techniques, such as hypothesis testing, measures of association and regression analysis. A description of these techniques goes beyond the scope of this book but can be found in any good marketing research textbook. The use of sophisticated statistical techniques depends on the researchers' objectives and the nature of the data gathered.

cross-tabulation
A method of analysing data that lets the analyst look at the responses to one question in relation to the responses to one or more other questions.

Exhibit 5.6
Hypothetical cross-tabulation between gender and brand of microwave popcorn purchased most frequently

Brand	Purchase by gender	
	Male	Female
Uncle Tobys	31%	48%
TV Time	12	6
Pop Rite	38	4
Act Two	7	23
Weight Watchers	4	18
Other	8	0

Recommendations

After data analysis has been completed, the researcher must prepare the report and communicate the conclusions and recommendations to management. This is a key step in the process. If the marketing researcher wants managers to carry out the recommendations, he or she must convince them that the results are credible and justified by the data collected.

Researchers are usually required to present both written and oral reports on the project. These reports should be tailored to the audience. They should begin with a clear, concise statement of the research objectives, followed by a complete, but brief and simple, explanation of the research design or methodology employed. A summary of major findings should come next. The conclusion of the report should also present recommendations to management.

Most people who enter marketing will become research users rather than research suppliers. Thus, they must know what to notice in a report. As with many other items we purchase, quality is not always readily apparent. Nor does a high price guarantee superior quality. The basis for measuring the quality of a marketing research report is the research proposal. Did the report meet the objectives established in the proposal? Was the methodology outlined in the proposal followed? Are the conclusions based on logical deductions from the data analysis? Do the recommendations seem prudent, given the conclusions?

Another criterion is the quality of the writing. Is the style crisp and lucid? It has been said that if readers are offered the slightest opportunity to misunderstand, they probably will. The report should also be as concise as possible.

Although the vast majority of marketing researchers are highly ethical, this profession, like every other, sometimes faces unethical practices and practitioners. The Ethics in marketing box provides such an example.

Scanner-based research

Scanner-based research is a system for gathering information from a single group of respondents by continuously monitoring the advertising, promotion and pricing they are exposed to and the things they buy. The variables measured are advertising campaigns, coupons, displays and product prices. The result is a huge database of marketing efforts and consumer behaviour. Scanner-based research is bringing ever closer the marketing research objectives of an accurate, objective picture of the direct causal relationship between different kinds of marketing efforts and actual sales.

The two main scanner research products are **BehaviorScan** and **InfoScan**. These products are sales-tracking systems for the consumer market.

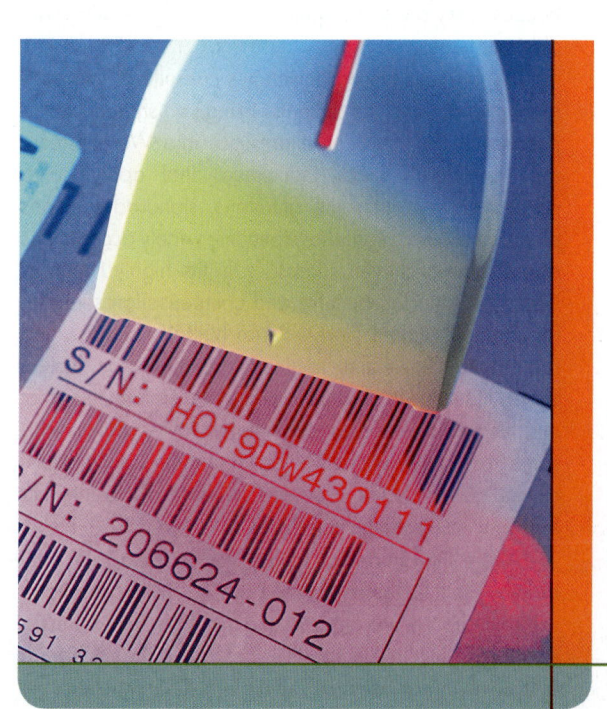

Scanner-based research helps marketers to identify how successful their marketing efforts actually are. For example, by tracking sample households' purchases, researchers can measure the relationship between an advertising or promotional campaign and actual scales.

4 Discuss the growing importance of scanner-based research

scanner-based research
A system for gathering information from a single group of respondents by continuously monitoring the advertising, promotion and pricing they are exposed to and the things they buy.

BehaviorScan
Scanner-based research program that tracks the purchases of 3000 households through store scanners.

InfoScan
A scanner-based sales-tracking service for the consumer packaged-goods industry.

Ethics IN MARKETING

It seems that I've heard this before

When Nissan Motor Co. USA decided to establish a workplace diversity program, it turned for guidance to one of the nation's leading human resources specialists: Towers Perrin. The New York consulting organisation had recently built a diversity practice to capitalise on companies' growing concerns about race and gender relations. Towers Perrin's pitch was that it would study an organisation in detail and then customise a program to fit the client's needs.

Towers Perrin launched its painstaking review of the giant Japanese carmaker's US unit. Charging up to US$360 an hour, the consultants conducted one-on-one interviews with 55 executives, analysed surveys of hundreds of additional workers, and reviewed organisation anti-discrimination policies and other internal documents. The project, which took four months to complete at a cost to the client of more than US$105 000, appeared to reflect Towers Perrin's credo: 'Prescription without diagnosis is malpractice.' But when the prescription arrived, Nissan USA officials say they were far from impressed. 'The recommendations were so broad, so generic, we didn't think it reflected what we thought we were going to get,' says spokesperson Kurt von Zumwalt. The 121-page report 'did not seem to be particularly tailored to Nissan'.

It wasn't. On the same day that Towers Perrin sent its written findings to Nissan, the consulting organisation submitted a strikingly similar report to French-owned Thomson Consumer Electronics, Inc., half a continent away in Indianapolis. Except for the companies' names, all nine major recommendations made to Thomson matched Nissan's word for word, as did all 54 accompanying 'tactics and objectives' and all 13 elements of a proposed implementation plan.

In offering its services, Towers Perrin had said its recommendations would be based on the organisation's specific needs, as gleaned from the data Towers Perrin would collect. 'No two organisations are identical,' the organisation wrote in its standard 35-page proposal. 'They are all as diverse as their workforces and the markets they serve.' Later in the proposal, the organisation added that 'no textbook solutions exist'.

Although each client's report contained a long section quoting from the interviews and other research, the recommendations didn't refer to any findings that were unique to either organisation. When Towers Perrin discussed employee polls, it described the results identically. In both instances, it said the polling showed that 'women and minorities believe there is little or no understanding by supervisors and managers of how to tap their potential or how to mentor them effectively'.

Nissan and Thomson weren't the only Towers Perrin clients that received nearly identical advice on workplace relations. The *Wall Street Journal* reviewed reports provided to 11 of the organisation's diversity clients. The vast majority of the advice given to seven clients was identical. Three clients received more individualised suggestions. One client cancelled its contract with the consultants before receiving a final report.

Privately held Towers Perrin, with revenue of just over US$1 billion, doesn't dispute that many of its reports use the same language. Indeed, Towers Perrin asserts, it is standard practice for the organisation and the industry to give clients with similar problems similar or identical advice. 'There are only a finite number of things you can do to make diversity work,' says Margaret Regan, current co-leader of Towers Perrin's global diversity practice. All of Towers Perrin's diversity clients, about 60 companies in recent years, received one of several 'templates', she says. Clients 'do not expect to get something very different from the next client in terms of recommendations'. One reason, she says, is that most clients come to the organisation precisely because they are at the same early stage of dealing with diversity issues.

Regan says the organisation's consultants compose recommendations for clients using a shared word-processing file. The consultants go 'into WordPerfect', she says, and select 'the pieces that apply' to a particular client. In some situations, standard solutions provided by consultants have become widely accepted as appropriate and even necessary. In the highly technical world of actuarial, benefits and compensation services, for example, where Towers Perrin built its expertise and reputation, consultants routinely use multi-organisation survey research to develop pay and pension systems that are then sold repeatedly. Similarly, law organisations sometimes provide virtually identical memos to different clients facing similar problems, without disclosing that the work has been recycled.[8]

Were the actions of Towers Perrin unethical? Why or why not? Is there anything wrong with consultants using a shared word-processing file from other similar studies to prepare a report? Is this any different from a lawyer giving an identical opinion to different clients for the same problem? Why or why not?

When should marketing research be conducted?

When managers have several possible solutions to a problem, they should not instinctively call for marketing research. In fact, the first decision to make is whether to conduct marketing research at all.

Some companies have been conducting research in certain markets for many years. Such organisations understand the characteristics of target customers and their likes and dislikes about existing products. Under these circumstances, further research would be repetitive and waste money. Managers rarely have such great trust in their judgement that they would refuse more information if it were available and free. But they might have enough confidence that they would be unwilling to pay very much for the information or to wait a long time to receive it. The willingness to acquire additional decision-making information depends on managers' perceptions of its quality, price and timing. Of course, if perfect information were available – that is, the data conclusively showed which alternative to choose – decision-makers would be willing to pay more for it than for information that still left uncertainty. Research should only be undertaken when the expected value of the information is greater than the cost of obtaining it.

5 Explain when marketing research should and should not be conducted

Connect it

Look back at the report about women on the Web at the beginning of the chapter. An organisation can use survey research, observations or experiments to conduct marketing research.

Unless an organisation has extensive knowledge of the problem at hand, which is based on research, it should probably conduct marketing research. Yet managers should also be reasonably sure that the cost of gathering the information will be less than the value of the data gathered.

Key marketing data often come from an organisation's own decision support system, which continually gathers data from a variety of sources and funnels it to decision-makers. It then manipulates the data to make better decisions. DSS data are often supplemented by marketing research information.

Summary

1 Explain the concept and purpose of a marketing decision support system.
Decision support systems make data instantly available to marketing managers and allow them to manipulate the data themselves to make marketing decisions. Four characteristics of decision support systems make them especially useful to marketing managers: they are interactive, flexible, discovery-oriented and accessible. Decision support systems give managers access to information immediately and without outside assistance. They allow users to manipulate data in a variety of ways and to answer 'what if' questions. And, finally, they are accessible to novice computer users.

Define it

audit 161
BehaviorScan 165
central-location telephone (CLT) facility 154
closed-ended question 158
computer-assisted personal interviewing 154
computer-assisted self-interviewing 154
computer disk by mail survey 155
convenience sample 162
cross-tabulation 164
database marketing 145
decision support system (DSS) 144
experiment 161
field service organisation 163
focus group 157
group dynamics 157
InfoScan 165
integrated interviewing 155
Internet 151
mall intercept interview 154
management decision problem 150
marketing intelligence 144
marketing research 145
marketing research objective 149
marketing research problem 149
measurement error 162
non-probability sample 162
observation research 160
open-ended question 158
primary data 152
probability sample 162
random sample 162
recruited Internet sample 156
research design 150
sample 162
sampling error 163
scaled-response question 158
scanner-based research 165
screened Internet sample 156
secondary data 150
survey research 153
universe 162
unrestricted Internet sample 155
World Wide Web (Web) 151

2 Define marketing research and explain its importance to marketing decision-making.

Marketing research is a process of collecting and analysing data for solving specific marketing problems. Marketers use marketing research to explore the profitability of marketing strategies. They can examine why particular strategies failed and analyse characteristics of specific market segments. Managers can use research findings to help keep current customers. Moreover, marketing research allows management to behave proactively rather than reactively by identifying newly emerging patterns in society and the economy.

3 Describe the steps involved in conducting a marketing research project.

The marketing research process involves several basic steps. First, the researcher and the decision-maker must agree on a problem statement or set of research objectives. The researcher then creates an overall research design to specify how primary data will be gathered and analysed. Before collecting data, the researcher decides whether the group to be interviewed will be a probability or non-probability sample. Field service organisations are often hired to carry out data collection. Once data have been collected, the researcher analyses them using statistical analysis. The researcher then prepares and presents oral and written reports, with conclusions and recommendations, to management. As a final step, the researcher determines whether the recommendations were implemented and what could have been done to make the project more successful.

4 Discuss the growing importance of scanner-based research.

A scanner-based research system enables marketers to monitor a market panel's exposure and reaction to such variables as advertising, coupons, store displays, packaging and price. By analysing these variables in relation to the panel's subsequent buying behaviour, marketers gain useful insight into the effectiveness of sales and marketing strategies.

5 Explain when marketing research should and should not be conducted.

Marketing research helps managers by providing data to make better marketing decisions. However, organisations must consider whether the expected benefits of marketing research outweigh its costs. Before approving a research budget, management also should ensure that adequate decision-making information doesn't already exist.

Review it

1 _____ is the process of planning, collecting and analysing data relevant to a marketing decision.
    a A decision support system
    b Marketing research
    c Marketing planning
    d A management information system

2 Which of the following is *not* one of the three basic roles of marketing research?
    a The descriptive role
    b The tracing role

    c   The diagnostic role
    d   The predictive role

3   The first step in the marketing research process must always be
    a   Identifying and formulating the problem/opportunity
    b   Planning the research design and gathering primary data
    c   Collecting data
    d   Specifying the sampling procedures

4   During which stage of the marketing research process is secondary data generally the most useful?
    a   Identifying and formulating the problem/opportunity
    b   Planning the research design and gathering primary data
    c   Collecting data
    d   Specifying the sampling procedures

5   Data that are collected for the first time and that are used to solve the particular problem under investigation by the organisation are called
    a   Research data
    b   Secondary data
    c   Primary data
    d   A database

6   Which of the following primary data collection techniques is the most popular and useful for obtaining facts, opinions and attitudes from people?
    a   Observation research
    b   Experiments
    c   On-line research
    d   Survey research

7   Which of the following methods of marketing research data collection does not rely on direct interaction with people?
    a   Observation research
    b   Experiments
    c   Reliability research
    d   Survey research

8   When marketing researchers alter variables such as price or package design and observe the effects of those alterations, they are likely using
    a   Observation research
    b   Experiments
    c   Validity research
    d   Survey research

9   A research error that occurs when a sample somehow does not represent the target population is called a
    a   Measurement error
    b   Frame error
    c   Sampling error
    d   Random error

10   When managers have several possible solutions to a problem, they should call for marketing research to help solve this dilemma.
    a   True
    b   False

Check the Answer Key to see how well you understood the material. More detailed discussion and writing questions and a video case related to this chapter are found in the Student Resources CD-ROM.

Apply it

1. The task of marketing is to create exchanges. What role might marketing research play in the facilitation of the exchange process?

2. Marketing research has traditionally been associated with manufacturers of consumer goods. Today, we are experiencing an increasing number of organisations, profit and non-profit, using marketing research. Why do you think this trend exists? Give some examples.

3. Write a reply to the following statement: 'I own a restaurant in the downtown area. I see customers every day whom I know on a first-name basis. I understand their likes and dislikes. If I put something on the menu and it doesn't sell, I know that they didn't like it. I also read the magazine *Modern Restaurants*, so I know what the trends are in the industry. This is all the marketing research I need to do.'

4. Give an example of
   a. The descriptive role of marketing research
   b. The diagnostic role of marketing research
   c. The predictive function of marketing research

5. Analyse the following methodologies and suggest more appropriate alternatives:
   a. A supermarket was interested in determining its image. It dropped a short questionnaire into the grocery bag of each customer before putting in the groceries.
   b. To assess the extent of its trade area, a shopping mall stationed interviewers in the car park every Monday and Friday evening. Interviewers walked up to persons after they had parked their cars and asked them for their postcodes.
   c. To assess the popularity of a new movie, a major film studio invited people to call a 1900 number and vote 'yes', they would see it again, or 'no', they would not. Each caller was billed a $2 charge.

6. You have been asked to determine how to attract more business studies students to your university. Write an outline of the steps you would take, including the sampling procedures, to accomplish the task.

7. Why are secondary data sometimes preferred to primary data?

8. In the absence of organisation problems, is there any reason to develop a marketing decision support system?

9. Discuss when focus groups should and should not be used.

10. Divide the class into teams of eight persons. Each team will form a focus group on the quality and number of services that your university provides to its students. One person from each group should be chosen to act as moderator. Remember, it is the moderator's job to facilitate discussion, not to lead the discussion. These groups should last approximately 45 minutes. If possible, the groups should be videotaped or recorded. Upon completion, each group should write a brief report of its results. Consider offering to meet with the academic registrar to share the results of your research.

11. Use the Internet and a Web browser, such as Lycos or Yahoo!, and type 'marketing research'. You will then have thousands of options. Pick a website that you find interesting and report on its content to the class.

12 Why has the Internet been of such great value to researchers seeking secondary data?

13 Go to www.roymorgan.com.au/monitor. Explain to the class the nature and scope of the Roy Morgan Internet Monitor. How can marketing researchers use the data from this research?

14 You are interested in home-building trends in Australia because your organisation (Fisher & Paykel; www.fp.com.au) is a major supplier of kitchen appliances. Go to www.abs.gov.au and describe what types of information at this site might be of interest to Fisher & Paykel.

15 What are the advantages and disadvantages of conducting surveys on the Internet?

16 Explain the three types of Internet samples and discuss why a researcher might choose one over the other.

17 Go to www.zoomerang.com/index.zgi and explain how the organisation's software lets you distribute questionnaires over the Internet.

18 Go to www.autonomy.com and explain what type of marketing research resources are offered at the site.

19 Go to www.acnielsen.com.au and determine what A.C. Nielsen is saying on the Web about their latest scanner-based technology.

20 Participate in a survey at one of the following URLs and report your experience to the class:
- GVU Semi-annual survey on Web usage: www.cc.gatech.edu/gvu/user_surveys
- Personality test: www.users.interport.net/~zang/personality.html
- Emotional intelligence test: www.utne.com/azEQ.tmpl
- Values and lifestyles (VALS) test: www.future.sri.com/VALS/presurvey.shtml
- Online transactions and privacy survey: www.hermes.bus.umich.edu/cgi-gin/spsurvey/questi.pl
- Various online surveys on topics such as politics and consumer trends: www.survey.net
- Various surveys: www.dssresearch.com/mainsite/surveys.htm

Try it

Corinne and Daniel Orset are thinking about opening an independent fast-food restaurant specialising in deli-style sandwiches and quiches. Daniel recently ran across some marketing research information, as described here.

Consumers claim that fast service is less important than the convenience of getting to the restaurant in the first place. Twenty-six per cent of adults surveyed by XYZ Marketing Research Organisation say that a convenient location is the most influential factor in their choice of fast-food restaurants. Men are more likely than women to value convenience, at 31 per cent compared to 23 per cent, and those aged 65 and older value it less than younger adults.

The thing average Australians value most highly after location is the fast food itself. Twenty-five per cent of respondents say that quality of food is the deciding factor in their choice of restaurant. This may mean they consider the food superior, but it could also mean that they appreciate the consistency of knowing they'll get the same thing every time, every place. Women, young adults and seniors are more likely than average to claim that quality is the key ingredient.

Only 12 per cent of adults say they make fast-food choices based on speed of service, and just eight per cent say price is the key. Adults under age 25 have lower than average incomes, and they are more likely than those with average incomes to cite price as the most important reason for their restaurant choices.

Middle-aged adults worry less about menu selection, maybe because they are often accompanied by children who tend to want the same thing every time. Just three per cent of those aged 35 to 44 claim that their choice is most influenced by children's preferences, yet the presence of offspring may explain why they are less likely than any other age group to care about selection and food quality.

They do care about money and time. This age group ranks second after young adults in valuing reasonable prices and second after 55 to 64-year-olds in caring about fast service. The middle-aged are also most likely to make decisions based on brand names, again possibly because of their children.

Questions

1. How might Corinne and Daniel use the preceding information?
2. Is this research performing a: (a) descriptive function; (b) diagnostic function; or (c) predictive function?
3. Is the preceding research basic or applied? Explain your answer.
4. The above research is part of a report by XYZ Marketing Research Organisation, which regularly conducts telephone surveys of a nationally representative sample of 1000 adults. Comment on the representativeness of their research.

Watch it

Burke Marketing Research: The right way to make the right decision

Accurate and timely information is the lifeblood of marketing decision-making. With good information, an organisation can increase sales and use its resources wisely. At Burke Marketing Research, planning, collecting and analysing data is an integral part of helping clients to make key decisions by answering important questions. What is the historic sales trend in the industry? What was the impact of a change in package design on sales? What if we change flavours? To answer questions like these, Burke has developed several research methods that examine and diagnose common marketing problems. The methods result from years of experience dealing with recurrent marketing problems across many industry and product categories. Some of these methods include PricePoint, STAGES and ICE, or Integrated Concept Evaluation System.

PricePoint is a research method designed for use within the communications and technology industry. It is ideal for new products or services that are so original that buyers cannot compare them with other products on the market. As part of the PricePoint research, Burke interviews potential buyers and describes and demonstrates the new product or service idea. After that, researchers ask key questions to measure perceptions about price and willingness to pay. These results are used in a model that can estimate demand for the new product at various price levels. In the face of brutal competition, Burke's clients receive the edge they need to make decisions about a new product based on possible demand. With tools like this, companies can then set solid pricing strategies.

Another useful research method Burke offers its clients is STAGES. This model was developed to learn how attitudes affect each of the five stages of the buying process: awareness, consideration, trial, adoption and customer loyalty. STAGES can answer important questions such as: How does awareness become a willingness to buy? Why do some buyers reject products and why do others become loyal customers? At Burke, researchers picture the purchase decision process as a funnel, where customers are lost at each stage. This loss occurs because customers lack awareness, have misperceptions, or don't have needs that match the product messages. The goal of STAGES is to help Burke's clients reduce the number of customers lost at each step in the buying process.

With STAGES, Burke can also respond to research findings that show that customers continuously evaluate products and services throughout the buying process but use different criteria at each stage. For example, a product must meet one set of requirements to be considered and another set for purchase on a trial basis. Once tried, there may be different requirements for a product to be adopted or bought repeatedly. Burke's customised STAGES model can identify the key attributes that drive each stage of a purchase, simulate these changes in attributes and predict the overall effect on purchase decisions.

PricePoint and STAGES are not, however, always used alone. Burke researchers can combine them to produce a more detailed analysis for a client. An integrated approach helps an organisation understand the ever-changing dynamics of the market so that it can seize the best business opportunity. One integrated approach employed by Burke is called ICE. This Integrated Concept Evaluation model combines several research methods to help clients select which product idea would best meet customers' needs. One of Burke's clients was a major communications organisation that wanted to explore consumer interest in several new product ideas. These concepts were so innovative there was no framework in place for comparing them to each other or to existing products, or for determining what price consumers would be willing to pay. The client needed information about the potential demand for each product concept under various pricing plans. In addition, the client wanted to be able to evaluate the specific benefits associated with each product. This information would be helpful in providing direction for future communications campaigns. The ICE research model used a combination of methods, including PricePoint and another method to evaluate benefits called Benefit Deficiency Analysis, to help the communications organisation map out a product development strategy.

To support all its customised models, Burke uses proven data collection methods such as focus groups, mail and telephone surveys, and mall intercepts. The completed research leads to results that, once interpreted, serve as the basis for the research analysis. This analysis is communicated clearly and concisely to the client in the research report, which in turn helps the organisation to make better decisions and develop better products and services to satisfy customers. In every business relationship, Burke picks the right research method to help clients make the right decisions.

Questions

1. Does Burke Marketing Research fulfil the roles of marketing research as described in the chapter? Explain.
2. In what ways does Burke assist its clients?
3. How does Burke improve the quality of decision making for its clients?
4. How does Burke keep its clients competitive?

Click it

Online reading

INFOTRAC® COLLEGE EDITION
For additional readings and review on decision support systems and marketing research, explore InfoTrac® College Edition, your online library. Go to: www.infotrac-college.com and search for any of the InfoTrac key terms listed below:
- observational marketing research
- marketing intelligence
- marketing research
- scanner-based research

Answer key

1. *Answer*: b, p. 145 *Rationale*: This is the definition of marketing research as given in the chapter. Marketing research is the main data source for management information systems and decision support systems.
2. *Answer*: b, p. 145 *Rationale*: Marketing research has three roles: descriptive, diagnostic and predictive.
3. *Answer*: a, pp. 148 *Rationale*: The problem/opportunity definition is always first and involves determining what information is needed and how that information can be obtained in an effective and efficient manner.
4. *Answer*: b, p. 150 *Rationale*: Although secondary data can be a valuable tool throughout the research process, it is particularly useful in the first step as it helps marketers to understand what information is already available and what is not.
5. *Answer*: c, p. 152 *Rationale*: The main advantage of primary data is that they will answer a specific research question that secondary data cannot answer.
6. *Answer*: d, p. 153 *Rationale*: Survey research techniques are the most popular. There are numerous survey techniques, including mail surveys, mall intercept interviews and focus groups.
7. *Answer*: a, p. 160 *Rationale*: Observation research involves watching people and their activities, using either people or machines.
8. *Answer*: b, p. 161 *Rationale*: Experiments are designed to alter one variable while holding another constant so that the researcher can observe changes. For example, an organisation might be interested in observing changes in sales that result from changing the amount of money spent on advertising.
9. *Answer*: c, p. 163 *Rationale*: A sampling error occurs when people in the target population either refused to cooperate or were not accessible to the researchers.
10. *Answer*: b, p. 145 *Rationale*: Managers should not instinctively conduct marketing research. Research should only be conducted when the expected value of the information gained from research is greater than the cost of obtaining it.

Cross-functional connections
SOLUTIONS

Questions

1 Why is marketing research perceived as being 'owned' by the marketing department?

There are probably a few general answers to this question. One, because the research is referred to as 'marketing' rather than 'market' or 'marketplace', it automatically denotes that it is part of the marketing department. In addition, the research has traditionally been conducted by the marketing department, reinforcing the notion that the marketing department owns it. Additionally, before the 1990s, the marketing department was the only formal link between the company and the customer. Because a primary focus of marketing research is the customer, the marketing department always owned it.

2 Where should marketing research be formally integrated across functional departments?

There are four main areas in which marketing research needs to be integrated formally within an organisation: (1) benchmarking studies; (2) customer visits; (3) customer satisfaction studies; and (4) forecasting. (The 'hows' and 'whys' of each of these areas are described in detail in the reading.)

3 What data differences exist across functions?

The historical data debate between marketing and other business functions centres on the qualitative versus quantitative format of the data. The data collected by marketers are perceived to be 'touchy-feely' data when compared to the 'hard' data utilised by other functional areas. In addition to unit sales and competitive offerings, marketing data look at customers' perceptions – something very 'soft' when compared to other functional data. For example, manufacturing can cite exact production output, cost and cycle data; and R&D has precise specifications for tensile strength, electrical usage and battery power. Add accounting data with their general accounting standards to the 'hard' data side of the picture, and it's not surprising that data differences cause cross-functional conflict within a firm.

Suggested reading

Gary S. LeVee, 'The Key to Understanding the Forecasting Process', *Journal of Business Forecasting*, Winter 1992–3, pp. 12–16.

Todd Vogel, 'At Xerox, They're Shouting "Once More into the Breach"', *Business Week*, 28 July 1990, pp. 62–3.

PART TWO CLOSING
MARKETING PLAN

Analysing marketing opportunities

The next step in preparing a marketing plan for the company you have already chosen is to get a thorough understanding in terms of marketing to customers. The following activities will help you to better understand the marketplace, which will increase your chances of success in developing an appropriate marketing mix.

Activities

We have provided you with questions and worksheets on the Student Resources CD-ROM to assist your progression. Go there after you have completed the 'Activities' section.

1. Identify the ANZIC code for your chosen company's industry. Perform a brief industry analysis of your firm's industry, based on the ANZIC code.
2. To whom does your company market (consumer, industrial, government, not-for-profit, or a combination of targets)? Within each market, are there specific segments or niches that your company can concentrate on? If so, which one(s) would you focus on and why? What are the factors used to create these segments?
3. Describe your company's target market segment(s). Use demographics, psychographics, geographic and economic factors, size, growth rates, trends, SIC codes and any other appropriate descriptors.
4. Describe the decision-making process that organisations go through when making a decision.
5. Are there critical issues that must be explored with primary marketing research before you can implement your marketing plan? These might include items such as customer demand, purchase intentions, customer perceptions of product quality, price perceptions and reaction to critical promotion.

Marketing miscues

Impulse Airlines was co-founded by former TNT and Mayne Nickless executive Gerry McGowan and his wife, Sue, in 1982 as a dedicated air-freight specialist and charter operator. At that stage, its main activity was the distribution and warehousing of newspapers and publications for the John Fairfax group. In 1993, Impulse acquired the assets of regional carrier Oxley and branched out into regional passenger services in northern New South Wales.

In 1998, at the National Aviation Press Club, Rod Eddington announced Ansett's Kendell-led recovery strategy. (Deregulation of the domestic trunk routes in 1990 had made it difficult for trunk operators to maintain unviable regional and country services. In March 1996, in conjunction with Ansett, Kendell operated up to 13 return flights daily between Sydney and the nation's capital, Canberra. Then, in 1998, the relationship expanded to other routes.)

McGowan was left with an uneasy feeling about the trunk route strategy and decided to develop the strategy in order to give Impulse more options. In June 2000, the airline became the first in seven years to fly jets on the nation's inter-city domestic trunk routes, becoming Australia's third domestic carrier. This entry was founded on a deep-seated belief that the Australian domestic industry required real and sustainable competition to ensure its long-term growth and viability. Impulse management also believed that an airline concentrating solely on the Australian market was needed.

Why did Impulse, a regional airline with a healthy profit base and consistent growth, branch out of its comfort zone into the jealously protected trunk market? They considered it a rite of passage. In

Part two closing
Marketing plan

the 18 years from 1982, they had grown progressively from being a dedicated freight company to providing regional passenger and freight services.

Despite suggestions to the contrary, the expansion into trunk route operations was an informed decision.

No one at Impulse was under any misapprehension about the immensity of the task or the risks involved. The airline market at that time was a duopoly, each member of which, directly or indirectly, enjoyed alliances with 90 per cent of Australia's travel agents and wholesalers. Vertical integration by the duopoly airline companies had paid off handsomely, allowing their dominance to extend to everything from the distribution and product network and computer reservations to airport facilities, freight and ground handling operations.

Impulse's decision to break away from the travel agency network inevitably attracted criticism from the agency industry and its representative organisation.

Impulse did not position itself as an anti-agent organisation, as has been suggested, but chose not to offer agents a fee if they wanted to sell Impulse fares. Impulse also knew that they operated on a much lower cost base than their larger competitors and so could afford to offer significantly reduced prices. The direct sell strategy they adopted reflected their determination to use new technology (such as the Internet) and introduce an uncomplicated and effective ticketing system at a cost they could afford. This rationale drove their decision to opt for a single unconditional fare for each route, starting with a Sydney–Melbourne service.

This tactic was vindicated by the market response. This, in turn, enabled the company to reach a break-even point earlier than expected. The management of Impulse believed that competition would bring base fares down, and within a relatively short time after Impulse began operating on trunk routes, this occurred. The major airlines continued to match the lowest discount rates available, but they could not guarantee the availability of those fares and still apply rigorous conditions due to their strategic alliances with their value chain members. Additionally, they attacked fares at the bottom end, while at the same time maintaining yields and profitability in the premium area, through enhancements and cheap travel and accommodation packages.

Where Impulse fares were higher than other airlines in the market, they were able to offer certainty to consumers that every seat on their domestic flights on a specific route carried the same standard price. There were no advance booking or overnight-stay requirements, nor any other conditions. Ultimately, this meant that Impulse turned its back on the multi-fare, yield management option used by other airlines and introduced a condition-free, one-fare, one-route strategy. Impulse's whole strategy was built around the cost benefits and efficiencies to be realised from innovation and from using the latest technology in their operations.

Where did Impulse Airlines' pulse go?

By September 2000, Impulse had four aircraft flying Australia's main trunk routes. Sales through Impulse's website quickly grew to 25 per cent of total revenue, and the proportion of passengers using the online facility increased daily. Impulse was determined to take full advantage of its Internet capability as a ticket-selling tool, which found favour with the small and medium-sized companies that liked the convenience and efficiency of using the rapid transaction facility.

However, increasing competition led Impulse to offer super-low prices on certain routes that would substantially undercut the $99 temporary one-way domestic airfare prices proposed by Virgin

Part two closing
Marketing plan

Blue, Qantas and Ansett. They did so in the belief that the market would appreciate that the new price offer was not a departure from their single fare strategy, which was to remain unchanged. It was offered as a complementary initiative designed to make profitable use of surplus capacity during slower sales periods.

Ultimately, Impulse discovered that the acid test for new competition is sustainability. However, for a fledgling business to graduate from a vulnerable, establishment phase to longevity, there must be a regulatory environment that provides protection from overly aggressive or unfair tactics by competitors.

By November 2000, the Olympics and increasing oil prices were having an impact on the domestic air travel market. Impulse was still buoyed by its success up to that time and had a fleet of five aircraft, with another three to be delivered in the December–January period and further aircraft in the January quarter. However, Impulse's directors had a question regarding the viability of four major players on the domestic trunk routes. At that time, they were reported as suggesting that some players would be likely to merge or amalgamate, and that an airline that focused solely on the bottom end of the market was sustainable.

Then, on 4 March 2001, Impulse unveiled its last discount Internet fare offering – a one-way ticket on the Sydney–Brisbane service, sold directly to on-line customers for the month of March. Passengers who booked directly through Impulse's website gained access to a limited number of seats on its services in both directions between Sydney and Brisbane, from $39 one way for individual flights secured before 18 March and for travel up until 8 April 2001.

Impulse was determined not to be beaten to the punch by any other airline, and to remain as the domestic airline price leader and price innovator in a highly competitive market. This still left their full economy fare rate at around 50 per cent of the price of Qantas and Ansett on flights to Brisbane and Melbourne from Sydney. On 1 May 2001, Impulse Airlines announced that it would withdraw from operating scheduled air services in Australia under its own brand and that Impulse and Qantas Airways had entered into a long-term commercial relationship. Gerry McGowan said the commercial relationship between Qantas and Impulse was a direct result of the increasingly competitive conditions in both the Australian and world aviation markets.

Impulse and a number of its institutional shareholders had decided the major trunk route market was too difficult for Impulse to continue operating on its own. As a result, Impulse would cease to operate services on the major trunk routes of Sydney–Melbourne and Sydney–Brisbane from 14 May.

On 22 May 2001, Impulse Airlines announced it would cease all interstate jet operations as of the close of services that day, although dedicated regional operations would continue until the following weekend. Impulse Airlines now operates as an aviation service provider to Qantas, Australia's largest domestic and international carrier.

Questions

1. Did Impulse really go into the market well informed?
2. Did the Olympics and increasing oil prices really mean the end for Impulse?

Sources: Address to National Aviation Press Club by Impulse Airlines' executive chairman Gerry McGowan, 19 July 2000; interview with Gerry McGowan, Impulse Airlines, National Nine Network, *Business Sunday*, 26 November 2000; 'Impulse Announces New Direct Hobart–Melbourne High-value Air Services': www.impulse.com.au/home/index.html (accessed 27 May 2002), 5 March 2001; 'Impulse Airlines to Cease Interstate Jet Operations Today', Impulse Airlines press release, 22 May 2001.

Part two closing
Critical thinking

Critical thinking
Staples.com: Reaping the benefits of a clicks-and-bricks strategy

Staples Inc., a US$9 billion retailer of office supplies, furniture and technology, is out to conquer the business-to-business market with its on-line business, Staples.com. At the core of Staples' e-business strategy is the technical interface that allows large corporate buyers to easily buy products and services from various vendors. Such marketing alliances and partnerships could allow Staples.com to sell virtually everything to small business owners – from notepads to insurance – as part of the company's Business Solutions Centre.

In late 1999, Staples Inc. named Kelly Mahoney as chief marketing officer at Staples.com, a new position within Staples. While the company is a bricks and mortar business as well as an on-line retailer, it was sending the signal that it recognised that the two businesses are distinct by dividing the company into two core businesses: retail and delivery, and the Staples.com Internet business. Mahoney's task was to develop the marketing program that would allow the company to maintain its current customer base, while establishing itself as a premier dot.com company. Staples is credited with inventing the office superstore concept. The largest operator of office supplies superstores in the world, the company employs over 46 000 people in its more than 1100 bricks-and-mortar stores, its mail order direct marketing business and its e-commerce business.

Founded in the mid-1980s, the company has grown quickly from its single store in Brighton, Massachusetts, in the United States. With headquarters in Framingham, Massachusetts, the company now has retail stores throughout the United States, Canada, the United Kingdom and Germany.

Major competitors

Until around the mid-1980s, the office product industry was dominated by independent speciality stores. However, three retailers – Staples, Office Depot and OfficeMax – entered the market and revolutionised the industry. These retailers combined low overhead costs with high-volume buying, bringing warehouse retailing to office products. Today, they remain the top three office supply retailers. Worldwide, the office supplies retail market is expected to grow at six to eight per cent annually. The North American market alone is valued at about US$200 billion. With annual sales of around US$10 billion, Office Depot operates around 900 stores in the United States, Canada, France and Japan. The number three office supply superstore, OfficeMax, has annual sales of around US$5 billion. OfficeMax has around 950 stores in the United States and Puerto Rico, with joint ventures in Japan, Brazil and Mexico.

Clicks and bricks

The office supplies superstores have entered the clicks-and-bricks domain with vigour. Websites for the three main competitors are among the most heavily visited retail sites on the Net. The on-line market for office supplies was estimated to be around US$100 million in 2000 and is expected to reach US$1.2 billion by 2003. Staples, Office Depot and OfficeMax are building on their existing brand names/brand recognition to create synergy between their bricks-and-mortar stores and their on-line sites. Other e-tailers in the office supplies market include Works.com, Onvia.com, BizBuyer.com and Officesupplies.com. Offerings of e-tail office suppliers vary from providing products on-line (e.g. Onvia) to linking buyers of products with sellers of products via bid solicitation from a database of vendors (e.g. BizBuyer).

© 2003 Nelson Australia Pty Limited

Part two closing

Critical thinking

E-commerce at Staples

Staples estimates that 70 per cent of its on-line business is incremental sales, with its revenue estimated in late 1999 to be around US$24 million. The dot.com business has become so successful that Staples Inc. now recognises it as a distinctive core business. In late 1999, the company issued a tracking stock that reflected the value it places on its e-commerce efforts. By 2003, Staples hopes to achieve revenues of US$1 billion from its dot.com endeavours. Success in e-commerce has allowed Staples to expand beyond its office products in meeting the needs of its business-to-business customers. It is becoming an invaluable component of its customers' businesses by providing all aspects of services such as high-speed Internet access, payroll management, financial services (e.g. 401(k) plans) and health insurance. Staples would receive commissions on services bought and sold. Staples expects to drive its dot.com business by establishing small business portals in which the company would not collaborate with existing service providers. Rather, Staples would serve as the technical interface between buyers and sellers. Thus, the company will sell its current physical products both in the stores and on-line. It will then enhance its offerings and build on its brand recognition by becoming an on-line service provider. Mahoney and her team must formulate a business-to-business marketing strategy that allows Staples to build on a brand that is known for convenience.

Questions

1 What is the difference between bricks-and-mortar stores and dot.com business?

2 How might Staples.com further penetrate the small-business marketplace?

3 How do clicks-and-bricks companies differ from pure e-tailers?

4 What are similar organisations in Australia and New Zealand?

Suggested reading

John E. Frook, 'Staples.com Takes on Office Depot', *Crain Communications, Inc.*, 10 April 2000, p. 1.
Robert D. Hot, 'Clicks Don't Need Mortar', *Business Week E.BIZ*, 5 June 2000, p. EB126.
Chris Reidy, 'B2B, That is Staples' Quest', *Boston Globe*, 18 February 2000, p. C3.
Ara C. Trembly and Susanne Sclafane, 'Staples.com to Offer Insurance Online', *National Underwriter*, 31 January 2000, p. 27.
Mike Troy, 'Office Supplies: Clicks-and-Mortar Dominates – for Now', *Discount Store News*, 13 December 1999, p. 57.
Mike Troy, 'Staples Maintains its Momentum', *Discount Store News*, 8 November 1999, p. 33.
Lauren Wiley, 'Staples.com Names Mahoney Marketing Chief', *Adweek*, 22 November 1999, p. 2.
www.officedepot.com
www.OfficeMax.com
www.staples.com

MANAGING THE MARKETING ELEMENTS: PRODUCT AND DISTRIBUTION DECISIONS

How organisations manage product, service and distribution decisions

PART THREE

Product and service concepts	Chapter 6
Developing and managing products	Chapter 7
Marketing channels and logistics decisions	Chapter 8

Cross-functional connections

Taking on the big guns

Product development and innovation is the lifeblood of any successful organisation, particularly one who has products in the highly competitive soft drink and confectionery markets. While there are the long-lived brands in these supermarket categories that provide companies like Cadbury Schweppes, Coca-Cola and Pepsi with a stable income, there is still the constant need to have new and innovative products in the market to keep customers interested and spending money. Changes in consumer demand and preferences also drive the need to develop and explore new products for organisations.

One example of this is the move by Coca-Cola into the flavoured milk market in Australia, following the lead of the US branch of the company. Changes in customer preferences away from the sugar-laden soft drink products to the lucrative nutritional beverages and diet options have seen a downturn in demand for the more traditional products offered by companies such as Coke. Coke has already made a strong stand in this market with their flagship water product Mount Franklin and their strong sales for Diet and caffeine-free Coke products. Even companies such as Cadbury Schweppes and Pepsi have begun investing in product development in this market with Pepsi announcing that in 2005 it will switch its marketing emphasis to its zero-calorie Diet Pepsi and other low-calorie and healthier products such as Splenda-sweetened Pepsi.

This trend away from sugared beverages is particularly evident in one New Zealand school near Penrose where they have taken the stance to become a 'water only' school (Fairfax New Zealand Limited 2005). No one is exempt from this rule (teachers and other staff included) and the school shop only sells water. However, children are encouraged to bring their own water bottles and to refill them rather than to buy water. None of this is good news for companies like Coca-Cola.

One person who understands the constant need for companies to innovate and to have new products is the manager of Australian Chocolate, Verne Stuber. In a product category that is highly competitive and very crowded, Mr Stuber has begun to realise his dream and produce high-quality Australian chocolate products. Swiss-born Stuber was disappointed when he came to live in Australia at the quality of the local chocolate products, so he set out to create and market a premium Australian Chocolate bar and now has three products, Verve, Red Ripper and Crikey. for sale.

Part three

Distribution and pressure from the big guns in confectionery are still his major hurdles for success; however, in spite of this the company is beginning to make headway. Consumer sampling is the key to his current success, with free trials of the products given out at chocolate fairs, to radio announcers, tastings at shopping centres, and even samples handed out on the main streets of Sydney and Melbourne. Crikey and Red Ripper have just won top medals at the Royal Easter Show in Sydney in 2005 and companies like Qantas are talking to Stuber about using his products on their planes. His plan is to have at least 20 different products in the marketplace and even if he only achieves a 2 per cent share of the Australian confectionery market with this product offering, this would mean about $40 million a year. If he can solve his distribution issues, compete with the multinationals and broaden his market base then Stuber may well achieve his goal which is to make Australian Chocolate famous for its product.

Questions for discussion

1 Why do firms have to invest in constant new product development?

2 What are some of the other companies that might be affected by the trend of customers to prefer diet, healthy and nutritional products?

3 What sorts of channels is Australian Chocolate currently using?

4 As a potential buyer of Australian Chocolate products, what would be your recommendations to Stuber about his current distribution strategy?

Product and service concepts

CHAPTER SIX

LEARNING OBJECTIVES

After studying this chapter, you should be able to

1. Define the term *product*
2. Classify consumer products
3. Discuss the importance of services to the economy
4. Define the terms *product item*, *product line* and *product mix*
5. Describe marketing uses of branding
6. Identify the differences between services and goods
7. Explain why services marketing is important to manufacturers
8. Describe marketing uses of packaging and labelling

McDonald's Healthy Choice

on-line

Are McDonald's promoting this change to their menu offering? Visit their websites to find out. How can you account for what you discover?

www.mcdonalds.com.au

In an attempt to meet the competition for healthier fast-food options provided by companies like Subway, McDonald's has introduced its range of Deli Choice items and Salads Plus options which include salads, freshly made sandwiches, fresh fruit, yoghurt and low-fat and vegetarian burger options. These lines are targeted at adult consumers, for some time an overlooked demographic with the fast-food chain, and have revitalised sales at McDonald's stores worldwide.

For McDonald's, the Salads Plus brand will provide a good-for-you image that is lacking in many of the company's food items. This approach is a deliberate attempt to upgrade its overall food quality and to develop new products that will attract consumer groups other than children. Its last adult-targeted Deluxe sandwich line proved to be an expensive disappointment. The Arch Deluxe burger was subsequently dropped from many stores, and the Fish Deluxe burger is being redesigned.

McDonald's management have taken the challenge of obesity very seriously and are attempting to incorporate a response to some of the issues involved in this pandemic sweeping the Western world into their menu options. Displays of nutritional information on packaging, in-store nutritional and calorie comparisons, low-sugar buns, a change to canola oil for cooking and an investment in healthier options will become common for the company in the future. They are already experimenting in the US with Happy Meals that contain carrot sticks instead of fries, new salad options and more fruit options to satisfy the demand for fresher, healthier fare.

Why would a company such as McDonald's – which already has a strong brand name and identity – change it's main menu offering? What are the positives and negatives of such a strategy? Do you think that McDonald's strategy is sound?

What is a product?

1 Define the term *product*

product
Everything, both favourable and unfavourable, that a person receives in an exchange.

core product
The problem-solving core benefits that customers are really buying when they obtain a product.

actual product
A product's parts, styling, brand name and packaging that combine to deliver the core product benefits.

The product offering, the heart of an organisation's marketing program, is usually the starting point in creating a marketing mix. A marketing manager cannot determine a price, design a promotion strategy or create a distribution channel until the firm has a product to offer. Moreover, an excellent distribution channel, a persuasive promotion campaign and a fair price have no value with a poor or inadequate product offering. You know, as a consumer, that there are many products in the marketplace that don't attract you because you can see no reason to purchase them – they don't offer any advantages or benefits over the products that you currently purchase.

A **product** may be defined as everything, both favourable and unfavourable, that a person receives in an exchange. A product may be a tangible good such as a pair of shoes, a service such as a haircut, an idea such as 'Don't Litter', a destination such as Queensland, a person such as Tiger Woods or Liz Ellis, or any combination of those attributes. Packaging, style, colour, options and size are some typical product features. Just as important are intangibles such as customer service, the seller's image, the manufacturer's reputation and the way consumers believe others will view the product.

To most people, the term *product* means a tangible good. However, services and ideas are also products. The marketing process identified in Chapter 1 is the same whether the product marketed is a good, a service, an idea or a combination of those attributes.

One way that product managers think about their products, in order to make sure they understand what their customers are really buying, is to break the product concept into three levels. This concept of layers of product can be represented as a series of concentric circles as shown in Exhibit 6.1. The innermost layer is known as the **core product**, which represents the essence of what the product really is, or the core benefit or service that a customer obtains when they buy the product (Kotler et al. 2001). For example, a person buying a BMW convertible is not buying a car or a means of transport (although the car would have to be able to get the owner from place to place reliably), rather, they are really looking for prestige and a status symbol. So the core product defines the core of benefits that the product will provide to customers and this may be different for different customer groups.

The next level of product is known as the **actual product** and this includes the secondary services or feature of the product that deliver the core benefits or services to the customer. Actual product attributes generally include things like the products parts, styling, brand name and packaging. For example, if you

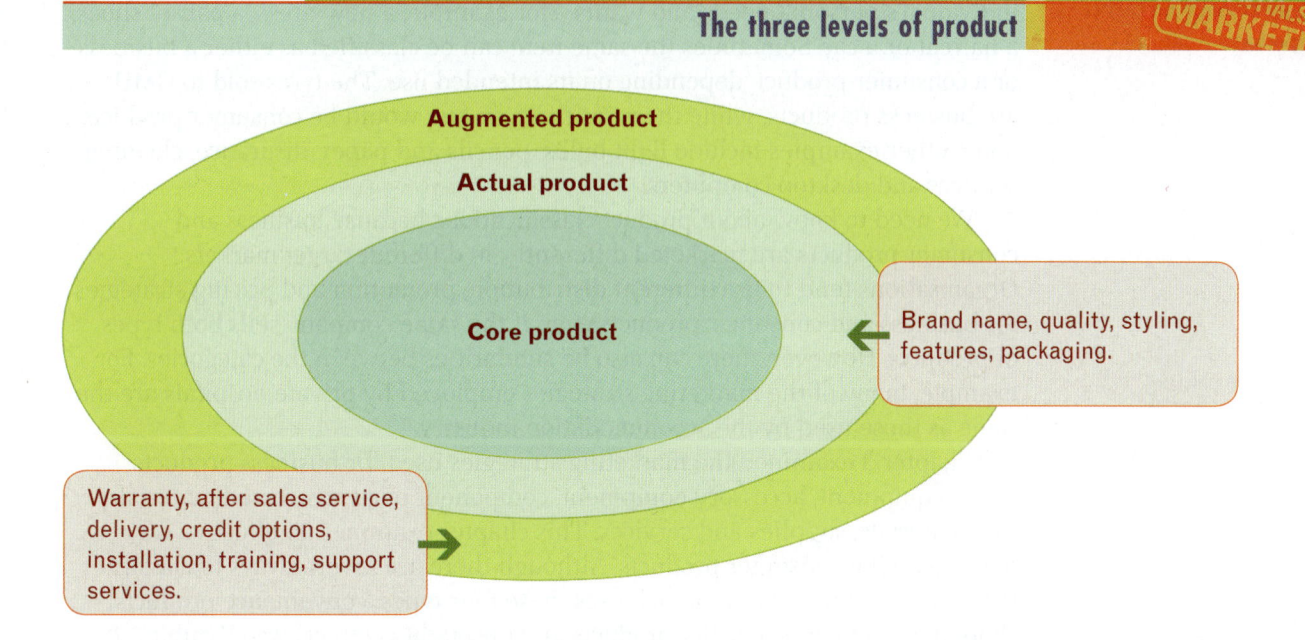

Exhibit 6.1 The three levels of product

- Augmented product
- Actual product
- Core product

Brand name, quality, styling, features, packaging. → (Actual product)

Warranty, after sales service, delivery, credit options, installation, training, support services. → (Augmented product)

were buying a BMW convertible this would be the actual product. The BMW brand name and all that this implies, the style and look of the car, the colour and features of the car, the car's engine performance, reliability, the special key ring and BMW seat covers all combine to deliver the core benefit which in this case may be prestige and status.

The final layer of product is the **augmented product**. This layer consists of all the additional customer services and benefits that support and surround the actual and core product elements. Quite often these augmented product attributes are where product differentiation is found and where companies can add value to their product offering. Augmented product attributes tend to include things like warranties and guarantees, support and training services, installation services, and so on. In the case of our BMW purchase this would include things like service options, delivery options, maybe driver training courses at a discount, roadside assist packages, free pick-up and delivery with detailing when the car is due for its first service, and so on.

augmented product
Additional customer services and benefits that are built around the core and actual products and support these offerings.

Types of products

Products can be classified as either business (industrial) or consumer products, depending on the buyer's intentions. The key distinction between the two types of products is their intended use. If the intended use is for business, the product is classified as a business or industrial product. As explained in Chapter 3, a **business product** is used to manufacture other goods or services, to facilitate an organisation's operations or to resell to other customers. For example, photocopy paper used by a business, tyres purchased from a tyre company to be used by GMH on their cars, insurance purchased by the organiser of a local sporting event, and grocery items bought by the local corner store from a wholesale warehouse are all business products.

2 Classify consumer products

business product (industrial product)
Product used to manufacture other goods or services, to facilitate an organisation's operations or to resell to other customers.

consumer product
Product bought to satisfy an individual's personal wants.

A **consumer product**, by contrast, is a product bought to satisfy an individual's personal needs and wants – for example, a new dress, a pair of shoes, a haircut or a car. Sometimes the same item can be classified as either a business or a consumer product, depending on its intended use. The tyres sold to GMH are business products, while the tyres that you buy would be consumer products. Some other examples include light bulbs, pencils and paper, insurance, cleaning services and desktop computers.

We need to know about product classifications because business and consumer products are marketed differently, to different target markets. Organisations tend to use different distribution, promotion and pricing strategies for business and consumer products even if the same company sells both types of products. However, there can also be similarities between the categories. For example, many of the marketing strategies employed by private hospitals are the same as those used by the accommodation industry.

Chapter 3 examined the marketing strategies used for business products: major equipment, accessory equipment, component parts, processed materials, raw materials, supplies and services. This chapter examines an effective way of categorising consumer products. Although there are several ways to classify them, the most popular approach uses these four types: convenience products, shopping products, speciality products and unsought products (see Exhibit 6.2). This approach classifies products according to how much effort is normally used to shop for them, and it also largely shapes how you can and may want to market the product. These classifications also help to predict the type of consumer behaviour a marketer can expect from their target market. Each of these types of products is discussed in more detail.

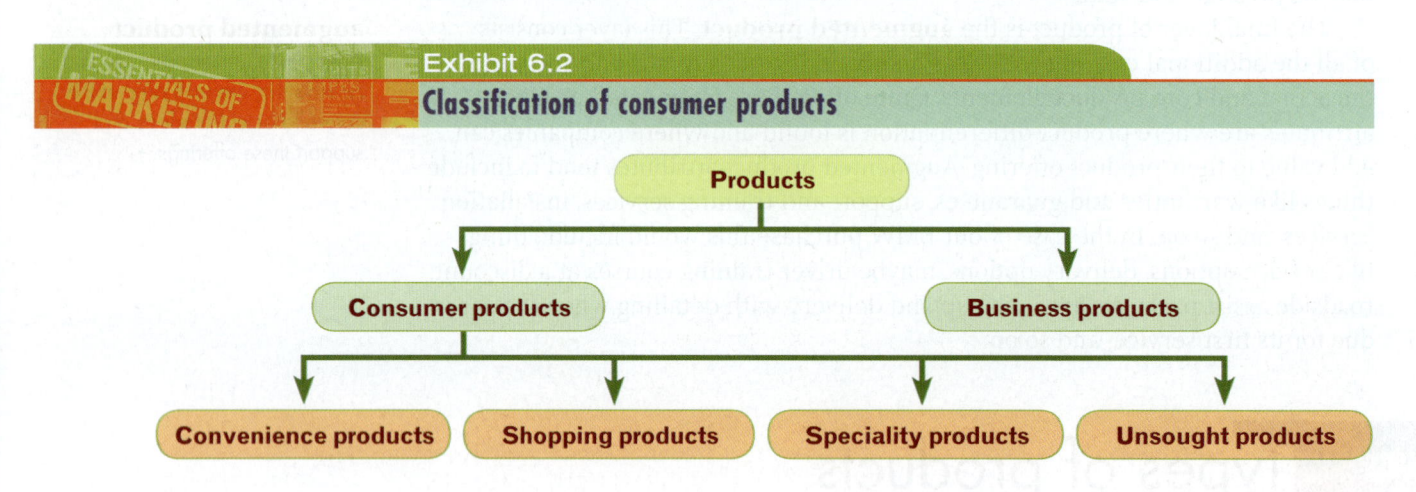

Exhibit 6.2
Classification of consumer products

Products
├── Consumer products
│   ├── Convenience products
│   ├── Shopping products
│   ├── Speciality products
│   └── Unsought products
└── Business products

Convenience products

convenience product
A relatively inexpensive item that merits little shopping effort.

A **convenience product** is a relatively inexpensive item that merits little shopping effort – that is, as a consumer you would be unwilling to shop extensively for such an item, preferring instead to use the most convenient retail outlet. Chocolate, soft drinks, combs, headache tablets, small hardware items, drycleaning and car washes, plus many others, generally fall into the convenience product category.

As a consumer, you tend to buy convenience products regularly, usually without much planning. Nevertheless, you would know the brand names of popular convenience products, such as Coca-Cola, Panadol, Fresh and Speedy

Drycleaning and Rexona deodorant. Convenience products normally require wide distribution in order to satisfy customers' needs and wants and to achieve the company's profit goals.

Shopping products

A **shopping product** is usually more expensive than a convenience product and is distributed in fewer stores. Consumers usually buy a shopping product only after comparing several brands or stores on the basis of style, practicality, price and, possibly, lifestyle compatibility. For these sorts of products, consumers would be willing to invest some effort into this process in order to get the desired product benefits. That is because these types of products are more important to them and possibly say something about them to others.

There are two types of shopping products: homogeneous shopping products and heterogeneous shopping products. Consumers perceive *homogeneous* shopping products as basically similar – for example, washers, dryers, refrigerators and televisions. With homogeneous shopping products, consumers would typically look for the lowest-priced brand that has the desired features.

In contrast, consumers perceive brands and types of *heterogeneous* shopping products as essentially different from each other – for example, furniture, clothing, housing and universities. Consumers may have trouble comparing heterogeneous shopping products because the prices, quality and features can vary greatly. The benefit of comparing heterogeneous shopping products is 'finding the best product or brand for me'; and that decision is often highly individual.

shopping product
Product that requires comparison shopping, because it is usually more expensive than a convenience product and found in fewer stores.

With homogeneous products such as televisions, consumers typically buy the lowest-priced brand that has the desired features.

Speciality products

speciality product
A particular item that consumers search extensively for and are very reluctant to accept substitutes for.

When consumers search extensively for a particular item and are very reluctant to accept substitutes, that item is known as a **speciality product**. Fine watches, luxury cars, gourmet restaurants or highly specialised forms of medical care are generally considered speciality products. Sometimes students get confused as to the difference between speciality products and shopping products (particularly heterogeneous shopping products). Generally, the main difference is that while all specialty products are also shopping products – that is, customers spend time and effort in searching for the right choice – not all shopping products are speciality products. Speciality products are those that are not purchased regularly and when they are, are purchased usually by a very specific target market. For example someone who owns and plays bagpipes may need to purchase a new bag for their instrument and this would be a specialty product purchase. Heterogeneous shopping products on the other hand are those that are generally purchased by a broader group of target consumers and most of us are likely to purchase them at some stage. In contrast we may never purchase a speciality item.

Marketers of speciality products tend to use selective, status-conscious advertising to maintain their product's exclusive image. Distribution is often limited to one or very few outlets in a geographic area, although this is not always the case for some service providers such as hairdressers and medical centres. In those cases, brand names and quality of service are very important, together with level of care and attention to customers.

Unsought products

unsought product
A product unknown to the potential buyer or a known product that the buyer does not actively seek.

A product unknown to the potential buyer, or a known product that the buyer does not actively seek, is referred to as an **unsought product**. New products fall into this category until advertising and distribution increase and cause consumers to become aware of them. Some products are always marketed as unsought items,

Exhibit 6.3
Examples of marketing mix decisions for different types of products

	Product	Price	Place/distribution		Promotion
Convenience	• Regularly purchased • Brand not so important	Low	Wide	Mass media	• Advertising • Sales promotion
Shopping	• Infrequent purchase • Requires some effort • Brand name can be important	Moderate/high	Controlled perhaps some speciality media, such as niche magazines	Mass media and	• Advertising • Sales promotion
Speciality	• Important to purchaser • Brand name critical	High	Restricted	Niche placements and selected media	• Direct mail advertising • Some personal selling
Unsought	• Niche products	Varies	Limited	Personal selling	• Advertising • Direct mail

especially products we need that we don't like to think about or care to spend money on. Insurance, burial plots, tax agents and similar items require active personal selling and highly persuasive advertising to gain consumer attention. Salespeople actively seek leads to potential buyers, because consumers usually don't seek out this type of product. The company must therefore go directly to them through a salesperson, or using direct mail or direct-response advertising.

Exhibit 6.3 summarises the types of products and the relevant marketing mix decisions that go with them.

Product items, lines and mixes

A company rarely sells a single product. More often, they sell a variety of products. A **product item** is a specific version of a product that can be designated as a distinct offering among an organisation's products. Schmackos dog treats are an example of a product item (see Exhibit 6.4).

A group of closely related product items is a **product line**. For example, the column in Exhibit 6.4 titled 'Petcare' represents one of Mars' product lines. Different product attributes, container sizes and shapes also distinguish items in a product line. Diet Coke, for example, is available in cans and various plastic and glass containers. Each size and each container are separate product items.

4 Define the terms *product item*, *product line* and *product mix*

product item
A specific version of a product that can be designated as a distinct offering among an organisation's products.

Exhibit 6.4
Mars Incorporated product lines and product mix

Snackfoods	Petcare	Main meals	Electronics
Kenman	Advance	Dolmio	MEI Cashflow
M&Ms	Dine	Kantong	MEI Easitrax
Maltesers	Golden Cob	Masterfoods	MEI Sodeco
Mars Bar	Good-O	Promite	
Milky Way	My Dog	Seeds of Change	
Mondo	Pedigree	Uncle Ben's	
Skittles	Schmackos		
Snickers	Trill		
Starburst	Whiskas		
Twix			

Depth of product lines

Source: Colgate-Palmolive website: www.colgate_palmolive.com.au.AQ

An organisation's **product mix** includes all the products it sells. All Mars' products constitute its product mix. Each product item in the product mix may require a separate marketing strategy. In some cases, however, product lines, and even entire product mixes, share some marketing strategy components. Toyota has promoted all of its product items and lines with its theme 'Oh what a feeling – Toyota!'

product line
A group of closely related product items.

product mix
All the products an organisation sells.

Pedigree is an excellent example of advertising economies. Without singling out a specific dog food product, Mars can promote its entire line of products with the single phrase 'We're for dogs'.

Organisations derive several benefits from organising related items into product lines, including the following:

- *Advertising economies*: Product lines provide economies of scale in advertising. Several products can be advertised under the umbrella of the line. Within the Mars group Masterfoods products have used the tag line, 'Enjoy the sweet taste of success', with their products and have incorporated successful personalities to promote various products (see their website for examples at www.masterfoods.com.au/tvc/).
- *Package uniformity*: A product line can benefit from package uniformity. All packages in the line may have a common look and still keep their individual identities. Again, within the Masterfoods line there is commonality of colour (red) and use of logo.
- *Standardised components*: Product lines allow firms to standardise components, thus reducing manufacturing and inventory costs. For example, many of the components Samsonite uses in its folding tables and chairs are also used in its patio furniture. GMH uses the same parts on many of the makes of its cars.
- *Efficient sales and distribution*: A product line enables sales personnel for companies such as Mars to provide a full range of choices to customers. Distributors and retailers are often more inclined to stock the company's products if it offers a full product line. Transportation and warehousing costs are likely to be lower for a product line than for a collection of individual items.
- *Equivalent quality*: Purchasers usually expect and believe that all products in a line are similar in quality. Consumers expect that all of Masterfoods' products and all of Revlon's cosmetics will be of similar quality.

Product mix width (or breadth) refers to the number of product lines an organisation offers. In Exhibit 6.4, for example, the width of Mars incorporated product mix is four product lines. **Product line depth** is the number of product items in a product line. As shown in Exhibit 6.4, the snack food and pet care product lines consist of many product items, while the electronics line is much smaller.

Firms increase the width of their product mix to manage market risk. To generate sales and boost profits, firms spread risk across many product lines rather than depend on only one or two. Firms also widen their product mix to capitalise on established reputations. By introducing new product lines, Kodak capitalised on its image as a leader in photographic products. Kodak's product lines now include film, processing, still cameras, movie cameras, paper and chemicals as well as digital cameras and printers. Gap Ltd, a company that mostly comprises apparel stores, now also offers its customers perfume, homewares and baby clothes, and other non-apparel-related merchandise.

Firms increase the depth of product lines to attract buyers with different preferences, to increase sales and profits by further segmenting the market, to capitalise on economies of scale in production and marketing, and to balance seasonal sales patterns.

Adjustments to product items, lines and mixes

Over time, firms change product items, lines and mixes to take advantage of new technical or product developments or to respond to changes in the environment. They may adjust by modifying or repositioning products, or extending or contracting product lines.

Product modifications

Marketing managers must decide if and when to modify existing products. **Product modification** changes one or more of a product's characteristics generally in the following ways:

- *Quality modification*: change in a product's dependability or durability. Reducing a product's quality may let the manufacturer lower the price and appeal to target markets unable to afford the original product. On the other hand, increasing quality can help the firm compete with rival firms. Increasing product quality can also result in increased brand loyalty, greater ability to raise prices or new opportunities for market segmentation. Eastman Kodak is considering launching a discount film called Colorburst that does not carry Kodak's well-recognised brand name in order to reach consumers who want to buy less expensive, lower quality film.[1] Conversely, in order to appeal to a more upscale market, Petersons Champagne House Limited sells its sparkling wines at a premium to members and through cellar door sales in order to differentiate itself from all the other wineries in Australia's Hunter Valley.[2]

- *Functional modification*: change in a product's versatility, effectiveness, convenience or safety. Sanitarium introduced a line of cereal/breakfast replacement drinks to extend its share of the breakfast cereal market and to attract busy people in the twenties to thirties age group who traditionally did not eat breakfast. Their aim was to condition these people over time to the idea of breakfast, through consumption of this convenient breakfast substitute, so that, in time, it would be replaced with more traditional breakfast cereals. Masterfoods is offering its sauce range in value-priced squeeze bottles with a 'No mess, stay clean' cap.

---

product mix width
The number of product lines an organisation offers.

product line depth
The number of product items in a product line.

product modification
Changing one or more of a product's characteristics.

- *Style modification*: aesthetic product change, rather than a quality or functional change. Clothing manufacturers commonly use style modifications to motivate customers to replace products before they have worn out.

Planned obsolescence is a term commonly used to describe the practice of modifying products so that those that have already been sold become obsolete before they actually need replacement. Some argue that planned obsolescence is wasteful; others that it is unethical. Marketers respond that consumers favour style modifications because they like changes in the appearance of goods such as clothing and cars. Marketers also contend that consumers, not manufacturers and marketers, decide when styles are obsolete.

planned obsolescence
The practice of modifying products so those that have already been sold become obsolete before they actually need replacement.

Repositioning

Repositioning, as Chapter 4 explained, is changing consumers' perceptions of a brand. For example, 'restaurant-style' has become a popular positioning for soup companies. Heinz has launched a line of gourmet soups for two, packaged in a vacuum-sealed bag, that are marketed as being as good as the traditional soups made by gourmet chefs.

Changing demographics, declining sales, competitor positioning or changes in the social environment often motivate firms to reposition established brands. The changing profile of customers and trends from overseas often give domestic marketers ideas about repositioning of products and brands. In 2005 Australia's major supermarkets will be adopting this very strategy. Companies like Coles and Woolworths/Safeway are planning to at least treble their house-branded goods, offering a range of products from cheap through to premium, all in an attempt to capture a greater share of the supermarket trade. Large manufacturers will find their sales either eroded or possibly they will end up producing these house-brands for the big retailers.[3] Playboy, one of the world's most well-known brands, is being repositioned to better reflect contemporary values and lifestyles. 'Our core customers have always been men, but we're trying now to extend the brand attributes to couples,' said Christie Hefner. 'Playboy is a classic ... brand, a brand that is sexy, romantic, fun and sophisticated. It should have a broader audience.'[4]

Product line extensions

Product line extension occurs when a company's management decides to add products to an existing product line in order to compete more broadly in the industry. Mercedes-Benz added 11 cars to its line of passenger vehicles between 1997 and 2000, including two 'mini' city cars and a sports utility vehicle.[5] Procter & Gamble extended its shampoo brand Pantene with its first anti-dandruff product – Pro V Anti-Dandruff – positioned distinctly for women.

product line extension
Adding additional products to an existing product line in order to compete more broadly in the industry.

Product line contraction

Does the world really need 31 varieties of Pantene shampoo? Or 52 versions of Colgate toothpaste? Procter & Gamble (P&G) has decided the answer is 'No'.[6] P&G is contracting product lines by eliminating unpopular sizes, flavours and other variations to make it easier for customers to find what they are looking for. After decades of introducing new-and-improved this, lemon-flavoured that and extra-jumbo-size the other thing, P&G has decided that its product lines are over-extended.[7] Likewise, Black & Decker has decided to delete a number of household products to concentrate on power tools.

Three main benefits are likely when a firm contracts overextended product lines:

- Resources become concentrated on the most important products.
- Managers no longer waste resources trying to improve the sales and profits of poorly performing products.
- New product items have a greater chance of being successful because more financial and human resources are available to manage them if total profitability has not been reduced.

Branding

The success of any business or consumer product depends in part on the target market's ability to distinguish one product from another. Branding is the main tool marketers use to distinguish their products from those of competitors.

A **brand** is a name, term, symbol, design or combination thereof that identifies a seller's products and differentiates them from competitors' products. A **brand name** is that part of a brand that can be spoken, including letters (GMH, YMCA), words (Ford) and numbers (WD-40, 7-Eleven). The elements of a brand that cannot be spoken are called the **brand mark** – for example, the well-known Mercedes-Benz and Qantas Airlines symbols.

Benefits of branding

Branding has three main purposes: product identification, repeat sales and new-product sales. The first and most important purpose is *product identification*. Branding allows marketers to distinguish their products from all others. Many brand names are familiar to consumers and indicate quality. In addition, strong brands also have value to company boards and accountants, where, like other commodities, they can be bought and sold. Brands are becoming increasingly global in an attempt to increase their potential markets and eventual profits. The companies who experienced the greatest growth in brand value in this annual survey (see Exhibit 6.5) were those that have built communities around their products and services creating 'cult brands' that enable customers to feel as if they own the brand. Those companies that deal in cutting edge technology also fared well.[8]

The fast food sector experienced an overall drop in brand value as a result of bad publicity and consumers focused on obesity and healthier eating. McDonald's healthier choice menu items enabled it to regain some brand value during 2004 while other competitors dropped substantially. Established brands like Coca-Cola and Microsoft are seeing the effect of the need to nurture ties with consumers rather than simply relying on their brand.[9] Exhibit 6.5 lists, in order, the top 10 brands globally.

In Australia, buoyant economic conditions and robust consumer sentiment has seen a strong performance in many brands. The biggest increases have been in the retail industry with financial services also doing well. In the top 25 Australian brands for the first time are Australia's rival airlines, Qantas and Virgin Blue. Many of the brands in this list are category leaders like Bunnings, Harvey Norman and Repco and the sheer size of their operations makes it difficult for competitors to rate. In Australia, Telstra is our most valuable brand,

---

5 Describe marketing uses of branding

brand
A name, term, symbol, design or combination thereof that identifies a seller's products and differentiates them from competitors' products.

brand name
That part of a brand that can be spoken, including letters, words and numbers.

brand mark
The elements of a brand that cannot be spoken.

followed by the big three banks (CBA, Westpac and ANZ) and then Woolworths/Safeway. NAB is number six and surprisingly, Billabong Surf & Leisure was the only manufacturing brand in the top 20, valued at number seven. Australia Post is listed as Number 11.[10]

brand equity
The value of company and brand names.

The term **brand equity** refers to the value of company and brand names. A brand that has high awareness, perceived quality and brand loyalty among customers has high brand equity. A brand with strong brand equity is a valuable asset.

Exhibit 6.5
What are the best brands?

Rank and brand 2004–03		Worldwide 2004 brand value (US$ billion)	Country of ownership	Comment
1/1	Coca-Cola	67.394	United States	Coke is still no. 1 though little innovation is seeing consumer's thirst diminish
2/2	Microsoft	61.372	United States	Microsoft is growing though virus plagues are taking some of the shine off
3/3	IBM	53.791	United States	The leader in defining e-business
4/4	GE	44.111	United States	New theme of imagination at work is working for GE
5/5	Intel	33.499	United States	No longer just inside PCs Intel is starting to shine in the wireless environment
6/7	Disney	27.113	United States	Still popular for family entertainment, but Pixar and Nickelodeon are stealing some market share
7/8	McDonald's	25.001	United States	The Big Mac has pulled out of a slump but still has a battle
8/6	Nokia	24.041	Finland	Tough times ahead for mobile giant with slipping market share
9/11	Toyota	22.673	Japan	Rock solid quality and the edge in hybrid cars sees Toyota on track
10/9	Marlboro	22,128	United States	The no.1 name in cigarettes has cut prices and beat back challenges of higher taxes and fewer smokers

Source: Adapted from 'The Best Global Brands', *Business Week*, 2 August 2004, p. 68.

Exhibit 6.6
Master brands in selected product categories

Photography	Kodak
Copiers	Xerox
Adhesive bandages	Band-Aid
Rum	Bundaberg
Soup	Campbell's
Biscuits	Arnott's
Crayons	Crayola
Heat flask	Thermos
Cooling box	Esky
Sailboard	Windsurfer
Petroleum jelly	Vaseline
Coffee	Starbucks

The term **master brand** has been used to refer to a brand so dominant in consumers' minds that they think of it immediately when a product category, use, attribute or customer benefit is mentioned.[11] Exhibit 6.6 lists the master brands in several product categories. How many other brands can you name in these 12 categories? Can you name any other product categories in which the master brands listed in Exhibit 6.6 compete? Probably not. To many consumers, Campbell's means soup; it doesn't mean high-quality food products.

What constitutes a good brand name? Most effective brand names have several of the following features. They:

- are easy to pronounce (by both domestic and foreign buyers)
- are easy to recognise
- are easy to remember
- are short
- are distinctive, unique
- describe the product
- describe product use
- describe product benefits
- have a positive connotation
- reinforce the desired product image
- are legally protectable in home and foreign markets of interest
- are translatable into other languages.

Obviously, no brand exhibits all of these characteristics. The most important issue is that the brand can be protected for exclusive use by its owner.

Many brands command substantial premiums in many markets around the world. For example, Gillette disposable razors sell for twice the price of local brands in India. When considering entering the global market, however, companies need to ensure that their brand names translate appropriately in other languages; there are many examples of situations where companies have misunderstood the literal translation for their brand name in a foreign country. On a more interesting note there is now a trend globally for children to be given brand names as a reflection of their parent's aspirations. Children with names like Armani, Timberlake, Chanel and even ESPN (an American cable sport channel) are becoming more common. On a more serious note though, there is a growing trend internationally for a lack of support and trust in American brands following the war in Iraq. See the Global perspectives box for a discussion about this phenomenon.

The second purpose of branding is repeat sales, and the best generator of *repeat sales* is satisfied customers. Branding helps consumers to identify products they wish to buy again and to avoid those they don't. **Brand loyalty**, a consistent preference for one brand over all others, is quite high in some product categories. Over half the users in product categories such as cigarettes, mayonnaise, toothpaste, coffee, headache remedies, photographic film, bath soap and tomato sauce are loyal to one brand. One annual *Monitor* poll conducted by Yankelovich Partners in the United States reported that 74 per cent of respondents 'find a brand they like, then resist efforts to get them to change'. Once consumers are convinced of the quality and value of a particular brand, it takes a lot of effort to change their minds.[14] Brand identity is essential to developing brand loyalty.

One of the other reasons that people develop loyalty to brands is that people have relationships with brands, much like the sorts of relationships people have with each other. There are two elements of an individual's relationship with

master brand
A brand so dominant in consumers' minds that they think of it immediately when a product category, use situation, product attribute or customer benefit is mentioned.

Kodak Herron
on-line
What elements on Kodak's website seem to encourage brand loyalty? Be sure to check the list of services. What about the elements on the Herron site? Why do you think so?
www.kodak.com.au
www.herron.com.au

brand loyalty
A consistent preference for one brand over all others.

Global PERSPECTIVES

Brands abroad under fire

A recent survey of international consumers by Global market Insite about their attitudes toward American Brands shows mounting distrust of things American. Almost 80 per cent of consumers say they distrust the US government while 50 per cent distrust US companies and 39 per cent distrust American people. These negative views have been largely formed as a result of the US war on terror in Iraq with consumers stating that American foreign policy shaped their perspective of their perception of US brands. Those brands that have drawn the most negative feelings are McDonald's, American Express, Barbie, Starbucks and American Airlines. Those seemingly insulated from the negative impact are Ralph Lauren, Kleenex, Calvin Klein and Kodak.[12]

However, on a more positive note, recent highly visible relief efforts mounted by major American companies – notably Coca-Cola, Starbucks and Microsoft, to the recent Asian tsunami appeal have begun to reverse the world's image of these global brands. Positive brand sentiment gained from tsunami relief efforts is beginning to pay off for these companies; however, one in five international consumers still state that they consciously avoid purchasing American brands as a way of displaying their discontent over recent American foreign policies and military action. The highest proportion of consumers who indicate intentions to boycott American brands come from Korea (45 per cent), Greece (40 per cent) and France (25 per cent).

In spite of the slow change in attitudes toward some American brands based on the tsunami relief efforts, for many brands this will not be enough to save them. Once a country's image has started to decline, international consumers tend to reject any data which doesn't confirm their negative prejudices. For many brands, America's reputation has fallen too far to be retrieved by a few good news stories. In America, the country's foreign policy plays a critical role in shaping international consumer views and it is therefore important that the US government supports and considers industry and other stakeholders when making these decisions.[13]

---

brand personality
The type of person or personality traits that the brand represents

a brand. First there is the relationship between the brand-as-person and the customer (much like a relationship between two people). Second there is the **brand personality**, which is the type of person that the brand represents. Brand personalities provide depth, feelings and liking to the relationship. To this end, brand personalities can take on many different elements from fun and irreverent, to serious and reliable and even sporty and outdoorsy. People cope with the stress and chaos of their lives by developing escape mechanisms, and brands can facilitate some of this process by being either an aspirational or trusted associate.[15] In the case of an aspirational relationship, escape might be in the form of a social lift to the customer, or in the case of a trusting relationship with a brand by providing information or knowledge on a subject that the person is interested in. These types of relationships based on brand personality can provide real competitive advantage to organisations.

Essentially there are five main dimensions of brand personality that marketers can consider when they develop their marketing and branding strategies. These are: *sincerity* (down to earth, honesty, wholesome); *excitement* (daring, spirited, cheerful, imaginative, up to date); *competence* (reliable, intelligent, successful); *sophistication* (upper class, charming); and *ruggedness* (outdoorsy, tough, sporty).[16] Within each of these dimensions, various personality traits can be targeted (such as imaginative, hard-working or successful) and then used to position a brand in a particular market segment. See Exhibit 6.7 for examples of products and their personality traits. By asking, 'What would this brand say to you if it were a person?' marketers can gain some feel for how their brand is likely to be received with their target audience and how effectively they are relating to their chosen customers. A brand that is trying to be sophisticated and classy for example, would have to be careful that is wasn't also seen as snobbish and condescending as this would turn off or repel some customers.

The third main purpose of branding is to *facilitate new product sales*. Companies with well-known brand names, such as those listed in Exhibits 6.5 and 6.6, will find it far easier when introducing new products to gain consumer attention and acceptance than those with unknown brands.

Exhibit 6.7 Brand personalities

Brand dimension	Traits	Suggested brands
Sincerity	Down to earth, family oriented, genuine, old-fashioned	Myer, Holden Commodore, Uncle Tobys, Johnson & Johnson
Excitement	Spirited, young, up to date, daring, independent	Boost Juice, Supre, Just Jeans, Barina, Pepsi, Bonds
Competence	Accomplished, influential, competent, intelligent, successful	*The Financial Review*, ING Financial Management, ABC TV
Sophistication	Glamorous, wealthy, upper class, charming	BMW, Oroton Lingerie, Argyle Diamonds
Ruggedness	Athletic, outdoorsy, masculine, tough, rugged	Timberland, Lee jeans, Rivers, Black & Decker, Ford

The Internet provides firms with alternatives for generating brand awareness, promoting a desired brand image, stimulating new and repeat brand sales, and enhancing brand loyalty and building brand equity. A number of packaged-goods firms, such as Procter & Gamble, Campbell's Soup and Kellogg, have a strong presence on-line.

Branding strategies

Firms face complex branding decisions. As Exhibit 6.8 illustrates, the first decision is whether to brand at all. Some firms actually use the lack of a brand name as a selling point. These unbranded products are called generic products. Firms that decide to brand their products may choose to follow a policy of using manufacturers' brands, private (distributor) brands, or both. In either case, they must then decide among a policy of individual branding (different brands for different products), family branding (common names for different products), or a combination of individual branding and family branding.

Generic products versus branded products

A **generic product** is typically a no-frills, no-brand-name, low-cost product that is simply identified by its product category. Brands such as Black & Gold and Homebrand are examples of generic brands. (Note that a generic product and a brand name that becomes generic, such as Esky, are not the same thing.) Generic products have captured significant market shares in some product categories, such as canned fruits, canned vegetables and paper products. These unbranded products are frequently identified only by simple packaging.

generic product
A no-frills, no-brand-name, low-cost product that is simply identified by its product category.

Exhibit 6.8
Major branding decisions

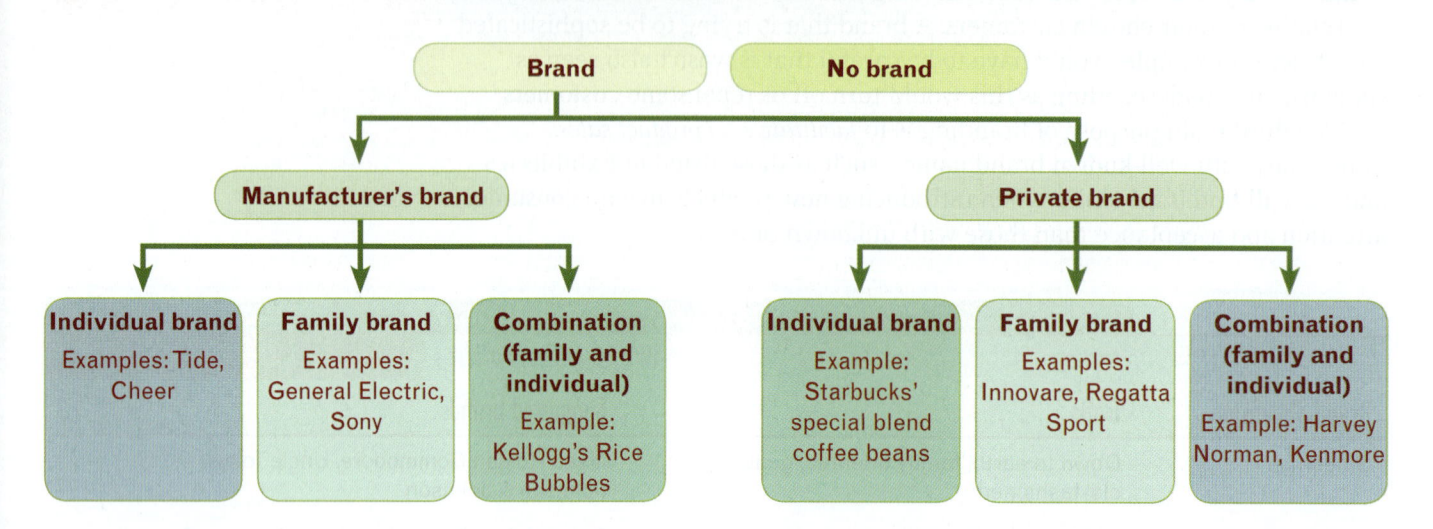

```
                    Brand                          No brand
                      |
        ┌─────────────┴─────────────┐
  Manufacturer's brand          Private brand
        |                             |
  ┌─────┼─────┐                 ┌─────┼─────┐
```

Manufacturer's brand:
- **Individual brand** — Examples: Tide, Cheer
- **Family brand** — Examples: General Electric, Sony
- **Combination (family and individual)** — Example: Kellogg's Rice Bubbles

Private brand:
- **Individual brand** — Example: Starbucks' special blend coffee beans
- **Family brand** — Examples: Innovare, Regatta Sport
- **Combination (family and individual)** — Example: Harvey Norman, Kenmore

The main appeal of generics is their low price. Generic grocery products are usually 30–40 per cent less expensive than manufacturers' brands in the same product category and 20–25 per cent less expensive than retailer-owned brands.

Pharmaceuticals make up another product category where generics have made inroads. When patents on successful pharmaceutical products expire, low-cost generics rapidly appear on the market. For example, when the patent on Merck's popular anti-arthritis drug Clinoril expired, its sales declined by 50 per cent almost immediately, even though the total market for Clinoril did not diminish. When you go to the chemist or doctor, you will usually be asked if you want the cheaper, generic brand of a particular medication.

Entrepreneurial Insights

Is the future in plastic?

A small company in the Lower Hutt region of New Zealand is leading the world with some of its innovations in plastic. The company's main philosophy is that their customer's success is their success and this approach plus a 'can-do' attitude has lead them to a 75 per cent increase in sales in the last year alone. Clavert Plastics makes some very interesting products. Riot shields for the NZ army and police, anti-personnel training aids like dummy mines for the NZ army and other international armies, environmentally conscious waste disposal units that were first trialled at the Sydney Olympics, and a new form of packaging for car parts that has revolutionised the automotive export industry.

The company takes the ideas and problems of its customers and designs solutions that not only solve the short-term needs, but are also immediately transferable to the larger industry. The development of plastic packaging for car parts has solved the problems that many countries have with transporting their products in wooden crates. These have to be fumigated before entering other countries and they are also heavy and not-reusable. The plastic crates that Clavert has designed are reusable, light and do not have the risk of contamination with pests. So here is a company that many of us will not hear about as their main focus is on industrial customers; however, they are leading the way in terms of product innovation and customer service – all characteristics that are essential in any successful organisation.[17]

Conversely, products in categories that traditionally have not been branded are now attempting to establish brand names that companies hope will build loyalty. For example, the All Blacks, the New Zealand national rugby union team, has realised the value and importance of the team and name as a brand.

Manufacturers' brands versus private brands

The brand name of a manufacturer – such as Kodak, Esky and Sara Lee – is called a **manufacturer's brand**, or *national brand*. The latter term is not always accurate, however, because many manufacturers serve only regional markets. The term *manufacturer's brand* more precisely defines the brand's owner.

A **private brand** is a brand name owned by a wholesaler or a retailer. Innovare (a Myer brand), River Gum Classics (Woolworths) and IGA (Independent Grocers Association) are all private brands. A Gallup survey, conducted for the Private Label Manufacturers Association in the United States, revealed that 83 per cent of consumers say they regularly buy less expensive retailer brands.[18] Private brands account for about 20 per cent of US supermarket sales, 8.6 per cent of pharmacy sales and over 9 per cent of mass merchandiser sales.[19]

Who buys private brands? According to one expert, 'the young, discerning, educated shopper is the private label buyer'. These individuals are willing to purchase private brands because they have confidence in their ability to assess quality and value. There are a number of issues related to the customer characteristics and to the store's management structure that impact the decision to stock manufacturers' brands or private brands. Many firms, such as Myer, Kmart and Woolworth's, offer a combination of both (see Exhibit 6.9).

manufacturer's brand
The brand name of a manufacturer.

private brand
A brand name owned by a wholesaler or a retailer.

Individual brands versus family brands

Many companies use different brand names for different products, which is referred to as **individual branding**. Companies use individual brands when their products vary greatly in use or performance. For example, it would not make sense to use the same brand name for a pair of dress socks and a cricket bat. Colgate-Palmolive targets different segments of the laundry detergent market with Dynamo, Cold Power, Fab, Gow's and Spree. The Accor hotel group also targets different market segments with the Novotel, Mercure, All Seasons and Ibis hotel categories.

On the other hand, a company that markets several different products under the same brand name is using a **family brand**. Sony's family brand includes radios, television sets, stereos and other electronic products. A brand name can only be stretched so far, however. Do you know the differences between Parkroyal, Centra, Intercontinental, Crowne Plaza, Holiday Inn, Express and Staybridge suites? Neither do most travellers, and yet they are all hotel brands owned by the BASS hotels and resorts group.

individual branding
Using different brand names for different products.

family brand
Marketing several different products under the same brand name.

Co-branding

Co-branding entails placing two or more brand names on a product or its package. There are three types of co-branding. *Ingredient branding* identifies the brand of a part that makes up the product. Examples of ingredient branding are Intel (a microprocessor) in a personal computer, such as Compaq, or a premium leather interior (Coach) in a car (Statesman). *Cooperative branding* is where two brands receive equal treatment and borrow on each other's brand equity, such as Citibank and Qantas, or American Express and Sheraton. Finally, there is *complementary branding*, where products are advertised or marketed together to suggest usage, such as a spirits brand (Bundaberg Rum) and a compatible mixer (Coke).

co-branding
Placing two or more brand names on a product or its package.

Exhibit 6.9
Comparing manufacturers' and private brands from the reseller's perspective

Key advantages of carrying manufacturer's brands	Key advantages of carrying private brands
⊙ Heavy advertising to the consumer by manufacturers such as Unilever helps to develop strong consumer loyalties.	⊙ A wholesaler or retailer can usually earn higher profits on its own brand. In addition, because the private brand is exclusive, there is less pressure to mark the price down to meet competition.
⊙ Well-known manufacturers' brands, such as Kodak and Fisher-Price, can attract new customers and enhance the dealer's (wholesaler's or retailer's) prestige.	⊙ A manufacturer can decide to drop a brand or a reseller at any time, or even to become a direct competitor to its dealers.
⊙ Many manufacturers offer rapid delivery, enabling the dealer to carry less stock.	⊙ A private brand ties the customer to the wholesaler or retailer. A person who wants Jeans West jeans must go to a Jeans West store.
⊙ If a dealer happens to sell a manufacturer's brand of poor quality, the customer may simply switch brands but remain loyal to the dealer.	⊙ Wholesalers and retailers have no control over the intensity of distribution of manufacturers' brands. Myer store managers don't have to worry about competing with other sellers of Innovare and Regatta Sport clothing brands. They know that these brands are sold only in Myer stores.

Co-branding is a useful strategy when a combination of brand names enhances the prestige or perceived value of a product or when it benefits brand owners and users. Co-branded Gold Coast theme parks and Fly Buys allow cardholders to earn points towards season passes, free admissions and in-park spending vouchers at the DreamWorld theme park.

Co-branding may also be used when two or more organisations wish to collaborate to offer a product. Mars confectionery and Mazda have teamed up in an attempt to boost awareness and consumer participation, targeting the 15–30-year-old market. In a recent competition, three Bravo Tribute 4WD cars were given away linked by the Mars theme of 'Work, rest and play'.[20]

European firms have been slower to adopt co-branding than have US firms. One reason is that European customers seem to be more reluctant than US customers to try new brands. European retailers also typically have less shelf space than their US counterparts and are less willing to give new brands a try.[21] Australian consumers appear to be more like their American counterparts, and co-branding is reasonably well accepted here.

Trademarks

trademark
The exclusive right to use a brand or part of a brand.

A **trademark** is the exclusive right to use a brand or part of a brand. Others are prohibited from using the brand without permission. A **service mark** performs the same function for services, such as H&R Block and Weight Watchers. Parts of a brand or other product identification may qualify for trademark protection. Some examples are:

- Shapes, such as the Chanel inlocking Cs, the Coca-Cola bottle and the Gucci 'G'.
- Ornamental colour or design, such as the logo on Nike tennis shoes, the black-and-copper colour combination of a Duracell battery, Levi's small tag on the left side of the rear pocket of its jeans, or the cut-off black cone on the top of Cross pens.
- Catchy phrases, such as the Commonwealth Bank's 'Which bank?', the Bank of Queensland's 'You wouldn't believe it … !' and XXXX's 'I can feel a fourex coming on.'
- Abbreviations, such as 'Bundy' and 'Coke'.

service mark
Trademark for a service.

A New York property company that purchased the Chrysler Building in Manhattan has even sought trademark registration for the building's elaborate exterior, its lobby's ceiling and even its elevator doors. Its distinctive pinnacle is already trademarked.[22] In 1977, General Electric Broadcasting Co. was one of the first companies to register a sound (the sound that a ship's bell clock makes) as a service mark.[23]

There are a range of laws governing the registration and use of trademark logos and sometimes it is difficult to determine whether a particular brand or package design infringes on another's trademark. GolfGear International's new product branding strategy described in the Ethics in marketing box illustrates this point.

Companies that fail to protect their trademarks face the problem of their product names becoming generic. A **generic product name** identifies a product by class or type and cannot be trademarked. Former brand names that were not sufficiently protected by their owners and were subsequently declared to be generic product names in US courts include aspirin, cellophane, linoleum, thermos, kerosene, monopoly, cola and shredded wheat.

Companies such as Rolls-Royce, Cross, Xerox, Levi Strauss, Frigidaire and McDonald's actively enforce their trademarks. Rolls-Royce, Coca-Cola and Xerox use newspaper and magazine ads stating that their names are trademarks and should not be used as descriptive or generic terms. Some ads threaten lawsuits against competitors that violate trademarks.

generic product name
Identifies a product by class or type and cannot be trademarked.

Ti-Gear: Owning up to a name — Ethics in Marketing

The name of GolfGear International Inc.'s new product offering, the 'Ti-Gear' wood, is raising a few eyebrows. On the one hand: 'They [GolfGear International] don't have Tiger [Woods'] authorisation, and we can't give further comment on the advice of our attorneys,' says Bev Norwood, spokesperson for Cleveland-based International Management Group, the sports agency working on behalf of Woods. On the other hand, the golf club is made with a patented 'forged titanium insert' intended to help the ball travel further.

GolfGear International's president and chairman, Don Anderson, noted in a written statement that his company has been using the name Titanium Gear since 1990 or 1991.

'[W]e shortened it to Ti-Gear: "Ti" is the symbol of Titanium, and "Gear" follows our family of products since we started in business nearly 10 years ago. The name ... clearly has nothing to do with Tiger Woods,' the statement read. He also noted that other GolfGear products use similar names that reflect their components, such as 'Carbon Gear'.

'Determining whether or not the use of a particular mark is likely to cause confusion with another mark is based on a number of factors. The fact that two marks may look or sound similar is important, but it's only one factor,' said Bart Lazar, a partner specialising in the protection and enforcement of trademark rights with the Seyfarth, Shaw, Fairweather and Geraldson law firm in Chicago. Among the criteria that would come into a trademark infringement case would be whether GolfGear knew of Tiger Woods at the time the company adopted the mark, and whether consumers are likely to be confused, Lazar said.[24]

Is the Ti-Gear brand a trademark violation? Is the branding strategy ethical? Discuss.

Despite severe penalties for trademark violations, trademark infringement lawsuits are not uncommon. One of the major battles is over brand names that closely resemble another brand name. Donna Karan filed a lawsuit against Donnkenny Inc., whose Nasdaq trading symbol – DNKY – was too close to Karan's DKNY trademark.[25] Polo Ralph Lauren is concerned about the potential confusion with a magazine named *Polo*, a 23-year-old publication aimed at equestrians. The company is worried that readers will mistake the magazine for something associated with the designer.[26]

Companies must also contend with fake or unauthorised brands, such as fake Levi jeans, Microsoft software, Rolex watches, Reebok and Nike footwear, and Louis Vuitton handbags.

In Europe, counterfeiters can be sued only if the brand, logo or trademark is formally registered. Until recently, a manufacturer's formal registration was required in each country in which a company sought protection. A company can now register its trademark in all European Union (EU) member countries with one application.[27] The increasing number of organisations targeting global customers and the increasing sophistication of both customers and marketing activities has seen an enormous growth in service brands. E-commerce is creating instant service brands like eBay, Amazon, Yahoo! and Google and the service environment itself is also becoming more brand oriented. Before we choose whether to buy a particular brand of coffee or shoes we decide first whether to shop at Coles, Myer or Target. The rise of service brands presents new challenges for providers of services and goods alike. Deregulation, e-commerce and globalisation are placing pressure on goods marketers to offer a closer relationship with customers and to deliver more value with the physical product offering, value that is, in the main, a service component. So before we can examine these issues in more detail, we need to first understand the essential differences between services and goods.

The importance of services

service
The result of applying human or mechanical efforts to people or objects.

A **service** is the result of applying human or mechanical efforts to people or objects. Services involve a deed, a performance or an effort that cannot be physically possessed. Today, the service sector substantially influences most Western economies. More than eight out of 10 workers currently produce services, such as transportation, retail trade and finance,[28] and the demand for services is expected to continue. According to the Australian Bureau of Statistics, service occupations will be responsible for all net job growth by the year 2006. Much of that demand reflects demographics. An ageing population needs nurses, home health care, physical therapists and social workers. Two-income families need childcare, house-cleaning and lawn mowing services. Also increasing will be the demand for information managers, such as computer engineers and systems analysts.

Services are important worldwide. In Great Britain, 73 per cent of workers are in service occupations, as are 57 per cent of German workers and 62 per cent of Japanese workers.[29]

The marketing process described in Chapter 1 is the same for all types of products, whether they are goods or services. Many ideas and strategies discussed throughout this book have been illustrated with service examples. However, services have four unique characteristics that distinguish them from goods, and marketing strategies need to be adjusted for these characteristics.

How services differ from goods

Services have four defining characteristics that distinguish them from goods. They are: *intangibility*, *inseparability*, *heterogeneity* and *perishability*. Each will now be discussed.

6 Identify the differences between services and goods

Intangibility

The basic difference between services and goods is that services are intangible. Because of their **intangibility**, they cannot be touched, seen, tasted, heard or felt in the same manner in which goods can be sensed. Services cannot be stored and are therefore often easy to duplicate.

The intangibility of services makes evaluating the quality before, or even after, the purchase harder than evaluating the quality of goods. In addition, when compared to goods, services tend to exhibit fewer search qualities. A **search quality** is a characteristic that can be easily assessed before purchase – for example, the colour of an appliance or of a car. Services also tend to exhibit more experience and credence qualities. An **experience quality** is a characteristic that can be assessed only after use, such as the quality of a meal in a restaurant or the actual experience of a holiday or of attending a concert. A **credence quality** is a characteristic that consumers often have difficulty assessing even after purchase because they don't have the necessary knowledge or experience to evaluate the service. Medical and consulting services are examples of services that exhibit credence qualities. How do you really know that the advice of the investment adviser is the best?

Those qualities also make it harder for marketers to communicate the benefits of an intangible service than to communicate the benefits of tangible goods. Thus, marketers often rely on tangible cues to communicate a service's nature and quality. For example, most business consulting firms have images that are easily recognised, using signature-like logos and colours that are clear and formal, in an attempt to create a more tangible sense of trust, experience and seriousness.

The physical facilities that customers visit, from which services are delivered, are also a critical, tangible part of the total service offering. Messages about the organisation are communicated to customers through such elements as the decor, the neatness of service areas, and the manners and dress of the service personnel. McDonald's has developed an outlet in Broome, Western Australia, which was designed to complement and be in harmony with the town's distinctive architecture. Corrugated iron was used extensively to ensure that the McDonald's outlet is in keeping with the ambience of the region. By designing its store to make shopping a pleasant experience, McDonald's has communicated that it is a quality organisation and wants to work with the community.

Inseparability

Goods are produced, sold and then consumed. In contrast, services are often sold, produced and consumed at the same time. In other words, their production and consumption are inseparable activities.

Inseparability means that, because consumers must be present during the production of services such as in haircuts or surgery, they are actually involved in the production of the services they buy. People may be inseparable from the service and so, too, the place and time of the service – for example, the tutor and

intangibility
Characteristic of services that cannot be touched, seen, tasted, heard or felt in the same manner in which goods can be sensed.

search quality
A characteristic that can be easily assessed before purchase.

experience quality
A characteristic that can be assessed only after use.

credence quality
A characteristic that consumers may have difficulty assessing even after purchase because they don't have the necessary knowledge or experience.

KPMG Horwath on-line

These corporate websites have strong logos that attempt to create a more tangible sense of trust for the customers of these firms. Compare the logos of these firms and comment on which of them you believe does this best and why.
www.kpmg.com.au
www.horwath.com.au

inseparability
Characteristic of services that allows them to be produced and consumed simultaneously.

students are inseparable from the tutorial, and the hairdresser is inseparable from the client and the salon.

Inseparability also means that services cannot normally be produced in a centralised location and consumed in decentralised locations, as goods typically are. Services are also inseparable from the perspective of the service provider. Thus, the quality of service that firms are able to deliver depends on the ability of their employees to satisfy customers' needs and wants. This is true even for self-service situations, such as automatic teller machines in banks. Even if provided remotely from the physical structure of the bank, consumers still associate positive and negative experiences when using the service with the service provider.

Heterogeneity

One great strength of McDonald's is its consistency. Whether customers order a Big Mac and French fries in Sydney, Tokyo, Salt Lake City or Moscow, they know exactly what they are going to get. This is not the case with many service providers. **Heterogeneity** means that services tend to be less standardised than goods. For example, physicians in a group practice or hairdressers in a hair salon differ in their technical and interpersonal skills. A given physician's or hairdresser's performance may even vary depending on the time of day, their physical health, or their moods and feelings on the day. Because services tend to be labour-intensive, and production and consumption are inseparable, consistent quality can be difficult to achieve.

Standardisation of the service process and staff training help to increase consistency and reliability. Limited-menu restaurants such as Pizza Hut and KFC offer customers high consistency from one visit to the next because of standardised operational procedures. Another way to increase consistency is to automate the process. Banks have reduced the inconsistency of teller services by providing automated teller machines. Airport x-ray surveillance equipment, and smart card technology on toll roads, have largely replaced the need for human intervention in these service processes.

Perishability

Perishability means that services cannot be stored, warehoused or inventoried. An empty hotel room or aircraft seat produces no revenue and that potential revenue is lost forever. Yet service organisations are often forced to turn away full-price customers during peak periods.

One of the most important challenges in many service industries is finding ways to synchronise supply and demand. The philosophy that some revenue is better than none has prompted many service providers such as hotels to offer discounts on weekends and during the off-season. Airlines, car rental agencies, movie theatres and restaurants also use discounts to encourage demand during non-peak periods.

Services marketing in manufacturing

7 Explain why services marketing is important to manufacturers

A comparison of goods and services marketing is beneficial, but in reality it is hard to distinguish clearly between manufacturing and service firms. Indeed, many manufacturing firms can point to customer service as a major factor in their success. For example, maintenance and repair services are important to buyers of photocopy machines.

Accor Hotels on-line

Find out about current specials that the Accor group of hotels is offering in your area by visiting the website. Are the discounts what you would expect? Do they seem to be available only on certain days or at certain times?
www.accorhotels.com.au

heterogeneity
Characteristic of services that makes them less standardised and uniform than goods.

perishability
Characteristic of services that prevents them from being stored, warehoused or inventoried.

Chapter 6 ■ ■ ■ Product and service concepts

By bundling computer hardware, software, maintenance and Internet services, Gateway can better position itself as a full-service provider in the computer market.

One reason that goods manufacturers stress customer service is that it can give them a strong competitive advantage, especially in industries in which goods are perceived as similar. In the car industry, for example, consumers perceive few quality differences between car brands.

Knowing that, General Motors has developed new guidelines for sales techniques and quality customer service, and will link dealer incentive payments to how well the guidelines are followed. Gateway now bundles a number of different services into the sale of a personal computer to consumers, including a wide range of software, maintenance and troubleshooting, and even its own Internet service.[30]

Regardless of whether an organisation is selling a good or a service, there needs to be careful consideration of how that good or service is delivered to the customer. For most products this involves some type of packaging. For physical goods, the packaging decisions and issues are reasonably easy to think about, but services also need to be packaged and this can be a more complex task for marketers. Let's look at packaging in more detail.

Mars on-line

Go to the Mars website and identify its product items, product lines and product mix. Do any of these surprise you? Why or why not? How wide do you think Mars' lines are?
www.mars.com.au

Packaging

Packages have always served a practical function. They hold contents together and protect goods as they move through the distribution channel. Packaging is also a container for promoting the product and making it easier and safer to use. In a service setting, packaging usually involves the bundling together of complementary services or goods that will facilitate the service encounter or make the service experience more rewarding. Examples might be for travel services, where hotel bookings, transfers, sightseeing trips, entry to attractions and transport are all arranged in one place or by one organisation. Essentially, packaging allows the product (whether it is a good or a service) to be delivered to the customer in the most efficient manner while protecting the integrity of the product.

8 Describe marketing uses of packaging and labelling

Hewlett Packard on-line

Find out about how Hewlett Packard facilitates recycling and refurbishing of its products by visiting its website. What role do environmental concerns play in HP's packaging?
www.welcome.hp.com/country/au/eng/welcome.htm

Packaging functions

The three most important functions of packaging are to contain and protect products, promote products, and facilitate the storage, use and convenience of products (this applies most to services). A fourth function of packaging that is becoming increasingly important is to facilitate recycling and reduce environmental damage.

Containing and protecting products

The most obvious function of packaging is to contain products that are liquid, granular or otherwise divisible. Packaging also enables manufacturers, wholesalers and retailers to market products in specific quantities, such as grams or litres.

Physical protection is another obvious function of packaging. Most products are handled several times between the time they are manufactured, harvested or otherwise produced, and the time they are consumed or used. Many products are shipped, stored and inspected several times between production and consumption. Some, like milk, need to be refrigerated. Others, like beer, are sensitive to light. Still others, like medicines and bandages, need to be kept sterile. Packages protect products from breakage, evaporation, spillage, spoilage, light, heat, cold, infestation and many other conditions. Old El Paso is using modified-atmosphere packaging for tortillas and other soft wraps, which are usually refrigerated. Oxygen-collecting films now in development could improve normal shelf-life for refrigerated pastas.[31]

Promoting products

Packaging does more than identify the brand, list the ingredients, specify features and give directions for use. A package differentiates a product from competing products and may associate a new product with a family of other products from the same manufacturer. Also in a culture that is increasingly 'self-service', packaging acts as a silent salesperson. Cider brand Strongbow has just launched and repackaged its brand, spending $4 million. The revamp included a new style of bottle, a new label featuring the well-known Knightshead logo and a new slogan, 'Drink fresh, think fresh'.[32]

Packages use designs, colours, shapes and materials to try to influence consumers' perceptions and buying behaviour. For example, marketing research indicates that health-conscious consumers are likely to think that any food is probably good for them as long as it comes in green packaging.

The new Strongbow Cider bottles are being used to promote this product as well as to contain and protect the quality of the contents.

Two top brands of low-fat foods – Snackwell's and Healthy Choice – use green packaging.[33] Kimberly-Clark Corp. and Kleenex recently introduced a wide array of more appealing boxes for their facial tissues. The idea is that if boxes are more attractive, people won't mind putting them in every room of the house. So far, the strategy appears to be working. In Australia, consumers spend about $92 million on premium-brand facial tissues a year, representing about 30 per cent of the market for facial tissues.[34]

Packaging has a measurable effect on sales, a fact that New Zealand-based organic milk producer Bio-Farm has noted. Their tried and tested packaging for their popular Country-Pet Plus yoghurt and other pet foods is testament to this. Bio-Farm says that the choice of packaging is critical: 'It communicates to the consumer the fresh, pure nature of our product for pets and the actual cartons are known to deliver the product in premium condition.'[35]

Facilitating storage, use and convenience

Wholesalers and retailers prefer packages that are easy to ship, store and stock on shelves. They also like packages that protect products, prevent spoilage or breakage, and extend the product's shelf life.

Consumers' requirements for convenience cover many dimensions. Consumers are constantly seeking items that are easy to handle, open and reclose, although some consumers want packages that are tamper-proof or child-proof. Consumers also want reusable and disposable packages. Surveys conducted in the United States by *Sales & Marketing Management* magazine revealed that consumers dislike – and avoid buying – leaky ice cream boxes, overly heavy or fat vinegar bottles, immovable pry-up lids on glass bottles, key-opener sardine cans and hard-to-pour cereal boxes. Such packaging innovations as zipper tear strips, hinged lids, tab slots, screw-on tops and pour spouts were introduced to solve those problems. As mentioned earlier in the case of services, packaging serves to facilitate the service experience and to make the entire process more efficient and effective for consumers.

Some firms use packaging to segment markets. For example, milk comes in packaging sizes from 250 millilitres, targeted to consumers who don't use a lot of milk, to three- and four-litre containers. Different-size packages appeal to heavy, moderate and light users. Salt is sold in package sizes ranging from a single serving to picnic size to giant economy size. Campbell's soup is packaged in single-serving cans aimed at the elderly and singles market segments. Beer and soft drinks are similarly marketed in various package sizes and types. Packaging convenience can increase a product's utility and, therefore, its market appeal and company earnings.

Facilitating recycling and reducing environmental damage

One of the most important packaging issues recently is compatibility with the environment. According to one study, 90 per cent of surveyed consumers say no more packaging material should be used than is necessary. The ability to recycle is also important.[36]

Some firms use their packaging to target environmentally concerned market segments. Brocato International markets shampoo and hair conditioner in bottles that are biodegradable in landfills. Procter & Gamble markets Sure Pro and Old Spice in 'eco-friendly' pump-spray packages that don't rely on aerosol propellants. Other firms that have introduced pump sprays include Johnson & Johnson (Pledge furniture polish), Reckitt & Coleman Household Products (Woolite rug cleaner), Rollout L.P. (Take 5 cleanser) and Richardson-Vicks (Vidal Sassoon hair spray).[37]

Labelling

An integral part of any package is its label and yet labelling is quite distinct from packaging. Labelling is about the information provided on the package relating to the contents, and often the chemical and nutritional makeup, of the product. Labelling generally takes one of two forms: persuasive or informational. **Persuasive labelling** focuses on a promotional theme or logo, and consumer information is secondary. The Intel logo and marketing strategy was clearly designed to strengthen brand identity and to become known as a brand instead of as a component parts manufacturer for computers. Note that the standard promotional claims – such as 'new', 'improved' and 'super' – are no longer very persuasive. Consumers have been saturated with 'newness' and thus discount these claims.

persuasive labelling
Focuses on a promotional theme or logo and consumer information is secondary.

Informational labelling, in contrast, is designed to help consumers make proper product selections and lower their cognitive dissonance after the purchase. The American company Sears attaches a 'label of confidence' to all its floor coverings. The label gives such product information as durability, colour, features, cleanability, care instructions and construction standards. Most major furniture manufacturers affix labels to their wares that explain the products' construction features, such as type of frame, number of coils and fabric characteristics. The Australia New Zealand Food Authority has mandated detailed nutritional information on most food packages and standards for health claims on food packaging. An important outcome of the *Australia New Zealand Food Regulations 1994* and the work of the Australian Competition and Consumer Commission (ACCC) is guidelines for using terms such as *low fat*, *light*, *reduced cholesterol*, *low sodium*, *low calorie* and *fresh*. The ANZFA website provides some interesting and useful information about labelling and the contents of food items (www.anzfa.gov.au).

informational labelling
Designed to help consumers make proper product selections and lower their cognitive dissonance after the purchase.

Many consumers are guided by labelling that is 'awarded' by organisations such as the Heart Foundation. However, the use of this type of labelling can be misleading. Marketers in New Zealand created a label called 'OK for Kids' in 1998 when the market became flooded with energy drinks such as Red Bull. The label was designed to help parents choose drinks that were suitable for their children. The problem with this classification (which is awarded by medical experts) lies in its interpretation by consumers. Some have taken the logo to mean 'more is better' and the result is increased incidences of gum disease and tooth decay in infants as a result of drinking fruit drinks high in sugar, in large volumes, because they are 'OK for Kids'. Thus, marketers need to be careful that their consumers understand and correctly interpret their labelling messages.

Universal product codes

The **universal product codes (UPCs)** that appear on many items in supermarkets and other high-volume outlets were first introduced in 1974. Because the numerical codes appear as a series of thick and thin vertical lines, they are often called bar codes. The lines are read by computerised optical scanners that match codes with brand names, package sizes and prices. They also print information on cash register tapes and help retailers to rapidly and accurately prepare records of customer purchases, control inventories and track sales. The UPC system and scanners are also used in single-source research (see Chapter 5).

universal product codes (UPCs)
Series of thick and thin vertical lines (bar codes), readable by computerised optical scanners, that represent numbers used to track products.

Connect it

Look back at the story that opens the chapter about McDonald's introducing a new line of healthier foods to its product line. McDonald's has chosen to take this approach partially in response to a global backlash about childhood obesity and partially to attract a more adult market. McDonald's has been criticised in the past for its high-fat foods and for not being honest about the ingredients and contents of its food products. With more and more adults wanting lower-fat, healthier foods, the Salads Plus brand should be an attractive partner for McDonald's. In addition, displaying nutritional data in store and on packaging is also allowing McDonald's to promote the benefits of their food items. A potential negative is that the emphasis on the Salads Plus brand may serve to confirm adult consumers' perceptions that McDonald's traditional menu items are less healthy. The company hopes to boost overall sales by attracting adult consumers – a market segment that has been a challenge in the past. Salads Plus has strong brand recognition as a low-fat product line, and given that more adults are becoming health-conscious, this strategy seems to be sound.

Summary

1 Define the term *product*.

A product is anything, desired or not, that a person or organisation receives in an exchange. The basic goal of purchasing decisions is to receive the tangible and intangible benefits associated with a product. Tangible aspects include packaging, style, colour, size and features. Intangible qualities include customer service, the retailer's image, the manufacturer's reputation and the social status associated with a product. An organisation's product offering is the crucial element in any marketing mix.

2 Classify consumer products.

Consumer products are classified into four categories: convenience products, shopping products, speciality products and unsought products. Convenience products are relatively inexpensive and require limited shopping effort. Shopping products are of two types: homogeneous and heterogeneous. Because of the similarity of homogeneous products, they are differentiated mainly by price and features. In contrast, heterogeneous products appeal to consumers because of their distinct characteristics. Speciality products possess unique benefits that are highly desirable to certain customers. Finally, unsought products are either new products or products that require active personal selling because they are generally avoided or overlooked by consumers.

3 Define the terms product item, product line and product mix.

A product item is a specific version of a product that can be designated as a distinct offering among an organisation's products. A product line is a group of closely related products offered by an organisation. An organisation's product mix includes all the products it sells. Product mix width refers to the number of product lines an organisation offers. Product line depth is the number of product

Define it

actual product 186
augmented product 187
brand 195
brand equity 196
brand loyalty 197
brand mark 195
brand name 195
brand personality 198
business product (industrial product) 187
co-branding 201
consumer product 188
convenience product 188
core product 186
credence quality 205
experience quality 205
family brand 201
generic product 199
generic product name 203
heterogeneity 206
individual branding 201
informational labelling 210
inseparability 205
intangibility 205
manufacturer's brand 201
master brand 197
perishability 206
persuasive labelling 210
planned obsolescence 194
private brand 201
product 186
product item 190
product line 190
product line depth 193
product line extension 194
product mix 191
product mix width 193
product modification 193
search quality 205
service 204
service mark 202
shopping product 189
speciality product 190
trademark 202
universal product codes (UPC) 210
unsought product 190

items in a product line. Firms modify existing products by changing their quality, functional characteristics or style. Product line extension occurs when a firm adds new products to existing product lines.

4 Describe marketing uses of branding.
A brand is a name, term or symbol that identifies and differentiates a firm's products. Established brands encourage customer loyalty and help new products to succeed in the market. Branding strategies require decisions about individual, family, manufacturers' and private brands.

5 Discuss the importance of services to the economy.
The service sector plays a crucial role in the Australian economy, employing about three-quarters of the workforce and accounting for more than 60 per cent of the gross domestic product.

6 Identify the differences between services and goods.
Services are distinguished by four characteristics: intangibility, inseparability, heterogeneity and perishability. Services are intangible in that they lack clearly identifiable physical characteristics, making it difficult for marketers to communicate their specific benefits to potential customers. The production and consumption of services are typically inseparable. Services are heterogeneous because their quality depends on such variables as the service provider, individual consumer, location, and so on. Finally, services are perishable in the sense that they cannot be stored or saved. As a result, synchronising supply with demand is particularly challenging in the service industry.

7 Explain why services marketing is important to manufacturers.
Although manufacturers are marketing mainly goods, the related services they provide often give them a competitive advantage – especially when competing goods are quite similar.

8 Describe marketing uses of packaging and labelling.
Packaging has four functions: containing and protecting products; promoting products; facilitating product storage, use and convenience; and facilitating recycling and reducing environmental damage. As a tool for promotion, packaging identifies the brand and its features. It also serves the critical function of differentiating a product from competing products and linking it with related products from the same manufacturer. The label is an integral part of the package, with persuasive and informational functions. In essence, the package is the marketer's last chance to influence buyers before they make a purchase decision.

Review it

1. A relatively inexpensive item that merits little shopping effort is a(n)
   a   Convenience product
   b   Shopping product
   c   Speciality product
   d   Unsought product
2. An item that consumers will search extensively for and are very reluctant to accept substitutes for is a(n)

- a Convenience product
- b Shopping product
- c Speciality product
- d Unsought product

3 A specific and distinct version of a product offered by an organisation is defined as a
- a Product item
- b Product category
- c Product line
- d Product mix

4 A modification of an existing product in which there is a change in the product's versatility or effectiveness is a
- a Line modification
- b Quality modification
- c Functional modification
- d Style modification

5 A brand name that is owned by a wholesaler or a retailer is known as a
- a Distributor's brand
- b Private brand
- c Manufacturer's brand
- d Generic brand

6 When a firm places two or more brand names on a product, it is known as
- a Individual branding
- b Unique branding
- c Co-branding
- d Family branding

7 An exclusive right to use a brand is a
- a Brand mark
- b Copyright
- c Trademark
- d Private brand

8 Services differ from goods in four main ways. These are
- a Search quality, perishability, heterogeneity and intangibility
- b Inseperability, heterogeneity, perishability and credence quality
- c Intangibility, perishability, heterogeneity and search quality
- d Intangibility, perishability, heterogeneity and inseperability

9 Organising related items into product lines often results in advertising efficiencies for the producer of these goods.
- a True
- b False

10 Packaging serves not only a practical function protecting products but also assists in promoting products by
- a Showing information on product ingredients
- b Using colour, shape and laterials to influence perception
- c Providing recycling options
- d All of the above

Check the Answer Key to see how well you understood the material. More detailed discussion and writing questions and a video case related to this chapter are found in the Student Resources CD-ROM.

Apply it

1. Form into groups of four or five students. From the following list of products, have the members of the group classify each product into the category (convenience, shopping, speciality, unsought) that they think fits best from their perspective as consumers (i.e. if they were buying the product): Coca-Cola (brand), car stereo, winter coat, pair of shoes, life insurance, blue jeans, hamburgers.

2. A local community organisation has asked you to give a talk about planned obsolescence. Rather than pursuing a negative approach by talking about how businesses exploit customers through planned obsolescence, you have decided to talk about the benefits of producing products that don't last forever. Prepare a one-page outline for that presentation.

3. A local supermarket would like to introduce their own brand of paper goods (paper towels, facial tissue, etc.) to sell alongside their current range. The company has hired you to generate a report outlining the advantages and disadvantages of doing so. Write the report.

4. Identify five outstanding brand names, and explain why each is included in your list. Comment also on the particular personalities of these brands – what do they say to you and their customers.

5. Form into small groups, and discuss the packaging of a product familiar to all members of your group. Make a brief presentation to your class describing the pros and cons of this package.

6. How have several snack food companies modified their product to serve the emerging needs of their customers?

7. What is the product mix offered at the following website? www.marriott.com.au

8. List the countries to which Levi Strauss & Co. markets through the following website. How do the product offerings differ between the United States, European and Australian selections? www.levi.com

Try it

The Baker family owns one of the largest barramundi farms in northern Western Australia, and is known for raising the best barramundi in the area. After graduating from university with a degree in marketing, Frank Baker returned to the farm with a lot of ideas on new ways to cash in on the farm's reputation. At the time, the family allowed the local supermarket to use the Baker name on their barramundi sold in the store. Frank, eager to put his degree to work, convinced his family that they could make money from their name by selling their barramundi products already packaged to supermarkets. After hearing the idea, the family met to formulate a plan to begin selling Baker Farms Barramundi.

Questions

1. What type of product is the Baker family selling? List your reasons.
2. What type of branding is the Baker family using? List your reasons.
3. How should Baker Farms Barramundi be packaged?
4. Assuming that the Baker family wishes to reposition its barramundi products, what would be an optimal strategy and what brand personality should they adopt and why?

Watch it

Ben & Jerry's taste and innovation

What's in a name? Everything, at Ben & Jerry's, makers of mouth-watering ice cream in smooth and chunky flavours. Produced in Vermont, in the United States, from local dairy products and spring water, Ben & Jerry's strong brand image is one of high quality, innovative flavours and barrel-of-laughs names. Products like Chunky Monkey, Vanilla Like It Oughta Be, Chubby Hubby and Chocolate Chip Cookie Dough delight the palate and underscore the whimsical image of the company. To honour Grateful Dead icon Jerry Garcia and to appeal to youthful audiences, the company created Cherry Garcia ice cream in 1987. And today their newest flavour is Dilbert: Totally Nuts, named for the hapless comic strip hero of today's workaday world.

But the names aren't only funny. They carry a lot of weight supporting the company's brand equity. They have also created value based on customer recognition of the brand and loyalty among customers who like both the ice cream and the company mandate to improve society and the environment. Actually, Ben & Jerry's social philosophy plays a major role in making the company name well known. For example, Phish Food, chocolate ice cream with fish-shaped chocolate chunks, is named for the Vermont-based rock band Phish. On each pint container of Phish Food, the band pledges, 'Our share of the proceeds from this pint goes to environmental efforts in the Lake Champlain Region of Vermont, so enjoy the good taste and karma.' In 1997, sales of Phish Food generated royalties of US$159 000.

Also in 1997, royalties in the amount of US$55 000 were paid on the sale of Doonesberry Sorbet. Pints of Doonesberry include the following message, signed by the cartoon strip's character Mike Doonesbury: 'P.S. All creator royalties go to charity, so your purchase represents an orderly transfer of wealth you can feel proud of.' Royalty funds from Doonesberry Sorbet go to education, AIDS treatment and prevention, reducing poverty, and human rights. Though premium ice cream is still the company favourite, Ben & Jerry's expanded the product mix because the original product was high in fat, and today's consumers wanted low-fat, healthier products with more nutritional value. So, product lines now include low-fat ice cream, low-fat and non-fat frozen yoghurts and fat-free sorbet. The idea is 'to blend flavour that tastes very fattening into ice cream that isn't'. All the product lines share the same marketing strategy, complete with offbeat humour and catchy names. For Ben & Jerry's 20th birthday, new low-fat flavours were introduced – Coconut Cream Pie Low Fat, S'Mores and Blackberry Cobbler. Within each product line, some flavours have become so well known that they constitute brands unto themselves. For example, Cherry Garcia is available in both the premium and frozen yoghurt categories. Catchy names and expanded product lines are not the only marketing strategies followed at Ben & Jerry's, where even the packaging is considered a promotional element. That's why all product lines are packaged in similarly designed and illustrated pint containers. Because consumers often believe that different product lines made by the same manufacturer are equal in quality, those who love the ice cream may try the yoghurt, especially because their packaging looks alike. To celebrate the company's 20th birthday, the pint package was redesigned to be fun and colourful and to have an appetising look. Packaging at Ben & Jerry's, however, also conveys important messages regarding the ingredients. In addition to the information on charitable contributions, the labels on pint cartons state: 'We oppose RBGH, Recombinant Bovine Growth Hormone. The family farmers who supply our milk and cream pledge not to treat their cows with RBGH ...' The company's overarching belief in social responsibility – whether it be the consumers' right to know what they are eating or the corporate call to social giving – is reflected and advertised in its package designs.

Packaging materials themselves have become a test case of the company's pledge to improve the environment. One goal is to make the transition to totally chlorine-free paper for pint containers because the bleaching process releases pollutants into the air. Although these kinds of measures seem on the surface to be great marketing hooks, still the public does not always favour company initiatives. Packaging for Peace Pops ice cream bars was redesigned and this message added: 'We package our Peace Pops in bags, not individual boxes, because it puts less trash in the landfill.' But sales declined as a result because customers wanted the packaging of their premium ice cream to reflect its high quality and high price. Reluctantly, the company changed packaging back to boxes. As a compromise, the new Peanut Butter & Jelly bar is in a plastic bag inside a chlorine-free box.

Questions

1 What are the tangible and intangible dimensions of Ben & Jerry's products?
2 Why did Ben & Jerry's develop several product lines?
3 Describe Ben & Jerry's brand equity.
4 What is the advantage of Ben & Jerry's using one marketing strategy for the entire product mix?

Suggested reading

Ben & Jerry's annual report

Ben & Jerry's website: www.benjerry.com

© 2003 Nelson Australia Pty Limited

Click it

Online reading

INFOTRAC® COLLEGE EDITION
For additional readings and review on **product and services concepts**, explore InfoTrac® College Edition, your online library. Go to: **www.infotrac-college.com** and search for any of the InfoTrac key terms listed below:
- core product
- product mix
- branding; brand loyalty
- generic product name
- persuasive labelling

Answer key

1. *Answer*: a, p. 188 *Rationale*: Convenience products are those that the consumer is unwilling to shop extensively for. Consumers buy these products regularly and are aware of brand names of such goods.
2. *Answer*: c, p. 190 *Rationale*: Speciality products are often expensive goods that try to maintain an exclusive image in the marketplace. Distribution is typically limited and brand names are very important.
3. *Answer*: a, p. 190 *Rationale*: A product item is a single product that can be designated as a distinct offering among an organisation's products.
4. *Answer*: c, p. 193 *Rationale*: A functional modification occurs when the firm changes a product's versatility, effectiveness, convenience or safety.
5. *Answer*: b, p. 201 *Rationale*: Private brands are those that are owned by distribution channel members such as retailers and wholesalers.
6. *Answer*: c, p. 201 *Rationale*: Co-branding is a strategy that is used when a combination of brand names enhances the prestige or perceived value of a product.
7. *Answer*: c, p. 202 *Rationale*: A trademark is the exclusive right to use a brand or a part of a brand and prohibits others from using a brand without permission.
8. *Answer*: d, pp. 205 *Rationale*: Services have four defining characteristics that distinguish them from goods.
9. *Answer*: a, p. 192 *Rationale*: Product lines do provide economies of scale in advertising since several products can be advertised under the umbrella of the line.
10. *Answer*: d, p. 208 *Rationale*: Packaging does more than just identify the brand, list ingredients and give directions for use. It also differentiates a product from its competition and attracts potential users.

CHAPTER SEVEN

Developing and managing products

LEARNING OBJECTIVES

After studying this chapter, you should be able to

1 Explain the importance of developing new products and describe the six categories of new products

2 Explain the steps in the new-product development process

3 Explain the concept of product life cycles

4 Explain the diffusion process through which new products are adopted

Every carmaker in the world is trying to figure out how to use the Internet to streamline the new-product development process, which traditionally can take four to six years and cost billions of dollars for a major launch. The Chrysler Group has reason to be trying harder than the rest. The company is losing money, and the Germans have arrived from the parent company to supervise a turnaround.

Part of Chrysler's answer to the pressure it faces is FastCar. The project is still in the early stages, but 200 workstations at Chrysler's Auburn Hills, Michigan, headquarters have been tied into the Web-based system.

FastCar allows the company to link the flow of information from at least six major information systems that until now have not been able to communicate seamlessly – finance has had its system, engineering had a different one, purchasing relied on a third, and so on. There were even smaller, largely secret 'shadow' systems. Because each arm of Chrysler had spent huge sums of money building information systems that suited its individual needs, headquarters could never force all of the departments onto one centrally controlled system. So far, the various arms of Chrysler are communicating over the Internet only in designing a large car for the 2004 model year.

The sheer scale and complexity of the auto industry is daunting for even the most intrepid Internet maven. The rule of thumb is that any given car has roughly 12 000 moving parts. Chrysler has 50 000 different components that it draws upon internally. Every screw, bolt and button has detailed specifications. When other variations are introduced (Do you want 16-inch or 17-inch tyres? What colour paint do you want?), there are billions of permutations for Chrysler vehicles. So, even though Internet-based collaboration is old hat for some newer, smaller companies, it's an enormous undertaking for the auto industry.

The whole point of FastCar is to keep everyone working on the same design at the same time. As designers go through hundreds of variations, colleagues at other arms of Chrysler can understand what is changing in real time. In the past, if the designers changed something, engineers would have to catch up later to see what effect that would have on manufacturing; finance would have to reassess the costs; and quality control would have to re-examine its own issues. By then, the designers could be on to the next iteration.

Now FastCar offers everyone what Chrysler calls a 'unified data model' or a 'single point of truth' that they can see in three dimensions. The goal of FastCar is to move from theme selection to design completion to mass manufacturing within two years, roughly half the current industry standard.

FastCar is not aimed only at Chrysler's internal processes. Chrysler says FastCar will eventually work seamlessly with Covisint, an industry consortium set up with General Motors, Ford Motor, Renault and Nissan. FastCar and Covisint fit together 'like lego blocks,' the company says.

Using Covisint's standards, FastCar hopes to send email messages to suppliers with hyperlinks to 3-D renderings of the parts or systems that are changing. Suppliers can use a personal computer or a laptop and don't need expensive workstations.

No one knows how fast the auto industry can migrate to Internet-based systems. It is the most wrenching period of change since Henry Ford introduced the assembly line nearly 90 years ago.

Aside from cutting the cost of each auto by as much as $1500, moving to newer Internet-based systems should make the industry much more responsive to fashion trends. Chris Cedergren, managing director of Nextrend, a consultancy in Thousand Oaks, California, argues that to survive, a carmaker will have to become more like a Calvin Klein or Ralph Lauren design house. 'They have to be able to get a concept from the design studio to the dealer's showroom in eighteen months and do it for 30 to 35 per cent less than it costs today,' says Cedergren. If the FastCar project succeeds, that type of speed, saving and flexibility could become standard operating procedure for an industry mired today in lags, costs and rigidity.

How has the Internet helped Chrysler to reduce the time it takes to design and develop a new car and at the same time dramatically reduce costs and increase flexibility? Could these processes be helpful to firms in other industries?

The importance of new products

New products are important to sustain growth and profits and to replace obsolete items. In the United States, 3M Corporation introduces about 500 new products each year.[1] In Australia, Woolworths' buying teams sort through more than 20 000 new products, line extensions and packaging rejigs each year, accepting just 2200, or 11 per cent. This means that every year Woolworths deletes 2000 lines. Eventually, nine out of 10 new listings fail, says Woolworths' chief buying manager.[2] Why this occurs is hard to predict. Product deaths usually occur due to market changes and a decline in the quality and quantity of consumer research. In the last year, Arnott's has considered about 25 new product concepts and plans to continue trialling and researching at least 12–15 new ideas a year – and that's just in the biscuit line!

Categories of new products

The term **new product** is somewhat confusing, because its meaning varies widely. Actually, there are several 'correct' definitions of the term. A product can be new to the world, to the market, to the producer or seller, or to some combination of these. There are six categories of new products:

- *New-to-the-world products* (also called *discontinuous innovations*): These products create an entirely new market. The telephone, television, computer and facsimile machine are commonly cited examples of new-to-the-world products.
- *New product lines*: These products, which the firm has not previously offered, allow it to enter an established market. For example, V energy drink, produced by Frucor Beverages of New Zealand, has allowed this company to enter the elusive youth culture market, which they were previously unable to do with plain soft drinks.[3]
- *Additions to existing product lines*: This category includes new products that supplement a firm's established line. Hallmark recently announced the addition of 117 new greeting cards – for pets. According to Hallmark's research, 75 per cent of pet owners give Christmas presents to their pets, and 40 per cent celebrate their pets' birthdays.[4]
- *Improvements or revisions of existing products*: The 'new and improved' product may be significantly or slightly changed. For example, Colgate's '2in1' toothpaste gives you a mouthwash and a toothpaste all in the one bottle. Most new products fit into this category. According to one expert, 'companies are making low-risk launches – a lot of line extensions, new colors and flavors'.[5]
- *Repositioned products*: These are existing products targeted at new markets or market segments. Frito Lay was successfully launched into the Australian market after four previous unsuccessful attempts. The company spent over $4 million in advertising this time, and the Australian market had also developed a taste for flat-cut potato chips.[6] The company aimed its products squarely at the pre-teen market and so far has been very successful, capturing a large share of the chip-eating market.

---

1 Explain the importance of developing new products and describe the six categories of new products

new product
Product new to the world, the market, the producer, the seller or some combination of these.

Apple on-line
Apple is constantly looking to adopt and create new products, such as their iPod. How does Apple's website support its new products? Find out at www.apple.com.au

- *Lower-priced products*: This category refers to products that provide performance similar to competing brands at a lower price. Many car manufacturers use this tactic in their marketing. For example, the Mazda Millennia aims directly at the same market as the BMW, and offers many similar features at a significantly reduced price.

Sometimes product's claim to be safer than an existing product raises ethical issues as the Ethics in marketing box indicates.

Ethics in Marketing: Less toxins, great taste

Vector Tobacco Ltd. recently introduced a new cigarette called Omni, with the slogan 'Reduced carcinogens, premium taste'. The ad says that Omni was created to 'significantly' cut levels of chemicals that are the 'major causes of lung cancer' in smokers. 'Now there's actually a reason to change brands,' it says.

The tobacco in the Omni cigarette is treated with a combination of chemicals, including palladium, a metal most commonly found in the catalytic converters of cars. Vector says that the treatment, combined with a new, carbon-filled filter, has resulted in a cigarette that tastes as good as competitors' brands but has lower levels of a number of toxic and cancer-causing compounds.

Vector says that its palladium catalyst reduces various cancer-causing compounds known as polycyclic aromatic hydrocarbons, or PAHs, by 15 to 60 per cent. It also cuts down on a tobacco-specific nitrosamine, known as NNK, that is considered an especially potent lung carcinogen. Levels of another nitrosamine, however, aren't reduced. The filter removes nearly all the benzene from the cigarette's smoke and also makes significant cuts in other chemicals, Vector scientist Robert Bereman says.

Vector acknowledges there is no scientific proof that these reductions will make its cigarettes any less dangerous than the average Marlboro or Camel. It has yet to complete any human or animal tests of the effects of smoking the new cigarettes. In an open letter to be published in magazines and newspapers, Vector's chief executive, Bennett S. LeBow, writes that 'there is no such thing as a safe cigarette, and we do not encourage anyone to smoke.' But, he adds: 'We strongly believe that if you do smoke, Omni is the best alternative.'

'We're doing what we have to do, to do the right thing,' Mr LeBow says. 'If we have this technology, we have to come out with it. I wouldn't be able to sleep at night if I were sitting on this.'

Vector's strategy is drawing fire from anti-smoking activists, public-health experts and some of its larger rivals in the cigarette business, who say the ads are misleading. 'Everything is designed to imply that this cigarette is safer, with Vector having no proof whatsoever that this is the case,' says Matthew L. Myers, President of the Campaign for Tobacco-Free Kids, a Washington advocacy group. 'That has the potential to cause serious harm to consumers.'

The whole notion of a less hazardous cigarette is controversial. Proponents say it would be wrong not to try to reduce the harm caused by smoking, which contributes to more than 400 000 deaths a year in the United States. But some anti-tobacco activists worry that the newfangled cigarettes will discourage smokers from quitting and possibly entice non-smokers to light up.

Is Omni a new product? If so, what category of new product does it fit into? Are Vector's claims for Omni legal and ethical?

The new-product development process

2 Explain the steps in the new-product development process

The management and technology consulting firm Booz, Allen and Hamilton, which has conducted a number of major studies of the new-product development process, has concluded that the companies most likely to succeed in developing and introducing new products are those that take the following actions:

1. Make the long-term commitment needed to support innovation and new-product development.
2. Use a company-specific approach, driven by corporate objectives and strategies, with a well-defined new-product strategy at its core.
3. Capitalise on experience to achieve and maintain competitive advantage.
4. Establish an environment – a management style, organisational structure and degree of top-management support – conducive to achieving company-specific new-product and corporate objectives.[7]

Most companies follow a formal new-product development process, usually starting with a new-product strategy. Exhibit 7.1 traces the seven-step process, which is discussed in detail in this section. The exhibit is funnel-shaped to highlight the fact that each stage acts as a screen. The purpose is to filter out unworkable ideas.

New-product strategy

A **new-product strategy** links the new-product development process with the objectives of the company, the business unit and the marketing department. A new-product strategy must be compatible with these objectives, and in turn, all three objectives must be consistent with one another.

New-product strategy is part of the organisation's overall marketing strategy. It sharpens the focus and provides general guidelines for generating, screening and evaluating new-product ideas. The new-product strategy specifies the roles that new products must play in the organisation's overall plan and describes the characteristics of products the organisation wants to offer and the markets it wants to serve.

Idea generation

New-product ideas come from many sources, including customers, employees, distributors, competitors, research and development, and consultants.

Mazda on-line
Visit the newsroom at Mazda to read about new product offerings. What categories of new products are presented?
www.mazda.com.au

new-product strategy
Linking the new-product development process with the objectives of the marketing department, the business unit and the corporation.

Nestlé on-line
Visit Nestlé's website and read about new-product offerings. What categories of new products are represented?
www.nestle.com.au

Exhibit 7.1 New-product development process

- New-product strategy
- Idea generation
- Idea screening
- Business analysis
- Development
- Test marketing
- Commercialisation
- New product

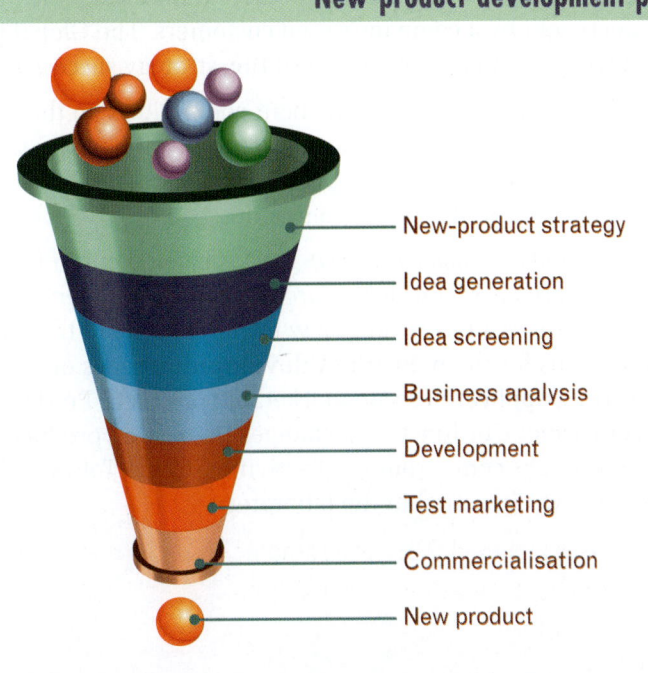

- *Customers*: The marketing concept suggests that customers' wants and needs should be the springboard for developing new products. Thermos, the vacuum bottle manufacturer, provides an interesting example of how companies tap customers for ideas. The company's first step in developing an innovative home barbecue grill was to send 10 members of its interdisciplinary new-product team into the field for about a month. Their assignment was to learn all about people's barbecue needs and to invent a product to meet them. The team conducted focus groups, visited people's homes in various cities and even videotaped barbecues.

- *Employees*: Marketing personnel – advertising and marketing research employees, as well as salespeople – often create new-product ideas, because they analyse and are involved in the marketplace. Firms should encourage their employees to submit new-product ideas and reward them if their ideas are adopted. The very successful introduction of Post-it® Notes started with an employee's idea. In 1974, the research and development department of 3M's commercial tape division developed and patented the adhesive component of Post-it® Notes. However, it was a year before an employee of the commercial tape division, who sang in a church choir, identified a use for the adhesive. He had been using paper clips and slips of paper to mark places in hymnbooks. But the paper clips damaged his books, and the slips of paper fell out. The solution, as we now all know, was to apply the adhesive to small pieces of paper and sell them in packages.

- *Distributors*: A well-trained sales team routinely asks distributors about needs that are not being met. Because they are closer to end users, distributors are often more aware of customer needs than are manufacturers. The inspiration for Rubbermaid's litter-free lunch box, named Sidekick, came from a distributor who suggested that Rubbermaid place some of its plastic containers inside a lunch box and sell the box as an alternative to plastic wrap and paper bags.

- *Competitors*: No firms rely solely on internally generated ideas for new products. A big part of any organisation's marketing intelligence system should be monitoring the performance of competitors' products. One purpose of competitive monitoring is to determine which, if any, of the competitors' products should be copied. Competitive monitoring may include tracking products sold by a company's own customers. The Global perspectives box illustrates how Coca-Cola has used this strategy successfully in Japan.

There is plenty of information about competitors on the World Wide Web. For example, AltaVista (www.altavista.com.au), Yahoo! (www.yahoo.com.au) and many other search engines are a powerful index tool that can be used to locate information about products and companies.

- *Research and development (R&D)*: R&D is carried out in four distinct ways. Basic research is scientific research aimed at discovering new technologies. Applied research takes these new technologies and tries to find useful applications for them. **Product development** goes one step further by converting applications into marketable products. Product modification makes cosmetic or functional changes in existing products. Many new-product breakthroughs come from R&D activities. Uncle Tobys' Roll-ups – real fruit, flat out – was invented in the laboratory.

product development
Marketing strategy that entails the creation of marketable new products; process of converting applications for new technologies into marketable products.

Chapter 7 — Developing and managing products

Monitoring competition pays off

Global PERSPECTIVES

In 1990, the Coca-Cola Company dominated the soft-drink market in Japan. Coke controlled 90 per cent of the carbonated drink market and over 30 per cent of the entire soft-drink market, including non-carbonated drinks.

But consumer preferences began changing rapidly. The demand for less sweet non-carbonated drinks rose quickly. Japanese companies such as Suntory, Ltd, Asahi Soft Drinks Co. and Calpis Food Industry Co. began attracting large numbers of purchasers with new products such as Asian teas, fruit-flavoured soft drinks, teas, coffees and fermented-milk drinks. Coke's market share began falling rapidly. According to one industry analyst, 'Coke used to have trouble with product development – with its speed and coming up with new localised products – but they've gotten faster and smarter.'[8]

Since 1994, Coke has reversed declining market share by introducing more than 30 new drinks, including an Asian tea called Sokenbicha, an English tea called Kochakaden, a coffee drink called Georgia and a fermented-milk drink called Lactia.

'Cola-Cola is mean and scary,' says one competitor. 'They have deep pockets, and these days they study us closely and challenge us with all these me-toos. That's something they never did before.'[9]

A Coca-Cola representative asked to respond to this charge said that the company does not follow a copy-cat strategy. Instead, it improved on competitors' product ideas and introduces superior products.

What category of new products is Cola-Cola Company introducing into Japan? Is their strategy of monitoring competitors' new products and introducing similar items ethical? Does it make good business sense?

Going direct to the customer to learn about people's preferences in cars is the latest strategy from the Ford Motor Company, which is aiming to achieve success with the launch of its new-model Ford Falcons and bigger, more powerful utes. Tapping customers can be a very effective method of generating new product ideas.

Levi's on-line

How does Levi's use its website to generate new-product ideas? Go to 'Cool stuff' and look at the 'Original spin' part of the website on www.levis.com.au

brainstorming
Getting a group to think of unlimited ways to vary a product or solve a problem.

screening
The first filter in the product development process, which eliminates ideas that are inconsistent with the organisation's new-product strategy or are obviously inappropriate for some other reason.

concept test
Test to evaluate a new-product idea, usually before any prototype has been created.

- *Consultants*: Outside consultants are always available to examine a business and recommend product ideas and you can locate many of them on the Internet by using a search engine and typing in 'marketing consultant'. The state and federal governments also provide advice and support for companies wanting to develop and market new products, as does Austrade for companies wanting to develop new export markets and products (www.austrade.gov.au).

Creativity is the wellspring of new-product ideas, regardless of who comes up with them. A variety of approaches and techniques have been developed to stimulate creative thinking. The two considered most useful for generating new-product ideas are brainstorming and focus group exercises. The goal of **brainstorming** is to get a group to think of unlimited ways to vary a product or solve a problem. Group members avoid criticism of an idea, no matter how ridiculous it may seem. Objective evaluation is postponed. The sheer quantity of ideas is what matters. An objective of focus group interviews is to stimulate insightful comments through group interaction. As noted in Chapter 5, focus groups usually consist of between seven and 10 people. Sometimes consumer focus groups generate excellent new-product ideas – for example, 'Dustbuster' vacuum cleaners and self-serve salad bars. In the industrial market, machine tools, keyboard designs, aircraft interiors and backhoe accessories have evolved from focus groups.

A study conducted in the United States by the Product Development and Management Association found that it took seven ideas to generate a new commercial product in 1995, down from 11 ideas in 1990. In 1967, it took 58 ideas for one new item. Today, companies do more work at the beginning of the development process (such as identifying final users) and can, in some cases, use computer-simulation tools to speed up the design stage.[10]

Idea screening

After new ideas have been generated, they pass through the first filter in the product development process. This stage, called **screening**, eliminates ideas that are inconsistent with the organisation's new-product strategy or are obviously inappropriate for some other reason. The new-product committee, the new-product department or some other formally appointed group performs the screening review. Most new-product ideas are rejected at the screening stage.

Concept tests are often used at the screening stage to rate concept (or product) alternatives. A **concept test** evaluates a new-product idea, usually before any prototype has been created. Typically, researchers get consumer reactions to descriptions and visual representations of a proposed product.

Concept tests are considered good predictors of success for line extensions. They have also been relatively precise predictors of success for new products that are not copycat items, are not easily classified into existing product categories and don't require major changes in consumer behaviour – such as Chicken Tonight bottled sauces, Cycle dog foods, and energy drinks. However, concept tests are usually inaccurate in predicting the success of new products that create new consumption patterns and require major changes in consumer behaviour – such as microwave ovens, videocassette recorders, computers and word processors.

Business analysis

New-product ideas that survive the initial screening process move to the **business analysis** stage, where preliminary figures for demand, cost, sales and profitability are calculated. For the first time, costs and revenues are estimated and compared. Depending on the nature of the product and the company, this process may be simple or complex.

The newness of the product, the size of the market and the nature of competition all affect the accuracy of revenue projections. In an established market such as soft drinks, industry estimates of total market size are available. Forecasting market share for a new entry is a bigger challenge.

Analysing overall economic trends and their impact on estimated sales are especially important in product categories that are sensitive to fluctuations in the business cycle. If consumers view the economy as uncertain and risky, they will put off buying durable goods such as major home appliances, cars and homes. Likewise, business buyers postpone major equipment purchases if they expect a recession.

These questions are commonly asked during the business analysis stage:

- What is the likely demand for the product?
- What impact would the new product probably have on total sales, profits, market share and return on investment?
- How would the introduction of the product affect existing products? Would the new product cannibalise existing products?
- Would current customers benefit from the product?
- Would the product enhance the image of the company's overall product mix?
- Would the new product affect current employees in any way? Would it lead to hiring more people or reducing the size of the workforce?
- What new facilities, if any, would be needed?
- How might competitors respond?
- What is the risk of failure? Is the company willing to take the risk?

Answering these and related questions may require studies of markets, competition, costs and technical capabilities. But at the end of this stage, management should have a good understanding of the product's market potential. This full understanding is important, because costs increase dramatically once a product idea enters the development stage.

The Entrepreneurial insights box provides a checklist that small businesses might use for evaluating new-product ideas.

> **business analysis**
> The second stage of the screening process where preliminary figures for demand, cost, sales and profitability are calculated.

Development

In the early stage of **development**, the R&D department or engineering department may develop a prototype of the product. During this stage, the firm should start sketching a marketing strategy. The marketing department should decide on the product's packaging, branding and labelling. In addition, it should map out preliminary promotion, price and distribution strategies. The technical feasibility of manufacturing the product at an acceptable cost should also be thoroughly examined.

> **development**
> Stage in the product development process in which a prototype is developed and a marketing strategy is outlined.

Entrepreneurial Insights

Checklist for evaluating new-product concepts

If a small business is lucky enough to have stable or increasing sales, new-product additions can boost profits and market share. Small-business managers must be careful, however, not to expand beyond the firm's financial capacities. A new product requires shelf space, investment in stock, perhaps spare parts, and maybe even a new salesperson – all of which require an extra financial commitment.

A new small business usually has only one chance to 'do it right'. A failure in introducing a new product can mean bankruptcy and perhaps the loss of a person's life savings. Conversely, for the owner of an established small business who suddenly finds that his or her source of livelihood has evaporated, the right new product can help to offset declining demand.

The product development process is generally the same for both large and small firms. However, many entrepreneurs must do most steps in the process themselves rather than rely on specialists or outside consultants.

Here's a simple checklist for evaluating new-product concepts for a small business. By adding up the points, a small-business owner can more accurately estimate success.

1 Contribution to before-tax return on investment:

More than 35 per cent	+2
25–35 per cent	+1
20–25 per cent	–1
Less than 20 per cent	–2

2 Estimated annual sales:

More than $10 million	+2
$2 million–$10 million	+1
$1 million–$1.99 million	–1
Less than $1 million	–2

3 Estimated growth phase of product life cycle:

More than three years	+2
Two or three years	+1
One or two years	–1
Less than one year	–2

4 Capital investment payback:

Less than one year	+2
One to two years	+1
Two to three years	–1
More than three years	–2

5 Premium-price potential:

Weak or no competition, making entry easy	+2
Mildly competitive entry conditions	+1
Strongly competitive entry conditions	–1
Entrenched competition that makes entry difficult	–2

This checklist is by no means complete, but a neutral or negative total score should give an entrepreneur reason to consider dropping the product concept.

The development stage can last a long time and thus be very expensive. Crest toothpaste was in the development stage for 10 years. It took 18 years to develop Minute Rice, 15 years to develop the Polaroid Colorpack camera, 15 years to develop the Xerox copy machine, and 55 years to develop television. Gillette spent six years and more than US$750 million developing the MACH 3 razor.[11] Preliminary efforts to develop a three-bladed razor began 28 years before the 1998 launch of MACH 3.[12]

The development process works best when all the involved areas (R&D, marketing, engineering, production and even suppliers) work together rather than sequentially, a process called simultaneous product development. The Internet is a useful tool for improving communications between marketing personnel, advertising agencies, graphic designers and others involved in developing products as was illustrated in the opening vignette. On the Internet, multiple parties from a number of different companies can meet regularly with new ideas and information at their fingertips, an inexpensive way to help get products to the shelf faster.[13]

Laboratory tests are often conducted on prototype models during the development stage. User safety is an important aspect of laboratory testing, which actually subjects products to much more severe treatment than is expected by end users. Part V of the *Trade Practices Act 1995* contains general consumer protection provisions, including issues about misleading advertising, deceptive conduct and general consumer safety. The Act makes it the manufacturer's responsibility to conduct 'reasonable testing programs' to ensure that their products conform to established safety standards.

Many products that test well in the laboratory are also tried out in homes or businesses. Examples of product categories well suited for such use tests include human and pet food products, household cleaning products, and industrial chemicals and supplies. These products are all relatively inexpensive, and their performance characteristics are apparent to users. For example, in the United States, at a Boston factory that Gillette Co. calls 'World Shaving Headquarters', about 200 male and 30 female employee volunteers evaluate potential new razors and blades each weekday morning. They report their assessment of features such as sharpness, smoothness and ease of handling.[14] In addition to employee feedback, research teams count razor strokes, clock the length of de-whiskerisation and observe split-face shaving, in which duelling products are tested on opposite sides of a subject's face.[15] Gillette also employs 2700 off-site shavers who evaluate products at home.

Most products require some refinement based on the results of laboratory and use tests. A second stage of development often takes place before test marketing.

Test marketing

After products and marketing programs have been developed, they are usually tested in the marketplace. **Test marketing** is the limited introduction of a product and a marketing program to determine the reactions of potential customers in a market situation. Test marketing allows management to evaluate alternative strategies and to assess how well the various aspects of the marketing mix fit together. Febreze, a spray that removes odours such as cigarette smoke or pet odours from garments, was test marketed in three cities in the United States, in 1996.[16] It has only recently been introduced into the Australian market.

The cities chosen as test sites should reflect market conditions in the new product's projected market area. Yet no 'magic city' exists that can universally represent market conditions, and a product's success in one city doesn't guarantee that it will be a nationwide hit. When selecting test market cities, researchers should therefore find locations where the demographics and purchasing habits mirror the overall market. The company should also have good distribution in test cities. Moreover, test locations should be isolated from the media. If the TV stations in a particular market reach a very large area outside that market, the advertising used for the test product may pull in many consumers from outside the market. The product may then appear more successful than it really is. Exhibit 7.2 provides a useful checklist of criteria for selecting test markets.

test marketing
The limited introduction of a product and a marketing program to determine the reactions of potential customers in a market situation.

Exhibit 7.2
Checklist for selecting test markets
In choosing a test market, many criteria need to be considered, especially the following:

- Similarity to planned distribution outlets
- Relative isolation from other cities
- Availability of advertising media that will cooperate
- Diversified cross-section of ages, religions, cultural-societal preferences, etc.
- No atypical purchasing habits
- Representative population size
- Typical per capita income
- Good record as a test city, but not overly used
- Not easily 'jammed' by competitors
- Stability of year-round sales
- No dominant television station; multiple newspapers, magazines and radio stations
- Availability of retailers that will cooperate
- Availability of research and audit services
- Freedom from unusual influences, such as one industry's dominance or heavy tourism

The high costs of test marketing

Test marketing frequently takes one year or longer and costs can exceed $1 million. Some products remain in test markets even longer. McDonald's spent 12 years developing and testing salads before introducing them. Despite the cost, many firms believe it is a lot better to fail in a test market than in a national introduction.

Because test marketing is so expensive, some companies don't test line extensions of well-known brands. For example, because the Nescafé brand is well known, Nestlé faced little risk in distributing its instant decaffeinated coffee nationally. Consolidated Foods' Kitchen of Sara Lee followed the same approach in the United States with its frozen croissants.

The high cost of test marketing is not purely financial. One unavoidable problem is that test marketing exposes the new product and its marketing mix to competitors before its introduction. Thus, the element of surprise is lost. Competitors can also sabotage, or 'jam', a testing program by introducing their own sales promotion, pricing or advertising campaign. The purpose is to hide or distort the normal conditions that the testing firm might expect in the market. Plax and Plaq, two mouthwash products, went head-to-head during their market trials conducted in South Australia. When one of the manufacturers heard of the other's market trial, they developed a new product and launched it in the trial market area during the trial period.

Alternatives to test marketing

Many firms are looking for cheaper, faster, safer alternatives to traditional test marketing. In the early 1980s, Information Resources Inc. in the United States pioneered one alternative: single-source research using supermarket scanner data (discussed in Chapter 5). A typical supermarket scanner test costs about $300 000. Another alternative to traditional test marketing is **simulated (laboratory) market testing**. Advertising and other promotional materials for several

AltaVista on-line

What can you find out on the Internet about test marketing? Use the AltaVista search engine and type in 'Test marketing'.
www.altavista.com.au

simulated (laboratory) market testing
Presentation of advertising and other promotional materials for several products, including a test product, to members of the product's target market.

products, including the test product, are shown to members of the product's target market. These people are then taken to shop at either a mock store or a real store, where their purchases are recorded. Shopper behaviour, including repeat purchasing, is monitored to assess the product's likely performance under true market conditions. Research firms offer simulated market tests for $25 000 to $100 000, compared to $1 million or more for full-scale test marketing.

Despite these alternatives, most firms still consider test marketing essential for most new products. The high price of failure simply prohibits the widespread introduction of most new products without testing. Sometimes, however, when risks of failure are estimated to be low, it is better to skip test marketing and move directly from development to commercialisation.

Commercialisation

The final stage in the new-product development process is **commercialisation**, the decision to market a product. The decision to commercialise the product sets several tasks in motion: ordering production materials and equipment, starting production, building inventories, shipping the product to field distribution points, training the sales team, announcing the new product to the trade, and promoting the product to potential customers.

commercialisation
The decision to market a product.

The time from the initial commercialisation decision to the product's actual introduction varies. It can range from a few weeks for simple products that use existing equipment, to several years for technical products that require custom manufacturing equipment.

The total cost of development and initial introduction can be staggering. Recall from the story at the beginning of this chapter that it now costs approximately US$10 million to develop a computer game from scratch and even then there is no guarantee of success.[17]

For some products, a well-planned Internet campaign can provide new-product information for people who are looking for the solutions that a particular new product offers. Attempting to reach customers when they need a product is much more cost-effective and efficient than communicating with a target market that may eventually have a need for the product.[18]

Despite the high cost of developing and testing new products, as mentioned in the opening section of this chapter, 90 per cent of all new products fail. Products fail for a number of reasons. One common reason is that they simply don't offer any discernible benefit compared to existing products.[19] Another commonly cited factor in new-product failures is a poor match between product features and customer desires. For example, there are telephone systems on the market with over 700 different functions, although the average user is happy with just 10 functions.[20] Other reasons for failure include overestimation of market size, incorrect positioning, a price too high or too low, inadequate distribution, poor promotion, or simply a product that is inferior to its competitors.

Failure can be a matter of degree. Absolute failure occurs when a company cannot recoup its development, marketing and production costs. The product actually loses money for the company. A relative product failure results when the product returns a profit but fails to achieve sales, profit or market-share goals.

High costs and other risks of developing and testing new products don't stop many companies, such as Colgate-Palmolive, Campbell's Soup, Arnott's and Unilever, from actively developing and introducing new products.

The most important factor in successful new-product introduction is a good match between the product and market needs – as the marketing concept would predict. Successful new products deliver a meaningful and perceivable benefit to a sizeable number of people or organisations and are different in some meaningful way from their intended substitutes.[21] Firms that routinely experience success in new-product introductions tend to share the following characteristics:

- A history of carefully listening to customers
- An obsession with producing the best product possible
- A vision of what the market will be like in the future
- Strong leadership
- A commitment to new-product development
- A team approach to new-product development.[22]

Product life cycles

3 Explain the concept of product life cycles

product life cycle
A concept that provides a way to trace the stages of a product's acceptance, from its introduction (birth) to its decline (death).

product category
All brands that satisfy a particular type of need.

The product life cycle (PLC) is one of the most familiar concepts in marketing. Few other general concepts have been so widely discussed. Although some researchers have challenged the theoretical basis and managerial value of the PLC, most believe it has great potential as a marketing management tool.

The **product life cycle** concept provides a way to trace the stages of a product's acceptance, from its introduction (birth) to its decline (death). As Exhibit 7.3 shows, a product progresses through four major stages: introduction, growth, maturity and decline. Note that the product life cycle illustrated does not refer to any one brand; rather, it refers to the life cycle for a product category or product class. A **product category** includes all brands that satisfy a particular type of need. Product categories include passenger cars, cigarettes, soft drinks and coffee.

The time a product spends in any one stage of the life cycle may vary dramatically. Some products, such as fad items, move through the entire cycle in weeks. Others, such as electric washing machines and dryers, stay in the maturity stage for decades. Exhibit 7.3 illustrates the typical life cycle for a consumer durable good, such as a washer or dryer. In contrast, Exhibit 7.4 illustrates typical life cycles for styles (such as formal, business or casual clothing), fashions (such as miniskirts or stirrup pants) and fads (such as leopard-print clothing). Changes in a product, its uses, its image or its positioning can extend that product's life cycle.

Exhibit 7.3
Four stages of the product life cycle

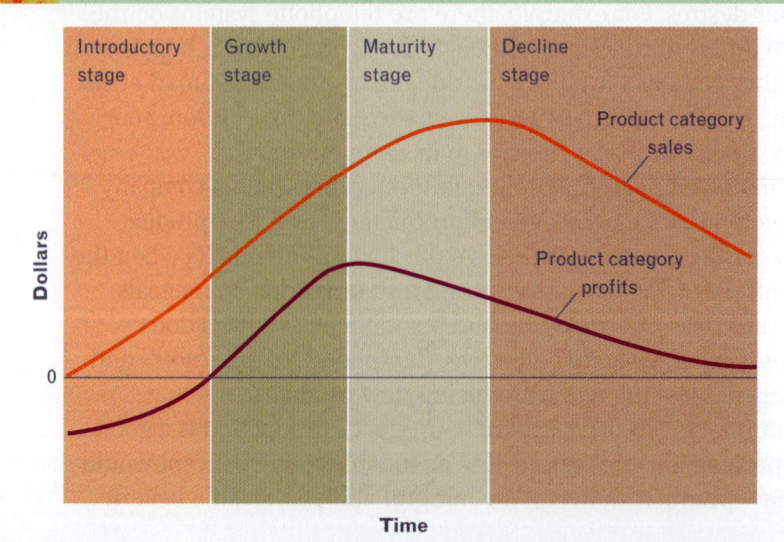

Exhibit 7.4
Product life cycles for styles, fashions and fads

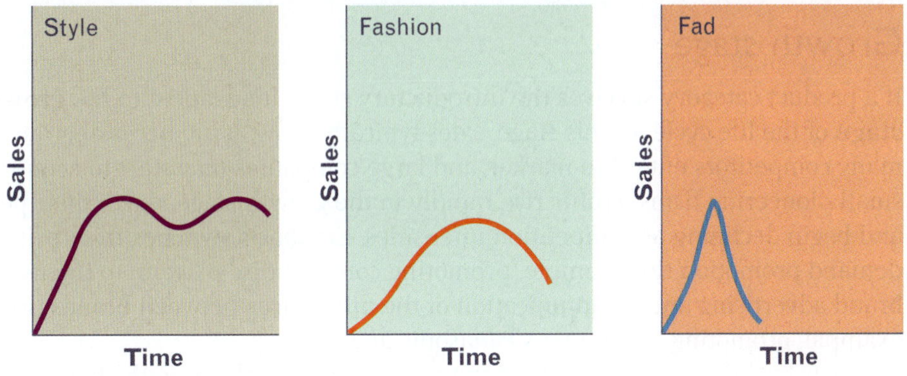

Style — Sales vs Time

Fashion — Sales vs Time

Fad — Sales vs Time

The product life cycle concept does not tell managers the length of a product's life cycle or its duration in any stage. It does not dictate marketing strategy. It is simply a tool to help marketers to forecast future events and suggest appropriate strategies.

Introductory stage

The **introductory stage** of the product life cycle represents the full-scale launch of a new product into the marketplace. Computer databases for personal use, room-deodorising air-conditioning filters and wind-powered home electric generators are all product categories that have recently entered the product life cycle. A high failure rate, little competition, frequent product modification and limited distribution typify the introduction stage of the PLC.

Marketing costs in the introductory stage are normally high for several reasons. High dealer margins are often needed to obtain adequate distribution, and incentives are needed to get consumers to try the new product. Advertising expenses are high because of the need to educate consumers about the new product's benefits. Production costs are also often high in this stage, as product and manufacturing flaws are identified and corrected, and efforts are undertaken to develop mass-production economies.

As Exhibit 7.3 illustrates, sales normally increase slowly during the introductory stage. Moreover, profits are usually negative because of research and development costs, factory tooling and high introduction costs. The length of the introductory phase is largely determined by product characteristics, such as the product's advantages over substitute products, the educational effort required to make the product known and management's commitment of resources to market the new item. A short introductory period is usually preferred to help reduce the impact of negative earnings and cash flows. As soon as the product gets off the ground, the financial burden should begin to diminish. Also, a short introduction helps to dispel some of the uncertainty regarding whether or not the new product will be successful.

Promotion strategy in the introductory stage focuses on developing product awareness and informing consumers about the product category's potential benefits. At this stage, the communication challenge is to stimulate primary demand – demand for the product in general, rather than for a specific brand. Intensive personal selling is often required to gain acceptance for the product among wholesalers and retailers. Promotion of convenience products often

introductory stage
The full-scale launch of a new product into the marketplace.

requires heavy consumer sampling and price discounting. Shopping and speciality products demand educational advertising and personal selling to the final consumer.

Growth stage

growth stage
The second stage of the product life cycle when sales typically grow at an increasing rate, many competitors enter the market, large companies may start acquiring small pioneering firms and profits are healthy.

If a product category survives the introductory stage, it advances to the **growth stage** of the life cycle. In this stage, sales typically grow at an increasing rate, many competitors enter the market, and large companies may start to acquire small pioneering firms. Profits rise rapidly in the growth stage, reach their peak, and begin declining as competition intensifies. Emphasis switches from primary demand promotion (for example, promoting compact disc players) to intensive brand advertising and communication of the differences between brands (for example, promoting Sony versus Panasonic and JVC).

Distribution becomes a major key to success during the growth stage, as well as in later stages. Manufacturers scramble to sign up dealers and distributors and to build long-term relationships. Without adequate distribution, it is impossible to establish a strong market position.

Maturity stage

maturity stage
A period during which sales increase at a decreasing rate.

A period during which sales increase at a decreasing rate signals the beginning of the **maturity stage** of the life cycle. New users cannot be added indefinitely, and sooner or later the market approaches saturation. Normally, this is the longest stage of the product life cycle. Many major household appliances are in the maturity stage of their life cycles.

For shopping products and many speciality products, annual models begin to appear during the maturity stage. Product lines are lengthened to appeal to additional market segments. Service and repair assume more important roles as manufacturers strive to distinguish their products from others. Product design changes tend to become stylistic (How can the product be made different?) rather than functional (How can the product be made better?).

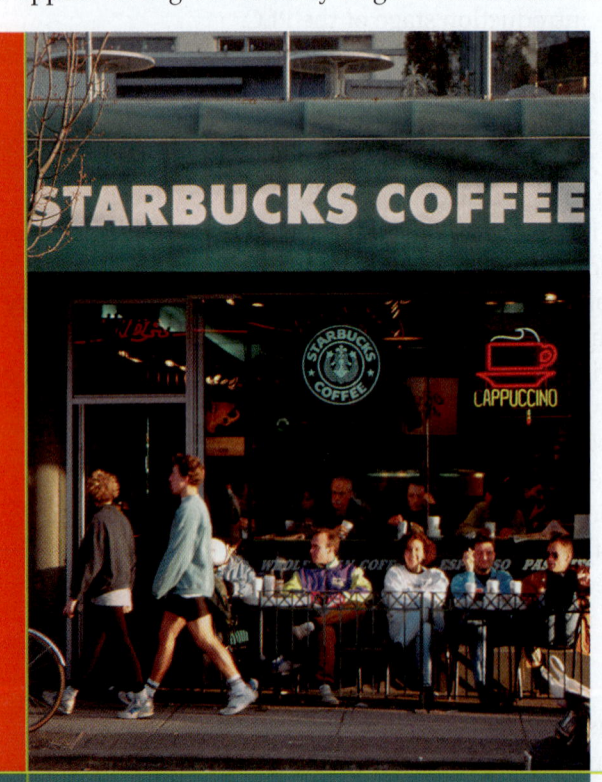

Mars on-line

Have a look at the Mars website and look at how the company has updated many of its products to compete in the maturity stage of the product life cycle. Note the repositioning of some products to maintain their appeal to the younger market segments.
www.mars.com.au

Coffee is an example of a product in the maturity stage where niche marketers have emerged. Starbucks, for example, targets its gourmet products at newer, younger, more affluent coffee drinkers.

As prices and profits continue to fall, marginal competitors start dropping out of the market. Dealer margins are reduced, resulting in less shelf space for mature items, lower dealer inventories and a general reluctance to promote the product. Thus, promotion to dealers often intensifies during this stage, in order to retain loyalty.

Heavy consumer promotion by the manufacturer is also required to maintain market share. Consider these well-known examples of competition in the maturity stage: the 'cola war' between Coke and Pepsi, the 'beer war' between Queensland's XXXX brand and Victoria's VB brand, and the 'burger war', which pitted market leader McDonald's against its challenger, Hungry Jack's.

Another characteristic of the maturity stage is the emergence of so-called niche marketers, which target narrow, well-defined and underserved segments of a market. Starbucks Coffee targets its gourmet line at the only segment of the coffee market that is growing: new, younger, more affluent coffee drinkers.

Decline stage

A long-run drop in sales signals the beginning of the **decline stage**. The rate of decline is governed by how rapidly consumer tastes change or substitute products are adopted. Many convenience products and fad items lose their market overnight, leaving large stocks of unsold items, such as designer jeans. Others die more slowly, like citizen band (CB) radios, analogue television sets and non-electronic wristwatches.

decline stage
A long-run drop in sales.

The acceptance and growth of the DVD is one example of this. Pioneer's AV general manager predicted that by the end of 2002, sales of DVDs would completely eclipse VHS sales, and this trend appeared to be consistent worldwide. At the end of 2002 nearly one-quarter of all Australian homes had a DVD player – more than double that of the year before. The falling price of the DVD, combined with its product advantages of clearer pictures, better sound, interactive menu navigation, and bonus material such as out-takes, commentaries, deleted scenes and alternative endings, have made this a popular new entertainment medium and led to the decline of VHS. This popularity has also spilled over into the movie rental market, where stores such as Video Ezy now devote much of their floor space to DVDs.[23]

Some firms have developed successful strategies for marketing products in the decline stage of the product life cycle. They eliminate all non-essential marketing expenses and let sales decline as more and more customers discontinue purchasing the products. Eventually, the product is withdrawn from the market.

Implications for marketing management

The product life cycle concept encourages marketing managers to plan so that they can take the initiative instead of reacting to past events. The product life cycle is especially useful as a predicting or forecasting tool. Because products pass through distinctive stages, it is often possible to estimate a product's location on the curve using historical data. Profits, like sales, tend to follow a predictable path over a product's life cycle. Exhibit 7.5 briefly summarises some typical marketing strategies during each stage of the product life cycle.

Exhibit 7.5
Typical marketing strategies during the product life cycle

Marketing mix strategy	Product life cycle stage			
	Introduction	**Growth**	**Maturity**	**Decline**
Product strategy	Limited number of models; frequent product modifications	Expanded number of models; frequent product modifications	Large number of models	Elimination of unprofitable models and brands
Distribution strategy	Distribution usually limited, depending on product; intensive efforts and high margins often needed to attract wholesalers and retailers	Expanded number of dealers; intensive efforts to establish long-term relationships with wholesalers and retailers	Extensive number of dealers; margins declining; intensive efforts to retain distributors and shelf space	Unprofitable outlets phased out
Promotion strategy	Develop product awareness; stimulate primary demand; use intensive personal selling to distributors; use samples and coupons for consumers	Stimulate selective demand; advertise brand aggressively	Stimulate selective demand; advertise brand aggressively; promote heavily to retain dealers and customers	Phase out all promotion
Pricing strategy	Prices are usually high to recover development costs	Prices begin to fall towards end of growth stage as result of competitive pressure	Prices continue to fall	Prices stabilise at relatively low level; small price rises are possible if competition is negligible

The spread of new products

4 Explain the diffusion process through which new products are adopted

Managers have a better chance of successfully marketing products if they understand how consumers learn about and adopt products. Even though you may have never before tried a new product, you can still ultimately become an **adopter** one day. An adopter is defined as a consumer who was happy enough with his or her trial experience with a product to want to use it again.

Diffusion of innovation

An **innovation** is a product perceived as new by a potential adopter. It really doesn't matter whether the product is 'new to the world' or some other category of new product. If it is new to a potential adopter, it is an innovation in that context. **Diffusion** is the process by which the adoption of an innovation spreads. Five categories of adopters participate in the diffusion process:

- *Innovators*: the first 2.5 per cent of all those who adopt the product. Innovators are eager to try new ideas and products, almost as an obsession. In addition to having higher incomes, they are more worldly and more active outside their community than non-innovators. They rely less on group norms and are more self-confident. Because they are well educated, they are more likely to get their information from scientific sources and experts. Innovators are characterised as being adventurous.

adopter
A consumer who was happy enough with his or her trial experience with a product to use it again.

innovation
A product perceived as new by a potential adopter.

diffusion
The process by which the adoption of an innovation spreads.

- *Early adopters*: the next 13.5 per cent to adopt the product. Although early adopters are not the very first, they do adopt early in the product's life cycle. Compared to innovators, they rely much more on group norms and values. They are also more oriented to the local community, in contrast to innovators' worldly outlook. Early adopters are more likely than innovators to be opinion leaders because of their closer affiliation with groups. The respect of others is a dominant characteristic of early adopters.
- *Early majority*: the next 34 per cent to adopt. The early majority weighs the pros and cons before adopting a new product. They are likely to collect more information and evaluate more brands than early adopters, therefore extending the adoption process. They rely on the group for information but are unlikely to be opinion leaders themselves. Instead, they tend to be opinion leaders' friends and neighbours. The early majority is an important link in the process of diffusing new ideas, because they are positioned between earlier and later adopters. A dominant characteristic of the early majority is deliberateness.
- *Late majority*: the next 34 per cent to adopt. The late majority adopts a new product because most of their friends have already adopted it. Because they also rely on group norms, their adoption stems from pressure to conform. This group tends to be older and below average in income and education. They depend mainly on word-of-mouth communication rather than on the mass media. The dominant characteristic of the late majority is scepticism.
- *Laggards*: the final 16 per cent to adopt. Like innovators, laggards don't rely on group norms. Their independence is rooted in their ties to tradition. Thus, the past heavily influences their decisions. By the time laggards adopt an innovation, it has probably become outmoded and replaced by something else. For example, they may have bought their first black-and-white TV set after colour television was already widely diffused. Laggards have the longest adoption time and the lowest socio-economic status. They tend to be suspicious of new products and alienated from a rapidly changing society. The dominant value of laggards is tradition. Marketers typically ignore laggards, who don't seem to be motivated by advertising or personal selling.

Exhibit 7.6 illustrates the diffusion of iPods globally. As you can see by the graph, iPod sales were good but not fantastic until about May 2003 when the third generation iPod was released which allowed a much larger audience of PC users to adopt the technology. Prior to this only Macintosh users could gain the benefits. It took Apple over a year and a half to hit the one million mark for sales. Only six months after this the second million was sold, and four months later (with the introduction of the iPod mini) another million units were sold. Importantly, Apple's sales milestones were achieved despite the continued introduction of cheaper alternatives by Creative, Dell and iRiver, among others. None of these companies' products appears to have significantly impacted the iPod's sales growth or undermined its perception as king of the digital music hill.[24]

Product characteristics and the rate of adoption

Five product characteristics can be used to predict and explain the rate of acceptance and diffusion of a new product:

- *Complexity*: the degree of difficulty involved in understanding and using a new product. The more complex the product, the slower is its diffusion. For instance, before many of their functions were automated, primarily hobbyists

3Com, Palm

on-line

Who do you think the adopters of PalmPilot organisers are? Read the 'Customer testimonials' on the 3Com website to help you decide who 3Com thinks are the innovators, the early majority and the late majority. What other clues on the site can help you to determine what kind of people are adopting PalmPilots?
www.palm.com.au/NewZealand/support/palmhandhelds.html

and professionals used 35mm cameras. They were just too complex for most people to learn to operate.

- *Compatibility*: the degree to which the new product is consistent with existing values and product knowledge, experience and current needs. Incompatible products diffuse more slowly than compatible products. For example, the introduction of contraceptives is incompatible in countries where religious beliefs discourage the use of birth control techniques.
- *Relative advantage*: the degree to which a product is perceived as superior to existing substitutes. For example, because it reduces cooking time, the microwave oven has a clear relative advantage over a conventional oven.
- *Observability*: the degree to which the benefits or other results of using the product can be observed by others and communicated to target customers. For example, fashion items and cars are highly visible and more observable than personal care items.
- *Trialability*: the degree to which a product can be tried on a limited basis. It is much easier to try a new toothpaste or breakfast cereal than a new car or personal computer. Demonstrations in showrooms and test drives are different from in-home trial use. To stimulate trials, marketers use free-sampling programs, tasting displays and small package sizes.

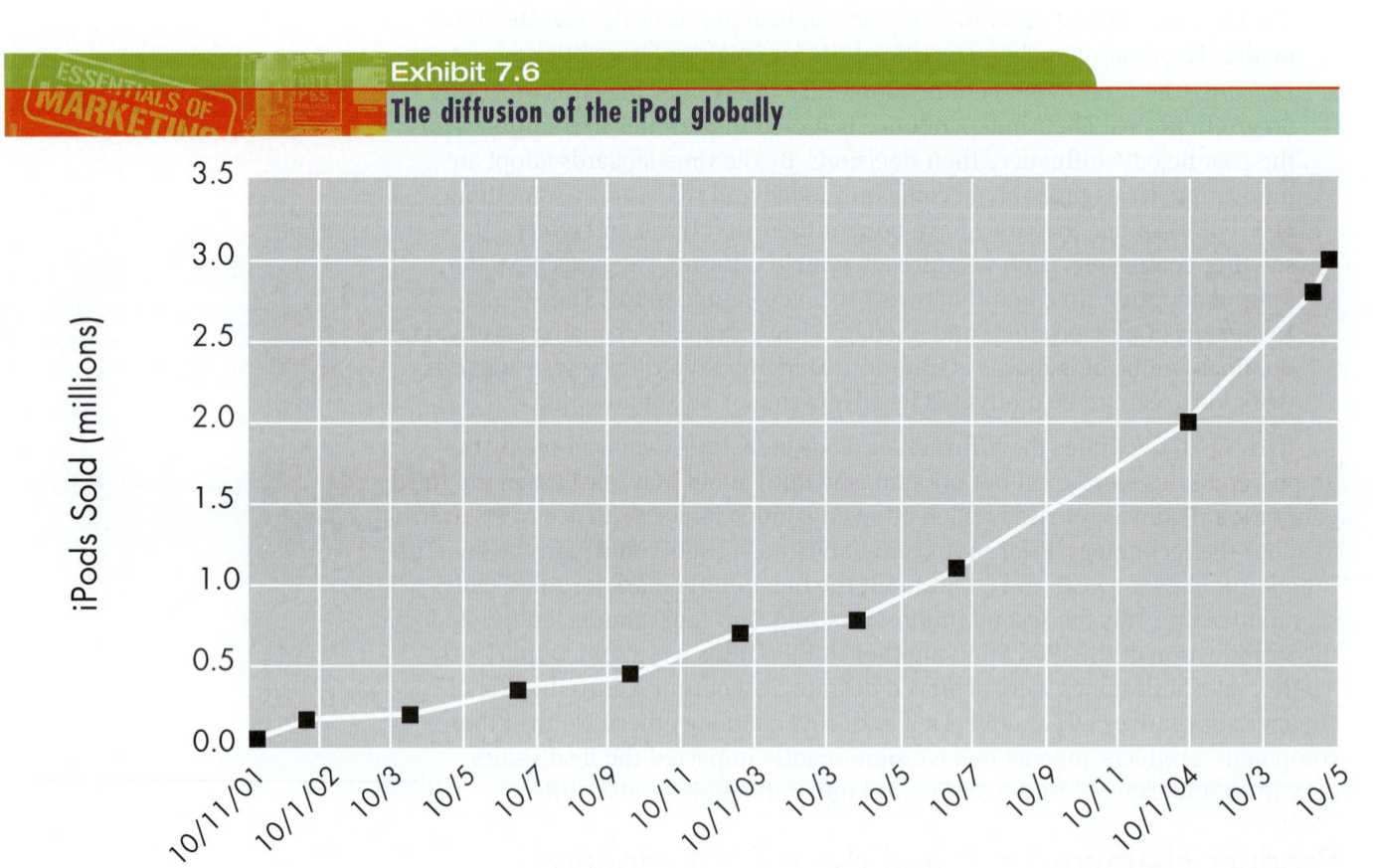

Exhibit 7.6

The diffusion of the iPod globally

Source: www.ilounge.com

Marketing implications of the adoption process

Two types of communication aid the diffusion process: word-of-mouth communication among consumers and **marketing communication** from marketers to consumers. *Word-of-mouth communication* within and across groups speeds the diffusion process. Opinion leaders discuss new products with their followers and with other opinion leaders. Marketers must therefore ensure that opinion leaders have the types of information desired in the media they use. Suppliers of some products, such as professional and health-care services, rely almost solely on word-of-mouth communication for new business.

The second type of communication aiding the diffusion process is *communication directly from the marketer to potential adopters*. Messages directed towards early adopters should normally use different appeals than messages directed towards the early majority, the late majority or the laggards. Early adopters are more important than innovators because they make up a larger group, are more socially active and are usually opinion leaders.

> **marketing communication**
> Information passed on from marketers to the public, including consumers, via a range of promotional activities.

Exhibit 7.7
Relationship between the diffusion process and the product life cycle

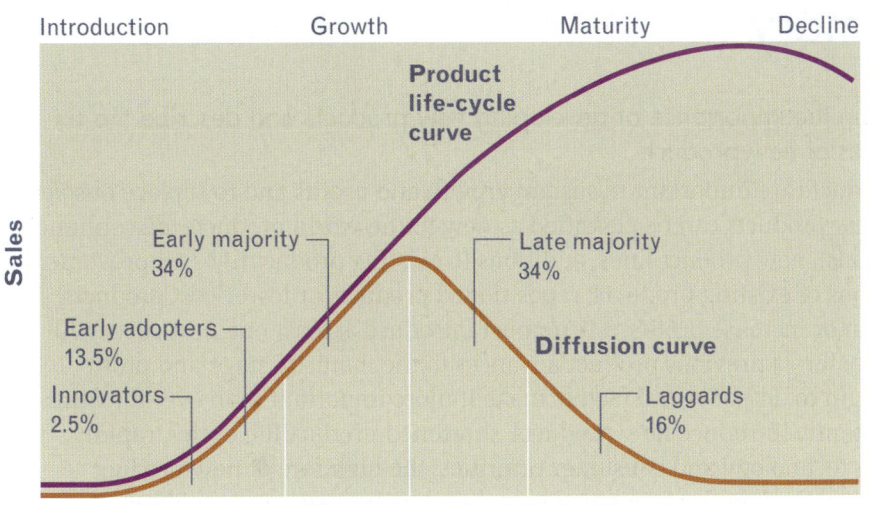

Diffusion curve: Percentage of total adoptions by category
Product life-cycle curve: Time

Stages: Introduction | Growth | Maturity | Decline

- Innovators 2.5%
- Early adopters 13.5%
- Early majority 34%
- Late majority 34%
- Laggards 16%

As the focus of a promotional campaign shifts from early adopters to the early majority and the late majority, marketers should study the dominant characteristics, buying behaviour and media characteristics of these target markets. Then they should revise messages and media strategy to fit. The diffusion model helps to guide marketers in developing and implementing promotion strategy. Exhibit 7.7 shows the relationships between the adopter categories and stages of the product life cycle. Note that the various categories of adopters first buy products in different stages of the product life cycle. Almost all sales in the maturity and decline stages represent repeat purchasing.

Connect it

Look back at the story at the beginning of the chapter about how the Chrysler group is using the Internet to streamline the new-product development process. You now know that involving design production, finance and other areas – including outside suppliers in the new-product development process – is called simultaneous product development. The process reduces product development time by keeping everyone up to date on design and development changes and allows a stamping engineer for example, to watch what is happening so that he or she can make sure the company's stamping plants (where multistorey-high presses stamp sheets of metal) can actually make the body that designers select. The Internet has been particularly helpful to Chrysler because the industry is very complex. Web technology has linked areas within the company that must communicate with one another and that previously had been using different information systems. In addition, the Covisint system will help coordinate activities with suppliers. Other firms such as Colgate Palmolive are also using the Internet to implement simultaneous product development processes.

Summary

1 Explain the importance of developing new products and describe the six categories of new products.

New products are important to sustain growth and profits and to replace obsolete items. New products can be classified as new-to-the-world products (discontinuous innovations), new product lines, additions to existing product lines, improvements or revisions of existing products, repositioned products or lower-cost products. To sustain or increase profits, a firm must introduce at least one new successful product before a previous product advances to the maturity stage and profit levels begin to drop. Several factors make it more important than ever for firms to consistently introduce new products: shortened product life cycles, rapidly changing technology and consumer priorities, the high rate of new-product failures, and the length of time needed to implement new-product ideas.

2 Explain the steps in the new-product development process.

First, a firm forms a new-product strategy by outlining the characteristics and roles of future products. Then new-product ideas are generated by customers, employees, distributors, competitors, and internal research and development personnel. Once a product idea has survived initial screening by an appointed screening group, it undergoes business analysis to determine its potential profitability. If a product concept seems viable, it progresses into the development phase, in which the technical and economic feasibility of the manufacturing process is evaluated. The development phase also includes laboratory and use testing of a product for performance and safety. Following initial testing and refinement, most products are introduced in a test market to evaluate consumer response and marketing strategies. Finally, test market successes are propelled into full commercialisation. The commercialisation process means starting up production, building inventories, shipping to distributors, training a sales team, announcing the product to the trade and advertising to consumers.

Chapter 7 Developing and managing products

3 Explain the concept of product life cycles.
All product categories undergo a life cycle with four stages: introduction, growth, maturity and decline. The rate at which products move through these stages varies dramatically. Marketing managers use the product life cycle concept as an analytical tool to forecast a product's future and devise effective marketing strategies.

4 Explain the diffusion process through which new products are adopted.
The diffusion process is the spread of a new product from its producer to ultimate adopters. Adopters in the diffusion process belong to five categories: innovators, early adopters, the early majority, the late majority and laggards. Product characteristics that affect the rate of adoption include product complexity, compatibility with existing social values, relative advantage over existing substitutes, visibility and trialability. The diffusion process is facilitated by word-of-mouth communication and communication from marketers to consumers.

Define it

adopter 236
brainstorming 226
business analysis 227
commercialisation 231
concept test 226
decline stage 235
development 227
diffusion 236
growth stage 234
innovation 236
introductory stage 233
marketing communication 239
maturity stage 234
new product 221
new-product strategy 223
product category 232
product development 224
product life cycle 232
screening 226
simulated (laboratory) market testing 230
test marketing 229

Review it

1 Which of the following types of new products are best described as existing products targeted at new markets?
   a Additions to existing product lines
   b Improvements or revisions of existing products
   c Repositioned products
   d New product lines

2 Evaluation of a new-product idea before any prototype is created is known as
   a Research and development
   b A concept test
   c Development
   d Brainstorming

3 During which stage of the new-product development process are preliminary figures for costs, sales and profits estimated?
   a Idea screening
   b Development
   c Business analysis
   d Test marketing

4 Which of the following characteristics of firms is not a common reason for successful new-product introductions?
   a Avoids team approaches to new product development
   b Avoids developing products that are not the best product possible
   c Has a history of carefully listening to customers
   d Has a vision of what the market may be like in the future

5 According to the diffusion process model, which of the following categories of adopters is the first group to accept a new product?
   a Innovators
   b Early adopters
   c Early majority
   d Laggards

6 Five characteristics affect the rate of acceptance of a new product. _____ is the degree to which a product is perceived as superior to existing substitutes.

    a Compatibility
    b Relative advantage
    c Complexity
    d Trialability

7 In the stage _____ of the product life cycle, sales grow at an increasing rate, many competitors enter the market and profits rise rapidly.
    a Introduction
    b Growth
    c Maturity
    d Decline

8 Primary demand promotion must occur during which of the following stages of the product life cycle?
    a Introductory
    b Growth
    c Maturity
    d Decline

9 The real purpose of using a formal new-product development process is to filter out unworkable product ideas.
    a True
    b False

10 The time a product spends in any one stage of the product life cycle does not typically vary from item to item.
    a True
    b False

Check the Answer Key to see how well you understood the material. More detailed discussion and writing questions and a video case related to this chapter are found in the Student Resources CD-ROM.

Apply it

1 List the advantages of simultaneous product development.

2 In small groups, brainstorm ideas for a new wet-weather clothing line. What type of product would potential customers want and need? Prepare and deliver a brief presentation to your class.

3 You are a marketing manager for Nike. Your department has come up with the idea of manufacturing a cricket bat for use in universities around the country. Assuming you are in the business analysis stage, write a brief analysis based on the questions in the business analysis section of the chapter.

4 What are the main disadvantages of test marketing and how might they be avoided?

5 Describe some products whose adoption rates have been affected by complexity, compatibility, relative advantage, observability and/or trialability.

6 What type of adopter behaviour do you typically follow? Explain.

7 Place the personal computer on the product life cycle curve, and give reasons for placing it where you do.

8 How could information from customer orders at the following site help the company's marketers to plan new-product developments? www.sizzler.com.au

9 How is customer input affecting the development of the product range at Nestlé? www.nestle.com.au

Try it

Joyce Strand removed the newest batch of home-spun wool from the dye bath where she was colouring it before knitting it into home-made jumpers and vests that she would later sell to the Highland Craft Store. To her surprise, she had added too much dye to the bath, and the wool had become a completely different colour than she expected. The darker dye had also accentuated the chunky nature of the home-spun wool, making some parts lighter than others. Although the colour and apparent texture were much different, the wool still had its soft feel, so Joyce decided to use it anyway. She made three jumpers and two vests from it, which she then took to the Highland Craft Store to let the customers decide whether they liked the new look.

The new look became a huge success in the store. Because of her recent success, Joyce began experimenting with other different colours and textures of wool that she makes into new items to sell at the store. Realising that innovation can be very profitable; Joyce now actively looks for new ways to please her customers.

Questions

1. How might Joyce ensure that proper attention is paid to developing new products?
2. What factors should she be aware of that might lead to product failure?
3. Prepare a list of criteria similar to those in the Entrepreneurial insights box in this chapter that might be used to evaluate Joyce's new-product ideas.

Watch it

AutoCite: Traffic ticket and parking system

For decades, the writing of a ticket was only the first step in a long manual process. An officer dropped off the ticket at the station, and from there it went to the records department for sorting and batching. It was then transmitted to the judicial system and data processing. The handwritten information was keypunched into the mainframe and then returned for filing. At each step, tickets were flagged for errors, but mistakes regularly surfaced, resulting in an inefficient process. This situation prompted companies such as Epson, Grid, Husky, Symbol and Telxon to market general-purpose, hand-held computers to police departments in the United States. But these devices required officers to wear a clumsy printer on their belts or strapped over their shoulders, and such computer configurations were not designed for fine management.

Enforcement Technology, Inc. (ETEC) recognised an unsatisfied need and set out to develop a new product that would deal the final blow to the bulky, inefficient computers. ETEC focused on developing a unique product that, once introduced, would outdate the competition. The new product, called AutoCite, is a portable, lightweight, hand-held computer with a built-in printer, specialised for issuing traffic tickets and parking fines.

ETEC's new product strategy was to carve out a market niche through specialisation. Competitors sold general-purpose computers – hardware only, requiring customers to purchase obligatory software from other companies. To distinguish AutoCite from other brands, ETEC produced a complete package of hardware and software. In addition, ETEC provided product training and totally maintained AutoCite at every level. Customers found it highly convenient to look to a single supplier for both sales and service. AutoCite's success encouraged ETEC to analyse other needs in the fining process and develop the technology to meet them. The result is a fully automated system of products that work in harmony. AutoCite is now updated to include a magnetic stripe and bar code reading capability so that information is entered automatically from the magnetic stripe on the back of a driver's licence. Using a pre-stored 'hotsheet', AutoCite alerts the officer with 'Wants or Warrants' keyed to the driver's licence number. AutoPROCESS processes fines through on-line court and hearing scheduling. AutoALARM is a false alarm management system, which includes fine issuance computers, window decal distribution, alarm permit updates and payments, and billing statements. The AutoCite Patrol Car System is an AutoCite unit that adapts to the notebook (laptop) computer in a patrol car to issue traffic tickets; it is particularly useful for issuing moving fines and preparing interviews and crime, accident and arrest reports. This product line is fully supported by ETEC's cash management and unpaid fine collection services. The company has parking enforcement centres to process in- and out-of-state tickets for its customers and has implemented a follow-up service to collect unpaid fines. But these services are only part of the benefits. Cities, universities and agencies are saving money in processing costs and recovery of unpaid fines. In one year, ETEC collected US$600 000 for the city of San Diego by taking a backlog of 60 000 fines and going back as far as two years for collections. Now ETEC processes about 3000 unpaid out-of-state parking fines each month for roughly US$50 000 in new revenue. With results like this, AutoCite can pay for itself within a year. Revenue generation is complemented by an additional benefit: the use of AutoCite has been shown to reduce the indirect costs associated with low staff productivity. Data entry, which used to eat into staff and clerical time, is now a memory in departments and agencies. And the error rate is smaller. There is also an intangible benefit – better employee morale. In Long Beach, California, officers have been pleased with ETEC's reliable computers and high-quality customer service. Their increased efficiency has led to greater job satisfaction, which in turn has positively affected morale on the entire police force. By creating a fully automated fine management process, ETEC has police departments and agencies in the United States and abroad singing its praises. Adopted by over 300 agencies in the United States, over 50 colleges and universities, and agencies in eight other countries, the AutoCite full-service solution for fine management is well positioned to build on its resounding success.

Questions

1. Describe the product development process for AutoCite.
2. Why has AutoCite been successful?
3. How did ETEC develop the product line?
4. What strategy should ETEC follow in introducing new products for law enforcement?

Suggested reading

Press Kit: Enforcement Technology, Inc.

© 2003 Nelson Australia Pty Limited

Chapter 7 Developing and managing products

Click it

Online reading

INFOTRAC® COLLEGE EDITION
For additional readings and review on developing and managing products, explore InfoTrac® College Edition, your online library. Go to: www.infotrac-college.com and search for any of the InfoTrac key terms listed below:
- test marketing
- product life cycle
- consumer adopter
- product diffusion

Answer key

1. *Answer*: c, p. 221 *Rationale*: Repositioned products are existing products targeted at new markets or market segments.

2. *Answer*: b, p. 226 *Rationale*: A concept test evaluates a new-product idea before a prototype is created by gathering consumer reactions to descriptions and visual representations of a proposed product.

3. *Answer*: c, p. 227 *Rationale*: Such figures are typically first calculated during business analysis. The newness of the product, the size of the market and the nature of competition all affect the accuracy of these projections.

4. *Answer*: a, p. 232 *Rationale*: Research has indicated that pursuing a team approach to new-product development is an important characteristic in a firm's success with new-product development.

5. *Answer*: a, p. 236 *Rationale*: Innovators are the most eager to try new products and are characterised as being adventurous.

6. *Answer*: b, p. 237-8 *Rationale*: Relative advantage is the degree to which a new product is seen as having a clear advantage over existing products.

7. *Answer*: b, p. 234 *Rationale*: Competition intensifies, sales grow rapidly and profits grow to their peak during the growth stage of the product life cycle.

8. *Answer*: a, p. 233 *Rationale*: Promotion expenses are often high in the introductory stage of the product life cycle because marketers must educate consumers about the new product's benefits.

9. *Answer*: a, p. 226 *Rationale*: The new-product development process provides guidelines to the firm for generating, screening and evaluating new-product ideas.

10. *Answer*: b, p. 232 *Rationale*: The time a product spends in any single stage of the product life cycle may vary dramatically. Some products move through an entire cycle in weeks; others stay in a single stage for decades.

Marketing channels and logistics decisions

CHAPTER EIGHT

LEARNING OBJECTIVES

After studying this chapter, you should be able to

1. Explain what a marketing channel is and why intermediaries are needed
2. Define the types of channel intermediaries and describe their functions and activities
3. Describe the channel structures for consumer and business-to-business products and discuss alternative channel arrangements
4. Discuss the issues that influence channel strategy
5. Explain channel leadership, conflict and partnering
6. Discuss logistics and supply chain management and their evolution into distribution practice
7. Discuss the concept of balancing logistics service and cost
8. Describe the integrated functions of the supply chain
9. Discuss new technology and emerging trends in logistics
10. Identify the special problems and opportunities associated with distribution in retail organisations
11. Identify the special problems and opportunities associated with distribution in service organisations
12. Identify the special problems and opportunities associated with distribution in an electronic environment

Shell Oil Products, a division of Shell Oil Company, used to buy all of its personal computers from Compaq Computers or IBM. In 1997, however, it switched its allegiance and its US$26 million in annual PC purchases to Dell Computer. The reason had less to do with the computers than with the way Dell sells them. Unlike Compaq and IBM, Dell sells directly to customers, eliminating distributors and resellers who bring up the price and lengthen the time it takes to get the hardware. On top of that, Dell only sells custom-made machines built to the customer's exact specifications. Its competitors build machines first and then wait for customers to order a particular model.

Dell Computer, which began as a mail-order company started out of founder Michael Dell's university dorm room, deploys a direct sales team to cut out the retailers, speciality stores and distributors who can drive prices up. The success of Dell's marketing model – selling through direct sales channels, building custom-made PCs and streamlining the distribution process – is well known and amply reflected in its stock price. Since 1990, Dell stock has increased by 29 600 per cent! In 2000, Dell had 7.4 per cent of the Australian market for PCs, worth approximately A$270 million.[1] Today, the US$13 billion company is the world's biggest direct seller of computers.

Dell Computer on-line

Visit Dell Computer's website. How is its site set up to sell in marketing channels directly to the customer? www.dell.com.au

To really understand Dell's eye-popping growth, you need only to look at how fully it exploits the model of selling custom-made machines directly to buyers. First, Dell has no finished stock because PCs are built on demand. As soon as a computer is built, it is immediately shipped off to the customer. The whole process from phone call to loading on to a delivery truck takes just 36 hours. Orders are instantly relayed to one of Dell's three plants in the United States, Malaysia or Ireland. After the order is received, a Dell PC can be custom-built to the customer's exact specifications, have its software installed, be tested and then packed in eight hours.

Second, Dell can ship machines with the latest high-margin components. Because it employs close relationships with component suppliers such as Intel for chips and Maxtor for hard drives, these components arrive just in time to be installed in its machines, virtually eliminating any raw materials stockpiling that can quickly become obsolete in the fast-changing computer industry. This saves money, too, because component prices tend to fall many times throughout the year.

Third, unlike IBM and Compaq, which use resellers to sell their PCs, Dell has direct contact with its customers. If customers start requesting an 40-gigabyte drive, Dell knows immediately what consumers are asking for and can make immediate procurement decisions. Additionally, knowing its customers gives Dell market intelligence the next time customers have hardware needs or want to upgrade their entire stock of computers. Fourth, selling directly means that Dell isn't being paid by resellers but by large organisations such as Boeing, Ford and Shell Oil. Not surprisingly, Dell receivables have a great credit rating – Dell typically has its money in the bank before the computer is even built.

Dell's latest drive is boosting sales over the Internet, the ultimate direct channel. The company is already the biggest on-line seller of computers, selling more than US$6 million in computers a day from its website. Dell has also become one of the first personal computer suppliers in China to conduct electronic commerce through its virtual store on the Internet.

Compaq and IBM are dabbling in direct sales, but risk losing relationships with dealers if they go too far. Compaq and IBM depend on resellers for 90 per cent of their sales, and resellers can easily retaliate if a supplier gets too aggressive with selling direct. Giving in to this reality, Compaq and IBM have been trying to make their three-step distribution process – manufacturer to distributor to reseller to customer – work as efficiently as the one-step model that Dell uses. Both have enlisted distributors to do part of the assembly of their computers as a way to lower costs. Distributors can also assemble customised PCs based on what customers want, as Dell does. However, because they must still pay dealers, they must either charge slightly more or accept lower profit margins.

What advantages does Dell receive from selling in marketing channels directly to the customer?

Could Compaq or IBM expand their use of direct channels, as did Dell, without alienating their current network of resellers?

What areas of distribution, such as stock, materials handling or transportation, could be streamlined to help Dell's competitors compete more effectively?

Similar questions will be addressed throughout the chapter discussion on marketing channels and logistics.

Marketing channels

The term *channel* comes from the Latin word *canalis*, which means canal. A marketing channel can be viewed as a large canal or pipeline through which products, their ownership, communication, financing and payment, and accompanying risk flow to the consumer. Formally, a **marketing channel** (also called a **channel of distribution**) is a group of organisations that agree to distribute a product from the point of product origin to the consumer, the final consumption destination.

Many different types of organisations participate in marketing channels. **Channel members** (also called intermediaries, resellers and middlemen) negotiate with one another, buy and sell products, and help the change of ownership between buyer and seller in the course of moving the product from the producer into the hands of the final consumer. As products move through the marketing channel, channel members provide economies to the distribution process in the form of specialisation and division of labour, overcoming discrepancies, and contact efficiency. These terms may sound a little daunting if you have not studied economics, so let's now investigate.

Providing specialisation and division of labour

Consider 10 people attempting to complete a project by themselves. They won't master any particular task making up the project and may take a long time to complete it. The concept of specialisation and division of labour tells us that if those same 10 people break the project down into 10 tasks, each selecting one task to become a specialist in, then they will create greater efficiency in time and costs incurred than if they developed the project individually.

Manufacturers achieve economies of scale with efficient equipment that is capable of producing large quantities of a single product. (You may have heard of 'production runs' or 'batches in production'.) Marketing channels can also attain economies of scale through specialisation and division of labour by aiding producers who lack the motivation, financing or expertise to market directly to end users or consumers. In some cases, as with most consumer convenience goods such as soft drinks, the cost of marketing directly to millions of consumers – taking and shipping individual orders – is prohibitive. For this reason, producers use channel members such as wholesalers and retailers to do what the producers are not equipped to do or what channel members are better prepared to do. Channel members can do some things more efficiently than producers can, because they have built good relationships with their customers. Therefore, their specialised expertise enhances the overall performance of the channel. This is why we don't see outlets owned by Kellogg or Levi Strauss.

Overcoming discrepancies

Marketing channels also aid in overcoming discrepancies of quantity, assortment, time and space created by economies of scale in production. For example, assume that Buttercup Bakeries can efficiently produce its McDonald's muffins at a rate of 5000 units in a typical day. Not even the most ardent muffin fan could consume that amount in a year, much less in a day. The quantity produced to achieve low unit costs has created a **discrepancy of quantity**, which is the difference between the amount of product produced and the amount an end user wants to buy. By storing the product and distributing it in the appropriate amounts,

---

1 Explain what a marketing channel is and why intermediaries are needed

marketing channel (channel of distribution)
Set of interdependent organisations that facilitate the transfer of ownership as products move from producer to business user or consumer.

channel members
All parties in the marketing channel that negotiate with one another, buy and sell products, and facilitate the change of ownership between buyer and seller in the course of moving the product from the manufacturer into the hands of the final consumer.

discrepancy of quantity
Difference between the amount of product produced and the amount a customer wants to buy.

discrepancy of assortment
Lack of all the items a customer needs to receive full satisfaction from a product or products.

marketing channels overcome quantity discrepancies by making products available in the quantities that consumers desire.

Mass production creates not only discrepancies of quantity but also discrepancies of assortment. A **discrepancy of assortment** occurs when a consumer does not have all of the items needed to receive full satisfaction from a product. For muffins to have maximum satisfaction, several other products are required to complete the assortment. At the very least, most people want a container and napkin. Others might want a plate, butter and syrup, or they might add orange juice, coffee, cream, milk, sugar, eggs and bacon or sausage to their order. Although Freshstart Bakeries Australia, part of the Goodman Fielder group, is a large company, it does not come close to providing all the things needed for the McDonald's range of products. To overcome discrepancies of assortment, marketing channels assemble in one place many of the products necessary to complete a consumer's needed assortment.

temporal (time) discrepancy
Difference between when a product is produced and when a customer is ready to buy it.

A **temporal (time) discrepancy** is created when a product is produced but a consumer is not ready to buy it. Marketing channels overcome temporal discrepancies by maintaining stocks in anticipation of demand. For example, manufacturers of seasonal merchandise such as Christmas decorations are in operation all year, even though consumer demand is concentrated during certain months of the year.

spatial (place) discrepancy
Difference between the location of the producer and the location of widely scattered markets.

Furthermore, because mass production requires many potential buyers, markets are usually scattered over large geographic regions, creating a **spatial (place) discrepancy**. Often, global or at least nationwide markets are needed to absorb the outputs of mass producers. Marketing channels overcome spatial discrepancies by making products available in locations convenient to consumers. For example, car manufacturers overcome spatial discrepancies by franchising dealerships close to consumers.

Providing contact efficiency

The third need fulfilled by marketing channels is to overcome contact inefficiency. Consider your extra costs if supermarkets, department stores and shopping centres or retailer did not exist. Suppose you had to buy your milk at a dairy and your meat at a live product market. Imagine buying your eggs and chicken at a hatchery and your fruits and vegetables at various farms. You would spend a great deal of time, money and energy just shopping for a few groceries. Channels simplify distribution by cutting the number of transactions required to get products from manufacturers to consumers and making an assortment of goods available in one location.

McDonald's on-line
Who is McDonald's in partnership with? Why does it need partners for food preparation and delivery?
www.mcdonalds.com.au/macpac.pdf

Consider another example, which is illustrated in Exhibit 8.1. Four students in your class each want to buy a television set. Without a retail intermediary such as Harvey Norman, television manufacturers LG, Samsung, Sony, Toshiba and Phillips would each have to make four contacts to reach the four buyers who are in the target market, totalling 20 transactions. However, each producer only has to make one contact when Harvey Norman acts as an intermediary between the producer and consumers, reducing the number of transactions to nine. Each producer sells to one retailer rather than to four consumers. In turn, your classmates buy from one retailer instead of from five producers.

This simple example illustrates the concept of contact efficiency. Manufacturers sell to millions of individuals and families around the world. Using channel intermediaries greatly reduces the number of required contacts. As a result, producers are able to offer their products cost-effectively and efficiently to consumers all over the world.

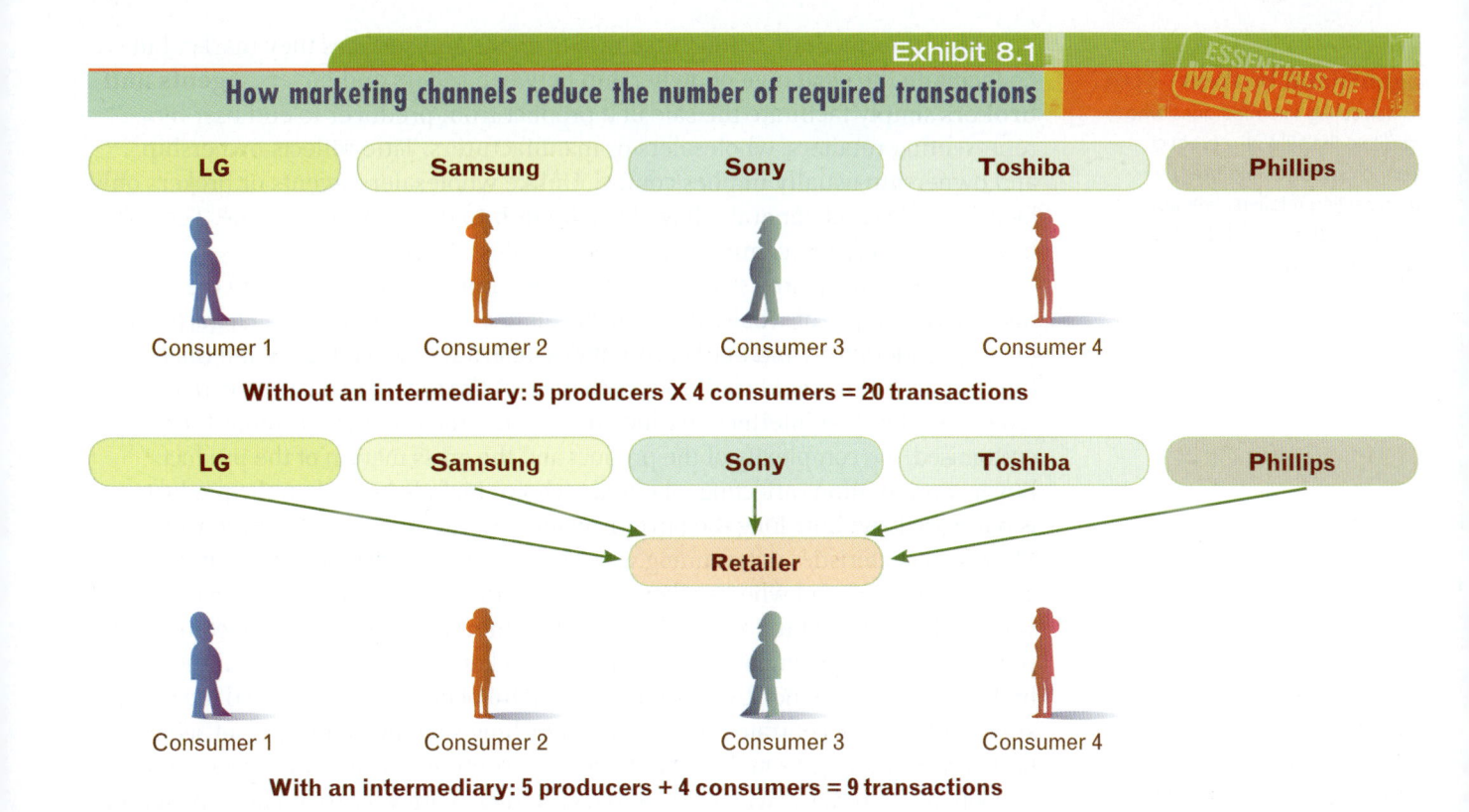

Exhibit 8.1 How marketing channels reduce the number of required transactions

LG — Samsung — Sony — Toshiba — Phillips

Consumer 1 — Consumer 2 — Consumer 3 — Consumer 4

Without an intermediary: 5 producers X 4 consumers = 20 transactions

LG — Samsung — Sony — Toshiba — Phillips
↓
Retailer
↓
Consumer 1 — Consumer 2 — Consumer 3 — Consumer 4

With an intermediary: 5 producers + 4 consumers = 9 transactions

Channel intermediaries and their functions

A marketing channel provides countless efficiencies in bringing a product to the consumer with other channel members. The next topic to consider is channel intermediaries and the specific functions they provide.

2 Define the types of channel intermediaries and describe their functions and activities

Types of channel intermediaries

Intermediaries in a channel negotiate with one another, facilitate the change of ownership between buyers and sellers, and physically move products from the manufacturer to the final consumer. The most prominent difference separating intermediaries is whether they take title to the product. Taking title means they own the merchandise and control the terms of the sale – for example, price and delivery date. **Retailers** and merchant wholesalers are examples of intermediaries who take title to products in the marketing channel and resell them. Retailers are firms that sell mainly to consumers. Retailers will be discussed in more detail later in this chapter.

Merchant wholesalers are organisations that facilitate the movement of products and services from the manufacturer to producers, resellers, governments, institutions and retailers. All merchant wholesalers take title to the goods they sell. Most merchant wholesalers operate one or more warehouses in which they receive goods, store them and later reship them. Customers are mostly small- or moderate-size retailers, but merchant wholesalers also market to manufacturers and institutional clients.

retailer
Channel intermediary that sells mainly to consumers.

merchant wholesaler
Institution that buys goods from manufacturers and resells them to businesses, government agencies, and other wholesalers or retailers and that receives and takes title to goods, stores them in its own warehouses and later ships them.

agents and brokers
Wholesaling intermediaries who facilitate the sale of a product from producer to end user by representing retailers, wholesalers or manufacturers and don't take title to the product.

Other intermediaries don't take title to goods and services they market but do facilitate the exchange of ownership between sellers and buyers. **Agents and brokers** simply facilitate the sale of a product from producer to end user by representing retailers, wholesalers or manufacturers. Title reflects ownership, and ownership usually implies control. Unlike wholesalers, agents or brokers only facilitate sales and generally have little input into the terms of the sale. They do, however, get a fee or commission based on sales volume.

Variations in channel structures are due in large part to variations in the numbers and types of wholesaling intermediaries. Generally, product characteristics, buyer considerations and market conditions determine which type of intermediary the manufacturer should use. Product characteristics that may dictate a certain type of wholesaling intermediary include whether the product is standardised or customised, the complexity of the product and the gross margin of the product. Buyer considerations affecting wholesaler choice include how often the product is purchased and how long the buyer is willing to wait to receive the product. Market characteristics determining wholesaler type include how many buyers are in the market and whether they are concentrated in a general location or are widely dispersed. Exhibit 8.2 shows these determining factors. A manufacturer that produces only a few engines a year for space rockets will probably use an agent or broker to sell its product. In addition, the handful of customers that need the product are most likely concentrated near rocket launching sites, again making an agent or broker more practical. On the other hand, a book publisher that prints thousands of books and has many widely dispersed customers with year-round demand for its product will probably use a merchant wholesaler.

Exhibit 8.2
Factors suggesting the type of wholesaling intermediary to use

Factor	Merchant wholesalers	Agents or brokers
Nature of product	Standard	Non-standard, custom
Technicality of product	Complex	Simple
Product's gross margin	High	Low
Frequency of ordering	Frequent	Infrequent
Time between order and receipt of shipment	Buyer desires shorter lead time	Buyer satisfied with long lead time
Number of customers	Many	Few
Concentration of customers	Dispersed	Concentrated

Source: Reprinted from Donald M. Jackson and Michael F. D'Amico, 'Products and Markets Served by Distributors and Agents', *Industrial Marketing Management*, February 1989, pp. 27–33. Copyright 1989, with permission from Elsevier Science.

Channel functions performed by intermediaries

Retailing and wholesaling intermediaries in marketing channels perform several essential functions that facilitate the flow of goods between producer and buyer. The three basic functions that intermediaries perform are summarised in Exhibit 8.3.

Transactional functions involve contacting and communicating with prospective buyers to make them aware of existing products and explain their features, advantages and benefits. *Logistical* functions include transporting, storing, sorting out, accumulating, allocating and assorting products into either homogeneous or heterogeneous collections. For example, grading agricultural products typifies the sorting-out process, whereas consolidation of many lots of super-fine wool from different sources into one lot illustrates the accumulation process. Other retailers perform the assorting function by assembling thousands of different items that match their customers' wants.

Exhibit 8.3 Marketing channel functions performed by intermediaries

Type of function	Description
Transactional functions	**Contacting and promoting:** contacting potential customers, promoting products and soliciting orders
	Negotiating: determining how many goods or services to buy and sell, type of transportation to use, when to deliver, and method and timing of payment
	Risk-taking: assuming the risk of owning stock
Logistical functions	**Physically distributing:** transporting and sorting goods to overcome temporal and spatial discrepancies
	Storing: overcoming discrepancies of quantity and assortment by
	Sorting out: breaking down a heterogeneous supply into separate homogeneous stocks
	Accumulation: combining similar stocks into a larger homogeneous supply
	Allocation: breaking a homogeneous supply into smaller and smaller lots ('breaking bulk')
	Assortment: combining products into collections or assortments that buyers want available at one place
Facilitating functions	**Researching:** gathering information about other channel members and consumers
	Financing: extending credit and other financial services to facilitate the flow of goods through the channel to the final consumer

The third basic channel function, *facilitating*, includes research and financing. Research provides information about channel members and consumers by getting answers to questions such as: 'Who are the buyers? Where are they located?' and 'Why do they buy?' Financing ensures that channel members have the money to keep products moving through the channel to the ultimate consumer.

A single company may provide one, two or all three functions. Consider the Metcash organisation, a distributor for IGA Distribution, Campbells Cash & Carry, and Australian Liquor Marketers. As an alcohol distributor, it provides transactional, logistical and facilitating channel functions. Australian Liquor Marketers (ALM) is the leading broad-range liquor wholesaler in Australia. It operates 16 distribution centres across Australia and New Zealand, carrying more than 8000 products to meet the wine, spirit and beer requirements of more than 13 000 licensed premises. ALM has an ongoing focus on improved customer service

Metcash Trading Limited Australasia
on-line
Metcash is a distribution organisation in the food and fast consumable items business. Why do such organisations exist?
www.metcash.com

Wool grading allows small lots to be combined, which enables a superior product to gain higher returns for the producers.

to its retail base and closer cooperation with suppliers to ensure an efficient value chain. Sales representatives contact local bars and restaurants to negotiate the terms of the sale, possibly giving the customer a discount for large purchases, and to determine when the alcohol will be delivered. At the same time, AML also provides a facilitating function by extending credit to the customer. AML provides logistical functions by accumulating the many types of alcohol from the manufacturing plant, storing them in its refrigerated warehouse and filling orders, which are heterogeneous collections for each particular customer.

Although individual members can be added to or removed from a channel, someone must still perform those essential functions. Producers, end users or consumers, channel intermediaries such as wholesalers and retailers, and sometimes non-member channel participants, can perform them. For example, if a manufacturer decides to eliminate its private fleet of trucks, it must still find a way to move the goods to the wholesaler. That task may be accomplished by the wholesaler, which may have its own fleet of trucks, or by a non-member channel participant such as an independent trucking firm. Non-members also provide many other essential functions that may have at one time been provided by a channel member. Research firms may perform the research function; advertising agencies, the promotion function; transportation and storage firms, the physical distribution function; and banks, the financing function.

Channel structures

3 Describe the channel structures for consumer and business-to-business products and discuss alternative channel arrangements

A product can take many routes to reach its consumer. Marketers search for the most efficient channel from the many alternatives available. Marketing a consumer convenience good such as Smarties differs from marketing a speciality good such as a Mercedes-Benz car. The two products require very different distribution channels. Likewise, the appropriate channel for a major equipment supplier such as Boeing Aircraft would be unsuitable for an accessory equipment producer such as Black & Decker. To illustrate the differences in typical marketing channels for consumer and business-to-business products like these, the next sections discuss the structures of marketing channels for each product type. Alternative channel structures are also considered.

Channels for consumer products

Exhibit 8.4 illustrates the four ways manufacturers can route products to consumers. Producers use the **direct channel** to sell directly to consumers. Direct marketing activities – including telemarketing, mail order and catalogue shopping, and forms of electronic retailing such as on-line shopping and shop-at-home television networks – are good examples of this type of channel structure. Home computer users can purchase Dell computers directly over the telephone or directly from Dell's Internet website. There are no intermediaries. Producer-owned stores and factory outlet stores – such as Brothers Neilsen, Rodger David and Eagle Boys Pizza – are other examples of direct channels. Direct marketing and factory outlets are discussed in more detail later in this chapter.

direct channel
Distribution channel in which producers sell directly to consumers.

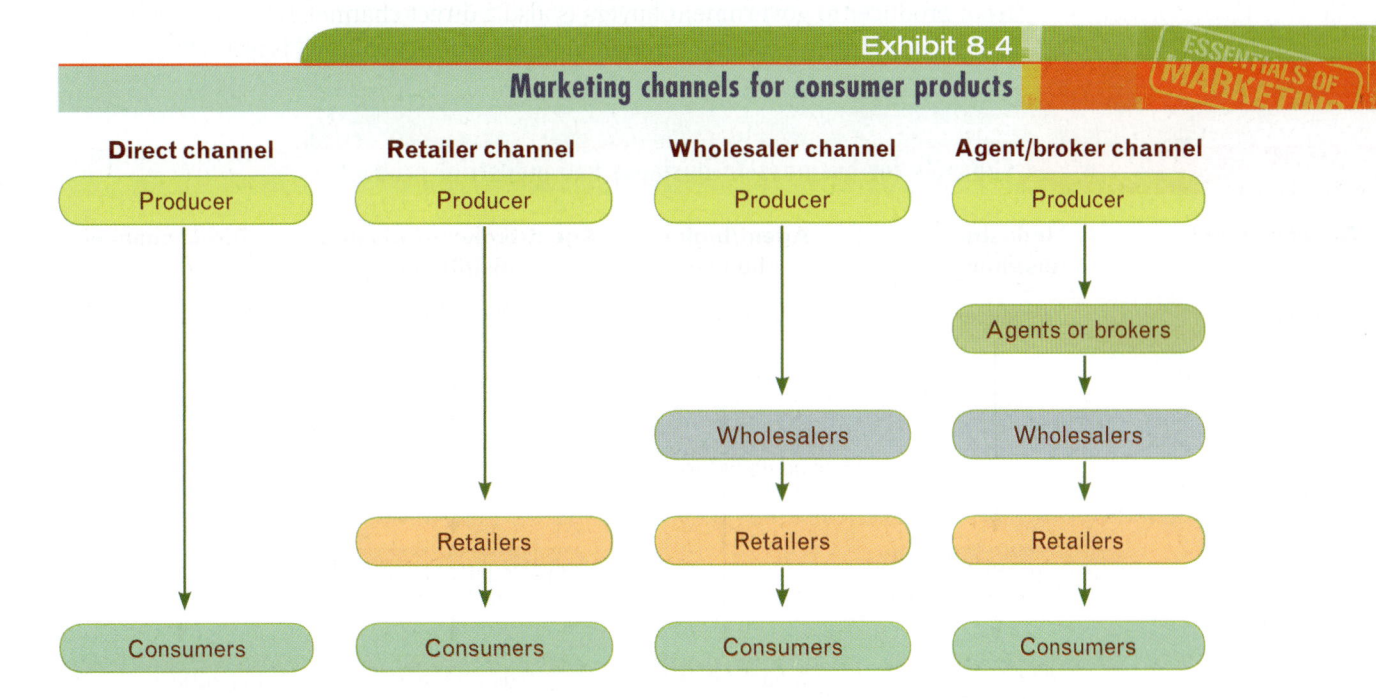

Exhibit 8.4
Marketing channels for consumer products

Direct channel	Retailer channel	Wholesaler channel	Agent/broker channel
Producer	Producer	Producer	Producer
			↓
			Agents or brokers
		↓	↓
		Wholesalers	Wholesalers
	↓	↓	↓
	Retailers	Retailers	Retailers
↓	↓	↓	↓
Consumers	Consumers	Consumers	Consumers

At the other end of the spectrum, *agent/broker channels* involve a complicated process. Agent/broker channels are typically used in markets with many small manufacturers and many retailers that lack the resources to find each other. Agents or brokers bring manufacturers and wholesalers together for negotiations, but don't take title to merchandise. Ownership passes directly to one or more wholesalers and then to retailers. Finally, retailers sell to the consumer of the product. A food broker represents buyers and sellers of grocery products. The broker acts on behalf of many different producers and negotiates the sale of their products to wholesalers that specialise in foodstuffs. These wholesalers in turn sell to grocers and convenience stores.

Most consumer products are sold through distribution channels similar to the other two alternatives: the retailer channel and the wholesaler channel. A *retailer channel* is most common when the retailer is large and can buy in large quantities directly from the manufacturer. Coles Myer, and car dealers such as GMH, are examples of retailers that often bypass a wholesaler. A *wholesaler channel* is often

on-line

What kind of marketing channel functions can be performed over the Internet? Why do you think so?

used for low-cost items that are purchased frequently, such as confectionery and magazines. For example, Mars sells confectionery to wholesalers in large quantities. The wholesalers then break down these quantities into smaller quantities to satisfy individual retailer orders.

Channels for business-to-business and industrial products

Exhibit 8.5 illustrates five channel structures that are common in business-to-business and industrial markets. First, direct channels are typical in business-to-business and industrial markets. Manufacturers buy large quantities of raw materials, major equipment, processed materials and supplies directly from other manufacturers. Manufacturers that require suppliers to meet detailed technical specifications often prefer direct channels. The direct communication required between GMH and its suppliers, for example, along with the tremendous size of the orders, makes anything but a direct channel impractical. The channel from producer to government buyers is also a direct channel. Because much of government buying is done through bidding, a direct channel is attractive.

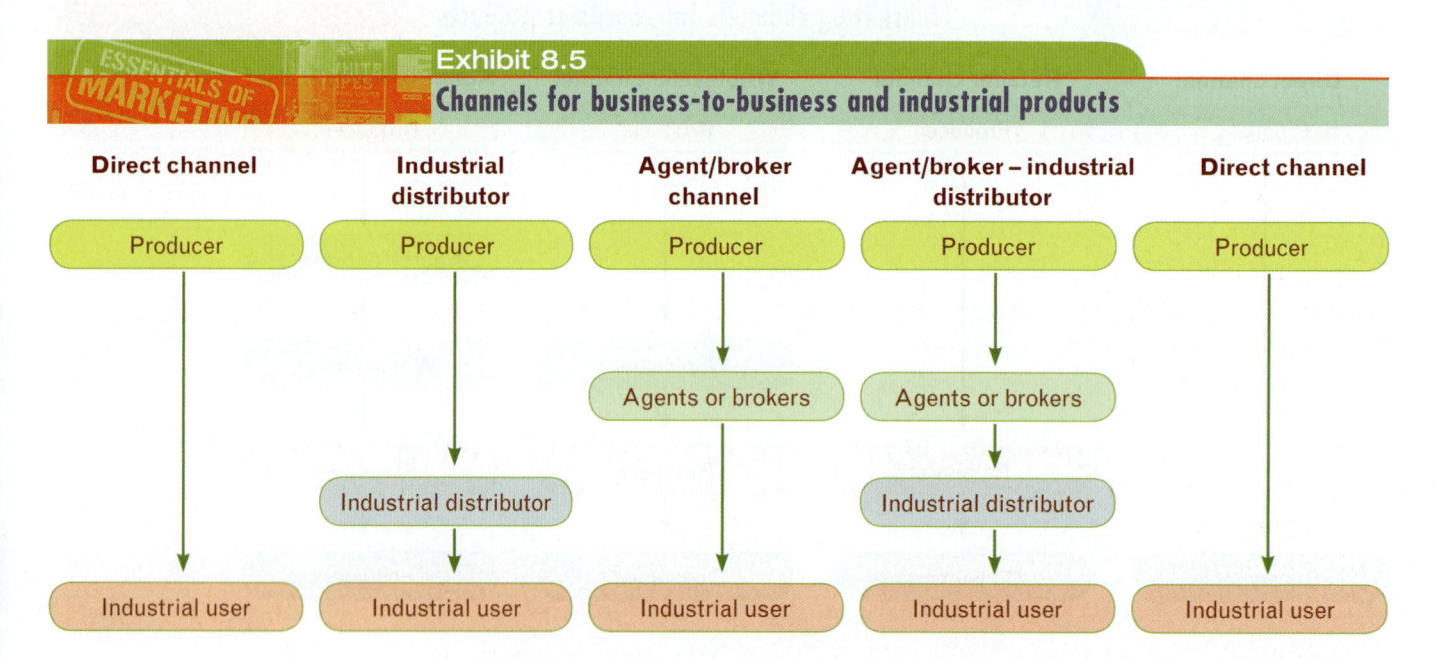

Exhibit 8.5
Channels for business-to-business and industrial products

Direct channel	Industrial distributor	Agent/broker channel	Agent/broker – industrial distributor	Direct channel
Producer	Producer	Producer	Producer	Producer
		Agents or brokers	Agents or brokers	
	Industrial distributor		Industrial distributor	
Industrial user	Industrial user	Industrial user	Industrial user	Industrial user

Companies selling standardised items of moderate or low value often rely on *industrial distributors*. In many ways, an industrial distributor is like a supermarket for organisations. Industrial distributors are wholesalers and channel members that buy and take title to products. Moreover, they usually keep stocks of their products and sell and service them. Often small manufacturers cannot afford to employ their own sales team. Instead, they rely on manufacturers' representatives or selling agents to sell to either industrial distributors or users.

Alternative channel arrangements

Rarely does a producer use just one type of channel to distribute its product. It usually employs several different or alternative channels, which include multiple channels, non-traditional channels, adaptive channels and strategic channel alliances.

Multiple channels

When a producer selects two or more channels to distribute the same product to target markets, this arrangement is called **dual distribution** (or **multiple distribution**). Whirlpool sells its washers, dryers and refrigerators directly to home and apartment builders and contractors, but it also sells these same appliances to retail stores that sell to consumers. Myer, a traditional retail outlet, now has a successful direct-mail channel. Producers with unique second brands may also employ multiple channels. For example, the Walt Disney Company routinely releases first-run animated films to movie theatres and then releases a sequel directly to the home-video market. Such sequels as *Aladdin and the King of Thieves* and *Pocahontas: Journey to a New World* follow up its theatre blockbusters. Similarly, computer maker Dell, which has traditionally sold PCs to consumers who ordered them over the telephone and the Internet, has forged new dealer channels to reach business markets.

dual distribution (multiple distribution)
Use of two or more channels to distribute the same product to target markets.

Non-traditional channels

Non-traditional channel arrangements often help to differentiate a firm's product from the competition. Manufacturers may decide to use non-traditional channels such as the Internet, mail-order channels or infomercials to sell their products instead of going through traditional retailer channels. Although non-traditional channels may limit a brand's coverage, they can give a producer serving a niche market a way to gain market access and customer attention without having to establish channel intermediaries. Non-traditional channels can also provide another avenue of sales for larger firms. For example, travellers can now purchase fast food from Pizza Hut, McDonald's and Hungry Jacks in many petrol stations across Australia. Similarly, in the United States, many Wal-Mart department stores now let customers order McDonald's burgers and fries as they check out. The order is sent from Wal-Mart's cash register to the McDonald's kitchen located within the store. The food is then whisked up to the departing customer.[3] Consumers looking for a new car can now purchase one over the Internet. The Entrepreneurial insights box discusses how entrepreneurial companies are transforming the way cars are sold.

Wine Trader on-line
Visit this home page and determine the types of channels used by this organisation.
www.winetrader.com.au

Adaptive channels

Many companies today realise that they don't have the capability to completely serve their customers in all situations. Innovative channel members have come to recognise that by sharing their resources with others in their channel, they can take advantage of profit-making opportunities. This concept of a flexible and responsive channel of distribution is called an **adaptive channel**. Adaptive channels are initiated when a firm identifies critical but rare customer requirements that they don't have the capability to fulfil. Once these requirements are identified, the firm can arrange with other channel members to help satisfy these requests. One such firm utilising the adaptive channel concept is Mitsubishi Electric air conditioning. Mitsubishi was having problems getting technicians to hold the stock necessary for repairs, even though its stock levels were quite high. To overcome this problem, Mitsubishi united with national couriers. Now, a technician who needs a part calls a toll-free number for the courier, and the parts are shipped and usually arrive the next day. This arrangement has helped Mitsubishi to eliminate warehousing costs and decrease stock levels.

adaptive channel
An alternative channel initiated when a firm identifies critical but rare customer requirements that they don't have the capability to fulfil.

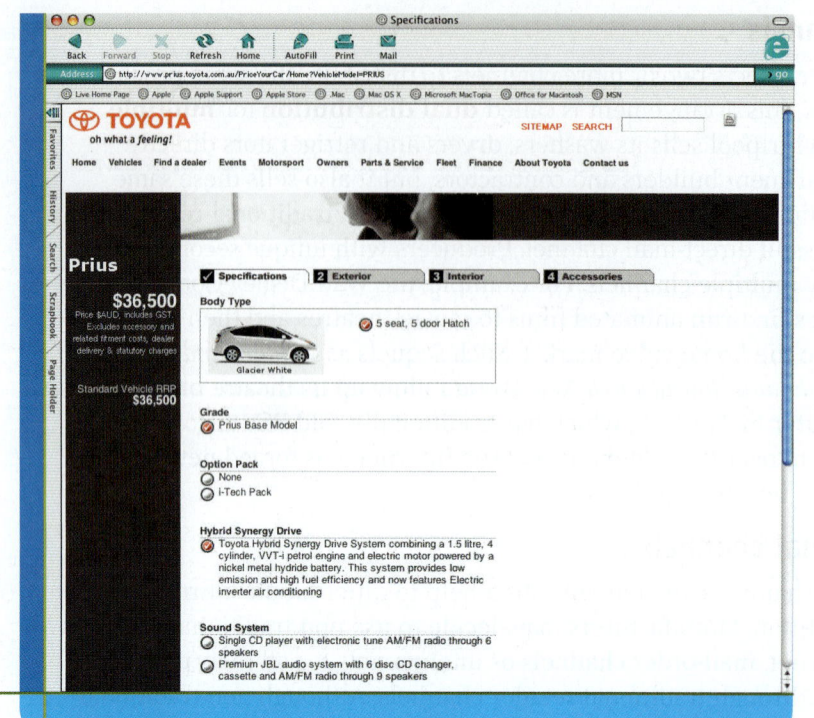

The Internet has had a drastic impact on retail channels in many industries, and now Internet purchasing is moving into the car industry. Would you buy a car over the Internet? Go to www.prius.toyota.com.au/PriceYourCar/Home?VehicleModel=PRIUS

strategic channel alliance
Cooperative agreement between business firms to use the other's already established distribution channel.

Strategic channel alliances

Producers often form **strategic channel alliances**, which use another manufacturer's already established channel. Alliances are used most often when the creation of marketing channel relationships may be too expensive and time consuming. Palmer's Tubemakers has a strategic alliance with Steelmark, with Palmer's producing the steel and Steelmark selling the product.[4]

Strategic channel alliances are also common for selling in global markets where cultural differences, distance or other barriers can inhibit channel establishment. US software giant Oracle has formed a strategic alliance with Japanese computer giant Fujitsu in the Asia–Pacific region. Under the alliance, Fujitsu distributes and markets Oracle's information management software on Fujitsu servers in Australia, China, Hong Kong, Thailand and Vietnam.[5]

Channel strategy decisions

4 Discuss the issues that influence channel strategy

Devising a marketing channel strategy requires several critical decisions. Marketing managers must decide what role distribution will play in the overall marketing strategy. In addition, they must be sure that the channel strategy chosen is consistent with product, promotion and pricing strategies. In making these decisions, marketing managers must analyse what factors will influence the choice of channel and what level of distribution intensity will be appropriate.

Factors affecting channel choice

Marketers must answer many questions before choosing a marketing channel. The final choice depends on analysis of several factors, which often interact. These factors can be grouped as market factors, product factors and producer factors.

Entrepreneurial Insights

CarsDirect.com: Driving car buyers to the Internet

CarsDirect.com is heating up the new car industry. The country's first direct broker of cars on the Internet has sent carmakers, on-line buying services and dealer groups scrambling to control the growing number of customers going on-line to shortcut the traditional process of shopping for new and used vehicles. The Internet start-up sparked a flurry of copycat websites dedicated to the direct-to-consumer purchase of cars, like CarOrder.com, DriveOff.com, Carpoint.com and Greenlight.com. But several have now gone out of business.

Backed by Michael Dell's personal investment firm, CarsDirect.com was conceived by Bill Gross, chairman of Idealab, a venture incubator that has also launched other Internet businesses, such as eToys, Tickets.com and Cooking.com. After becoming frustrated with his own efforts at buying a car on-line, Gross realised that current Internet options for car buying were not only inadequate but did nothing to leverage available technology on behalf of the consumer. At the time of his search, on-line car sites functioned only as lead generators for local dealers, requiring him to close the sale of his car the old-fashioned way: haggling at the dealership with the untrustworthiest of people, a car salesperson.

His vision, CarsDirect.com, sells cars entirely through the Internet, allowing consumers to bypass traditional car dealers in their negotiations. As a car broker, CarsDirect.com offers Web buyers a car at a fixed price based on recent average selling prices. Then, CarsDirect.com works through its network of existing dealers to get the car at that price. Since CarsDirect.com doesn't hold franchise agreements with any car manufacturers, consumers enjoy an impartial and unbiased shopping experience as well as an unrivalled selection. In contrast, buying cars the old-fashioned way makes consumers travel from car dealer to car dealer looking for the models they are interested in or the best price.

Car buyers visiting CarsDirect.com can research a car by searching the site's extensive database, which provides objective information on price, performance and options for more than 2500 different makes and models – virtually every production vehicle available in the United States. CarsDirect.com's research tools let buyers compare the features of vehicles and see in seconds the manufacturer's suggested retail price, the invoice and, most importantly, the price CarsDirect can get for them. If a consumer wants to buy, payment is arranged completely on-line to close the deal. Financing options are provided through CarsDirect.com's financial partner Bank One, one of the nation's largest banks and a major automotive lender. Then, the buyer can arrange for delivery of the vehicle at home of the office or pick it up from a local automotive retailer.

With on-line auto sales expected to exceed 5 per cent of total sales soon, there are still big hurdles ahead for car brokers like CarsDirect.com. General Motors, for instance, recently warned its 7700 dealers to cease and desist from using on-line car-buying sites like CarsDirect.com. The largest obstacle, however, is the myriad of state franchise laws that protect car dealers and restrict direct sales of automobiles. Car brokers have found that no two states' franchise laws are the same, and many include rules that are arcane or impractical. Texas, the nation's second biggest automotive market, has the most restrictive dealer-protection laws in the country. There, only state-licensed dealers can sell cars. Brokering of cars to consumers by anyone other than a dealer is strictly prohibited. As a result, car brokers have had to redesign their direct-sales model around Texas laws. CarsDirect.com, for instance, currently does not offer cars to residents of Texas. Often, instead of trying to bypass dealers, Internet car brokers are forming alliances with dealers or reworking their strategies to become more dealer-friendly to comply with state law.

Market factors

Among the most important market factors affecting the choice of distribution channel are target customer considerations. Specifically, marketing managers should answer the following questions: Who are the potential customers? What do they buy? Where do they buy? When do they buy? How do they buy? Additionally, the choice of channel depends on whether the producer is selling to consumers or to industrial customers. Industrial customers' buying habits are very different from those of consumers. Industrial customers tend to buy in larger quantities and require more customer service. Consumers usually buy in very small quantities and sometimes don't mind if they get no service at all, as in a discount store.

Geographic location and size of the market are also important to channel selection. As a rule, if the target market is concentrated in one or more specific areas, then direct selling through a sales team is appropriate. When markets are more widely dispersed, intermediaries are less expensive. The size of the market also influences channel choice. Generally, a very large market requires more intermediaries. Coles Myer has to reach millions of consumers with its many brands of household goods. It needs many intermediaries, including wholesalers and retailers.

Product factors

Products that are more complex, customised and expensive tend to benefit from shorter and more direct marketing channels. These types of products sell better through a direct sales team. Examples include pharmaceuticals, scientific instruments, commercial aircraft and mainframe computer systems. On the other hand, the more standardised a product is, the longer its distribution channel can be and the greater the number of intermediaries that can be involved. For example, the formula for chewing gum is about the same from producer to producer, with the exception of flavour and shape. Chewing gum is also very inexpensive. As a result, the distribution channel for chewing gum tends to involve many wholesalers and retailers.

The product's life cycle is also an important factor in choosing a marketing channel. In fact, the choice of channel may change over the life of the product. When photocopiers were first available, a direct sales team typically sold them. Now, however, photocopiers can be found in several places, including warehouse outlets, electronic superstores and direct-order catalogues. As products become more common, the number of intermediaries and channels increases.

Another factor is the delicacy of the product. Perishable products such as vegetables and milk have a relatively short life span. Fragile products such as china and crystal require a minimum amount of handling. Therefore, both require short marketing channels.

Producer factors

Several factors pertaining to the producer are important to the selection of a marketing channel. In general, producers with large financial, managerial and marketing resources are better able to use channels that are more direct. Those producers have the ability to hire and train their own sales force, warehouse their own goods and extend credit to their customers. Smaller or weaker firms, on the other hand, must rely on intermediaries to provide these services for them. Compared to producers with only one or two product lines, producers that sell several products in a related area are able to choose channels that are more direct. Sales expenses then can be spread over more products.

A producer's desire to control pricing, positioning, brand image and customer support also tends to influence channel selection. For example, firms that sell products with exclusive brand images, such as designer perfumes and clothing, usually avoid channels in which discount retailers are present. Manufacturers of upscale products, such as Gucci (handbags) and Godiva (chocolates), may sell their wares only in expensive stores in order to maintain an image of exclusivity. Many producers have opted to risk their image, however, and test sales in discount channels. Polaroid cameras, for example, can be found in chemists, as well as in discount stores.

Levels of distribution intensity

Organisations have three options for intensity of distribution: intensive distribution, selective distribution or exclusive distribution (see Exhibit 8.6).

Exhibit 8.6 Intensity of distribution levels

Intensity level	Distribution intensity objective	Number of intermediaries in each market	Examples
Intensive	Achieve mass market selling; popular with health and beauty aids and convenience goods that must be available everywhere	Many	Coca-Cola, Pepsi-Cola, Frito-Lay potato chips, Twisties, Paracetamol
Selective	Work closely with selected intermediaries who meet certain criteria; typically used for shopping goods and some speciality goods	Several	Hewlett-Packard printers, Bamboo surfboards, Nikon cameras, Levi's jeans
Exclusive	Work with a single intermediary for products that require special resources or positioning; typically used for speciality goods and major industrial equipment	One	Lotus cars, Rolex watches, Cash Converters franchises

Intensive distribution

Intensive distribution is distribution aimed at maximum market coverage. The manufacturer tries to have the product available in every outlet at which potential customers might want to buy it. If buyers are unwilling to search for a product (as is true of convenience goods and operating supplies), the product must be very accessible to buyers. A low-value product that is purchased frequently may require a lengthy channel. For example, confectionery is found in almost every type of retail store imaginable. It is typically sold to retailers in small quantities by a food or confectionery wholesaler. The Wrigley Co. could not afford to sell its chewing gum directly to every service station, corner shop, supermarket and discount store. The cost would be too high.

Most manufacturers pursuing an intensive distribution strategy sell to a large percentage of the wholesalers willing to stock their products. Retailers' willingness (or unwillingness) to handle items tends to control the manufacturer's ability to achieve intensive distribution. A retailer already carrying 10 brands of chewing gum may show little enthusiasm for one more brand.

intensive distribution
Form of distribution aimed at having a product available in every outlet at which target customers might want to buy it.

Selective distribution

Selective distribution is achieved by screening dealers to eliminate all but a few in any single area. KleenMaid uses a selective distribution system by choosing a select handful of appliance dealers in a geographic area to sell its line of washing machines and dryers and other appliances. Likewise, Hugo Boss clothing is sold only in select retail outlets. Because only a few retailers are chosen, the consumer must seek out the product. Shopping goods and some speciality products are distributed selectively. Accessory equipment manufacturers in the business-to-business market also tend to follow a selective distribution strategy.

Several screening criteria are used to find the right dealers. An accessory equipment manufacturer such as NEC may seek firms that are able to service its products properly. A television manufacturer such as Phillips may look for

selective distribution
Form of distribution achieved by screening dealers to eliminate all but a few in any single area.

service ability and a quality dealer image. If the manufacturer expects to move a large volume of merchandise through each dealer, it will choose only those dealers that seem able to handle such volume. As a result, many smaller retailers may not be considered.

Exclusive distribution

exclusive distribution
Form of distribution that establishes one or a few dealers within a given area.

The most restrictive form of market coverage is **exclusive distribution**, which entails only one or a few dealers within a given area. Because buyers may have to search or travel extensively to buy the product, exclusive distribution is usually confined to consumer speciality goods, a few shopping goods and major industrial equipment. Products such as Rolls-Royce cars and Kencraft Marine boats are distributed under exclusive arrangements. Sometimes exclusive territories are granted by new companies (such as franchisers) to obtain market coverage in a particular area. Limited distribution may also serve to project an exclusive image for the product.

Retailers and wholesalers may be unwilling to commit the time and money necessary to promote and service a product unless the manufacturer guarantees them an exclusive territory. This arrangement shields the dealer from direct competition and enables it to be the main beneficiary of the manufacturer's promotion efforts in that geographic area. With exclusive distribution, channels of communication are usually well established, because the manufacturer works with a limited number of dealers rather than many.

Exclusive distribution has been part of retailing for years. In the toy industry, toy maker Hasbro makes Luke and Wampa Star Wars collector dolls only for Target stores. It makes other figures in the Star Wars series exclusively for other retailers, including Toys 'R' Us.

Although exclusivity has its advantages, it also can have its pitfalls. An exclusive network may not be large enough, for example, if demand is brisk. Manufacturers and retailers run the risk of angering customers who can't get the product. In addition, the producer's insistence on exclusivity might put the channel in financial jeopardy during times of weak demand. Toyota's Lexus division uses an exclusive distribution strategy to create a distinctive image for its high-priced cars. Toyota dealers struggled initially because of the car's small niche market, low resale demand and, ironically, infrequent need for follow-up service and repair. After several years, however, Toyota dealerships have become very strong competitors by promoting quality and service.

> **Exclusive distribution on-line**
> Why would exclusive distribution limited be considered an example of exclusive distribution? What other products can you think of that may be exclusive?
> www.exclusive.noelmedia.com/indexie.html

Channel relationships

5 Explain channel leadership, conflict and partnering

A marketing channel is more than a set of institutions linked by economic ties. Social relationships play an important role in building unity among channel members. The basic social dimensions of channels are power, control, leadership, conflict and partnering.

Channel power, control and leadership

channel power
The capacity of a particular marketing channel member to control or influence the behaviour of other channel members.

Channel power is a channel member's capacity to control or influence the behaviour of other channel members. **Channel control** occurs when one channel member affects another member's behaviour. To achieve control, a channel member assumes channel leadership and exercises authority and power. This member is termed the **channel leader**, or **channel captain**. In one marketing channel, a manufacturer may be the leader because it controls new product designs and product availability. In another, a retailer may be the channel leader because it wields power and control over the retail price, stock levels and after-sale service. Read about how some retailers are wielding their power in the Ethics in marketing box.

Channel conflict

Inequitable channel relationships often lead to **channel conflict**, which is a clash of goals and methods among the members of a distribution channel. In a broad context, conflict may not be bad. Often it arises because staid, traditional channel members refuse to keep pace with the changing environment. Removing an outdated intermediary may result in reduced costs for the entire supply chain.

Sources of conflicts among channel members can be due to many different situations and factors. Conflict often arises because channel members have conflicting goals. Athletic footwear retailers want to sell as many shoes as possible in order to maximise profits, regardless of whether the shoe is manufactured by Nike, Adidas or Saucony, but the Nike manufacturer wants a certain sales volume and market share in each market.

Conflict can also arise when channel members fail to fulfil expectations of other channel members, such as when a franchisee does not follow the rules set down by the franchiser or when communication links break down between channel members. For example, if a manufacturer reduces the length of warranty coverage and fails to communicate this change to dealers, then conflict may occur when dealers make repairs with the expectation that they will be reimbursed by the manufacturer. Further, ideological differences and different perceptions of reality can also cause conflict among channel members. For example, retailers may believe 'the customer is always right' and offer a very liberal return policy. Wholesalers and manufacturers may feel that people 'try to get something for nothing' or don't follow product instructions carefully. Their differing views of allowable returns will undoubtedly conflict with the retailers'.

Conflict within a channel can be either horizontal or vertical. **Horizontal conflict** occurs among channel members on the same level – such as two or more different wholesalers or two or more different retailers – that handle the same manufacturer's brands. This type of channel conflict is found most often when manufacturers practise dual or multiple distribution strategies. There was considerable channel conflict after computer manufacturers began distributing their computers beyond the traditional computer resellers and to discount stores, department stores, warehouse clubs and giant electronic superstores, such as Harvey Norman and Chandlers X Site. Horizontal conflict can also occur when channel members on the same level feel the manufacturer is treating them unfairly.

Many regard horizontal conflict as healthy competition. Vertical conflict is much more serious. **Vertical conflict** occurs between different levels in a marketing channel, most typically between manufacturer and wholesaler and manufacturer and retailer. Producer versus wholesaler conflict occurs when the producer chooses to bypass the wholesaler to deal directly with the consumer or retailer. For example, conflict arose when a gearbox manufacturer was in dispute with a car assembly plant. Several intermediaries suffered as car production ground to a halt.

channel control
A situation that occurs when one marketing channel member intentionally affects another member's behaviour.

channel leader (channel captain)
Member of a marketing channel that exercises authority and power over the activities of other channel members.

channel conflict
A clash of goals and methods between distribution channel members.

horizontal conflict
Channel conflict that occurs among channel members on the same level.

vertical conflict
Channel conflict that occurs between different levels in a marketing channel, most typically between manufacturer and wholesaler or between manufacturer and retailer.

Ethics in Marketing

Video piracy

As discussed in the chapter, new Internet and computer technology has been largely responsible for advances in supply chain management. However, the new technology and the Internet are also creating serious supply chain problems for the entertainment industry. For example, the invention of mp3 music files, which can be swapped on the Internet and burned onto compact discs, had a dramatic effect on traditional music sales. The music industry was forced to sue Napster, the leading music file-swapping website, which eventually filed for bankruptcy, for copyright infringement and to develop both new distribution channels and new technologies to prevent music swapping.

Similarly, new technology now allows consumers to make and swap digital copies of television shows and movies. For instance, digital video recorders (DVRs) allow consumers to record their favourite television shows and movies via traditional cable, broadcast satellite and Internet connections. With DVRs, consumers can watch their favourite programs when it is convenient and even pause live programming. As adoption of the technology increases, DVRs could have an impact on television advertising sales and program scheduling. The industry is more concerned, however, about SonicBlues's introduction of ReplayTV 4000, which not only enables consumers to automatically skip commercials but also allows them to send copies over the Internet to other Replay users.

Consumers can also obtain copies of their favourite movies and television shows by going on-line with one of two popular software programs that make it easy to swap video files on the Internet – Morpheus and Kazaa. With more than forty million users between the two, experts say that more than one million users are downloading copies of their favourite television shows at any given time. Available downloads include every *Simpsons* episode ever recorded, film classics such as *Breakfast at Tiffany's*, and episodes of HBO's *The Sopranos* and *Sex and the City*. Finally, digital video cameras with FireWire are even making it easy to share copies of movies currently being shown in theatres.

All of these new technologies are leading to a dramatic increase in video piracy. Movie theatres around the globe are reporting heavy losses as a result. In fact, the Motion Picture Association of America claims that consumers illegally copy 350 000 films a day on the Internet. Other piracy experts put the number closer to a million a day. What's more, experts predict the trend will grow as technology improves and Internet speed increases.

To protect its product, the television industry has sued SonicBlue, claiming that ReplayTV 4000 illegally jeopardises the industry's two main revenue sources: advertising and subscription fees. SonicBlue claims that copyright laws give consumers a 'fair use' right to share – an argument the courts rejected in the Napster trial. Further, the company contends that it is creating innovative products that give consumers more control over how they use the entertainment.

The film industry has also sued StreamCast Networks, the distributor of Morpheus, for copyright infringement. StreamCast argues that the software enables people to share home movies that are in the public domain.

Regardless of the outcome of these lawsuits, the entertainment industry is examining the future of its distribution channels. Television studios are looking for a way to use electronic tags within a broadcast to prevent copying and are asking the federal government to require that all television sets, receivers and computers be capable of reading the tags. For the tags to be effective, the studios would have to cease all non-digital broadcasts – a move that could eliminate free television, forcing consumers to use a cable or satellite company for program access.

In contrast, in an effort to satisfy consumers, MGM, Sony, Paramount, Universal and Warner Bros. studios have started a joint venture called Moviefly to provide consumers with a secure reliable way to 'rent' movies on the Internet. Of course, if successful, the joint venture would eliminate cable and satellite companies from the pay-per-view distribution channel.

What other distribution options does the entertainment industry have? Will new technology give the industry a way to protect its products, or will the industry be forced to reinvent the way it operates? How do you think television programs and movies will be distributed in the future?

Dual distribution strategies can also cause vertical conflict in the channel. For example, mobile telephone carriers, such as Telstra and Optus, traditionally sold mobile phone service through local dealers, usually their own outlets. Faced with increased competition from new carriers and an increasing range of products available on the market, carriers began distribution to other channel outlets, as well as offering special prices and telemarketing to reach potential customers in their homes. Local dealers, which were loyal to the carriers, felt the carriers were now trying to squeeze them out of business. Similarly, manufacturers that are experimenting with selling to customers directly over the Internet are also creating conflict with their traditional retailing intermediaries.

Producers and retailers may also disagree over the terms of the sale or other aspects of the business relationship. Conflict often arises when a retailer sells below the recommended price set by the producer or when the discounts received by the retailer are changed in mid-promotion of a product.

Channel partnering

Regardless of the locus of power, channel members rely heavily on one another. Even the most powerful manufacturers depend on dealers to sell their products; even the most powerful retailers require the products provided by suppliers. In sharp contrast to the adversarial relationships of the past between buyers and sellers, contemporary management thought emphasises the development of close working partnerships among channel members. **Channel partnering**, or **channel cooperation**, is the joint effort of all channel members to create a supply chain that serves customers and creates a competitive advantage. Channel partnering is vital if each member is to gain something from other members. By cooperating, retailers, wholesalers, manufacturers and suppliers can speed up stock replenishment, improve customer service and reduce the total cost of the marketing channel.

Channel alliances and partnerships can be traced, in part, directly to attempts by firms to use the intellectual, material and marketing resources of their business partners worldwide to make entry into far-flung markets easier and more cost effective. The growth of channel partnering is also due to the growth of an information infrastructure that fosters cooperation and sharing of information in national as well as global markets.[6] A comparison between companies that approach the marketplace unilaterally and those that engage in channel cooperation and form partnerships is detailed in Exhibit 8.7.

channel partnering (channel cooperation)
The joint effort of all channel members to create a supply chain that serves customers and creates a competitive advantage.

Exhibit 8.7
Transaction- versus partnership-based firms

Transaction-based	Partnership-based
Short-term relationships	Long-term relationships
Multiple suppliers	Fewer suppliers
Adversarial relationships	Cooperative partnerships
Price dominates	Value-added services dominate
Minimal investment from suppliers	High investment for both buyer and supplier
Minimal information sharing	Extensive product, marketing and logistics information sharing
Firms are independent	Firms are interdependent with joint decision-making
Minimal interaction between respective functional areas	Extensive interaction between buyer and supplier functional areas

Source: From David Frederick Ross, *Competing Through Supply Chain Management: Creating Market-winning Strategies Through Supply Chain Partnerships* (New York: Chapman & Hall, 1998), p. 61. Reprinted by permission of Kluwer Academic publishers.

Collaborating channel partners meet the needs of consumers more effectively by ensuring the right products reach shelves at the right time and at a lower cost, boosting sales and profits. Forced to become more efficient in a highly competitive environment, retailers and their vendors have turned many formerly adversarial relationships into partnerships. Many wholesalers are establishing technological links with their outlets in order to minimise the amount of stock held by those outlets and to ensure speedier payments. Electronic systems create a just-in-time (JIT) system (to be discussed later in this chapter) with electronic ordering and payment systems.

Logistics decisions and supply chain management

6 Discuss logistics and supply chain management and their evolution into distribution practice

Now that you are familiar with the structure and strategy of marketing channels, it is important also to understand the means by which products physically move through a channel of distribution, or the supply chain. **Logistics** is a term borrowed from the armed forces that describes the process of strategically managing the efficient flow and storage of raw materials, in-process stock and finished goods from point of origin to point of consumption. An integral part of marketing strategy, logistics represents 'place' in the marketing mix (product, price, promotion and place) and encompasses the logistical processes involved in getting the right product to the right place at the right time.

The **supply chain** is the connected chain of all of the business entities, both internal and external to the company, that perform or support the logistics function. It incorporates all of the logistical activities associated with moving goods from the raw-materials stage through to the end user. These include sourcing and procurement of raw materials, production scheduling, order processing, stock management, transportation, warehousing, customer service, the information systems necessary to monitor these activities, and the external partners, such as vendors, carriers and third-party companies.[7]

logistics
The process of strategically managing the efficient flow and storage of raw materials, in-process stock and finished goods from point of origin to point of consumption.

supply chain
The connected chain of all the business entities, both internal and external to the company, that perform or support the logistics function.

Woolworths has managed its supply chain to coordinate and integrate all logistic functions into a seamless process.

Supply chain management, or **integrated logistics**, coordinates and integrates all of these activities performed by supply chain members into a seamless process. This continuously evolving management philosophy seeks to unify the competencies and resources of business functions both within the firm and outside in the firm's allied channel partners. The result is a highly competitive, customer-satisfying supply system focused on developing innovative solutions and synchronising the flow of goods, services and information to create enhanced customer value.[8] Bernard J. LaLonde, professor emeritus of logistics at Ohio State University in the United States, defines supply chain management as: 'The delivery of enhanced customer and economic value through synchronised management of the flow of physical goods and associated information from sourcing to consumption.'[9] Exhibit 8.8 depicts the supply chain process.

An important element of supply chain management is that it is completely customer driven. In the mass-production era, manufacturers produced standardised products that were 'pushed' down through the supply channel to consumers. In contrast, in today's marketplace, the customers, who expect to receive product configurations and services matched to their unique needs, are driving products.[10]

supply chain management (integrated logistics)
Management system that coordinates and integrates all of the activities performed by supply chain members from source to the point of consumption that results in enhanced customer and economic value.

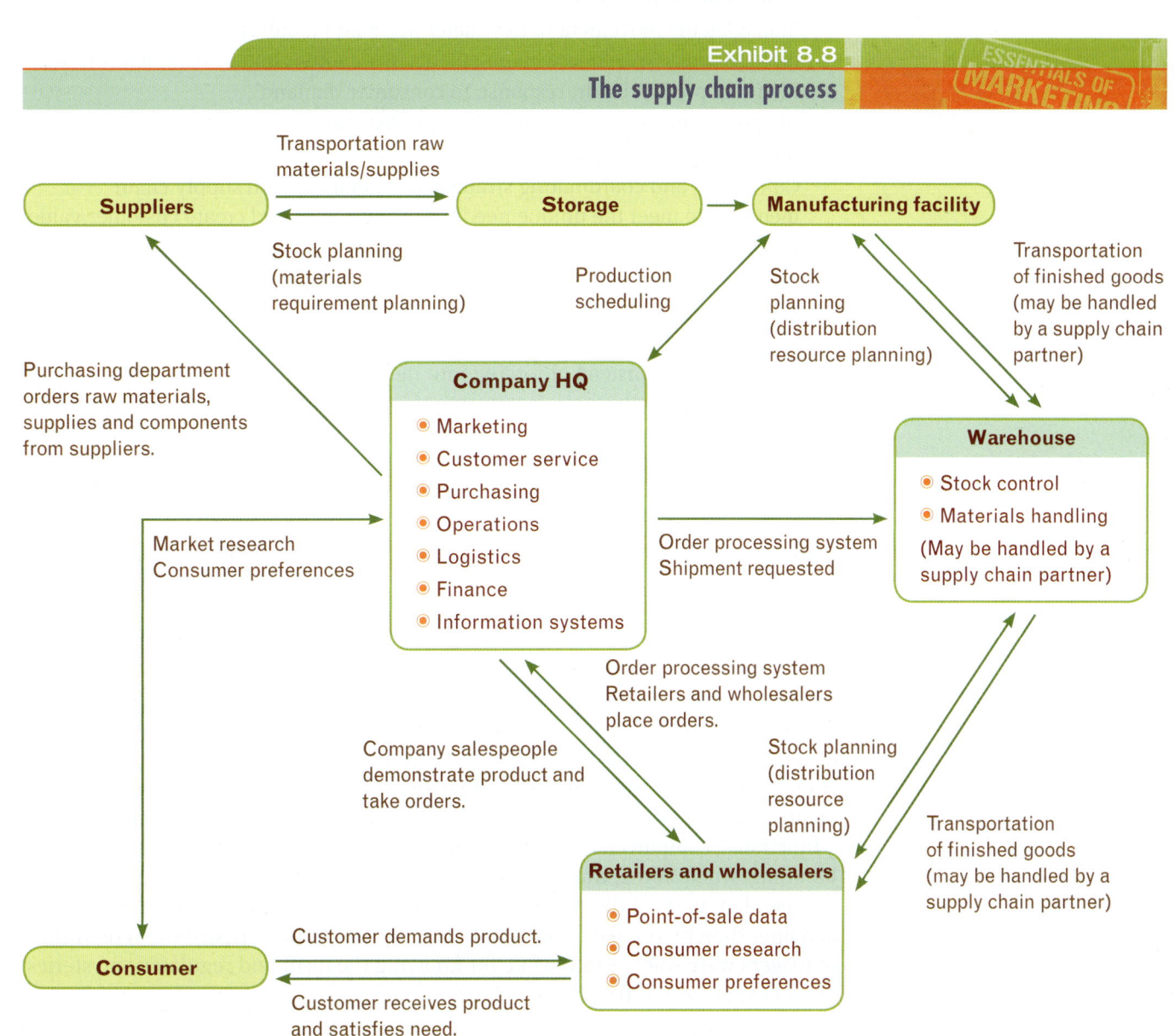

Exhibit 8.8 The supply chain process

This reversal of the flow of demand from a 'push' to a 'pull' has resulted in a radical reformulation of market expectations and traditional marketing, production and distribution functions. Through the channel partnership of suppliers, manufacturers, wholesalers and retailers along the entire supply chain, who work together towards the common goal of creating customer value, supply chain management allows companies to respond with the unique product configuration and mix of services demanded by the customer. Today, supply chain management plays a dual role: first, as a *communicator* of customer demand that extends from the point of sale all the way back to the supplier; and second, as a *physical flow process* that engineers the timely and cost-effective movement of goods through the entire supply pipeline.[11]

Supply chain management includes the following activities:

- Managing the movement of information and customer requirements up and down the supply chain (this is more frequently being conducted electronically with emails, rfid tags and the like)
- Managing the movement and storage of raw materials and parts from their sources to the production site
- Managing the movement of raw materials, semi-manufactured products and finished products within and among plants, warehouses and distribution centres
- Planning production in response to consumer demand
- Planning and coordinating the physical distribution of finished goods to intermediaries and final buyers
- Cultivating and coordinating strategic partnerships with supply chain members to meet the unique needs of the customer and create customer value.

In summary, supply chain management logisticians are responsible for directing raw materials and parts to the production department and the finished or semi-finished product through warehouses and eventually to the intermediary or end user. Above all, supply chain management begins and ends with the customer. Instead of forcing into the market products that may or may not sell quickly, supply chain management logisticians react to actual customer demand. By doing so, the flows of raw materials, finished products and packaging materials are minimised at every point in the supply chain, resulting in lower costs and increased customer value.

The evolution of integrated logistics and supply chain management

Although the concept of an integrated supply chain has only recently been given top priority by corporate management, its roots go back to a process simply called *physical distribution*.[12] In the early 1900s, the focus was on moving agricultural products to market. For businesses, production output was cascaded, or pushed, down the channel with the focus on transporting and storing finished goods from the manufacturer to the next member in the channel. Until the late 1950s, business saw physical distribution as a sub-set of marketing and viewed it from a functional, compartmentalised perspective. Thus, warehousing, materials handling, wholesaling, transportation and stock control were distinct and independent parts of the distribution process. The process only concerned those activities directly related to physically moving the product. Distribution or 'traffic' managers were solely responsible for knowing the tariff and regulatory mysteries of moving outbound freight.

Beginning in the early 1960s, there was a shift from physical distribution as the focus to an entire system of activities working with and relying on one another. A systems approach and a total cost perspective marked this era of *logistics management*. Costs along the entire logistics system were analysed and streamlined in an attempt to balance physical distribution service with cost. Management was consolidated for both inbound (raw materials for production) and outbound (finished goods to final consumers) transportation, warehousing, stock control and materials handling.

In the early 1970s, the concept of logistics management was broadened to include the customer as the primary focus of the firm. Customer service, of which physical distribution is a component, became a significant issue. Minimising cost gave way to maximising profits and using logistics as a way to create customer value and satisfy the customer. The more progressive companies began migrating from a stock 'push' to a customer 'pull' channel as power began to move downstream to the customer.

As the 1980s ended, logistics began to be considered as a key means of differentiation for a firm, and a critical component in marketing and corporate strategy. Globalisation of markets and advances in information technology had significant influences on supply chain partnering. During this phase, the concept of an integrated supply chain, sharing information and working together to satisfy the customer emerged as the focus of distribution. Such concepts as integrated logistics, supply chain management, global logistics and information technology became important to the success of a firm. Advocates of this distribution focus realise that significant productivity increases can only come from managing supply chain relationships, information and material flow across enterprise borders – that is, becoming a truly integrated supply chain that shares information and works together for the common goal of increasing customer value.

The future of logistics lies in a deeper understanding of customers' behavioural processes and their perceptions of a firm's logistics systems. Specifically, what are the reactions of customers when aspects of logistics are changed? As the boundaries between supply chain partners partially disappear, an absolute need for understanding all components of the supply chain is inevitable. Firms that are able to bring about greater cooperation of supply chain partners and to span the boundaries to create a value-enhanced experience for customers will be successful.

Exhibit 8.9 provides a summary of the evolution of logistics thought from a management perspective.

Benefits of supply chain management

Companies are increasingly recognising the tremendous payoff potential of successful supply chain management, such as Coles Myer's use of the supply chain to achieve a dominant position in the retail marketplace, Dell Computer's reconfiguring the supply chain to respond almost immediately to customer orders, and the bold measures taken by Woolworth's to virtually eliminate standing stock in the supply chain.

The benefits of an integrated supply chain are many. A study by the Center for Transportation Studies at the Massachusetts Institute of Technology in the

Exhibit 8.9
Evolution of integrated logistics and supply chain management

Distribution phase	Period	Characteristics
Farm to market	Up to the 1940s	Distribution attention centred on transporting products from the farm to point of sale
Segmented functions	1940s to 1950s	Independent departments focused on moving finished goods to the next member of the channel; stock 'push' orientation
Integrated functions	1960s to early 1970s	Recognised inbound transportation as part of the logistics system; focus on streamlining costs along entire logistics system
Customer focus	1970s to mid-1980s	The customer regarded as the primary focus of the firm; movement towards stock 'pull' orientation
Logistics as differentiator	Early 1980s to 2000	Logistics as a key means of competitive differentiation and a critical component of the strategy of the firm; integration of all members of the supply chain; the emergence of concepts such as integrated logistics and supply chain management and a heightened awareness of globalisation; information technology important to success; marked stock 'pull' from the customer
Behavioural and boundary	2000 and beyond	Search for deeper understanding of behavioural issues, spanning specifically customer perceptions of a firm's logistics systems and their related behaviours; greater interfunctional cooperation and coordination across the boundaries of supply chain partners

Source: From John L. Kent, Jr and Daniel J. Flint, 'Perspectives on the Evolution of Logistics Thought', *Journal of Business Logistics*, vol. 18, no. 2, 1997. Reprinted by permission of the Council of Logistics Management.

United States found that the most commonly reported bottom-line benefits centre on reduced costs in stock management, transportation, warehousing and packaging; improved service through techniques such as time-based delivery and make-to-order; and enhanced revenues, which result from such supply-chain-related achievements as higher product availability and more customised products. The companies studied by the centre recorded a number of impressive supply chain accomplishments:

- A 50 per cent reduction in stock
- A 40 per cent increase in on-time deliveries
- A 27 per cent decrease in cumulative cycle times (length of time from customer placing order to customer receiving order)
- A doubling of stock turns coupled with a ninefold reduction in out-of-stock rates
- A 17 per cent increase in revenues.[13]

Another study, by A.T. Kearney, looked at supply chain management from another angle – specifically, the costs of not paying careful attention to the supply chain process. The Kearney consultants found that supply chain inefficiencies, such as late deliveries, stagnant stocks and the higher costs they produce, could waste as much as 25 per cent of a company's operating costs. Assuming even a relatively low profit margin of 3–4 per cent, a 5 per cent reduction in supply chain waste could double a company's profitability. Another recent study found that best-practice supply chain management companies enjoyed a 45 per cent total supply chain cost advantage over their median competitors. Specifically, their supply chain costs as a percentage of revenues were 3–7 per cent less than the median, depending on the industry.

Balancing logistics service and cost

Logistics service is the package of activities performed by a supply chain member to ensure that the right product is in the right place at the right time. Customers are rarely interested in the activities themselves; instead, they are interested in the results or the benefits they receive from those activities – namely, efficient distribution. At the most basic level, customers demand availability, timeliness and quality. Specifically, customers expect product availability at the time of order, minimal effort required to place the order, prompt and consistent delivery, and undamaged goods when they are finally received.

Most logistics managers try to set their service level at a point that maximises service yet minimises cost. To do so, they must examine the total cost of all parts of the supply chain – sourcing and procurement of raw materials, warehousing and materials handling, stock control, order processing and transportation – using the *total cost approach*. The basic idea of the total cost approach is to examine the relationship of factors such as cost of raw materials, number of warehouses, size of finished-goods stock and transportation expenses. Of course, the cost of any single element should also be examined in relation to the level of customer service. Thus, the supply chain is viewed as a whole, not as a series of unrelated activities.

Ideally, the logistics manager would like to optimise overall logistics performance so that overall logistics costs are minimised while the desired level of supply chain service is maintained. Consequently, implementing the total cost approach requires tradeoffs. For example, a supplier that wants to provide next-day delivery to its customers and also to minimise transportation costs must make a tradeoff between the desired level of service (expensive next-day delivery) and the transportation goal (minimal costs).

Often the high cost of air transportation can be justified under the total cost approach. Rapid delivery may drastically reduce the number of warehouses required at distant locations. Therefore, the savings in stock and warehouse expenses, as shown in Exhibit 8.10, may more than justify the higher cost of using air freight. The Limited, a US company, uses a quick-response logistics infrastructure to respond to market information collected from actual point-of-sale data that tracks consumer preferences. Premium air transportation is used for time-sensitive fashions to ensure immediate market availability, whereas basic articles of clothing are shipped by less costly means. The savings from reduced stock levels make this a cost-effective solution.[14]

New breeds of logistics managers, however, are decreasing their emphasis on reducing logistics costs to the lowest possible level. Instead, they are favouring the exploitation of logistics capabilities to increase customer satisfaction and maintain customer demand. According to the Global Logistics Research Team at Michigan State University in the United States, many firms are using their logistics capabilities to achieve business success. These firms are developing competencies that are 'superior to competition in terms of satisfying customer expectations and requirements'. They define world-class logistical competencies to include:

- Devising logistics service strategies to meet the specific requirements of customers as a way to position and differentiate themselves from the competition
- Integrating all members of the supply chain to achieve internal logistical operating excellence and development of external supply chain relationships
- Determining and responding quickly to changing logistical requirements
- Constant monitoring of all internal and external aspects of the supply chain to ensure that the right product is in the right place at the right time.[15]

7 Discuss the concept of balancing logistics service and cost

logistics service
Interrelated activities performed by a member of the supply chain to ensure that the right product is in the right place at the right time.

Exhibit 8.10
How using air freight lowers logistics cost under the total cost approach

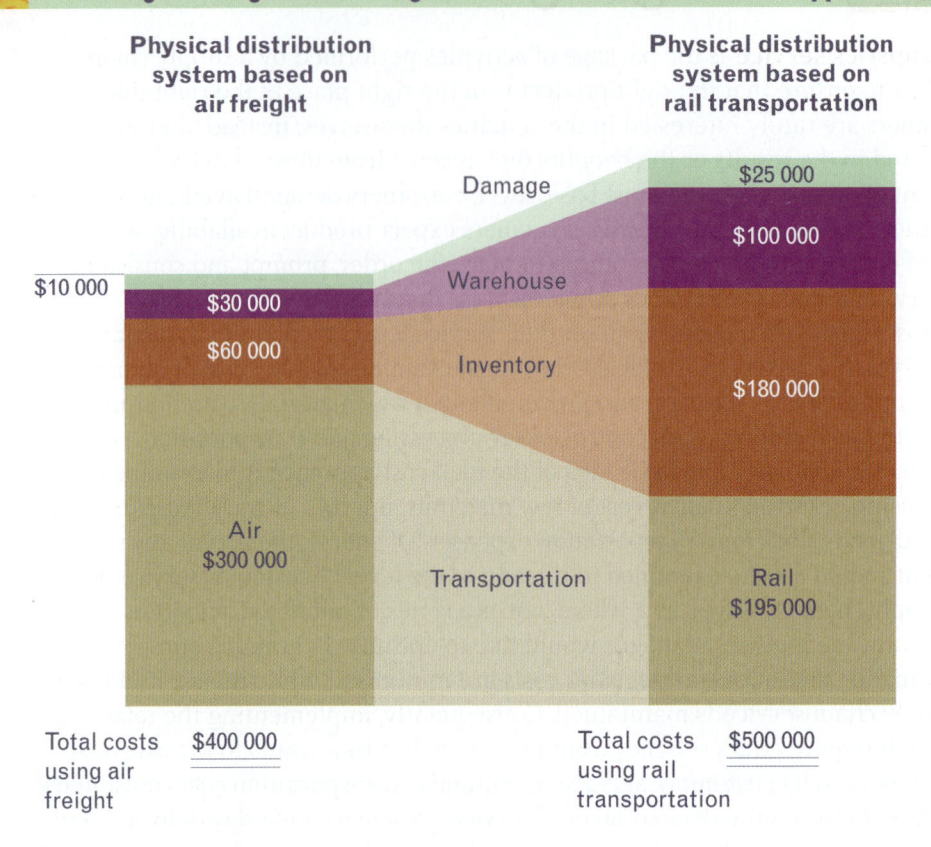

Physical distribution system based on air freight		Physical distribution system based on rail transportation
	Damage	$25 000
$10 000		$100 000
$30 000	Warehouse	
$60 000	Inventory	$180 000
Air $300 000	Transportation	Rail $195 000
Total costs using air freight: $400 000		Total costs using rail transportation: $500 000

For example, warehousing facilities are increasingly providing value-added services that go well beyond mere storage. In the past, overnight delivery was considered an extra service for a warehouse to provide. Today, warehouses are more likely to engage in product-transformation services, such as custom palletisation, kitting, repackaging, or even final assembly of a product.[16] A recent study by KPMG Management Consulting found that there is a growing belief among executives that the supply chain can contribute to corporate success as much as or more than branding. Specifically, these companies believe that an efficiently managed supply chain can result in service excellence and this, ultimately, may mean more to customers than branding.[17]

Integrated functions of the supply chain

8 Describe the integrated functions of the supply chain

The logistics supply chain consists of several interrelated and integrated functions: (1) procuring supplies and raw materials; (2) scheduling production; (3) processing orders; (4) managing stocks of raw materials and finished goods; (5) warehousing and materials management; and (6) selecting modes of transportation. These components are shown in Exhibit 8.11. Although these components are discussed separately, they are, of course, highly interdependent.

Integrating and linking all the logistics functions of the supply chain is the **logistics information system**. Today's supply chain logisticians are at the forefront of information technology. Information technology is not just a functional

logistics information system
Information technology that integrates and links all the logistics functions of the supply chain.

affiliate of supply chain management. Rather it is the enabler, the facilitator, the linkage that connects the various components and partners of the supply chain into an integrated whole. Electronic data interchange, on-board computers, satellite and mobile communications systems, materials-handling and warehouse-management software, enterprise-wide systems solutions and the Internet are among the information enablers of successful supply chain management.[18]

The **supply chain team**, in concert with the logistics information system, orchestrates the movement of goods, services and information from the source to the consumer. Supply chain teams typically cut across organisational boundaries, embracing all parties who participate in moving product to market. The best supply chain teams also move beyond the organisation to include the external participants in the chain, such as suppliers, transportation carriers and third-party logistics suppliers. Members of the supply chain communicate, coordinate and cooperate extensively.[19]

supply chain team
Entire group of individuals who orchestrate the movement of goods, services and information from the source to the consumer.

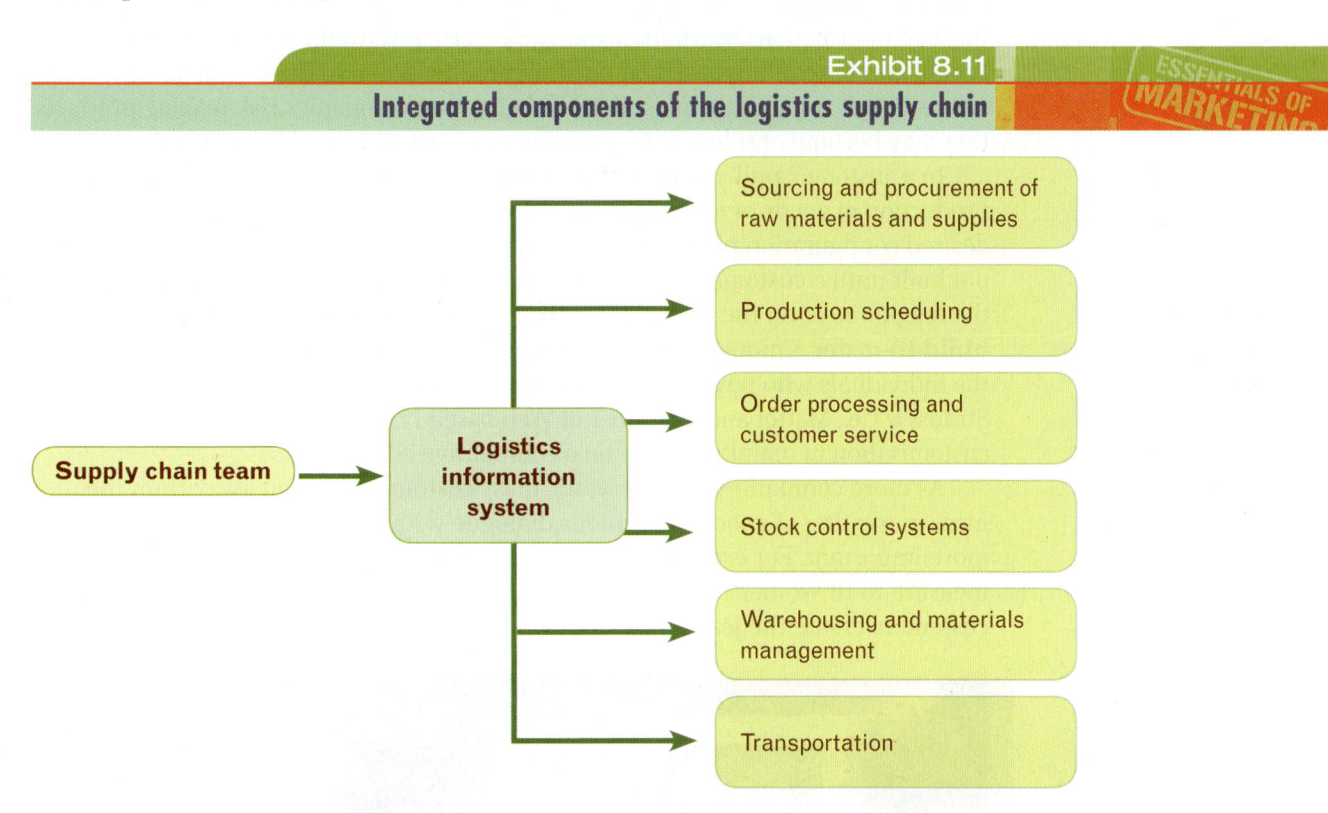

Exhibit 8.11
Integrated components of the logistics supply chain

Supply chain team → Logistics information system →
- Sourcing and procurement of raw materials and supplies
- Production scheduling
- Order processing and customer service
- Stock control systems
- Warehousing and materials management
- Transportation

Sourcing and procurement

One of the most important links in the supply chain is that between the manufacturer and the supplier. Purchasing professionals are on the front lines of supply chain management. Purchasing departments plan purchasing strategies, develop specifications, select suppliers, and negotiate price and service levels.

The goal of most sourcing and procurement activities is to reduce the cost of raw materials and supplies. Purchasing professionals traditionally rely on tough negotiations to get the lowest price possible from suppliers of raw materials, supplies and components. However, the traditional approach of simply negotiating the lowest price doesn't always fit well with the philosophy of supply chain management. In its position at the top of the supply chain, purchasing is crucial to the success of the manufacturer's relationship with its customers down the line. Yet purchasing efforts rarely look towards the bottom of the chain to the customers.[20]

Perhaps the biggest contribution purchasing can make to supply chain management is in the area of vendor relations. Companies can use the purchasing function to strategically manage suppliers in order to reduce the total cost of materials and services. Through enhanced vendor relations, buyers and sellers can develop cooperative relationships that reduce costs and improve efficiency with the aim of lowering prices and enhancing profits.[21] By integrating suppliers into their companies' businesses, purchasing managers have become better able to streamline purchasing processes, manage stock levels and reduce overall costs of the sourcing and procurement operations.[22]

Production scheduling

In traditional mass-market manufacturing, production begins when forecasts call for additional products to be made or stock control systems signal low stock levels. The firm then makes product and transports it to their own warehouses or those of intermediaries, where it waits to be ordered from retailers or customers. Production scheduling based on pushing product down to the consumer obviously has its disadvantages, the most notable being that companies risk making products that may become obsolete or that consumers don't want in the first place.

In a customer 'pull' manufacturing environment, which is growing in popularity, production of goods or services is not scheduled until the customer specifying the desired configuration places an order. For example, at Dell, a personal computer is not built until a customer selects the desired configuration and places an order over the telephone or on the Internet. This process, known as **mass customisation** or **build-to-order**, uniquely tailors mass-market goods and services to the needs of the individuals who buy them. Companies as diverse as BMW, Dell Computer, Levi Strauss & Co., Mattel and a number of Web-based businesses are adopting mass customisation to maintain or obtain a competitive edge.

As more companies move towards mass customisation and away from the mass marketing of goods, continuous dialogue with the customer becomes ever more important. For example, in the United States, Levi Strauss & Co. has made measure-to-fit women's jeans for several years. With the help of a sales assistant, customers create the jeans they want by picking from six colours, three basic models, five different leg openings and two types of fly. Each customer is measured for a correct fit. Then their order is entered into a Web-based terminal linked to the stitching machines in the factory. Two to three weeks later, the jeans arrive in the mail. A bar-code tag sealed to the pocket lining stores the measurements for simple reordering.[23]

mass customisation (build-to-order)
Production method whereby products are not made until an order is placed by the customer; products are made according to customer specifications.

Mass customisation is a way for companies to meet each individual customer's needs. Levi Strauss & Co. has been using this type of build-to-order strategy in the manufacture of women's jeans. The custom order is transmitted to production at the point of sale and the measured-to-fit jeans arrive two to three weeks later.

Just-in-time manufacturing

An important manufacturing process common today among manufacturers is just-in-time manufacturing. Borrowed from the Japanese, **just-in-time production (JIT)**, sometimes called *lean production*, requires manufacturers to work closely with suppliers and transportation providers to get required items to the assembly line or factory floor at the precise time they are needed for production. For the manufacturer, JIT means that raw materials arrive at the assembly line in guaranteed working order just in time to be installed, and finished products are generally shipped to the customer immediately after completion. For the supplier, JIT means supplying customers with products in just a few days, or even a few hours, rather than weeks. For the ultimate consumers, JIT means lower costs, shorter lead times and products that more closely meet their needs.

JIT benefits manufacturers most by reducing their raw materials stocks. For example, at some of Dell's assembly plants, computer components are often delivered just minutes before they are needed. Chips, boards and drives are kept in trucks backed up into bays located about 20 metres from the beginning of the production line. On average, the time it takes between when Dell buys parts and sells them as a finished product is only eight days.[24]

Additionally, JIT creates shorter lead times, or the time it takes to get parts from a supplier after an order has been placed. Manufacturers also enjoy better relationships with suppliers and can decrease their production and storeroom costs. Because there is little safety stock and therefore no margin for error, the manufacturer cannot afford to make a mistake. As a result, a manufacturer using JIT must be sure it receives high-quality parts from all vendors and must be confident that the supplier will meet all delivery commitments. Finally, JIT tends to reduce the amount of paperwork.

Many companies have adopted JIT II, an updated form of just-in-time manufacturing. JIT II involves the sharing of up-to-the-minute internal, proprietary data such as sales forecasts with suppliers. In addition, agents of suppliers may be allowed to set up an office in the manufacturer's facility and may be asked to replace purchasing agents and to place orders for themselves.

just-in-time production (JIT)
Redefining and simplifying manufacturing by reducing stock levels and delivering raw materials just when they are needed on the production line.

Order processing

The order is often the catalyst that brings the supply chain in motion, especially in the build-to-order environments of leading computer manufacturers such as Dell and, now, Compaq. The **order processing system** processes the requirements of the customer and sends the information into the supply chain via the logistics information system. The order goes to the manufacturer's warehouse, where it is checked whether the product is in stock. If the product is in stock, the order is fulfilled and arrangements are made to ship. If the product is not in stock, a replenishment request is triggered that finds its way to the factory floor.

The role of proper order processing in providing good service cannot be overemphasised. As an order enters the system, management must monitor two flows: the flow of goods and the flow of information. Often the best-laid plans of marketers can get entangled in the order processing system. Obviously, good communication among sales representatives, office personnel, and warehouse and shipping personnel is essential to correct order processing. Shipping incorrect merchandise or partially filled orders can create just as much dissatisfaction as stock outs or slow deliveries. The flow of goods and information must be continually monitored so that mistakes can be corrected before an invoice is prepared and the merchandise shipped.

order processing system
System whereby orders are entered into the supply chain and filled.

electronic data interchange (EDI)
Information technology that replaces the paper documents that usually accompany business transactions, such as purchase orders and invoices, with electronic transmission of the needed information to reduce stock levels, improve cash flow, streamline operations, and increase the speed and accuracy of information transmission.

Order processing is becoming more automated using computer technology known as **electronic data interchange (EDI)**. The basic idea behind EDI is to replace the paper documents that usually accompany business transactions, such as purchase orders and invoices, with electronic transmission of the needed information. Companies that use EDI can reduce stock levels, improve cash flow, streamline operations, and increase the speed and accuracy of information transmission. EDI is also believed to create a closer relationship between buyers and sellers.

It should not be surprising that retailers have become major users of EDI. For Coles Myer and the like, logistics speed and accuracy are crucial competitive tools in an overcrowded retail environment. Many big retailers are helping their suppliers to acquire EDI technology so that they can be linked in the system. EDI works hand in hand with retailers' *efficient consumer response* programs, which are designed to have the right products on the shelf, in the right styles and colours, through improved inventory, ordering and distribution techniques. More discussion of retailers' use of EDI techniques occurs later in this chapter.

Stock control

stock control system
Method of developing and maintaining an adequate assortment of products to meet customer demand.

Closely interrelated to the procurement, manufacturing and ordering processes is the inventory control system. A **stock control system** develops and maintains an adequate assortment of materials or products to meet a manufacturer's or a customer's demands.

Inventory decisions, for raw materials and finished goods, have a big impact on supply chain costs and the level of service provided. If too many products are kept in stock, costs increase – as do risks of obsolescence, theft and damage. If too few products are kept on hand, then the company risks product shortages and angry customers, and ultimately lost sales. A study by Procter & Gamble found that out-of-stock products reduced consumer purchases by more than 3 per cent per shopping trip, and 48 per cent of their products were out of stock at least once a month, costing the company valuable sales and customer satisfaction.[25] The goal of stock management, therefore, is to keep stock levels as low as possible while maintaining an adequate supply of goods to meet customer demand.

materials requirement planning (MRP)
Stock control system that manages the replenishment of raw materials, supplies and components from the supplier to the manufacturer.

distribution resource planning (DRP)
Stock control system that manages the replenishment of goods from the manufacturer to the final consumer.

Managing stock from the supplier to the manufacturer is called **materials requirement planning (MRP)** or materials management. This system also encompasses the sourcing and procurement operations, signalling purchasing when more raw materials, supplies or components will need to be replenished for the production of more goods. Systems that manage the finished goods inventory from the manufacturer to end user are commonly referred to as **distribution resource planning (DRP)**. Both inventory systems use various inputs – such as sales forecasts, available stock, outstanding orders, lead times and mode of transportation to be used – to determine what actions must be taken to replenish goods at all points in the supply chain. Demand in the system is collected at each level in the supply chain, from the retailer back up the chain to the manufacturer. With the use of electronic data interchange, the transmission speed of the information can be greatly accelerated, thereby enhancing the quick-response needs of today's competitive marketplace. Exhibit 8.12 provides an example of stock replenishment using distribution resource planning from the retailer to the manufacturer.

Enhanced versions of DRP have emerged, especially in the retailing and supermarket industries, under the names of *continuous replenishment* (CR), *efficient consumer response* (ECR) and *vendor-managed inventory* (VMI). Although these systems are beyond the scope of this discussion, all are designed to increase the speed by which stock needs can be communicated throughout the supply chain by utilising information technology to migrate from pushing product down the supply chain to pulling stock on to retailers' shelves, driven by actual customer demand. The mechanics of CR, ECR and VMI focus on increasing the flow and sharing of sensitive information across the distribution pipeline, which, in turn, accelerates the flow of product from the manufacturer to the point of sale.

Exhibit 8.12 Stock replenishment example

Sleep Right Mattress Retail Store

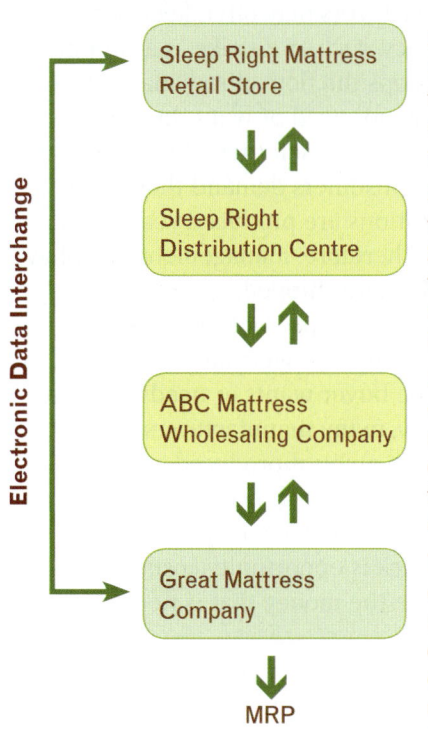

Sleep Right is planning a promotion on the Great Mattress Company's Gentle Rest mattress. Sales forecast is for 50 units to be sold. Sleep Right has 10 open Gentle Rest orders with its distribution centre. New mattresses must be delivered in two weeks in time for the promotion.

Sleep Right Distribution Centre

Sleep Right's Distribution Centre is electronically notified of the order of 50 new Gentle Rest mattresses. It currently has 20 Gentle Rest mattresses in stock and begins putting together the transportation plans to deliver these to the Sleep Right store. Delivery takes one day. It orders 40 new mattresses from its mattress wholesaler to make up the difference.

ABC Mattress Wholesaling Company

ABC Mattress Wholesaling Company is electronically notified of Sleep Right Distribution Centre's order of 40 new Gentle Rest mattresses. It currently does not have any of these in stock but electronically orders 40 from the Great Mattress Company's factory. Once it receives the new mattresses, it can have them delivered to the Sleep Right Distribution Centre in two days.

Great Mattress Company

The Great Mattress Company electronically receives ABC's order and forwards it to the factory floor. Production of a new mattress takes 20 minutes. The total order of 40 mattresses can be ready to be shipped to ABC in two days. Delivery takes one day. Raw material supplies for this order are electronically requested from Great Mattress's supply partners, who deliver the needed materials just-in-time to its stitching machines.

↓ MRP

Electronic Data Interchange

Just-in-time manufacturing processes have had a significant impact on reducing stock levels. Because JIT requires supplies to be delivered at the time they are needed on the factory floor, little stock is needed. With JIT, the purchasing firm can reduce the amount of raw materials and parts it keeps on hand by ordering more often and in smaller amounts. Lower stock levels due to JIT also can give firms a competitive edge through the flexibility to halt production of existing products in favour of ones gaining popularity with consumers. Additional savings come from less capital being tied up in stock and from the reduced need for storage facilities.[26]

In a true supply chain management environment where all members of the supply chain are working closely together, companies are substituting information for stock. Chrisco recently partnered with UPS Worldwide Logistics to develop a more efficient process for sending its routers to Europe. Of the tonnes of routers it ships to European markets each week, Chrisco needed to know where each box was at all times and have the ability to reroute an order to fill an urgent request. Using its knowledge of international plane, train and trucking schedules, UPS can send and track Chrisco's routers from the company's distribution facility to anywhere in the world. The partnership with UPS saves Chrisco precious dollars once tied up in stock.

Warehousing and materials handling

Supply chain logisticians oversee the constant flow of raw materials from suppliers to manufacturer and finished goods from the manufacturer to the ultimate consumer. Although JIT manufacturing processes may eliminate the need to warehouse many raw materials, manufacturers may often keep some safety stock on hand in the event of an emergency, such as a strike at a supplier's plant or a catastrophic event that temporarily stops the flow of raw materials to the production line. Likewise, the final user may not need or want the goods at the same time the manufacturer produces and wants to sell them. Products such as grain and corn are produced seasonally, but consumers demand them year-round. Other products such as Christmas decorations are produced year-round, but consumers don't want them until summer. Therefore, management must have a storage system to hold these products until they are shipped.

Storage is what helps manufacturers to manage supply and demand, or production and consumption. It provides time utility to buyers and sellers, which means that the seller stores the product until the buyer wants or needs it. Even when products are used regularly, not seasonally, many manufacturers store excess products in case the demand surpasses the amount produced at a given time. Storing additional product does have disadvantages, however, including the costs of insurance on the stored product, taxes, obsolescence or spoilage, theft, and warehouse operating costs. Another drawback is opportunity costs – that is, the lost opportunities of using for something else the money that is tied up in stored product.

A **materials-handling system** moves stock into, within and out of the warehouse. Materials handling includes the following functions:

- Receiving goods into the warehouse or distribution centre
- Identifying, sorting and labelling the goods
- Dispatching the goods to a temporary storage area
- Recalling, selecting or picking the goods for shipment (may include packaging the product in a protective container for shipping).

The goal of the materials-handling system is to move items quickly with minimal handling. With a manual, non-automated materials-handling system, a product may be handled more than a dozen times. Each time it is handled, the cost and risk of damaging it increase; each lifting of a product stresses its package. Consequently, most manufacturers today have moved to automated systems. Scanners quickly identify goods entering and leaving a warehouse through bar-coded labels affixed to the packaging. Automatic storage and

materials-handling system
Method of moving stock into, within and out of the warehouse.

retrieval systems store and pick goods in the warehouse or distribution centre. Automated materials-handling systems decrease product handling and ensure accurate placement of product, as well as improve the accuracy of order picking and the rates of on-time shipment. For example, a manufacturer and marketer of health-care products used a sophisticated materials-handling system to reduce product handling and keep costs to a minimum. As goods are received into the warehouse, bar-coded labels are affixed to the pallets of incoming product, which are then placed on a fully automated conveyor to be sent to the storage area. There, truck operators scan the labels, while an on-board, radio-controlled computer tells the operator exactly where to drop off the load. When the items to fill an order are picked off the shelves and placed in a carton, another bar-coded label is applied and the carton is placed on the conveyor system. Automatic scanners posted throughout the intricate conveyor system read each bar code and divert each carton to the proper shipping lane. This automated system gives the manufacturer a high degree of control over how orders are handled, placed, picked and sequenced for shipping.

Transportation

Transportation typically accounts for between 5 and 10 per cent of the price of goods.[27] Supply chain logisticians must decide which mode of transportation to use to move products from supplier to producer and from producer to buyer. These decisions are, of course, related to all other logistics decisions. The five main modes of transportation are railroads, road transportation, pipelines, water transportation and airways. Logistics managers generally choose a mode of transportation based on several criteria:

- *Cost*: the total amount a specific carrier charges to move the product from the point of origin to the destination.
- *Transit time*: the total time a carrier has possession of goods, including the time required for pick-up and delivery, handling, and movement between the point of origin and the destination.
- *Reliability*: the consistency with which the carrier delivers goods on time and in acceptable condition.
- *Capability*: the ability of the carrier to provide the appropriate equipment and conditions for moving specific kinds of goods, such as those that must be transported in a controlled environment (for example, under refrigeration).
- *Accessibility*: the carrier's ability to move goods over a specific route or network.
- *Traceability*: the relative ease with which a shipment can be located and transferred.

The mode of transportation used depends on the needs of the shipper, as they relate to the six criteria described above. Exhibit 8.13 compares the advantages and problems of the basic modes of transportation on these criteria.

In many cases, especially in a JIT manufacturing environment, the transportation network replaces the warehouse or eliminates the expense of holding stocks because goods are timed to arrive the moment they are needed on the assembly line or for shipment to customers. Dell Computer has gone even further to trim inventory of parts by taking delivery of components just minutes before they are needed.[28]

Exhibit 8.13
Criteria for ranking modes of transportation

	Highest				Lowest
Relative cost	Air	Truck	Rail	Pipe	Water
Transit time	Water	Rail	Pipe	Truck	Air
Reliability	Pipe	Truck	Rail	Air	Water
Capability	Water	Rail	Truck	Air	Pipe
Accessibility	Truck	Rail	Air	Water	Pipe
Traceability	Air	Truck	Rail	Water	Pipe

Trends in logistics

9 Discuss new technology and emerging trends in logistics

TNT Tracking System on-line

View the on-line video on the range of offering by one logistics company.
www.pallecontnt.com/files/cable/intro2.wmv

outsourcing (contract logistics)
Manufacturer's or supplier's use of an independent third party to manage an entire function of the logistics system, such as transportation, warehousing or order processing.

Several technological advances and business trends affect the logistics industry today. Three of the most outstanding trends are increased automation, outsourcing of logistics functions and electronic distribution.

Automation

Computer technology has boosted the efficiency of logistics dramatically. One of the main goals of automation is to bring up-to-date information to the logistics manager's desk. For instance, logisticians have long referred to the transportation system as the 'black hole', where products and materials fall out of sight until they reappear some time later in a factory, store or warehouse. Now carriers have systems that track freight, monitor the speed and location of carriers, and make routing decisions on the spur of the moment. The majority of trucking companies now use computers to help plan routes, and some have computers on board each truck to monitor location by satellite. Such systems help transportation firms to compete in today's demanding economy. With retailers and manufacturers keeping fewer stocks, deliveries must often be made at exact times to avoid shutting down a factory or forcing a store to run out of a popular product.

The rapid exchange of information that automation brings to the distribution process helps each supply chain partner to plan more effectively. The links among suppliers, buyers and carriers open up opportunities for joint decision-making. As more companies compete in global markets, timely information becomes even more important. For example, some 17 500 UPS employees in the United States are now equipped with 'ring scanners' – small, electronic devices worn on their index finger and wired to a small computer on their wrists. When a handler holds a package, the ring shoots a pattern of photons at a bar code on the package. Within moments, its location flashes to customers trolling the Internet. The Internet service can also zap the signature of whoever signs for a shipment anywhere in the world.[29]

Outsourcing logistics functions

External partners are becoming increasingly important in the efficient deployment of supply chain management. **Outsourcing**, or **contract logistics**, is a rapidly growing segment of the distribution industry in which a manufacturer

TNT helps its clients to be more self-sufficient in processing and tracking shipments. TNT customers can take more ownership of their logistics functions without having to invest in customised logistics technology

or supplier turns over the entire function of buying and managing transportation or another function of the supply chain, such as warehousing, to an independent third party. Many manufacturers are turning to outside partners for their logistics expertise in an effort to focus on the core competencies that they do best. Partners create and manage entire solutions for getting products where they need to be, when they need to be there. Logistics partners offer staff, an infrastructure and services that reach consumers virtually anywhere in the world. Because a logistics provider is focused, clients receive service in a timely, efficient manner, thereby increasing customers' level of satisfaction and boosting their perception of added value to a company's offerings.

Third-party contract logistics allows companies to reduce stock, locate it at fewer plants and distribution centres, and still provide the same or even better service levels. The companies then can refocus investment on their core business. Whirlpool, in the United States, decided to use a third-party logistics provider after realising it was spending too much on moving products – costs that were cutting into profits. On a single day, two or more Whirlpool trucks might make stops to pick up goods from a supplier when a single truck could have done the job. Whirlpool decided that outsourcing was the best option, allowing the company to concentrate on what it does best: making appliances. The company selected Ryder Dedicated Logistics, which soon untangled and coordinated the transport routes. Ryder now runs warehouses for Whirlpool and collects data that let it analyse supplier performance and spot new cost-cutting opportunities.[30]

Many firms are taking outsourcing one step further by allowing business partners to take over the final assembly of their product or its packaging in an effort to reduce inventory costs, speed up delivery or better meet customer requirements. Ryder assembles and packages 22 different combinations of shrink-wrapped boxes that contain the ice trays, drawers, shelves, doors and other accessories for the various refrigerator models Whirlpool sells. Before, Whirlpool would install the accessories in the refrigerators at the plant – a source of considerable factory-floor confusion.[31] IBM allows some of its distributors to do more of the final product assembly. Today, about 31 per cent of its US desktop personal computers are assembled by 11 business partners, many of which may install non-IBM components. One reseller actually assembles some of its IBM

Woolworths on-line

What restrictions does the Woolworths organisation place upon its vendors? Is this equitable for both parties to the value chain?
www.woolworths.com.au/vendors/downloads/brochure.pdf

orders in a warehouse right next to IBM's factory in North Carolina, saving on distribution costs.[32] For Nike's new athletic-equipment division, contract logistics provider Menlo Logistics inflates basketballs, soccer balls and footballs, which come in half-inflated because they take up less room. The logistics company also puts the balls in colourful packages and sticks on price tags for some sports retailers.[33]

Channel and distribution decisions

10 Identify the special problems and opportunities associated with distribution in retail organisations

retailing
All the activities directly related to the sale of goods and services to the ultimate consumer for personal, non-business use.

In this section three key areas – namely the retail sector, the service sector and the electronic sector – are discussed in relation to the impact on the community and the differing types of decisions organisations need to make due to the form of retail, the degree of the service component mix, and the impact of the electronic environment.

The role of retailing

Retailing is recognised as having enhanced the quality of our daily lives through the activities directly related to the sale of products (goods and services) to the ultimate consumer for personal, non-business use. When we shop for groceries, hair styling, clothes, books and many other products, we are involved in retailing. The millions of goods and services provided by retailers mirror the needs and styles of our society. Accordingly, we will find different types of retail environments in different countries and even in different regions within a country.

Retailing affects all of us directly or indirectly. The retailing industry is one of the largest employers in Australia and New Zealand. Supermarkets and grocery stores account for almost one quarter of the total retail trade income. Small business accounts for 95 per cent of total retail business but for nearly 40 per cent of total retail income. Large business accounts for less than 1 per cent of total retail business but for 41 per cent of total retail income, which clearly indicates that a few large organisations dominate the industry.

Classification of retail operations

A retail establishment can be classified according to its *ownership, level of service, product assortment* and *price*. Specifically, retailers use the latter three variables to position themselves in the competitive marketplace. (As noted in Chapter 4, on segmentation and targeting, positioning is the strategy used to influence how consumers perceive one product in relation to all competing products.) These three variables can be combined in several ways to create distinctly different retail operations. Exhibit 8.14 lists the main types of retail stores discussed in this chapter and classifies them by level of service, product assortment, price and gross margin.

Ownership

independent retailers
Retailers owned by a single person or partnership and not operated as part of a larger retail institution.

Retailers can be broadly classified by form of ownership: independent, part of a chain, or franchise outlet. Retailers owned by a single person or partnership and not operated as part of a larger retail institution are **independent retailers**. Around the world, most retailers are independent, operating one or a few stores in their community. Local florists, shoe stores, and ethnic and some food markets typically fit this classification.

Exhibit 8.14
Types of stores and their characteristics

Type of retailer	Level of service	Product assortment	Price	Gross margin
Department store	Moderately high to high	Broad	Moderate to high	Moderately high
Speciality store	High	Narrow	Moderate to high	High
Supermarket	Low	Broad	Moderate	Low
Chemist	Low to moderate	Medium	Moderate	Low
Convenience Store	Low	Medium to narrow	Moderately high	Moderately high
Full-line discount store	Moderate to low	Medium to broad	Moderately low	Moderately low
Discount speciality store	Moderate to low	Medium to broad	Moderately low to low	Moderately low
Off-price retailer	Low	Medium to narrow	Low	Low
Restaurant	Low to high	Narrow	Low to high	Low to high

Chain stores are owned and operated as a group by a single organisation. Under this form of ownership, the head office handles many of the administrative tasks for the entire chain. The head office also buys most of the merchandise sold in the stores.

Franchises are owned and operated by individuals but are licensed by a larger supporting organisation. Franchising combines the advantages of independent ownership with those of the chain store organisation. Franchising is discussed in more detail later in the chapter.

Level of service

The level of service that retailers provide can be classified along a continuum, from full service to self-service. Some retailers, such as exclusive clothing stores, offer high levels of service. They provide alterations, credit, delivery, consulting, liberal return policies, layby, gift-wrapping and personal shopping. Discount stores usually offer fewer services. Retailers such as factory outlets offer virtually no services. Vending machines offer no service but do provide convenience.

Product assortment

The third basis for positioning or classifying stores is by the breadth and depth of their product line. Speciality stores – for example, McGills book stores, Foot Locker and Wendy's ice cream shops – are the most concentrated in their product assortment, usually carrying single or narrow product lines but in considerable depth. On the other end of the spectrum, full-line discounters typically carry broad assortments of merchandise with limited depth. For example, Target, and discount outlets such as Silly Solly's and Dimmeys, have a product range from auto parts to household items and dog food. However, these outlets tend to carry only one or two brands of dog food, whereas a supermarket may carry as many as 10 different brands.

chain stores
Stores owned and operated as a group by a single organisation.

franchise
The right to operate a business or to sell a product.

McGills on-line
How has this organisation taken on overseas retailers such as Amazon? What market is this retailer focusing on?
www.mcgills.com.au

Blundstone on-line

What does Blundstone retail? Does the Web presence improve its retail efforts? Why, or why not?
www.blundstone.com.au

Other retailers, such as factory outlet stores, may carry only part of a single line. Blundstones, a major manufacturer of work boots, sells only certain items of its own brand in its many outlet stores. Discount speciality stores such as Hardwarehouse carry a broad assortment in concentrated product lines, such as building and hardware supplies.

In keeping with this concept of classification by product type, Australian and New Zealand government bodies have developed the Australian and New Zealand Standard Industry Classification system. Exhibit 8.15 shows the first two levels of the classification system relevant to the retail industry and which are coded by product classification.

Exhibit 8.15
Types of retail activity based on product assortment

Industry class ANZSIC code	Description	Management units %	Employment %	Total income %	Floor space %
511	Supermarket and grocery stores	25.2	2.2	2.3	4.1
512	Specialised food retailing – total	5.6	4.4	3.9	6.7
521	Department stores	34.1	0.1	0.1	1.4
522	Clothing and soft goods retailing – total	14.5	6.1	6.4	12.5
523	Furniture, houseware and appliance retailing – total	5.1	4.5	6.6	8.0
524	Recreational goods retailing – total	3.8	5.1	4.7	9.2
525	Other personal and household goods retailing – total	4.8	4.3	6.6	12.9
526	Household equipment repair services – total	5.0	6.5	10.3	18.5
531	Motor vehicle retailing – total	14.8	6.3	5.6	na
532	Motor vehicle services – total	2.2	3.8	4.4	na
	Total retail trade	1.9	1.3	1.5	3.5

Source: ABS, Cat. No. 8622.0

Price

Price is a fourth way to position retail stores. Traditional department stores and speciality stores typically charge the full 'recommended retail price'. In contrast, discounters, factory outlets and off-price retailers use low prices as a major lure for shoppers.

Gross margin is how much the retailer makes as a percentage of sales after the cost of the products and the cost of selling them (cost of goods sold) is subtracted. The level of gross margin and the price level generally match. For example, a traditional jewellery store has high prices and high gross margins.

gross margin
Amount of money the retailer makes as a percentage of sales after the cost of goods sold is subtracted.

A factory outlet has low prices and low gross margins. Markdowns on merchandise during sale periods and price wars among competitors, in which stores lower prices on certain items in an effort to win customers, cause gross margins to decline. When Impulse Airlines entered the domestic air travel business in Australia in June 2000, a fierce price war ensued. By the time the price war was in full swing, the price of a flight from Sydney to Brisbane was down to 30 per cent of the original cost of a flight, at which level an airline could not make a profit.

Main types of retail operations

Retail operations can be discussed in terms of types of retail centres and types of retail outlets. We will first discuss the retail outlets and then explore how the amalgamation of different store types allows us to classify the retail centres as having different attributes and catchments.

Retail outlets

There are many different types of retail outlets and these vary from country to country. In Australia, there are a range of retail outlets with each offering different product assortment, type of service and price level, according to its customers' shopping preferences.

The common range of retail outlets in Australia include:

- *Department stores*: Housing several departments under one roof, a **department store** carries a wide variety of shopping and speciality goods, including apparel, cosmetics, housewares, electronics and sometimes, furniture. Purchases are generally made within each department rather than at one central checkout area. Each department is treated as a separate buying centre to achieve economies in promotion, buying, service and control.
- *Speciality stores*: Speciality store formats allow retailers to refine their segmentation strategies and tailor their merchandise to specific target markets. A **speciality store** is not only a type of store but also a method of retail operations – namely, specialising in a given type of merchandise. A typical speciality store carries a deeper but narrower assortment of speciality merchandise than does a department store. Generally, speciality stores' knowledgeable sales assistants offer more attentive customer service. The format has become very powerful in the apparel market and other areas. Benetton, Victoria's Secret, The Body Shop, Foot Locker and Wallace Bishop are several successful chain speciality retailers.
- *Supermarkets*: are large, departmentalised, self-service retailer that specialises in food and some non-food items. Supermarkets evolved to meet the demand for one stop shopping. As stores seek to meet consumer demand for one-stop shopping, conventional supermarkets are being replaced by bigger superstores, which are usually twice the size of supermarkets.
- *Convenience stores*: are a miniature supermarket, carrying only a limited range of high-turnover convenience goods. These self-service stores are typically located near residential areas and are open extended trading hours, seven days a week. Convenience stores offer exactly what their name implies: convenient location, long hours, fast service. However, prices are usually higher than at a supermarket.

department store
A store housing several departments under one roof.

speciality store
Retail store specialising in a given type of merchandise.

supermarket
A large, departmentalised, self-service retailer that specialises in food and some non-food items.

convenience store
A miniature supermarket, carrying only a limited line of high-turnover convenience goods.

discount store
A retailer that competes on the basis of low prices, high turnover and high volume.

full-line discount store
A retailer that offers consumers very limited service and carries a broad assortment of well-known, nationally branded 'hard goods'.

mass merchandising
Retailing strategy using moderate to low prices on large quantities of merchandise and lower service to stimulate high turnover of products.

speciality discount store
Retail store that offers a nearly complete selection of single-line merchandise and uses self-service, discount prices, high volume and high turnover.

category killers
Term often used to describe speciality discount stores because they so heavily dominate their narrow merchandise segment.

- *Discount stores*: are a retailer that competes based on low prices, high turnover and high volume. Discounters can be classified into three major categories: full-line discount retailers, speciality discount retailers and category killers.

Aussie Shopper on-line
What are these organisations offering to the retail environment? Will their current actions change the retail behaviour of their customers?
www.aussieshopper.com.au

Myer/Grace Bros is one of the retail department store chains controlled by the Coles Myer group offering different product ranges and mixes for the various target markets.

non-store retailing
Shopping without visiting a store.

automatic vending
The use of machines to offer goods for sale.

Non-store retailing

The retailing methods discussed so far has been in-store methods, where customers must physically shop at stores. In contrast, **non-store retailing** is shopping without visiting a store. Because consumers demand convenience, non-store retailing is currently growing faster than in-store retailing. The main forms of non-store retailing are **automatic vending**, direct marketing and electronic marketing. A more detailed discussion of this topic will be covered later in Chapter 9.

Channels and distribution decisions – services

11 Identify the special problems and opportunities associated with distribution in service organisations

The fastest-growing part of our economy is the service sector. Although distribution in the service sector is difficult to visualise, the same skills, techniques and strategies used to manage stock can also be used to manage service availability – for example, hospital beds, bank accounts or airline seats. The quality of the planning and execution of distribution can have a major impact on costs and customer satisfaction.

Discount speciality stores usually offer single-line merchandising and self-service. This provides them with high-volume sales and allows them to offer discount prices and to remain viable.

One thing that sets service distribution apart from traditional manufacturing distribution is that, in a service environment, production and consumption are simultaneous. In manufacturing, a production setback can often be remedied by using safety stock or a faster mode of transportation. Such substitution is not possible with a service. The benefits of a service are also relatively intangible – that is, you can't normally see the benefits of a service, such as a doctor's physical examination. A consumer can, however, normally see the benefits provided by a product – for example, a vacuum cleaner removing dirt from the carpet.

Because service industries are so customer-oriented, customer service is a priority. Service distribution focuses on three main areas:

- *Minimising waiting times*: Minimising the amount of time customers wait in line to deposit a cheque, wait for their food at a restaurant or wait in a doctor's office for an appointment is a key factor in maintaining the quality of service. People tend to overestimate the amount of time they spend waiting in line, researchers report, and unexplained waiting seems longer than explained waits. To reduce anxiety among waiting customers, some restaurants give patrons pagers that allow them to roam around or go to the bar. Banks sometimes install electronic boards displaying share values or sports scores. Car rental companies reward repeat customers by eliminating their waiting time altogether.[34] Airports have designed comfortable waiting areas with televisions and children's play areas for those waiting to board planes.[35]
- *Managing service capacity*: For a product manufacturer, stock acts as a buffer, enabling it to provide the product during periods of peak demand without extraordinary effort. Service firms don't have this luxury. If they don't have the capacity to meet demand, they must either turn down some prospective customers, let service levels slip or expand capacity. For example, at tax time an accounting firm may have so many customers desiring its services that it either has to turn business away or add temporary offices or staff. Popular restaurants risk losing business when seating is unavailable or the wait is too long.

Dimmeys on-line

More and more discount stores are relocating to be near other discount and speciality stores. Does Dimmeys promote itself as a discount store? Why would this be a good strategy for the off-price and discount stores?
www.dimmeys.com.au

Virgin Blue
on-line

Visit the Virgin Blue site. What can you do at this site? Was it convenient to book a flight using this site? What other services are provided?
www.virginblue.com.au

○ *Improving delivery through new distribution channels*: Like manufacturers, service firms are now experimenting with different distribution channels for their services. These new channels can increase the time that services are available (such as using the Internet to disseminate information and services 24 hours a day) or add to customer convenience (such as pizza delivery, walk-in medical clinics, or a drycleaner located in the supermarket). Many banks are experimenting with mobile bank branches. Many ATMs are located in high-traffic locations, such as supermarkets. In addition, telephone and Internet banking are generating more and more inbound calls daily.

The Internet is fast becoming an alternative channel through which to deliver services. Consumers can now purchase plane tickets, plan holidays, book hotel rooms, pay bills, purchase books and music, and receive electronic news.

Channels and distribution decisions – electronic

12 Identify the special problems and opportunities associated with distribution in an electronic environment

electronic distribution
Distribution technique that includes any kind of product or service that can be distributed electronically, whether over traditional forms such as fibre-optic cable or through satellite transmission of electronic signals.

TV Shopping Network
on-line

To which type of customer do you think this site is targeted? What range of products does it offer?
www.tvsn.com.au

Electronic distribution is the most recent development in the logistics arena. Broadly defined, **electronic distribution** includes any kind of product or service that can be distributed electronically, whether over traditional forms such as fibre-optic cable or through satellite transmission of electronic signals. Woolworths has developed for potential vendors a program of the protocols they need to adhere to in order to operate within the Woolworths organisation. This information can be retrieved from the address given in the on-line box and shows the relevancies of logistics developed to one of Australia's larger companies.

Electronic retailing

Electronic retailing includes the 24-hour, shop-at-home television networks and on-line retailing.

Shop-at-home networks

The shop-at-home television networks are specialised forms of direct-response marketing. These shows display merchandise, with the retail price, to home viewers. Viewers can phone in their orders directly on a toll-free line and shop with a credit card. The shop-at-home industry in Australia has quickly grown into a billion-dollar business with a loyal customer following. Shop-at-home networks have the capability of reaching nearly every home that has free-to-air or pay TV.

The best-known shop-at-home network is TVSN (TV Shopping Network). Home shopping networks are now branching out with new products to appeal to audiences that are more affluent.

On-line retailing

On-line retailing is a two-way, interactive service available to consumers with personal computers and access to the Internet. Internet service providers, such as bigpond.com and Telnet, typically provide shopping services or virtual shopping malls for subscribers. Retailers can also set up their own site on the World Wide Web for on-line shoppers to find. Coles Myer, for example, operates its own website (www.colesmyer.com.au) where it sells its clothes and accessories on-line.

In the year to November 2000, on-line consumer sales increased 66 per cent. This represents 1.3 million Australians who purchased products for their own use over the Internet. Retail products expected to sell well over the Internet include books, computer hardware and software, music and videos, toys, consumer electronics and even wines.[36]

Despite its potential convenience, on-line shopping has had a slow start. Although the number of consumers purchasing goods on-line has increased dramatically, on-line shopping has not been greatly successful as buyers still like touching the goods they are going to buy, as well as the social interaction, and are concerned about the security and the privacy of their personal information on-line.[37] However, many on-line merchants are thriving. Selling books, music, software and flowers on-line are a few bright spots in terms of sales and visits. Amazon.com has become one of the world's most successful booksellers via the Internet. On-line shoppers can search Amazon's database of over one million titles, read on-line reviews and receive email alerts about their favourite subjects and authors. CDNow's Internet site offers more than 500 000 music- and entertainment-related products, including CDs, vinyl, cassettes, music videos, movies, DVDs, digital music downloads and special product offerings. It enables custom-made CDs, where the customers pick their own songs, and offers site navigation in eight languages.[38]

Connect it

As you complete this chapter, you should be able to see how marketing channels operate and how physical distribution is necessary to move goods from the manufacturer to the final consumer.

Companies can choose from several different marketing channels to sell their products or sell in several channels. For example, as the opening story discussed, computer manufacturers can use direct channels, like Dell has done, or indirect channels using one or more resellers. Computer manufacturers Compaq and IBM have been experimenting with direct channels. Dell and Gateway also utilise the Internet as a distribution channel for their products.

Summary

1 Explain what a marketing channel is and why intermediaries are needed.
Marketing channels are composed of members that perform negotiating functions. Some intermediaries buy and resell products; other intermediaries aid the exchange of ownership between buyers and sellers without taking title. Non-member channel participants do not engage in negotiating activities and function as an auxiliary part of the marketing channel structure. Intermediaries are often included in marketing channels for three important reasons. First, the specialised expertise of intermediaries may improve the overall efficiency of marketing channels. Second, intermediaries may help overcome discrepancies by making products available in quantities and assortments desired by consumers and business buyers, and at locations convenient to them. Third, intermediaries reduce the number of transactions required to distribute goods from producers to consumers and end users.

2 Define the types of channel intermediaries and describe their functions and activities.

The most prominent difference separating intermediaries is whether they take title to the product, such as retailers and merchant wholesalers. Retailers are firms that sell mainly to consumers. Merchant wholesalers are those organisations that facilitate the movement of products and services from the manufacturer to producers, resellers, governments, institutions and retailers. Agents and brokers, on the other hand, don't take title to goods and services they market but do facilitate the exchange of ownership between sellers and buyers. Channel intermediaries perform three basic types of functions. Transactional functions include contacting and promoting, negotiating and risk-taking. Logistical functions performed by channel members include physical distribution, storing and sorting functions. Finally, channel members may perform facilitating functions such as researching and financing.

3 Describe the channel structures for consumer and business-to-business products and discuss alternative channel arrangements.

Marketing channels for consumer and business-to-business products vary in degree of complexity. The simplest consumer product channel involves direct selling from producers to consumers. Businesses may sell directly to business or government buyers. Marketing channels grow more complex as intermediaries become involved. Consumer product channel intermediaries include agents, brokers, wholesalers and retailers. Business product channel intermediaries include agents, brokers and industrial distributors. Marketers often use alternative channel arrangements to move their products to the consumer. With dual distribution or multiple distributions, they choose two or more different channels to distribute the same product. Non-traditional channels help to differentiate a firm's product from those of competitors or provide a manufacturer with another avenue for sales. Adaptive channels are flexible and responsive channels of distribution initiated when a firm identifies critical but rare customer requirements that they don't have the capability to fulfil. Once the requirements are identified, arrangements with other channel members are made to help satisfy these requests. Finally, strategic channel alliances are arrangements that use another manufacturer's already established channel.

4 Discuss the issues that influence channel strategy.

When determining marketing channel strategy, the marketing manager must determine what market, product and producer factors will influence the choice of channel. The manager must also determine the appropriate level of distribution intensity. Intensive distribution is distribution aimed at maximum market coverage. Selective distribution is achieved by screening dealers to eliminate all but a few in any single area. The most restrictive form of market coverage is exclusive distribution, which entails only one or a few dealers within a given area.

5 Explain channel leadership, conflict and partnering.

Power, control, leadership, conflict and partnering are the main social dimensions of marketing channel relationships. Channel power refers to the capacity of one channel member to control or influence other channel members. Channel control occurs when one channel member intentionally affects another member's behaviour. Channel leadership is the exercise of authority and power. Channel

Chapter 8 ■ ■ Marketing channels and logistics decisions

conflict occurs when there is a clash of goals and methods among the members of a distribution channel. Channel conflict can be either horizontal, among channel members at the same level, or vertical, among channel members at different levels of the channel. Channel partnering is the joint effort of all channel members to create a supply chain that serves customers and creates a competitive advantage. Collaborating channel partners meet the needs of consumers more effectively by ensuring that the right products reach shelves at the right time and at a lower cost, boosting sales and profits.

6 Discuss logistics and supply chain management and their evolution into distribution practice.

Logistics is the process of strategically managing the efficient flow and storage of raw materials, in-process stock and finished goods from point of origin to point of consumption. The supply chain connects all of the business entities, both internal and external to the company, that perform or support the logistics function. Supply chain management, or integrated logistics, coordinates and integrates all of these activities performed by supply chain members into a seamless process that delivers enhanced customer and economic value through synchronised management of the flow of goods and information from source to consumer. The concept of supply chain management evolved from the physical distribution of agricultural goods in the early 1900s, which focused on pushing products to market. Today, logistics and supply chain management are viewed as a key means of differentiation for a firm and a critical component in marketing and corporate strategy. The focus is on pulling products into the marketplace and partnering with members of the supply chain to work together and share information with the goal of enhancing customer value.

7 Discuss the concept of balancing logistics service and cost.

Today, logistics service is recognised as an area in which a firm can distinguish itself from the competition. Many logisticians strive to achieve an optimal balance of customer service and total distribution cost. Important aspects of service are availability of product, timeliness of deliveries, and quality (accuracy and condition) of shipments. In evaluating costs, logistics managers examine all parts of the supply chain – sourcing and procurement of raw materials, warehousing and materials handling, stock control, order processing and transportation – using the total cost approach. Many logisticians are decreasing their emphasis on reducing logistics costs to the lowest possible level in favour of exploiting logistics capabilities to increase customer satisfaction and maintain customer demand.

8 Describe the integrated functions of the supply chain.

The logistics supply chain consists of several interrelated and integrated functions: (1) procuring supplies and raw materials; (2) scheduling production; (3) processing orders; (4) managing stocks of raw materials and finished goods; (5) warehousing and materials handling; and (6) selecting modes of transportation. Integrating and linking all the logistics functions of the supply chain is the logistics information system. Information technology connects the various components and partners of the supply chain to make an integrated whole. The supply chain team, in concert with the logistics information system, orchestrates the movement of goods, services and information from the source to the consumer. Supply chain teams typically cut across organisational boundaries, embracing all parties that participate in moving product to market. Procurement deals with the purchase of raw materials, supplies and components according to production scheduling. Order processing monitors the flow of goods and information (order entry and order handling). Stock control systems regulate when and how much to buy (order timing and order quantity). Warehousing provides storage of goods until needed by the customer, while the materials-handling system moves stock into, within and out of the warehouse. Finally, the main modes of transportation include railroads, roads, pipelines, waterways and airways.

9 Discuss new technology and emerging trends in logistics.

Several trends are emerging in today's logistics industry. Technology and automation are bringing up-to-date distribution information to the decision-maker's desk. Technology is also linking suppliers, buyers and carriers for joint decision-making and has created a new electronic distribution channel. Many companies are saving money and time by outsourcing third-party carriers to handle some or all aspects of the distribution process.

10 Identify the special problems and opportunities associated with distribution in retail organisations.

Retailing plays a vital role in the economy for two main reasons. First, retail businesses contribute to our high standard of living by providing a vast number and diversity of goods and services. Second, retailing employs a large part of the working population. Further, many different kinds of retailers exist. A retail **establishment** can be classified according to its ownership, level of service, product assortment and price. On the basis of ownership, retailers can be broadly differentiated as independent retailers, chain stores or franchise outlets. The level of service retailers provide can be classified along a continuum of high to low. Retailers also classify themselves by the breadth and depth of their product assortment: some retailers have concentrated product assortments, whereas others have extensive product assortments. Last, general price levels also classify a store, from discounters offering low prices to exclusive speciality stores where high prices are the norm. Retailers use these latter three variables to position themselves in the marketplace. The main types of retail stores in Australia are department stores, speciality retailers, supermarkets, chemists, convenience stores and discount stores. Additionally, non-store retailing has three main categories: automatic vending, direct retailing and direct marketing. Finally, there are three main trends evident in retailing today: adding entertainment; retailers offering more convenience and efficiency to consumers; and using the information collected about customers at the point of sale to develop customer management programs, including customer relationship marketing, loyalty programs and developing clientele.

11 Identify the special problems and opportunities associated with distribution in service organisations.

Managers in service industries use the same skills, techniques and strategies to manage logistics functions as managers in goods-producing industries. The distribution of services focuses on three main areas: minimising waiting times, managing service capacity, and improving delivery through new distribution channels.

12 Discuss non-store retailing techniques.

Non-store retailing, which is shopping outside a store setting, has three main categories. Automatic vending uses machines to offer products for sale. In direct retailing, the sales transaction occurs in a home setting, typically through door-to-door sales or party plan selling. Direct marketing refers to the techniques used to get consumers to buy from their homes or place of business. Those techniques include direct mail, catalogues and mail order, telemarketing, and electronic retailing, such as home shopping channels and on-line shopping over the Internet.

Review it

1. Which of the following is *not* another name for a channel member?
   a. Intermediary
   b. Reseller
   c. Middleman
   d. All of the above are names for channel members

2. Marketing channels overcome _____ by maintaining stocks in anticipation of future demand for products.
   a. Discrepancies of quantity
   b. Discrepancies of assortment
   c. Temporal discrepancies
   d. Spatial discrepancies

3. Channels can help to simplify distribution by reducing the number of transactions required to get products from manufacturers to consumers. This need that is fulfilled by a distribution channel is
   a. Providing specialisation of labour
   b. Providing division of labour
   c. Overcoming discrepancies
   d. Providing contact efficiency

4. Which of the following types of channels would most likely be used when there are many manufacturers and many retailers who often lack the resources to find each other?
   a. Direct channel
   b. Agent/broker channel
   c. Retailer channel
   d. Wholesaler channel

5. The concept of a flexible and responsive channel of distribution is called a(n):
   a. Multiple channel
   b. Non-traditional channel
   c. Adaptive channel
   d. Strategic channel alliance

6. _____ is distribution that is aimed to maximise marketplace coverage.
   a. Intensive distribution
   b. Selective distribution
   c. Strategic distribution
   d. Exclusive distribution

7. According to the evolution of integrated logistics, what distribution phase are marketers in today?
   a. The segmented functions phase
   b. The integrated functions phase
   c. The customer focus phase
   d. The logistics as differentiator phase

Define it

adaptive channel 257
agents and brokers 252
automatic vending 286
category killers 285
chain stores 283
channel conflict 263
channel control 263
channel leader (channel captain) 263
channel members 249
channel partnering (channel cooperation) 265
channel power 262
convenience store 285
department store 285
direct channel 255
discount store 285
discrepancy of assortment 250
discrepancy of quantity 249
distribution resource planning (DRP) 276
dual distribution (multiple distribution) 257
electronic data interchange (EDI) 276
electronic distribution 288
exclusive distribution 262
franchise 283
full-line discount store 285
gross margin 284
horizontal conflict 263
independent retailers 282
intensive distribution 261
just-in-time production (JIT) 275
logistics 266
logistics information system 272
logistics service 271
marketing channel (channel of distribution) 249
mass customisation (build-to-order) 274
mass merchandising 285
materials requirement planning (MRP) 276
materials-handling system 278
merchant wholesaler 251
non-store retailing 286
order processing system 275
outsourcing (contract logistics) 280
retailer 251

retailing 282
selective distribution 261
spatial (place)
　discrepancy 250
speciality discount store 285
speciality store 285
stock control system 276
strategic channel alliance 258
supermarket 285
supply chain 266
supply chain management
　(integrated logistics) 267
supply chain team 273
temporal (time)
　discrepancy 250
vertical conflict 263

8 Some independent channel members can perform channel duties more efficiently than can the manufacturer of the product.
　a True
　b False

9 Merchant wholesalers always take title to the goods that they sell.
　a True
　b False

10 The product life cycle can have a significant impact on the producer's choice of a distribution channel.
　a True
　b False

11 Which of the following is *not* an example of non-store retailing?
　a Direct mail
　b Automatic vending
　c Discount stores
　d Telemarketing

Check the Answer Key to see how well you understood the material. More detailed discussion and writing questions and a video case related to this chapter are found in the Student Resources CD-ROM.

Apply it

1 Describe the most likely marketing channel structure for each of these consumer products: chocolate bars, Tupperware products, non-fiction books, new cars, farmers' market produce and stereo equipment. Construct alternative channels for these same products.

2 Discuss the reasons intermediaries are important to the distribution of most goods. What important functions do they provide?

3 Amazon.com successfully uses a direct channel to sell books and music to consumers over the Internet. How has Amazon affected traditional book retailers with bricks-and-mortar buildings? How have other booksellers countered Amazon's competitive advantage in its direct channel?

4 Decide which distribution intensity level – intensive, selective or exclusive – is used for the following products and why: Rolex watches, Land Rover four-wheel drives, M&Ms, special edition Barbie dolls, Colgate toothpaste.

5 You are hired to design an alternative marketing channel for a firm specialising in the manufacturing and marketing of novelties for university student organisations. In a memo to the president of the organisation, describe how the channel operates.

6 Discuss the benefits of supply chain management. How does the implementation of supply chain management result in enhanced customer value?

7 Discuss the tradeoffs between logistics service and cost. How can the high cost of expensive air transportation to enhance service be offset? How does logistics service affect customer satisfaction?

8 Discuss the impact of just-in-time production on the entire supply chain. Specifically, how does JIT affect suppliers, procurement planning, stock levels, mode of transportation selected and warehousing? What are the benefits of JIT to the consumer?

9 Assume that you are the logistics manager for a producer of high-tech, expensive computer components. Identify the most suitable method(s) of transporting your product in terms of cost, transit time, reliability, capability, accessibility and traceability. Now assume you are the logistics manager for a producer of milk. How does this change your choice of transportation?

10 Assume that you are the marketing manager of a hospital. Write a report indicating the distribution functions that concern you. Discuss the similarities and dissimilarities of distribution for services and for goods.

11 Visit the website of Logistics Bureau at www.logisticsbureau.com.au. What logistics functions can this third-party logistics supplier provide? How does its mission fit in with the supply chain management philosophy?

12 Discuss the possible marketing implications of the recent trend towards the clustering of major discount stores. In particular, which type of organisation combines a supermarket and a full-line discount store?

13 Identify a successful retail business in your community. What marketing strategies do you think it adopted that have led to its success?

14 You want to convince your boss, the owner of a retail store, of the importance of store atmosphere. Write a memo citing specific examples of how store atmosphere affects your own shopping behaviour.

15 You have been asked to write a brief article about the way consumer demand for convenience and efficiency is influencing the future of retailing. Write the outline for your article.

16 Your retail clothing company is considering expanding into East Timor. What information about the country and its customs should you collect before opening a store in East Timor?

17 Form a team of three classmates to identify the different retail stores in your city or town where DVD players, CD players and TVs are sold. Team members should visit all the different stores between them and describe the products and brands that are sold in each. Prepare a report describing the differences in brands and products sold at each of the stores and the differences in the stores' characteristics and service levels. For example, which brands are sold in Myer/Grace Bros and Kmart versus Harvey Norman and Dick Smith versus independent, speciality outlets? Suggest why different products and brands are distributed through different types of stores.

18 How much does the most powerful computer with the fastest modem, most memory, largest monitor, biggest hard drive and all the available peripherals cost at the website below? Now configure a more affordable computer and compare the differences in features and prices. www.dell.com

19 Should retailers market their printed catalogues on-line?

Try it

Peterson House has owned and operated a small sparkling wine organisation in the Hunter Valley region of Australia for about 10 years (www.petersonhouse.com.au/about.htm#company). Peterson House has also experimented with preparing and selling several sparkling wine varieties. For the most part the wine is sold locally at the cellar door, by mail order, or through the Peterson House Society club membership. Peterson's most recent product has been a huge success locally, and several enquiries have come from other distributors about the possibilities of selling the product regionally and perhaps nationally. No research has been conducted to determine the level or scope of demand for the wine.

Questions

1. What should Peterson House do to help the firm decide how best to market the new wine?
2. Should Peterson House sign a contract with one of the distributors to sell the wine, or should the firm try to sell the product directly to one or more of the major distributors?

Ron Johnson is developing a retail strategy to open up his new athletic footwear and sports equipment store. He has decided to carry Nike and Converse as his two lines of athletic footwear. This will give him top-of-the-line merchandise (Nike) and a lower priced, high-quality alternative (Converse). He obtained permission from one of his former university lecturers to hold brainstorming sessions in a couple of his classes.

From these sessions, he identified the following evaluative criteria customers might use in selecting particular athletic footwear to purchase: (1) attractiveness/style/colour; (2) brand name; (3) comfort; (4) price; (5) endorsement; and (6) quality. He also determined that location, friends' recommendations, brands carried and store atmosphere are important in selecting a place to purchase athletic footwear.

Questions

1. What type of retailing strategy should Ron use?
2. Which elements of the retailing mix are relatively more important?

Watch it

Burton Snowboards: Going global

Burton Snowboards, which we first met in Chapter 1, is a designer and manufacturer of premier snowboarding equipment and since its somewhat humble start in 1977, the company has grown from a single workshop in Vermont into an international retailer. Higher sales require a more involved distribution system, so in 1992 Burton relocated its offices to Burlington, Vermont. Because Burlington offered easy access to an international airport, a larger workforce and more business services, Burton expected to achieve better distribution of its products from its new headquarters.

In conjunction with smaller offices in Austria and Japan, the Burlington office links Burton to retailers and consumers in the United States and abroad.

Although Burton does all its manufacturing in Vermont, it has warehouses in Vermont, New York, Europe and Asia.

In order to reach the maximum number of customers, Burton uses dual distribution. This means that it sells the same products to snowboarders through direct and indirect marketing channels. One outlet in its direct marketing strategy is its headquarters in Burlington, where Burton sells to about 100 customers a day. The headquarters houses the manufacturing facility, offices and a factory showroom, whose retail store sells everything Burton makes, from hard goods to soft goods. The hard-goods line includes snowboards, bindings, boots, board and travel bags, and backpacks, and the soft goods are five categories of specially designed clothing made from highly breathable and highly waterproof insulated fabrics. Direct marketing of products is also handled through mail order, catalogue shopping and on-line Internet retailing. The latest addition to the company's direct marketing efforts, the Burton website, gives a detailed description of all the products and explains the many different kinds of snowboards and gear available each season.

Internet users can then order the catalogue from the American, European or Japanese offices. The Internet and Burton's dual distribution strategy have made it easy for customers around the world to buy Burton products, but this has not always been so. Prior to 1985, Burton was sending snowboards to Europe based on individual requests, but the company finally realised that it could simplify distribution by cutting the number of transactions required to get products from the factory to the rider. In response to this need, the Burton Snowboard Company decided to develop a marketing channel using intermediaries, dealers and distributors who buy and resell the products.

Burton intermediaries provide the specialised expertise necessary for efficient product education and distribution. Distributors and dealers communicate with new and repeat customers to create awareness of Burton's product features, advantages and benefits. Perhaps more importantly, however, intermediaries ensure that the right quantities, proportions and assortments of products are available at one location so that riders have the right number and kind of items they need when they need them. After all, having a great snowboard doesn't mean much unless you have the bindings to go with it. Burton's supply chain connects all the business entities that move company products to the right place at the right time, and this chain allows Burton to avoid discrepancies that could reduce customer satisfaction, cost the company repeat business or compromise its reputation.

To support its extensive distribution network, Burton uses a supply chain information system to track every stock item throughout the world and to monitor ordering, delivery and bill payment. When the company first decided to use intermediaries, Jake Burton, the company founder and owner, had to choose a marketing channel strategy that took the particulars of the market, his company and its products into consideration. He had to ask the question, 'Where are the potential snowboarders?' The answer to that primary question has been constantly evolving since it was first asked. When the company started, it advertised in major publications and filled orders as they came in directly to the Vermont office. As the popularity of snowboarding increased to the point of being accepted at most American ski resorts, national distribution began to make more sense. When Burton saw the untapped potential of the European market, he opened up shop in Austria. By the late 1990s, Burton Snowboards was doing business in 27 countries.

Product factors also influenced the company channel decisions. Burton snowboards are highly customised, varying in length, type of ride (freestyle, freeride or carving) and graphic design. For such specialised products, a shorter, more direct marketing channel is preferable. The type of manufacturer also influences channel selection. Jake Burton's investment in Burton Snowboards is reflected in the distribution strategy the company has pursued. Because he personally spent years developing the sport of snowboarding and the products that go with it, Burton wanted to control his company's pricing, positioning, brand image and customer support initiatives.

Another issue affecting Burton's channel strategy was the level of distribution intensity – that is, the number of outlets available to customers for buying snowboards and other Burton products. Jake Burton chose selective distribution, screening dealers to eliminate all but a few retailers in any single area and having the company's outside sales team and internal distribution management staff work closely with this focused group of American retailers. In Europe, the challenge of screening prospective distributors was more difficult, so Jake Burton carefully selected only dealers that were dedicated to the sport of snowboarding.

Burton Snowboards has risen to be the industry leader in its market, and its multi-pronged distribution strategy that uses both direct and indirect channels is what allows the company to provide top-of-the-line snowboards, bindings, boots and clothing to snowboarders worldwide.

Questions

1 Describe Burton Snowboards' dual distribution.
2 What advantages does Burton gain from using a channel of distribution?
3 How do marketing channels help Burton to overcome discrepancies?
4 Using Exhibit 8.6, explain the intensity of distribution levels. Why did Burton choose selective distribution?

Suggested reading

Reade Bailey, 'Jake Burton, King of the Hill', *Ski*, February 1998, pp. 67–8.

Burton Snowboards Press Kit.

Burton website: www.burton.com.

© 2002 Nelson Australia Pty Limited

Click it

Online reading

INFOTRAC® COLLEGE EDITION

For additional readings and review on marketing channels and logistics decisions, explore InfoTrac® College Edition, your online library. Go to: www.infotrac-college.com and search for any of the InfoTrac key terms listed below:
- marketing channel
- consumer product channels
- industrial distributor
- electronic distribution
- exclusive distribution
- mass customisation

Answer key

1. *Answer:* d, p. 251-2 *Rationale:* A channel member is any organisation that helps producers to move goods to their final consumers.
2. *Answer:* c, p. 250 *Rationale:* A temporal discrepancy is created when a product is produced but a consumer is not yet ready to buy it.
3. *Answer:* d, p. 250 *Rationale:* Increasing the number of channel members in a marketing system is a way to overcome contact inefficiency, making an assortment of goods possible at a single location.
4. *Answer:* b, p. 252 *Rationale:* An agent/broker channel is often very complicated and the agents or brokers typically act on behalf of many producers at once.
5. *Answer:* c, p. 257 *Rationale:* Adaptive channels are flexible and typically involve close relationships between channel members so that customer requests can be more easily satisfied.
6. *Answer:* a, p. 261 *Rationale:* With intensive distribution, the manufacturer tries to have the product available in every outlet in which a potential customer might look for it.
7. *Answer:* d, p. 270 *Rationale:* Since the 1980s, logistics has been viewed as a key way for a firm to differentiate itself from its competitors.
8. *Answer:* a, p. 249 *Rationale:* Marketing channels can often perform functions more efficiently than producers, by obtaining economies of scale through specialisation and division of labour.
9. *Answer:* a, p. 251 *Rationale:* Merchant wholesalers help facilitate exchange in a distribution channel and always take title to the goods they distribute.
10. *Answer:* a, p. 260 *Rationale:* The product life cycle is an important factor in choosing a marketing channel and thus causes channels to change over the life of a product in the marketplace.
11. *Answer:* c, p. 285 *Rationale:* Discount stores are an example of traditional in-store retailing.

Cross-functional connections
SOLUTIONS

Questions

1 Why do firms have to invest in constant new product development?

Innovation is the lifeblood of any successful organisation, particularly those who have products in the highly competitive markets. There is constant need to have new and innovative products in the market to keep customers interested and to extend product life cycles. Further, consumer tastes and preferences change and organisations need to be aware of these changes and have new product on the market to meet the modified or new needs.

2 What are some of the other companies that might be impacted by the trend of customers to prefer diet, healthy and nutritional products?

Clearly, to respond to this question the first issue is to look at what are determined as not healthy or non-nutritional products from the customer's perspective. This has been seen most prevalently in the fast food market. Companies such as McDonald's are reacting to legal challenges and changes in market perception as to the quality and value of the food. Similarly, the frozen dinner market is now conscious of calories, fat content and the number of carbohydrates in the total meal. There are many more examples, especially in the industries of drinks, fitness, weight loss, and speciality and organic foods.

3 What sorts of channels is Australian Chocolate currently using?

Australian chocolate is currently selling and giving away chocolate at fairs, via mass media commentators, tastings at shopping centres and direct negations with large organisations such as Qantas, which can be classified as a direct channel. However, as the demand increases other intermediaries will enter the channel in some form of adaptive channel.

4 As a potential buyer of Australian Chocolate products, what would be your recommendations to Mr Stuber about his current distribution strategy?

In response to this question students should consider marketing theory of innovation commercialisation, product life cycle and the diffusion of innovation theory with its associated categorisation of adopter participants.

PART THREE CLOSING
MARKETING PLANNING ACTIVITIES

Managing the marketing elements of product and distribution

Developing a marketing plan is one of the key tools used by marketers to ensure that their marketing strategy for a particular product has a greater chance of success. A marketing plan has many sections. At the end of each of the five parts of this book you are asked to complete portions of the marketing plan according to the sections or topics that have been covered in that part. Don't be concerned about how the plan will come together until you have completed all five parts. In fact, the marketing plan won't look like a marketing plan until it is completed at the end of Part 5.

By now, you should have completed the activities for the marketing plan at the end of Parts 1 and 2. If you are progressing through the text in this manner, you would already have addressed the idea of the consumer decision-making process, and investigated how organisations conduct research on the marketplace and how they segment the market so that specific markets can be targeted to make effective use of resources while maximising their principal objectives.

We have provided you with questions and worksheets on the Student Resources CD-ROM to assist your progression. Go there after you have completed the 'Activities' section.

Activities

Part 3 discussed two of the 4Ps – namely, products and place (distribution). This part of the text investigated the product and distribution decision processes that organisations adopt in order to be effective in the marketplace.

To continue our development of the marketing plan, we will now address questions on the elements of distribution and product. Once again, you should be able to provide further insight into your selected organisation's current situation. You should also be able to address the issues of product and place (distribution) from the organisation's marketing mix. Below are some questions you should be able to answer:

- Describe the product offering provided by the organisation.
- What are the main competing products to that offered by your selected organisation?
- What are the product's features and benefits – for example, branding, packaging, warranties, guarantees, and so on?
- What is the product's current life cycle stage?
- How is the distribution managed?
- Is there more than one distribution channel?
- How are these channels integrated, and what markets do they serve?

Managing the marketing elements: Integrated marketing communication and pricing decisions

How organisations integrate the promotion and pricing elements to maximise their ability to appeal to customers

PART FOUR

Integrated marketing communication (IMC)	Chapter 9
Promotions mix	Chapter 10
Pricing concepts	Chapter 11

Cross-functional connections

Integrated marketing communications requires integrated business functions

Customers perceive messages about a firm's goods and services through many sources, only one of which is the advertising message. Customers make judgements about goods and services, comparing the price, the packaging, the distribution methods and even the features with other goods and services of a similar type. It is therefore critical that marketers carefully integrate all of the marketing elements to ensure a consistent message is heard, read and perceived by the customer. In addition, marketers need to consider the various methods of communicating with customers to ensure the most appropriate combination of methods is selected. Communication methods include advertising, personal selling, sales promotion, direct marketing and publicity. Finally, marketing activities don't occur in isolation within a firm. In order to ensure maximum coordination and cooperation, all functional areas of a firm need to be advised and possibly included in the planning stages of any marketing activity. This process of bringing together the marketing mix elements, business functions and full consideration of the various methods of communicating with customers is known as *integrated marketing communications*.

Customers consider both tangible and intangible elements of a good or service when they make judgements about its suitability. One of the main intangible elements considered is the product quality. This is an issue that touches the heart of a firm's operational processes. Marketers love to emphasise a product's superior quality when communicating with potential customers. For example, Singapore Airlines clearly depicts quality service in its advertisements.

When a company's communications strategy focuses on promoting quality features, pressure is placed on research and development, manufacturing and human resources to deliver on quality. Firms that over-promise or raise expectations beyond their ability to deliver will find it difficult to achieve customer satisfaction and may end up losing customers who are dissatisfied. Unfortunately, issues that mean quality to a scientist or an engineer in a manufacturing or a research and development department may not readily translate to perceptions of quality by the customer. Certainly, quality issues are simpler to manage for tangible goods than they are for intangible services. If a firm's communications program entices the consumer to try a good or service, the good or service must then be consistent with the consumer's expectations of the quality. The only way to ensure this consistency is with a strong integration of business functions.

Too frequently, marketers have developed award-winning communications campaigns for a new product only to see the product fail in the market. A few years ago a new car was introduced, backed by a superior marketing communications effort. One of the television ads was even nominated for the highly regarded Clio award for excellence in advertising. Unfortunately, the car didn't receive equally superior quality ratings within the car industry. Thus, the company had an award-winning advertising campaign with a mediocre product. It was no surprise that sales of the car weren't strong!

The need for interaction between marketing and manufacturing doesn't stop with the product introduction campaign, however. At any point in a product's life cycle, marketing may decide to promote the product. For example, Goodman Fielder – the manufacturer of Uncle Tobys products – may decide to offer a price discount over a two- or three-week period, to advertise heavily and/or to offer coupons in a freestanding insert for one of its Uncle Tobys products. From marketing's perspective, the hope is that a consumer will try the product because of the heavy marketing communications effort (and keep using the product even after the communications effort has stopped).

PART FOUR

Marketing at Goodman Fielder would need to work closely with manufacturing when planning such an extensive product promotion. Otherwise, manufacturing would be producing the product at its traditional level, which would be inconsistent with marketing's promotional sales plan. An integrated marketing communications program that generates high demand for a product is only as good as the product's availability. A well-orchestrated marketing campaign can create a powerful purchasing stimulus.

Personal selling is one component of integrated marketing communications where considerable interaction among functions occurs. Salespeople have to possess intimate knowledge of the products they present to potential consumers, as well as good interpersonal skills. For example, a salesperson for Thomson Learning publishers has to understand the topics covered in a particular textbook in order to be able to talk knowledgeably with lecturers in that subject. Eli Lilly Pharmaceuticals might recruit a science graduate to promote its prescription drugs to doctors. Not only could the science graduate talk knowledgeably to the potential customer (doctor), but he or she could also interact knowledgeably with the research and development team that developed the new drug.

In an attempt to further integrate all business functions, some firms now require research and development engineers and manufacturing specialists to talk directly with their customers. Not surprisingly, such an external emphasis is in direct contrast with the technical orientation of research and development and manufacturing employees. However, this interaction helps to ensure that all functional areas within the firm are focused on the customer.

Firms such as Motorola and Intuit expect that their engineers will go on sales calls. These engineers may visit customers with a marketing person as part of a sales call, or the visit may be distinct from a sales call and may involve watching the customer use the product. There seems to be no better way of developing and manufacturing innovative, cutting-edge products than to have the people who work directly with the product also working in close contact with the end user.

Sales departments also work closely with finance, accounting and human resources sections with regard to compensation systems for sales staff and to monitor customer activity and purchasing patterns. The clear linkage among finance, accounting, human resources and marketing with regard to a firm's selling strategy is exemplified in IBM's focus on profits and customer satisfaction. IBM follows a variable commission strategy that ties a salesperson's commission to margins on the company's products. Sixty per cent of the commission is tied to profit margin, while the other 40 per cent is linked to customer satisfaction. Customer satisfaction is measured by the customer's perception of how well the IBM sales team has helped it to achieve its own company objectives.

A successful integrated marketing communications program is dependent on marketing working closely with research and development and manufacturing with regard to quality and availability. Simultaneously, marketing has to interact closely with finance, accounting and human resources in order to establish appropriate goals and objectives for its marketing communications programs. It is the sum of the external messages and internal operations that produces a satisfied customer.

Questions for discussion

1. Why are the company's marketing communications of particular concern to research and development and manufacturing?

2. Why is it important to consider all elements of the marketing mix and the communications methods in the development of a communications program?

3. Why should the marketing department work closely with areas such as finance, accounting and human resources?

Integrated marketing communication (IMC)

CHAPTER NINE

Learning Objectives

After studying this chapter, you should be able to

1. Discuss the role of promotion in the marketing mix
2. Discuss the elements of the promotional mix
3. Describe the communication process
4. Explain the goals and tasks of promotion
5. Discuss the AIDA concept and its relationship to the promotional mix
6. Describe the factors that affect the promotional mix
7. Define personal selling
8. Discuss the key differences between relationship selling and traditional selling
9. Define direct marketing

So what is the 'tween' market? Officially it is those kids aged between six and 13 who are increasingly of interest to global marketers. Why? Because this group are not classed as teenagers and they also have disposable income and, it appears, quite specific fashion and purchasing tastes. They also represent a large market for magazine purchases. This market segment, particularly girls, are seen to be having a greater say in family decision-making and they are also aspirational – they want to be teenagers and like the kids they see on television in *Neighbours*, *Home and Away* and some of the American soaps. These girls can't get enough of celebrity information, slumber party ideas, fashion and make-up tips and all within a parent-friendly environment. This is definitely an attractive market segment for magazine marketers.

The leading tween magazine in Australia at present is *Total Girl*. It has a readership of 274 000 children aged between six and 13 and its website receives more than 1.5 million hits a month. Interestingly the male tween market has not seen the same degree of growth as the female market. It seems that male tweens are more 'fad-driven' whereas the girls are more interested in variety.

Total Girl on-line

Total Girl now has 94 000 opt in members on-line. Have a look at their website and comment on the promotional tools they are using there to attract and keep visitation levels high.
www.totalgirl.com.au

In order to keep this fickle group of readers interested in continuing their magazine purchases, the marketing team attempts to create interactivity with games and competitions, as well as information on celebrities, gossip, sporting information, celebrity boys and even community events. It seems not all tweens are into shopping and girly pursuits. Sales promotions play a major role in the marketing of the magazine with interactive competitions and give-aways planned throughout the year to stimulate and surprise readers. The current competition requires readers to send in a video of themselves singing and dancing to win a three-day training session by Australian celebrities in singing, dance or acting.

As well as sales promotions, the magazine also relies heavily on advertising on commercial television as well as subscription TV channels such as Nickelodeon and the Cartoon Network. Where possible the magazine also tries for publicity, particularly in relation to the winners of their main competitions. You can imagine that 20 young tweens spending time with Australian entertainment celebrities to learn the secrets of future success would make quite an interesting news and current events story. The magazine also engages in shopping centre promotions during holiday times, bringing celebrities to the readers and attempting to maintain the interest and high levels of involvement. Behind the scenes, personal selling is used to attract advertisers in the magazine and to set up and arrange special celebrity articles, exposees and competitions.

As you can see, *Total Girl* places considerable emphasis on promotion in their marketing mix. What is the role of promotion in the marketing mix? What types of promotional tools are available to companies, and what factors influence the choice of tool? How is the promotion plan created? These questions are answered in this section, so stick around.

The role of promotion in the marketing mix

1 Discuss the role of promotion in the marketing mix

promotion
Communication by marketers that informs, persuades and reminds potential buyers of a product in order to influence an opinion or elicit a response.

promotional strategy
Plan for the optimal use of the elements of promotion: advertising, public relations, direct marketing, personal selling and sales promotion.

differential advantage
One or more unique aspects of an organisation that cause target consumers to patronise that firm rather than competitors.

Few goods or services, no matter how well developed, priced or distributed, can survive in the marketplace without effective promotion. **Promotion** is communication by marketers that informs, persuades and reminds you, the potential buyer, of a product in order to influence your opinion or elicit a response.

Promotional strategy is a plan for the optimal use of the elements of promotion: advertising, public relations, personal selling and sales promotion (the promotional mix). As Exhibit 9.1 shows, the marketing manager determines the goals of the company's promotional strategy in light of the firm's overall goals for the marketing mix – product, place (distribution), promotion and price. Using these overall goals, marketers combine the elements of the promotional mix into a coordinated plan. The promotion plan then becomes an integral part of the marketing strategy for reaching the target market.

The main function of a marketer's promotional strategy is to convince target customers that the goods and services offered provide a differential advantage over the competition. A **differential advantage** is the set of unique features of a company and its products that are perceived by the target market as significant and superior to the competition. Such features can include high product quality, rapid delivery, low prices, excellent service or a feature not offered by the competition. For example, Revlon's Age Defying makeup with Botafirm promises

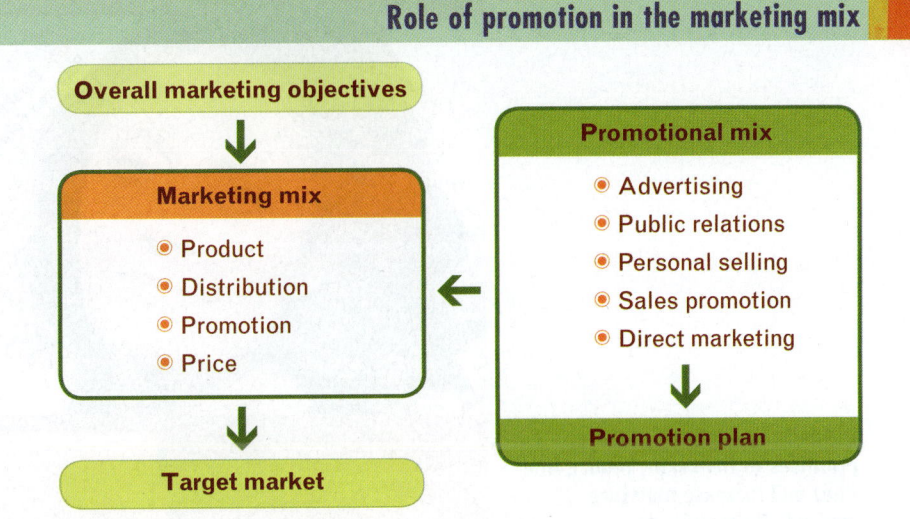

Exhibit 9.1 Role of promotion in the marketing mix

Overall marketing objectives → **Marketing mix**: Product, Distribution, Promotion, Price → **Target market**

Promotional mix: Advertising, Public relations, Personal selling, Sales promotion, Direct marketing → **Promotion plan**

to reduce fine lines and increase moisture content of the skin all in a foundation. By effectively communicating this differential advantage through its advertising, Revlon can stimulate demand for its revolutionary products. Promotion is therefore a vital part of the marketing mix, informing consumers of a product's benefits and thus helping to position the product in the marketplace. Most promotional strategies use several ingredients – which may include personal selling, direct marketing, advertising, sales promotion and public relations – to reach the target market. That combination is called the **promotional mix**. The proper promotional mix is the one that management believes will meet the needs of the target market and fulfil the organisation's overall goals. Each of the elements of the promotional mix will now be introduced briefly.

Personal selling

Personal selling is a purchase situation in which two or more people communicate in an attempt to influence each other. In this situation, both the buyer and seller have specific objectives they wish to accomplish. The buyer may need to minimise costs or assure a quality product, for example, while the salesperson may need to maximise revenue and profits.[1]

Traditional methods of **personal selling** include a planned presentation to one or more prospective buyers for the purpose of making a sale. Whether it takes place face-to-face or over the phone, personal selling attempts to persuade the buyer to accept a point of view or convince the buyer to take some action. For example, a car salesperson may try to persuade a car buyer that a particular model is superior to a competing model in certain features, such as petrol consumption, roominess and interior styling. Once the buyer is somewhat convinced, then the salesperson may attempt to elicit some action from the buyer, such as a test drive or a purchase.

In some selling situations, a relationship develops between a salesperson and a buyer. This concept is more typical with business- and industrial-type goods, such as heavy machinery or computer systems, than with consumer goods. Personal selling and relationship selling are discussed later in this chapter.

promotional mix
Combination of promotion tools – including advertising, direct marketing, public relations, personal selling and sales promotion – used to reach the target market and fulfil the organisation's overall goals.

personal selling
Planned presentation to one or more prospective buyers for the purpose of making a sale.

Revlon's age-defying make-up promises to firm skin, reduce fine lines and increase moisture content. By effectively communicating this differential advantage through advertising, Revlon can stimulate demand for its product.

The promotional mix

2 Discuss the elements of the promotional mix

Direct marketing

direct marketing (direct-response marketing)
Techniques used to get consumers to make a purchase from their home, office or other non-retail setting.

Direct marketing, sometimes called **direct-response marketing**, refers to the techniques used to get consumers to make a purchase from their home, office or other non-retail setting. Those techniques include direct mail, catalogues and mail order, telemarketing and electronic retailing. Shoppers using these methods are less bound by traditional shopping situations. Time-strapped consumers and those who live in rural or suburban areas are most likely to be direct-response shoppers, because they value the convenience and flexibility that direct marketing provides.

Advertising

advertising
Impersonal, one-way mass communication about a product or organisation that is paid for by a marketer.

Almost all companies selling a good or a service use some form of advertising, whether it is in the form of a multimillion-dollar campaign or a simple classified ad in a newspaper. **Advertising** is any form of paid communication in which the sponsor or company is identified. Traditional media – such as television, radio, newspapers, magazines, books, direct mail, billboards and transit cards (advertisements on buses and taxis and at bus stops) – are most commonly used to transmit advertisements to consumers. Marketers, however, are finding many new ways to send their advertisements, most notably through such electronic means as the Internet, computer modems, mobile phones and fax machines.

One of the primary benefits of advertising is its ability to communicate to a large number of people at one time. The cost per contact, therefore, is typically very low. Advertising has the advantage of being able to reach the masses (for example, through national television networks), but it can also be microtargeted to small groups of potential customers, such as television ads on a targeted pay-TV network or through print advertising in a trade or specialised magazine such as *Renovator's Guidebook*.

Although the cost per contact in advertising is very low, the total cost to advertise is typically very high. For example, to launch the brand to the Australian market in 2001, Renault unleashed a $20 million assault on the market with a new TV campaign.[2] Few small companies can match this level of spending for a national campaign. Chapter 10 examines advertising in greater detail.

Advertising costs can sometimes be prohibitive for smaller companies. For example, few small companies can match the $20 million spent by Renault on their Australian campaign for their new cars.

Sales promotion

Sales promotion consists of all marketing activities – other than personal selling, advertising and public relations – that stimulate consumer purchasing and dealer effectiveness. Sales promotion is generally a short-run tool used to stimulate immediate increases in demand. Sales promotion can be aimed at end consumers, trade customers or a company's employees. Sales promotions include free samples, contests, premiums, trade shows, vacation give-aways and coupons. A major promotional campaign might use several of these sales promotion tools. For example, MasterFoods' recently held a promotion to increase the sales of their products and to increase trial of their barbecue spices particularly, by giving away a Ford car loaded with barbecue equipment[3]. Further, in order to grab customers' attention, they also used Glen McGrath (the Australian cricketer) in the promotion and the lucky winner could also win a backyard barbecue with him and their mates.

Often marketers use sales promotion to improve the effectiveness of other ingredients in the promotional mix, especially advertising and personal selling. Research shows that sales promotion complements advertising by yielding faster sales responses. In 2001, Pizza Hut launched an integrated cross-promotion with Network Ten's reality program *Big Brother*. The promotion saw the launch of secret product lines, $100 000 in cash give-aways, *Big Brother* meal deals, packaging and leaflet tie-ins.[4] The campaign was designed to go beyond the standard sponsorship, with viewers who rang to vote on the fate of *Big Brother* participants being given the option to be connected directly to Pizza Hut's call centre. 'Given that 70 per cent of our sales are made from the phone it makes sense for us to get involved with this program,' said marketing manager Greg Creed.[5] This theme was continued through the *BB* series with other companies cashing in on the publicity and high exposure to the fickle 18–35 market. Sales promotion is discussed in more detail in Chapter 10.

sales promotion
Marketing activities – other than personal selling, advertising and public relations – that stimulate consumer buying and dealer effectiveness.

Arnott's on-line
Arnott's lists its promotions on its website. What do you think are the advantages and disadvantages of this? Visit the site to get more information.
www.arnotts.com.au

Public relations

public relations (PR)
Marketing function that evaluates public attitudes, identifies areas within the organisation that the public may be interested in, and executes a program of action to earn public understanding and acceptance.

Concerned about how they are perceived by their target markets, organisations often spend large sums to build a positive public image. **Public relations (PR)** is the marketing function that evaluates public attitudes, identifies areas within the organisation that the public may be interested in, and executes a program of action to earn public understanding and acceptance. PR helps an organisation to communicate with its customers, suppliers, shareholders, government officials, employees and the community in which it operates.

Marketers use PR not only to maintain a positive image but also to educate the public about the company's goals and objectives, introduce new products and help support the sales effort. The distinguishing feature of PR and other forms of marketing communication is that PR is non-paid-for communication and, as such, the marketer has little control over where and how the information is presented to the various stakeholders. Non-paid-for communication refers to the fact that the marketer doesn't have to pay to have their news release or story presented to the public; this decision is made by the media or journalists involved.

Sir Richard Branson, the well-known and controversial owner of the Virgin group of companies, uses public relations continually to support his company's products and brand image. Only recently he captured the attention of the media at the Sydney launch of his Virgin Mobile Telephony Company. Sir Richard flew into the press conference hanging from a helicopter to save Australians from their evil phone contractors.[6] In a further PR twist, his sales director and creative director bared all to create a series of billboard ads featuring streakers to complement their company catchline, 'Unplan your life'.

publicity
Public information about a company, good or service appearing in the mass media as a news item.

A solid public relations program can generate favourable publicity. **Publicity** is public information about a company, good or service appearing in the mass media as a news item. The organisation is not generally identified as the source of the information. This form of communication is not always generated by the company the information is about. Journalists, customers and others can also generate publicity (both good and bad) about an organisation.

For example, the Australian wine industry received favourable publicity and an increase in sales after several medical studies found a link between good health and the moderate consumption of red wine. This incident underscores a peculiar reality of marketing: no matter how many millions are spent on advertising, nothing sells a product better than publicity. Although an organisation doesn't pay for this kind of mass-media exposure, publicity should not be viewed as free. Preparing news releases, staging special events and persuading media personnel to print or broadcast them costs money. Public relations and publicity are examined further in Chapter 10.

Integrated marketing communications

Ideally, marketing communications from each promotional mix element (personal selling, advertising, sales promotion and public relations) should be integrated – that is, the message reaching the consumer should be the same regardless of whether it is from an advertisement, a salesperson in the field, a magazine article or a coupon in a newspaper insert.

From the consumer's standpoint, a company's communications are already integrated. Consumers don't think in terms of the four elements of promotion: advertising, sales promotion, public relations and personal selling. Instead, everything is an 'ad'. The only people who can separate these communications elements are the marketers themselves. Unfortunately, many marketers neglect this fact when planning promotional messages and fail to integrate their communication efforts from one element to the next.

Adopting the concept of **integrated marketing communications (IMC)** helps to protect companies from disjointed approaches to communication. IMC is the method of carefully coordinating all promotional activities – media advertising, sales promotion, personal selling, public relations, as well as direct marketing, packaging and other forms of communication – to produce a consistent, unified message that is customer-focused.[7] Following the concept of IMC, marketing managers carefully work out the roles that various promotional elements will play in the marketing mix. Timing of promotional activities is coordinated and the results of each campaign are carefully monitored to improve future use of the promotional mix tools. Typically, a marketing communications director is appointed who has overall responsibility for integrating the company's marketing communications.

Movie marketing campaigns benefit greatly from an integrated marketing communications approach. Those campaigns that are most integrated generally have more impact and make a bigger impression on potential movie-goers, leading to higher box office sales. An integrated marketing approach, for example, was used in the United States for the release of *Godzilla* by TriStar Pictures and Sony Pictures Entertainment in 1998. To heighten the anticipation for the film and its monster star, the movie's producers kept *Godzilla* under wraps until the day the film opened. Consumers only saw the film's signature green colour and the line 'Size does matter'. The first previews for the movie arrived a full year in advance, proclaiming the day *Godzilla* would be revealed. Outdoor advertising compared the yet-to-be-seen monster's 23-storey size to famous urban landmarks in the United States such as the Empire State Building in New York. Sales promotional support for the movie included: Dreyer's Grand Ice Cream, which created a special flavour, Godzilla Vanilla, with vanilla chunks in the shape of the monster; a sweepstakes sponsored by Duracell that gave the winner a swimming pool shaped like Godzilla's foot; a Kodak television spot that blended movie footage to dramatise a young man's efforts to photograph Godzilla with a disposable camera; and Taco Bell, which paired Godzilla with its talking chihuahua. Commemorative tickets were also issued to those who bought seats at the first screening of the film on opening day, autographed by the film's makers and accompanied by Taco Bell coupons.[8]

integrated marketing communications (IMC)
The method of carefully coordinating all promotional activities to produce a consistent, unified message that is customer-focused.

Outdoor advertising was a key part in the integrated marketing campaign Sony put together to promote its feature film *Godzilla*. Newspaper and magazine ads could not convey the monster's size, but buses worked just fine.

Marketing communication

3 Describe the communication process

communication
Process by which we exchange or share meanings through a common set of symbols.

Promotional strategy is closely related to the process of communication. **Communication** is the process by which we exchange or share meanings through a common set of symbols. When a company develops a new product, changes an old one, or simply tries to increase sales of an existing good or service, it must communicate its message to potential customers. Marketers communicate information about the firm and its products to the target market and various publics through its promotion programs. Pepsi commercials, for example, send messages to their target audience of kids through the use of entertainment and sports figures, such as pop singer Britney Spears and basketball star Shaquille O'Neal. Marketers are always looking for a way to communicate more effectively with an increasingly uninterested and overexposed audience. The latest trend in shopping centre communications is tabletop ads – see the Entrepreneurial insights box for more information about this form of communication.

Entrepreneurial Insights

The totally integrated realm of the shopping centre

Australian company Creatable Media has developed an innovative and creative way to communicate with over 50 million people per year, and that's just in Australia and New Zealand. Tabletop advertising uses high colour and 3D tabletops in food courts in large shopping centres to advertise products and services for a wide range of clients. Over 170 million people visit shopping centres in Australia and New Zealand each year and about 30 per cent of these visit the food courts. Even better is that when they are at the food court, most people spend at least 15 minutes at a table and this makes them a captive and attentive audience particularly those eating alone.[9]

Most out of home media offers only two to three seconds of exposure, whereas this medium gives advertisers a concentrated period of time to get their message across with a minimum of external interference. See-through plastic food trays (also produced by Creatable) help to ensure that part of the message is always visible. This extended exposure means that advertisers can provide more detail about their products, which is great for products like health messages, new products, recipe ideas, community information and retail deals that are a bit more complicated.[10]

The other exciting part of this medium is that is a great way to get to youth and those under 25. The food court and shopping malls play a large part in the day-to-day life of many of Australia's and New Zealand's youth and this is a perfect way to get their attention. Companies who use this medium in conjunction with TV advertising can capture the creative images and visuals from their other promotional material and use it again on tabletops to create synergy and gain recall in their target audiences.

The shopping centre market has only recently been identified as a huge potential market for many promotional messages, and the proximity to the point-of-purchase for many products makes interactive and technologically advances methods appropriate. Seventy per cent of purchase decisions are made at the point-of-purchase, so mall or shopping centre adverting makes good sense. Options for marketers currently include the tabletop advertising already discussed, mini-billboards, backlight light boxes, parking lot billboards, shopping trolley ads and PR stunts and gimmicks.

It is often the interactive sales promotion and PR gimmicks that increase sales and get customer attention. At Westfield centres, scooters roam the halls offering sample products, while in centre court action ranges from concerts, competitions and model searches to video gaming sessions. The real key to using this forum for communications is to integrate the messages and to use a range of media to get the message across.[11] And you thought you were just shopping and hanging out with your friends when you visited the mall?

Communication can be divided into two main categories: interpersonal communication and mass communication. **Interpersonal communication** is direct, face to face communication between two or more people. When communicating face to face, people see the other person's reaction and can respond almost immediately. A salesperson speaking directly with a client is an example of marketing communication that is interpersonal.

Mass communication refers to communicating to large audiences. A great deal of marketing communication is directed to consumers as a whole, usually through a mass medium such as television, radio or newspapers. When a company advertises, it generally doesn't personally know the people with whom it is trying to communicate. Furthermore, the company is unable to respond immediately to consumers' reactions to its message. Instead, the marketing manager must wait to see whether people are reacting positively or negatively to the mass-communicated promotion. Any clutter from competitors' messages or other distractions in the environment can reduce the effectiveness of the mass communication effort.

interpersonal communication
Direct, face-to-face communication between two or more people.

mass communication
Communication to large audiences.

The communication process

Marketers are both senders and receivers of messages. As *senders*, marketers attempt to inform, persuade and remind the target market to adopt courses of action compatible with the need to promote the purchase of goods and services. As *receivers*, marketers attune themselves to the target market in order to develop the appropriate messages, adapt existing messages and spot new communication opportunities. In this way, marketing communication is a two-way, rather than one-way, process.[12] The two-way nature of the communication process is shown in Exhibit 9.2.

The sender and encoding

The **sender** is the originator of the message in the communication process. In an interpersonal conversation, the sender may be a parent, a friend or a salesperson. For an advertisement or press release, the sender is the company itself.

sender
Originator of the message in the communication process.

Exhibit 9.2
Communication process

Noise
- Other advertisements
- News articles
- Other store displays

Sender
- Marketing manager
- Advertising manager
- Advertising agency

Encoding the message
- Advertisement
- Sales presentations
- Store display
- Coupon
- Press release

Message channel
- Media
- Salesperson
- Retail store
- Local news show

Decoding the message
- Receiver's interpretation of message

Receiver
- Customers
- Viewers/listeners
- News media
- Clients

Message channel
- Market research
- Sales results
- Change in market share

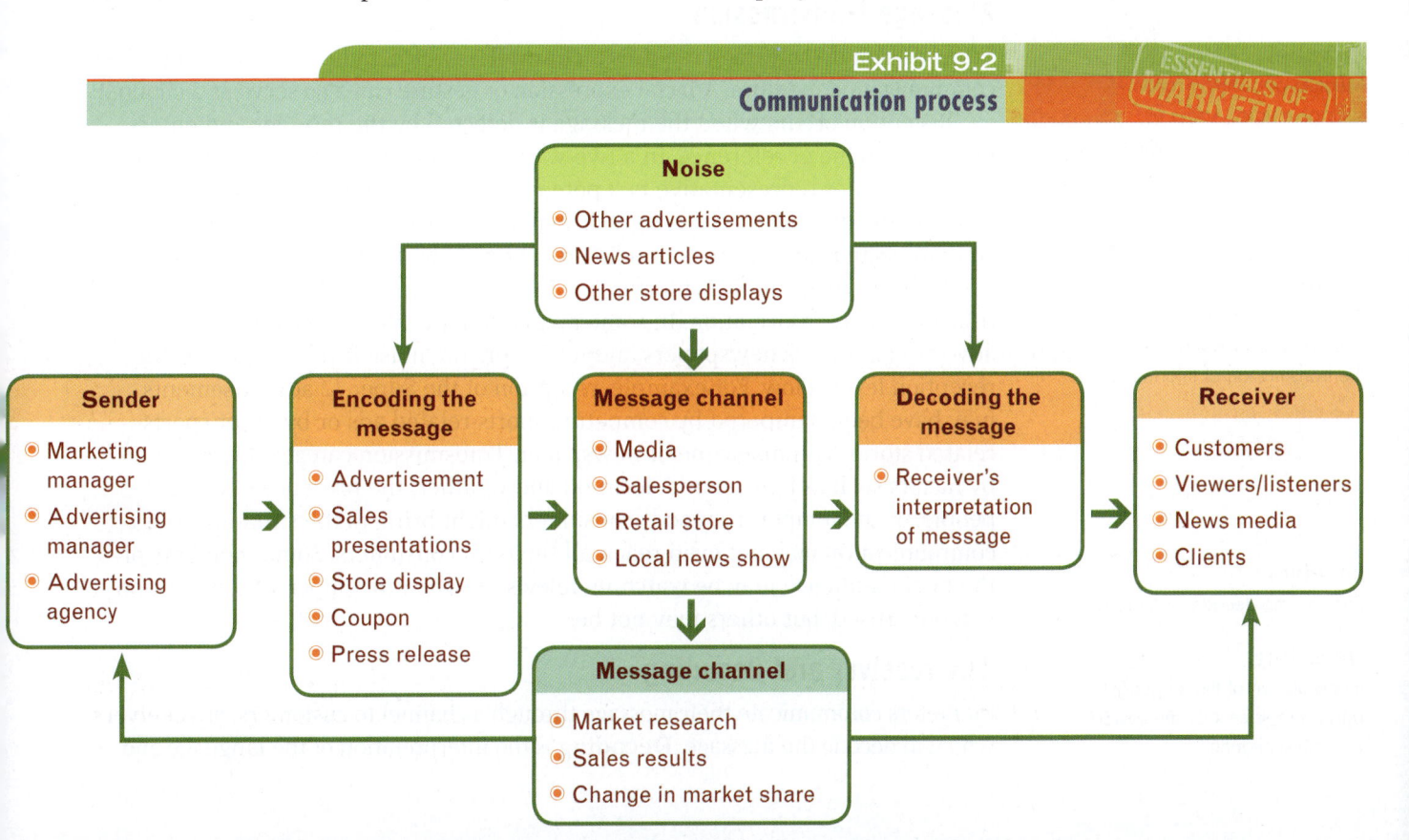

Every communication needs a sender and a receiver. The Brumbies rugby team sends messages promoting both the team and the sport to sports fans. Can its corporate sponsors also be senders along with the team? Why or why not?

encoding
Conversion of the sender's ideas and thoughts into a message, usually in the form of words or signs.

channel
Medium of communication – such as a voice, radio or newspaper – for transmitting a message.

noise
Anything that interferes with, distorts or slows down the transmission of information.

receiver
Person who decodes a message.

decoding
Interpretation of the language and symbols sent by the source through a channel.

Encoding is the conversion of the sender's ideas and thoughts into a message, usually in the form of words or signs. Microsoft might encode its message into an advertisement, or a Microsoft salesperson might encode the promotional message as a sales presentation.

A basic principle of encoding is that what matters is not what the source says but what the receiver hears. One way of conveying a message that the receiver will hear properly is to use concrete words and pictures. For example, television and print advertising announcing the start of the new Super 12 Rugby competition a few years ago gave detailed information about when the games would begin. Print advertising concentrated on detailed biographies of players, teams, colours and rules.

Message transmission

Transmission of a message requires a **channel** – a voice, radio, newspaper or other communication medium. A facial expression or gesture can also serve as a channel.

Reception occurs when the message is detected by the receiver and enters his or her frame of reference. In a two-way conversation, such as a sales pitch given by a sales representative to a potential client, reception is normally high. In contrast, the desired receivers may or may not detect the message when it is mass communicated, because most media are cluttered by 'noise'.

Noise is anything that interferes with, distorts or slows down the transmission of information. In some media that are overcrowded with advertisers, such as newspapers and television, the noise level is high and the reception level is low. For example, reception of the Super 12 advertisements may have been hampered by competing sports-related ads or by other sports-related stories in a magazine or newspaper. Transmission can also be hindered by factors such as light, sound, location and weather; the presence of other people; or the temporary moods consumers might bring to the situation. Mass communication may not even reach all the right consumers. Some members of the target audience may be watching television when the Super 12 competition was advertised, but others may not be.

The receiver and decoding

Marketers communicate their message through a channel to customers, or **receivers**, who will decode the message. **Decoding** is the interpretation of the language and symbols sent by the source through a channel. Common understanding between two communicators, or a common frame of reference, is required for effective communication. Therefore, marketing managers must ensure a proper match between the message to be conveyed and the target market's attitudes and ideas.

Even though a message has been received, it won't necessarily be properly decoded – or even seen, viewed or heard – because of selective exposure, distortion and retention (refer to Chapter 2).[13] Even when people receive a message, they tend to manipulate, alter and modify it to reflect their own biases, needs, knowledge and culture. Factors that can lead to miscommunication are differences in age, social class, education, culture and ethnicity. Further, because people don't always listen or read carefully, they can easily misinterpret what is said or written.

Bright colours and bold graphics have been shown to increase consumers' comprehension of marketing communication. However, even these techniques are not foolproof. A classic example of miscommunication occurred when Lever Brothers mailed out samples of its new dishwashing liquid, Sunlight, which contained real lemon juice. The package clearly stated that Sunlight was a household cleaning product. However, many people saw the word sunlight, the large picture of lemons, and the phrase 'with real lemon juice' and thought the product was a lemon juice drink.

Feedback

In interpersonal communication, the receiver's response to a message is direct **feedback** to the source. Feedback may be verbal, as in saying 'I agree', or non-verbal, as in nodding, smiling, frowning or gesturing.

Because mass communicators, like those in relation to the Super 12 competition, are often cut off from direct feedback, they must rely on market

feedback
Receiver's response to a message.

Exhibit 9.3
Strategic criteria for selecting various elements of the promotional mix using the example of direct marketing.

	Direct marketing	Personal selling	Advertising	Sales promotion	Public relations
Mode of communication	Indirect and personal	Direct and face to face	Indirect and non-personal	Usually indirect and non-personal	Usually indirect and non-personal
Communicator control over situation	Moderate	High	Low	Moderate to low	Moderate to low
Amount of feedback	Moderate	Much	Little	Little to moderate	Little
Speed of feedback	Varies	Immediate	Delayed	Varies	Delayed
Direction of message	Mostly one-way	Two-way	One-way	Mostly one-way	One-way
Control over message content	Yes	Yes	Yes	Yes	No
Identification of sender	Yes	Yes	Yes	Yes	No
Speed in reaching the audience	Fast	Slow	Fast	Fast	Usually fast
Message flexibility	Same message to different target groups	Tailored to prospective buyer	Same message to audiences	Same message to varied target audiences	Usually no direct control over message

research or analysis of sales trends, such as ticket sales, for indirect feedback. The Super 12 competition might use such measurements as the percentage of television viewers or magazine readers who recognise, recall or state that they have been exposed to the competition's message. Indirect feedback enables mass communicators to decide whether to continue, modify or drop a message.

The communication process and the promotional mix

The four elements of the promotional mix differ in their ability to affect the target audience and whether they communicate with the consumer directly or indirectly. The message may flow one way or two ways. Feedback may be fast or slow, a little or a lot. Likewise, the communicator may have varying degrees of control over message delivery, content and flexibility. Exhibit 9.3 outlines the strategic criteria by which marketing managers might evaluate the various promotional mix elements, in this case direct marketing, with respect to mode of communication, the marketer's control over the communication process, the amount and speed of feedback, direction of message flow, the marketer's control over the message, identification of the sender, speed in reaching large audiences

Exhibit 9.4
Advantages and disadvantages of the elements in the promotional mix

Element	Advantages	Disadvantages
Advertising	Creates awareness Informs a large audience Low cost per exposure	Is intrusive Expensive to produce Suffers from clutter Impersonal and therefore not persuasive Not seen as credible
Personal selling	Personalised and allows for customisation of the message Most persuasive tool Good for complex products or products that need demonstration and explanation Can develop relationships	Most expensive from of promotion Can be intrusive for customers Has other management problems associated due to dealing with people
Sales promotion	Stimulates immediate response Can create value Good for creating awareness and product trial Creates excitement and interest Good for trade promotions	Can add to clutter Can erode brand equity if overused Has only a short-term benefits
Public Relations	Can create good will Can place messages in the media in a more credible fashion than advertising Can ad value to brand image Communicates with a range of publics	Hard to measure effectiveness Little control over placement in mass media No direct short term benefits
Internet and interactive marketing	Allows interactivity Good for stimulating trial Can be flexible Allows specific targeting and message tailoring Allows access to additional support information to enhance consumer buying processes Highly creative	Can be hard to create a strong brand image Hard to measure effectiveness Can be hampered by technological limitations Clutter Can restrict potential audience (have to have a computer with Internet access – poor reach) Privacy issues
Direct marketing	Can be highly targeted Excellent for reaching niche audiences Can customise and create one-on-one communication Offers means for customer feedback	Effectiveness depends on accuracy of database Not always seen as credible and can be discarded Expensive to large audiences

Source: Burnett, J and Moriarty, S, 1998, *Introduction to Marketing Communications*, Prentice Hall, New Jersey, p. 114.

and message flexibility. Exhibit 9.4 then provides a summary of the main advantages and disadvantages of each of the elements.

From Exhibit 9.3, you can see that most elements of the promotional mix use indirect and impersonal channels of communication with a target market, providing only one direction of message flow. For example, advertising, public relations and sales promotion are generally impersonal, one-way means of mass communication. Because they provide no opportunity for direct feedback, they cannot adapt easily to consumers' changing preferences, individual differences and personal goals.

Personal selling, on the other hand, is personal, two-way communication. The salesperson is able to receive immediate feedback from the consumer and adjust the message in response. Personal selling, however, is very slow in dispersing the marketer's message to large audiences. Because a salesperson can only communicate to one person or a small group of people at one time, it is a poor choice if the marketer wants to send a message to many potential buyers. From Exhibit 9.4 you can see that there are other issues that marketers also need to consider when choosing the elements to use in their promotional mix. Things like cost per audience reach, effectiveness and the influence of clutter also need to be considered.

The goals and tasks of promotion

Promotion can perform one or more of three tasks: *inform* the target audience, *persuade* the target audience or *remind* the target audience. Often a marketer will try to accomplish two or more of these tasks at the same time. For example, Hungry Jack's may be opening a new fast-food outlet. They may use promotion to inform the local community that they will be opening soon. In addition, they may wish to persuade customers to change their existing fast-food eating options and to try Hungry Jack's. Finally, they will also want to remind their customers who live in the area to visit the new store, which may be more conveniently located. Exhibit 9.5 lists the three tasks of promotion and some examples of each.

4 Explain the goals and tasks of promotion

Exhibit 9.5
Promotion tasks and examples

Informative promotion
- Increasing the awareness of a new brand, product class or product attribute
- Explaining how the product works
- Suggesting new uses for a product
- Building a company image

Persuasive promotion
- Encouraging brand switching
- Changing customers' perceptions of product attributes
- Influencing customers to buy now
- Persuading customers to call

Reminder promotion
- Reminding consumers that the product may be needed in the near future
- Reminding consumers where to buy the product
- Maintaining consumer awareness
- Informing

Hungry Jack's on-line

Visit the Hungry Jack's website to see what promotional activity the company is undertaking.
www.hungryjacks.com.au

Informative promotion may seek to convert an existing need into a want or to stimulate interest in a new product. It is generally more prevalent during the early stages of the product life cycle. People typically won't buy a product service or support a non-profit organisation until they know its purpose and its benefits to them. Informative messages are important for promoting complex and technical products such as cars, computers and investment services. Informative promotion is also important for a 'new' brand being introduced into an 'old' product class – for example, a new brand of detergent entering the well-established laundry detergent product category dominated by well-known brands such as Omo and Dynamo. The new product cannot establish itself against more mature products unless potential buyers are aware of it, and understand its benefits and its positioning in the marketplace.

Persuading

Persuasive promotion is designed to stimulate a purchase or an action – for example, to drink more Coca-Cola or to use H&R Block tax services. Persuasion normally becomes the main promotion goal when the product enters the growth stage of its life cycle. By this time, the target market should have general product awareness and some knowledge of how the product can fulfil their wants. Therefore, the promotional task switches from informing consumers about the product category to persuading them to buy the company's brand rather than the competitor's. At this time, the promotional message emphasises the product's real and perceived differential advantages, often appealing to emotional needs such as love, belonging, self-esteem and ego satisfaction.

Persuasion can also be an important goal for very competitive mature product categories such as many household items, soft drinks, beer and banking services. In a marketplace characterised by many competitors, the promotional message often encourages brand switching and aims to convert some buyers into loyal users. For example, to persuade new customers to switch their home loan accounts, a bank's marketing manager may offer an alternative home loan with no transaction fees, lower interest rates, more flexible payment options or some other benefit to customers.

Reminding

Reminder promotion is used to keep the product and brand name in the public's mind. This type of promotion prevails during the maturity stage of the life cycle. It assumes that the target market has already been persuaded of the merits of the goods or services. Its purpose is simply to trigger a memory. Colgate toothpaste, Omo laundry detergent, Fosters beer and many other consumer products often use reminder promotion.

Promotional goals and the AIDA concept

5 Discuss the AIDA concept and its relationship to the promotional mix

The ultimate goal of any promotion is to get someone to buy a good or service or, in the case of non-profit organisations, to take some action (for example, donate blood). A classic model for reaching promotional goals is called the **AIDA concept**.[14] The acronym stands for Attention, Interest, Desire and Action – the stages of consumer involvement with a promotional message. This model is most appropriate for purchases classified as mid- to high-involvement decision-making. Low-involvement purchases tend to be more simplistic.

This model proposes that consumers respond to marketing messages in a cognitive (thinking), affective (feeling) and conative (doing) sequence. First, the promotion manager attracts a person's attention by a greeting and approach (in personal selling) or loud volume, unusual contrasts, bold headlines, movement, bright colours, and so on (in advertising and sales promotion). Next, a good sales presentation, demonstration or advertisement creates interest in the product and then, by illustrating how the product's features will satisfy the consumer's needs or desires. Finally, a special offer or a strong closing sales pitch may be used to obtain purchase action.

The AIDA concept assumes that promotion propels consumers along the following four steps in the purchase-decision process:

1. *Awareness*: The advertiser must first achieve awareness with the target market. A firm cannot sell something if the market doesn't know that the good or service exists. When New Zealand firm Bio-Farm introduced its Country Pet–Pet Plus Yoghurt, it not only used milk carton packaging commonly used for human food products (to reduce any quality concerns), but it also heavily publicised the introduction of the product with ads on TV, on outdoor billboards, in consumer magazines and at point-of-purchase displays in supermarkets.

2. *Interest*: Simple awareness of a brand seldom leads to a sale. The next step is to create interest in the product. A print ad or TV commercial cannot actually tell pet owners whether their pets will like the yoghurt; it can only tell them why the product is good for their pets and why they should try it. Thus, Bio-Farm might send samples of the product to pet owners to create interest in the new brand.

3. *Desire*: Even though owners (and their pets) may like Country Pet–Pet Plus Yoghurt, they may not see any advantage over competing brands, especially if owners are brand loyal. Therefore, Bio-Farm must create brand preference by explaining the product's differential advantage over the competition. Specifically, it has to show that pets' health will be greatly enhanced with the product and that this brand is superior to all others. Although pet owners may come to prefer the Bio-Farm brand to other brands, they still may not have developed the desire to buy the new brand. At this stage, Bio-Farm might offer the consumer additional reasons to buy its product, such as easy-to-open, hygienic packaging that keeps the product fresh; additional vitamins and minerals that healthy pets need; or the results of a taste test.

4. *Action*: Some members of the target market may now be convinced to buy the Bio-Farm pet yoghurt but have yet to make the purchase. Displays in grocery stores, coupons, premiums and trial-size packages can often push the complacent shopper into making a purchase.

Most buyers involved in high-involvement purchase situations pass through the four stages of the AIDA model on the way to making a purchase. The promoter's task is to determine where on the purchase ladder most of the target consumers are located and to design a promotion plan to meet their needs. For example, if Bio-Farm had determined that about half of its buyers are in the preference or conviction stage but have not bought its brand of pet yoghurt for some reason, the company may mail cents-off coupons to pet owners to prompt them to buy.

AIDA concept
Model that outlines the process for achieving promotional goals in terms of stages of consumer involvement with the message; the acronym stands for Attention, Interest, Desire and Action.

The AIDA concept does not explain how all promotions influence purchase decisions. The model suggests that promotional effectiveness can be measured in terms of consumers progressing from one stage to the next. However, the order of stages in the model, as well as whether consumers go through all the steps, has been much debated. For example, purchase can occur without interest or desire, perhaps when a low-involvement product is bought on impulse. Regardless of the order of the stages or consumers' progression through these stages, the AIDA concept helps marketers by suggesting which promotional strategy will be most effective.[15]

AIDA and the promotional mix

Exhibit 9.6 depicts the relationship between the promotional mix and the AIDA model. It shows that, although advertising does have an impact in the later stages, it is most useful in creating awareness about goods or services. In contrast, personal selling reaches fewer people at first. Salespeople are more effective at creating customer interest for merchandise or a service and at gaining desire. For example, advertising may help a potential computer purchaser to gain knowledge and information about competing brands, but the salesperson in an electronics store may be the one who actually encourages the buyer to decide that a particular brand is the best choice. The salesperson also has the advantage of having the computer physically there to demonstrate its capabilities to the buyer.

Sales promotion and direct marketing's greatest strengths are in creating strong desire and purchase intent. Coupons and other price-off promotions are techniques used to persuade customers to buy new products. Frequent-buyer sales promotion programs, popular among retailers, allow consumers to accumulate points or dollars that can later be redeemed for goods. Frequent-buyer programs tend to increase purchase intent and loyalty and encourage repeat purchases. The Fly Buys scheme is Australia's leading customer loyalty program. Over two million households collect Fly Buys points which they redeem or exchange for various awards. In the case of direct marketing, generally very targeted offers are made to a small number of consumers who have been previously shown to have an interest in the product category. This greatly increases the likelihood of a desired response.

Exhibit 9.6
When the elements of promotion are most useful

	Attention	Interest	Desire	Action
Personal selling	Somewhat effective	Very effective	Very effective	Somewhat effective
Advertising	Very effective	Very effective	Somewhat effective	Not effective
Sales promotion	Somewhat effective	Somewhat effective	Very effective	Very effective
Public relations	Very effective	Very effective	Very effective	Not effective
Direct marketing	Very effective	Very effective	Somewhat effective	Very effective

Public relations has its greatest impact in building awareness about a company, good or service. Many companies can attract attention and build goodwill by sponsoring community events that benefit a worthy cause, such as anti-drug and learn-to-swim programs. Such sponsorships project a positive image of the firm and its products into the minds of consumers and potential consumers. Good publicity can also help to develop consumer desire for a product. Book publishers push to get their titles listed on the bestseller lists of major publications, such as *Australian Bookseller & Publisher* or, internationally, the *New York Times*. Authors also make appearances on talk shows and at bookstores to personally sign books and speak to fans. Similarly, movie marketers use pre-release publicity to raise the profile of their movies and to increase initial box office sales. For example, most major motion picture studios have their own websites with multimedia clips and publicity photos of their current movies to attract viewers. Furthermore, movie promoters will include publicity gained from reviewers' quotes and award nominations in their advertising.

Factors affecting the promotional mix

Promotional mixes vary a great deal from one product and one industry to the next. Normally, advertising and personal selling are used to promote goods and services, supported and supplemented by sales promotion. Public relations helps to develop a positive image for the organisation and the product line. However, a firm may choose not to use all four promotional elements in its promotional mix, or it may choose to use them all in varying degrees. The particular promotional mix chosen by a firm for a product or service depends on several factors: nature of the product, stage in the product life cycle, target market characteristics, type of buying decision, available funds for promotion, and use of either a push or a pull strategy.

6 Describe the factors that affect the promotional mix

Nature of the product

Characteristics of the product itself can influence the promotional mix. For example, a product can be classified as either a business product or a consumer product (refer to Chapter 3). As business products are often custom-made to the buyer's exact specifications, they are often not well suited to mass promotion. Therefore, producers of most business goods, such as computer systems or industrial machinery, rely more heavily on personal selling than on advertising. Informative personal selling is common for industrial installations, accessories, and component parts and materials. Advertising, however, still serves a purpose in promoting business goods. Advertisements in trade media may be used to create general buyer awareness and interest. Moreover, advertising can help to locate potential customers for the sales team. For example, print media advertising often includes coupons soliciting the potential customer to 'fill this out for more detailed information'.

On the other hand, because consumer products generally are not custom-made, they don't require the selling efforts of a company representative who can tailor them to the user's needs. Thus, consumer goods are promoted mainly through advertising to create brand familiarity. Broadcast advertising, newspapers and consumer-oriented magazines are used extensively to promote consumer goods, especially non-durables. Sales promotion, the brand name and the product's packaging are about twice as important for consumer goods as for business products. Persuasive personal selling is important at the retail level for shopping goods such as cars and appliances.

The costs and risks associated with a product also influence the promotional mix. As a general rule, when the costs or risks of using a product increase, personal selling becomes more important. Items that are a small part of a firm's budget (supply items) or of a consumer's budget (convenience products) don't require a salesperson to close the sale. In fact, inexpensive items cannot support the cost of a salesperson's time and effort unless the potential volume is high. On the other hand, expensive and complex machinery, new buildings, cars and new homes represent a considerable investment. A salesperson must assure buyers that they are spending their money wisely and not taking an undue financial risk.

Social risk is an issue as well. Many consumer goods are not products of great social importance because they don't reflect social position. People don't experience much social risk in buying a loaf of bread or a chocolate bar. However, buying some shopping products and many speciality products such as jewellery and clothing does involve a social risk. Many consumers depend on sales personnel for guidance and advice in making the 'proper' choice.

Stage in the product life cycle

The product's stage in its life cycle is a big factor in designing a promotional mix (see Exhibit 9.7). During the *introduction stage*, the basic goal of promotion is to inform the target audience that the product is available. Initially, the emphasis is on the general product class – for example, desktop computer systems. This emphasis gradually changes to awareness of specific brands, such as Dell, IBM, Apple and Compaq. Typically, both extensive advertising and public relations inform the target audience of the product class or brand and heighten awareness levels. Sales promotion encourages early trial of the product, and personal selling gets retailers to carry the product.

When the product reaches the growth stage of the life cycle, the promotion blend may shift. Often a change is necessary because different types of potential

Exhibit 9.7
Product life cycle and the promotional mix

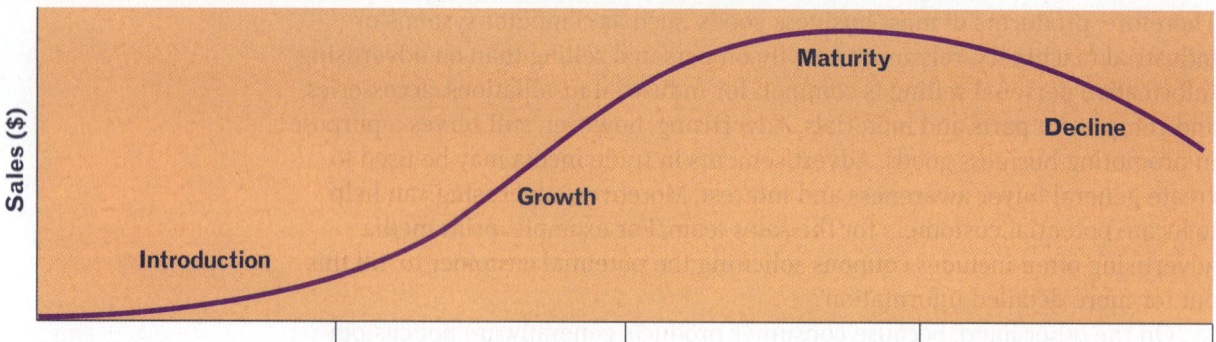

Time				
Pre-introduction publicity; small amounts of advertising near introduction	Heavy advertising and public relations to build awareness; sales promotion to induce trial; personal selling to obtain distribution	Heavy advertising and public relations to build brand loyalty; decreasing use of sales promotion; personal selling to maintain distribution	Advertising slightly decreased – more persuasive and reminder in nature; increased use of sales promotion to build market share; personal selling to maintain distribution	Advertising and public relations drastically decreased; sales promotion and personal selling maintained at low levels

Stages shown on curve: Introduction, Growth, Maturity, Decline (Sales $ vs Time)

buyers are targeted. Although advertising and public relations continue to be major elements of the promotional mix, sales promotion can be reduced because consumers need fewer incentives to purchase. The promotional strategy is to emphasise the product's differential advantage over the competition. Persuasive promotion is used to build and maintain brand loyalty to support the product during the growth stage. By this stage, personal selling has usually succeeded in getting adequate distribution for the product.

As the product reaches the *maturity stage* of its life cycle, competition becomes fiercer, and thus persuasive and reminder advertising is more strongly emphasised. Sales promotion comes back into focus as product sellers try to increase their market share.

All promotion, especially advertising, is reduced as the product enters the *decline stage*. Nevertheless, personal selling and sales promotion efforts may be maintained, particularly at the retail level.

Target market characteristics

A target market characterised by widely scattered potential customers, highly informed buyers and brand-loyal repeat purchasers generally requires a promotional mix with more advertising and sales promotion and less personal selling. Sometimes, however, personal selling is required even when buyers are well informed and geographically dispersed. Although industrial installations and component parts may be sold to extremely competent people with extensive education and work experience, salespeople must still be present to explain the product and work out the details of the purchase agreement.

Often firms sell goods and services in markets where potential customers are hard to locate. Print advertising can be used to find them. The reader is invited to call for more information or to mail in a reply card for a detailed brochure. As the calls or cards are received, salespeople are sent to visit the potential customers.

Type of buying decision

The promotional mix also depends on the type of buying decision – for example, a routine decision or a complex decision. For routine consumer decisions such as buying toothpaste or soft drinks, the most effective promotion calls attention to the brand or reminds the consumer about the brand. Advertising and, especially, sales promotion are the most productive promotion tools to use for routine decisions.

If the decision is neither routine nor complex, advertising and public relations help to establish awareness of the good or service. Suppose a man is looking for a bottle of wine to serve to his dinner guests. As a beer drinker, he is not familiar with wines, yet he has seen advertising for Wolf Blass wines and has also read an article in a popular magazine about the wine maker, Wolf Blass. He may be more likely to buy this brand because he is already aware of it.

In contrast, consumers making complex buying decisions are more extensively involved. They rely on large amounts of information to help them reach a purchase decision. Personal selling is most effective in helping these consumers decide. For example, consumers thinking about buying a car usually depend on a salesperson to provide the information they need to reach a decision. Print advertising may also be used for high-involvement purchase decisions because it can often provide a large amount of information to the consumer.

Sydney Morning Herald
Courier-Mail
on-line

What can you tell about the target market for the Sydney Morning Herald and the Courier-Mail from their respective websites? How will this information influence any promotions either paper would want to do?
www.smh.com.au
www.couriermail.news.com.au

Consumers making complex buying decisions often depend on the salesperson to provide important product information. Purchasing a car is one such example. Can you think of others?

Available funds

Money, or the lack of it, may easily be the most important factor in determining the promotional mix. A small, undercapitalised manufacturer may rely heavily on free publicity if its product is unique. If the situation warrants a sales team, a financially strained firm may turn to manufacturers' agents, who work on a commission basis with no advances or expense accounts. Even well-capitalised organisations may not be able to afford the advertising rates of publications such as *Home Beautiful*, *Women's Weekly* and the *Sydney Morning Herald*. The price of a high-profile advertisement in these media could support a salesperson for a year.

When funds are available to permit a mix of promotional elements, a firm will generally try to optimise its return on promotion dollars while minimising the cost per contact, or the cost of reaching one member of the target market. In general, the cost per contact is very high for personal selling, public relations and sales promotions such as sampling and demonstrations. On the other hand, for the number of people national advertising reaches, it has a very low cost per contact.

Usually there is a tradeoff among the funds available, the number of people in the target market, the quality of communication needed and the relative costs of the promotional elements. A company may have to forgo a full-page, colour advertisement in *Gourmet Traveller* magazine in order to pay for a personal selling effort. Although the magazine ad will reach more people than personal selling, the high cost of the magazine space is a problem.

Push and pull strategies

push strategy
Marketing strategy that uses aggressive personal selling and trade advertising to convince a wholesaler or a retailer to carry and sell particular merchandise.

The last factor that affects the promotional mix is whether a push or a pull promotional strategy will be used. Manufacturers may use aggressive personal selling and trade advertising to convince a wholesaler or a retailer to carry and sell their merchandise. This approach is known as a **push strategy** (see Exhibit 9.8).

Exhibit 9.8 Push strategy versus pull strategy

Push strategy

Manufacturer promotes to wholesaler → Wholesaler promotes to retailer → Retailer promotes to consumer → Consumer buys from retailer

Orders to manufacturer

Pull strategy

Manufacturer promotes to consumer → Consumer demands product from retailer → Retailer demands product from wholesaler → Wholesaler demands product from manufacturer

Orders to manufacturer

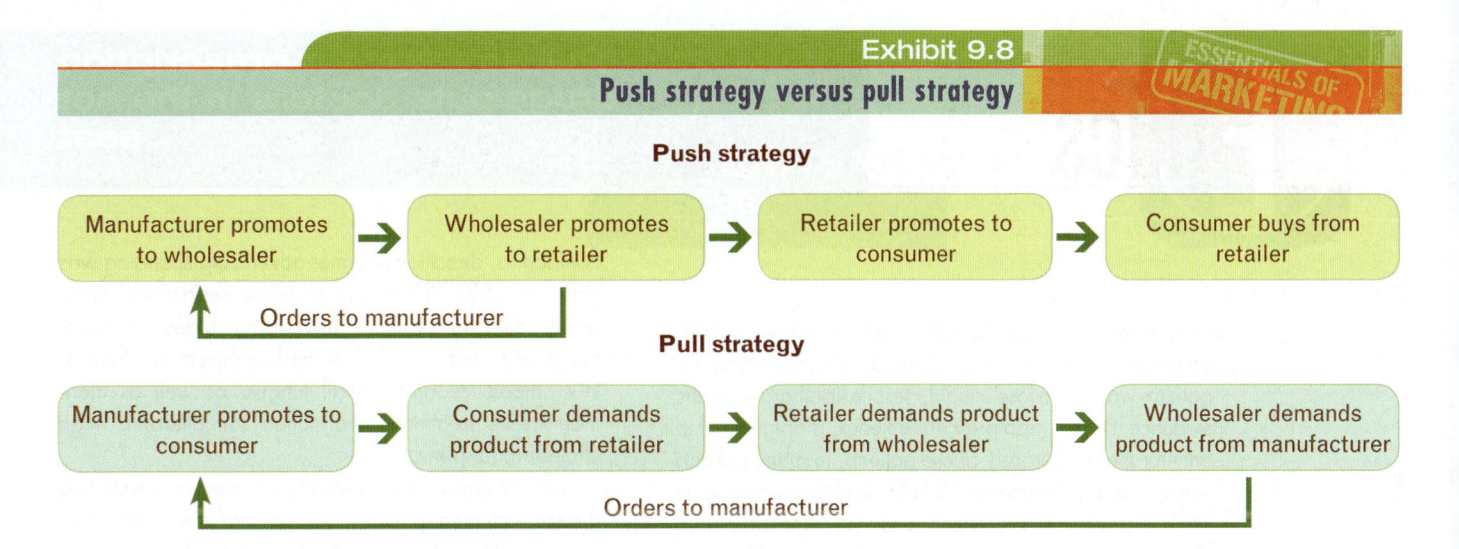

The wholesaler, in turn, must often push the merchandise forward by persuading the retailer to handle the goods. The retailer then uses advertising, displays and other forms of promotion to convince the consumer to buy the 'pushed' products. This concept also applies to services. For example, Queensland Tourism often targets promotions to travel agencies selling its Sunlover Holidays packages. These agents in turn tell their customers about the benefits of holidaying in Queensland.

At the other extreme is a **pull strategy**, which stimulates consumer demand to obtain product distribution. Rather than trying to sell to the wholesaler, the manufacturer using a pull strategy focuses its promotional efforts on end consumers or opinion leaders. For example, in the United States, Colgate-Palmolive sent 30 million samples of its new Colgate Total toothpaste to dental practitioners throughout the country to create demand.[16] As consumers begin demanding the product, the retailer orders the merchandise from the wholesaler. The wholesaler, confronted with rising demand, then places an order for the 'pulled' merchandise from the manufacturer. Consumer demand pulls the product through the channel of distribution (see Exhibit 9.7). Heavy sampling, introductory consumer advertising, cents-off campaigns and coupons are part of a pull strategy. Using a pull strategy, Queensland Tourism entices travellers to visit by advertising heavily in consumer magazines or offering discounts on hotels or airfares.

Rarely does a company use a pull or a push strategy exclusively. Instead, the mix will emphasise one of these strategies. For example, pharmaceutical companies generally use a push strategy, through personal selling and trade advertising, to promote their pharmaceuticals and therapies to doctors. Sales presentations and advertisements in medical journals give physicians the detailed information they need to prescribe medication to their patients. Most pharmaceutical companies supplement their push promotional strategy with a pull strategy targeted directly to potential patients through advertisements in consumer magazines and on television. Many doctors, however, are concerned with the increasing amount of direct-to-consumer advertising that prompts many patients to demand drugs they either don't need or that may cause adverse reactions. Read the Ethics in marketing box to learn more about this controversial promotional practice.

pull strategy
Marketing strategy that stimulates consumer demand to obtain product distribution.

Herron on-line

Is Herron using its website for direct-to-consumer advertising? What makes you think as you do? How is the company promoting its latest drugs on its website? What is your opinion of how Herron is informing consumers about or promoting its products?
www.herron.com.au

Ethics IN MARKETING

Pull strategy for prescription drugs puts doctors in the hot seat

During the diet-drug debacle, doctors wrote millions of prescriptions for the Fenphen drug combination for patients wanting to lose weight, despite little hard scientific evidence. Doctors also prescribed Redux, a drug intended only for the dangerously obese patients, to many patients who wanted to trim five or 10 kilos. And they wrote some 15 000 to 20 000 prescriptions for the impotency drug Viagra when it first appeared on the market for many men who were not clinically impotent but wanted a boost. Fenphen and Redux were eventually called off the market, whereas Viagra was found to be potentially dangerous for men with certain types of heart disease.

In the fallout, doctors are under attack for prescribing the drugs too much, too readily and to the wrong patients. Doctors contend it isn't all their fault. Prodded by an explosion in direct-to-consumer advertising of prescription drugs, patients pressure their physicians for quick treatments. Prozac, the most widely prescribed drug in the world, is often prescribed to patients who are only mildly depressed. Likewise, many patients pressure their family physicians and paediatricians for antibiotics to treat flu symptoms, even though antibiotics are ineffective against viral-type infections.

Prescription drug advertising has become a billion-dollar consumer media tidal wave since the US Food and Drug Administration (FDA) loosened its rules on pharmaceutical advertising. The biggest boom came after the FDA allowed drug companies to advertise on television as long as the ad mentioned major side effects and directed viewers to a print ad and website for detailed disclosures. In the early 1990s, prescription drug marketers spent only about US$160 million on direct-to-consumer advertising, mostly in consumer magazines. That figure jumped to US$350 million in 1995 to match industry spending on advertising directed to physicians. By 1998, US pharmaceutical companies' direct-to-consumer advertising spending was close to US$1 billion due to fewer restrictions. As a result, direct-to-consumer advertising today confronts the public with such squeamish subjects as herpes, HIV, impotence and toenail fungus, as well as more mainstream treatment information for allergies, high cholesterol and migraines.

Many physicians dislike the increase in advertising directed at their patients, saying that the information is given to patients in limited form. Patients then diagnose themselves and come to their physicians with a particular therapy in mind without knowing its drawbacks or even if the drug is right for them. Drug advertising also tends to present the pharmaceutical products as wonder drugs. Ads for allergy medicine are particularly dramatic, offering allergy sufferers visions of happiness and serenity.

On the other hand, many believe the benefits of direct-to-consumer advertising of prescription drugs far outweigh its disadvantages. Drug advertising leads to more informed patients who are able to ask better questions while with their physicians. Further, consumers are presented with information concerning treatments they might have never known existed. Drug ads may also help consumers to determine whether they have a medical problem. Many serious medical conditions remain undiagnosed because people don't know about the symptoms or don't regularly see a doctor. For example, it is estimated that only half of the 16 million Americans with diabetes know they have the disease. In the end, proponents claim, the doctor makes the prescribing decision based on what is best for the patient.[17]

What is your opinion on direct-to-consumer advertising of prescription drugs? Do you believe there should be restrictions on what drug advertisers can do? How can doctors cope with the increased pressure from patients due to drug advertising?

Personal selling

7 Describe personal selling

As mentioned in the beginning of the chapter, *personal selling* is interpersonal communication between a sales representative and one or more prospective buyers in an attempt to influence prospective buyers in a purchase situation.

Personal selling offers several advantages over other forms of promotion:

- Personal selling provides a detailed explanation or demonstration of the product. This capability is especially needed for complex or new goods and services.
- The sales message can be varied according to the motivations and interests of each prospective customer. Moreover, when the prospect has questions or raises objections, the salesperson is there to provide explanations. In contrast, advertising and sales promotion can only respond to the objections the marketing manager thinks are important to customers.
- Personal selling is generally directed only to qualified prospects, though in some cases sales personnel do make 'cold calls', which may result in unqualified prospects being approached. Other forms of promotion include more unavoidable waste because many people in the audience are not prospective customers.
- Personal selling costs can be controlled by adjusting the size of the sales team (and resulting expenses) in one-person increments. On the other hand, advertising and sales promotion must often be purchased in fairly large amounts.

Personal selling might work better than other forms of promotion given certain customer and product characteristics. Generally speaking, personal selling becomes more important as the number of potential customers decreases, as the complexity of the product increases and as the value of the product grows (see Exhibit 9.9). When there are relatively few potential customers and the value of the good or service is relatively sufficient, the time and travel costs of personally visiting each prospect are justifiable. For highly complex goods, such as business jets or private communication systems, a salesperson is needed to determine the prospective customer's needs, explain the product's basic advantages, and propose the exact features and accessories that will meet the client's needs.

Exhibit 9.9 Comparison of personal selling and advertising/sales promotion

Personal selling is more important if ...	Advertising and sales promotion are more important if ...
The product has a high value.	The product has a low value.
It is a custom-made product.	It is a standardised product.
There are few customers.	There are many customers.
The product is technically complex.	The product is simple to understand.
Customers are concentrated.	Customers are geographically dispersed.
Examples: insurance policies, custom windows, aircraft engines.	Examples: soap, magazine subscriptions, cotton T-shirts.

Relationship selling

Traditional marketing theory and practice concerning personal selling focused almost entirely on a planned presentation to prospective customers for the sole purpose of making the sale, and then moving on to the next prospect. Whether it took place face to face during a personal sales call or by selling over the telephone (telemarketing), traditional personal selling methods attempted to persuade the buyer to accept a point of view or convince them to take some action. Once the customer was somewhat convinced, then the salesperson used a variety of techniques in an attempt to elicit a purchase. Although this type of sales approach has not disappeared entirely, it is being used less and less often by professional salespeople.

8 Discuss the key differences between relationship selling and traditional selling

relationship selling (consultative selling)
Sales practice of building, maintaining and enhancing interactions with customers in order to develop long-term satisfaction through mutually beneficial partnerships.

In contrast, modern views of personal selling emphasise the relationship that develops between a salesperson and a buyer. **Relationship selling**, or **consultative selling**, is a multi-stage process that emphasises personalisation and empathy as key ingredients in identifying prospects and developing them as long-term, satisfied customers. The focus is on building mutual trust between buyer and seller with the delivery of anticipated, long-term, value-added benefits to the buyer.[18] Relationship or consultative salespeople therefore become consultants, partners and problem-solvers for their customers. They strive to build long-term relationships with key accounts by developing trust over time. The focus shifts from a once-off sale to a long-term relationship in which the salesperson works with the customer to develop solutions for enhancing the customer's bottom line. Thus, relationship selling emphasises a win-win outcome.[19]

The end result of relationship selling tends to be loyal customers who purchase from the company time after time. A relationship selling strategy focused on retaining customers costs a company less than if it were constantly prospecting and selling to new customers. One consulting firm estimates that if a small to mid-size company were to increase its customer retention rate by just 5 per cent, its profits would double in about 10 years. Further, the average Fortune 500 company could instantly double its revenue growth with that same 5 per cent boost in retention.[20]

Relationship selling is more typical with selling situations for industrial-type goods – such as heavy machinery or computer systems, and services, such as airlines and insurance – than for consumer goods, although it is possible, as Sanitarium discovered. Sanitarium, through its Weet-Bix brand, has joined forces with the Australian Cricket Board (ACB), the Wallabies and the Active Australia Council to promote sport involvement and, in particular, triathlons to Australian children. Children join the sports club and receive personalised coaching tips from Australian cricketers and rugby players. They have opportunities to enter competitions to win tickets to games, and they also get other prizes and sports packs. In addition, through the Active Australia Council, they are promoting kids' TRYathlon to encourage children to get into sport, have fun, meet other kids, get healthy and ultimately to eat Weet-Bix to have the energy to do so. This arrangement benefits all the participating organisations, providing the ACB and the Wallabies with much-needed financial investments and Sanitarium with exposure to a large group of people from all age groups and walks of life, with whom it would not otherwise have close contact.[21]

Source: Robert M. Peterson, Patrick L. Schul and George H. Lucas, Jr, 'Consultative Selling: Walking the Walk in the New Selling Environment', National Conference on Sales Management, *Proceedings*, March 1996.

Exhibit 9.10
Key differences between traditional selling and relationship selling

Traditional personal selling	Relationship selling
Sell products (goods and services)	Sell advice, assistance and counsel
Focus on closing sales	Focus on improving the customer's bottom line
Limited sales planning	Consider sales planning as top priority
Spend most contact time telling customers about product	Spend most contact time attempting to build a problem-solving environment with the customer
Conduct 'product-specific' needs assessment	Conduct discovery in the full scope of the customer's operations
'Lone wolf' approach to the account	Team approach to the account
Proposals and presentations based on pricing and product features	Proposals and presentations based on profit-impact and strategic benefits to the customer
Sales follow-up is short term, focused on product delivery	Sales follow-up is long term, focused on long-term relationship enhancement

Exhibit 9.10 lists the key differences between traditional personal selling and relationship or consultative selling. These differences will become more apparent as we explore the personal selling process later in the chapter.

Advances in electronic commerce on the Internet, however, are threatening the buyer–seller relationship as more and more companies are choosing to conduct business and purchase supplies and materials through a computer screen rather than face to face with a salesperson. This will be discussed more later in this chapter when we talk about electronic marketing.

More and more companies are expanding their marketing and selling efforts into global markets. Salespeople selling in foreign markets should tailor their presentation and closing styles to each market. Different personalities and skills will be successful in some countries and absolute failures in others. For example, if a salesperson is an excellent closer and always focused on the next sale, doing business in Latin America might be difficult. The reason is that in Latin America, people want to take a long time building a personal relationship with their suppliers.[22] Read about other global dos and don'ts of selling in the Global perspectives box.

Global dos and don'ts in selling

Global PERSPECTIVES

Most large companies with operations on foreign soil are employing locals to sell their products – international buyers are often cold to Americans and other Westerners trying to peddle their wares. So the Westerner who finds him- or herself trying to sell internationally had better be prepared.

Most selling skills that are successful in the West also will work overseas. However, knowing how to act in certain cultures can be the difference between closing the deal and losing a customer. There are certain things Westerners take for granted that could easily cost them a deal overseas. A simple thumbs-up sign that we give every day could offend a customer in another country. Here, from many international business experts, are some things to watch out for in certain countries and regions around the world.

Arab countries: Don't use your left hand to hold, offer or receive materials, because Arabs use their left hand to touch toilet paper. If you must use your left hand to write, apologise for doing so. Handshakes in Arab countries are a bit limp and last longer than typical Western handshakes.

China: Never talk business on the first meeting – it's disrespectful. Don't refuse tea during a business discussion. Always drink it, even if you're offered a dozen cups a day. Never begin to eat or drink before your host does. Also, printed materials presented to Chinese business leaders should be in black and white, because colours have great significance for the Chinese. The Chinese tend to be meticulous, looking to create long-term relationships with a supplier before agreeing to buy anything. Chinese are more intradependent and tend to include more people in a deal. Most deals in China are finalised in a social setting, either over drinks or dinner. Additionally, getting to know the businessperson's family will personalise and strengthen the relationship.

European countries: Western and Eastern Europeans reshake hands whenever they are apart for even a short period of time, such as during lunch.

France: Don't schedule a breakfast meeting – the French tend not to meet until after 10 a.m. Since the French knowledge of wine is far greater than that of most other Westerners, avoid giving wine or wine-related gifts to French clients. The French also prefer gifts that are of French origin.

Germany: Don't address a business associate by his or her first name, even if you have known each other for years. Always wait for an invitation to do so. Also, breakfast meetings are unheard of here, too. Salespeople should expect a sober, rigid business climate and negotiations that lack flexibility and compromise.

Central and South America: People here don't take the clock too seriously – scheduling more than two appointments in one day can prove disastrous.

Latin Americans also tend to use a lighter, lingering handshake. Negotiations with Central and South American customers typically include a great deal of bargaining. Personal relationships are also important in Central and South America, so salespeople should make face-to-face contact with their clients during meetings and presentations.

Japan: Don't bring up business on the golf course – always wait for your host to take the initiative. Don't cross your legs in Japan – showing the bottom of the foot is insulting. Japanese businesspeople shake hands with one firm gesture combined with a slight bow, which should be returned. Japanese prefer designer-label gifts. Also, the higher the position of the recipient, the more elaborately wrapped the gift should be.

Mexico: Don't send a bouquet of red or yellow flowers as a gift – Mexicans associate those colours with evil spirits and death. Instead, send a box of premium chocolates. Including a small gift for the client's children creates a positive impression.

Vietnam: When meeting a Vietnamese woman, wait for her to extend a hand first – she may simply nod or bow slightly, the most common form of greeting in Vietnam. Vietnamese don't like to be touched or patted on the back or shoulders in social situations.

Miscellaneous: The thumbs-up gesture is considered offensive in the Middle East, rude in Australia and a sign of 'OK' in France. It's rude to cross your arms while facing someone in Turkey. In the Middle East don't ask, 'How's the family?' – it's considered too personal. In most Asian countries, staring directly into a person's eyes is considered discourteous.[23]

After closing a sale, it is important that salespeople follow up with the customer, as this increases the chances of customer satisfaction. Dell Computer Corporation is one company that is committed to enhancing its customers' satisfaction through effective follow-up and customer support. Dell developed an extensive extranet system, called Premier Pages, that is designed to give Dell's contract customers product, pricing and service information at the touch of a mouse. Each Dell customer gets its own password-protected Premier Page found at an unlisted URL on the Web. Access includes product information, pricing structures, an employee-purchase plan (which gives customers' employees discounts on Dell products bought for personal use), on-line product ordering and up-to-date purchase-history reports. The costs to Dell have been justified in customer satisfaction alone. One customer in the United States estimated saving US$2 million on technical support costs thanks to Premier Pages. Another customer reported that it redeployed most of its procurement people and uses the remaining ones more efficiently.[24]

Direct marketing

9 Define direct marketing

As mentioned earlier, *direct marketing* refers to techniques used to get consumers to make a purchase from their home, office or other non-retail setting. Techniques used in direct marketing include direct mail, catalogues and mail order, telemarketing and electronic retailing. These forms of direct marketing offer customers increased convenience and flexibility, and at the same time can allow marketers to directly target particular needs of specific customers.

Personal retailing

personal retailing
Representatives selling products door-to-door, office-to-office or through party plans.

In **personal retailing**, representatives sell products door-to-door, office-to-office or through party plans. Companies such as Avon, Tupperware, Mary Kay

Cosmetics, Mia Lingerie, The Pampered Chef, Usbourne Books and World Book Encyclopaedia depend on these techniques. Even personal computers are now being sold through personal retailing methods.

Most personal retailers seem to favour party plans these days in lieu of door-to-door canvassing. Party plans call for one person, the host, to gather as many prospective buyers as possible. Most parties are a combination of social affair and sales demonstration. For example, Mia, an Australian-based direct sales apparel manufacturer, sells its fashionable women's lingerie through party plans with friends and acquaintances (see Exhibit 9.6).

The sales of personal retailers have suffered as more women have entered the workforce. Working women are not home during the day and have little time to attend selling parties. Although most direct sellers such as Avon and Tupperware still advocate the party plan method, the realities of the marketplace have forced them to be more creative in reaching their target customers. Direct sales representatives now hold parties in offices, parks and even parking lots. Others hold informal gatherings in which shoppers can just drop in at their convenience, or offer self-improvement classes. Many direct retailers are also turning to direct mail, telephone and Internet orders to find new avenues to their customers and increase sales.

Nuskin International Amway on-line

Have a look at the website of Nuskin International, which has offices all over the world, and see how it uses the personal retailing approach to target its customers. What are your views on this particular company? Compare its operations and activities to those of Amway, which is similar in nature. What do you think about the two companies and why?
www.nuskin.com.au
www.amway-au.com

Exhibit 9.11
Mia Lingerie chooses to sell its product range via the direct market approach of party plans

Tupperware Mia Lingerie on-line

Do these sites show how personal selling is the key to the retail experience? What other techniques are used to separate personal retailing from store retailing?
www.tupperware.com.au
www.mialingerie.com

Amway, the personal seller of shampoos, detergents, toothpaste and other household products, is one company that has benefited from overseas expansion. Amway mobilised its diverse sales force to expand its interests into other countries. Today, Amway peddles its products in more than 80 countries and territories.[25]

Direct mail

Direct mail can be the most efficient or the least efficient retailing method, depending on the quality of the mailing list and the effectiveness of the mailing piece. With direct mail, marketers can precisely target their customers according to demographics, geographics and even psychographics. Good mailing lists come from an internal database or are available from list brokers. Today, direct mailers are even using DVDs in place of letters and brochures to deliver their sales message to consumers.

Direct mailers are becoming more sophisticated in their targeting of the 'right' customer. Using statistical methods to analyse census data, lifestyle and financial information, and purchase and credit history, direct mailers can pick out those most likely to buy their products. For example, a direct marketer such as Dell Computer might use this technique to target 500 000 people with the right spending patterns, psychographics and preferences. Without it, Dell could easily mail millions of solicitations annually and only reach one in 20 as potential buyers.

Catalogues and mail order

Consumers can now buy just about anything through the mail, from the mundane such as books, CDs and clothing, to the outlandish, such as the US$5 million diamond-and-ruby-studded bra available through the Victoria's Secret catalogue. Although women have made up the bulk of catalogue shoppers in the past, the percentage of male catalogue shoppers has increased in recent years.

Telemarketing

telemarketing
The use of the telephone to sell directly to consumers.

Telemarketing is the use of the telephone to sell directly to consumers. It consists of outbound sales calls, usually unsolicited, and inbound calls – that is, orders through toll-free 1800 numbers or fee-based 1900 numbers.

Outbound telemarketing is an attractive direct-marketing technique because of rising postage rates and decreasing long-distance phone rates. Skyrocketing field sales costs have also put pressure on marketing managers to use outbound telemarketing. Searching for ways to keep costs under control, marketing managers are discovering how to pinpoint prospects quickly, zero in on serious buyers and keep in close touch with regular customers. Meanwhile, they are reserving expensive, time-consuming, in-person calls for closing sales. However, this outbound telemarketing came under scrutiny during 2001 with the enactment of the Commonwealth *Privacy Act 2000*.

Inbound telemarketing programs, which use 1800 and 1900 numbers, are mainly used to take orders, generate leads and provide customer service. Inbound 1800 telemarketing has successfully supplemented direct-response TV, radio and print advertising for more than 25 years. The more recently introduced 1900 numbers, which customers pay to use, are gaining popularity as a cost-effective way for companies to target customers. One of the main benefits of 1900 numbers is that they allow marketers to generate qualified responses. Although the charge may reduce the total volume of calls, the calls that do come through are from customers who have a true interest in the product.

Electronic retailing

Electronic retailing includes the 24-hour, shop-at-home television networks and on-line retailing.

Shop-at-home networks

The shop-at-home television networks are specialised forms of direct-response marketing. These shows display merchandise, with the retail price, to home viewers. Viewers can phone in their orders directly on a toll-free line and shop with a credit card. The shop-at-home industry in Australia has quickly grown into a billion-dollar business with a loyal customer following. Shop-at-home networks have the capability of reaching nearly every home that has free-to-air or pay TV.

The best-known shop-at-home network is TVSN (TV Shopping Network). Home shopping networks are now branching out with new products to appeal to audiences that are more affluent.

On-line retailing

On-line retailing is a two-way, interactive service available to consumers with personal computers and access to the Internet. Internet service providers, such as bigpond.com and Telnet, typically provide shopping services or virtual shopping malls for subscribers. Retailers can also set up their own site on the World Wide Web for on-line shoppers to find. Coles Myer, for example, operates its own website (www.colesmyer.com.au) where it sells its clothes and accessories on-line.

In the year to November 2000, on-line consumer sales increased 66 per cent. This represents 1.3 million Australians who purchased products for their own use over the Internet. Retail products expected to sell well over the Internet include books, computer hardware and software, music and videos, toys, consumer electronics and even wines.[26]

Despite its potential convenience, on-line shopping has had a slow start. Although the number of consumers purchasing goods on-line has increased dramatically, on-line shopping has not been greatly successful as buyers still like touching the goods they are going to buy, as well as the social interaction, and are concerned about the security and the privacy of their personal information on-line.[27] However, many on-line merchants are thriving. Selling books, music, software and flowers on-line are a few bright spots in terms of sales and visits. Amazon.com has become one of the world's most successful booksellers via the Internet. On-line shoppers can search Amazon's database of over one million titles, read on-line reviews, and receive email alerts about their favourite subjects and authors. CDNow's Internet site offers more than 500 000 music- and entertainment-related products, including CDs, vinyl, cassettes, music videos, movies, DVDs, digital music downloads and special product offerings. It enables custom-made CDs, where the customers pick their own songs, and offers site navigation in eight languages.[28]

TV Shopping Network on-line

To which type of customer do you think this site is targeted? What range of products does it offer?
www.tvsn.com.au

Connect it

Companies in the highly competitive publishing industry don't use just one element of the promotional mix to promote their many brands of magazines. Rather, they use a mix of promotional elements: advertising, public relations and publicity, and sales promotion. Effective promotion is crucial to the success of these companies as their target markets are often fickle and transitory. As you read the next chapter, keep in mind that marketers try to choose the mix of promotional elements that will best promote their good or service. Rarely will a marketer rely on just one method of promotion.

Summary

1 Discuss the role of promotion in the marketing mix.
Promotion is communication by marketers that informs, persuades and reminds potential buyers of a product in order to influence an opinion or elicit a response. Promotional strategy is the plan for using the elements of promotion – personal selling, advertising, sales promotion and public relations – to meet the firm's overall objectives and marketing goals. Based on these objectives, the elements of the promotional strategy become a coordinated promotion plan. The promotion plan then becomes an integral part of the total marketing strategy for reaching the target market along with product, distribution and price.

2 Discuss the elements of the promotional mix.
The elements of the promotional mix include personal selling, advertising, sales promotion and public relations. Personal selling typically involves direct communication, in person or by telephone; the seller tries to initiate a purchase by informing and persuading one or more potential buyers. More current notions of personal selling focus on the relationship developed between the seller and buyer. Advertising is a form of impersonal, one-way mass communication paid for by the source. Sales promotion is typically used to back up other components of the promotional mix by motivating employees and stimulating consumer and business-customer purchasing. Finally, public relations is the function of promotion concerned with a firm's public image. Firms cannot buy good publicity, but they can take steps to create a positive company image.

3 Describe the communication process.
The communication process has several steps. When an individual or an organisation has a message it wishes to convey to a target audience, it encodes that message using language and symbols familiar to the intended receiver and sends the message through a channel of communication. Noise in the transmission channel distorts the source's intended message. Reception occurs if the message falls within the receiver's frame of reference. The receiver decodes the message and usually provides feedback to the source. Normally, feedback is direct for interpersonal communication and indirect for mass communication.

4 Explain the goals and tasks of promotion.

The fundamental goals of promotion are to induce, modify or reinforce behaviour by informing, persuading and reminding. Informative promotion explains a good's or service's purpose and benefits. Promotion that informs the consumer is typically used to increase demand for a general product category or to introduce a new good or service. Persuasive promotion is designed to stimulate a purchase or an action. Promotion that persuades the consumer to buy is essential during the growth stage of the product life cycle, when competition becomes fierce. Reminder promotion is used to keep the product and brand name in the public's mind. Promotions that remind are generally used during the maturity stage of the product life cycle.

5 Discuss the AIDA concept and its relationship to the promotional mix.

The AIDA model outlines the four basic stages in the purchase decision-making process, which are initiated and propelled by promotional activities: (1) awareness; (2) interest; (3) desire; and (4) action. The components of the promotional mix have varying levels of influence at each stage of the AIDA model. Advertising is a good tool for increasing awareness and knowledge of a good or service. Sales promotion is effective when consumers are at the purchase stage of the decision-making process. Personal selling is most effective in developing customer interest and desire.

6 Describe the factors that affect the promotional mix.

Promotion managers consider many factors when creating promotional mixes. These factors include the nature of the product, product life cycle stage, target market characteristics, the type of buying decision involved, availability of funds, and feasibility of push or pull strategies. Because most business products tend to be tailored to the buyer's exact specifications, the marketing manager may choose a promotional mix that relies more heavily on personal selling. On the other hand, consumer products are generally mass produced and lend themselves more to mass promotional efforts such as advertising and sales promotion. As products move through different stages of the product life cycle, marketers will choose to use different promotional elements. For example, advertising is emphasised more in the introductory stage of the product life cycle than in the decline stage. Characteristics of the target market, such as geographic location of potential buyers and brand loyalty, influence the promotional mix, as does the issue of whether the buying decision is complex or routine. The amount of funds a firm has to allocate to promotion may also help to determine the promotional mix. Small firms with limited funds may rely more heavily on public relations, whereas larger firms may be able to afford broadcast or print advertising. Finally, if a firm uses a push strategy to promote the product or service, the marketing manager may choose to use aggressive advertising and personal selling to wholesalers and retailers. If a pull strategy is chosen, then the manager often relies on aggressive mass promotion, such as advertising and sales promotion, to stimulate consumer demand.

7 Describe personal selling.

Personal selling is direct communication between a sales representative and one or more prospective buyers in an attempt to influence each other in a purchase situation. Broadly speaking, all businesspeople use personal selling to promote

Define it

advertising 310
AIDA concept 321
channel 316
communication 314
decoding 317
differential advantage 308
direct marketing (direct-
   response marketing) 310
encoding 316
feedback 317
integrated marketing
   communications (IMC) 313
interpersonal 315
mass communication 315
noise 316
personal retailing 332
personal selling 309
promotion 308
promotional mix 309
promotional strategy 308
publicity 312
public relations (PR) 312
pull strategy 327
push strategy 326
receiver 317
relationship selling
   (consultative selling) 330
sales promotion 311
sender 315
telemarketing 334

themselves and their ideas. Personal selling offers several advantages over other forms of promotion. Personal selling allows salespeople to thoroughly explain and demonstrate a product. Salespeople have the flexibility to tailor a sales proposal to the needs and preferences of individual customers. Personal selling is more efficient than other forms of promotion because salespeople target definite prospects and avoid wasting efforts on unlikely buyers. Personal selling affords greater managerial control over promotion costs. Finally, personal selling is the most effective method of closing a sale and producing satisfied customers.

8 Discuss the key differences between relationship selling and traditional selling.
Relationship selling is the practice of building, maintaining and enhancing interactions with customers in order to develop long-term satisfaction through mutually beneficial partnerships. Traditional selling, on the other hand, is transaction-focused. That is, the salesperson is most concerned with making once-off sales and moving on to the next prospect. Salespeople practising relationship selling spend more time understanding a prospect's needs and developing solutions to meet those needs.

9 Define direct marketing.
Direct marketing is direct response marketing that is used to target consumers in non-traditional retail settings – such as their own homes or via the Internet. Direct marketing can use a number of different techniques such as personal retailing, direct mail, catalogues, interactive television and Internet marketing.

Review it

1. Most promotional strategies use several ingredients. Which of the following is *not* one of the elements of the promotional mix?
    a   Personal selling
    b   Informative promotion
    c   Sales promotion
    d   Public relations

2. Any form of paid communications in which a product or company is identified is the definition of
    a   Advertising
    b   The promotional mix
    c   Sales promotion
    d   Publicity

3. _____ communication is direct, face-to-face communication; _____ communication refers to communicating to large audiences.
    a   Interpersonal; mass
    b   Mass; interpersonal
    c   Encoded; decoded
    d   Decoded; encoded

4. With which element of the promotional mix does the communication sender receive the greatest amount of feedback?
    a   Advertising
    b   Personal selling
    c   Public relations
    d   Sales promotion

5 Influencing customers to buy a product now is accomplished with _____ promotion.
   a Informative
   b Advocacy
   c Persuasive
   d Reminder

6 The first step for the marketer following the AIDA concept for reaching promotional goals is
   a Awareness
   b Action
   c Desire
   d Interest

7 Which of the elements of the promotional mix is most effective in stimulating action in the target market?
   a Advertising
   b Personal selling
   c Sales promotion
   d Public relations

8 Products with high value are usually best suited to using _____ as the primary element of the promotional mix.
   a Advertising
   b Personal selling
   c Sales promotion
   d Direct marketing

9 A promotion strategy designed to stimulate consumer demand to obtain product distribution is called a push strategy.
   a True
   b False

10 One of the main benefits of direct marketing is that it can offer increased convenience and flexibility to customers.
   a True
   b False

Check the Answer Key to see how well you understood the material. More detailed discussion and writing questions and a video case related to this chapter are found in the Student Resources CD-ROM.

Apply it

1 What is a promotional strategy? Explain the concept of a differential advantage in relation to promotional strategy.
2 Why is understanding the target market a crucial aspect of the communication process?
3 Discuss the importance of integrated marketing communications. Give some current examples of companies that are and are not practising integrated marketing communications.
4 Why might a marketing manager choose to promote his or her product using persuasion? Give some current examples of persuasive promotion.
5 Discuss the role of personal selling and advertising in promoting industrial products. How does their role differ in promoting consumer products?

6. What are the key differences between relationship selling and traditional methods of selling? What types of products or services do you think would be conducive to relationship selling?

7. You have decided to engage in a direct mail campaign for your local pizza shop. Explain why this type of campaign is likely to work, what you need to ensure its success and how you would go about designing the campaign.

8. Most of you would know someone who uses Amway products. Interview this person and then discuss why they prefer to purchase their products using this retail method rather than more traditional in-store options.

9. Choose a partner from class and go together to interview the owners or managers of several small businesses in your city or town. Ask them what their promotional objectives are and why. Are they trying to inform, persuade or remind customers to do business with them? Also determine whether they believe they have an awareness problem or whether they need to persuade customers to come to them instead of to competitors. Ask them to list the characteristics of their primary market, the strengths and weaknesses of their direct competitors, and how they are positioning their store to compete. Prepare a report to present in class summarising your findings.

10. Visit www.pm-a.com. What statements does this website make about the buying power, size and growth of the Hispanic market in the United States? Why are these statistics important for marketing communication and promotion strategy in the United States?

11. Visit www.fujixerox.com.au. In what ways does this website generate a sense of personal selling?

Try it

Morgan's is a retail clothing store offering high-quality, reasonably priced merchandise. Its target markets include students at the local university and working individuals, primarily in the age range 18 to 35. The location is about five kilometres from the campus in an upscale strip shopping centre next to a small, local shopping complex. For several years the owner has been using several students as part-time salespersons and assistant managers. He has been able to find good workers, but turnover is high and training new employees takes a lot of time. Also, his sales training has consisted mostly of asking new students to review the reports of former student employees. To reduce these problems he has considered hiring a university graduate full time and fewer part-time students. The full-time employee should reduce turnover and the need for repeated training and be able to help him develop a better sales training approach. He pays the students between $10 and $16 per hour, depending on their experience. University graduates would have to be paid between $44 000 and $54 000 per year plus benefits.

Questions

1. What factors must be considered in making this decision?
2. Should the owner hire a university graduate as a full-time employee? Why?

Watch it

Boyne USA Resorts' *Lifestyles* magazine: Promoting the ultimate playground

Boyne USA Resorts' *Lifestyles* magazine has a circulation of 500 000. Through direct mail, newsstand distribution and trade show exposure, the magazine reaches an audience from Montana to Michigan and from Washington to Utah. Boyne USA Resorts is the largest privately owned resort corporation in the United States and has a very diverse audience. In many ways, *Lifestyles* epitomises Boyne's integrated approach to communication about available services. All promotional activities – media advertising, sales promotion, personal selling, public relations, as well as direct marketing – have a consistent, unified message.

This integrated approach to promotion can be seen in every issue of *Lifestyles*, which informs the target audience of skiers and golfers, persuades them to come to a Boyne resort, and reminds them of special events and sales promotions. *Lifestyles* articles advertise all the amenities of the resorts: the inns, condominiums and vacation homes; the superb quality of the slopes, crosscountry skiing trails and manicured golf courses; other activities such as hiking, cycling and fishing; and the gourmet restaurants. The section entitled 'Distinctive Resort Properties for Sale' lists available real estate for sale and invites readers to contact a Boyne real estate professional who will work one to one with prospective buyers. Also highlighted in *Lifestyles* is the Boyne team of convention planners, who offer companies a wide choice of tastefully decorated facilities and conferences for six to 600 people. *Lifestyles* also describes Boyne's special events, which are carefully orchestrated to build good public relations nationwide.

By identifying areas of public interest and offering programs to generate public awareness, Boyne USA maintains a positive image and educates the public about its goal to be a premier ski and golf resort. The company's special events calendar at the Michigan resorts is full. Ski with the Greats is a popular event, with celebrities on hand to hold clinics, compete in a challenge race and award prizes at the après-ski party. At the Hawaiian Tropic, contestants from around the state come to Boyne Mountain to compete in an evening gown and swimsuit competition, a fashion show, a limbo dance and a Mr Boyne contest, all of which culminate in a party with live entertainment. Dannon Winterfest, put on in conjunction with the Dannon Company, has tents and inflatables set up around Boyne Mountain with product sampling, a dance contest, an après-ski party and merchandise giveaways. And the World Pro Snowboard Tour features international racers who compete for US$250 000 in prize money. These events give the resorts lots of publicity, and regardless of how much advertising is done, nothing generates more excitement about Boyne USA than extensive media coverage. In addition to informing readers about the resorts, *Lifestyles* persuades them to visit. 'Want your ten-year-olds to spend more time outside? Get them a FREE Gold Season Pass to Boyne USA Resorts!' This promotion offers a complimentary pass that entitles 10-year-olds to unlimited skiing and snowboarding at Boyne Mountain and Boyne Highlands. Another powerful way to draw skiers to the resorts is to make skiing affordable. As the *Lifestyles* article explains, 'No longer will non-skiers be able to use the expense of skiing or snowboarding as an excuse to remain couch potatoes this winter. For just US$29, beginners will get a 90-minute lesson, equipment, and a beginner area lift ticket.' The promotions information in *Lifestyles* is regularly updated on the Boyne website to remind holiday-makers about special events, skiing and golfing packages, and clothing or equipment. A key element in the promotional mix for Boyne USA resorts is *Lifestyles* magazine's pull strategy to stimulate consumer demand. The scenic photos of the slopes and golf courses, lovely inns and sumptuous dining entice readers to learn more about the resorts, and deep discounts on weekday packages encourage readers to call travel agencies, use the toll-free number or email for information. Once visitors arrive at the resorts, this pull strategy is supported by a push strategy through the personal selling of real estate, clothing and equipment, and conventions. At Boyne, the push strategy is more about relationships and trust, so salespeople are viewed as consultants who help the resort connect with its guests. For example, meeting planners work diligently with key customers to develop long-term relationships, and carefully planned family events, such as Take Your Daughter to the Slopes Day or Ski Free with Lodging, make skiing affordable and so build customer loyalty.

Lifestyles is just the beginning of Boyne USA's well-coordinated promotion strategy, a strategy that is customer-focused to bring holiday-makers back to the ultimate playground year after year.

Questions

1. Using Exhibit 9.1, what is the role of promotion in Boyne USA's marketing mix?
2. How does *Lifestyle* magazine encompass all of Boyne's promotional activities?
3. Using Exhibit 9.5, explain the three tasks of promotion at Boyne USA resorts.
4. How do push and pull strategies affect Boyne's promotional mix?

Suggested reading

Boyne USA Resorts, *Lifestyles* magazine, Winter 1997–98, Spring – Summer 1998.

Boyne USA website: www.boyneusa.com.

© 2003 Nelson Australia Pty Limited

Click it

Online reading

INFOTRAC® COLLEGE EDITION
For additional readings and review on integrated marketing communications (IMC), explore InfoTrac® College Edition, your online library. Go to: www.infotrac-college.com and search for any of the InfoTrac key terms listed below:
- promotional strategy
- personal selling
- sales promotion
- marketing ethics
- marketing communication
- relationship selling

Answer key

1. *Answer*: b, p. 309 *Rationale*: The promotional mix includes personal selling, sales promotion, advertising and public relations.
2. *Answer*: a, p. 310 *Rationale*: This is the proper definition of advertising.
3. *Answer*: a, pp. 315 *Rationale*: A salesperson speaking directly with a client is an example of interpersonal communication; advertising is an example of mass communication.
4. *Answer*: b, p. 317, 329 *Rationale*: Because of the two-way message flow in personal selling, feedback is the greatest and the quickest for any of the promotional mix elements.
5. *Answer*: c, p. 320 *Rationale*: Persuasive promotion is designed to stimulate a purchase or action of the customer.
6. *Answer*: a, p. 321 *Rationale*: A firm cannot sell anything until the target market knows that the good or service exists, through promotion to stimulate awareness.
7. *Answer:* c, p. 322 *Rationale*: Sales promotion's greatest strength is in creating desire and purchase intent.
8. *Answer*: b, p. 324 *Rationale*: When a product has high value, the costs associated with personal selling become more justifiable.
9. *Answer*: b, p. 327 *Rationale*: This statement describes a pull strategy.
10. *Answer*: a, p. 322 *Rationale*: Direct marketing techniques allow customers to make purchases directly from their home or workplace or other non-retail setting.

Promotions mix

CHAPTER TEN

LEARNING OBJECTIVES

After studying this chapter, you should be able to

1. Discuss the effect advertising has on market share, consumers, brand loyalty and perception of product attributes
2. Identify the main types of advertising
3. Describe the advertising campaign process
4. Describe media evaluation and selection techniques
5. Define and state the objectives of sales promotion
6. Discuss the most common forms of consumer sales promotion
7. List the most common forms of trade sales promotion
8. Discuss the role of public relations in the promotional mix

It's after midnight and the dance clubs are jumping – music is pulsating, lights are flashing, people are dancing and the bar is littered with little silver and blue cans. Yes, Red Bull is in the house – and has absolutely no intention of leaving the party.

Red Bull, exported from Austria, has created and dominated the energy drink category with marketing savvy, guerrilla tactics and unusual distribution methods. Dietrich Mateschitz, the owner of Red Bull International, created the caffeine-charged beverage in 1987, based on a popular health tonic he discovered in Thailand. After spreading into neighbouring countries including Hungary, Slovenia, Germany and Switzerland, Red Bull charged the US market, virtually creating the energy drink market and taking it by the horns.

Initially, Red Bull was the drink of choice for extreme athletes and all-night ravers, but the taurine-based energy drink has gained a larger following and can now be found on supermarket shelves in almost every state. According to Red Bull's website at www.redbull.com.au, 'Taurine is a conditionally essential amino acid, which naturally occurs in the body. But in times of extreme physical exertion, the body no longer produces the required amounts and a relative deficiency results.' Hence, a need is defined and Red Bull races to fill it.

Red Bull on-line

See the latest promotional efforts from Red Bull and look at the different approaches and promotional effects used. Based on what you see, what target groups is this company focusing on and why do you think this? redbull.com.au

In less than three years, Red Bull has spawned a hot new beverage category and boosted sales from a base of US$12 million to US$42 million in 1998 and US$75 million in 1999, according to Beverage Marketing Corporation. Now Coke, Anheuser Busch and Pepsi are looking to get a piece of the action, and some predict that sales of energy drinks in the United States could top US$500 million in the next few years.

But with 70 per cent of the market share, Red Bull executives feel confident that they can continue leading the category by employing the same marketing techniques that put them on the map in the first place.

The company's consistent strategy has been to 'open up' a market by securing unusual distribution channels. Red Bull initially began its US charge in Santa Monica, California, by piggybacking with established distributors that deliver a number of brands. As the drink became more popular, Red Bull narrowed its distribution methods by contacting smaller distributors and insisting that they sell only Red Bull. Otherwise, Red Bull sets up warehouses and hires college students to deliver its product. Results have been incredible – in a new market, Red Bull generally breaks even within the first three months and shows a profit after six.

Another tactic that Red Bull employs is hiring hip locals 'who embody the spirit of Red Bull' in target areas to drive around in a Red Bull logoed car, hand out samples and educate consumers about the product.

Sales teams also visit targeted on-site accounts – trendy nightclubs and bars. After an initial purchase of a few cases, Red Bull supplies the bar with a branded cooler and other POP (point-of-purchase) items. The sales teams also work to get the drink into convenience stores near colleges, gyms, health-food stores and supermarkets.

While Red Bull relies heavily on sampling events at bars and nightclubs, alternative sports have proved to be a natural fit for the product. Red Bull underwrites a number of extreme sports competitions and sponsors about three dozen athletes like kayaker Tao Berman, who set a world record by paddling over a 98-foot waterfall. Another unique event Red Bull sponsors is a DJ Academy. The latest one, held in New York City and taught by such mix masters as MJ Cole and Shadow Boy, was offered to 60 aspiring DJs from around the world.

Once established in a market, Red Bull employs more traditional advertising. Current ads portray an animated bull character and carry the tag 'Red Bull gives you wings'. The ads run on late-night TV and on popular alternative radio shows.

How do marketers like Red Bull decide what type of advertising message should be conveyed to prospective consumers? How do marketers decide which media to use? How do public relations and publicity benefit a marketer's promotional plan? Answers to these questions and many more will be found as you read through this chapter.

Effects of advertising

1 Discuss the effect advertising has on market share, consumers, brand loyalty and perception of product attributes

Advertising is defined as any form of non-personal, paid communication in which the product or company is identified. It is a popular form of promotion, especially for consumer packaged goods and services. Advertising spending increases annually, with an estimated global advertising expenditure in 2004 of A$370 billion and a prediction of global spending in the order of A$400 billion by the end of 2005.[1] Europe is expected to have the fastest growth in advertising expenditure during 2004 with Asia–Pacific expenditure predicted to overtake all others by 2010. Currently advertising expenditures in the Asia–Pacific region are around $75.6 billion.[2] This measure includes advertising expenditure from 12 countries, including China, Hong Kong, New Zealand, Singapore and Indonesia, as well as Australia. In pure dollar terms, China leads the group in terms of expenditure, with Australia coming in fourth. While impressive, this figure represents only about 16 per cent of that spent in the United States each year (US$176 billion predicted for 2006).[3]

Although total advertising expenditures seem large, the industry itself is very small. There are only about 10 000 jobs in total advertising industry in Australia in 943 agencies. Interestingly 839 of these agencies (89 per cent) employ fewer than 20 people on average. In addition there are a further 1000 people working in media services, such as radio and television, magazines and newspapers, and direct-mail firms.[4] This makes the Australian industry somewhat limited.

The amount of money budgeted for advertising by some firms is staggering. In Australia, companies in the retail and auto sectors generally lead the top spenders list. Of growing importance to advertising spend are technology companies, such as Hewlett Packard, Dell and Microsoft. Mobile communications are also an important category with Telstra, Vodafone and Optus committing large sums to advertising. This category of advertising alone accounted for $180 million dollars in 2004.[5] For example, Toyota Australia spent $5 million on promoting their Camry Sportivo car in 2004 (that's just for one car!), while they spent only $77 million on their whole product range for that same year – still a lot of money. Coles Myer spent about $165 million, Vodaphone $26 million and McDonald's spent about $50 million on advertising.[6]

Spending on advertising varies by industry. For example, the game and toy industry has one of the highest ratios of advertising dollars to sales. For every dollar of merchandise sold in the toy industry, about 15 cents is spent on advertising the toy to consumers. Other consumer goods manufacturers that spend heavily on advertising in relation to total sales include book publishers, sugar and confectionery products manufacturers, watchmakers, perfume and cosmetic manufacturers, detergent makers, and wine and liquor companies.[7]

There are four major effects of advertising that marketers aim for. These are to maintain brand awareness and subsequently market share, to attempt to influence the attitudes of consumers, to encourage brand loyalty and finally to change the importance of various brand attributes. Each of these effects will now be discussed in more detail.

Advertising and market share

Today's most successful brands of consumer goods, such as Dove soap and Coca-Cola, were built by heavy advertising and marketing investments long ago. For these brands, advertising dollars are spent on maintaining brand awareness and market share.

New brands with a small market share tend to spend proportionately more for advertising and sales promotion than those with a large market share, typically for two reasons. First, beyond a certain level of spending for advertising and sales promotion, diminishing returns set in. That is, sales or market share begins to decrease no matter how much is spent on advertising and sales promotion. This phenomenon is called the **advertising response function**. Understanding the

advertising response function
Phenomenon in which spending for advertising and sales promotion increases sales or market share up to a certain level but then produces diminishing returns.

advertising response function helps marketers to use budgets wisely. A market leader such as Samboy potato chips may spend proportionally less on advertising than newcomer Frito-Lay's brand. Frito-Lay spends more on its brand in an attempt to increase awareness and market share. Samboy, on the other hand, spends only as much as needed to maintain market share; anything more would reap diminishing benefits. Because Samboy has already captured the attention of the majority of the target market, it needs only to remind customers of its product.

The second reason that new brands tend to require higher spending for advertising and sales promotion is that a certain minimum level of exposure is needed to measurably affect purchase habits. If Frito-Lay advertised its chips in only one or two publications and bought only one or two television spots, it certainly would not achieve the exposure needed to penetrate consumers' perceptual defences, obtain awareness and comprehension, and ultimately affect their purchase intentions. Instead, Frito-Lay was introduced through advertising in many different media for a sustained period of time.

Advertising and the consumer

Advertising affects everyone's daily life and influences many purchases. Consumers turn to advertising for information as well as entertainment value. The average person is exposed to hundreds of advertisements a day from many types of advertising media. In just the television media alone, researchers estimate that the average person spends over four hours a day watching TV.[8] Advertising affects the TV programs people watch, the content of the newspapers they read, the politicians they elect, the medicines they take and the toys their children play with. Consequently, the influence of advertising on a country's socio-economic system has been the subject of extensive debate among economists, marketers, sociologists, psychologists, politicians, consumerists and many others.
Although advertising cannot change consumers' deeply rooted values and attitudes, it may succeed in transforming a person's negative attitude towards a product into a positive one.[9] When prior evaluation of the brand is negative, serious or dramatic advertisements are more effective in changing consumers' attitudes. Humorous ads, on the other hand, have been shown to be more effective in shaping attitudes when consumers already have a positive image of the advertised brand.[10]

Advertising and brand loyalty

Consumers with a high degree of brand loyalty are least susceptible to the influences of advertising for competing goods or services. For example, new competitors have found it hard to dislodge Telstra after deregulation of the long-distance telephone industry. After relying on Telstra for a lifetime of service, many loyal customers have shown little response to advertising by competing companies.

Advertising also reinforces positive attitudes towards brands. When consumers have a neutral or favourable frame of reference towards a product or brand, advertising often positively influences them for it. When consumers are already highly loyal to a brand, they may buy more of it when advertising and promotion for that brand increase.[11]

Advertising and product attributes

Advertising can affect the way consumers rank a brand's attributes, such as colour, taste, smell and texture. For example, in the past a shopper may have selected a brand of luncheon meat based on taste and variety of cuts available. However, advertising may influence that consumer to choose luncheon meat on the basis of other attributes, such as kilojoules and fat content. Luncheon meat marketers such as Don Smallgoods and Healthy Choice now stress the amount of kilojoules and fat when advertising their products.

Car advertisers also understand the influence of advertising on consumers' rankings of brand attributes. Car ads have traditionally emphasised such brand attributes as roominess, speed and low maintenance. Today, however, car marketers have added safety to the list. Safety features such as anti-lock brakes, power door locks and air bags are now a standard part of the message in many carmakers' ads.

Main types of advertising

When planning an advertising campaign, firms generally choose between either institutional or product advertising. The type of advertising used depends on the firm's promotional objectives. For example, if the goal of the promotion plan is to build up the image of the company or the industry, *institutional advertising* may be used. By contrast, if the advertiser wants to enhance the sales of a specific good or service, *product advertising* is used. Each of these forms of advertising will now be explained in detail.

2 Identify the main types of advertising

This ad for Amway Corporation is a good example of institutional advertising. Notice how the ad focuses on the corporation as a whole rather than on any specific products marketed by the corporation.

Australians put a lot of trust in Panadol.*

Panadol provides more than just effective temporary relief from pain and fever. It gives the added confidence of being less likely to affect people who suffer from asthma[1,†]. It's also gentle on the stomach. And just for good measure, Panadol now has a new 3 Way Safety Seal System™. It's just another reason why Australians can trust Panadol.

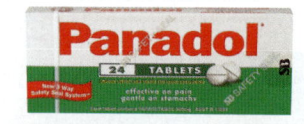

Panadol
24 TABLETS

Australia's most trusted pain reliever[2].

SB SmithKline Beecham Panadol contains paracetamol. Prolonged use could be harmful. Use only as directed. If symptoms persist, see your doctor. *Panadol is a registered Trade Mark of SmithKline Beecham (Australia) Pty Limited. 1. Jenkins C. AJT 2000;7(2):55-61. 2. Analgesics tracking. The Leading Edge, August 2000. †Up to 5% of aspirin sensitive asthmatics are cross-sensitive to paracetamol. ASMI6873 SOMKLI0453

Panadol had to spend a good deal of money on its corporate advertising in an effort to regain consumer trust after a problem with product tampering.

Institutional advertising

institutional advertising
Form of advertising designed to enhance a company's image rather than promote a particular product.

Advertising has historically been product-oriented; however, modern corporations market multiple products and need a different type of advertising. **Institutional advertising**, or corporate advertising, promotes the corporation as a whole and is designed to establish, change or maintain the corporation's identity. It usually does not ask the audience to do anything but maintain a favourable attitude towards the advertiser and its goods and services. Ford Motor Company in the United States recently embarked on a corporate campaign to promote the Ford brand as a whole rather than one specific model. The US$30 million campaign, which features Ford employees, is designed to tout the carmaker's accomplishments in safety, security and protecting the environment. The ultimate goal of the corporate campaign is to build a relationship with consumers based on trust.[12] Toyota in New Zealand has also been using this style of campaign very successfully. This form of advertising is also very common for non-profit organisations such as Greenpeace and the Heart Foundation.

A form of institutional advertising called **advocacy advertising** is typically used to safeguard against negative consumer attitudes and to enhance the company's credibility among consumers who already favour its position.[13] Often, corporations use advocacy advertising to express their views on controversial issues. At other times, firms' advocacy campaigns react to criticism or blame, sometimes in direct response to criticism by the media. Other advocacy campaigns may try to ward off increased regulation, damaging legislation or the outcome of a lawsuit. McDonald's had to do some quick work to safeguard their credibility in New South Wales in 2001, when they were accused of taking advantage of children. Apparently a local McDonald's outlet had arranged a deal with a primary school where McDonald's food would be supplied in the tuckshop and the school would get a percentage of the profits. Advocacy groups concerned with advertising to children were outraged, saying: '[The] children had few defences against marketing and were a "captive audience" in this situation.'[14] Panadol had a similar situation recently when sabotage of their product required it to be recalled from shelves for some time. The company then had to attempt to satisfy consumers that the product was safe to use by detailing their new safety measures and procedures.

advocacy advertising
Form of advertising in which an organisation expresses its views on controversial issues or responds to media attacks.

Product advertising

Unlike institutional advertising, **product advertising** promotes the benefits of a specific good or service. The product's stage in its life cycle often determines which type of product advertising is used. There are three main categories of product advertising that firms consider. These are: pioneering advertising, competitive advertising and comparative advertising. Each of these will be discussed in more detail.

product advertising
Form of advertising that promotes the benefits of a specific good or service.

Pioneering advertising

Pioneering advertising is intended to stimulate primary demand for a new product or product category. Heavily used during the introductory stage of the product life cycle, pioneering advertising offers consumers in-depth information about the benefits of the product class. Pioneering advertising also seeks to create interest. Food companies, which introduce many new products, often use pioneering advertising. Gillette used pioneering advertising to introduce its revolutionary three-bladed MACH3 shaver to consumers. The company embarked on a US$300 million global ad campaign capitalising on the high-tech theme of the product. The pioneering ad campaign's goal was to attract men seeking an even better shave than was possible with premium razors on the market.[15]

pioneering advertising
Form of advertising designed to stimulate primary demand for a new product or product category.

Competitive advertising

Firms use competitive or brand advertising when a product enters the growth phase of the product life cycle and other companies begin to enter the marketplace. Instead of building demand for the product category, the goal of **competitive advertising** is to influence demand for a specific brand. Often promotion becomes less informative and appeals more to emotions during this phase. Advertisements may begin to stress subtle differences between brands, with heavy emphasis on building recall of a brand name and creating a favourable attitude towards the brand. Car advertising has long used very competitive messages, drawing distinctions based on such factors as quality, performance and image.

competitive advertising
Form of advertising designed to influence demand for a specific brand.

comparative advertising
Form of advertising that compares two or more specifically named or shown competing brands on one or more specific attributes.

Dominos Pizza Hut
on-line

In Australia and New Zealand, both Dominos and Pizza Hut are competing directly for the same market. Have a look at their websites and see if you can see any evidence of comparative advertising. Also comment on both websites and which you think is more attractive and appeals to you more. Discuss this with your class mates and think about why you prefer one site over the other.
www.dominos.com.au
www.pizzahut.com.au

Comparative advertising

Comparative advertising directly or indirectly compares two or more competing brands on one or more specific attributes. Some advertisers even use comparative advertising against their own brands. Products experiencing sluggish growth or those entering the marketplace against strong competitors are more likely to employ comparative claims in their advertising. Products that are high in search qualities (see Chapter 6) also benefit from this style of advertising.

When thinking of comparative advertisements, ads comparing products directly by name first spring to mind. For example, Sanitarium Health Food compared the sugar content of Weet-Bix with Kellogg's NutriGrain. Subaru 'apologised' for the road test results between models of Subaru, Porsche and BMW. But comparative advertising need not be so obvious. More subtle means can also be used, including indirect references to a competitor's colours, imagery or actors, or claims such as '50 per cent bigger' and 'the strongest'. In fact, any means can be used that conveys a comparative message.

An ad for AAPT's Smartchat phone services used plastic animals calling to mind the wildlife ads of its competitor, Optus. An ad for Country Cup noodles used 'kids on a see-saw' to compare the fat content with 'the noodles your kids are currently eating' and dressed the overweight child in the same yellow and red colours of the market leader, Maggi. Neither of these ads named their competitor; however, the ads themselves left no doubt in consumers' minds about whom they were targeting. The main principle involved in comparative advertising is that the comparisons have to be valid and not misleading. Many marketers shy away from using comparative ads for fear that competitors will take legal action against them. The most common form of attack is to challenge the validity of the comparison on the basis that it is false or misleading and deceptive in breach of sections 52 and 53 of the *Trade Practices Act 1974*.[16]

In Australia, all advertising content is regulated through the *Trade Practices Act* and the *Australian Broadcasting Authority Act*. The Australian Broadcasting Authority (ABA) has also developed the Children's Television standards, which include a section on advertising to children. Complaints by individuals about misleading or untruthful ads are handled by the Australian Competition & Consumer Commission (ACCC) and the Department of Fair Trading in each state.

Interestingly, in the United States until the 1970s, comparative advertising was allowed only if the competing brand was veiled and unidentified. In 1971, however, the Federal Trade Commission (FTC) fostered the growth of comparative advertising by saying that it provided information to the customer and that advertisers were more skilful than the government in communicating this information. Federal rulings prohibit advertisers from falsely describing competitors' products and allow competitors to sue if ads show their products or mention their brand names in an incorrect or false manner. These rules also apply to advertisers making false claims about their own products. These laws also apply in Australia and are managed by the *Trade Practices Act*.

Recently, Glaxosmithkline, the British-owned maker of Panadol, was at loggerheads with pharmaceutical company Herron over comparative advertising it claims is misleading to consumers. The consumer health-care giant had asked the Federal Court to ban Herron ads which boast that the company is Australian-owned, claiming they may mislead consumers into thinking all Herron products are made in Australia: 'The reason for our complaint is that the most recent Herron TV commercials make, for the first time, comparative advertising claims we believe are misleading for consumers. The depiction of Panadol as foreign-owned – our parent company is British – in the commercials leads consumers to believe Panadol products are all imported, which is an insult to the 400 workers responsible for producing and marketing Panadol from our plant in Sydney.' During the airing of these ads, Panadol's share of the $90 million painkiller market reportedly dropped and Herron's sales jumped by 7 per cent. Unfortunately for Panadol, the court ruled in favour of Herron and the ads continued.[17]

In some other nations, particularly newly capitalised countries in Eastern Europe, claims that seem exaggerated by our standards are commonplace, while in others the hard-sell tactics found in our comparative ads are taboo. Until the 1980s, Japanese regulations all but prohibited comparative ads; ads that failed to compare objectively were considered slanderous. Nevertheless, although the Japanese have traditionally favoured a soft-sell advertising approach, consumers are witnessing a trend towards comparative ads. Germany, Italy, Belgium and France don't permit advertisers to claim that their products are best or better than competitors' products, which are common claims in our advertising. In fact, the French are so adamant about comparative ads that a Paris court banned a Philip Morris ad campaign comparing second-hand smoke to eating biscuits for violating comparative advertising laws, even though no specific brands of biscuits were mentioned in the ad.[18]

advertising campaign
Series of related advertisements focusing on a common theme, slogan and set of advertising appeals.

Steps in creating an advertising campaign

An **advertising campaign** is a series of related advertisements focusing on a common theme, slogan and set of advertising appeals. It is a specific advertising effort for a particular product that extends for a defined period of time. Management of advertising begins with understanding the steps in developing an advertising campaign and then making the important decisions relating to each step. Exhibit 10.1 traces the steps in this process.

3 Describe the advertising campaign process

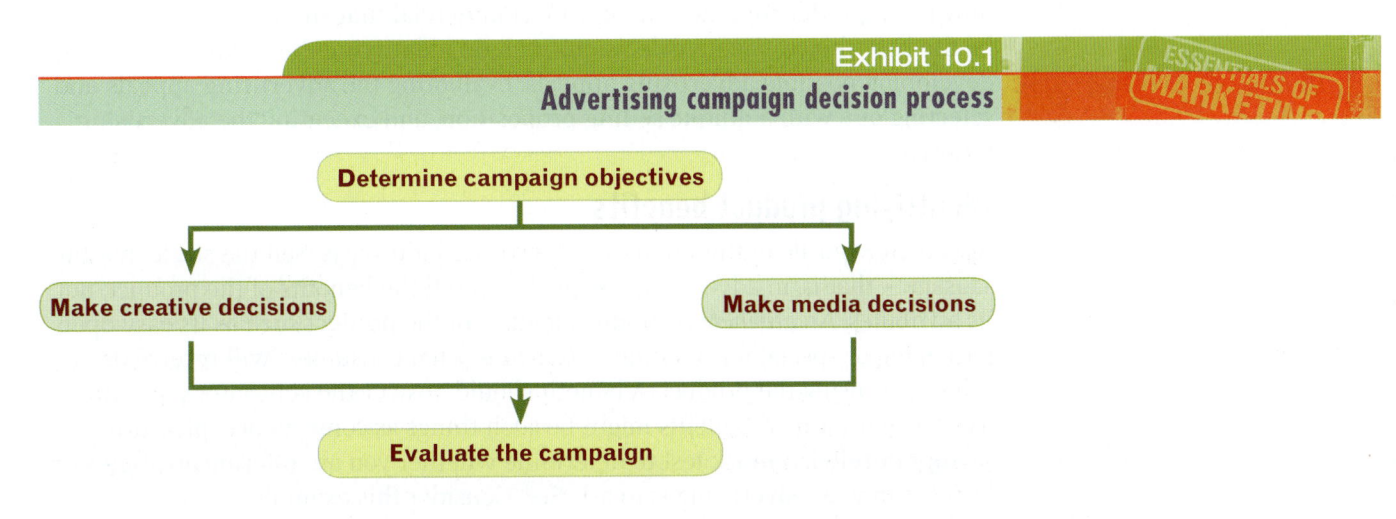

Exhibit 10.1
Advertising campaign decision process

Determine campaign objectives
↓
Make creative decisions → Make media decisions
↓
Evaluate the campaign

The advertising campaign process is set in motion by a promotion plan. The promotion planning process identifies the target audience, determines the overall promotional objectives, sets the promotion budget and selects the promotional mix. Advertising, which is usually part of the promotional mix, is used to encode a selling message to the target market. The advertisement is then conveyed to the target market, or receivers of the message, through such advertising vehicles as broadcast or print media.

Determine campaign objectives

The first step in the development of an advertising campaign is to determine the advertising objectives. An **advertising objective** identifies the specific communication task a campaign should accomplish for a specified target audience during a specified period of time. The objectives of a specific advertising campaign depend on the overall corporate objectives and the product being advertised.

advertising objective
Specific communication task a campaign should accomplish for a specified target audience during a specified period.

The DAGMAR approach (Defining Advertising Goals for Measured Advertising Results) is one method of setting objectives. According to this method, all advertising objectives should precisely define the target audience, the desired percentage change in some specified measure of effectiveness, and the time frame in which that change is to occur. For example, the objectives of an advertising campaign for Gillette's MACH3 shaving system might be to achieve 90 per cent awareness within the first six months of introduction as a result of sending free shavers to a sample of the target audience.

Make creative decisions

The next step in developing an advertising campaign is to make the necessary creative and media decisions. Note in Exhibit 10.1 that both creative and media decisions are made at the same time. Creative work cannot be completed without knowing which **medium**, or message channel, will be used to convey the message to the target market. For example, creative planning will likely differ for an ad to be displayed on an outdoor billboard versus that placed in a print medium, such as a newspaper or magazine. However, in this chapter media decisions are addressed after creative decisions.

medium
Channel used to convey a message to a target market.

In many cases, the advertising objectives dictate the medium and the creative approach to be used. For example, if the objective is to demonstrate how fast a product operates, then a TV commercial that shows this action may be the best choice. Creative decisions include identifying the product's benefits, developing possible advertising appeals, evaluating the advertising appeals and selecting one with a unique selling proposition, and executing the advertising message.

Identifying product benefits

A well-known rule of thumb in the advertising industry is 'Sell the sizzle, not the sausage' – that is, in advertising the goal is to sell the benefits of the product, not its attributes. An *attribute* is simply a feature of the product such as its easy-open packaging or special formulation. A *benefit* is what consumers will receive or achieve by using the product. A benefit should answer the consumer's question, 'What's in it for me?' Benefits might be such things as convenience, pleasure, savings or relief. A quick test to determine whether you are offering attributes or benefits in your advertising is to ask 'So?' Consider this example:

Attribute: 'The Gillette MACH3 shaving system has three blades aligned progressively nearer to the face, each coated with a microscopic layer of carbon, mounted on a forward-pivoting shaver to automatically adjust to the curves and contours of a man's face.' 'So ...?'

Benefit: 'So, you'll get a closer, smoother and safer shave than ever before with fewer strokes and less irritation.'[19]

Market research and intuition are usually used to unearth the perceived benefits of a product and to rank consumers' preferences for these benefits. Gillette's rival Schick is advertising its razors on the basis of safety. Schick's research shows that safety is among the top three attributes men look for in a razor. As a result, its advertising campaign touts the benefits of a safe shave rather than a close shave.[20]

Developing and evaluating advertising appeals

An **advertising appeal** identifies a reason for a person to buy a product. Developing advertising appeals, a challenging task, is usually the responsibility of the creative people in the advertising agency. Advertising appeals typically play on consumers' emotions, such as fear or love, or address some need or want the consumer has, such as a need for convenience or the desire to save money, or some combination of these.

advertising appeal
Reason for a person to buy a product.

Advertising campaigns can focus on one or more advertising appeals. Often the appeals are quite general, thus allowing the firm to develop a number of sub-themes or mini-campaigns using both advertising and sales promotion. Several possible advertising appeals are listed in Exhibit 10.2.

Exhibit 10.2
Common advertising appeals

Profit	Lets consumers know whether the product will save them money, make them money, or keep them from losing money
Health	Appeals to those who are body-conscious or who want to be healthy
Love or romance	Is used often in selling cosmetics and perfumes
Fear	Can centre around social embarrassment, growing old or losing one's health; because of its power, it requires advertiser to exercise care in execution
Admiration	Is the reason that celebrity spokespeople are used so often in advertising
Convenience	Is often used for fast-food outlets and microwave foods
Fun and pleasure	Are the key to advertising holidays, beer, amusement parks and more
Vanity and egotism	Are used most often for expensive or conspicuous items such as cars and clothing
Environmental consciousness	Centres on protecting the environment and being considerate of others in the community

Choosing the best appeal from those developed normally requires market research. Criteria for evaluation may include desirability, exclusiveness or believability. The appeal first must make a positive impression on and be desirable to the target market. It must also be exclusive or unique; consumers must be able to distinguish the advertiser's message from competitors' messages. Most important, the appeal should be believable. An appeal that makes extravagant claims not only wastes promotional dollars but also creates ill will for the advertiser.

unique selling proposition
Desirable, exclusive and believable advertising appeal selected as the theme for a campaign.

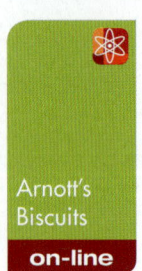

Arnott's Biscuits
on-line

How does Arnott's Biscuits use its parrot symbol to promote its biscuits on the company's website? Do you think it is still an effective advertising tool? Why or why not?
www.arnotts.com.au

The advertising appeal selected for the campaign becomes what advertisers call its **unique selling proposition**. The unique selling proposition usually becomes the campaign's slogan. Gillette's MACH3 advertising campaign aimed at men carries the slogan 'Three blades, fewer strokes, less irritation'. This is also MACH3's unique selling proposition, implying that its razor's high-tech features are important and can help to reduce discomfort caused by shaving.[21]

Effective slogans often become so ingrained that consumers can immediately conjure up images of the product just by hearing the slogan. For example, most consumers can easily name the companies and products behind these memorable slogans or even hum the jingle that goes along with some of them: '… helps you work, rest and play', 'Which bank?', 'Ring around the collar' and 'Oh What a feeling …!' Advertisers can also have great impact with the symbols used in their ads. For example, it took a little Aussie cattle dog called Kane to make small Korean cars a household name, from Dae *who*? to Daewoo. Advertisers often revive old slogans or jingles in the hope that the nostalgia will create good feelings with consumers. Sanitarium recently embarked on a campaign to revitalise the market appeal of their Weet-Bix brand. Their research showed that whatever their new message was, the ad should carry at least some of the familiar and very popular jingle, 'Aussie kids are Weet-Bix kids'.[22] Similarly, after a decade-long absence from national television, the well-known Arnott's parrot has recently appeared in television ads to highlight their plain biscuits (Scotch Finger Biscuits and Milk Arrowroot).[23]

Executing the message

Message execution is the way the advertisement conveys its information. In general, the AIDA plan is a good blueprint for executing an advertising message. Any ad should immediately draw the reader's, viewer's or listener's attention. The advertiser must then use the message to hold the consumer's interest, create desire for the good or service and, ultimately, motivate action: a purchase.

The style in which the message is executed is one of the most creative elements of an advertisement. Exhibit 10.3 lists some examples of executional styles used by advertisers. Executional styles often dictate what type of media is to be employed to convey the message. Scientific executional styles lend themselves well to print advertising where more information can be conveyed. On the other hand, demonstration and musical styles are more likely found in broadcast advertising.

Injecting humour into an advertisement is a popular and effective executional style. Humorous executional styles are more often used in radio and television advertising than in print or magazine advertising, where humour is less easily communicated. Humorous ads are typically used for lower-risk, routine purchases such as lollies and soft drinks than for higher-risk purchases or those that are expensive, durable or flamboyant.[24] Mars, for example, recently used humour in its television advertising using animated M&M characters. The ads led to a 3 per cent increase in sales and better 'likeability' for the M&Ms brand.[25]

Executional styles for foreign advertising are often quite different from those we are accustomed to in Australia. Sometimes they are sexually oriented or aesthetically imaginative. For example, European advertising avoids the direct-sell approaches common in many Australian ads and instead is more indirect, more symbolic and, above all, more visual. Nike, known for 'in-your-face' advertising and irreverent slogans such as 'Just Do It', discovered that its brash

Exhibit 10.3
Ten common executional styles for advertising

Slice-of-life	Is popular when advertising household and personal products; depicts people in normal settings, such as at the dinner table.
Lifestyle	Shows how well the product will fit in with the consumer's lifestyle. Volkswagen ads showing two silent young men on an aimless Sunday drive in a VW Golf appeal to the lifestyle of Generation Xers.
Spokesperson/ testimonial	Can feature a celebrity, company official or typical consumer making a testimonial or endorsing a product: swimming star Grant Hackett eats Uncle Tobys muesli bars and Ian Thorpe watches Channel 7.
Fantasy	Creates a fantasy for the viewer built around use of the product, such as Levi's spot of jean-clad strangers on an elevator, who eye each other, share the same daydream – falling in love, marriage, raising a family – and then silently go their separate ways.
Humorous	Advertisers often use humour in their ads, such as the 'Bugger' ads that have been very successful for Toyota.
Real/animated product symbols	Create a character that represents the product in advertisements, such as the Energizer bunny, the Daewoo dog or the Bundy Rum bears.
Mood or image	Builds a mood or image around the product, such as peace, love or beauty. DeBeers ads depicting shadowy silhouettes wearing diamond engagement rings and diamond necklaces portray passion and intimacy while extolling that a 'diamond is forever'.
Demonstration	Shows consumers the expected benefit. Many consumer products use this technique. Laundry detergent spots are famous for demonstrating how their product will clean clothes whiter and brighter.
Musical	Conveys the message of the advertisement through song. Examples are Mercedes-Benz ads depicting historical car shots while strains of Marlene Dietrich's 'Falling in Love Again' are heard in the background, and the song 'Get What You Give' by the New Age Radicals for Mitsubishi.
Scientific	Uses research or scientific evidence to give a brand superiority over competitors. Pain relievers such as Bayer and Panadol use scientific evidence in their ads.

advertising did not appeal to Europeans. A television commercial of Satan and his demons playing soccer against a team of Nike endorsers was a hit in America. However, many European stations refused to run it, saying it was too scary and offensive to show in prime time, when children were watching.[26]

Japanese advertising is known for relying on fantasy and mood to sell products. Ads in Japan notoriously lack the emphatic selling demonstrations found in much Western advertising, limit the exposure of unique product features and avoid direct comparisons to competitors' products. Japanese ads often feature cartoon characters or place the actors in irrelevant situations. For example, one advertisement promotes an insect spray while showing the actor having teeth extracted at a dentist's surgery. One explanation of Japan's preference for soft-sell advertising is cultural: Japanese consumers are naturally suspicious of someone who needs to extol the virtues of a product. Additionally, unlike advertising agencies in the United States and Australia, which consider working for competing companies to be unethical, Japan's larger ad agencies customarily maintain business relationships with competing advertisers. Ads are less hard-hitting so as not to offend other clients.[27]

Global advertising managers are increasingly concerned with the issue of standardisation versus customisation of their advertising appeals and executional styles when delivering advertising messages around the world. Read about this dilemma in the Global perspectives box.

Global PERSPECTIVES

Global challenges for advertisers

One of the hottest debates for global advertising professionals today is whether to customise or standardise advertising. On one side of the fence are those who believe the advertisement's appeals and execution style should be tailored to each country or region to be most effective. Because cultures perceive and react to advertising differently, this school of though advocates that the advertiser must know something about the intended audience's culture in order to communicate effectively.

Kodak, for instance, favours a customised approach to advertising in China because consumer tastes and values vary between mainland China and the more progressive Taiwan and Hong Kong. In Taiwan and Hong Kong, which are quickly catching up to the United States and Europe in sales volume, Kodak targets a young, innovative audience. In mainland China, which is comparatively far behind technologically except in a few urban centres, the approach will be more lifestyle-oriented.

Some would disagree with this distinction, however, and would advocate a single advertising campaign for all countries. Following this standardised approach, an advertiser would develop one advertising campaign, appeal and execution style, and deliver this same message, translated into the language of each country, to all target markets. Supporters of this approach insist that consumers everywhere have the same basic needs and desires and can therefore be persuaded by universal advertising appeals. Furthermore, they say, standardised advertising campaigns create unified brand images worldwide and the advertiser eliminates the inefficiencies of trying to reinvent the meaning of its brand in every country. Athletic shoemaker Reebok recently embarked on a US$100 million global ad campaign in an attempt to make its message more cohesive throughout the world. In the past, Reebok sent out confusing messages – it was known as a running shoe in the United Kingdom and a fashion statement in the United States. Moreover, Reebok generally was seen as a women's fitness and aerobics sneaker, not an ideal image for winning over male consumers.

Possibly the best answer to this dilemma is to use a mixture of standardisation and customisation – that is, standardising the message while paying attention to local differences in the execution of the message. For example, Unilever uses a standardised appeal when promoting its Dove soap but it uses models from Australia, France, Germany and Italy to appeal to women in those places. Although this mixture of standardisation and customisation seems to be successful for many global marketers, it only works as long as the message truly plays to a worldwide audience. For example, because parents around the world are deeply concerned about the welfare of their children, advertising for children's products generally represents an area of universal concern or agreement. Fisher-Price, therefore, is effective using a standardised approach because no matter where they live, parents want the best for their children. Similarly, IBM was successful with its 'Solutions for a Small Planet' campaign because people all over the world have similar information and computing needs. The global imagery of the campaign is achieved through the use of the same footage in each country. The difference is the use of local subtitles to translate the 'foreign' language of the commercial.

Although efficiencies can be achieved by producing a single advertising campaign and message for worldwide use, the approach only makes sense if it does not run counter to social mores, ethnic issues or religious taboos. For example, a food commercial showing hungry children licking their lips would be taboo in a country where exposing the tongue is considered obscene. Similarly, an ad portraying a young couple running barefoot, hand-in-hand down a beautiful, sandy beach would be offensive in a country in which naked feet are never to be seen by the public.[28]

Some of the marketers discussed here have been successful using a global approach to advertising, but not every product or service is suited for a unified advertising message. What types of products do you think would benefit from a standardised approach to advertising? What types would fare better using a tailored approach?

Making media decisions

As mentioned at the beginning of the chapter, Asia–Pacific advertisers spend over $75 billion annually on media advertising. Where does all this money go? In Australia the average total advertising expenditure is approximately A$20.5 billion, of which about 36.5 per cent, or $7.5 billion, is spent in media monitored by national reporting services – magazines, newspapers, outdoor, radio, television, Yellow Pages and the Internet. The remaining 63.5 per cent, or $13 billion, is spent in unmonitored media, such as direct mail, trade exhibits, cooperative advertising, brochures, coupons, catalogues and special events. Exhibit 10.4 breaks down the $20.5 billion spent in advertising by media type.

4 Describe media evaluation and selection techniques

Exhibit 10.4 Advertising by media type

Medium	Per cent of spend	Total spend
Main media	36.5	$ 7 472 304 000
Direct marketing	35.1	$ 7 199 935 916
Promotional marketing	25.1	$ 5 136 040 882
Sponsorship of sport	3.3	$ 681 537 439

Source: Australian Federation of Advertising: www.afa.org.au.

Media type

Advertising media are channels that advertisers use in mass communication. The six main advertising media are newspapers, magazines, radio, television, outdoor media, and the Internet and World Wide Web. Exhibit 10.5 summarises the advantages and disadvantages of these main channels. In recent years, however, alternative media vehicles have emerged that give advertisers innovative ways to reach their target audience and avoid advertising clutter.

Newspapers

The advantages of newspaper advertising include geographic selectivity and timeliness. Because copywriters can usually prepare newspaper ads quickly and at a reasonable cost, local merchants can reach their target market almost daily. However, because newspapers are generally a mass-market medium, they may not be the best vehicles for marketers trying to reach a very narrow market. For example, local newspapers are not the best media vehicles for reaching purchasers of speciality steel products or even tropical fish. These target consumers comprise very small, specialised markets. Newspaper advertising also encounters a lot of distractions from competing ads and news stories; thus, one company's ad may not be particularly visible.

The largest source of newspaper ad revenue is local retailers, classified ads and cooperative advertising. In **cooperative advertising**, the manufacturer and the retailer split the costs of advertising the manufacturer's brand. One reason manufacturers use cooperative advertising is the impracticality of listing all their dealers in national advertising. Also, co-op advertising encourages retailers to devote more effort to the manufacturer's lines.

cooperative advertising
Arrangement in which the manufacturer and the retailer split the costs of advertising the manufacturer's brand.

Exhibit 10.5
Advantages and disadvantages of main advertising media

Medium	Advantages	Disadvantages
Newspapers	Geographic selectivity and flexibility; short-term advertiser commitments; news value and immediacy; year-round readership; high individual market coverage; co-op and local tie-in availability; short lead time	Little demographic selectivity; limited colour capabilities; low pass-along rate; may be expensive
Magazines	Good reproduction, especially for colour; demographic selectivity; regional selectivity; local market selectivity; relatively long advertising life; high pass-along rate	Long-term advertiser commitments; slow audience build-up, limited demonstration capabilities; lack of urgency; long lead time
Radio	Low cost; immediacy of message; can be scheduled on short notice; relatively little seasonal change in audience; highly portable; short-term advertiser commitments; entertainment carry-over	No visual treatment; short advertising life of message; high frequency required to generate comprehension and retention; distractions from background sound; commercial clutter
Television	Ability to reach a wide, diverse audience; low cost per thousand; creative opportunities for demonstration; immediacy of messages; entertainment carry-over; demographic selectivity with pay-TV stations	Short life of message; some consumer scepticism about claims; high campaign cost; little demographic selectivity with network stations; long-term advertiser commitments; long lead times required for production; commercial clutter
Outdoor media	Repetition; moderate cost; flexibility; geographic selectivity	Short message; lack of demographic selectivity; high 'noise' level distracting audience
Internet and World Wide Web	Fastest-growing medium; ability to reach a narrow target audience; relatively short lead time required for creating Web-based advertising; moderate cost	Difficult to measure ad effectiveness and return on investment; ad exposure relies on 'click-through' from banner ads; not all consumers have access to the Internet

Magazines

Compared to the cost of other media, the cost per contact in magazine advertising is usually high. However, the cost per potential customer may be much lower, because magazines are often targeted to specialised audiences and thus reach more potential customers. The most frequent types of products advertised in magazines include cars, apparel, computers and alcohol.

One of the main advantages of magazine advertising is its market selectivity. Magazines are published for virtually every market segment. For example, *PC Week* is a leading computer magazine; *Working Mother* targets one of the fastest-growing consumer segments; *Sports Illustrated* is a successful all-around sporting publication; *Marketing News* is a trade magazine for the marketing professional; and *The Source* is a niche publication geared to young urbanites with a passion for hip-hop music.

Radio

Radio has several strengths as an advertising medium: selectivity and audience segmentation, a large out-of-home audience, low unit and production costs, timeliness and geographic flexibility. Local advertisers are the most frequent users of radio advertising, contributing over three-quarters of all radio ad revenues. Like newspapers, radio also lends itself well to cooperative advertising.

Radio advertising is enjoying a resurgence in popularity. As consumers become more mobile and pressed for time, other media such as network television and newspapers struggle to retain viewers and readers. Radio listening, however, has grown in step with population increases mainly because its immediate, portable nature meshes so well with a fast-paced lifestyle. The ability to target specific demographic groups is also a major selling point for radio stations, attracting advertisers who are pursuing narrowly defined audiences that are more likely to respond to certain kinds of ads and products. Moreover, radio listeners tend to listen habitually and at predictable times, with the most popular radio listening hours during 'drive time', when commuters form a vast captive audience.[29]

Television

Because television is an audiovisual medium, it provides advertisers with many creative opportunities. Television broadcasters include network television, independent stations, pay television and a relative newcomer, direct broadcast satellite television. The ABC, The Nine Network, The Seven Network, Network Ten and SBS comprise network television in Australia, which reaches a wide and diverse market. Conversely, pay TV and direct broadcast satellite systems, such as Foxtel and Austar, offer consumers a multitude of channels devoted exclusively to particular audiences – for example, women, children, nature lovers, senior citizens, Christians, sports fans, fitness enthusiasts and movie enthusiasts. Because of its targeted channels, pay TV is often characterised as 'narrowcasting' by media buyers.

Advertising time on television can be very expensive, especially for network stations and popular pay-TV stations. A 30-second spot during a Network Ten regular prime-time mid-week show goes for between $17 000 and $25 000, whereas the same spot sold for $49 000 during the final episode of the Australian version of *Big Brother*.[30] Rates can be even more expensive during prime-time or live-broadcast television events such as grand finals and other sporting events.

A relatively new form of television advertising is the **infomercial**, a 30-minute or longer advertisement. Infomercials are an attractive advertising vehicle for many marketers because of the cheap air time and the relatively small production cost. Advertisers say the infomercial is an ideal way to present complicated information to potential customers, which other advertising vehicles typically don't allow time to do. In the United States, the Arthritis Foundation recently traded in its annual telethon for an infomercial for their fund-raising. The infomercial sold subscriptions for *Arthritis Today*, membership to the foundation, and various resources, including a guide called '101 Tips for Better Living' and a videotape on exercises for arthritis sufferers.[31]

Outdoor media

Outdoor or out-of-home advertising is a flexible, low-cost medium that may take a variety of forms. Examples include billboards, skywriting, giant inflatables, mini-billboards in shopping centres and on bus stop shelters, signs in sports arenas, lighted moving signs in bus terminals and airports, and ads painted on the sides of cars, trucks, buses or even water towers. Another aspect of outdoor advertising, which took off in Australia during the 2000 Olympics, was building wraps, where entire buildings are 'wrapped' in the ad to create maximum impact and exposure. Outdoor advertising reaches a broad and diverse market. Therefore, it is normally limited to promoting convenience products, cars and some services such as banking, hospitals, accommodation and travel – though this is by no means a restricted list of products. In fact, in Australia we are seeing many innovative uses of outdoor advertising for things such as women's lingerie (the Triumph and Wonderbra ads), government messages (the GST and medical health cover), medical insurers (MBF and Medibank Private), funeral directors, and many other types of products and services.

Channel 7 ABC on-line

What kind of advertising is done on the i7 website? Compare this to the ABC site. What differences do you notice? Why do you think a television network would choose not to sell ad space on its website?
www.i7.com.au
www.abc.net.au

infomercial
Thirty-minute or longer advertisement that looks more like a TV talk show than a sales pitch.

One of the newest media on offer in the outdoor field is digital outdoor, which is somewhat of a cross between outdoor and TV. This system is generally used in high-transit areas such as train and bus stations where sensors cut off ads as the train or bus approaches.[32] The 2000 Olympics saw a boom in outdoor advertising in Australia, with revenues up by 40 per cent in 2001. However, outdoor advertising still only accounts for between 3 per cent and 7 per cent of total ad spending in Australia compared to about 15 per cent in Europe.[33]

The main advantage of outdoor advertising over other media is that its exposure frequency is very high, yet the amount of clutter from competing ads is very low. Outdoor advertising also has the ability to be customised to local marketing needs. Outdoor advertising has been growing in recent years mainly due to the fragmentation of other media, more exposure as people spend more time commuting, and improved billboard quality through the use of computers.[34] Outdoor advertising is also becoming more innovative. For example, when Nike wrapped three sides of the Maritime Trade Towers at the southern approach to Sydney's Harbour Bridge during the 2000 Olympics, it certainly made an impact and changed many people's view of wrapping as a medium as it had previously only been used to beautify construction sites.

The Internet and the World Wide Web

The World Wide Web and the Internet have undoubtedly shaken up the advertising world. With worldwide ad revenue anticipated to be US$28 billion by 2005, up from US$4.3 billion in 1999, the Internet has established itself as a solid advertising medium.[35] By 2005 it is expected that at least 8 per cent of the total US spend on advertising will be on-line and this same trend appears to be being followed by Australia and New Zealand. Traditional marketers in the United States nearly tripled their Internet advertising spending to an average of around US$750 000 from 1997 to 1998. Additionally, whereas only 38 per cent of companies were advertising on the Internet in 1997, 68 per cent were doing so in 1998. Although on-line advertising has made significant gains since the early 1990s, it still makes up only a small portion of companies' total advertising budgets.

In spite of these impressive figures and the fact that Australia has one of the highest penetration rates for the Internet in the world, Australian companies have been slow to join the race to use on-line advertising. Australian on-line advertising amounts to just US$5 per capita (equal to Latin America), compared to the United States, which has about US$100 per capita to spend.[36] The two top barriers to Internet advertising, according to a survey conducted by the Association of National Advertisers, are the difficulty of tracking return on investment and the lack of reliable and accurate measurement information.[37]

Popular Internet sites and search engines such as Netscape and Yahoo!, as well as on-line service providers such as America Online, generally sell advertising space, called 'banners', to major consumer product and service companies to promote their goods and services. Internet surfers click on these banners, which link them to the advertiser's site. New forms of Web advertising are starting to transcend the static company logo and message in a banner ad. Using technologies such as Shockwave and Java, advertisers are developing Web ads that incorporate interactivity, electronic commerce, sound and animation. For example, a banner ad from John Hancock Mutual Life Insurance Company lets users input their children's ages to find out how much money they need to invest each month for a university education.[38]

A recent survey on the effectiveness of on-line banner ads concluded that they actually work as well at boosting brand and advertising awareness as their TV or magazine counterparts. On-line ads also boost the likelihood that a consumer will want to buy a product, just as traditional ads do. Best of all, on-line ads are even more memorable than commercials on TV, the survey data show. More people could recall seeing banner ads than having seen a TV ad after one exposure.[39]

However, on-line media pose a daunting challenge for advertisers because consumers have more control over the marketing relationship than they have had with traditional advertising media. With traditional media, consumers passively view commercials during their favourite sitcom or avoid commercials by pushing a button on a remote-control device. Surfers on the Internet, however, generally have to find the marketer rather than the other way around. In spite of this experts predict that by the end of 2005, most consumers will be exposed to 950 on-line marketing messages a day and that the problem of clutter will be a major challenge for on-line marketing activity.[40]

Some have likened the Internet to an electronic trade show and a virtual flea market – a trade show in that it can be thought of as a giant international exhibition hall where potential buyers can enter at will and visit prospective sellers; a flea market in the sense that it possesses the fundamental characteristics of openness, informality and interactivity similar to a community marketplace.[41] Ebay.com.au is an example of this. One website actually pays consumers to view ads that have been automatically targeted to fit their interests. Users must peruse each Web ad to its last page, then click on a special symbol to receive credit. Ad viewers can choose to have their earnings transferred to an on-line bank account, credited as frequent flyer points, or applied to a product purchase or a charitable donation. They can even use their earnings to credit their Visa card account.[42]

Another challenge for on-line and Internet advertisers is measuring the effectiveness of their electronic advertisement or site. Although there are methods already in use that can count the number of visitors to an advertiser's website, advertisers don't know how their site ranks compared to the competition. Also lacking are the kinds of in-depth demographic and psychographic information about Web page users that television, magazines, radio and newspapers provide about their viewers and subscribers.[43] The lack of consistency between various measures is also a problem experienced by on-line marketers. The Internet and the World Wide Web provide countless opportunities for entrepreneurs and small business start-ups and provide an inexpensive way for marketers to reach a global market.

Alternative media

To cut through the clutter of traditional advertising media, advertisers are now looking for new ways to promote their products. Alternative vehicles include fax machines, video-shopping carts in grocery stores, computer screen savers, CD-ROMs, interactive kiosks in department stores, and advertisements run before movies at the cinema and on rented videocassettes. In fact, just about anything can become a vehicle for displaying advertising. Walt Disney promoted its movies *Mulan* and *Armageddon* by placing ads on the dividers shoppers use to separate their groceries from another person's at the checkout aisle.[44]

Media selection considerations

Promotional objectives and the type of advertising a company plans to use strongly affect the selection of media. An important element in any advertising campaign is the **media mix**, the combination of media to be used. Media mix decisions are typically based on cost per contact, reach, frequency and target audience considerations. The Entrepreneurial insights box highlights a creative and innovative use of media and appeal that has been hugely successful for the Land Transport Safety Authority of New Zealand. Their campaigns have won them awards both at home and overseas for their creativity and innovative use of media.

Cost per contact is the cost of reaching one member of the target market. Naturally, as the size of the audience increases, so does the total cost. Cost per contact enables an advertiser to compare media vehicles such as television versus radio, or magazines versus newspapers, or more specifically the *Australian* versus the *Australian Financial Review*. An advertiser debating whether to spend local advertising dollars for TV spots or radio spots could consider the cost per contact of each. The advertiser might then pick the vehicle with the lowest cost per contact to maximise advertising punch for the money spent.

media mix
Combination of media to be used for a promotional campaign.

cost per contact
Cost of reaching one member of the target market.

Entrepreneurial Insights

If you drink and don't drive you're a legend!

Every year hundreds of people die and families and friends experience enormous pain and suffering, all because people put the lives of others at risk by driving dangerously and without consideration. In New Zealand the Land Transport Safety Authority in conjunction with Clemenger have been constantly using creative advertising to find new ways to influence a safety culture on their roads. For their efforts they have now won a number of awards both at home 2003 Axis Awards and abroad (2003 CAAANZ media awards winner). Independent assessment of the effectiveness of these campaigns shows that since 1995 as many as 300 lives have been saved on New Zealand roads.

One of the more recent campaigns also incorporates a creative use of alternative media as well as traditional television, billboard and static toilet door sign media. In an attempt to particularly target 17–21-year-old men with the message that it is not safe to drink and drive, Clemenger, in conjunction with Vodafone, arranged to have Vodafone cell display change to read RUOK2DRIV? Whenever the phone entered a bar in the Wellington or Auckland CBDs. This timely and relevant medium was an effective way to get the attention of this difficult target group at exactly the time when they were likely to be considering driving. This approach combined with graphic TVCs showing the link between drink driving and road crashes, and static posters with prophetic statements on billboards near night clubs and in toilets has been very effective.[45]

reach
Number of target consumers exposed to a commercial at least once during a specific period, usually four weeks.

Reach is the number of different target consumers who are exposed to a commercial at least once during a specific period, usually four weeks. The media plans for product introductions and attempts at increasing brand awareness usually emphasise reach. For example, an advertiser might try to reach 70 per cent of the target audience during the first three months of the campaign. Because the typical ad is short-lived, and because often only a small portion of an ad may be perceived at one time, advertisers repeat their ads so that consumers will remember the message. Exhibit 10.6 provides a glimpse of the average reach by television of people in Sydney in 2000. The graph shows that the average weekly reach for Monday to Friday between 6 p.m. and 10.30 p.m. is 89 per cent of the Sydney population.

Frequency is the number of times an individual is exposed to a message. Average frequency is used by advertisers to measure the intensity of a specific medium's coverage.

frequency
Number of times an individual is exposed to a given message during a specific period.

Exhibit 10.6
TV audience reach of people in Sydney, 2000

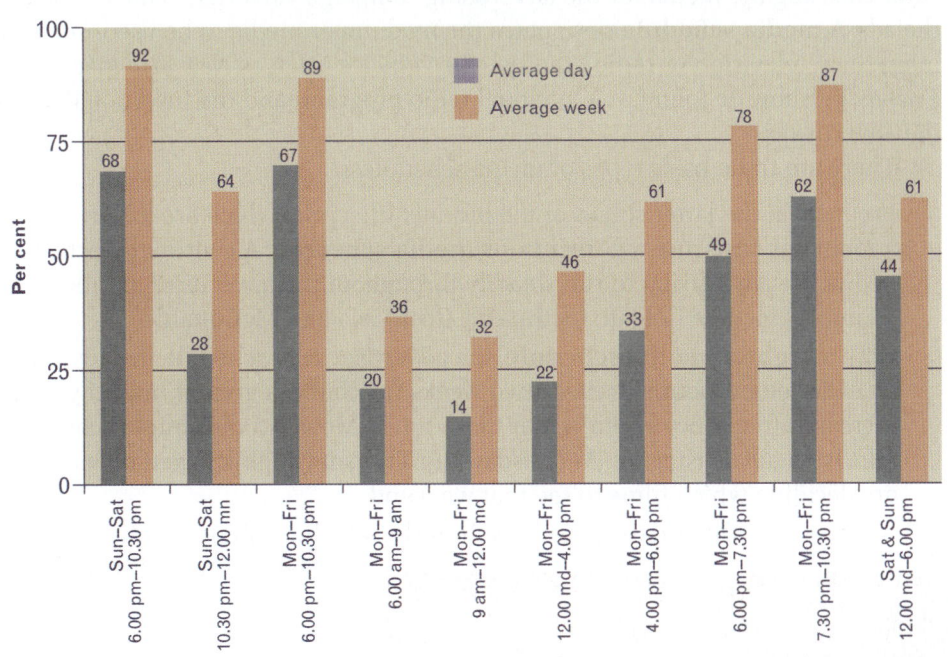

Time slot	Average day	Average week
Sun–Sat 6.00 pm–10.30 pm	68	92
Sun–Sat 10.30 pm–12.00 mn	28	64
Mon–Fri 6.00 pm–10.30 pm	67	89
Mon–Fri 6.00 am–9 am	20	36
Mon–Fri 9 am–12.00 md	14	32
Mon–Fri 12.00 md–4.00 pm	22	46
Mon–Fri 4.00 pm–6.00 pm	33	61
Mon–Fri 6.00 pm–7.30 pm	49	78
Mon–Fri 7.30 pm–10.30 pm	62	87
Sat & Sun 12.00 md–6.00 pm	44	61

Source: A.C. Nielsen.

Exhibit 10.7
Selected cable television network viewer profiles

Nickelodeon	Targeted at children 5–12 years of age, with cartoons and targeted shows 24 hours a day. Twenty per cent reach among this age group in Australia.
Arena	Aimed at 25–54-year-old professionals, offering a range of entertainment from movies to fashion and music. Aimed at time-poor, media-savvy market.
Lifestyle Channel	Aimed at active lifestylers looking for inspiration and ideas to enrich their lives.
FX	Targeted solely at women, offering a range of movies, drama and talk shows.
Fox8	Aimed at 13–30-year-olds, offering sitcoms and sport.

Source: www.austar.com.au.

audience selectivity
Ability of an advertising medium to reach a precisely defined market.

media schedule
Designation of the media, the specific publications or programs, and the insertion dates of advertising.

continuous media schedule
Media scheduling strategy, used for products in the latter stages of the product life cycle, in which advertising is run steadily throughout the advertising period.

flighted media schedule
Media scheduling strategy in which ads are run heavily every other month or every two weeks, to achieve a greater impact with an increased frequency and reach at those times.

pulsing media schedule
Media scheduling strategy that uses continuous scheduling throughout the year coupled with a flighted schedule during the best sales periods.

Media selection is also a matter of matching the advertising medium with the product's target market. If marketers are trying to reach teenage females, they might select *Girlfriend* magazine. If they are trying to reach consumers interested in health issues, they may choose *Good Medicine* magazine. A medium's ability to reach a precisely defined market is its **audience selectivity**. Some media vehicles, such as general newspapers and network television, appeal to a wide cross-section of the population. Others – such as *Popular Mechanics*, *Hot Property*, MTV and Christian radio stations – appeal to very specific groups. Viewer profiles for a sampling of popular cable networks are presented in Exhibit 10.7.

Media scheduling

After choosing the media for the advertising campaign, advertisers must schedule the ads. A **media schedule** designates the medium or media to be used (such as magazines, television or radio), the specific vehicles (such as *New Idea* magazine, *Friends* TV show or John Laws' national radio program) and the insertion dates of the advertising.

There are three basic types of media schedules:

- Products in the latter stages of the product life cycle, which are advertised on a reminder basis, use a **continuous media schedule**. A continuous schedule allows the advertising to run steadily throughout the advertising period. Examples include Colgate toothpaste, Coca-Cola and McDonald's.
- With a **flighted media schedule**, the advertiser may schedule the ads heavily every other month or every two weeks to achieve a greater impact with an increased frequency and reach at those times. Movie studios might schedule television advertising on Wednesday and Thursday nights, when moviegoers are deciding which films to see that weekend.
- A variation is the **pulsing media schedule**, which combines continuous scheduling with flighting. Continuous advertising is simply heavier during the best sale periods. A retail department store may advertise on a year-round basis but place more advertising during holiday sale periods such as Easter, Christmas and back-to-school.

This ad for Valentine's Day chocolates is an example of a seasonal advertising strategy. Besides Valentine's Day, what other times of year do you think Ferrero Rocher would benefit from concentrated advertising? How could these be a part of an IMC?

- Certain times of the year call for a **seasonal media schedule**. Products such as Codral cold tablets and Banana Boat suntan lotion, which are used more during certain times of the year, tend to follow a seasonal strategy. Advertising for champagne is concentrated during the weeks of Christmas and New Year, whereas health clubs concentrate their advertising in January to take advantage of New Year resolutions.

seasonal media schedule
Media scheduling strategy that runs advertising only during times of the year when the product is most likely to be used.

Evaluating the ad campaign

Evaluating an advertising campaign can be the most demanding task facing advertisers. How do advertisers know whether the campaign led to an increase in sales or market share or elevated awareness of the product? Most advertising campaigns aim to create an image for the good or service instead of asking for action, so their real effect is unknown. So many variables shape the effectiveness of an ad that, in many cases, advertisers must guess whether their money has been well spent. Despite this grey area, marketers spend a considerable amount of time studying advertising effectiveness and its probable impact on sales, market share or awareness.

Testing ad effectiveness can be done either before or after the campaign. Before a campaign is released, marketing managers use pre-tests to determine the best advertising appeal, layout and media vehicle. After advertisers implement a campaign, they often conduct tests to measure its effectiveness. Several monitoring techniques can be used to determine whether the campaign has met its original goals. Even if a campaign has been highly successful, advertisers still typically do a post-campaign analysis. They assess how the campaign might have been more efficient and what factors contributed to its success.

Sales promotion

In addition to using advertising, public relations and personal selling, marketing managers can use sales promotion to increase the effectiveness of their promotional efforts. *Sales promotion* is marketing communication activities, other than advertising, personal selling and public relations, in which a short-term incentive motivates consumers or members of the distribution channel to purchase a good or service immediately, either by lowering the price or by adding value.

Advertising offers the consumer a *reason* to buy; sales promotion offers an *incentive* to buy. Both are important, but sales promotion is usually cheaper than advertising and easier to measure. A major national TV advertising campaign may cost over $2 million to create, produce and place. In contrast, a newspaper coupon campaign or promotional contest may cost only about half as much. It is hard to figure exactly how many people buy a product as a result of seeing a TV ad. However, with sales promotion, marketers know the precise number of coupons redeemed or the number of contest entries.

Sales promotion is usually targeted towards either of two distinctly different markets. **Consumer sales promotion** is targeted at the ultimate consumer market. **Trade sales promotion** is directed at members of the marketing channel, such as wholesalers and retailers. Sales promotion has become an important element in a marketer's integrated marketing communications program (see Chapter 9). Sales promotion expenditures have been steadily increasing over the last several years as a result of increased competition,

consumer sales promotion
Sales promotion activities to the ultimate consumer.

trade sales promotion
Sales promotion activities targeted at a channel member, such as a wholesaler or retailer.

the ever-expanding array of available media choices, consumers and retailers demanding more deals from manufacturers, and the continued reliance on accountable and measurable marketing strategies. In addition, product and service marketers who have traditionally ignored sales promotion activities, such as electric companies and restaurants, have discovered the marketing power of sales promotion. In fact, AMR Interactive estimates that Australian marketers spent approximately $6 billion a year on sales promotions in 2000 and this figure has increased steadily to approximately to about 7 billion in 2005.[46]

5 Define and state the objectives of sales promotion

The objectives of sales promotion

Sales promotion usually works best in affecting consumer behaviour rather than attitudes. Immediate purchase is the goal of sales promotion, regardless of the form it takes. Therefore, it seems to make more sense when planning a sales promotion campaign to target customers according to their general behaviour. For example, is the consumer loyal to your product or to your competitor's? Does the consumer switch brands readily in favour of the best deal? Does the consumer buy only the least expensive product, no matter what? Does the consumer buy any products in your category at all?

The objectives of a sales promotion depend on the general behaviour of target consumers (see Exhibit 10.8). For example, marketers who are targeting loyal users of their product actually don't want to change behaviour. Instead, they need to reinforce existing behaviour or increase product usage. An effective tool for strengthening brand loyalty is the frequent buyer program that rewards consumers for repeat purchases. Other types of promotions are more effective with customers who are prone to brand switching or who are loyal to a competitor's product. The cents-off coupon, free sample or eye-catching display in a store will often entice shoppers to try a different brand. Consumers who don't use the product may be enticed to try it through the distribution of free samples.

Exhibit 10.8
Types of consumers and sales promotion goals

Type of buyer	Desired results	Sales promotion examples
Loyal customers People who buy your product most or all of the time	Reinforce behaviour, increase consumption, change purchase timing	● Loyalty marketing programs, such as frequent buyer cards or frequent shopper clubs ● Bonus packs that give loyal consumers an incentive to stock up or premiums offered in return for proofs of purchase
Competitor's customers People who buy a competitor's product most or all of the time	Break loyalty, persuade to switch to your brand	● Sampling to introduce your product's superior qualities compared to its brand ● Sweepstakes, contests or premiums that create interest in the product
Brand switchers People who buy a variety of products in the category	Persuade to buy your brand more often	● Any promotion that lowers the price of the product, such as coupons, price-off packages and bonus packs ● Trade deals that help to make the product more readily available than competing products
Price buyers People who consistently buy least expensive brand	Appeal with low prices or supply added value that makes price less important	● Coupons, price-off packages, refunds or trade deals that reduce the price of the brand to match that of the brand that would have been purchased

Source: From Don E. Schultz, William A. Robinson and Lisa A. Petrison, *Sales Promotion Essentials*, 2nd edn. Reprinted by permission of NTC Publishing Group, United States.

Once marketers understand the dynamics occurring within their product category and have determined the particular consumers and consumer behaviours they want to influence, they can then go about selecting promotional tools to achieve these goals.

Tools for consumer sales promotion

Marketing managers must decide which consumer sales promotion devices to use in a specific campaign. The methods chosen must suit the objectives to ensure success of the overall promotion plan. Popular tools for consumer sales promotion are coupons and rebates, premiums, loyalty marketing programs, contests and sweepstakes, sampling and point-of-purchase promotion.

Coupons and rebates

A **coupon** is a certificate that entitles consumers to an immediate price reduction when they buy the product. Coupons are a particularly good way to encourage product trial and repurchase. They are also likely to increase the amount of a product bought.

Coupon distribution has been steadily declining in recent years as packaged-goods marketers attempt to wean consumers off coupon clipping. Although approximately 268 billion coupons are distributed through free-standing newspaper inserts a year in the United States, only about 2 per cent, or about five billion, are actually redeemed by consumers.[47] Part of the problem is that coupons are often wasted on consumers who have no interest in the product – for example, dog food coupons that reach people who don't have a dog. Another problem is that most coupons expire before the consumer has the opportunity to use them. Additionally, coupons are more likely to encourage repeat purchases by regular users of a product than to encourage non-users to try the brand.[48]

Because of their high cost and disappointing redemption rates, many marketers are re-evaluating their use of coupons. Procter & Gamble, for example, has halved its coupon distribution and shifted to a lower-price strategy. Similarly, Kraft has opted to distribute a single, all-purpose coupon good on any of its cereal brands. Other marketers are also experimenting with on-line coupons over the Internet. Marketers such as Greater Union (www.greaterunion.com.au), which requires registration of members before then offering coupon discounts on tickets, and Sanity (www.sanity.com) have both experienced increased redemption rates.

In addition, marketers are provided with detailed anonymous information about how, where and when consumers downloaded and used the coupons. Internet coupon campaigns can complement established promotional programs, reach more consumers, and help marketers to gain valuable knowledge about their customers. This is the case with the current Sanity promotion in conjunction with Kellogg: customers log in their PIN found on the back of selected cereal packets, which then allows them to print a $5 discount voucher for Sanity products. This cross-promotion between the two companies will be supported by a national TV and radio campaign, and in-store pointers, and comes hot on the heels of a similar initiative by biscuit manufacturer Arnott's in 2001, which reportedly contributed to a 15 per cent sales boost.[49]

Another bright spot for couponing is the trend towards in-store couponing, where coupons are most likely to affect customer buying decisions. Instant coupons on product packages, coupons distributed from on-shelf coupon-

6 Discuss the most common forms of consumer sales promotion

coupon
Certificate that entitles consumers to an immediate price reduction when they buy the product.

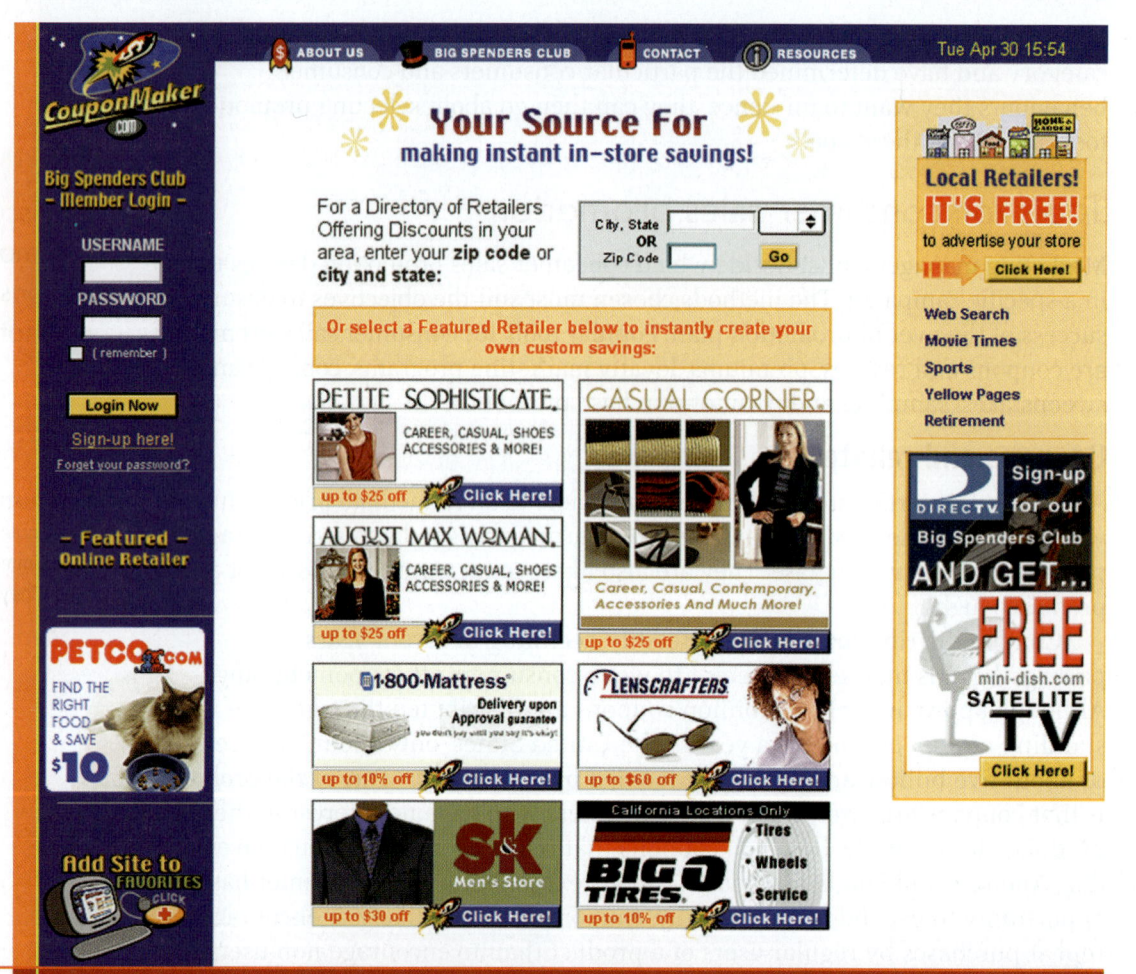

Faced with declining redemption of coupons, marketers are experimenting with new kinds of discounts. Many retailers offer websites that allow customers to print their own coupons. This process also gives these companies valuable information about coupon users.

rebate
Cash refund given for the purchase of a product during a specific period.

dispensing machines, and electronic coupons issued at the checkout counter are achieving much higher redemption rates. Redemption of instant coupons, for example, is about 17 times that of traditional newspaper coupons, suggesting that consumers are making more in-store purchase decisions.[50]

Rebates are similar to coupons in that they offer the purchaser a price reduction; however, because the purchaser must mail in a rebate form and usually some proof of purchase, the reward is not as immediate. Traditionally used by food and cigarette manufacturers, rebates now appear on all types of products, from computers and software to film and baby seats. Consumers who purchased MYOB (a small business accounting package) were recently offered a rebate on the latest upgrade software. Similarly, US Robotics offered a US$50 cash-back, mail-in rebate for several modem models.

Manufacturers prefer rebates over coupons for several reasons. Rebates allow manufacturers to offer price cuts directly to consumers. Manufacturers have more control over rebate promotions because they can be rolled out and shut off quickly. Further, because buyers must fill out forms with their names, addresses and other data, manufacturers use rebate programs to build customer databases. Perhaps the best reason of all to offer rebates is that although rebates are particularly good at enticing purchase, most consumers never bother to redeem them. Redemption rates for rebates run between 5 and 10 per cent.[51]

Premiums

A **premium** is an extra item offered to the consumer, usually in exchange for some proof that the promoted product has been purchased. Premiums reinforce the consumer's purchase decision, increase consumption and persuade non-users to switch brands. Ideally they should involve the brand itself to reinforce the link between the brand and the incentive. Premiums such as telephones, tote bags and umbrellas are available when consumers buy cosmetics, magazines, bank services, rental cars, and so on. Premiums can also include more products for the regular price, such as two-for-the-price-of-one bonus packs or packages that include more of the product. Kellogg was hugely successful in its promotion of Pop Tarts, which added two more pastries to the current six in a package without increasing the price. Kellogg used the promotion to boost market share it had lost to private-label brands of pastries and new competitors.[52]

Probably the best example of the use of premiums is the McDonald's Happy Meal, where children are rewarded with a small toy with their meal. The fast-food marketer's lucrative pact with Ty Inc., marketer of Beanie Babies in the United States, has made the annual Happy Meal and Teenie Beanie Babies combo a hot commodity. Demand was so high during the 1998 Teenie Beanie Babies promotion that many McDonald's outlets ran out of food items and the premiums lasted only days or, at best, two weeks in most stores.[53] McDonald's also routinely promotes Disney movies through Happy Meal premiums tied to films such as *101 Dalmations*, *Flubber*, *Mulan* and *Monsters Inc.*

premium
Extra item offered to the consumer, usually in exchange for some proof of purchase of the promoted product.

Loyalty marketing programs

Loyalty marketing programs, or **frequent buyer programs**, reward loyal consumers for making repeat purchases. Popularised by the airline industry in the mid-1980s through frequent flyer programs, loyalty marketing enables companies to strategically invest sales promotion dollars in activities designed to capture greater profits from customers already loyal to the product or company.[54] One study concluded that if a company retains an additional 5 per cent of its customers each year, profits would increase by at least 25 per cent. What's more, improving customer retention by a mere 2 per cent can decrease costs by as much as 10 per cent.[55]

The objective of loyalty marketing programs is to build long-term, mutually beneficial relationships between a company and its key customers. The Fly Buys program at Coles Myer stores, for example, rewards spending with discounts, rebates for tickets to theme parks and for airline travel, and much more (see www.flybuys.com.au).

On-line versions of loyalty programs are also popping up. Computer users will soon be able to earn frequent flyer points by surfing the Internet. Users will be awarded points for using the Web search engine Yahoo! to visit certain websites or to buy from several retailers over the Internet. Consumers can then transfer their points into an airline frequent flyer account or a hotel frequent-stay account.[56]

loyalty marketing program
Promotional program designed to build long-term, mutually beneficial relationships between a company and its key customers.

frequent buyer program
Loyalty program in which loyal consumers are rewarded for making multiple purchases of a particular good or service.

Contests and sweepstakes

Contests and sweepstakes are generally designed to create interest in the good or service, often to encourage brand switching. Contests are promotions in which participants use some skill or ability to compete for prizes. A consumer contest usually requires entrants to answer questions, complete sentences or write a paragraph about the product and submit proof of purchase. Winning a sweepstakes, on the other hand, depends on chance or luck, and participation is free. Sweepstakes usually draw about ten times more entries than contests do.

When setting up contests and sweepstakes, sales promotion managers must make certain that the award will appeal to the target market. In the United States, Guinness Import Company sponsors an annual essay contest that gives an actual Irish pub to the winner. The contest invites consumers to write a 50-word essay on 'Why Guinness Is My Perfect Pint'.[57] The key to successful sweepstakes is once again to involve the brand as part of the competition to reinforce the linkage between the two.

Sampling

Consumers generally perceive a certain amount of risk in trying new products. Many are afraid of trying something they won't like (such as a new food item) or spending too much money and getting little reward. **Sampling** allows the customer to try a product risk-free. Recent research on sampling effectiveness indicates that among those consumers who had never before purchased the product, 71 per cent indicated that the free sample would encourage them to try a product. Additionally, 67 per cent said they have switched brands because they were satisfied with a free sample.[58]

Sampling can be accomplished by directly mailing the sample to the customer, delivering the sample door to door, packaging the sample with another product, or demonstrating or sampling the product at a retail store. In a novel twist to run-of-the-mill sampling programs, premium ice-cream brand Movenpick took its products into hair salons and the home in a push to encourage a trial of the product. It was noted that when salon clients were waiting for their hair colour to process, they were a captive audience. Selected salons were supplied with 100-millilitre tubs of Movenpick Swiss Premium ice cream and a brochure outlining flavours and availability. The product was also offered to residents through a home-sampling program. People were a little surprised when offered a tub of ice cream, but they were appreciative of the product and very receptive to the concept, and the idea has turned into real sales.[59]

sampling
Promotional program that allows the consumer the opportunity to try the product or service for free.

Contests are a long-standing way to attract attention to a product. Guinness Beer's essay contest in the United States received a response far greater than the company had anticipated and was more successful than any previous promotional campaign.

Sampling at special events is a popular, effective and high-profile distribution method that permits marketers to piggyback on to fun-based consumer activities – including sporting events, fairs and festivals, and beach events. Lindt's aggressive sampling promotion of its premium, but affordable, chocolate has proven to be very successful for it. Lindt spend approximately $1 million annually in sampling and it believes the 60 per cent increase in sales is due to this strategy. The way Lindt sees it, when it puts the product in the consumer's mouth they fall in love with it.[60]

Distributing samples to specific location types where consumers regularly meet for a common objective or interest, such as health clubs, churches or doctors' surgeries, is one of the most efficient methods of sampling. If someone visits a health club regularly, chances are he or she is a good prospect for a health-food product or vitamin supplement. Likewise, patients of doctors who specialise in diabetes management are excellent candidates for trial samples of sugar-free snacks, diagnostic kits or other diabetes-related products. Additionally, the credibility of their being distributed at the health club or the doctor's surgery implies a powerful third-party endorsement.[61]

Point-of-purchase promotion

Point-of-purchase promotion includes any promotional display set up at the retailer's location to build traffic, advertise the product or induce impulse buying. Point-of-purchase promotions include shelf 'talkers' (signs attached to store shelves), shelf extenders (attachments that extend shelves so that products stand out), ads on grocery carts, end-of-aisle and floor-stand displays, television monitors at supermarket checkout counters, in-store audio messages and audiovisual displays. One big advantage of point-of-purchase promotion is that it offers manufacturers a captive audience in retail stores. Up to 70 per cent of all purchase decisions are made in the store, according to research conducted by the Point-of-Purchase Advertising Institute in the United States, with 88 per cent of food purchase decisions made in-store.[62] Therefore, point-of-purchase works better for impulse products – those products bought without prior decision by the consumer – than for planned purchases. Fifty-two per cent of soft-drink sales and 31 per cent of chip and snack sales are attributable to in-store point-of-purchase promotions.[63]

point-of-purchase display
Promotional display set up at the retailer's location to build traffic, advertise the product or induce impulse buying.

Tools for trade sales promotion

Whereas consumer promotions *pull* a product through the channel by creating demand, trade promotions *push* a product through the distribution channel by encouraging the trade to stock and sell the product (see Chapter 8). When selling to members of the distribution channel, manufacturers use many of the same sales promotion tools used in consumer promotions – such as sales contests, premiums and point-of-purchase displays. Several tools, however, are unique to manufacturers and intermediaries:

- *Trade allowances*: A **trade allowance** is a price reduction offered by manufacturers to intermediaries such as wholesalers and retailers. The price reduction or rebate is given in exchange for doing something specific, such as allocating space for a new product or buying something during special periods. For example, a local dealer could receive a special discount for running its own promotion on Nokia mobile telephones.
- *Push money*: Intermediaries receive **push money** as a bonus for pushing the manufacturer's brand through the distribution channel. Often the push money is directed towards a retailer's salespeople. Through its Retail Masters

7 List the most common forms of trade sales promotion

trade allowance
Price reduction offered by manufacturers to intermediaries, such as wholesalers and retailers.

push money
Money offered to channel intermediaries to encourage them to 'push' products – that is, to encourage other members of the channel to sell the products.

incentive program, US cigarette marketer Philip Morris rewards participating retailers with cash payouts based on sales and display of Philip Morris cigarette brands. Retailers earn extra money by restricting displays of competing cigarette brands and offering a free Philip Morris cigarette to smokers of other brands to promote brand switching.[64]

- *Training*: Sometimes a manufacturer will train an intermediary's personnel if the product is rather complex – as frequently occurs in the computer and telecommunication industries. For example, if a large department store purchases an NCR computerised cash register system, NCR may provide free training so that the salespeople can learn how to use the new system.

- *Free merchandise*: Often a manufacturer offers retailers free merchandise in lieu of quantity discounts. For example, a breakfast cereal manufacturer may throw in one case of free cereal for every 20 cases ordered by the retailer. Occasionally, free merchandise is used as payment for trade allowances normally provided through other sales promotions. Instead of giving a retailer a price reduction for buying a certain quantity of merchandise, the manufacturer may throw in extra merchandise 'free' (that is, at a cost that would equal the price reduction).

- *Store demonstrations*: Manufacturers can also arrange with retailers to perform an in-store demonstration. Food manufacturers often send representatives to grocery stores and supermarkets to let customers sample a product while shopping. Cosmetics companies also send their representatives to department stores to promote their beauty aids by performing facials and makeovers for customers.

- *Business meetings, conventions and trade shows*: Trade association meetings, conferences and conventions are an important aspect of sales promotion and a growing, multi-billion-dollar market. At these shows, manufacturers, distributors and other vendors have the chance to display their goods or describe their services to customers and potential customers. The cost per potential customer contacted at a show is estimated to be only 25–35 per cent of that of a personal sales call. Trade shows have been uniquely effective in introducing new products; they can establish products in the marketplace more quickly than can advertising, direct marketing or sales calls. Companies participate in trade shows to attract and identify new prospects, serve current customers, introduce new products, enhance corporate image, test the market response to new products, enhance corporate morale and gather competitive product information.

Trade promotions are popular among manufacturers for many reasons. Trade sales promotion tools help manufacturers to gain new distributors for their products, obtain wholesaler and retailer support for consumer sales promotions, build or reduce dealer stocks, and improve trade relations. These types of promotions are also useful in maintaining or developing good relationships with manufacturers, which is in line with the relationship marketing approach discussed in Chapter 6. Car manufacturers annually sponsor dozens of car shows for consumers. Many of the displays feature interactive computer stations where consumers enter vehicle specifications and get a printout of prices and local dealer names. In return, the local car dealers get the names of good prospects. The shows attract many consumers, providing dealers with increased store traffic as well as good leads.

Public relations

Public relations is the element in the promotional mix that evaluates public attitudes, identifies issues that may elicit public concern, and executes programs to gain public understanding and acceptance. Like advertising and sales promotion, public relations is a vital link in a progressive company's marketing communication mix. Marketing managers plan solid public relations campaigns that fit into overall marketing plans and focus on targeted audiences. These campaigns strive to maintain a positive image of the firm in the eyes of the public. Before launching public relations programs, managers evaluate public attitudes and company actions. Then they create programs to capitalise on the factors that enhance the firm's image and minimise the factors that could generate a negative image.

Many people associate public relations with publicity. *Publicity* is part of public relations and is the effort to capture media attention – for example, through articles or editorials in publications or through human-interest stories on radio or television programs. Corporations usually initiate publicity through a press release that furthers their public relations plans. A company about to introduce a new product or open a new store may send press releases to the media in the hope that the story will be published or broadcast. Savvy publicity can often create overnight product sensations. Talk show host Rosie O'Donnell made *Sesame Street*'s Tickle Me Elmo doll the most sought after toy of the 1996 Christmas shopping season in the United States. Similarly, books that were picked to be in Oprah's Book Club became instant bestsellers, flying off the shelves of bookstores the world over.

Donating products or services to worthy causes also creates favourable publicity. Many firms use this approach during major environmental crises or when there are worldwide media focusing on a particular issue. The plight of the people of East Timor saw many companies donating time, products and services to help rebuild communities; even the army donated people and resources to the task. Closely related to donation is cause-related marketing, where companies donate money or services to community causes. Examples include Pura Milk's 'Big Brother, Big Sister' campaign, Panadol's donation of 10 cents for every packet of Panadol sold to the Royal Flying Doctor Service, and Kellogg's Kids' Help Line.

Public relations departments may perform any or all of the following functions:

- *Press relations*: placing positive, newsworthy information in the news media to attract attention to a product, a service or a person associated with the firm or institution.
- *Product publicity*: publicising specific products or services.
- *Corporate communication*: creating internal and external messages to promote a positive image of the firm or institution.
- *Public affairs*: building and maintaining national or local community relations.
- *Lobbying*: influencing legislators and government officials to promote or defeat legislation and regulation.
- *Employee and investor relations*: maintaining positive relationships with employees, shareholders and others in the financial community.
- *Crisis management*: responding to unfavourable publicity or a negative event.

8 Discuss the role of public relations in the promotional mix

Major public relations tools

Several tools are commonly used by public relations professionals, including new product publicity, product placement, consumer education, event sponsorship and issue sponsorship. A relatively new tool public relations professionals are using in increasing numbers is a website on the Internet. Although many of these tools require an active role on the part of the public relations professional, such as writing press releases and engaging in proactive media relations, many of these techniques create their own publicity.

New product publicity

Publicity is instrumental in introducing new products and services. Publicity can help advertisers to explain what is different about their new product by prompting free news stories or positive talk about it. During the introductory period, an especially innovative new product often needs more exposure than conventional, paid advertising affords. Public relations professionals write press releases or develop videos in an effort to generate news about their new product. They also jockey for exposure of their product or service at major events, on popular television and news shows, or in the hands of influential people.

Savvy game marketer id Software, Inc., maker of the popular computer games *Doom* and *Quake*, distributes early versions of its games free over the Internet, creating word-of-mouth excitement among its followers of young males that helps to sell follow-up sequels. The test version for *Quake II* was downloaded more than a million times. The game marketer further enticed followers by releasing manuals, game photos and commentary from the game's programmers. As a result, websites dedicated to *Quake* play were abuzz with discussion of the new, soon-to-be-released version.[65]

Product placement

Marketers can also garner publicity by making sure their products appear at special events or in movies or television shows. This particular strategy has been seen to be successful at targeting wealthy potential luxury product markets, particularly in relation to watches, jewellery, clothing and cars.[66] In 1982, a short, ugly creature with an extendable neck (ET) and the voice of Debra Winger boosted sales of M&Ms by a stratospheric 70 per cent and helped create the product placement industry. In the film *Goldeneye*, the car that James Bond drove – a BMW Z3 – sold out of all BMW dealers' outlets worldwide before they even hit the showroom floor; and after Mike Meyers shouted 'Get your hand off my Heiny, baby!' in the film *The Spy Who Shagged Me*, sales of Heineken beer rose by 17 per cent.[67] But successful product placement is about more than celebrity endorsement. It's also about matching the product and the image of the celebrity and/or medium, and about breaking through the clutter and reinforcing the placement with follow-on advertising and point-of-sale strategies to remind customers.

Companies reap invaluable product exposure through product placement, usually at a fraction of the cost of paid-for advertising. Often, the fee for exposure is in merchandise. For example, The Gap outfitted 3500 traders, specialists and clerks of the New York Stock Exchange in khaki pants and casual shirts for the exchange's first casual workday.[68] Exposure of controversial products such as cigarettes and cigars, however, can invite unwanted criticism, as you will see in the Ethics in marketing box.

Do you really know what you are buying?

Ethics IN MARKETING

Consumers are becoming more and more conscious of the impact of their consumption on both the environment and on other individuals. In an attempt to become more ethical and responsible, people are turning more and more to organic food, free-range meat and eggs, sustainably harvested timber, animal friendly cosmetics, environmentally friendly energy and even choosing ethically accredited investments. Of course, marketers have seen this trend and have noted the potential profits in aligning their operations and products to this more conscious market segment, but are all these marketers ethical themselves in how they approach this issue?

It is well known that the Body Shop has immaculate credentials as an ethical and socially conscious organisation, supporting global causes such as AIDS research and adopting fair production practices for their products that support and develop third world communities, but not all organisations are so noble. The latest development in the US are Sustainable Slopes. This is a classification for ski resorts and is intended to indicate that the ski area has agreed to meet a code of environmental ethics. However, according to experts this claim is little more than a marketing gimmick for the 177 member resorts as there is no third party organisation established to oversee or control this title.

Marketers have long struggled with claims that they use advertising unethically to achieve goals of increased sales and profits and it looks like the latest interest by consumers in ethical business practices and in supporting organisations that are environmentally friendly have opened the way for some unethical organisations to enter this market. Fortunately consumers are not stupid and those that take on this approach will soon find themselves in the hot seat.[69]

Consumer education

Some major firms believe that educated consumers are better, more loyal customers. Financial planning firms often sponsor free educational seminars on money management, retirement planning and investing in the hope that the consumer will choose its organisation for his or her future financial needs. Likewise, computer hardware and software firms, realising that many consumers feel intimidated by new technology and recognising the strong relationship between learning and purchasing patterns, sponsor computer seminars and free in-store demonstrations. In a pre-launch public relations push for its 1999 3-Series line, BMW of North America sponsored an instructional driving and educational tour in six major US cities as a way to increase sales more cost-efficiently than traditional advertising. The tour, called the Ultimate Driving Experience, targets prospective purchasers and current owners near the end of their leases. One event during the tour invites high-school students and their parents to special weekend programs teaching driver safety.[70]

Event sponsorship

Public relations managers can sponsor events or community activities that are sufficiently newsworthy to achieve press coverage; at the same time, these events also reinforce brand identification. Sporting, music and arts events remain the most popular choices of event sponsors, although many are now turning to more specialised events such as tie-ins with schools, charities and other community service organisations. For example, Mercedes-Benz has sponsored the Australian Fashion Week since 1997. This has been so successful that the company is copying

Consumer education can not only influence the buying decision but also can result in better, more loyal customers. BMW's instructional driving tour is a way to show off its cars' capabilities to prospective purchasers and current owners without mounting expensive advertising campaigns.

the idea globally and is negotiating with New York Fashion Week for a similar deal. While the association was not aimed primarily at selling cars, it also gives Mercedes the brand image they want to communicate – a dynamic and youthful image – to new target groups of customers.[71]

Marketers can also create their own events tied around their product. Publicity surrounding IBM's highly publicised chess match between its Deep Blue supercomputer and Russian chess master Garry Kasparov reaped the equivalent of more than US$100 million worth of favourable and free publicity. IBM's Internet site, which covered the competition live, drew one million viewers at the height of the match, making it one of the most highly trafficked events ever on the World Wide Web.[72]

Issue sponsorship

Corporations can build public awareness and loyalty by supporting their customers' favourite issues. Education, health care and social programs get the largest share of corporate funding. Firms often donate a percentage of sales or profits to a worthy cause that their target market is likely to favour. For example, pantyhose maker Hanes supports national breast cancer organisations in the United States and prints instructions for breast self-examinations on packages of pantyhose.

'Green marketing' has also become an important way for companies to build awareness and loyalty by promoting a popular issue. Large numbers of consumers, mostly older, female and highly educated, profess a preference for, and are willing to pay more for, products made by environmentally friendly companies.[73] By positioning their brands as ecologically sound, marketers can convey concern for the environment and society as a whole. Burger King and McDonald's no longer use Styrofoam cartons to package their burgers in an effort to decrease waste in landfills. In a similar effort, there are a number of resorts in Australia that claim to be environmentally friendly and that are designed to appeal to the consumers' desire to save the environment. The resorts use air-conditioning systems that have a non-ozone-depleting refrigerant, rainwater is collected for watering the landscape, skylights allow natural light into the buildings, waste is recycled, and so on.

Internet websites

Internet websites as public relations tools are a relatively new phenomenon in the marketing arena. Whereas many marketers initially used their websites as a way to advertise their products or services, public relations professionals now feel these sites are an excellent vehicle to post news releases on products, product enhancements, strategic relationships and financial earnings. Corporate press releases, technical papers and articles, and product news help to inform the press, customers, prospects, industry analysts, shareholders and others of the firm's products and services and their applications. The website can also be an open forum for new product ideas and product improvements, and can be used to obtain feedback on the website's usefulness to viewers. Additionally, a self-help desk at the website can also list the most common questions and answers to assist with customer support and satisfaction.[74]

Several companies are also experimenting with Internet chat rooms as a competitive advantage and as a way to provide enhanced customer service. Merrill Lynch routinely sponsors moderated chat seminars hosted by expert employees. Recently, senior investment strategists at Merrill Lynch addressed international investing, and members of its tax advisory group explored the implications of current tax legislation during a live chat event. Egghead, the software retailer, holds chat sessions on weekdays in its on-line store, offering customers instant advice about software and helping them with their purchases.[75]

Managing unfavourable publicity

Although the majority of marketers try to avoid unpleasant situations, crises do happen. Intel faced this reality after consumers became aware of an obscure flaw in its Pentium chip. In our free-press environment, publicity is not easily controlled, especially in a crisis. **Crisis management** is the coordinated effort to handle the effects of unfavourable publicity, ensuring fast and accurate communication in times of emergency.

A good public relations staff is perhaps more important in bad times than in good. Critics chastised Panadol when they had an incident recently involving product tampering, saying that the company was too slow in informing the media and customers about the dangers and risks, and about what the company was doing to rectify the situation. The company was also late in reassuring the public that they were taking preventive action and instigating recall of the product. All public relations professionals can learn valuable lessons from this and other corporate blunders when emergencies arise. Companies must have a communication policy firmly in hand before a disaster occurs, because timing is uncontrollable.

crisis management
Coordinated effort to handle the effects of unfavourable publicity or of another unexpected, unfavourable event.

A good public relations and crisis management plan helped to steer Ansett Airlines through a crisis they faced in early 2001, when on three occasions planes were grounded due to maintenance problems. Interestingly, Ansett launched an advertising campaign to communicate their corporate image and received criticism from some quarters about their choice of budget allocation – why not spend the money on better maintenance procedures rather than advertising? So why did they do it this way? They suggested that the driving force was the need to come out of the crisis a stronger airline, and that they felt they had to take the immediate opportunity; there was a very strong feeling internally that they had done a good job of dealing with what was going on, and the staff were very motivated. The other key issue was that they still had considerable support from their customers, corporate accounts and partner airlines.[76] Of course, all this was in vain when the company went into receivership late in 2001 and then folded in early 2002.

Connect it

As you finish reading this chapter, think back to the opening story about the advertising campaign for Red Bull. The promotional team for Red Bull goes through the same creative steps as other large marketers – from determining what appeal to use to choosing the appropriate executional style. Great effort is also expended in deciding which medium will best reach the desired target markets. Red Bull takes into account such things as audience selectivity of the medium, cost per contact, frequency and reach. Red Bull also complements its traditional media advertising with effective sales promotion and sponsorships that target teens.

Summary

1 Discuss the effect advertising has on market share, consumers, brand loyalty and perception of product attributes.

First, advertising helps marketers to increase or maintain brand awareness and, subsequently, market share. Typically, more is spent to advertise new brands with a small market share than to advertise older brands. Brands with a large market share use advertising mainly to maintain their share of the market. Second, advertising affects consumers' daily lives as well as their purchases. Although advertising can seldom change strongly held consumer values, it may transform a consumer's negative attitude towards a product into a positive one. Third, when consumers are highly loyal to a brand, they may buy more of that brand when advertising is increased. Last, advertising can also change the importance of a brand's attributes to consumers. By emphasising different brand attributes, advertisers can change their appeal in response to consumers' changing needs or try to achieve an advantage over competing brands.

2 Identify the main types of advertising.

Advertising is any form of non-personal, paid communication in which the product or company is identified. The two main types of advertising are institutional advertising and product advertising. Institutional advertising is not product-oriented; rather, its purpose is to foster a positive company image among the general public, investment community, customers and employees. Product advertising is designed mainly to promote goods and services, and it is classified into three main categories: pioneering, competitive and comparative. A product's place in the product life cycle is a major determinant of the type of advertising used to promote it.

3 Describe the advertising campaign process.

An advertising campaign is a series of related advertisements focusing on a common theme and common goals. The advertising campaign process consists of several important steps. Promotion managers first set specific campaign objectives. They then make creative decisions, often with the aid of an advertising agency, centred on developing advertising appeals. Once creative decisions have been made, media are evaluated and selected. Finally, the overall campaign is assessed through various forms of testing.

4 Describe media evaluation and selection techniques.

Media evaluation and selection make up a crucial step in the advertising campaign process. The main types of advertising media include newspapers, magazines, radio, television, outdoor advertising such as billboards and bus panels, and the Internet and World Wide Web. Recent trends in advertising media include fax, video shopping carts, computer screen savers, and cinema and video advertising. Promotion managers choose the advertising media mix on the basis of the following variables: cost per contact, reach, frequency and characteristics of the target market. After choosing the media mix, a media schedule designates when the advertisement will appear and the specific media it will appear in.

5 Define and state the objectives of sales promotion.

Sales promotion combines those marketing communication activities, other than advertising, personal selling and public relations, in which a short-term incentive motivates consumers or members of the distribution channel to purchase a good or service immediately, either by lowering the price or by adding value. The main objectives of sales promotion are to increase trial purchases, consumer inventories and repeat purchases. Sales promotion is also used to encourage brand switching and to build brand loyalty. Sales promotion supports advertising activities.

6 Discuss the most common forms of consumer sales promotion.

Consumer forms of sales promotion include coupons and rebates, premiums, loyalty marketing programs, contests and sweepstakes, sampling and point-of-purchase displays. Coupons are certificates entitling consumers to an immediate price reduction when they purchase a product or service. Coupons are a particularly good way to encourage product trial and brand switching. Similar to coupons, rebates provide purchasers with a price reduction, although it is not immediate. To receive a rebate, consumers must generally mail in a rebate form with a proof of purchase. Premiums offer an extra item or incentive to the consumer for buying a product or service. Premiums reinforce the consumer's purchase decision, increase consumption and persuade non-users to switch

Define it

advertising appeal 355
advertising campaign 353
advertising objective 354
advertising response
  function 347
advocacy advertising 351
audience selectivity 366
comparative advertising 352
competitive advertising 351
consumer sales
  promotion 367
continuous media
  schedule 366
cooperative advertising 359
cost per contact 364
coupon 369
crisis management 379
flighted media schedule 366
frequency 365
frequent buyer program 371
infomercial 361
institutional advertising 350
loyalty marketing
  program 371
media mix 364
media schedule 366
medium 354
pioneering advertising 351
point-of-purchase display 373
premium 371
product advertising 351
pulsing media schedule 366
push money 373
reach 364
rebate 370
sampling 372
seasonal media schedule 367
trade allowance 373
trade sales promotion 367
unique selling
  proposition 356

brands. Rewarding loyal customers is the basis of loyalty marketing programs. Loyalty programs are extremely effective at building long-term, mutually beneficial relationships between a company and its key customers. Contests and sweepstakes are generally designed to create interest, often to encourage brand switching. Because consumers perceive risk in trying new products, sampling is an effective method for gaining new customers. Finally, point-of-purchase displays set up at the retailer's location build traffic, advertise the product and induce impulse buying.

7 List the most common forms of trade sales promotion.
Manufacturers use many of the same sales promotion tools used in consumer promotions, such as sales contests, premiums and point-of-purchase displays. In addition, manufacturers and channel intermediaries use several unique promotional strategies: trade allowances, push money, training programs, free merchandise, store demonstrations, and meetings, conventions and trade shows.

8 Discuss the role of public relations in the promotional mix.
Public relations is a vital part of a firm's promotional mix. A company fosters good publicity to enhance its image and promote its products. Popular public relations tools include new product publicity, product placement, consumer education, event sponsorship, issue sponsorship and Internet websites. An equally important aspect of public relations is managing unfavourable publicity in a way that is least damaging to a firm's image.

Review it

1. Consumers are typically exposed to hundreds of ads each day. Researchers estimate that the average person spends _____ hours per day watching TV.
   a One
   b Two
   c Three
   d Four

2. Which of the following is not one of the three basic types of advertising?
   a Service advertising
   b Product advertising
   c Institutional advertising
   d Advocacy advertising

3. Advertising that is intended to stimulate primary demand for a new product is called
   a Advocacy advertising.
   b Pioneering advertising
   c Competitive advertising
   d Comparative advertising

4. The goal of _____ advertising is to influence demand for a specific brand.
   a Comparative
   b Institutional
   c Competitive
   d Pioneering

5　The first step in any advertising campaign decision process must be to
　a　Determine campaign objectives
　b　Make creative decisions
　c　Make media decisions
　d　Evaluate the campaign

6　Which of the following types of media has the main advantage of being low in cost with high levels of intimacy and short lead times required for scheduling?
　a　Newspapers
　b　Radio
　c　Magazines
　d　Television

7　An important consideration when selecting media is the number of target customers who will be exposed to a commercial. This is known as
　a　Media mix
　b　Cost per contact
　c　Frequency
　d　Reach

8　The primary objective of sales promotion is to influence
　a　Attitudes
　b　Behaviour
　c　Beliefs
　d　Knowledge

9　The element of the promotional mix that is designed to help gain public acceptance and understanding of issues important to the firm is known as
　a　Advertising
　b　Public relations
　c　Sales promotion
　d　Direct marketing

10　Trade sales promotion is targeted towards the ultimate consumer of a product.
　a　True
　b　False

Check the Answer Key to see how well you understood the material. More detailed discussion and writing questions and a video case related to this chapter are found in the Student Resources CD-ROM.

Apply it

1　How can advertising, sales promotion and publicity work together? Give an example.

2　Discuss the reasons why new brands with a smaller market share spend proportionately more on advertising and sales promotion than brands with a larger market share.

3　At what stage in a product's life cycle are pioneering, competitive and comparative advertising most likely to occur? Give a current example of each type of advertising.

4　What is an advertising appeal? Give some examples of advertising appeals you have observed recently in the media.

5   What are the advantages of radio advertising? Why is radio expanding as an advertising medium?

6   You are the advertising manager of a sailing magazine, and one of your biggest potential advertisers has questioned your rates. Write the firm a letter explaining why you believe your audience selectivity is worth the extra expense for advertisers.

7   Discuss how different forms of sales promotion can erode or build brand loyalty. If a company's objective is to enhance customer loyalty to its products, what sales promotion techniques would be most appropriate?

8   As the new public relations director for a sportswear company, you have been asked to set public relations objectives for a new line of athletic footwear to be introduced to the teen market. Draft a memo outlining the objectives you propose for the footwear's introduction and your reasons for them.

9   Reports have just surfaced that your company, a fast-food chain, sold contaminated food products that have made several people seriously ill. As your company's public relations manager, devise a plan to handle the crisis.

10 Identify an appropriate media mix for the following products:
    a   Burial services
    b   *Who Weekly* magazine
    c   Whipper snippers
    d   Foot odour killers
    e   'Drink responsibly' campaigns by beer brewers

11 Design a full-page magazine advertisement for a new brand of soft drink. The name of the new drink, as well as its package design, are at your discretion. On a separate sheet, specify the benefits stressed or appeals made in the advertisement.

12 Form a three-person team. Divide between you the responsibility for getting newspaper advertisements and menus for several local restaurants. While you are at the restaurants to obtain copies of their menus, observe the atmosphere and interview the manager to determine what he or she believes are the primary reasons people choose to dine with them. Pool your information and develop a table comparing the restaurants in terms of convenience of location, value for money, food variety and quality, atmosphere, and so on. Rank the restaurants in terms of their appeal to students. Explain the basis of your rankings. What other market segment would be attracted to the restaurants and why? Do the newspaper advertisements emphasise the most effective appeal for a particular restaurant? Explain.

13 What associations and organisations are listed with the National Women's Justice Network? How would you try to appeal to some of the diverse interests of these groups if you were an advertiser trying to reach these consumers? www.nwjc.org.au.

14 How does sponsorship of the Kids' Help Line help this corporation's public relations effort? www.kelloggs.com.au

Try it

Quality of service is increasingly the basis for deciding where to do business. Customers are five times more likely to return to a particular business if they perceive that it is providing higher-quality service than the competition. The

Student Copy Centre is a local business competing with Kinko's and a couple of other national franchise copy centres. Its owner, Mack Bayles, has just attended a Small Business Administration workshop on customer service. He learned that when people say they expect good customer service, they most often mean they want prompt and accurate service from friendly, knowledgeable and courteous employees. The presenter also emphasised that all market segments, even the most price-conscious, expect good customer service. Mack wants to use this knowledge to develop an effective advertising campaign. Mack has no idea what his customers think about either his copy business or that of his competitors. He decides, therefore, to ask his customers to complete a brief survey while in his store. From his survey he learns that the Student Copy Centre is considered friendlier and more courteous than the major competitors, but is rated lower on speed of service.

Questions

1. What should Mack do before developing his advertising campaign?
2. Should Mack use comparative ads?
3. What advertising appeal would be most effective for Mack? Why?

Watch it

Red Roof Inns: Ads to charm, disarm and deliver

During the 1970s and 1980s, when budget lodging was far less competitive than it is today, billboards broadcasting 'Sleep Cheap' grabbed the attention of road-weary business travellers in the United States and brought them to the nearest Red Roof Inn. In addition to saying 'low cost', however, 'Sleep Cheap' also said 'low level', and occupancy rates at Red Roof Inns started to decline nationwide. Hired to reverse this image was the W.B. Doner advertising agency, whose philosophy was best articulated by its founder, Brod Doner: 'Ads are created to charm, disarm and deliver.' For the Red Roof account, Brod wanted creativity that would persuade, motivate and make something happen. The Doner Agency realised that advertising copy cannot change consumers' deeply rooted values and attitudes, but it could succeed in transforming a person's negative attitude about Red Roof's economy lodging into a positive one. Advertising could affect the way consumers ranked Red Roof's primary attribute – prices lower than the competition for the same economy hotel room – and thus motivate them to try spending the night at a Red Roof Inn. As part of a comprehensive promotion plan, an advertising campaign was set in motion to transmit the sales message to the target market. The Doner agency, in conjunction with Red Roof Inns executives, decided that the advertising campaign would target business travellers on a limited expense account who most likely arrive late at night and leave early the next morning. The specific communication in the advertising campaign mirrored Red Roof's corporate objective to increase market share in the budget lodging market. The whole point of the advertising was to convey the idea that a hotel room doesn't have to be expensive to be good. After all, 'Why pay [US]$70 when you can have the same good night's sleep for [US]$30 less at Red Roof Inn?' the commercials asked.

The advertising campaign then moved into the creative and media decision phase. The Doner team stuck to its core philosophy: although highly creative ads win accolades from peers in the advertising business, the bottom line is to sell products and services to the client. And the results have to be measurable. 'Sleep Cheap' was replaced by 'Hit the Roof', which was featured primarily in television spots. In addition to television, Doner's integrated marketing approach used radio, billboards, direct mail, print and the Internet to drive home the same message of value.

The initial creative effort came alive in a television commercial centred on one simple concept – spending US$70 for a night's stay in a hotel room is throwing money away. To make the concept visual, a business traveller stood at the top of Hoover Dam while a celebrity spokesperson literally threw the traveller's wallet from the dam into the raging waters below. Such an outrageous act provoked humour *and* underscored a well-known adage in advertising – sell the benefit. The message here was clear: what the consumer receives by staying at Red Roof Inns is money in his or her pocket. Put another way, a stay at Red Roof Inns saves a customer wasting their hard-earned cash. Red Roof Inns was trying to differentiate itself on price, but more importantly on value. Making claims of better value was not enough to universally boost business, so another TV spot was designed to increase occupancy rates at Red Roof during the slow period of January to March. The same celebrity, now well associated with Red Roof Inns, handed a telephone to a business customer and urged him to call and compare Red Roof's rates with those offered by other budget lodging chains such as Hampton Inn. The competitors' rates were consistently US$5 to US$10 a night higher. The same tag line, 'Hit the Roof', continued to reinforce the same unified message of value. Building on the success of prior campaigns, the Doner agency again selected humour as the creative style to execute the message. The commercial generated awareness by challenging viewers to call and compare rates. It sparked viewer interest in learning about room rates; it peaked viewer desire to save money; and, it is hoped, it resulted in a stay at Red Roof. The Doner agency has handled the Red Roof Inns account for over 12 years, and the advertising appeal has remained consistent the whole time. The appeal plays on the customer's desire for thrift, convenience and a nice place to stay.

Both the initial and subsequent ad campaigns produced measurable results. When the ad campaigns were evaluated, market share was shown to have increased despite heavy competition, and occupancy rates during slack periods had improved. Brod Doner's advertising mantra – ads that charm, disarm and deliver – has certainly made today's business travellers 'Hit the Roof'.

Questions

1 Using Exhibit 10.1, describe the advertising campaign decision process for Red Roof Inns.
2 Why did the Doner Agency identify the benefits of Red Roof Inns in the TV commercial?
3 Describe the advertising appeal used in the campaign.
4 How does Red Roof's advertising campaign follow AIDA as discussed early in this chapter?

Selected reading

John DeCerchio, 'Osmosis, Fiat Passed Doner Philosophy', *Advertising Age*, 3 March 1997, pp. C6–7.

John McDonough, 'W.B. Doner, 60th Anniversary', *Advertising Age*, 3 March 1997, pp. C1–2.

Video by Learnet Inc.: A Case Study in Advertising Strategy: Red Roof Inn.

Website: www.redroof.com.

© 2003 Nelson Australia Pty Limited

Click it

Online reading

INFOTRAC® COLLEGE EDITION
For additional readings and review on promotions mix, explore InfoTrac® College Edition, your online library. Go to: www.infotrac-college.com and search for any of the InfoTrac key terms listed below:
- institutional advertising
- outdoor advertising
- infomercial
- loyalty marketing programs

Answer key

1. *Answer*: d, p. 348 *Rationale*: During each hour of network television, the average consumer is exposed to 18 minutes of commercial advertising.

2. *Answer*: a, p. 349 *Rationale*: Services are advertised in a fashion that is consistent with products. Therefore, a separate category doesn't exist for service advertising.

3. *Answer*: b, p. 351 *Rationale*: Pioneering advertising is designed to generate awareness and create interest in new product offerings.

4. *Answer*: c, pp. 351 *Rationale*: Competitive advertising tends to rely more on emotional appeals and be less informative as it tries to encourage the target audience to consider a specific brand.

5. *Answer*: a, p. 353-4 *Rationale*: Campaign objectives are set first to identify the specific communication tasks a campaign should accomplish for a specified target audience during a specified period of time.

6. *Answer*: b, p. 360 *Rationale*: Radio has high selectivity, low cost per person reached and can provide flexible and short-notice scheduling opportunities that allow marketers to take advantage of immediate environmental conditions.

7. *Answer*: d, p. 364 *Rationale*: Reach is a measure of how many target customers will be exposed to an advertising message at least once and is generally expressed as a percentage of the total market.

8. *Answer*: b, p. 367 *Rationale*: Immediate purchase is the goal of sales promotion, regardless of the form it takes.

9. *Answer*: b, p. 375 *Rationale*: Public relations is the element of the promotional mix that evaluates public attitudes, identifies issues that may elicit public concern, and executes programs to gain public acceptance and understanding.

10. *Answer*: b, p. 373 *Rationale*: Trade sales promotion is directed at members of the distribution channel, such as wholesalers and retailers.

Pricing concepts

CHAPTER ELEVEN

Learning Objectives

After studying this chapter, you should be able to

1. Discuss the importance of pricing decisions to the economy and to the individual organisation
2. List and explain a variety of pricing objectives
3. Explain the role of demand in price determination
4. Describe cost-oriented pricing strategies
5. Demonstrate how the product life cycle, competition, distribution and promotion strategies, customer demands, the Internet and extranets, and perceptions of quality can affect price
6. Describe the procedure for setting the right price
7. Identify the legal and ethical constraints on pricing decisions
8. Explain how discounts, geographic pricing and other special pricing tactics can be used to fine-tune the base price

In the 2004–05 cricket season in Australia, one mobile network provider '3' is banking on the loyalty of supporters and fans by charging sports fans a base rate of $3.00 per month to stay up to date on the scores. This service also includes automatic SMS alerts to exciting action, near live video of the action.

The organisation also offerers additional information that can be downloaded to the mobile phone devices including music, games, sports news, movie trailers, surfcam, resturant guides, comedy clips, and news and finance information as well as other services.

'This season we have not only built on our cricket content offering, but have also introduced a Sports Pack, which gives customers unlimited access to cricket and other sporting content including tennis, Soccer, V8 Supercar racing and golf – all for just $3.00 per month.

'In future it will also offer sports fans basketball, action sports, horse racing, AFL, Rugby League, Rugby and UEAF Championship League.'

3 is banking on the sports fans needing to remain up to date with their sports and having the opportunity to use the technology on offer to watch and rewatch video streams of their favourite or exciting part of games and share these with friends.[1]

The interesting aspect of this new use of technology is that the sporting organisation should be able to claim the same types of deals that television and radio broadcasters pay to have rights to present the sport action in the respective countries.

For 3 this means either getting access to the video streaming directly from the various sports offical bodies or piggybacking from the broadcast media.

However, the most interesting aspect of this whole new venture is that 3 is charging a premium for the service and then charging for the use of the technology. For example, if the fan has opted to be notifed of an exciting sports event they will most likely be paying for the SMS and then paying again to connect to the video streaming of the event.

The rules of pricing are changing and this is just one example. Product pricing is getting more and more complex.

The 3 concept illustrates the notion of how demand and supply determine price. How does cost fit into the pricing equation? Can price influence the perceived quality of a product? How does competition affect price?

The importance of price

1 Discuss the importance of pricing decisions to the economy and to the individual organisation

Price means one thing to the consumer and something else to the seller. To the consumer, it is the cost of something given away in return for some other good or service. To the seller, price is an indication of revenue, the primary source of profits. In the broadest sense, price allocates resources in a free-market economy. With so many ways of looking at price, it's no wonder that marketing managers find the task of setting prices a challenge.

What is price?

Price is what is given up in an exchange to get a good service. Often this exchange helped with money, and price in such exchanges is the money associated with the exchange. However, price may also include lost time while waiting to get the good or service. For example, you may have experienced waited long periods on the telephone or in queues at counters to access

price
What is given up in an exchange to acquire a good or service.

'3' on-line
Find out more about how 3 works by visiting its website. Would you be willing to book this service? Which of 3's services would you be willing to try? Can you think of other markets 3 can enter?
www.three.com.au

Successful retailers such as Target understand that 'perceived reasonable value' is important to consumers.

$39.99

This gorgeous 16 piece Blue Leaves handpainted dinner set would make any dining experience a delight.

⊙ Target.

services. Thus, your price for these services must include the time spent waiting for them. Price also might include such things as 'lost dignity' – for example, queuing for unemployment benefits and relying on charity to get food and clothing.

Consumers are people like you who are interested in getting a 'reasonable price', which means 'perceived reasonable value' at the time of the exchange. You may regret purchasing the product after taking it home or consuming the good or service, but this is most likely because of the product not meeting your expected level of enjoyment or satisfaction from the utility of the product. Thus, a product may not be seen as good value after the purchase. In these circumstances, the price for the good or service may seem high after the exchange but reasonable at the time of the exchange. Remember, the price paid is based on the satisfaction consumers *expect* to receive from a product and not necessarily on the satisfaction they *actually* receive.

Price can relate to anything that you perceive as having value, not just money. When goods and services are exchanged for each other – for example, swapping CDs – the trade is called barter.

The importance of price to marketing managers

Prices are the key to revenues, which in turn are the key to profits for an organisation. **Revenue** is the price charged to customers multiplied by the number of units sold. Revenue is what pays for every activity of the company: production, finance, sales, distribution, and so on. What's left over (if anything) is **profit**. Managers usually strive to charge a price that will earn a fair profit.

To earn profit, managers must choose a price that isn't too high or too low – a price that equals the perceived value to target consumers. If a price is set too high in consumers' minds, the perceived value will be less than the cost, and sales opportunities will be lost. Many mainstream purchasers of cars, sporting goods, CDs, tools, wedding gowns and computers are buying 'used or pre-owned' items to get a better deal. Pricing a new product too high may give some shoppers the necessary incentive to change products or to buy second-hand. For example, you may want to buy tickets to see Limp Bizkit and find the prices too high, and choose to see a movie instead.

Lost sales mean lost revenue. Conversely, if a price is too low, it may be perceived as a great value for the consumer, but the organisation loses revenue it could have earned. Setting prices too low may not even attract as many buyers as managers might think. It is a recognised phenomenon that when prices for perceived high quality products are set too low the buying public perceive the product to be old stock, inferior or damaged. Retailers have also experienced situations where product such as hair shampoo can be taken out of discount bins, and place them on the shelf at a higher price, only to see an increase in sales volume and flowing on revenue. Retailers that place too much emphasis on discounts may not be able to meet the expectations of full-price customers.

Trying to set the right price is one of the most stressful and pressure-filled tasks of the marketing manager, as trends in the consumer market attest:

- Confronting a flood of new products, potential buyers carefully evaluate the price of each one against the value of existing products.
- The increased availability of bargain-priced private and generic brands has put downward pressure on overall prices.
- Many firms are trying to maintain or regain their market share by cutting prices. For example, IBM has regained some PC market share from Compaq by aggressively cutting prices.[2]

revenue
The price charged to customers multiplied by the number of units sold.

profit
Revenue minus expenses.

In the organisational market, where customers include governments and businesses, buyers are also becoming more price-sensitive and better informed. In the consumer market, people like yourself are using the Internet to compare prices between organisations and are making wiser purchasing decisions. Computerised information systems enable the organisational buyer to compare price and performance with great ease and accuracy. Improved communication and the increased use of telemarketing and computer-aided selling have also opened up many markets to new competitors. Finally, competition in general is increasing, so some installations, accessories and component parts are being marketed like indistinguishable commodities.

Pricing objectives

To survive in today's highly competitive marketplace, companies need pricing objectives that are specific, attainable and measurable. Realistic pricing goals then require periodic monitoring to determine the effectiveness of the company's strategy. For convenience, pricing objectives can be divided into three categories: profit-oriented, sales-oriented and status quo.

2 List and explain a variety of pricing objectives

Profit-oriented pricing objectives

Profit-oriented objectives include profit maximisation, satisfactory profits and target return on investment. A brief discussion of each of these objectives follows.

Profit maximisation

Profit maximisation means setting prices so that total revenue is as large as possible relative to total costs. (A more theoretically precise definition and explanation of profit maximisation appears later in the chapter.) Profit maximisation does not always signify unreasonably high prices. Both price and profits depend on the type of competitive environment a firm faces, such as being in a monopoly position (being the only seller) or selling in a much more competitive situation. Also, remember that a firm cannot charge a price higher than the product's perceived value. In an ideal world, product deliverers will keep producing product until the cost of producing the last item is the same as the revenue received for that item. Economic theory tells us at this point profits are maximised. However, many firms don't have the necessary data to determine this position and therefore to maximise profits.

Sometimes managers say that their company is trying to maximise profits – in other words, trying to make as much money as possible. Although this goal may sound impressive to shareholders, it isn't good enough for planning. The statement, 'We want to make all the money we can' is vague and lacks focus. It gives management licence to do just about anything it wants to do.

Satisfactory profits

Satisfactory profits are a reasonable level of profits. Rather than maximising profits, many organisations strive for profits that are satisfactory to the shareholders and management – in other words, a level of profits consistent with the level of risk an organisation faces. In a risky industry, a satisfactory profit may be 35 per cent. In a low-risk industry, it might be 7 per cent. To maximise profits, a small-business owner might have to keep his or her store open seven days a week. However, the owner might not want to work so hard and might be satisfied with less profit.

Target return on investment

The most common profit objective is a target **return on investment (ROI)**, sometimes called the firm's return on total assets. ROI measures the overall effectiveness of management in generating profits with its available assets. The higher the firm's return on investment, the better off the firm is. Many companies use target return on investment as their main pricing goal.

Return on investment is calculated as follows:

$$\text{Return on investment (ROI)} = \frac{\text{net profit after tax}}{\text{total assets}}$$

return on investment (ROI)
Net profit after taxes divided by total assets.

Assume that Company A had assets of $4.5 million, net profits of $550 000 and a target ROI of 10 per cent. This was the actual ROI:

$$\text{ROI} = \frac{550\,000}{4\,500\,000}$$
$$= 12.2 \text{ per cent}$$

As you can see, Company A has exceeded its target, which indicates that the company prospered in that year.

While it is good to see Company A exceed its expected return on investment, the company should not be happy with this result until it is compared with the industry average. The industry average allows managers to see if their performance was exceptional or whether the conditions in the competitive environment, risk in the industry, economic conditions and other environmental factors allowed all competitors to perform as well.

An organisation with a target ROI can predetermine its desired level of profitability. The marketing manager can use the standard, such as 10 per cent ROI, to determine whether a particular price and marketing mix are feasible. However, the manager must also weigh the risk of a given strategy even if the return is in the acceptable range.

Sales-oriented pricing objectives

Sales-oriented pricing objectives are based either on market share or on dollar or unit sales. The effective marketing manager should be familiar with these pricing objectives.

Market share

Market share is the organisation's percentage of total sales for that industry. Sales can be reported in dollars or in number of units. It is very important to know whether market share is expressed in revenue or units, because the results may be different. Many organisations believe that maintaining or increasing market share is an indicator of the effectiveness of their marketing mix. Larger market shares can mean higher profits, thanks to greater economies of scale, market power and ability to compensate top-quality management. However, many businesses with low market share survive and even prosper. These businesses succeed with a low market share by competing in industries with slow growth and few product changes or stable markets. Otherwise, they must vie in an industry that makes frequently bought items, such as fast-moving consumer goods (FMCG).

market share
A company's product sales as a percentage of total sales for that industry.

Sales maximisation

Rather than strive for market share, sometimes companies try to maximise sales. The objective of maximising sales is to ensure that sales are rising, and ignores profits, competition and the marketing environment. As you may expect, this isn't a good strategy in the long term. However, if your business had a poor cash flow, you may consider redeeming payments from creditors and maximising sales in the short term. Sales maximisation can also be used effectively on a temporary basis to sell off excess stock. It isn't uncommon to find Christmas cards, ornaments, and so on discounted at 50–70 per cent off retail prices after the holiday season. In addition, management can use sales maximisation for year-end sales to clear out old models before introducing the new ones.

Status quo pricing objectives

Status quo pricing seeks to maintain existing prices or to meet the competition's prices. This third category of pricing objectives has the major advantage of requiring little planning. It is essentially a passive policy. Often, firms competing in an industry with an established price leader simply meet the competition's prices. These industries typically have fewer price wars than those with direct price competition.

In other cases where the market may be more volatile, or the product may not be totally substitutable, it isn't uncommon for managers to check competitors' products and prices to monitor the market.

The demand determinant of price

Kraft General Foods on-line
Visit the Maxwell House site. Does it emphasise taste in its Web advertising? If so, how?
www.kraftfoods.com.au/maxwellhouse/products.cfm

status quo pricing
Pricing objective that maintains existing prices or meets the competition's prices.

3 Explain the role of demand in price determination

After marketing managers establish pricing goals, they must set specific prices to reach those goals. The price they set for each product depends mostly on two factors:

- the demand for the good or service; and
- the cost to the seller for that good or service.

When pricing goals are mainly sales-oriented, demand considerations usually dominate. Other factors, such as distribution and promotion strategies, perceived quality and stage of the product life cycle, can also influence price.

The nature of demand

demand
The quantity of a product that will be sold in the market at various prices for a specified period.

Demand is the quantity of a product that will be demanded by the market at various prices for a specified period. The quantity of a product that people will buy depends on its price. Usually it can be said that the higher the price, the fewer goods or services consumers will demand. Conversely, the lower the price, the more goods or services they will demand (see Exhibit 11.1).

Elasticity of demand

elasticity of demand
Consumers' responsiveness or sensitivity to changes in price.

elastic demand
Situation in which consumer demand is sensitive to changes in price.

inelastic demand
Situation in which an increase or a decrease in price won't significantly affect demand for the product.

To appreciate demand analysis, you should understand the concept of elasticity. **Elasticity of demand** refers to consumers' responsiveness or sensitivity to changes in price. **Elastic demand** occurs when consumers buy more or less of a product when the price changes. Conversely, **inelastic demand** means that an

Chapter 11 Pricing concepts

increase or a decrease in price won't significantly affect demand for the product. When demand is inelastic, sellers can raise prices and increase total revenue. Often, items that are relatively inexpensive but convenient tend to have inelastic demand. **Unitary elasticity** means that an increase in sales exactly offsets a decrease in prices so that total revenue remains the same. Thus, the slope of the demand curve can measure the elasticity of the demand curve. When the line is at 45 degrees sloping downwards to the right, it is said to be unitary or equal to 1 because as you increase price by one unit you decrease demand by one unit. When a small change in price creates a big change in demand, then the slope is more horizontal and the demand curve will give a value of less than 1 and is called elastic. Finally, if the demand curve is more vertical then the change in one unit of price will cause little change in demand for the product and this is called inelastic.

unitary elasticity
Situation in which total revenue remains the same when prices change.

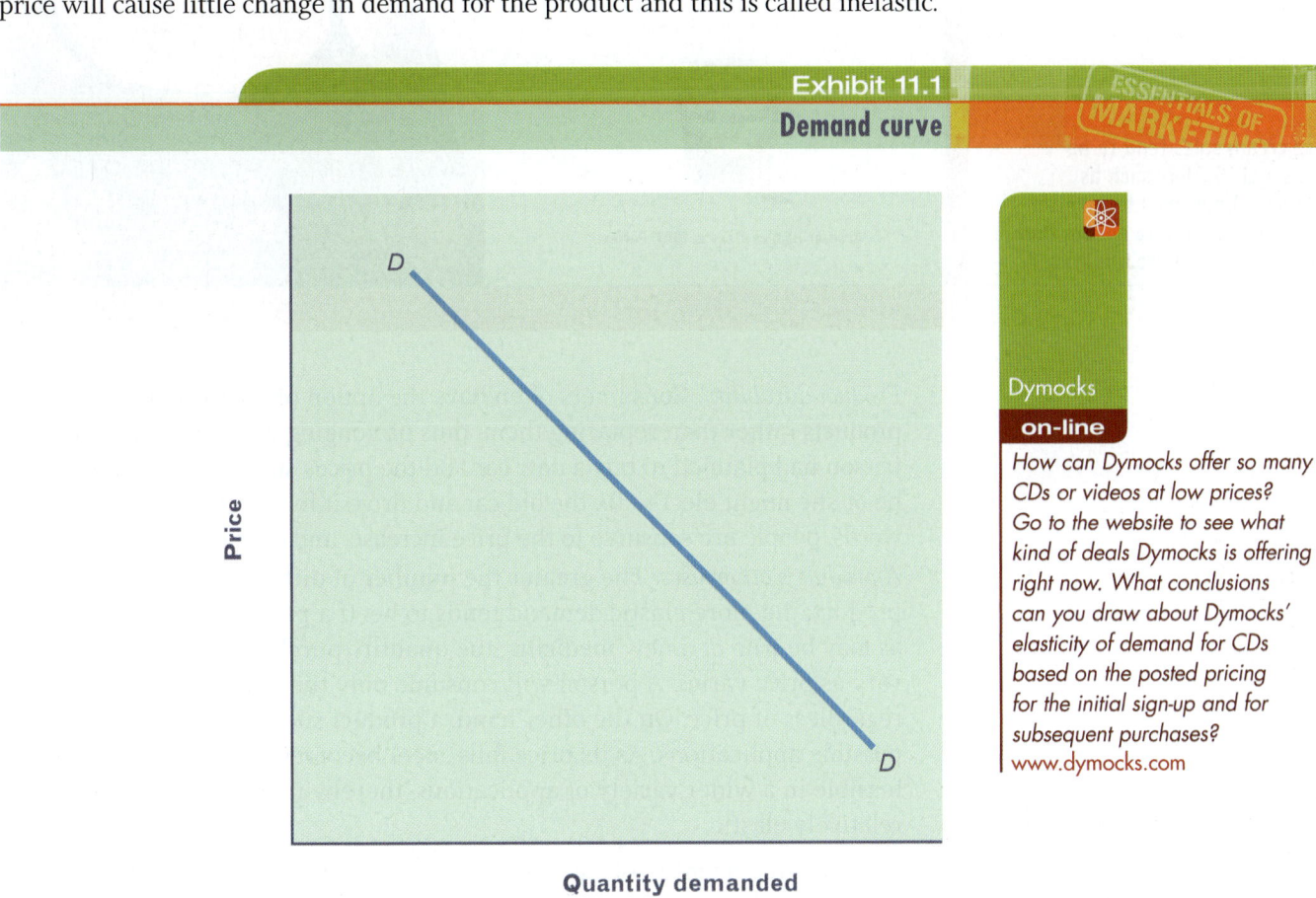

Exhibit 11.1
Demand curve

(Graph: Price on y-axis, Quantity demanded on x-axis, downward-sloping line from D to D)

Dymocks on-line
How can Dymocks offer so many CDs or videos at low prices? Go to the website to see what kind of deals Dymocks is offering right now. What conclusions can you draw about Dymocks' elasticity of demand for CDs based on the posted pricing for the initial sign-up and for subsequent purchases?
www.dymocks.com

Factors that affect elasticity

Several factors affect elasticity of demand, including the following:

- *Availability of substitutes*: When many substitute products are available, the consumer can easily switch from one product to another, making demand elastic and the same is true in reverse.
- *Price relative to purchasing power*: If a price is so low that it is an inconsequential part of an individual's budget, demand will be inelastic. For example, if the price of salt doubles, consumers won't stop putting salt and pepper on their eggs, because salt is cheap.

Lemonade stand site on-line
Play the game and see what happens to the demand when the price rises or falls.
www.lemonadegame.com/

Ice cream sales tend to be seasonal. Outlets such as Häagen-Dazs need to monitor sales and pricing to ensure that seasonal trends are minimised.

- *Product durability*: Consumers often have the option of repairing durable products rather than replacing them, thus prolonging their useful life. If a person had planned to buy a new car and the prices suddenly began to rise, he or she might elect to fix the old car and drive it for another year. In other words, people are sensitive to the price increase, and demand is elastic.
- *A product's other uses*: The greater the number of different uses for a product, the more elastic demand tends to be. If a product has only one use, as may be true of a new medicine, the quantity purchased probably won't vary as price varies. A person will consume only the prescribed quantity, regardless of price. On the other hand, a product such as steel has many possible applications. As its price falls, steel becomes more economically feasible in a wider variety of applications, thereby making demand relatively elastic.

supply
The quantity of a product that will be offered to the market by a supplier at various prices for a specified period.

Supply is the quantity of a product that will be offered to the market by a supplier or suppliers at various prices for a specified period. Unlike the falling demand curve, the supply curve slopes upwards and to the right. At higher prices, producers will obtain more resources and produce more product for the market (see Exhibit 11.2).

How demand and supply establish prices

At this point, let us combine the concepts of demand and supply to see how competitive market prices are determined. So far, the premise is that if the price is X, then consumers will purchase Y amount of a product. How high or low will prices actually go? How many units will be produced? How many products will be consumed? The demand curve cannot predict consumption, nor can the supply curve alone forecast production. Instead, we need to look at what happens when supply and demand interact – as shown in Exhibit 11.3, on page 398.

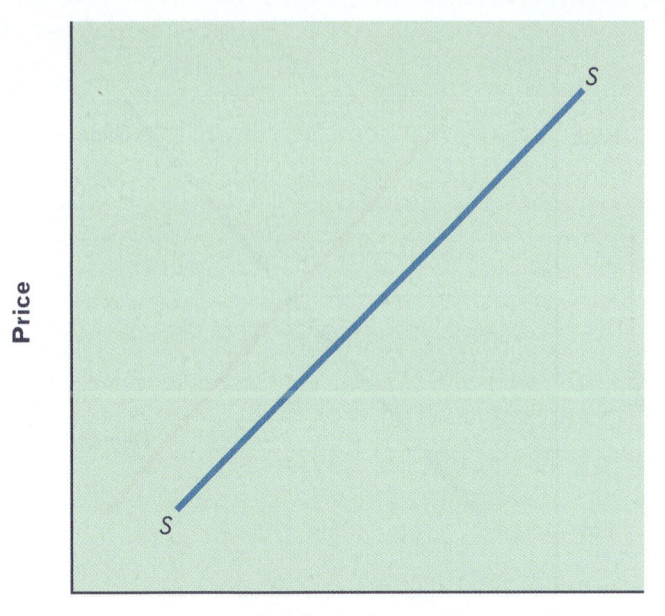

Exhibit 11.2
Supply curve

[Graph showing an upward-sloping supply curve with Price on the y-axis and Quantity supplied on the x-axis, labelled S to S]

The cost determinant of price

Sometimes companies minimise or ignore the importance of demand and decide to price their products largely or solely based on costs. Prices determined strictly based on costs may be too high for the target market, thereby reducing or eliminating sales. On the other hand, cost-based prices may be too low, causing the firm to earn a lower return than it should. However, understanding costs should be part of any price determination, if only to recognise the floor price below which a good or service must not be priced in the long run.

Costs may seem simple, but it is actually a multifaceted concept, especially for producers of goods and services. **Variable costs** are those that differ with changes in the level of output; an example of a variable cost is the cost of buying materials. In contrast, a **fixed cost** doesn't change as output is increased or decreased. Examples include rent and executives' salaries.

In order to compare the cost of production to sales, it is helpful to calculate costs per unit, or average costs. **Average variable cost (AVC)** equals total variable costs divided by quantity of output. **Average fixed cost (AFC)** is the fixed cost of production divided by the quantity of output. **Average total cost (ATC)** also equals total costs divided by output. **Marginal cost (MC)** is the change in total costs associated with a one-unit change in output. The cost relationships are summarised as:

- AVC plus AFC equals ATC.
- MC falls for a while and then turns upwards, in this case with the fourth unit. At that point, diminishing returns set in, meaning that less output is produced for every additional dollar spent on variable input.

4 Describe cost-oriented pricing strategies

variable costs
Costs that vary with changes in the level of output.

fixed cost
Cost that does not change as output is increased or decreased

average variable cost (AVC)
Total variable costs divided by quantity of output.

average fixed cost (AFC)
Total fixed cost divided by the quantity of output.

average total cost (ATC)
Total costs divided by quantity of output.

marginal cost (MC)
Change in total costs associated with a one-unit change in output.

Exhibit 11.3
Demand and supply curve

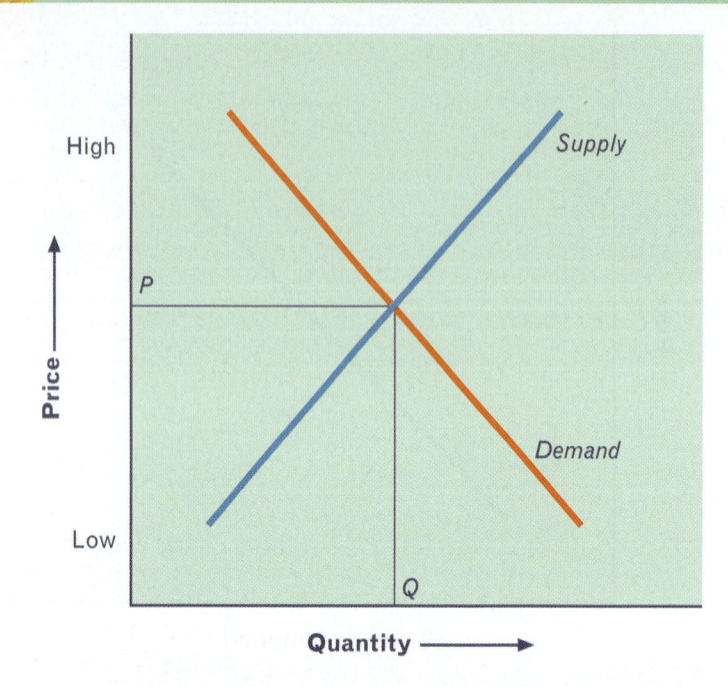

- MC intersects both AVC and ATC at their lowest possible points.
- When MC is less than AVC or ATC, the incremental cost will continue to pull the averages down. Conversely, when MC is greater than AVC or ATC, it pulls the averages up, and ATC and AVC begin to rise.
- The minimum point on the ATC curve is the least-cost point for a fixed-capacity firm, although it isn't necessarily the most profitable point.

Costs can be used to set prices in a variety of ways. The first two methods discussed here – mark-up pricing and formula pricing – are relatively simple. The other three – profit maximisation pricing, break-even pricing and target-return pricing – make use of the more complicated concepts of cost.

Mark-up pricing

Mark-up pricing, the most popular method used by wholesalers and retailers to establish a selling price, doesn't directly analyse the costs of production. Instead, **mark-up pricing** is the cost of buying the product from the producer, plus amounts for profit and for expenses not otherwise accounted for. The total determines the selling price. For example, a retailer will add a percentage, often based on experience, to the cost of the merchandise to determine the retail price. Many small retailers mark up merchandise 100 per cent over cost. (In other words, they double the cost.) This tactic is called **keystoning**.

Some other factors that influence mark-ups are the merchandise's appeal to customers, past response to the mark-up (an implicit demand consideration which influences future experience and decisions), the item's promotional value, the seasonality of the goods, their fashion appeal, the product's traditional selling price, and competition. Most retailers avoid any set mark-up because of such considerations as promotional value and seasonality. Sometimes businesses charge different mark-ups to different customers. One example of this practice is trade prices versus retail price where tradespeople receive a different price due to their profession.

mark-up pricing
Cost of buying the product from the producer plus amounts for profit and for expenses not otherwise accounted for.

keystoning
Practice of marking up prices by 100 per cent, or doubling the cost.

The biggest advantage of mark-up pricing is its simplicity. The primary disadvantage is that it ignores demand and may result in overpricing or underpricing the merchandise.

Profit maximisation pricing

Producers tend to use more complicated methods of setting prices than distributors use. One is **profit maximisation**, which occurs when marginal revenue equals marginal cost. You learned earlier that marginal cost is the change in total costs associated with a one-unit change in output. Similarly, **marginal revenue (MR)** is the extra revenue associated with selling an extra unit of output. As long as the revenue of the last unit produced and sold is greater than the cost of the last unit produced and sold, the firm should continue manufacturing and selling the product.

profit maximisation
When marginal revenue equals marginal cost.

marginal revenue (MR)
The extra revenue associated with selling an extra unit of output or the change in total revenue with a one-unit change in output.

Ethics in Marketing: Many governments are hooked on tobacco revenue

Four million people will die this year from lung cancer and other smoking-related causes, according to the World Health Organization. By 2030, the agency predicts, the annual loss of life will more than double, making cigarettes the leading cause of premature death around the globe, outstripping malaria, AIDS and other scourges.

Yet, some countries make more money from a pack of smokes than do the tobacco companies. More than 70 per cent of the average retail price of Marlboro cigarettes in the European Union goes into government pockets. In Brazil, the government's take is about 65 per cent. Tobacco taxes account for about 6 per cent of federal government tax revenue in Germany. For the roughly two dozen governments that still manufacture cigarettes, dependence on tobacco revenue can be even higher. China, whose government is the world's largest cigarette maker, derives about 13 per cent of its annual income from tobacco sales and taxes.

All that can make governments reluctant to take aggressive action against smoking. In Japan, where the government owns two-thirds of the country's largest cigarette maker, Japan Tobacco, Inc., the Health Ministry dropped plans for specific targets to reduce tobacco use after complaints from tobacco interests.

Because smokers are hooked on cigarettes, they are less responsive to price increases than consumers of many other goods. That means that in the short to medium term, tax revenue would increase as consumption declines. In the United States, a 10 per cent increase in cigarette price translates to a 4 per cent drop in consumption. In developing countries, where people have less disposable income, the World Bank estimates that a 10 per cent price increase would reduce consumption by 8 per cent, on average.

A study by Teh-wei Hu, a health economist at the University of California at Berkeley, and Zhengzhong Mao, of the West China University of Medical Sciences, concludes that a 25 percent cigarette-tax increase in China would reduce consumption there by 4.57 billion packs and boost central-government revenue by 24.74 billion yuan.

Worldwide, the public-health benefits of tax increases would be significant, the World Bank says. A recent bank report estimates that a sustained 10 per cent in the real price of cigarettes around the globe would prompt 40 million people to quit and deter many others from starting to smoke, saving about 10 million lives while, at the same time, boosting government revenue by an average of 7 per cent.[3]

Should governments get out of the tobacco business? Why or why not? Do you think that the government should increase taxes on cigarettes 100 per cent or more? Why or why not? Consider the 2002 tax increase in New York City. A more direct alternative is to ban smoking altogether. Is this feasible?

Break-even pricing

break-even analysis
Method of determining what sales volume must be reached before total revenue equals total costs.

Now let's take a closer look at the relationship between sales and cost. **Break-even analysis** determines what sales volume must be reached before the company breaks even (its total costs equal total revenue) and no profits are earned.

The typical break-even model assumes a given fixed cost and a constant average variable cost. Suppose that Universal Sportswear has fixed costs of $2000 and that the cost of labour and materials for each unit produced is 50 cents. Assume that it can sell up to 6000 units of its product at $1 without having to lower its price.

Exhibit 11.4(a) illustrates Universal Sportswear's break-even point. As Exhibit 11.4(b) indicates, Universal Sportswear's total variable costs increase by 50 cents every time a new unit is produced, and total fixed costs remain constant at $2000 regardless of the level of output. Therefore, 4000 units of output give Universal Sportswear $2000 in fixed costs and $2000 in total variable costs (4000 units @ 50 cents), or $4000 in total costs.

Revenue is also $4000 (4000 units @ $1), giving a net profit of zero dollars at the break-even point of 4000 units. Notice that once the firm gets past the break-even point, the gap between total revenue and total cost gets wider and wider, because both functions are assumed to be linear.

Exhibit 11.4
Costs, revenues and break-even for Universal Sportswear

(a) Break-even point

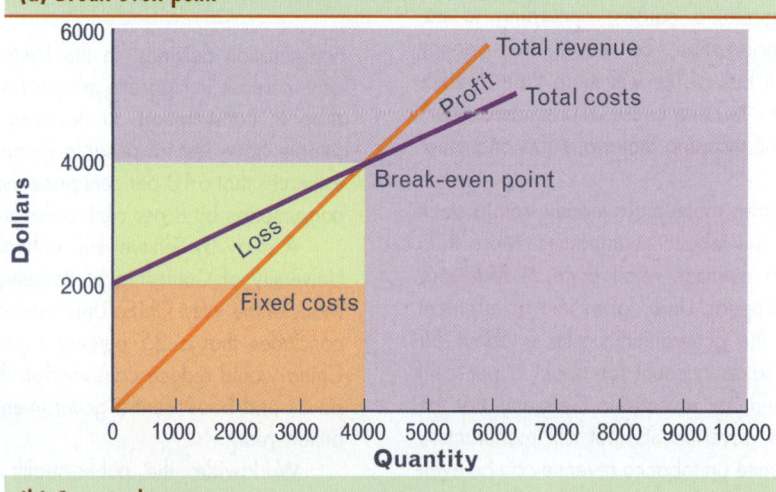

(b) Costs and revenues

Output	Total fixed costs	Average variable costs	Total variable costs	Average total costs	Average revenue (price)	Total revenue	Total costs	Profit or loss
500	$2000	$0.50	$ 250	$4.50	$1.00	$ 500	$2250	($1750)
1000	2000	0.50	500	2.50	1.00	1000	2500	(1500)
1500	2000	0.50	750	1.83	1.00	1500	2750	(1250)
2000	2000	0.50	1000	1.50	1.00	2000	3000	(1000)
2500	2000	0.50	1250	1.30	1.00	2500	3250	(750)
3000	2000	0.50	1500	1.17	1.00	3000	3500	(500)
3500	2000	0.50	1750	1.07	1.00	3500	3750	(250)
*4000	2000	0.50	2000	1.00	1.00	4000	4000	0
4500	2000	0.50	2250	.94	1.00	4500	4250	250
5000	2000	0.50	2500	.90	1.00	5000	4500	500
5500	2000	0.50	2750	.86	1.00	5500	4750	750
6000	2000	0.50	3000	.83	1.00	6000	5000	1000

*Break-even point

The formula for calculating break-even quantities is simple:

$$\text{Break-even quantity} = \frac{\text{total fixed costs}}{\text{fixed cost contribution}}$$

Fixed cost contribution is the price minus the average variable cost. Average variable cost divided by the quantity of output. Therefore, for Universal Sportswear:

$$\text{Break-even} = \frac{\$2000}{(\$1.00 - 50c)}$$
$$= 4000 \text{ units}$$

The advantage of break-even analysis is that it provides a quick estimate of how much the firm must sell to break even and how much profit can be earned if a higher sales volume is obtained. If a firm is operating close to the break-even point, it may want to see what can be done to reduce costs or increase sales. Moreover, in a simple break-even analysis, it isn't necessary to calculate marginal costs and marginal revenues, because price and average cost per unit are assumed constant. In addition, because accounting data for marginal cost and revenue are frequently unavailable, it is convenient not to have to depend on that information.

Break-even analysis isn't without several important limitations. Sometimes it is hard to know whether a cost is fixed or variable. If labour wins a tough enterprise bargaining agreement, are the resulting expenses a fixed cost? Are middle-level executives' salaries fixed costs? More important than cost determination is the fact that simple break-even analysis ignores demand. How does Universal Sportswear know it can sell 4000 units at $1? Could it sell the same 4000 units at $2 or even $5? Obviously, this information would profoundly affect the firm's pricing decisions.

Scentwise on-line
How is this company able to sell perfumes at such low prices? Does it have any fixed costs?
www.scentwise.com.au

Other determinants of price

Other factors besides demand and costs can influence price. For example, the stage of the product's life cycle, the competition, the product distribution strategy, promotion strategy and perceived quality can all affect pricing.

Stages in the product life cycle

As a product moves through its life cycle (see Exhibit 11.5 and Chapter 7), the demand for the product and the competitive conditions tend to change:

- *Introductory stage*: Management usually sets prices high during the introductory stage. One reason is that it hopes to recover its development costs quickly. In addition, demand originates in the core of the market (the customers whose needs ideally match the product's attributes) and thus is relatively inelastic. On the other hand, if the target market is highly price-sensitive, management often finds it better to price the product at the market level or lower.
- *Growth stage*: Prices generally begin to stabilise as the product enters the growth stage. There are several reasons. First, competitors have entered the market, increasing the available supply. Second, the product has begun to appeal to a broader market, often lower-income groups. Finally, economies of scale are lowering costs, and the savings can be passed on to the consumer in the form of lower prices.

5 Demonstrate how the product life cycle, competition, distribution and promotion strategies, customer demands, the Internet and extranets, and perceptions of quality can affect price

- *Maturity stage*: Maturity usually brings further price decreases as competition increases and inefficient, high-cost firms are eliminated. Distribution channels become a significant cost factor, however, because of the need to offer wide product lines for highly segmented markets, extensive service requirements and the sheer number of dealers necessary to absorb high-volume production. The manufacturers that remain in the market towards the end of the maturity stage typically offer similar prices. Usually only the most efficient remain. At this stage, price increases are usually cost-initiated, not demand-initiated. Nor do price reductions in the late phase of maturity stimulate much demand. Because demand is limited and producers have similar cost structures, the remaining competitors will probably match price reductions.
- *Decline stage*: The final stage of the life cycle may see further price decreases as the few remaining competitors try to salvage the last vestiges of demand. When only one firm is left in the market, prices begin to stabilise. In fact, prices may eventually rise dramatically if the product survives and moves into the speciality goods category, as horse-drawn carriages and vinyl records have done.

Exhibit 11.5
The product life cycle

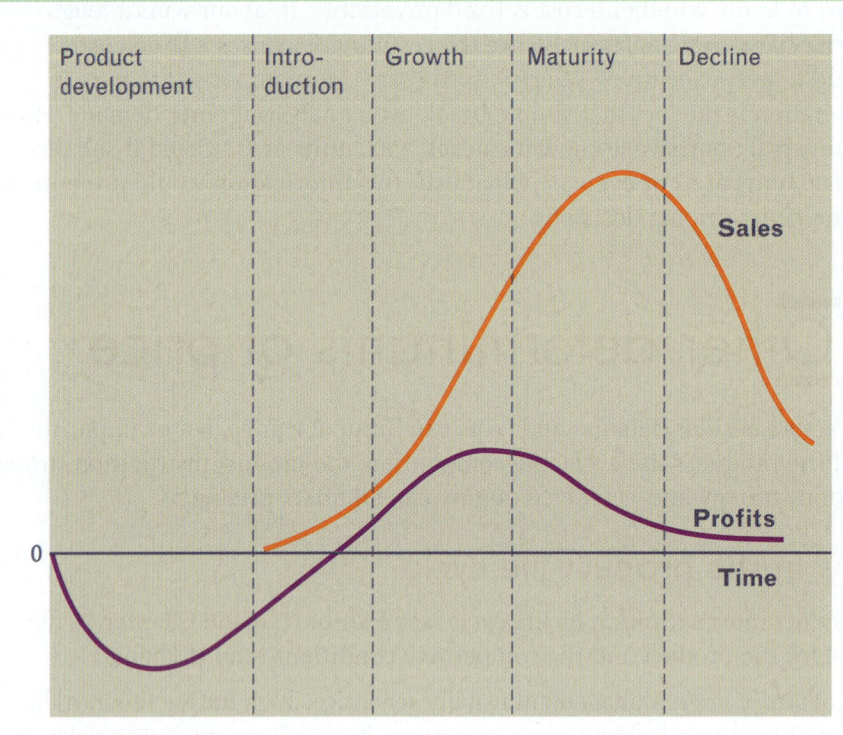

Virgin Blue on-line
What market is Virgin Blue after? Does competition among the airlines mean that the market is efficient?
www.virginblue.com.au

The competition

Competition varies during the product life cycle, of course, and at times may strongly affect pricing decisions. Although a firm may not have any competition at first, the high prices it charges may induce another firm to enter the market. Intense competition can sometimes lead to price wars. What pulls companies into such self-defeating price wars? Often, they make the mistake of measuring their success by market share rather than by profitability – but something more is at play.

CDs were once the most common medium for listening to recorded voice and music, but are being replaced by hard disk recorders like iPod – similar to the experiences of cassette tapes and vinyl records.

The deregulation of the Australian domestic airline market in the mid-1980s has resulted in a number of price wars. Some companies were forced out of the market, or had to consolidate with other airline businesses to stay in operation. When Sir Richard Branson set up Virgin Blue, he did so with the realisation that the competition would make it difficult to establish a sound base in the marketplace and would attempt to drive his business out of the market.

Sometimes governments will intervene to control actions of competitors that could lead to price wars. Price wars often begin when one company offers a 'sale'. However, that's not so easily done in France, as the Global perspectives box reveals.

Distribution strategy

An effective distribution network can often overcome other minor flaws in the marketing mix. For example, although consumers may perceive a price as being slightly higher than normal, they may buy the product anyway if it is being sold at a convenient retail outlet.

Adequate distribution for a new product can often be attained by offering a larger-than-usual profit margin to distributors. A variation on this strategy is to give dealers a large trade allowance to help offset the costs of promotion and further stimulate demand at the retail level.

Foot Locker on-line

Does Foot Locker focus on the price or the convenience of buying the product? Does Foot Locker see price as an important aspect of the buying process?
www.footlocker.com.au/launch.cfm

Global PERSPECTIVES

Want to have a sale in France? Hey, not so fast there

Mark this down: the French government says holiday sales can begin on 6 January. In France, the government not only owns the airlines, runs the railways and operates a bank, it is also in charge of post-Christmas sales.

Price cutting after the holidays is common practice around the world, but here it is the political heirs of Louis XIV who determine when and how merchandise can be discounted. By law, stores are allowed to offer merchandise below cost only twice a year – during the post-Christmas period and in the six-week summer sale season. A law passed in 1996 set even stricter terms for what constitutes a sale: the goods must have been bought by the stores at least 30 days before, not brought in and instantly marked down.

About 2000 inspectors from the Competition, Consumption and Repression of Fraud Directorate go to the stores, making sure that the labels on sale products are genuine discounts, that only previously offered merchandise is on sale and that the time limit has been adhered to. Every year, dozens of fines are issued to stores that start their sales early. Violators of the starting date or merchandise rules can be fined US$5000 to US$20 000. 'If a government inspector came in the day before a sale can begin and we had articles on sale, we would have been charged a fine,' said a spokeswoman for Le Bon Marché, a major department store.

The regulation of sales is just one visible example of how the French approach to capitalism diverges sharply from the approach taken by its Anglo-Saxon neighbours and allies. The law 'is to avoid too much competition between merchants', said Bernard Chartier of the city administration office in Paris, which is responsible for setting the kick-off date for the sale season. The date is carefully selected in consultation with merchant and consumer associations. French consumer groups, not a strong lobby in any case, focus their efforts on making sure the items offered are really on sale and not shoddy merchandise brought in just for the discount period. Little concern has been apparent over whether consumers should be allowed to pay less during the rest of the year if a retailer wishes to lower prices. By some estimates, half of all French consumer purchases are made during the two sale seasons.[4]

Should Australia adopt the French law? Why or why not? Do you feel that the law hurts competition? Why do you think that French consumers aren't more upset by this law?

The impact of the electronic environment

Internet
Worldwide telecommunications network allowing access to data, pictures, sound and files throughout the world.

extranet
A private electronic network that links a company with its suppliers and customers.

wireless link
A radio or infra-red link between two or more electronic devices.

The **Internet**, **extranet** and **wireless links** are connecting people, machines and organisations around the globe – and connecting sellers and buyers as never before. This link is enabling buyers to compare products and prices, quickly and easily, putting both buyers and sellers in better bargaining positions. At the same time, the technology allows sellers to collect detailed data about customers' buying habits and preferences, so that they can tailor their products and prices.

The first signs of this new fluid pricing can be found on the Internet. Unfortunately, the promise of pricing efficiencies for Internet retailers and lower costs for consumers has run headlong into reality. Flawed pricing strategies have taken much of the blame. Too many merchants offered deep discounts that made profits all but impossible to achieve. Other e-retailers have felt the consumer backlash against price discrimination, as the Internet has given shoppers the ability to better detect price discrepancies and bargains. Organisations must now figure out how to manage and merge the pricing of products in an on-line or electronic environment with traditional product pricing.

Chapter 11 Pricing concepts

Commerce on-line

Visit Commerce Online. Search for "buy a camera" for New Zealand. Are there other considerations besides price that influence your decision? What are they, and how important are they in your selection? Why?
www.commerce.com

Shopping over the Internet is on the rise, and as part of that trend Internet auctions are becoming increasingly popular. At sites like www.ebay.com.au, consumers can purchase anything from computers to collectibles. How interested would you be in participating in an Internet auction, either as a buyer or a seller?

'Before the Internet existed, retail was a very competitive, difficult, low-margin business,' says Austan Goolsbee, an economist at the University of Chicago. 'With the advent of Internet retailers, there was a brief moment in which they and others believed they had broken the iron chain of low margins and high competition in retail by introducing the Internet. However, electronic retail is now looking like retail off-line – very competitive, profit margins squeezed. In all, a very tough place to be.'

Setting prices on the Internet was expected to offer retailers several advantages. To start with, it would be far easier to raise or lower prices in response to demand. Further, on-line prices could be changed in far smaller increments, and as frequently as a merchant desired, making it possible to fine-tune pricing strategies. But, the real payoff was supposed to be better information on how price-conscious customers are. For instance, knowing that customer A doesn't care whether an Oscar-nominated DVD in her shopping basket costs $21.95 or $25.95 would leave an enterprising merchant free to charge the higher price on the spot. By contrast, knowing that customer B is going to put author John Le Carre's latest thriller back on the shelf unless it's priced at $20, rather than $28, would open an opportunity for a bookseller to make the sale by cutting the price in real time.

The idea was to charge exactly what the market will bear. But putting this into practice has turned out to be exceptionally difficult, in part because the electronic environment has also empowered consumers to compare prices (value) from other merchants.

Another outcome of the electronic environment is that it has made it easier for consumers to complain. For example, Amazon.com faced a problem when customers learned they had paid different prices for the same DVD movies as a result of a marketing test in which the retailer varied prices to gauge the effect on demand. After complaints from irate consumers, who learned from on-line chat boards that they had paid higher prices, Amazon announced it would refund the difference between the highest and lowest prices in the test.

While the electronic environment has helped drive down prices by making it easier for consumers to shop for the best bargain, it also makes it possible for on-line merchants to monitor each other's prices and adjust them in concert without overtly colluding. As long as the number of retailers in a given market is relatively small, it is now much simpler for merchants to signal each other by changing prices for short periods – long enough for their competitors to notice, but not long enough for consumers. USA airlines have long used on-line reservation systems to signal fare changes to each other.

'On-line markets may not be as cutthroat as is commonly expected,' says Hal Varian, dean of the school of information management and systems at the University of California at Berkeley. Recent research supports the notion that on-line merchants' prices are lower than bricks-and-mortar prices, but have increased prices over that of the bricks-and-mortar counterpart though the use of additional charges such as postage, handling and insurance. That runs against early conventional wisdom of Internet shopping – that consumers were only a click away from lower prices offered by a competing merchant.

One area where the electronic environment is having a major impact on pricing is the bargaining power between buyers and sellers in the business-to-business (B2B) markets. As bargaining power evens out, organisations are reaching price agreements more quickly and then disseminating this information throughout the channel of distribution. Manufacturers are creating private networks, or extranets, that link them with their suppliers and customers. These systems make it possible to get a handle on inventory, costs and demand at any given moment, and, after bargaining with suppliers, adjust prices instantly. In the past, a significant cost, known as the 'menu cost', was associated with changing prices. For a company with a large product line, it could take months for price adjustments to filter down to distributors, retailers and salespeople. Streamlined distribution channels and networks reduce cost and time.

Equally in the retail market such activities as Internet auctions allow B2C and C2C activities to cause 'disintermediation' – a buzzword meaning buyers and sellers connecting directly and avoiding intermediaries. This creates efficiencies similar to direct bartering or flea markets without using coveted weekends or worrying about the weather. Plus, bidding itself can be fun and exciting. A few of the most popular consumer auction sites are www.ebay.com.au; www.auctions.amazon.com; and www.auctions.yahoo.com.

Promotion strategy

Price is often used as a promotional tool to increase consumer interest. The weekly grocery section of the newspaper, for instance, advertises many products with special low prices. Some hotels on the Gold Coast are offering accommodation for $5 a night per person. The only condition is that the guests purchase their meals at the hotel. This works because costs are fixed and an empty room receives no revenue. Therefore, the revenue gained on the sale of food items improves the hotel's overall cost base and even makes revenue for the hotel.

Pricing can be a tool for trade promotions as well. For example, Levi's Dockers (casual men's slacks) are very popular with white-collar men aged 25 to 45, a growing and lucrative market. Sensing an opportunity, rival pants maker Bugle Boy began offering similar pants at cheaper wholesale prices, which gave retailers a bigger gross margin than they got with the Dockers. Levi Strauss either had to lower its prices or risk losing $400 million annually in Docker sales. Although Levi Strauss intended its cheapest Dockers to retail for $35, it started selling Dockers to retailers for $18 a pair. Retailers could then advertise Dockers at a very attractive retail price of $25.

Demands of large customers

Large customers of manufacturers such as Coles and Woolworths often make specific pricing demands that the suppliers must agree to. They want suppliers to guarantee their stores' profit margins by ensuring that the combination of the product cost and the mark-up margin will still allow a price to be set that is acceptable to the buyers.

In the past, when a garment maker sold to a store, the two parties would agree on a retail price; then, at the end of the season, the supplier would rebate some of the cost of markdowns. Discounts and markdowns were less common then than they are today: department stores could afford plenty of sales help to push products. However, as stores cut labour costs, they came to rely on promotional markdowns and sales to move goods – with suppliers covering profit-margin shortfalls.

Retailers often sell the balance of their seasonal stock at the end of the season at lower prices, and manufacturers make up the shortfall in profits that retailers experience.

The relationship of price to quality

Consumers tend to rely on a high price as a predictor of good quality when there is great uncertainty involved in the purchase decision. Reliance on price as an indicator of quality seems to exist for all products, but it reveals itself more strongly for some items than for others.[5] Among the products that benefit from this phenomenon are coffee, stockings, aspirin, salt, floor wax, shampoo, clothing, furniture, perfume, jewellery, whisky and many services. If the consumer obtains additional information – for example, about the brand or the store – then reliance on price as an indicator of quality decreases.[6] In the absence of other information, people typically assume that prices are higher because the products contain better materials, because they are made more carefully or, in the case of professional services, because the provider has more expertise. In other words, consumers assume that 'You get what you pay for'.

In general, consumers tend to be more accurate in their price–quality assessments for non-durable goods (such as ice cream, frozen pizza or oven cleaner) than for durable goods (such as DVD players, scooters or mountain bikes).[7]

Knowledgeable merchants consider these consumer attitudes when devising their pricing strategies. **Prestige pricing** is the charging of a high price to help promote a high-quality image. A successful prestige pricing strategy requires a retail price that is reasonably consistent with consumers' expectations. No one goes shopping for a Tag Heuer watch and expects to pay only $20. In fact, demand would fall drastically at such a low price.

Consumers also expect private or store brands to be cheaper than national brands. However, if the price difference between a private brand and a nationally distributed manufacturer's brand is *too* great, consumers tend to believe that the private brand is inferior. On the other hand, if the savings aren't big enough, there is little incentive to buy the private brand. One study of scanner data found that

prestige pricing
Charging a high price to help promote a high-quality image.

if the price difference between the national brand and the private brand was less than 10 per cent, people tended not to buy the private brand. If the price difference was greater than 20 per cent, consumers perceived the private brand to be inferior.[8]

In sum, the most recent research has shown that in many countries, people use a well-known brand name as their primary indicator of quality. If the product doesn't have this feature, then price, followed by the physical appearance of the item, is used to judge quality. After a well-known brand name, price and physical appearance, consumers use the reputation of the retailer as an indicator of quality.[9]

Let's now consider the process for setting price.

How to set a price on a product

Setting the right price on a product is a four-step process (see Exhibit 11.6):

1. Establish pricing goals.
2. Estimate demand, costs and profits.
3. Choose a price strategy to help determine a base price.
4. Fine-tune the base price with pricing tactics.

The first three steps are discussed next; the fourth step is discussed later in the chapter.

6 Describe the procedure for setting the right price

Exhibit 11.6 Steps in setting the right price on a product

- Establish pricing goals
- Estimate demand, costs and profit
- Choose a price strategy to help determine a base price
- Fine-tune the base with pricing tactics
- Results lead to the right price

Establish pricing goals

The first step in setting the right price is to establish pricing goals. Recall that pricing objectives fall into three categories: profit-oriented, sales-oriented and status quo. These goals are derived from the firm's overall objectives.

A good understanding of the marketplace and of the consumer can sometimes tell a manager very quickly whether a goal is realistic. For example, if firm A's objective is a 20 per cent target return on investment (ROI), and its product development and implementation costs are $5 million, the market must be rather large or must support the price required to earn a 20 per cent ROI. Assume that company B has a pricing objective that all new products must reach at least 15 per cent market share within three years after their introduction. A thorough study of the environment may convince the marketing manager that the competition is too strong and the market share goal can't be met.

Managers must work through all pricing objectives and tradeoffs when setting a price for a product. A profit maximisation objective may require a bigger initial investment than the firm can or wants to commit. Reaching the desired market share often means sacrificing short-term profit to ensure that long-term profit goals are met. Meeting the competition is the easiest pricing goal to implement. However, managers cannot afford to ignore demand and costs, the life cycle stage or other considerations. When creating pricing objectives, managers must consider these tradeoffs in light of the target customer and the environment.

Estimate demand, costs and profits

Earlier it was explained that total revenue is a function of price and quantity demanded and that quantity demanded depends on elasticity. After establishing pricing goals, managers should estimate total revenue at a variety of prices. Next, they should determine corresponding costs for each price. They are then ready to estimate how much profit, if any, and how much market share can be earned at each possible price. These data become the heart of the developing price policy. Managers can study the options in light of revenues, costs and profits. In turn, this information can help to determine which price can best meet the firm's pricing goals.

Choose a price strategy

price strategy
Basic, long-term pricing framework, which establishes the initial price for a product and the intended direction for price movements over the product life cycle.

The basic, long-term pricing framework for a good or service should be a logical extension of the pricing objectives. The marketing manager's chosen **price strategy** defines the initial price and gives direction for price movements over the product life cycle.

The price strategy sets a competitive price in a specific market segment, based on a well-defined positioning strategy. Changing a price level from premium to super premium may require a change in the product itself, the target customers served, the promotional strategy or the distribution channels. Thus, changing a price strategy can require dramatic alterations in the marketing mix. A carmaker cannot successfully compete in the super-premium category if the car looks and drives like an economy car.

An organisation's freedom in pricing a new product and devising a price strategy depends on the market conditions and the other elements of the marketing mix. If the organisation launches a new item resembling several others already on the market, its pricing freedom will be restricted. To succeed, the business will probably have to charge a price close to the average market price. In contrast, a business that introduces a totally new product with no close substitutes will have considerable pricing freedom.

The three basic strategies for setting a price on a good or service are price skimming, penetration pricing and status quo pricing. A discussion of each type follows.

Price skimming

Price skimming is sometimes called a 'market-plus' approach to pricing, because it denotes a high price relative to the prices of competing products. Sony produces many unique products. They often use a skimming policy to recoup revenue for the innovative product released on the market.

The term price *skimming* is derived from the phrase 'skimming the cream off the top'. Organisations often use this strategy for new products when the target market perceives the product as having unique advantages. As a product progresses through its life cycle, the organisation may lower its price to successfully reach larger market segments. Economists have described this type of pricing as 'sliding down the demand curve'. Not all companies slide down the curve. Genentech's TPA, a drug that clears blood clots, was still priced at US$2200 a dose four years after its introduction, despite competition from a much lower-priced competitor.

Price skimming works best when the market is willing to buy the product even though it carries an above-average price. If, for example, some purchasing agents feel that Caterpillar equipment is far superior to competitors' products, then Caterpillar can charge premium prices successfully. Firms can also effectively use price skimming when a product is legally protected, when it represents a technological breakthrough or when it has blocked entry in some other way to competitors. Managers may follow a skimming strategy when production cannot be expanded rapidly because of technological difficulties, shortages or constraints imposed by the skill and time required to produce a product. As long as demand is greater than supply, skimming is an attainable strategy.

A successful skimming strategy enables management to recover its product development or 'educational' costs quickly. (Often, consumers must be 'taught' the advantages of a radically new item, such as high-definition TV.) Even if the market perceives an introductory price as too high, managers can easily correct the problem by lowering the price. Firms often feel it is better to test the market at a high price and then lower the price if sales are too slow. They are tacitly saying, 'If there are any premium-price buyers in the market, let's reach them first and maximise our revenue per unit.' Successful skimming strategies are not limited to products. Well-known athletes, entertainers, lawyers and hairstylists are experts at price skimming. Naturally, a skimming strategy will encourage competitors to enter the market.

price skimming
Pricing policy whereby a firm charges a high introductory price, often coupled with heavy promotion.

Penetration pricing

Penetration pricing is at the other end of the spectrum from skimming. **Penetration pricing** means charging a relatively low price for a product as a way to reach the mass market. The low price is designed to capture a large share of a substantial market, resulting in lower production costs. If a marketing manager has made obtaining a large market share the firm's pricing objective, penetration pricing is a logical choice.

Penetration pricing does mean lower profit per unit. Therefore, to reach the break-even point, it requires higher volume sales than would a skimming policy. If reaching a high volume of sales takes a long time, then the recovery of product development costs will also be slow. As you might expect, penetration pricing tends to discourage competition.

A penetration strategy tends to be effective in a price-sensitive market. Price should decline more rapidly when demand is elastic, because the market can

penetration pricing
Pricing policy whereby a firm charges a relatively low price for a product initially as a way to reach the mass market.

be expanded through a lower price. In addition, price sensitivity and greater competitive pressure should lead to a lower initial price and a relatively slow decline in the price later.

For many years, Fuji and Kodak have been battling it out in international markets, but in the United States the picture was quite different. Kodak and Fuji treated that market like a cosy, mutually profitable duopoly. Both enjoyed large margins. Kodak controlled over 80 per cent of the film market, and distant number two Fuji always priced its film just a little bit lower. Then in 1997, Fuji began slashing prices by as much as 25 per cent. When consumers saw that the familiar red, white and green boxes were a dollar or two cheaper, they switched brands.

Penetration pricing can also be very effective in international marketing, as described in the Global perspectives box.

Global Perspectives

Irish airline flies high just like Southwest Airlines

Europe's grand old airlines have hit a rough patch of air these days, and Michael O'Leary is proud to be a big part of their problem.

The chief executive of Ryanair Holdings didn't set out to rattle the once cosy world of European aviation. Ten years ago, when he was financial adviser to Irish tycoon Tony Ryan, he was asked by Ryan for some thoughts on fixing the struggling family-owned carrier. O'Leary's advice: 'Shut the bloody thing down.'

Instead, Ryan persuaded O'Leary to visit Southwest Airlines in Dallas and learn how the pioneer of low-cost air travel makes a big profit. There, under the Texas sun, O'Leary found cut-price religion. He agreed to run Ryanair, in the process taking on some of the biggest names in aviation.

Today, Ryanair stands foremost among a handful of European budget airlines, rewriting the rules and battering venerable flag carriers. Passengers grumble that flying Ryanair is like riding a bus, but they are doing it by the busload. Ryanair carries seven million passengers in 11 countries each year – Britain, France and Italy, among them – ranking its traffic volume above that of Ireland's state-owned Aer Lingus. That makes Ryanair Europe's first start-up to surpass a national carrier.

Ryanair's rise from Irish puddle-jumper to continental contender is more than one airline's growth story. The Gaelic upstart and its followers such as London-based EasyJet are fundamentally shifting the economics of flying around Europe. Some promotional Ryanair fares are as cheap as £1 ($2.40) to fly from one European city to another; the majority of the carrier's tickets are in the same price range as old-line carriers' bargain fares. But while major airlines make most of their money from premium travellers and offer discounts mainly to fill unsold seats, Ryanair is able to turn a profit at discount-fare levels.

The carrier, which today bases most of its flights in London, can make money on bargain fares because it pares costs to the bone and then keeps cutting. Frequent flyer plan? Forget about it. Want a snack or drink on board? You buy it. And Ryanair won't serve peanuts because prying them out from between the seat cushions takes too long (and, hence, costs too much money). In its no-frills fervour, Ryanair even refuses to use those extendable boarding corridors at airports because it's quicker to park a plane at the gate, roll stairs up to the front and back doors, and let passengers hustle across the tarmac. The result: Ryanair can break even with its planes almost half empty – its average flight is 75 per cent full, better than most major European carriers.

What type of pricing strategy is Ryanair following? What might Europe's traditional airlines, like British Airways and Lufthansa, do to counteract Ryanair's success? What other problems might Ryanair face in following this pricing strategy?

Status quo pricing

The third basic price strategy a firm may choose is status quo pricing, or meeting the competition. It means charging a price identical to or very close to the competition's price. Although status quo pricing has the advantage of simplicity, its disadvantage is that the strategy may ignore demand or cost or both. However, meeting the competition may be the safest route to long-term survival if the firm is comparatively small.

The legality and ethics of price strategy

Some pricing decisions are subject to government regulation. Before marketing managers establish any price strategy, they should know the laws that limit their decision-making. Among the issues that fall into this category are unfair trade practices, price fixing, price discrimination and predatory pricing.

7 Identify the legal and ethical constraints on pricing decisions

Unfair trade

The Australian **Trade Practices Act**, managed by the ACCC, and the New Zealand fair trading Acts, managed by the Commerce Commission, ensure that unfair trade practices don't occur to exclude anyone from the market. In particular, there are sections to ensure that the retail price for some products is maintained regardless of the producer or buyer.

Trade Practices Act
Law that prohibits wholesalers and retailers from selling below cost.

Price fixing or collusion

Price fixing is an agreement between two or more firms on the price they will charge for a product. Suppose two or more executives from competing firms meet to decide how much to charge for a product, or which of them will submit the lowest bid on a certain contract. Such practices are illegal under the trade practices and fair trading Acts. Offenders have received fines and sometimes prison terms. Price fixing is one area where the law is quite clear, and is vigorously enforced.

Recently, the petrol companies were reviewed to ensure collusion was not occurring, and, in the 1990s, the courier business was found to be acting in a way that contravened the Act and large fines were enforced.

price fixing
An agreement between two or more firms on the price they will charge for a product.

Price discrimination

There are certain times when price discrimination is acceptable:
- A firm can charge different prices to different customers if the prices represent manufacturing or quantity discount savings.
- Price variations are justified if they are designed to meet fluid product or market conditions. Examples include the deterioration of perishable goods, the obsolescence of seasonal products, a distress sale under court order and a legitimate going-out-of-business sale.
- A reduction in price may be necessary to stay even with the competition. Specifically, if a competitor undercuts the price quoted by a seller to a buyer, the law authorises the seller to lower the price charged to the buyer for the product in question.

Predatory pricing

predatory pricing
The practice of charging a very low price for a product with the intent of driving competitors out of business or out of a market.

Predatory pricing is the practice of setting a price for one product so low that it drives a competitor out of the market. There is a fine line between predatory pricing and strong competition. When there were four domestic carriers in the airline industry in Australia, there was fierce competition. Prices dropped dramatically due to the competition for a limited number of the flying public. However, these prices were not set to drive the competition out of the market, but in a desperate attempt to capture a share of the market. Unfortunately, it didn't work and two airlines failed.

Tactics for fine-tuning the base price

8 Explain how discounts, geographic pricing and other special pricing tactics can be used to fine-tune the base price

base price
The general price level at which the company expects to sell the good or service.

quantity discount
Price reduction offered to buyers buying in multiple units or above a specified dollar amount.

cumulative quantity discount
A deduction from list price that applies to the buyer's total purchases made during a specific period.

non-cumulative quantity discount
A deduction from list price that applies to a single order rather than to the total volume of orders placed during a certain period.

cash discount
A price reduction offered to a consumer, an industrial user or a marketing intermediary in return for prompt payment of a bill.

functional discount (trade discount)
Discount to wholesalers and retailers for performing channel functions.

After managers understand both the legal and the marketing consequences of price strategies, they should set a **base price**, the general price level at which the company expects to sell the good or service. The general price level is correlated with the pricing policy: above the market (price skimming), at the market (status quo pricing) or below the market (penetration pricing). The final step, then, is to fine-tune the base price.

Fine-tuning techniques are short-run approaches that don't change the general price level. They do, however, result in changes within a general price level. These pricing tactics allow the firm to adjust for competition in certain markets, meet ever-changing government regulations, take advantage of unique demand situations, and meet promotional and positioning goals. Fine-tuning pricing tactics include various sorts of discounts, geographic pricing and special pricing tactics.

Discounts, allowances, rebates and value pricing

A base price can be lowered through the use of discounts and the related tactics of allowances, rebates and value pricing. Managers use the various forms of discounts to encourage customers to do what they wouldn't ordinarily do, such as paying cash rather than using credit, taking delivery out of season, or performing certain functions within a distribution channel. A summary of the most common tactics follows:

- *Quantity discounts*: When buyers get a lower price for buying in multiple units or above a specified dollar amount, they are receiving a **quantity discount**. A **cumulative quantity discount** is a deduction from list price that applies to the buyer's total purchases made during a specific period; it is intended to encourage customer loyalty. In contrast, a **non-cumulative quantity discount** is a deduction from list price that applies to a single order rather than to the total volume of orders placed during a certain period. It is intended to encourage orders in large quantities.
- *Cash discounts*: A **cash discount** is a price reduction offered to a consumer, an industrial user or a marketing intermediary in return for prompt payment of a bill. Prompt payment saves the seller carrying charges and billing expenses and allows the seller to avoid bad debt.
- *Functional discounts*: When distribution channel intermediaries, such as wholesalers or retailers, perform a service or function for the manufacturer, they must be compensated. This compensation, typically a percentage discount from the base price, is called a **functional discount** (or **trade discount**). Functional discounts vary greatly from channel to channel, depending on the tasks performed by the intermediary.

- *Seasonal discounts*: A **seasonal discount** is a price reduction for buying merchandise out of season. It shifts the storage function to the purchaser. Seasonal discounts also enable manufacturers to maintain a steady production schedule year-round. An unusual form of discount may be referred to as a social responsibility discount. This is a discount given for ethical, socially responsible or humanitarian purposes.

  seasonal discount
  A price reduction for buying merchandise out of season.

- *Promotional allowances*: A **promotional allowance** (also known as a **trade allowance**) is a payment to a dealer for promoting the manufacturer's products. It is both a pricing tool and a promotional device. As a pricing tool, a promotional allowance is like a functional discount. If, for example, a retailer runs an ad for a manufacturer's product, the manufacturer may pay half the cost. If a retailer sets up a special display, the manufacturer may include a certain quantity of free goods in the retailer's next order.

  promotional allowance (trade allowance)
  Payment to a dealer for promoting the manufacturer's products.

- *Rebates*: A **rebate** is a cash refund given for the purchase of a product during a specific period. The advantage of a rebate over a simple price reduction for stimulating demand is that a rebate is a temporary inducement that can be taken away without altering the basic price structure. A manufacturer that uses a simple price reduction for a short time may meet resistance when trying to restore the price to its original, higher level.

  rebate
  Cash refund given for the purchase of a product during a specific period.

Value-based pricing

Value-based pricing is a pricing strategy that has grown out of the quality movement. Instead of figuring prices based on costs or competitors' prices, it starts with the customer, considers the competition and then determines the appropriate price. The basic assumption is that the firm is customer-driven, seeking to understand the attributes customers want in the goods and services they buy and the value of that bundle of attributes to customers. A marketer using value-based pricing must also determine the value of competitive offerings to customers. Customers determine the value of a product (not just its price) relative to the value of alternatives. In value-based pricing, therefore, the price of the product is set at a level that seems to the customer to be good value compared with the value offered by other options.

value-based pricing
The price is set at a level that seems to the customer to be a good price compared to the prices of other options.

Geographic pricing

Because many sellers ship their wares to a nationwide or even a worldwide market, the cost of freight can greatly affect the total cost of a product. Sellers may use several different geographic pricing tactics to moderate the impact of freight costs on distant customers. Following are the most common methods of geographic pricing:

- *FOB origin pricing*: **FOB origin pricing** is a price tactic that requires the buyer to absorb the freight costs from the shipping point. The further buyers are from sellers, the more they pay, as transportation costs generally increase with the distance merchandise is shipped.

  FOB origin pricing
  Price tactic that requires the buyer to absorb the freight costs from the shipping point (free on board).

- *Uniform delivered pricing*: If the marketing manager wants total costs, including freight, to be equal for all purchasers of identical products, the firm will adopt uniform delivered pricing, or 'postage stamp' pricing. With **uniform delivered pricing**, the seller pays the actual freight charges and bills every purchaser an identical, flat freight charge.

  uniform delivered pricing
  Price tactic in which the seller pays the actual freight charges and bills every purchaser an identical, flat freight charge.

zone pricing
Modification of uniform delivered pricing that divides the total market into segments or zones and charges a flat freight rate to all customers in a given zone.

freight absorption pricing
Price tactic in which the seller pays all or part of the actual freight charges and does not pass them on to the buyer.

basing-point pricing
Price tactic that charges freight from a given (basing) point, regardless of the city from which the goods are shipped.

- *Zone pricing*: A marketing manager who wants to equalise total costs among buyers within large geographic areas – but not necessarily all of the seller's market area – may modify the base price with a zone-pricing tactic. **Zone pricing** is a modification of uniform delivered pricing. Rather than placing all of Australia under a uniform freight rate, the firm divides it into segments or zones and charges a flat freight rate to all customers in a given zone. Most parcel delivery services structure their pricing on this basis.
- *Freight absorption pricing*: In **freight absorption pricing,** the seller pays all or part of the actual freight charges and does not pass them on to the buyer. The manager may use this tactic in intensely competitive areas or as a way to break into new market areas.
- *Basing-point pricing*: With **basing-point pricing**, the seller designates a location as a basing point and charges all buyers the freight cost from that point, regardless of the city from which the goods are shipped. Thanks to several adverse court rulings, basing-point pricing has waned in popularity. Freight fees charged when none were actually incurred, called *phantom freight*, have been declared illegal.

Special pricing tactics

Unlike geographic pricing, special pricing tactics are unique and defy neat categorisation. Managers use these tactics for various reasons – for example, to stimulate demand for specific products, to increase store patronage and to offer a wider variety of merchandise at a specific price point. Special pricing tactics include flexible pricing, professional services pricing, leader pricing, bait pricing, odd–even pricing, price bundling and two-part pricing. A brief overview of each of these tactics follows, along with a manager's reasons for using that tactic or a combination of tactics to change the base price.

Flexible pricing

flexible pricing (variable pricing)
Price tactic in which different customers pay different prices for essentially the same merchandise bought in equal quantities.

Flexible pricing (or **variable pricing**) means that different customers pay different prices for essentially the same merchandise bought in equal quantities. This tactic is often found in the sale of shopping goods, speciality merchandise and most industrial goods except supply items. Car dealers, many appliance retailers, and manufacturers of industrial installations, accessories and component parts commonly follow the practice. It allows the seller to adjust for competition by meeting another seller's price. Thus, a marketing manager with a status quo pricing objective might readily adopt the tactic. Flexible pricing also enables the seller to close a sale with price-conscious consumers. If buyers show promise of becoming large-volume shoppers, flexible pricing can be used to lure their business. The obvious disadvantages of flexible pricing are the lack of consistent profit margins, the potential ill will of high-paying purchasers, the tendency for salespeople to automatically lower the price to make a sale, and the possibility of a price war among sellers.

Professional services pricing

Professional services pricing is used by people with lengthy experience, training and often certification by a licensing board – for example, lawyers, doctors and family counsellors. Professionals sometimes charge customers at an hourly rate, but sometimes fees are based on the solution of a problem or performance of an act (such as an eye examination) rather than on the actual time involved.

Professional services are priced using a variety of methods.

A surgeon may perform a heart operation and charge a flat fee of $5000. The operation itself may require only four hours, resulting in a hefty $1250 hourly rate. The surgeon justifies the fee because of the lengthy education and internship required to learn the complex procedures of a heart operation. Lawyers also sometimes use flat-rate pricing, such as $500 for completing a divorce and $50 for handling a traffic offence. Those who use professional pricing have an ethical responsibility not to overcharge a customer. Because demand is sometimes highly inelastic, such as when a person requires heart surgery or a daily insulin shot to survive, there may be a temptation to charge 'all the traffic will bear'.

Leader pricing

Leader pricing (or **loss-leader pricing**) is an attempt by the marketing manager to attract customers by selling a product near or even below cost, hoping that shoppers will buy other items once they are in the store. This type of pricing appears weekly in the newspaper advertising of supermarkets, speciality stores and department stores. Leader pricing is normally used on well-known items that consumers can easily recognize as bargains at the special price. The goal is not necessarily to sell large quantities of leader items, but to try to appeal to customers who might shop elsewhere.

leader pricing (loss-leader pricing)
Price tactic in which a product is sold near or even below cost in the hope that shoppers will buy other items once they are in the store.

Bait pricing

In contrast to leader pricing, which is a genuine attempt to give the consumer a reduced price, bait pricing is deceptive. **Bait pricing** tries to get the consumer into a store through false or misleading price advertising and then uses high-pressure selling to persuade the consumer to buy merchandise that is more expensive. This practice contravenes the *Trade Practices Act*.

bait pricing
Price tactic that tries to get consumers into a store through false or misleading price advertising and then uses high-pressure selling to persuade consumers to buy more expensive merchandise.

Odd–even pricing

Odd–even pricing (or **psychological pricing**) means pricing at odd-numbered prices to connote a bargain and pricing at even-numbered prices to imply quality. For years, many retailers have used this tactic to price their products in odd numbers – for example, $99.95 or $49.95 – in order to make consumers feel that they are paying a lower price for the product. Some retailers favour odd-numbered prices because they believe that $9.99 sounds much less imposing to customers than $10.00. Other retailers believe that the use of an odd-numbered price signals to consumers that the price is at the lowest level possible, thereby encouraging them to buy more units. Neither theory has ever been conclusively proven, although one study found that consumers perceive odd-priced products as being on sale.[10] Even-numbered pricing is sometimes used to denote quality. Examples include a fine perfume at $200 a bottle, a good watch at $1000 or a fur coat at $5000. The demand curve for such items would also be saw-toothed, except that the outside edges would represent even-numbered prices and, therefore, elastic demand.

> **odd–even pricing (psychological pricing)**
> Price tactic that uses odd-numbered prices to connote bargains and even-numbered prices to imply quality.

Price bundling

Price bundling is marketing two or more products in a single package for a special price. Examples include the sale of maintenance contracts with computer hardware and other office equipment, packages of stereo equipment, packages of options on cars, weekend hotel packages that include a room and several meals, and airline holiday packages. Microsoft now offers 'suites' of software that bundle spreadsheets, word processing, graphics, electronic mail, Internet access and groupware for networks of microcomputers. Price bundling can stimulate demand for the bundled items if the target market perceives the price as a good value. Businesses such as hotels and airlines sell a perishable commodity (hotel rooms and airline seats) with relatively constant fixed costs. Bundling can be an important income stream for these businesses because the variable cost tends to be low – for example, the cost of cleaning a hotel room or putting one more passenger on an airplane. Therefore, most of the revenue can help cover fixed costs and generate profits. The car industry has a different motive for bundling. People buy cars only every three to five years. Thus, selling options is a somewhat rare opportunity for the car dealer. Price bundling can help the dealer sell a maximum number of options. A related price tactic is **unbundling**, or reducing the bundle of services that comes with the basic product. Rather than raise the price of hotel rooms, some hotel chains have started charging registered guests for parking. To help hold the line on costs, some department stores require customers to pay for gift wrapping.

> **price bundling**
> Marketing two or more products in a single package for a special price.

> **unbundling**
> Reducing the bundle of services that comes with the basic product.

Two-part pricing

Two-part pricing means establishing two separate charges to consume a single good or service. Tennis clubs and health clubs charge a membership fee and a flat fee each time a person uses certain equipment or facilities. In other cases they charge a base rate for a certain level of usage, such as 10 squash games per month, and a surcharge for anything over that amount. Consumers sometimes prefer two-part pricing because they are uncertain about the number and the types of activities they might use at places like an amusement park. Also, the people who use a service most often pay a higher total price. Two-part pricing can increase a seller's revenue by attracting consumers who wouldn't pay a

> **two-part pricing**
> Price tactic that charges two separate amounts to consume a single good or service.

high fee even for unlimited use. For example, a health club might be able to sell only 100 memberships at $700 annually with unlimited use of facilities, for total revenue of $70 000. However, perhaps it could sell 900 memberships at $200 with a guarantee of using the squash courts 10 times a month. Every use over 10 would require the member to pay a $5 fee. Thus, membership revenue would provide a base of $180 000, with some additional usage fees coming in throughout the year.

Connect it

Cost determines the floor below which a price should not be set in the long run. A price set solely on cost may be too high and therefore not attract customers. Conversely, a price based on cost alone that is too low results in lost revenues and profits.

Price can have an impact on perceived quality, depending on a number of issues, such as the type of product, advertising and the consumer's personality. A well-known brand is usually more important than price in consumers' quality perceptions.

Competition can help hold down prices in the marketplace. A firm without competition that charges a high price will soon find competitors attracted to that market. As competitors enter the market, prices typically fall, because firms compete for market share by lowering prices.

Summary

1 Discuss the importance of pricing decisions to the economy and to the individual firm.

Pricing plays an integral role in the economy by allocating goods and services among consumers, governments and businesses. Pricing is essential in business because it creates revenue, which is the basis of all business activity. In setting prices, marketing managers strive to find a level high enough to produce a satisfactory profit.

2 List and explain a variety of pricing objectives.

Establishing realistic and measurable pricing objectives is a critical part of any firm's marketing strategy. Pricing objectives are commonly classified into three categories: profit-oriented, sales-oriented and status quo. Profit-oriented pricing is based on profit maximisation, a satisfactory level of profit or a target return on investment. The goal of profit maximisation is to generate as much revenue as possible in relation to cost. Often, a more practical approach than profit maximisation is setting prices to produce profits that will satisfy management and shareholders. The most common profit-oriented strategy is pricing for a specific return on investment relative to a firm's assets. The second type of pricing objective is sales-oriented, and it focuses on either maintaining a percentage share of the market or maximising dollar or unit sales. The third type of pricing objective aims to maintain the status quo by matching competitors' prices.

3 Explain the role of demand in price determination.

Demand is a key determinant of price. When establishing prices, a firm must first determine demand for its product. A typical demand schedule shows an inverse relationship between quantity demanded and price: when price is lowered, sales increase; and when price is increased, the quantity demanded falls. However, for prestige products, there may be a direct relationship between demand and price: the quantity demanded will increase as price increases.

Marketing managers must also consider demand elasticity when setting prices. Elasticity of demand is the degree to which the quantity demanded fluctuates with changes in price. If consumers are sensitive to changes in price, demand is elastic; if they are insensitive to price changes, demand is inelastic. Thus, an increase in price will result in lower sales for an elastic product and little or no loss in sales for an inelastic product.

4 Describe cost-oriented pricing strategies.

The other main determinant of price is cost. Marketers use several cost-oriented pricing strategies. To cover their own expenses and obtain a profit, wholesalers and retailers commonly use mark-up pricing: they tack an extra amount on to the manufacturer's original price. Another pricing technique is to maximise profits by setting price where marginal revenue equals marginal cost. Still another pricing strategy determines how much a firm must sell to break even and uses this amount as a reference point for adjusting price.

5 Demonstrate how the product life cycle, competition, distribution and promotion strategies, customer demands, the Internet and extranets, and perceptions of quality can affect price.

The price of a product normally changes as it moves through the life cycle and as demand for the product and competitive conditions change. Management often sets a high price at the introductory stage, and the high price tends to attract competition. The competition usually drives prices down, because individual competitors lower prices to gain market share.

Adequate distribution for a new product can sometimes be obtained by offering a larger-than-usual profit margin to wholesalers and retailers. The Internet enables consumers to compare products and prices quickly and efficiently. Extranets help to control costs and lower prices. Price is also used as a promotional tool to attract customers. Special low prices often attract new customers and entice existing customers to buy more. Demands of large customers can squeeze the profit margins of suppliers.

Perceptions of quality also can influence pricing strategies. A firm trying to project a prestigious image often charges a premium price for a product. Consumers tend to equate high prices with high quality.

6 Describe the procedure for setting the right price.

Setting the right price on a product is a process with four main steps: (1) establishing pricing goals; (2) estimating demand, costs and profits; (3) choosing a price policy to help determine a base price; and (4) fine-tuning the base price with pricing tactics.

A price strategy establishes a long-term pricing framework for a good or service. The three main types of price policies are price skimming, penetration pricing and status quo pricing. A price-skimming policy charges a high introductory price, often followed by a gradual reduction. Penetration pricing offers a low introductory price to capture a large market share and attain economies of scale. Finally, status quo pricing strives to match competitors' prices.

7 Identify the legal and ethical constraints on pricing decisions.

The *Trade Practices Act* helps to monitor four main areas of pricing: unfair trade practices, price fixing, predatory pricing and price discrimination.

8 Explain how discounts, geographic pricing and other special pricing tactics can be used to fine-tune the base price.

Several techniques enable marketing managers to adjust prices within a general range in response to changes in competition, government regulation, consumer demand, and promotional and positioning goals. Techniques for fine-tuning a price can be divided into three main categories: discounts, allowances, rebates and value pricing; geographic pricing; and special pricing tactics.

The first type of tactic gives lower prices to those that pay promptly, order a large quantity or perform some function for the manufacturer. Value-based pricing starts with the customer, considers the competition and costs, and then determines a price.

Geographic pricing tactics – such as FOB origin pricing, uniform delivered pricing, zone pricing, freight absorption pricing, and basing-point pricing – are ways of moderating the impact of shipping costs on distant customers.

A variety of special pricing tactics stimulate demand for certain products, increase store patronage, and offer more merchandise at specific prices.

Review it

1. The price charged on a product multiplied by the number of units sold is
   a. Profit
   b. Cost of goods sold
   c. Gross margin
   d. Revenue

2. Which of the following pricing objectives requires the least planning and is considered a passive policy?
   a. Profit-oriented
   b. Demand-oriented
   c. Sales-oriented
   d. Status quo

3. _____ occurs when total revenue increases in response to a decrease in price.
   a. Profit
   b. Unitary elasticity
   c. Inelastic demand
   d. Elastic demand

4. During which stage of the product life cycle do prices decline as competition intensifies and high-cost firms are eliminated?
   a. Introduction
   b. Growth
   c. Maturity
   d. Decline

Define it

average fixed cost (AFC) 397
average total cost (ATC) 397
average variable cost (AVC) 397
bait pricing 417
base price 414
basing-point pricing 416
break-even analysis 400
cash discount 414
cumulative quantity discount 414
demand 394
elastic demand 394
elasticity of demand 394
extranet 404
fixed cost 397
flexible pricing (variable pricing) 416
FOB origin pricing 415
freight absorption pricing 416
functional discount (trade discount) 414
inelastic demand 394
Internet 404
keystoning 398
leader pricing (loss-leader pricing) 417
marginal cost (MC) 397
marginal revenue (MR) 399
market share 393
mark-up pricing 398
non-cumulative quantity discount 414
odd–even pricing (psychological pricing) 418
penetration pricing 411
predatory pricing 414
prestige pricing 408
price 390
price bundling 418
price fixing 413
price skimming 411
price strategy 410
profit 391
profit maximisation 399
promotional allowance (trade allowance) 415
quantity discount 414
rebate 415
return on investment (ROI) 393
revenue 391
seasonal discount 415
status quo pricing 394
supply 396

two-part pricing 418
unbundling 418
Trade Practices Act 413
uniform delivered pricing 415
unitary elasticity 395
value-based pricing 415
variable costs 397
wireless link 404
zone pricing 416

5 The first step in setting the right price for a product is always to
   a Estimate demand, costs and profits
   b Fine-tune base prices with pricing tactics
   c Establish pricing goals
   d Choose a price strategy to help determine a base price

6 A price reduction offered in return for prompt payment of a bill is a
   a Quantity discount
   b Cash discount
   c Functional discount
   d Promotional allowance

7 A pricing tactic used by marketers to attract customers to a store by selling products near or below cost is called
   a Price bundling
   b Bait pricing
   c Leader pricing
   d Everyday low pricing (EDLP)

8 When many substitute products are available in the marketplace for customers, demand for an individual product in that category tends to be elastic.
   a True
   b False

Check the Answer Key to see how well you understood the material. More detailed discussion and writing questions and a video case related to this chapter are found in the Student Resources CD-ROM.

Apply it

1 Why is pricing so important to the marketing manager?

2 Explain the concepts of elastic and inelastic demand. Why should managers understand these concepts?

3 Your firm has based its pricing strictly on cost in the past. As the newly hired marketing manager, you believe this policy should change. Write the CEO a memo explaining your reasons.

4 Why is it important for managers to understand the concept of break-even points? Are there any drawbacks?

5 Divide the class into teams of five. Each team will be assigned a different grocery store from a different chain. (An independent is fine.) Appoint a group leader. The group leaders should meet as a group and pick 15 nationally branded grocery items. Each item should be specifically described as to brand name and size of the package. Each team will then proceed to its assigned store and collect price data on the 15 items. The team should also gather price data on 15 similar store brands and 15 generics, if possible. Each team should present its results to the class and discuss why there are price variations between stores, national brands, store brands and generics. As a next step, go back to your assigned store and share the overall results with the store manager. Bring back the manager's comments and share them with the class.

6   How does the stage of a product's life cycle affect price? Give some examples.

7   A manufacturer of office furniture decides to produce antique-style roll-top desks, but formatted for personal computers. The desks will have built-in surge protectors, a platform for raising or lowering the monitor, and a number of other features. The quality, solid-oak desks will be priced far below comparable products. The marketing manager says, 'We'll charge a low price and plan on a high volume to reduce our risks.' Comment.

8   Janet Oliver, owner of a mid-priced dress shop, notes: 'My pricing objectives are simple: I just charge what my competitors charge. I'm happy because I'm making money.' React to Janet's statement.

9   You are contemplating a price change for an established product sold by your firm. Write a memo analysing the factors you need to consider in your decision.

10 What is the difference between price policy and a price tactic? Give an example.

11 Develop a price line strategy for each of these firms:
    a a campus bookstore
    b a restaurant
    c a video-rental firm

12 You are contemplating a price change for an established product sold by your firm. Write a memo analysing the factors you need to consider in your decision.

13 How does technological change influence the nature of pricing?

14 What pricing strategy does Microsoft seem to be using for the software offered via the following Web page? www.microsoft.com/msdownload

15 What kind of pricing strategies are the following three telecommunication competitors offering?
    www.telstra.com.au
    www.optus.com.au
    www.aapt.com.au.

Try it

Scentwise is a small Australian distributor of a line of quality women's perfumes to intermediate- and high-priced department and speciality stores. It has recently decided to add a new lower-priced line to its product mix in order to capture a slightly different segment of the market. The new product is called 'Aussie Scent'. For an exercise, assume that a recent market test revealed the following estimated total demand for the product at the quoted prices.

Price ($)	Number of units
15.00	25 000
20.00	20 000
22.50	19 000
25.00	11 000
27.50	10 000

The accounting department figured that the average variable cost for the new perfume would be $13 per unit. Fixed costs are estimated at $40 000.

Questions

1. Assuming that the market research studies are accurate, what price should be charged for the perfume?
2. What kind of market research study could have been done to determine the demand schedule for the perfume? Assume that fixed costs are $140 000 rather than $40 000. Should the company have produced for the short run? For the long run?
3. Discuss the advantages and disadvantages of break-even analysis.
4. What is the break-even point for this perfume? Of what significance is that point?

Watch it

Toronto Blue Jays: Ballpark pricing

The opening pitch of 1999 marked the start of the Toronto Blue Jays' 23rd season in the American League for a 162-game schedule. In 1998, the Jays scored 88 wins against 74 losses and 1 tie, and brought in their first winning season since 1993. For home games, the Jays play in the world's most advanced retractable-roof stadium, with seating for 50 516. It is luxuriously called the Sky Dome, and the club invested US$5 million in it for preferred supplier status and a Sky Box.

With a winning record like this and a state-of-the-art ballpark, the Jays feel their tickets are great value because of the satisfaction fans can expect to receive from the ball game. Their pricing structure is based on the perceived value of a game, the entertainment, the love of baseball and the action – not just the money. Every season the Blue Jays have to balance two key economic factors when determining their ticket prices: the demand for seats by baseball fans and the skyrocketing costs of running a major league baseball club.

Despite this balancing act, the front office does not expect consumers to be really sensitive to fluctuations in price. This was particularly true of the 1999 season, when the fans were expected to turn out in great numbers in spite of rising ticket prices. This inelastic demand for Blue Jays tickets can be attributed in large part to the fact that the team played so well in 1998, but also to the fact that loyal Blue Jays fans could never stay away. They are simply willing to pay the price to support their team.

Another reason for the inelastic demand for Blue Jays tickets is that there is no locally available substitute. Sports fans can support any number of sports (baseball to tennis) or watch amateurs play; but for major league baseball in Toronto, the Blue Jays are the only game in town. The purchasing power of Torontonians is also an important factor in the inelastic demand for Blue Jays tickets. The Blue Jays front office provides a wide range of ticket options (preferred or general seating, a season's subscription or a single ticket), so that even if their prices were to increase, most residents in the Toronto area could still easily afford the same category of ticket, or a lower category ticket, and so would not miss a game.

For the Blue Jays, pricing strategies are not just a financial necessity; they are also a promotional tool used to increase fan attendance. At all Saturday home games and non-holiday weekday games, senior citizens and young people up to

14 years old can purchase tickets (except the most expensive ones) for half price. Season ticket holders receive special benefits: the same seats for every game, guaranteed tickets for post-season games played at home, a complimentary Toronto Blue Jays media guide and calendar, and the convenience of entering the Sky Dome on game day without having to wait in line at the ticket window.

Group ticket sales also receive special treatment: preferred seating; personal services from the group sales staff; and promotional posters, pocket schedules and stickers. These perks help persuade large groups (500 or more) to use a game as a social event, a fund-raiser, or a way to promote a business, a social group or a sports organisation.

Ticket sales provide a large portion of the Blue Jays' revenue, but merchandising is also responsible for a significant percentage. A wide selection of Blue Jays souvenirs and gifts is sold at the ballpark, at Blue Jays Bullpen Souvenir Stores and at finer department stores across Canada. In addition to these retail outlets, free catalogues are available by calling a toll-free number, and the complete line of Jays merchandise is available online from a wholly owned Jays subsidiary. Caps, jumpers and jackets, like those worn on the field by the players, and accessories, novelties and collectibles are all available for sale.

The Blue Jays merchandising machine uses a prestige pricing strategy; charging high prices to promote the Jays' high-quality image. Consumers are willing to pay a high price for official, authentic merchandise that has been approved by the Blue Jays and by Major League Baseball.

Inelastic ticket demand and the prestige pricing of merchandise are fuelled by the success of the team. Because the Toronto Blue Jays are a winning team, their loyal fans are willing to pay the price to see them play.

Questions

1. What considerations are included in the Jays' ticket pricing structure?
2. Why is demand for Blue Jays tickets inelastic?
3. How do the Jays use price as a promotional tool?
4. What pricing strategy is used for Blue Jays merchandise?

Suggested reading

Toronto Blue Jays website: www.bluejays.ca.

Click it

Online reading

INFOTRAC® COLLEGE EDITION

For additional readings and review on pricing concepts, explore InfoTrac® College Edition, your online library. Go to: www.infotrac-college.com and search for any of the InfoTrac key terms listed below:
- AVC (average variable cost)
- keystoning
- distribution strategy
- trade practices act

Answer key

1. *Answer*: d, p. 391 *Rationale*: Revenue is the key to profits for the organisation. It is calculated by multiplying the number of units sold by the price customers paid for the product.

2. *Answer*: d, p. 394 *Rationale*: Status quo pricing objectives are based on maintaining existing prices or meeting the prices of competitors.

3. *Answer*: d, p. 394 *Rationale*: Elasticity of demand is a concept that deals with consumers' sensitivity to price changes. Elastic demand means that total revenue increases when price decreases.

4. *Answer*: c, p. 402 *Rationale*: Maturity usually brings price declines, and later in the stage these declines are often not sufficient to stimulate additional demand.

5. *Answer*: c, p. 409 *Rationale*: The first step in setting prices is to establish pricing goals. Remember, pricing objectives fall into one of three categories: profit-oriented, sales-oriented, and status quo.

6. *Answer*: b, p. 414 *Rationale*: A cash discount is an incentive offered to customers for prompt payment, which helps the seller to save carrying charges and billing expenses.

7. *Answer*: c, p. 417 *Rationale*: This tactic lowers prices to levels at or below cost to encourage customers to visit a store with hope that the shoppers will buy other items once they are inside the store.

8. *Answer*: a, p. 395 *Rationale*: Availability of substitutes is a key factor that affects the elasticity of demand for any product.

Cross-functional connections SOLUTIONS

Questions

1 Why are the companies marketing communications of particular concern to research and development and manufacturing?

Marketers have a tendency to refer to product quality in their communications with potential customers. This product quality is also reflected in the pricing of the product. However, it is not the marketing department that has its hands on the development and production of the actual product. Usually, this is the job of the research and development and manufacturing groups who provide the physical product marketing presents to their customers. If a customer is dissatisfied with the product's quality, then it is typically the hands-on group who are blamed for the low-quality product. It is rare to hear of the marketing group being chastised for creating demand for a high-quality product when in reality it should have been creating demand for a low-quality product. Finance and accounting are concerned about margins for products. If marketing has priced a product low and/or spent large sums of money on marketing communications, a company's financial executives still expect to see profitable outcomes.

2 Why is it important to consider all elements of the marketing mix and the communications methods in the development of a communications program?

Marketing communication is about more than just promotion. All marketing activities of the firm communicate something to the customer. The price of a product, for example, gives customers information about the product's value and relative positioning against competitors. The same is true for the product's packaging and styling. Quite often, customers make judgements about a product's value from these visual cues. The distribution network chosen for the product also communicates something to the customer about relative positioning and value. Products that are only sold in exclusive outlets are perceived as quite different from those available in discount outlets, for example. It is important, therefore, that all these elements of the promotional mix be coordinated with the promotional plan in order to present a coherent and well-considered message to the potential customers.

3 Why should the marketing department work closely with areas such as finance, accounting and human resources?

One of the main benefits of these departments working closely together is the ability to facilitate cross-functional communications where all groups have access to the same information at the same time. This improves not only the speed but also the accuracy of information processing. The improved speed of communications can also advantage customers whose orders can be sent electronically and simultaneously to all departments that will perform activities in the order and will allow all involved to begin fulfilling necessary tasks to get the order out the door. In addition, close cooperation between these groups allows a greater understanding of the roles each performs and, further, allows better customer relations.

PART FOUR CLOSING
MARKETING PLAN

Integrating price and IMC into the marketing plan

Developing a marketing plan is one of the key tools used by marketers to ensure that their marketing strategy for a particular product that they provide to the market has a greater chance of success. A marketing plan has many sections. At the end of each of the five parts of this book you are asked to complete portions of the marketing plan according to the sections or topics that have been covered in that part. Don't be concerned about how the plan will come together until you have completed all five parts. In fact, the marketing plan won't look like a marketing plan until it is completed at the end of Part 5.

By now, you should have completed the activities for the marketing plan at the end of Parts 1, 2 and 3. If you are progressing through the text in this manner, you would already have addressed the idea of the consumer decision-making process, and investigated how organisations conduct research on the marketplace and how they segment the market such that specific markets can be targeted to make effective use of the organisational resources while maximising its principal objectives.

We have provided you with questions and worksheets on the Student Resources CD-ROM to assist your progression. Go there after you have completed the 'Activities' section.

Activities

Part 4 discussed the two remaining Ps from the 4Ps – namely, price and promotion. This part of the text investigated how organisations manage and integrate the various marketing activities to maximise their appeal to customers. In this part, we investigated how pricing and promotion can be used to influence the customer in the decision process to select one product over another.

As noted earlier, the marketing plan process isn't easy and does take time. In addressing the questions below, you will build up a marketing plan for the organisation for your selected product.

Once again, you should be able to provide further insight into the description of the organisation's current situation. You should also be able to address the issues of pricing and promotional aspects from the organisation's marketing mix. Below are some questions you should to be able to answer:

- What promotional effort is used by the organisation for your selected product?
- What is the organisation's promotional message?
- What media do they use to get the message across?
- What type of costs do you think the organisation incurs for the promotion it conducts? (You may need to contact a local media consultant or identify a standard rates list from the media outlets.)
- What types of promotional activities are used – for example, direct sales, public relations, mass advertising, and so on?
- What are the pricing strategies being adopted for the product you selected?
- Does the competition affect the pricing of your organisation's product? If so, how?
- What is the elasticity of demand for the product?
- What do you surmise to be the fixed and variable costs for the development and sale of the product?
- What pricing tactics are being adopted by the organisation for the product?
- What risk does the organisation experience in the development of the product?
- Is this a fixed or variable cost? How do organisations deal with the risk factors?

Part four closing
Marketing miscues

Marketing miscues

Advertising in foreign countries often leads to embarrassing situations for US multinational marketers. In a spot that ran briefly on Peruvian television, Africans are seen getting ready to devour some white tourists until they are appeased by Nabisco's Royal Pudding.

Nabisco initially responded that although the commercial was 'inconsistent' with company values, the Peruvian audience saw it as 'a fantasy situation that was humorous in nature, and effectively communicated people's preference for Royal Desserts over all else'.

After realising that its explanation of local taste tests as justification for a racially insensitive ad was, to say the least, weak, Nabisco quickly moved to consolidate control of its international advertising under Foote, Cone & Belding in New York in an effort to keep ad campaigns more uniform. Ann Smith, Nabisco's director of marketing and communications, stated that the company wanted to 'ensure that the quality of our ads meets the standards we set for our brands'. The spot, she adds, was 'a mistake'.

In a separate but similar incident, a sketch on a popular Peruvian television show featured a Michael Jackson character complaining that his 'son', played with a black face and having a tail, looks 'too black', prompting him to beg a doctor to bleach the boy's skin and cut off his tail. The show was sponsored by such major corporations as Chesebrough-Pond's, Proctor & Gamble, PepsiCo and Quaker Oats. To add to the insult, the characters of the popular show are featured in a commercial for Goodyear Tyre & Rubber Co. shuffling around and stating that 'Goodyear tyres are as strong as a black man's lips'. Goodyear quickly pulled the ad after its US executives saw it and fired the Lima, Peru, agency that produced the tyre ad. It also promptly issued an unsolicited apology to the NAACP even though the ad ran only in Peru for one week. Although the company determined it would be impractical to impose central review of all international advertising from its US base, as Nabisco did, it stepped up sensitivity training for local managers and suppliers around the world.

Like a number of multinational companies, Nabisco and Goodyear were forced to address concerns about how to adapt sales pitches to foreign markets without violating domestic sensibilities. Such situations shed light not only on how far some ad agencies will go to create striking messages but also on how a lack of internal controls at agencies can cause problems. Because local units of international ad agencies aren't typically required to consult with parent companies when creating ads for domestic audiences, racially insensitive or otherwise controversial ads, such as those for Nabisco's Royal Pudding and Goodyear tyres, sometimes slip through.

Questions

1. What steps can a multinational company take, in addition to issuing ad guidelines, to ensure that embarrassing promotional situations like those discussed don't occur?

2. Assume that you are the international advertising manager for a large consumer products company. Write a brief list of ad standards pertaining to creative and media selection to which your foreign ad agencies would be required to adhere.

Sources: '1997: Ad Follies', *Advertising Age*, 22 December 1997, p. 14; 'Tire Maker's Racist TV Ad Causes International Blowout', *Michigan Chronicle*, 22 December 1997, p. 6-A; Pichayaporn Utumporn, 'Ad with Hitler Causes a Furor in Thailand', *Wall Street Journal*, 5 June 1998, p. B8; Leon E. Wynter, 'Global Marketers Learn to Say No to Bad Ads', *Wall Street Journal*, 1 April 1998, p. B1.

© 2003 Nelson Australia Pty Limited

Part four closing
Proactive pricing

Proactive pricing

Pricing is one of the most complex and yet most important marketing mix decisions that a firm can make. Firms that approach pricing decisions proactively are in a better position to avoid any surprises or problems. Proactive pricing requires firms to consider the effects of pricing decisions on the value perceptions of buyers. This means that they must understand how pricing works. What will happen to customers if prices are raised or lowered? What will competitors do? How will shareholders react, and so on? Pricing has complex impacts on a range of interested parties in a firm – customers, suppliers, salespeople, distributors, competitors and shareholders. Unfortunately, most managers don't have accurate information on the degree to which pricing changes will affect these groups and, ultimately, sales.

In addition, it is important for marketers also to understand that consumers' responses to price changes involve perceptions of value, product quality, branding and comparison of alternative choices. Most buyers don't have complete information about alternative choices, and most are not capable of perfectly processing the available information to arrive at their 'best choice'. Price setters must therefore have a detailed understanding of their buyers' perceptions of pricing information and the factors that impact on those perceptions. Once the buyers' perceptions have been analysed, it is also important to understand price elasticity. This refers to the amount of change in demand for a product or service that corresponds to a specific change in price. For example, an elasticity of '-2' would mean that if you increased the price by 1 per cent, then sales (demand) would decrease by 2 per cent and the same would apply for a reverse situation. Research into price elasticity has found that the reactions to price changes are greater for small brands than for large brands.

Reactions to prices (elasticity) were also greater when prices were increased than when they were decreased. This means that prices increases would result in a more negative reaction by buyers than the same degree of price decrease. Finally, price reactions were greater where there was more intense competition between alternative products. While it may be difficult to determine the exact effect of price changes, these results have been supported over time in a number of different countries and may offer marketing managers some starting points for pricing decisions.

In summary, then, proactive pricing requires that firms have a designated pricing strategy (as opposed to pricing tactics – raising or lowering prices), which considers the overall business strategy (where the firm is heading), the benefits offered by the product/service, and the relative value of the product/service to buyers. In addition, it requires that pricing tactics – timing, and the degree and direction of price changes – also be considered in line with these other elements. Successful pricing requires accurate and timely information about customers, competitors, costs and the firm's objectives. Most importantly, marketers need to know how pricing works and how customers perceive prices.

Part four closing
Marketing plan

Questions

1. Why do you think companies don't adopt this concept of proactive pricing?

2. How might an understanding of price elasticity assist a marketer in determining pricing tactics?

3. Why is it important for marketers to consider the organisational objectives when making strategic pricing decisions?

Sources: Adapted from K. Munroe, 'Price Proactive for Best Results', *B&T Marketing and Media*, 4 May 2001; J. Dawes, 'How Will a Price Change Affect Your Sales?' *B&T Marketing and Media*, 27 October 2000.

Suggested activities

Go to the pricing game website at www.olin.wustl.edu/faculty/pazgal/prc_game.htm and take the challenge with a group of fellow students to see who can make the most money from their bistro using the pricing principles outlined both in this case and in Chapter 11.

Suggested reading

A. Ehrenberg and L. England, 'Generalising a Pricing Effect', *Journal of Industrial Economics*, vol. 39, September 1990, pp. 47–68.

J. Scriven and A. Ehrenberg, 'Patterns of Response to Price Changes', Australian and New Zealand Marketing Conference, Sydney, 29 November–1 December 1999.

THE WORLD OF MARKETING

Other factors that influence customers and the organisation's marketing efforts

PART FIVE

Global marketing	Chapter 12
Marketing strategy	Chapter 13

Cross-functional connections

Johnasen, Browne & Cooper-Smith – Architects

Background: The key personalities and culture

Johnasen, Browne & Cooper-Smith is a small architectural practice based in the inner Brisbane suburb of Paddington. The firm was originally a sole practice operated by Brien Johnasen who has an enviable reputation for authentic conservation and heritage restoration architectural services. In fact, Johnasen has been a perennial winner of architectural awards for the restoration of many inner-city Brisbane buildings that had originally been constructed using convict labour. It was these particular projects that led Johnasen to form a strategic alliance in 1985 with Russell Browne, another highly reputed conservation architect who was based in Sydney.

Like Johnasen, Browne was a sole practitioner and he had accumulated a substantial body of expertise in the restoration of early settlement buildings. Browne was also a regular guest lecturer in conservation architecture at several universities in Sydney, Brisbane, Melbourne and Hobart. Although they formalised their alliance by naming their respective practices Johnasen Browne Architects (in Brisbane) and Browne Johnasen Architects (in Sydney), the day-to-day operations continued as sole practices with part-time and contract staff introduced as work was available.

One contract architect became a regular over a five-year period and in 1988 Johnasen offered Paul Cooper-Smith a 10 per cent shareholding in his practice as an acknowledgement of Cooper-Smith's loyalty and forbearance when work was erratic. It was also an acknowledgement by Johnasen that he needed to expand the practice to capitalise on additional expertise and to share some of the increasingly time-consuming management tasks. An additional bonus was the perception of a more significantly sized practice created by the new name Johnasen, Browne & Cooper-Smith – Architects.

Cooper-Smith brought to the practice an added dimension of architectural services. Although he was highly inspired by conservation and heritage architecture, he was also a keen supporter of 'sympathetic infill' architecture. This involved the design and building of new 'sympathetic' buildings between existing heritage buildings and was a lucrative market for the small practice because most clients for infill buildings were committed to unobtrusive buildings with elegant, period-based interiors. This led to a further strategic alliance with Carole Baker-Herbert, a recently graduated architect.

Baker-Herbert is from an old establishment family in Brisbane and had developed a passion for heritage interior design. There was little that she didn't know about historical interiors – the colour schemes, artefacts, drapes and floor coverings. It was a passion and she spent many late nights sewing the intricate fabrics and designs that she then personally installed in clients' buildings. On weekends, Baker-Herbert would most likely be found browsing through antique and bric-a-brac shops looking for that special artefact or painting that would complete a client's room.

The established management and marketing practices

Although they worked on independent projects, with their own 'informal' teams, both Johnasen and Cooper-Smith endeavoured to ensure that they maintained their individual billable weekly hours at 30–40 hours, thereby ensuring that the amount of time available for effective practice management was always desperately short. Despite this, they both had thoroughly autocratic approaches to management.

PART FIVE

Every item of correspondence was scrutinised by both before it went into the postal system, every tender document and quotation had to be endorsed by both, and every client invoice was examined. Their part-time office administrator was always trying to secure their assistance and attention to overdue items. This caused substantial delays, one of the most troublesome of which was that clients often weren't invoiced for work until 60 or 90 days had elapsed. Most clients would then take an additional 60 to 90 days before any approach was made to humbly ask for payment. (Johnasen and Cooper-Smith considered it unprofessional to ask clients for money.) It was only when the bank threatened to dishonour payments because their overdraft was in excess of approved limits that the two partners would follow up with clients. The perpetual cash flow difficulties experienced by the practice also affected the available options for staffing, equipment and marketing.

Virtually all projects secured by the practice resulted from either government-funded conservation projects or by word of mouth from previous clients. This resulted in considerable peaks and troughs in the workflows. When a government-funded project was secured, it frequently meant that progress payments were taken up with reducing their bank overdraft to give them liquidity to employ part-time and casual expertise.

The only advertising and promotion that occurred was a small and unpretentious sign on the front of each project while construction was under way, and the occasional press article in the Sunday newspaper or other media coverage of architectural awards. No promotion materials existed with the exception of a benign photo album that contained a motley collection of project photographs and some press clippings relating to awards that Johnasen had won. Neither Johnasen nor Cooper-Smith had business cards, and whenever a potential client asked for one, they would hand-prepare a card using their best architectural printing and proudly pass it over – almost a piece of historical art in its own right.

Cooper-Smith had just completed a small interior refit for a client who ran a public relations consultancy and who was in a similar position in terms of embarrassed cash flow. After discussion with Johnasen, they decided to accept a proposal from the client for a contra deal, whereby they would work out the fee by conducting a public relations SWOT analysis on Johnasen, Browne and Cooper-Smith. This was to result in some brochures, a letterhead, stationery, business cards and a proposal to manage their public relations activities.

After Cooper-Smith accepted his minority shareholding in the practice, he progressively developed spreadsheet programs on his computer to upgrade the manual office procedures that had been used. This included a hybrid accounts system and a database of historical information relevant to each new project. He also started preparing his proposals and tender documents on a word processor. When the part-time office administrator began to encounter frustrations with not being able to get access to much of the information that Cooper-Smith had on his computer, he convinced Johnasen that it was time for the practice to make a transition from manual to electronic records and processing.

Unfortunately, Johnasen wasn't computer-literate and he passively resisted using the computer that was purchased for his use. Johnasen also found it difficult to follow and use Cooper-Smith's hybrid systems and he progressively became more alienated from the financial information relating to the practice management. He was also feeling that things were getting out of control and took to reading current management books and attending Royal Australian Institute of Architects practice management seminars and discussions. On a flight to Sydney for a meeting with Browne, Johnasen started a SWOT

Cross-functional connections

analysis of the practice. He was very perturbed by the number of weaknesses and threats that he had listed down and concluded that he needed to get some outside assistance in order to deal with the dilemma the practice was facing.

Upgrading the administrative and management systems

A client of Johnasen had used a general management consultant to carry out an evaluation of the administrative and management systems and to restructure their company. Johnasen was very impressed by what he heard, and after discussing the issue with Cooper-Smith he arranged a meeting with the consultant.

After they accepted a proposal from the consultant, steady progress was made with evaluating the existing systems and processes. This was despite passive resistance from Cooper-Smith, who appeared to believe that most of the proposed changes had already been put in place but hadn't been effective because Johnasen was resistant to change and refused to familiarise himself with the computerised systems Cooper-Smith had developed and installed. Underlying this resistance was concern about a discussion with Johnasen about the soon-to-expire lease on their office premises. Cooper-Smith had expressed an opinion that they should merge with another practice to become a heritage and conservation division of that practice and move into more modern inner-city premises. This would modernise the image of what they did and allow them to capitalise on other architectural work when heritage and conservation projects weren't available. Johnasen was furious about the suggestion and reminded Cooper-Smith that it was 'his' practice and that he hadn't worked for so many years to see it dissolved.

The underlying tensions between the two partners, together with the failure of a major client to continue with the second phase of a project, resulted in the consultant being asked to scale back her involvement. The consultant decided to cease operating with the partners and made the following recommendations to them:

- They needed to free up time to work on their business. The suggested way to achieve this was for both partners to allocate an initial eight hours each per week and for their hourly fees to be increased to cover this time. (The hourly charge-out rates were below those recommended by the Royal Australian Institute of Architects.)
- Immediate attention had to be given to reducing outstanding debtors to the practice, and future invoicing had to be done every month and follow-up for payments done after 30 days.
- Decisions had to be made about the services mix that the practice was going to offer, and appropriate management structures and marketing strategies put in place to pursue the delivery of those services.
- To alleviate the strains that were developing between Johnasen and Cooper-Smith, consideration should be given to offering associate partnerships to two existing staff members – one of whom was Carole Baker-Herbert. Much of the day-to-day management activities should be carried out by the associates so as to leave quality time available for Johnasen and Cooper-Smith to concentrate on the strategic and marketing activities that needed to be addressed.

Both partners undertook to commit to implementing the consultant's recommendations.

Potential market opportunities

Johnasen, Browne and Cooper-Smith have identified three potential markets they need to consider to determine their services mix:

1. Remain small and rely on the status quo. Because the practice has been established on heritage and conservation architectural services, this is the specialist niche market that differentiates Johnasen, Browne

Part Five

and Cooper-Smith from most other architectural practices. Johnasen was recently a member of a committee advising the relevant minister on the drafting of heritage conservation legislation which is to be introduced into the Queensland Parliament. He was invited on to the committee because of his extensive expertise, and while this is a complimentary acknowledgement, it also introduces a possible conflict of interest given the dependency of Johnasen, Browne and Cooper-Smith on government-funded heritage conservation projects. It is widely speculated in the profession that the pending legislation will introduce substantial restrictions on the renovation and restoration of heritage-listed buildings. Because there are only a small number of architects who have the expertise to be engaged for work in this highly specialised area, there has been disquiet that Johnasen, Browne and Cooper-Smith are likely to benefit substantially from the proposed legislation.

2. Merge with a larger practice and become a specialist division. Pursuing a niche market is a major inhibitor because potential clients perceive Johnasen, Browne and Cooper-Smith as providing only heritage and conservation services. There is considerable potential to increase the 'sympathetic infill' services, and other compatible services such as specialised heritage replication residential and commercial projects. However, the erratic project work and cash flow that Johnasen, Browne and Cooper-Smith experiences severely limit its capacity to undertake an increased number of projects – especially those projects that require an increase in and a different mix of professional skills. A potential solution is to merge with another small practice that has complementary services and capabilities. This would enable the heritage and conservation services to be provided under a division within a larger practice rather than being the sole emphasis for the entire practice.

3. Explore opportunities for work in Southeast Asia. Browne has just returned from a spiritual pilgrimage to Thailand where he spent three weeks at a number of Buddhist temples. He has returned very excited by news that substantial opportunities will soon become available because of a planned long-term restoration of three temples. The monks were very interested in his professional knowledge and the work that he, Johnasen and Cooper-Smith have done. Browne has been invited, initially, to act as a project adviser and to be considered as the project architect.[1]

Questions for discussion

1. If you were the partners of Johnasen, Browne and Cooper-Smith, what market segments would you focus on? Why?
2. Why are costs so important to Johnasen, Browne and Cooper-Smith in developing a pricing strategy?
3. Why is the implementation of a marketing plan so important for Johnasen, Browne and Cooper-Smith?
4. How should Johnasen, Browne and Cooper-Smith communicate and promote the services that they offer?
5. If the activities in Southeast Asia become a reality, how would this affect the service offering provided by Johnasen, Browne and Cooper-Smith?

Source: Department of Human Resource Management and Employment Relations, Faculty of Business, University of Southern Queensland.

Global marketing

CHAPTER TWELVE

LEARNING OBJECTIVES

After studying this chapter, you should be able to

1 Discuss the importance of global marketing
2 Describe the external environment facing global marketers
3 List the basic elements involved in developing a global marketing mix
4 Discuss the challenges of expanding retailing operations into global markets
5 Consider how e-marketing is affecting global marketing

One of the many strategic decisions that an organisation will make is whether to compete internationally. Today, global revolutions are under way in many areas of our lives: management, politics, communications and technology. The word 'global' has assumed a new meaning, referring to a boundless mobility and competition in social, business and intellectual arenas. We discuss some of the reasons for this expanded access and the removal of barriers to global trade. For many organisations, however, **global marketing** (marketing to target markets worldwide) is not an option; rather, it is a business imperative.

A company should consider entering the global marketplace only after its management has a solid grasp of the global environment. Some relevant questions are: 'What are our options in selling abroad?', 'How difficult is global marketing?' and 'What are the potential risks and returns?' Concrete answers to these questions would probably encourage many firms not selling overseas to venture into the international arena. Foreign sales could be an important source of profits.

Companies decide to 'go global' for many reasons. Perhaps the most stimulating reason is to earn more profits. Managers may feel that international sales will result in higher profit margins or more added-on profits. A second

global marketing
Marketing that targets markets throughout the world.

stimulus is that a firm may have a unique product or technological advantage not available to other international competitors. Such advantages should result in major business successes abroad. In other situations, management may have exclusive market information about foreign customers, marketplaces or market situations not known to others. Although exclusivity can provide an initial incentive for international marketing, managers must realise that competitors can be expected to catch up with the information advantage of the firm. Finally, saturated domestic markets, excess capacity and potential for economies of scale can also be motivators to 'go global'. Economies of scale mean that average per-unit production costs fall as output is increased. These issues and strategic decisions faced by organisations considering entering the international marketplace are discussed next.

In this chapter, we explore the benefits and importance of international and global marketing, the external environments impact on global marketing, the challenges in developing the 4Ps for global markets and lastly the impact of the electronic environment on global marketing.

Benefits of global marketing

1 Discuss the importance of global marketing

global vision
Recognising and reacting to international marketing opportunities, being aware of threats from foreign competitors in all markets, and effectively using international distribution networks.

Metal Storm on-line

Go to the Metal Storm website and read about its latest market success, the new counter-terrorist technology of an access denial weapon. This is a great example of a company reacting to its environments and taking advantage of marketing opportunities quickly.
www.metalstorm.com

Managers must develop a **global vision**, not only to recognise and react to international marketing opportunities but also to remain competitive at home. Often an organisation's toughest domestic competition comes from foreign companies. Moreover, a global vision enables a manager to understand that customer and distribution networks operate worldwide, blurring geographic and political barriers and making them increasingly irrelevant to business decisions. Having a global vision means recognising and reacting to international marketing opportunities, being aware of threats from foreign competitors in all markets, and effectively using international distribution networks.

Over the past 25 years, world trade has climbed from US$200 billion a year to US$7.3 trillion. From the 1990 to the 21st century, the trade grew at 4.5 per cent and most recently at 14 per cent. Countries and companies that were never considered major players in global marketing are important, some of them showing great skill. Today, marketers face many challenges to their customary practices. Product development costs are rising, the life of products is becoming shorter, and new technology is spreading around the world faster than ever. But marketing winners relish the pace of change rather than fearing it.

A young company with a global vision that has capitalised on new technology is Brisbane-based Metal Storm Ltd. This Australian weapons technology company has offices in Washington DC in the United States. The company is attracting unprecedented attention from defence organisations around the world with its revolutionary 100 per cent electronic ballistics technology, which has no known conventional equivalent. Metal Storm's main international market is the United States, with over $50 million in exports to that country in 2001.[2] Adopting a global vision can be very lucrative for an organisation when it gets all the decisions correct, but as we will see later in this section, some disastrous mistakes have been made, even by large multinational companies.

Importance of global marketing

Australia and New Zealand, like many countries, depend on international commerce for ongoing trade revenue and commercial returns. For example, France, the United Kingdom and Germany all derive more than 19 per cent of their gross domestic product (GDP) from world trade, while the United States derives about 12 per cent. Australia and New Zealand derive 16.7 per cent and 33 per cent, respectively, of GDP.[3] (This has recently been converted to GDE, a chain volume series developed in Australia and New Zealand.) These figures support the fact that the impact of international business on many countries' economies is important and generally exports for Australia and New Zealand have increased annually.

The major trading partners for both countries Australia and New Zealand are shown in Exhibits 12.1 and 12.2. Both countries have a majority of their international trade in raw materials, food and live animals, representing for Australia a total of $115.5 billion and for New Zealand $24.5 billion.[4] With this reliance on international trade, it is easy to see why global marketing would be a major strategic decision for these countries and their associated organisations.

Exhibit 12.1
New Zealand exports by destination

Rank	Code (2)	Destination Name	2004 $ (million)	2005 P $ (million)	% Change
1	AU	Australia	6 262	6 528	4.2
2	US	United States of America	4 046	4 530	12.0
3	JP	Japan	3 151	3 457	9.7
4	CN	People's Republic of China	1 486	1 651	11.1
5	GB	United Kingdom	1 413	1 480	4.8
	99	**All merchandise exports**	**28 797**	**31 195**	**8.3**

12 months ended April

(1) Statistics are compiled according to the New Zealand Standard Classification of Countries 1999.

Symbol: P provisional (Statistics for the latest three months are provisional)

Source: Statistics New Zealand.

Exhibit 12.2
Australia's exports by country and country group

	Exports 2002-03 $m	Exports 2003-04 $m	Imports 2002-03 $m	Imports 2003-04 $m	Balance of trade 2003-04 $m
China (excl. SARs & Taiwan Prov.)	8 803	9 912	13 789	15 339	-5 427
Japan	21 727	19 798	16 337	16 101	3 697
New Zealand	8 127	8 080	5 019	5 056	3 024
United Kingdom	7 234	5 132	5 769	5 430	-298
Untied States of America	10 365	9 453	22 494	19 945	-10 492

Source: International trade in goods and services, Australia (5368.0)

External environment facing global marketers

2 Describe the external environment facing global marketers

A global marketer or a firm considering global marketing may have to deal with many issues often caused by the external environment, and many of the same environmental factors that operate in the domestic market also exist internationally. These factors include culture, economic and technological development, political structure, demographic makeup and natural resources. We will examine them in turn.

Culture

Central to any society is the common set of values shared by its citizens that establish what is socially acceptable. Culture underlies the family, the educational system, religion and the social class system. The network of social organisations generates overlapping roles and status positions. These values and roles have a tremendous effect on people's preferences and thus on marketers' options. Inca Kola, a fruity, greenish-yellow carbonated drink, is the largest-selling soft drink in Peru. Despite being compared to 'liquid bubble gum', the drink has become a symbol of national pride and heritage. The drink was invented in Peru and contains only fruit indigenous to the country. A local consumer of about a six-pack per day says, 'I drink Inca Kola because it makes me feel like a Peruvian.' He tells his young daughter, 'This is our drink, not something invented overseas. It is named for your ancestors, the great Inca warriors.'[5]

Culture may influence product preferences as in the Inca Kola story, or influence the marketing mix in other ways. Culture also influences perception and, often, knowing what not to do is as important as knowing what to do. For example, in India it is considered a violation of sacred hospitality to discuss business in the home or on a social occasion. Similarly, when a person from India offers to 'visit at any time', it is an honest invitation to visit at a time suitable to the guest and not just a polite expression, as we might use it. Failure to understand the meanings of these customs have led to some serious misunderstandings between people of different cultures.

Gift giving can also create problems. Sometimes gifts are expected and the failure to supply them is seen as insulting. At other times, however, the mere offer of such a token is considered offensive. In the Middle East, for example, hosts are insulted if guests bring food and drink to their homes, as they believe this implies that they are poor hosts. This isn't the case in Australia and New Zealand, where an international visitor who is asked to 'bring a plate' to a party may interpret this to mean that their host doesn't have enough crockery. In parts of Latin America, cutlery or handkerchiefs should not be given as gifts, as they imply cutting off the friendship, and giving clocks to a Chinese person is seen as offensive.[6]

Even packaging plays a major role in marketing decisions in international markets. In many parts of Asia, the way a gift is presented is as important as the gift itself. For example, in Japan a small present of charcoal, purchased at a Japanese department store, to be put in the bath to improve the skin, comes in an elaborate package. The charcoal with a sticker affixed is placed in a cup, which is placed in a cloth bag that is tied and then enveloped in shredded paper. The shredded paper is then nestled in a small wicker basket. The basket is encased in plastic and then tied with string. A note then explains that the whole package should be wrapped in gift paper, secured with another sticker and a bow, and then placed in a shopping bag. All together, 10 layers of packaging.

Language is another important aspect of culture. Marketers must take care when translating product names and instructions, slogans and promotional messages not to convey the wrong meaning. For example, Mitsubishi Motors had to rename its Pajero model in Spanish-speaking countries because the term describes a sexual activity. Toyota Motors' MR2 model dropped the number 2 in France because the combination sounds like a French swearword.[7] The literal translation of Coca-Cola in Chinese characters means 'Bite the wax tadpole'.

Each country has its own customs and traditions that determine business practices and influence negotiations with foreign customers. In many countries, personal relationships are more important than financial considerations. For instance, skipping social engagements in Mexico may lead to lost sales. Negotiations in Japan often include long evenings of dining, drinking and entertaining, and only after a close personal relationship has been formed do business negotiations begin. The Japanese go through an elaborate ritual when exchanging business cards. An American businesswoman had no idea about this important cultural tradition. She came into a meeting and tossed some of her business cards across the table at a group of stunned Japanese executives. One of them turned his back on her and walked out. The deal didn't go through.[8]

Here a Western businessman accepts a business card from an Asian businesswoman with both hands, in the Asian tradition.

An area where businesspeople often find it difficult to know what is right in different cultures is the notion of time. There are no overriding rights or wrongs about a particular pace of life. They are simply different. Not understanding a culture's notion of time can sometimes lead to situations that are awkward and embarrassing, or, in extreme cases, to a loss of business. Exhibit 12.3 offers six lessons for global marketers about cultural differences regarding the concept of time.

Exhibit 12.3
Six lessons about the cultural notion of time

Lesson 1: Be punctual.

Learn to translate appointment times. What is the appropriate time to arrive for an appointment with a professor? With a government official? For a party? When should you expect others to show up, if at all? Should we expect our hosts to be upset of we arrive late – or promptly? Are people expected to assume responsibility for their lateness?

Lesson 2: Understand the line between work time and social time.

What is the relationship between work time and down time? Some questions have easy answers: How many hours are there in the working day? Other questions are more difficult to answer. For example, how much of the working day is spent on-task and how much time is spent socialising, chatting and being pleasant? For Australians in a big city, the typical ratio is in the neighbourhood of about 80:20; about 80 per cent of work time is spent on-task and about 20 per cent is used for fraternising, chitchatting and the like. But many countries deviate sharply from this formula. In countries such as India and Nepal, for example, be prepared for a balance closer to 50:50. When you are in Japan, the distinction between work and social time can often be meaningless.

Lesson 3: Study the rules of the waiting game.

When you arrive in a foreign culture, be sure to ask about the specifics of the version of the waiting game. Are their rules based on the principle that time is money? Who is expected to wait for whom, under what circumstances and for how long? Are some players exempt from waiting?

Lesson 4: Learn to reinterpret 'doing nothing'.

How do your hosts treat pauses, silences or doing nothing at all? Is appearing chronically busy a quality to be admired or pitied? Is doing nothing a waste of time? Is constant activity seen as an even bigger waste of time? What must it be like to live in a country such as Brunei, where people start their day by asking: What isn't going to happen today?

Lesson 5: Ask about accepted sequences.

Be prepared for what time frames to expect. Each culture sets rules about the sequence of events. Is it work before play or vice versa? Do people take all of their sleep at night or is there a siesta in the mid-afternoon?

Lesson 6: Are people on clock time or event time?

This may be the most slippery lesson of all. A move from clock time to event time requires a complete shift of consciousness. It entails the suspension of industrialised society's temporal golden rule: time is money.

Source: From 'Robert Levine, 'Re-learning to Tell Time', *American Demographics*, January 1998. Reprinted with permission from *American Demographics* magazine. © 1998 PRIMEDIA Intertec, Stamford, CT.

Fortunately, some habits and customs seem to be the same throughout much of the world. A study of 37 743 consumers from 40 different countries found that 95 per cent brushed their teeth daily.[9] Other activities that majorities worldwide engage in include reading a newspaper, listening to the radio, taking a shower and washing their hair.

Economic and technological development

A second major factor in the external environment facing the global marketer is the level of economic development in the countries where it operates. In general, complex and sophisticated industries are found in developed countries, and more basic industries are found in less developed nations. Higher average family incomes are found in the more developed countries than in the less developed markets. Larger incomes mean greater purchasing power and demand not only for consumer goods and services but also for the machinery and workers required to produce consumer goods.

To appreciate marketing opportunities (or the lack of them), it helps to examine the five stages of economic growth and technological development: traditional society, pre-industrial society, takeoff economy, industrialising society, and fully industrialised society.

The traditional society

Countries in the traditional stage are in the earliest phase of development. A traditional society is largely agricultural, with a social structure and value system that provide little opportunity for upward mobility. The culture may be highly stable, and economic growth may not get started without a powerful, disruptive force. Therefore, to introduce single units of technology into such a country is probably wasted effort. In Ghana, for instance, a tollway 25 kilometres long and six lanes wide, intended to modernise distribution, does not connect to any city or village or other road.

The pre-industrial society

The second stage of economic development, the pre-industrial society, involves economic and social change and the emergence of a middle class with an entrepreneurial spirit. Nationalism may begin to rise, along with restrictions on multinational organisations. Countries such as Madagascar and Uganda are in this stage. Effective marketing in these countries is very difficult because they lack the modern distribution and communication systems that Western marketers often take for granted. Peru, for example, did not establish a television network until 1975.

The takeoff economy

The takeoff economy is the period of transition from a developing to a developed nation. New industries arise and a generally healthy social and political climate emerges. Kenya and Vietnam have entered the takeoff stage. Although politics in Kenya are not considered particularly healthy, there are significant areas of economic growth. Oil exploration is increasing and Kenya is set to become the world's largest exporter of tea.[10] In an effort to develop its economy, Vietnam offers large tax breaks to foreign investors who promise jobs. Gold Medal Footwear, which has its headquarters in Taiwan, employs 500 young workers in Danang and hopes to raise the number to 2500.

The industrialising society

The fourth phase of economic development is the industrialising society. During this era, technology spreads from sectors of the economy that powered the takeoff to the rest of the nation. Mexico, China, India and Brazil are among the nations in this phase of development. Countries in the industrialising stage start to produce capital goods and consumer durable products. These industries also foster economic growth. As a result, a large middle class begins to emerge, and the demand for luxuries and services grows.

One of the fastest growing economies in the world today (about 10 per cent per year) is China. This has resulted in per capita incomes quadrupling in only the last decade and a half.[11] A population of 1.2 billion is producing a GDP of over US$1.2 trillion a year. This new industrial giant will be the world's largest manufacturing zone, the largest market for such key industries as telecommunications and aerospace, and one of the largest users of capital.

Rapidly growing large markets such as China create enormous opportunities for Western global marketers. One tempting market, for example, is the 21 million babies born in China each year. One-child families are the rule, so parents spare few expenses in bringing up their baby. The Walt Disney Company is in department stores in a dozen or so Chinese cities with the Disney Babies line of T-shirts, rattles and crib linens – all emblazoned with likenesses of baby Mickey Mouse and other characters.

The fully industrialised society

The fully industrialised society, the fifth stage of economic development, is an exporter of manufactured products, many of which are based on advanced technology. Examples include cars, computers, aircraft, oil exploration equipment and telecommunications gear. Britain, Japan, Germany, France, Canada, Australia, New Zealand, Singapore, Taiwan and the United States fall into this category.

The wealth of the industrialised nations creates tremendous market potential. Therefore, industrialised countries trade extensively. Also, industrialised nations usually ship manufactured goods to developing countries in exchange for raw materials such as petroleum, precious metals and bauxite.

Political structure

Political structure is a third important variable facing global marketers. Government policies run the gamut from no private ownership and minimal individual freedom to little central government and maximum personal freedom. As rights of private property increase, government-owned industries and centralised planning tend to decrease. But rarely will a political environment be at one extreme or the other. India, for instance, is a republic with elements of socialism, monopoly capitalism and competitive capitalism in its political ideology.

Many countries are changing from a centrally planned economy to a market-oriented one. Eastern European nations such as Hungary and Poland have also been moving quickly with market reforms. Many reforms have increased foreign trade and investment. For example, in Poland, foreigners are now allowed to invest in all areas of industry, including agriculture, manufacturing and trade. Poland even gives companies that invest in certain sectors some tax advantages.

Changes leading to market-oriented economies are not restricted to Eastern Europe and Russia. Many countries in Latin America are also trying market reforms. Countries such as Brazil and Mexico are reducing government control over many sectors of the economy. They are also selling state-owned companies to foreign and domestic investors and removing trade barriers that have protected their markets against foreign competition. Brazil has now overtaken Italy and Mexico to become the 10th-largest car manufacturer in the world. India has recently opened up its market of 900 million consumers. While India's per capita average annual income is quite low (US$330), an estimated 250 million-plus Indians have enough income to be considered middle class.[12]

Another trend in the political environment is the growth of nationalist sentiments among citizens who have strong loyalties and devotion to their country. Failure to appreciate emerging nationalist feelings can create major problems for multinational firms. In 1995, Hindus in India smashed Pepsi bottles and burned Pepsi posters. And the country's first Kentucky Fried Chicken, in Bangalore, was targeted by protesters claiming to defend Indian culture against Western encroachment.

Another potential cloud on the horizon for some types of companies doing business abroad is the threat of nationalisation. Some countries have nationalised (taken ownership of) certain industries or companies, such as airlines in Italy and Bull Computer in France, to infuse more capital into their development. Industries are also nationalised to allow domestic corporations to sell vital goods below cost. For example, for many years France has been supplying coal to users at a loss.

Legal considerations

Closely related to and often intertwined with the political environment are legal considerations. Nationalistic sentiments of the French led to a 1996 law that requires pop music stations to play at least 40 per cent of their songs in French. (French teenagers love American and English rock and roll.[13]) Christian Bellanger, president of a popular Paris station called Skyrock, said the law was totalitarian and useless. The major (French) recording companies don't produce enough good French music to fill the schedule.[14] The measure is being policed by the government's watchdog audiovisual committee, the Conseil Supérieur de l'Audiovisuel. With the help of computers, the official ear will be tuned to about 1300 radio stations, which risk losing their broadcast licences if they break the law.

In April 1998, the Chinese State Council ordered all direct-sales operations to cease immediately. Alarmed by a rise in pyramid schemes by some direct sellers and uneasy about the big sales meetings that direct sellers hold, Beijing gave all companies that held direct-selling licences until 31 October 1998 to convert to retail outlets or shut down altogether. The move threatened Avon's China sales, about US$75 million a year, and put Avon, Amway and Mary Kay's combined China investment of roughly US$180 million at risk. It also created problems for Sara Lee Corporation and Tupperware Company, which had recently launched direct-sales efforts in China.[15]

However, since 1998 Hong Kong and China have become more marketing-oriented and the direct marketing effort that is now considered appropriate for China tends to focus on business-to-business activities.

Many legal structures are designed to either encourage or limit trade. Some examples are:

- *Tariff*: tax levied on the goods entering a country. For example, many Australian and New Zealand products such as lamb, wool and beef are subject to high import tariffs in the United States. These tariffs are designed to protect local industries but make it difficult for countries such as Australia and New Zealand to compete. Until recently, Australia had high tariffs on the importation of Canadian salmon, but these have been lifted following an appeal from the Canadians to the World Trade Organization (WTO). Tariffs have tended to

---

Direct Marketing of Asia

on-line

At this site, we see that direct marketing is now growing in China, but in this case the structure isn't pyramid selling as originally discouraged by the Chinese government. What type of products do you see as being acceptable for direct marketing in China?
www.dm-asia.com

decrease around the world as a barrier to trade, but they have often been replaced by non-tariff barriers, such as quotas, boycotts and other restrictions.

- *Quota*: a limit on the amount of a specific product that can enter a country. The United States has strict quotas for imported textiles, sugar and many dairy products. The United States and China have strict quotas on the amount of Australian beef they will import, and wool and lamb products are also often subjected to strict quotas. Quotas are often sought as a means of protection from foreign competition. For example, Harley-Davidson convinced the US government to place quotas on large motorcycles imported to the United States. These quotas gave the company the opportunity to improve its quality and to compete with Japanese motorcycles.
- *Boycott*: the exclusion of all products from certain countries or companies. Governments use boycotts to exclude companies from countries with which they have a political dispute. Several Arab nations boycotted Coca-Cola because it maintained distributors in Israel.
- *Exchange control*: laws compelling a company earning foreign exchange from its exports to sell it to a control agency, usually a central bank. A company wishing to buy goods abroad must first obtain foreign exchange from the control agency. Generally, exchange controls limit the importation of luxuries. For instance, Avon Products drastically cut back new production lines and products in the Philippines because exchange controls prevented the conversion of pesos to dollars to ship back to the home office. The pesos had to be used in the Philippines. China restricts the amount of foreign currency each Chinese company is allowed to keep from its exports. Therefore, Chinese companies must usually get government approval to release funds before they can buy products from foreign companies.
- *Market grouping*: also known as a common trade alliance, it occurs when several countries agree to work together to form a common trade area that enhances trade opportunities. The best-known market grouping is the European Union (EU), whose members are Austria, Belgium, France, Germany, Italy, Luxembourg, the Netherlands, Denmark, Ireland, Finland, Spain, Sweden, the United Kingdom, Portugal and Greece. The EU has been evolving for nearly four decades, and yet, until recently, many trade barriers existed among the member nations. Since 2004, new members include Cyprus, Czech Republic, Estonia, Hungary, Latvia, Lithuania, Malta, Poland, Slovakia and Slovenia.
- *Trade agreement*: an agreement to stimulate international trade. Not all government efforts are meant to stifle imports or investment by foreign corporations. The Uruguay Round of trade negotiations, which created the WTO, is an agreement to dramatically lower trade barriers worldwide. Adopted in 1994, the agreement was signed by 117 nations in Marrakesh, Morocco. It is the most ambitious global trade agreement ever negotiated. The agreement reduces tariffs by one-third worldwide. This, in turn, should raise global income by US$235 billion annually by 2005. Perhaps most notable is the recognition of the new global realities. For the first time, there is an agreement covering services, intellectual property rights and trade-related investment measures such as exchange controls.

The Uruguay Round makes several major changes in world trading practices:

- *Entertainment, pharmaceuticals, integrated circuits and software*: New rules will protect patents, copyrights and trademarks for 20 years. Computer programs receive 50 years' protection and semiconductor chips receive

10 years' protection. But many developing nations will have a decade to phase in patent protection for drugs. France, which limits the number of American movies and TV shows that can be shown, refused to liberalise market access for the US entertainment industry.

- *Financial, legal and accounting services*: Services come under international trading rules for the first time, potentially creating a vast opportunity for these competitive industries. It will now be easier to admit managers and key personnel into a country. Licensing standards for professionals, such as doctors, cannot discriminate against foreign applicants. That is, foreign applicants cannot be held to higher standards than domestic practitioners.
- *Agriculture*: Europe will gradually reduce farm subsidies, opening new opportunities for such farm exports as wheat and corn. Japan and Korea will begin to import rice. But growers of US sugar, citrus fruit and peanuts will have their subsidies trimmed.
- *Textiles and apparel*: Strict quotas limiting imports from developing countries will be phased out over 10 years, possibly causing job losses in many Western countries' clothing trade. But retailers and consumers will be the big winners, because quotas now add US$15 billion a year to clothing prices.
- *A new trade organisation*: The World Trade Organization replaced the old General Agreement on Tariffs and Trade (GATT), which was created in 1948. The old GATT agreements provided extensive loopholes that enabled countries to avoid the trade-barrier reduction agreements. It was like obeying the law if you wanted to! Today, all WTO members must fully comply with all agreements under the Uruguay Round. The WTO also has an effective dispute settlement procedure with strict time limits to resolve disputes.

The new service agreement under the Uruguay Round requires member countries to create adequate penalties against counterfeiting and piracy. China, which joined the WTO in 2001, has done little to control its rampant piracy problem. US producers of records, books, motion pictures and software lose about US$2.5 billion a year to Chinese piracy.[16] Chinese authorities have destroyed 800 000 pirated audio and videocassettes and more than 40 000 software programs. Some US$3 million worth of fines have been levied in connection with 9000 cases of trademark violation. Yet the government failed to close 29 known plants pirating music and computer CDs. These production facilities have politically connected backers.[17]

The move towards an increasingly global business environment is wonderfully illustrated by the Euro. The first economic union to create a common currency, the European Monetary Union represents a US$6.4 trillion economy.

Demographic makeup

Three of the most densely populated nations in the world are China, India and Indonesia. But that fact alone isn't particularly useful to marketers. They also need to know whether the population is mostly urban or rural, because marketers may not have easy access to rural consumers. In Belgium, about 90 per cent of the population lives in an urban setting, whereas in Kenya almost 80 per cent of the population lives in a rural setting. Belgium is thus the more attractive market.

Just as important as population is personal income within a country. The wealthiest countries in the world include Japan, the United States, Switzerland, Sweden, Canada, Germany and several of the Arab oil-producing nations. At the other extreme are countries such as Mali and Bangladesh, with a fraction of the per capita purchasing power of the United States. However, a low per capita income isn't in itself enough reason to avoid a country. In countries with low per capita incomes, wealth isn't evenly distributed. There are pockets of upper- and middle-class consumers in just about every country of the world. In some cases, such as India, their number is surprisingly large.

The most significant global economic news of the past decade is the rise of a global middle class. From Shekou, China, to Mexico City and countless cities in between, there are traffic jams, bustling bulldozers and people hawking tickets to various events. These are all symptoms of a growing middle class. In China, per capita incomes are rising rapidly.[18] Developing countries, excluding Eastern Europe and the former Soviet Union, should grow about 5 per cent annually over the next decade.

Growing economies demand professionals. In Asia, accountants, stock analysts, bankers and even middle managers are in short supply. Rising affluence also creates demand for consumer durables such as refrigerators, VCRs and cars. As Central Europe's middle class grows, Whirlpool expects its sales to grow over 6 per cent annually.[19] Companies such as Lever & Kitchen and Gillette offer an array of products at different price points to attract and keep customers as they move up the income scale. The percentage of the world's population that lives in industrialised nations has been declining since 1960, because the population of industrialised nations has grown slowly and that of developing nations has grown rapidly. In this decade, more than 90 per cent of the world's population growth will occur in developing countries and only 10 per cent in the industrialised nations.

Natural resources

A final factor in the external environment that has become more evident in the past decade is the shortage of natural resources. For example, petroleum shortages have created huge amounts of wealth for oil-producing countries such as Norway, Saudi Arabia and the United Arab Emirates. Consumer and industrial markets have blossomed in these countries. Other countries – such as Indonesia, Mexico and Venezuela – were able to borrow heavily against oil reserves in order to develop more rapidly. On the other hand, industrial countries such as Japan, the United States and much of Western Europe experienced rampant inflation in the 1970s and an enormous transfer of wealth to the petroleum-rich nations. But during much of the 1980s and 1990s, when the price of oil fell, the petroleum-rich nations suffered. Many were not able to service their foreign debts when their oil revenues were sharply reduced. However, Iraq's invasion of Kuwait in 1990 led to a rapid increase in the price of oil and focused attention on the dependence of industrialised countries on oil imports. The price of oil once again declined following the defeat of Iraq, but the dependence of many countries on foreign oil will likely remain high and Australia and New Zealand are no exceptions to this.

Petroleum isn't the only natural resource that affects international marketing. Warm climate and lack of water mean that many of Africa's countries will remain importers of foodstuffs. Japan depends heavily on the United States for timber and logs and on Australia for its beef and other raw materials. The list could go on, but the point is clear. Vast differences in natural resources create international dependencies, huge shifts of wealth, inflation and recession, export opportunities for countries with abundant resources, and even a stimulus for military intervention.

Having considered the environmental factors the next issue for global marketers is to consider the global marketing mix.

The global marketing mix

To succeed, firms seeking to enter into foreign trade must still adhere to the principles of the marketing mix. Information gathered on foreign markets through research is the basis for the four Ps of global marketing strategy: product, place (distribution), promotion and price. Marketing managers who understand the advantages and disadvantages of different ways to enter the global market and the effect of the external environment on the firm's marketing mix have a better chance of reaching their goals.

3 List the basic elements involved in developing a global marketing mix

The first step in creating a marketing mix is developing a thorough understanding of the global target market. Often this knowledge can be obtained through the same types of marketing research used in the domestic market (see Chapter 5). However, global marketing research is conducted in vastly different environments. Conducting a survey can be difficult in developing countries, where telephone ownership is rare and mail delivery slow or sporadic. Drawing samples based on known population parameters is often difficult because of the lack of data. In some cities in South America, Mexico and Asia, street maps are unavailable, streets are unidentified and houses are unnumbered. Moreover, the questions a marketer can ask may differ in other cultures. In some cultures, people tend to be more private than in many Western countries and don't like to respond to personal questions in surveys. For instance, in France, questions about one's age and income are considered especially rude.

Product and promotion

With the proper information, a good marketing mix can be developed. One important decision is whether to alter the product or the promotion for the global marketplace. Other options are to radically change the product or to adjust either the promotional message or the product to suit local conditions.

One product, one message

The strategy of global marketing standardisation, which was discussed earlier, means developing a single product for all markets and promoting it the same way all over the world. For instance, Procter & Gamble uses the same product and promotional themes for Head and Shoulders shampoo in China as it does

MTV on-line

This website brings teenagers from around the world together to share common interests through global media. What age group do you think the site is targeted towards? Is this consistent with the suggested 18 year olds?
www.mtv.com

in other countries around the world, including Australia and New Zealand. The advertising draws attention to a person's dandruff problem, which stands out in a nation of black-haired people. Head and Shoulders is now the best-selling shampoo in China despite costing over 300 per cent more than local brands.

Kodak is enjoying success in China with film sales up 50 per cent since 1996. It uses the 'Kodak moments' campaign theme to build brand awareness. One unique promotional tool is the use of scratch cards with the purchase of film. These cards are very popular with Chinese consumers, but only if the card gives a guaranteed instant win.[20]

Global media – especially satellite and cable TV networks such as Cable News Network International, MTV Networks and British Sky Broadcasting – make it possible to beam advertising to audiences unreachable a few years ago. 'Eighteen year olds in Paris have more in common with 18 year olds in New York than with their own parents,' says William Roedy, director of MTV Europe. Almost all of MTV's advertisers run unified, English-language campaigns in the 28 nations the firm reaches. The audiences 'buy the same products, go to the same movies, listen to the same music, sip the same colas. Global advertising merely works on that premise.'[21] Although teens throughout the world prefer movies above all other forms of television programming, they are closely followed by music videos, stand-up comedy and then sport.

Both Nike and Reebok spend over US$100 million a year in promotion outside the United States. Each company practises global marketing standardisation to keep its messages clear and its products desirable. Both companies have exploited basketball's surging popularity around the world. Nike sends LeBron James of the Cleveland Cavaliers to Europe and Asia touting its products. Reebok counters by sending basketball superstar Shaquille O'Neal overseas as its ambassador. One of the main appeals of sneakers is their American style; therefore, the more American an advertising commercial, the better it is. The tag lines – whether in Italy, Germany, Japan or France – all read the same way in English: 'Just do it' and 'Planet Reebok'. Nike has found, however, that its brashness doesn't always go over well in other countries. A TV commercial of Satan and his demons playing soccer against a team of Nike endorsers was a hit in America, but deemed as too offensive to be shown in prime time in Europe.

Even a one-product, one-message strategy may call for some changes to suit local needs, such as variations in the product's measurement units, package sizes and labelling. Pillsbury, for example, changed the measurement unit for its cake mixes because adding 'cups of' has no meaning in many developing countries. Also, in developing countries, packages are often smaller so that consumers with limited incomes can buy them. For instance, cigarettes, chewing gum and razor blades may be sold individually instead of in packages.

Unchanged products may fail simply because of cultural factors. The game *Trivial Pursuit* failed in Japan. It seems that getting the answers wrong can be seen as a loss of face. Any type of war game tends to do very poorly in Germany, despite the fact that Germany is by far the world's biggest game-playing nation. A successful game in Germany has plenty of details and thick rulebooks. *Monopoly* remains the world's favourite board game; it seems to overcome all cultural barriers. The game is available in 25 languages, including Russian, Croatian and Hebrew.[22]

Product invention

In the context of global marketing, product invention can be taken to mean either creating a new product for a market or drastically changing an existing product. For the Japanese market, Nabisco had to remove the cream filling from its Oreo biscuits because Japanese children thought they were too sweet. Ford thinks it can save billions on its product development costs by developing a single small-car chassis and then altering its styling to suit different countries. Campbell Soup invented a watercress and duck gizzard soup that is now selling well in China. It is also considering a cream of snake soup. Frito-Lay's most popular potato chip in Thailand is prawn flavoured. In Australia, McDonald's has recently introduced toasted cheese and tomato sandwiches and fish and chips to the menu – both to cater to Australian tastebuds.

Rather than creating a new product, companies can take the strategy of buying smaller local firms and maintaining their existing product and market mix. This is the strategy used by Coca-Cola in India when they purchased Thums Up cola, which now outsells Coke by a four-to-one margin in most Indian markets.

Consumers in different countries use products differently. For example, in many countries, clothing is worn much longer between washings than in Australia or New Zealand, so a more durable fabric must be produced and marketed. For Peru, Goodyear developed a tyre that contains a higher percentage of natural rubber and has better treads than tyres manufactured elsewhere in order to handle the tough Peruvian driving conditions. Rubbermaid has sold millions of open-top wastebaskets in America; Europeans, picky about garbage peeking out of bins, wanted bins with tight lids that snap into place.

Australia has taken a major role over the years in the development of many products that other countries now use and sell as their own. Exhibit 12.4 lists some of them.

Message adaptation

Another global marketing strategy is to maintain the same basic product but alter the promotional strategy. Bicycles are mainly pleasure vehicles in Australia; however, in many parts of the world they are a family's main mode of transportation. Thus, promotion in these countries should stress durability and efficiency. In contrast, Australian or New Zealand advertising may emphasise escaping and having fun.

Harley-Davidson decided that its American promotion theme, 'One steady constant in an increasingly screwed-up world', wouldn't appeal to the Japanese market. The Japanese ads combine American images with traditional Japanese ones, such as American riders passing a geisha in a rickshaw, and Japanese ponies nibbling at a Harley motorcycle. Waiting lists for Harleys in Japan are up to six months long.

Foster's beer, the third most widely distributed lager in the world, associates the Australian kangaroo with the packaging of the Foster's lager bottle.

Exhibit 12.4
Australian inventions

- Refrigeration
- Heart pacemaker
- Aircraft inventions:
  - The 'black box' flight recorder (also claimed by the United States)
  - Interscan aircraft landing system
  - Aircraft radar distance measuring equipment
  - Inflatable escape slide
- Photocopier (liquid xerographics)
- Utility truck (i.e. the pickup truck)
- Interactive computer systems
- The wire-driven torpedo
- The bionic ear (cochlear implant)
- The portable cardboard wine cask
- Permanent press fabric
- Microsurgery
- Differential gears
- Atomic absorption spectroscopy
- Military tank (concept only)
- The car radio
- Police car radio
- Ready-mix concrete
- The lawn mower
- In vitro fertilisation and frozen embryo implantation
- The clothes hoist
- The orbital engine
- Favco crane
- Wave-piercing catamaran
- Self-twist yarn spinning
- Speed packer garbage collector
- Michell thrust bearing (for screw propellers)
- Artificial rain
- Mechanised brick production
- Snake bite antivenene
- The Owen machine gun
- Mills cross radiotelescope
- The laser lighthouse
- Sports ergometer
- Contour farming
- Agricultural machinery:
  - Harvester
  - Sunshine harvester
  - Stripper harvester
  - Sugar cane harvester
  - Stump-jump plough
  - Chaff cutter
  - Drill cultivator
  - Rotary hoe
  - Shearing machines
  - Infra-red chicken brooder
- Guided anti-aircraft weapons
- Ikara anti-submarine torpedo/missile system
- Furniture castors
- Soundproof windows
- Beamed radar
- Snail killer
- Modern milking machine
- Tubular sheet metal
- Periscope rifle
- Totalisator betting system
- Processes for extracting precious metals:
  - Lister's zinc/lead process
  - Bromocyanide process for extracting gold
- Water meter (direct measurement)
- Spun concrete pipe
- Exploding bullets
- Automatic lid for jugs
- Superefficient solar cell
- Optically variable plastic banknotes
- Superlightweight fabrics
- Superlightweight composite machine parts
- Rare earth supermagnet motors
- 3D prototyping
- Australians also made essential contributions to the invention/discovery of:
  - Powered flight
  - Penicillin/antibiotics
  - Teratogenic effects of thalidomide and rubella
  - X-ray crystallography

In a new effort to increase its international presence, Foster's Brewing is targeting many fast-growing markets around the world. But breaking with its promotion strategy at home, the brewer is positioning the unique Australian nature of Foster's beer. It has recently launched the Aussie bar concept, where five different Australian-themed bars will be established around the world to showcase Australia's fun and friendly party style. Foster's is now the third most widely distributed international lager worldwide, with more than 100 million cases of Foster's consumed around the world each year. Prior to the Aussie bar theme, Foster's promotional campaign in North America focused on Australian humour and the outback themes, quite different from the more sophisticated image created at home.

Global consistency in brand packaging and advertising image portrayal, in both above- and below-the-line programs, builds upon the brand's strengths. Also, stringent controls are in place to ensure the Foster's experience remains consistent around the world. This experience guarantees a consistent, high-quality product and brand support that makes Foster's Lager instantly recognisable and familiar to beer drinkers the world over.

Global marketers find that promotion is a daunting task in some countries. For example, commercial television time is readily available in Canada but severely restricted in Germany. Until recently, marketers in Indonesia had only one subscription TV channel with few viewers (120 000 in a nation of 180 million people). Because of this limited television audience, several marketers, such as the country's main Toyota dealer, had to develop direct-mail campaigns to reach their target markets.

Some cultures view a product as having less value if it has to be advertised. In other nations, claims that seem exaggerated by Australian standards are commonplace. On the other hand, Germany doesn't permit advertisers to state that their products are 'best' or 'better' than those of competitors, a description commonly used in Australian advertising. The hard-sell tactics and sexual themes so common in Australian and New Zealand advertising are taboo in many countries. For example, in the Middle East, pictures of women in print advertisements have been covered with censor's ink.

Language barriers, translation problems and cultural differences have generated numerous headaches for international marketing managers. Consider these examples:

- A toothpaste claiming to give users white teeth was especially inappropriate in many areas of Southeast Asia, where the well-to-do chew betel nuts and black teeth are a sign of higher social status.
- Procter & Gamble's Japanese advertising for Camay soap nearly devastated the product. In one commercial, a man meeting a woman for the first time immediately compared her skin to that of a fine porcelain doll. Although the ad had worked in other Asian countries, in Japan the man came across as rude and disrespectful.

Product adaptation

Another alternative for global marketers is to slightly alter a basic product to meet local conditions. Additional pizza toppings offered by Domino's in Japan include corn, curry, squid and spinach, and in Australia they include ham and pineapple. When Lewis Woolf Griptight, a British manufacturer of infant accessories such as dummies (or pacifiers), moved into the US market, it found subtle differences between British and American parents. Elizabeth Lee,

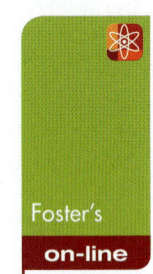

Foster's on-line

How does Foster's ensure consistency in its beer product and branding around the world?
www.fosters.com.au/corporate/brands/fosters/branding.asp

marketing manager, noted, 'There are subtle differences, but many problems are the same. Whether a cup spills in America or in Madagascar or in the UK, mums aren't going to like it,' she said. 'We didn't need to redo all the research to find out that people didn't want cups that spill, but we still had to do research on things like colour and packaging.'[23] The brand name Kiddiwinks is a British word for 'children'. In the United States, the name was changed to Binky because of positive parental reactions in marketing research tests.

Pricing

Once marketing managers have determined a global product and promotion strategy, they can select the remainder of the marketing mix. Pricing presents some unique problems in the global sphere. Exporters must not only cover their production costs, but also consider transportation costs, insurance, taxes and tariffs. When deciding on a final price, marketers must also determine what customers are willing to spend on a particular product. Marketers also need to ensure that their foreign buyers will pay them. Because developing nations lack mass purchasing power, selling to them often poses special pricing problems. Sometimes a product can be simplified in order to lower the price. However, the firm must not assume that low-income countries are willing to accept lower quality. Although the nomads of the Sahara are very poor, they still buy expensive fabrics to make their clothing. Their survival in harsh conditions and extreme temperatures requires this expense. Additionally, certain expensive luxury items can be sold almost anywhere.

Distribution

Solving promotional, price and product problems doesn't guarantee global marketing success. The product still has to get adequate distribution. For example, Europeans don't play sport as much as Australians and New Zealanders, so they don't visit sporting-goods stores as often. Realising this, Reebok started selling its shoes in about 800 traditional shoe stores in France. In one year, the company doubled its French sales. Harley-Davidson had to open two company-owned stores in Japan to get distribution for its Harley clothing and clothing accessories.

The Japanese distribution system is considered the most complicated in the world. Imported goods wind their way through layers of agents, wholesalers and retailers. For example, a bottle of 96 aspirins costs about $40 because the bottle passes through at least six wholesalers, each of whom increases the selling price. The result is that the Japanese consumer pays the world's most exorbitant prices. These distribution channels seem to be based on historical and traditional patterns of socially arranged tradeoffs, which Japanese officials claim are very hard for the government to change. Today, however, the system seems to be changing because of pressure from the Japanese consumer. Japanese shoppers are now placing low prices ahead of quality in their purchasing decisions. The retailer who can cut distribution costs, and therefore the retail price, gets the sale. For example, Kojima, a Japanese electronics superstore chain like the Australian and New Zealand Harvey Norman stores, had to bypass GE's Japanese distribution partner Toshiba to import its merchandise at a good price. Toshiba's distribution system required refrigerators to pass through too many hands before they reached the retailer. Kojima went directly to GE headquarters in the United States and persuaded the company to sell it refrigerators, which were then shipped directly to Kojima. It is now selling GE refrigerators for about $1600, which is half the price of a typical Japanese model.

Retail institutions in other countries also may differ from what a company is used to in its domestic market. The terms 'department store' and 'supermarket' may refer to types of retail outlets that are very different from those found in New Zealand and Australia. Japanese supermarkets, for example, are large multi-storey buildings that sell not only food but also clothing, furniture and home appliances. Department stores are even larger outlets that emphasise foodstuffs and operate a restaurant on the premises. For a variety of reasons, our commonly recognisable retail outlets don't exist or are impractical in developing countries. For example, consumers may not have the storage space to keep food for several days. Refrigerators, when available, are usually small and don't allow for bulk storage. Attempting to build new retail outlets can be a frustrating battle. In Germany's Ruhr Valley, the discounter All Kauf SB-Warenhaus GmbH has struggled to build a store for 15 years on land that it owns. Local authorities are blocking construction, however, because they are afraid the store will hurt local retailers.[24]

Channels of distribution and the physical infrastructure are also inadequate in many developing nations. In China, for example, most goods are carried on poles or human backs, in wheelbarrows and handcarts, or, increasingly (and this is an important advance), on bicycles.

Channels and distribution decisions – global markets

The world is indeed becoming a friendlier place for marketers. The surging popularity of free-market economics, such as the European Union, over the past decade or so has swept away many barriers. As a result, businesses are finding that the world market is more appealing than ever. Thus, global marketing channels and management of the supply chain are important to Australian and New Zealand organisations that export their products or manufacture abroad.

Developing global marketing channels

Executives should recognise the unique cultural, economic, institutional and legal aspects of each market before trying to design marketing channels in foreign countries. Manufacturers introducing products in global markets face a tough decision: what type of channel structure to use. Specifically, should the product be marketed directly, mostly by the organisation's salespeople, or through independent foreign intermediaries such as agents and distributors? Using the organisation's salespeople generally provides more control and less risk than using foreign intermediaries. However, setting up a sales team in a foreign country also entails a greater commitment, both financially and organisationally.

Marketers should be aware that the channel structure abroad might not be very similar to channels in Australia or New Zealand. For example, organisations wishing to sell goods into Asia frequently must go through three layers of wholesalers and sub-wholesalers: the national or primary wholesalers, the secondary or regional wholesalers, and the local wholesalers.

The channel types available in foreign countries usually differ as well. The more developed a nation is economically, the more specialised its channel types. Therefore, a marketer wishing to sell in Germany or Japan will have several channel types to choose from. Conversely, developing countries such as India, Thailand and Indonesia have limited channel types available; there are typically few mail-order channels, vending machines, or specialised retailers and wholesalers.

By creating a channel that circumvented Japan's inefficient and expensive retail distribution system, Amway has become one of the country's most profitable companies. As a result, Amway has many more distributors in Japan than it does in the United States.

Marketers must also be aware of 'grey' marketing channels in many foreign countries, in which products are distributed through unauthorised channel intermediaries.

Global logistics and supply chain management

As global trade becomes a more decisive factor in success or failure for organisations of all sizes, a well-thought-out global logistics strategy becomes ever more important. Uncertainty regarding shipping usually tops the list of reasons why companies, especially smaller ones, resist international markets. Even companies that have scored overseas successes often are vulnerable to logistical problems. Large companies have the capital to create global logistics systems, but smaller companies often must rely on the services of carriers and freight forwarders to get their products to overseas markets. Read about one company's successful strategy for global distribution in the Global perspectives box.

Global PERSPECTIVES

Columbia Sportswear: A European distribution centre with a French Flair
by Thomas A. Foster

The Oregon-based sportswear company finds France's labour rules are a perfect fit for its new European distribution centre operation.

Columbia Sportswear Company, the 67-year-old manufacturer of a broad range of apparel based in Portland, Oregon, USA, sells its products in more than 60 countries and to more than 12 000 retailers worldwide. Global sales were above $1 billion during 2004. The 450 million consumers in the ever-expanding European Union represent a burgeoning market for the sportswear company, especially because of the Europeans' shared passion for skiing, hiking and other outdoor sports.

In fact, the large and diverse European marketplace has emerged as a critical component of the company's growth strategy, and for good reason. Its 2004 annual sales in Europe totalled $170.3 million last year, up 26 per cent over 2003. Particularly important to Columbia's European operations is its distribution centre, which serves as the hub for all of its shipping and receiving throughout Western Europe.

Columbia's original European distribution centre was located in the Netherlands, where the company outsourced its distribution operations to a third-party logistics provider. During the contract period with the 3PL, Columbia's European sales volume grew so rapidly that its space requirements expanded from one to two and eventually to three different buildings. While growing sales were welcome, the multiple building operation set definite limits on the distribution efficiency that could be achieved.

'When it came time to negotiate another agreement, we decided that it was time for us to invest in a place that would allow us to manage our European distribution operations as they grew,' says Dan Dougherty, Columbia's director of technical services. 'If we stayed with the 3PL, we knew that we would constantly be resizing our operation and having to move our inventory.'

The decision to build and operate its own distribution centre was made in late 1990s, but the bigger question was where should this new distribution centre be located? Columbia understood that the decision would play a huge role in the future of its European operations. To identify the optimal location, Columbia launched a comprehensive search that encompassed many European countries.

The company's criteria were specific. It wanted a location that could provide:

- A central location relative to the rest of Western Europe, including proximity to key customers and ports;
- Ample land: approximately 50 acres, with room for expansion and in an area that is suited to high-volume distribution activity; and
- A highly skilled labour pool with sufficient flexibility to handle Columbia's two busy seasons: August–September for pre-Christmas, and January–March for summer.

'Each site we looked at had good things to recommend it, but we found everything we were looking for in Nord-Pas-de-Calais,' says Dougherty. Nord-Pas-de-Calais offered solutions to all of Columbia's needs, including experienced and technically skilled labour, a close proximity to much of Western Europe, and an expanse of undeveloped land that enabled the company to build a 270 000 square-foot facility. Building construction was completed in 2002 followed by equipment installation and testing. The first orders were shipped from the distribution centre January 2003.

The Cambrai site not only met all of the stated criteria, but also came with the considerable value-added support of Northern France Experts (NFX), which promotes economic development in northern France. Among other assistance, NFX helped Columbia find the optimal vendors and contractors for building the facility, negotiate potential financial incentives and identify the best sources for high-performing labour.

Inbound and outbound transportation

As with most apparel companies today, the vast majority of Columbia's manufacturing is in Asia. The great distances involved mean fairly long lead times, but the supply chain runs very smoothly.

'Our sourcing and planning people in Asia are able to tell us exactly when a purchase order will be finished in the factory, when the goods will ship, how long they will be in transit and when they will arrive in the port,' says Dougherty. He explains that several hundred inbound ocean containers each year come through the ports of LeHavre, Antwerp and the French port of Dunkerque near the Belgian border.

'We are often able to schedule inbound containers far enough in advance that we can use river barge to move the containers from the ports to a terminal near our distribution centre,' he says. 'Barge is a less expensive mode to dray in the containers. If we need the containers more quickly, we just truck them in directly.'

The distribution centre's close proximity to highways allows for quick transport and delivery time throughout the rest of Europe, including the new EU states in Eastern Europe that Columbia is beginning to serve. France's transportation infrastructure is one of the best in Europe and boasts the largest road network. The country has more than 589 000 miles of road network, including 6 820 miles of freeways, fully interconnected with Western Europe.

Unlike many companies in Europe that outsource its transportation to forwarders or 3PLs, Columbia's shipping is handled entirely by its own transportation management department that is housed at the distribution centre. It manages its own transportation contracts and routes each shipment. Orders are shipped to retailer's distribution centre or directly to stores. Columbia prepays all freight.

'We are fortunate to have a very experienced transportation manager who knows the whole European market very well,' says Dougherty. 'We have been able to control the cost and increase the level of service better than we could by outsourcing this to a forwarder.'

The company uses as many as 16 different carriers of all types including express, less-than-truckload and full truckload to handle everything from single parcels to multiple pallets. The transportation department even does its own pool shipping to the United Kingdom. Full truckloads are shipped across the English Channel to a parcel carrier terminal where pallets are deconsolidated into individual shipments.

'It would certainly be simpler to hand off all of our shipments to a single freight company, but we believe we get better service and lower costs managing the freight ourselves.'

The Cambrai distribution centre is well situated for its outbound truck shipments. It is very near the Belgian border on the A2 motorway that is a major truck route linking Brussels and Paris. The distribution centre is only 90 minutes' drive north of Paris and an hour south of Lille and Brussels.

Columbia's pan-European distribution strategy has always been to serve the entire market out of one facility. Even as its business has mushroomed, the strategy remains the same and the Cambrai distribution centre continues to meet the need.

'When we moved into this facility, 70 per cent of our shipping points were in northwestern Europe and were within a transit time of a day or two,' says Dougherty. 'As we grow our business in more distant areas such as Scandinavia, the Baltic States and southern Italy, we still are able to meet our customer service requirements out of this distribution centre. Our farthest regular service points in eastern Europe are still only about a three-day transit time.'

Distribution centre operations

The Cambrai site is 48 acres, which by European standards is quite large. The size allows for considerable expansion in the future, and it is in an industrial zone with similar operations. Adjacent companies include a grocery distribution centre a printing company and several small manufacturers.

Columbia designed its 25 000 square-metre distribution centre to meet is specific distribution needs. The building is 250 metres long by 100 metres wide. Receiving is on one end, and shipping is on the other end. Stock keeping is in the middle and occupies most of the building.

Cases that come in off the container are put on a conveyer into stock keeping. The stock put-away is a manual system using pushcarts on three levels of the storage area. Picking is done the same way. Items that are picked are placed on conveyers that can handle cases and cartons and interpack footwear cartons. Picked items go to a sorter area that goes to a processing area for any retail services needed for an order. The sortation system also supports a repacking operation for less-than-case quantities. The remnant cases are moved via an automatic stacker crane to slots for easy retrieval for the next less-than-case order. Orders are moved by conveyor to 16 shipping areas on the floor that represent separate carriers, countries or major customers. The orders are marshalled and palletised in the shipping area and loaded on trucks. A small portion of expedited orders, samples and other special shipments are moved by air, mainly through Paris's Charles de Gaulle International Airport, which is about 90 minutes away.

As well as the facility runs, Columbia's success is already forcing the company to think about expansion. It has enjoyed double-digit growth every year in its apparel lines, and is now expanding its footwear business.

'The cube requirement for footwear and different processing needs takes more storage space.' Says Dougherty, 'These demands are already pushing the limits of our building. Fortunately, expansion would not be a major challenge.'

With full expansion, the outside building dimensions will eventually have a total footprint of 80 000 square meters.

Good labour relations

For Columbia, the flexibility of France's skilled workforce has been critically important. Besides the typical distribution operations in the warehouse, Columbia's workers add considerable value to product for individual customers. The retail services performed include customizing the product and packaging, which can be as simple as attaching price tickets or as complicated as making a special assortment packs of products for specific customers.

'We have a unionised workforce, but we have a very positive relationship with them. They help us improve the efficiency of the facility,' says Dougherty

Columbia has also benefited from the 35-hour working week that is now part of France's labour regulations. These same regulations allow a system called modulation where employees can work fewer hours during off seasons, and more hours during busy seasons, all while paying workers a consistent salary year-round. Thus, the 35-hour working week is actually flexible. The working week must be in a range between 28 hours to 44 hours for up to 10 weeks.

'As long as we are in that range and don't exceed the annual number of hours, we pay each worker a monthly salary that includes no overtime premiums,' says Dougherty. 'This arrangement works extremely well for us because our business is very seasonal. We are able to move the hours to meet our peak periods and have fewer hours in the slow periods. As a result, we have a much smaller per cent of temporary workers than we do in our US operation.'

While some industries have complained about France's 35-hour working week, businesses with seasonality have come to appreciate it. These businesses traditionally incur considerable costs in hiring temporary workers, training them and then letting them go when the peak demand cools. France's modulation system allows companies like Columbia to schedule the workforce when the need it, avoid paying wages when workers are not needed, and during these slow times, still retain valuable workers and the investment in training. In addition to facilitating the planning process, this workforce flexibility also allows Columbia to minimise training costs, because fewer temporary workers are required during busy seasons.

'There is a great labour pool, and we are impressed with the work ethic of our French employees,' says Dougherty. 'For a total investment of $30 million, Columbia believes we've put the centre of our European operations in safe hands that will allow us to develop our business in Europe.'

Source: *Global Logistics & Supply Chain Strategies*, March 2005[25]

One of the most critical global logistical issues for importers of any size is coping with the legalities of trade in other countries. Shippers and distributors must be aware of the permits, licences and registrations they may need to acquire and, depending on the type of product they are importing, the tariffs, quotas and other regulations that apply in each country. Another important factor to consider is the transportation infrastructure in a country. For example, in China, post offices aren't equipped for bulk mailings and they don't deliver parcels to residential addresses. To address this problem, Germany's Bertelsmann Book Club created its own crew of 70 bicycle-riding deliverymen in Shanghai to deliver books to book club members.[26]

Other emerging countries have similar situations. In Nigeria, for example, a crumbling road system, ageing trucks and safety concerns forced Nestlé to rethink its traditional distribution methods. Instead of operating a central warehouse, the company built small warehouses across the country. For safety reasons, trucks carrying Nestlé goods are allowed to travel only during daylight hours, frequently under armed guard.[27]

Global retailing

It is no accident that retailers are now testing their store concepts on a global basis. With the battle for market share among domestic retailers showing no sign of abating, and growth prospects dismal, mature retailers are looking for growth opportunities in the growing consumer economies of other countries. American and European retailers have made quite an impact on the global market.

4 Discuss the challenges of expanding retailing operations into global markets

Several events have made expansion across national borders more feasible. First, the spread of communication networks and mass media has homogenised tastes and product preferences to some extent around the world. As a result, the casual lifestyle and the products that symbolise it, such as Levi's jeans and Nike sportswear, have become more appealing. Second, the development of free trade areas such as the North American Free Trade Agreement (NAFTA) and the formation of the European Union (EU) have facilitated the expansion of retail activities within these zones. Last, high growth potential in underserved markets is also luring retailers into Asia. China contains a quarter of the world's population and now allows retailers to access the Chinese market. Although the majority of China's population still lacks adequate consumer spending power, projections indicate that the country's economy will eclipse all others in the next 25 years.[28]

Before taking the plunge into the international retailing arena, the soundest advice retailers can heed is to do their homework. Analysts from consulting firm Accenture count among the prerequisites for going global a secure and profitable position domestically, a long-term perspective as many foreign operations take longer to set up and longer to turn a profit, and a global strategy that meshes with the retailer's overall corporate strategy. Retailers should first determine what their core competency is – whether it be low prices, a distinctive fashion look or excellent customer service – and determine whether this differentiation is what the local market wants.

However, in addition to keeping their core strengths when going global, retailers also need to make adjustments skilfully. Therefore, a major part of a retailer's advance 'homework' is to understand what products will sell in foreign locales. Colour preferences, taste preferences, service expectations, the preferred cut of a garment and shoppers' physiques vary worldwide, as does customer acceptance of foreign brands or private-label merchandise. Differences also dictate the placement of goods within a retail store. In some cultures, for example, men's and women's clothing should not be displayed for sale adjacent to each other.

Impact of the electronic environment

5 Consider how the Internet is affecting global marketing

In many respects, 'going global' is easier now than it has ever been in the past. Opening an e-commerce site on the Internet immediately puts a company in the international marketplace, but does not make it an international or global marketing organisation. However, the promise of borderless commerce and the electronic economy is still being somewhat restrained by old habits. For example, even though more than 61 per cent of Australians and 47 per cent of New Zealanders own computers, only 46 per cent have access to the Internet and less than 20 per cent have actually made purchases on-line. It seems that while Australia is a leader in Internet access, it lags behind much of the rest of the world in on-line purchases. Organisational consumers are a different story, with e-commerce being a main part of many business transactions in both Australia and New Zealand.

In Germany, it is typically cheaper to buy books from Amazon.com in the UK rather than from the local site. Why? Germany, France and several other European countries allow publishing cartels through which groups of book publishers can legally dictate retail prices to booksellers – both on-line and on the ground.

Scandinavians, like the Japanese, are reluctant to use credit cards, the currency of the Internet, and the French have an aversion to revealing the private information that Net retailers usually ask for. French websites tend to be decidedly different from their Australian, New Zealand and even US counterparts.

One of the main problems with organisational trade via the Internet (B2B) is the complexity of tariffs, trade laws, taxes, regulations and exchange rates that need to be factored into the terms and conditions of sale on the site. These complexities can make some forms of trade impossible in the electronic medium. Quite often, organisational buyers will use the Internet to find information and obtain contact details, and then start negotiations using more traditional methods. This will slowly change, but at present, depending on the industry, some of these barriers are insurmountable.

FNAC.com on-line
Visit this popular French website and compare it to yahoo.com.au. Do you notice any cultural differences with the type of information presented and the layout of the site? www.fnac.com

Chapter 12 — Global marketing

Connect it

This chapter opens with a review of the benefits of global and international marketing. However, to understand the global market it is necessary to have an appreciation for the differing external factors that influence the way global and international markets are marketed. With this appreciation marketers can move forward in their planning and consider the 4Ps in the various forms necessary to take the product to the world. Finally the chapter closes with consideration of the electronic environment and how it is impacting on the global marketing processes.

Summary

1 Discuss the importance of global marketing.

Businesspeople who adopt a global vision are better able to identify global marketing opportunities, to understand the nature of global networks and to engage foreign competition in domestic markets.

2 Describe the external environment facing global marketers.

Global marketers face the same environmental factors as they do domestically: culture, economic and technological development, political structures, demography and natural resources. Cultural considerations include societal values, attitudes and beliefs, language, and customary business practices. A country's economic and technological status depends on its stage of industrial development: traditional society, pre-industrial society, takeoff economy, industrialising society or fully industrialised society. The political structure is shaped by political ideology and such policies as tariffs, quotas, boycotts, exchange controls, trade agreements and market groupings. Demographic variables include population, income distribution and population growth rate.

3 List the basic elements involved in developing a global marketing mix.

A firm's main consideration is how much it will adjust the four Ps – product, promotion, place (distribution) and price – within each country. One strategy is to use one product and one promotion message worldwide. A second strategy is to create new products for global markets. A third strategy is to keep the product basically the same but alter the promotional message. A fourth strategy is to slightly alter the product to meet local conditions.

Further manufacturers introducing products in foreign countries must decide what type of channel structure to use – in particular, whether the product should be marketed through direct channels or through foreign intermediaries. Marketers should be aware that channel structures in foreign markets might be very different from those they are accustomed to in Australia and New Zealand. Global distribution expertise is also emerging as an important skill for logistics managers as many countries are removing trade barriers.

With increased competition and slow domestic growth, mature retailers are looking for growth opportunities in the developing consumer economies of other

Define it

global marketing 439
global vision 440

countries. The homogenisation of tastes and product preferences around the world, the lowering of trade barriers and the emergence of underserved markets have made the prospects of expanding across national borders more feasible for many retailers. Retailers wanting to expand globally should first determine what their core competency is and determine whether this differentiation is what the local market wants. Retailers also need to skilfully make adjustments in product mix to meet local demands.

4 Consider how the electronic environment is affecting global marketing.
Simply setting up a website can open the door for international sales. International carriers such as UPS can help to solve logistics problems. Language translation software can help an e-commerce business to become multilingual. Yet cultural differences and old-line rules, regulations and taxes hinder rapid development of e-commerce in many countries.

Review it

1. A limit on the amount of a specific product that can enter a country is a
   a   Tariff
   b   Quota
   c   Boycott
   d   Trade agreement

2. Tariffs are a tax that is levied on goods by the country where they are produced.
   a   True
   b   False

3. Global marketing is important to most developed countries.
   a   True
   b   False

4. Which of the following is *not* an external environmental factor?
   a   Political structure
   b   Culture
   c   Organisational capacity
   d   Natural resources

5. Developing a thorough understanding of global target markets is an important first step in developing a global marketing plan. However, the following problems impede global market research:
   a   People may not respond to questions for cultural reasons
   b   Telephone ownership can be rare
   c   There may be nomail system
   d   All of the above

6. When an economy is in a period of transition from developing to developed nation it is called a
   a   Transitional economy
   b   An industrialising economy
   c   Traditional society
   d   Takeoff economy

7   Culture impacts on international marketing. Which of the following is *not* a cultural consideration?
    a   Language
    b   Packaging
    c   Gift giving
    d   Media habits

8   Electronic marketing in the global environment does not include which of the following?
    a   Internet
    b   SMS
    c   Email
    d   Wireless technology

9   Global marketing has a motto, one product one message. It this true or false?
    a   True
    b   False

10 When making decisions about distribution in a global marketing campaign, marketers need to consider which of the following in their channel considerations?
    a   Culture, legal, economic and climatic conditions
    b   Culture, legal, economic and institutional aspects of the market
    c   Legal, political, environmental and technical ability of the market
    d   Culture, legal and social aspects of the market

Check the Answer Key to see how well you understood the material. More detailed discussion and writing questions and a video case related to this chapter are found in the Student Resources CD-ROM.

Try it

1   Many marketers now believe that teenagers in developed countries are becoming 'global consumers'. That is, they all want to buy the same goods and services. Do you think this is true? If so, what has brought about this outcome?

2   Suppose you are the marketing manager for a consumer products firm that is about to undertake its first expansion abroad. Write a memo for your staff reminding them of the role that culture will play in the new venture. Give examples.

3   Divide into six teams. Each team will be responsible for one of the following industries: entertainment; pharmaceuticals; computers and software; financial, legal or accounting services; agriculture; and textiles and apparel. Interview one or more executives in each of these industries to determine how the Uruguay Round and the EU trade regulations have affected and will affect their organisations. If a local firm cannot be contacted in your industry, use the library and the Internet to prepare your report.

4   What are the main barriers to international trade? Explain how government policies may be used either to restrict or to stimulate global marketing.

5   How does the website called 'The Paris Pages' (www.paris.org) handle language and translation issues?

Apply it

Yucca, also known as cassava or manioc, is a plant that produces a starchy root that is a subsistence staple for farmers in the Amazon and other tropical areas. The processed root is also widely used as animal feed, but in its raw form, yucca is poisonous (a natural source of cyanide). Despite its bland taste and toxic potential, yucca has inspired Gerald Ritthaler to start a new venture. Ritthaler is determined to turn the lowly yucca into an upscale 'natural' snack in the form of the beloved chip. He has bought land in Venezuela, purchased an abandoned government yucca flourmill and imported chip-making production equipment from Michigan, in the United States. His new company, Ritz Foods, packages the yucca chips in a glossy, black, seven-ounce bag that retails for US$3.79. Ritthaler has already obtained a vending machine contract and is now trying to get into stores via food distributors. The chips have received an enthusiastic response from Linda Palermo, the manager and owner of The Boy's Farmers Market in Florida, where the unusual chips are selling well.

However, there is already competition. Dana Alexander, Inc., has produced a fancy, multicolour root mix called Terra Chips, which is 10 per cent yucca (and also happens to come in glossy black bags). Additionally, Frito-Lay is marketing fat-free chips and toying with the idea of 'alternative roots'. Ritthaler is undeterred, citing the immense size of the potato-chip market.

Questions

1. What is an appropriate mission statement for Ritz Foods?
2. What specific objective would you suggest that it achieve?
3. What are the strengths, weaknesses, opportunities and threats in this situation?
4. What strategic growth options can Ritz Foods pursue?
5. What should the target market be, and should Ritthaler consider an international marketing strategy? Why?
6. What are the elements of Ritz Foods' marketing mix, and how would these differ with an international strategy? Describe a brief strategy for each of the four Ps for both the domestic and international markets.

Watch it

Comedian Mark Lundholm marketing recovery

Been there. Done that. That's what gives stand-up comic Mark Lundholm the edge. His comic routines tell about his experience as an alcoholic, drug addict, drug dealer, tax evader, cheque forger and prison inmate. He makes audiences laugh and cry with his personal memories about living in a cardboard box and pointing a loaded gun to his mouth to commit suicide.

As for his days of living on the streets of Oakland, California, Lundholm says, 'There's a pecking order on the street that is unbelievable. How big you are, how long you've been there and who you know – those things are the important things. Who you know is more important than who you are on the street.'

So why would anybody pay to hear what Lundholm calls comedy for the chemically challenged? Drug and alcohol addiction are so widespread today that despite positive efforts like the Just Say No program, alcohol and drug abuse are rising. When Lundholm performs at prisons, treatment centres and recovery meetings such as Alcoholics Anonymous (AA), audience members can truly identify with Lundholm's stories and so can their friends and families.

The population affected by substance abuse cuts across race, age, gender, and social and economic levels.

To those who suffer from addiction, Lundholm shares hope and the joy of fulfilment found in recovery through the powerful force of laughter. Yet parts of the show aren't funny at all. 'I'd be lying by omission if I went in and did 90 minutes of comedy,' explains Lundholm. He admits freely to audiences that his addiction cost him his wife, his daughter and his drycleaning business. His own recovery began in an Oakland drug rehabilitation centre in 1988, and the turmoil of his own life serves as material for his three comic shows: 'An Evening of 12-Step Humour', 'The Insanity Remains' and 'I'm Not Judgin', I'm Just Sayin''. Whenever his 'close to the bone originality' hits too close to home, Lundholm replies, 'I'm not judging, I'm just saying'. This catch phrase drew so many laughs that it became the name of a show. But people in recovery aren't the only ones who laugh at Lundholm's routines. He plays the comedy club circuit as well and appeals to 'normies', as he calls non-alcoholics. Although the routines revolve around the 12-step program of AA, they embrace enough of life's highs and lows for even 'normies' to be entertained. Every joke, every story is punctuated with animation: hands waving, feet flying, face contorted into a hundred deviations. Lundholm hits on the trials and tribulations of growing up with parents of the 1950s: 'Mark, back away from that TV, you're going to ruin your eyes.' Jokes aim at all types of relationships, roles and human peculiarities.

Now Lundholm performs at established comedy clubs such as Comedy Central, Zanies and Funny-Bone, but he began his career by opening shows for well-known Russian comic Yakov Smirnoff. Lundholm's booking agent and personal manager, Jimmy Goings, sells the one-man show directly to comedy venues and also provides entertainment consulting and production services to organisations conducting events.

A website, videocassettes, tapes, T-shirts and a book also promote Lundholm as a comedian. In general, an entertainer's fees grow as name recognition grows, and Lundholm is no exception. As he continues to travel and play the nightclub circuit, higher fees can be negotiated, but he still donates his time to reach people in recovery. Performing 46 weeks a year nationally and internationally, Lundholm usually includes recovery venues such as the Betty Ford Center, hospitals, halfway houses and prisons. When performing at a comedy club, he will speak at no charge at a high school in the area about the dangers of drug abuse. Lundholm takes his timely message to teenagers who can really benefit from it.

And this volunteer work has paid off. Solid public relations and much goodwill have come from this commitment to recovery. When writing reviews, the press regularly covers both the nightclub act and the performances at rehabilitation centres and schools. Good public relations, along with good material, have helped Lundholm to build his reputation as a comedian and to distinguish himself from the multitude of very funny, stand-up comics in the entertainment world. That's how Mark Lundholm markets recovery.

Questions

1 What is Lundholm's mission?
2 What is Lundholm's differential advantage?
3 Who are the target market segments? What benefits do they receive?
4 Describe Lundholm's marketing mix.

Click it

Online reading

INFOTRAC® COLLEGE EDITION
For additional readings and review on global marketing, explore InfoTrac® College Edition, your online library. Go to: www.infotrac-college.com and search for any of the InfoTrac key terms listed below:
- global marketing
- tarrif
- product invention
- free-trade agreement

Answer key

1 *Answer*: b, p. 448 *Rationale*: A quota is a tool used by a government to limit the amount of imports in a specific industry or sector in an effort to help domestic producers.

2 *Answer*: b, p. 447 *Rationale*: Tariffs are a tax that is levied on goods entering a country to help control import levels.

3 *Answer*: a, p.440 *Rationale*: Global marketing offers organisations advantages in production and economic viability.

4 *Answer*: c, p.442 *Rationale*: Organisational capacity is the only variable that looks inwards to the organisation while all other factors look to the external environment that the organisation cannot control.

5 *Answer*: d, p.451 *Rationale*: Global marketing research can be different in foreign countries due to differences in culture, geography and mail and telephone systems.

6 *Answer*: d, p.445 *Rationale*: When a country emerges from a developing country to one that is developed it is recognised as a takeoff economy due to its economic growth, and healthy social and political climate.

7 *Answer*: d, p.442-4 *Rationale*: Language, packaging and gift giving are cultural factors that must be understood as part of the cultural factors when considering trade with different countries to ones own.

8 *Answer*: d, p.462 *Rationale*: Wireless technology is limited to local areas and the proximity of a wireless connection all other answers and communication modes available to global marketers.

9 *Answer*: b, p.452 *Rationale*: One of the first decisions a global marketer needs to make is whether to adopt a standardised or differentiated marketing strategy. A differentiated strategy would require a seperate message and maybe a modified product.

10 *Answer*: b, p.457 *Rationale*: Marketing managers need to consider the cultural, economic, legal and institutional aspects of each market before trying to design marketing channels in foreign countries.

Marketing strategy

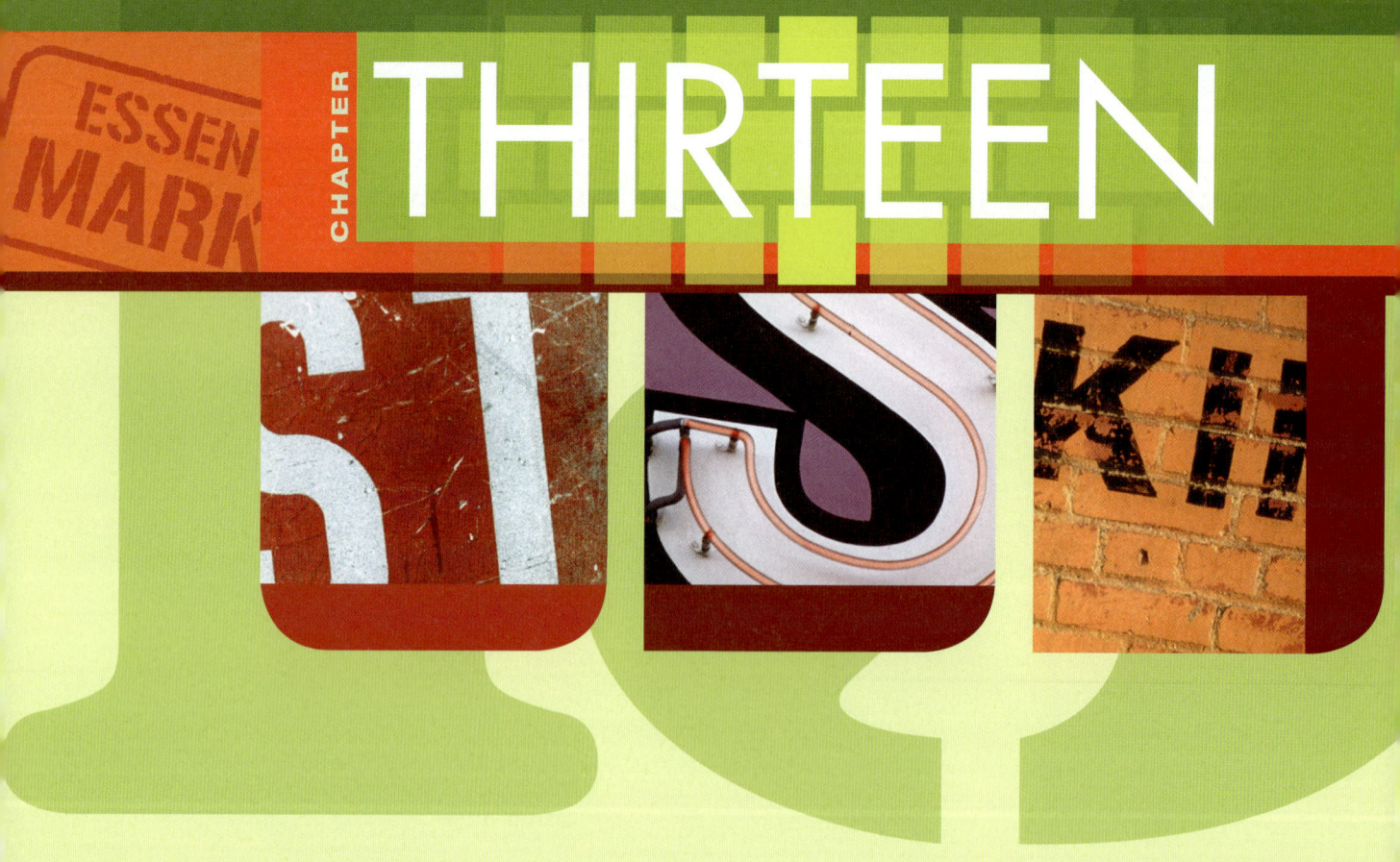

CHAPTER THIRTEEN

LEARNING OBJECTIVES

After studying this chapter, you should be able to

1. Discuss the three levels of strategy
2. Explain the four competing business orientations that impact marketing strategy
3. Understand the importance of strategic planning
4. Discuss the importance of writing a marketing plan and define its elements
5. Describe the criteria for stating good marketing objectives
6. Discuss the external environment of marketing and explain how it affects an organisation
7. Describe the sociocultural factors that affect marketing
8. Explain the importance to marketing managers of multiculturalism and growing ethnic markets
9. Identify consumer and market reaction to the state of the economy
10. Identify the impact of technology on an organisation
11. Discuss the political and legal environment of marketing
12. Explain the basis of foreign and domestic competition
13. Describe the elements of the marketing mix
14. Explain why implementation, evaluation and control of the marketing plan are necessary
15. Describe the role of ethics and ethical decisions in business
16. Discuss corporate social responsibility

Sports shoes: The shocking truth

Sports shoes are not designed to help the average punter and may do more harm than good, says an Australian podiatrist. Speaking at the 2001 Australian Conference of Science and Medicine in Sport, Simon Bartold from the University of South Australia said it was a myth that shoes with softer mid-soles provide better cushioning.

'To a large degree shoe design doesn't make a lot of difference,' said Mr Bartold, a research fellow within the School of Health Sciences. 'The perfect model we should be working on already exists – the foot.'

The problem, he says, is that many sports shoe manufacturers have spent considerable amounts of money marketing certain products and are unwilling to change their marketing focus.

'What you are dealing with is a very unusual crossover between hard-core science and a commercial product, and it's an unholy marriage.'

Biomechanics, the science behind sports shoe manufacture, is a very active area of research both inside and outside manufacturers' laboratories.

But don't give up on sports shoes yet.

New Balance on-line

How does New Balance utilise its website to build brand identity? What clues do you see on the site that New Balance appeals to an older target market? Compare New Balance's website to Nike's. Which is more youth-oriented? How did you reach this conclusion?
www.newbalance.com.au
www.nike.com

'There is a widespread acknowledgement now that things have to change,' said Mr Bartold, who, in addition to his work at the university, advises a sports shoe company. Research that was done on shoes for an athlete for the 2000 Olympic Games showed he could increase his time by between 0.5 per cent and 3 per cent, which may be the difference between gold and silver. And while footwear as an ergonomic aid is not necessary for the average weekend jogger, the wrong shoe, regardless of cost, can potentially cause injury. In the future, Mr Bartold believes we will see radically different running shoes on shop shelves, with considerably less bulk and flexibility where the foot flexes.[1]

And yet companies such as Nike and New Balance are spending about $1 thousand million a year to advertise their athletic shoes.[2] Fortunately for New Balance,
it is becoming the Nike of the baby-boom generation, says Mike Kormas, president of Footwear Market Insights. He notes that the average age of an American Nike consumer is 25, the average age of a Reebok consumer is 33 and the average age of a New Balance consumer is 42.

Although a youngster tends to buy more sneakers than a middle-aged person, the older-age niche is less fickle about fashion, which reduces development and stocking costs. With fewer models and fewer expensive updates, the company believes it can risk skimping on marketing and big-name endorsers. Changing demographics can pose threats and offer opportunities to companies and is only one of a number of factors in the external environment that can impact on an organisation's decisions in the product development phase.

Does the external environment affect the marketing mix of most companies? What other uncontrollable factors in the external environment might impact on New Balance? Read this chapter to find out how to answer these questions.

About this chapter

In this chapter, we examine the way organisations plan and manage their marketing activities. First, we consider the different marketing orientations and their role in influencing the strategies adopted by an organisation. Next, we reflect on the role of marketing in the organisation's overall strategic plan and the four stages in the marketing process used to develop the constructs to draft the marketing plan. The components of the marketing plan, and the implementation and control processes adopted to ensure that the goals of the marketing program are addressed, follow from this discussion. Finally, we consider issues involved with social and ethical behaviour and its impact and influence upon corporate social responsibility.

An organisational overview of strategy

1 Discuss the three levels of strategy

corporate strategy
The highest level of the strategic hierarchy that deals with the overall direction of the organisation.

There are three levels of strategy that together form a 'hierarchy of strategy' within an organisation. At the highest level is the **corporate strategy**. Areas of interest at this level include decisions about the types of business the firm will be in, and the allocation of key company resources to different divisions. For example, Goodman Fielder (GF) operates in five major business areas: baking Australia, baking New Zealand, commercial, Uncle Tobys and Meadow Lea Foods.[3]

The second level of strategy, **business strategy**, is normally associated with strategic business units (SBUs). An SBU comprises related products that satisfy the needs of a particular market. For example, GF separates its food-related consumer goods products into the following SBUs: margarine, cooking oils, mayonnaise, dressings, table sauces, meal solutions, Asian cuisine, vinegars, Indian cuisine, marinades, pasta sauces, breakfast cereals, cake mixes, bread mixes, soups, retail flour, desserts, nutritious snacks, cereal snacks, muesli bars, fruit snacks, fruit bars, biscuit and cheese snacks, pasta packaged meals, sauces, cake and dessert mixes, baking powder and baking soda, custard powder, yeasts, cornflour, oat products, vinegar, and herbs and spices.

The third and final level of strategy, **functional strategy**, supports the corporate- and business-level strategies by pulling together various activities necessary to gain the desired competitive advantage. Traditionally, each functional area performs specialised aspects of the organisation's tasks. Functional areas may include marketing, accounting or finance, manufacturing, product development and others. For example, the functional-level marketing strategy resolves questions concerning which products deliver customer satisfaction and value, what price to charge, how to distribute these products, and what type of marketing communication activities should be engaged in; whereas the functional-level manufacturing strategy would decide what products manufacturing can make, at what rate to produce them and how best to make the products (that is, the best combination of labour and capital).

The effective formulation and implementation of corporate- and business-level strategies, however, depend on functional groups working in partnership with one another. Crossing functional boundaries is referred to as managing horizontally and requires a significant level of coordination among business functions. Effective horizontal management therefore would require that a marketing manager would need to take a keen interest in, say, financial issues and that an operational manager would need to have some understanding of the firm's customers, and so on throughout the various functional areas.

Today's business environment has put considerable pressure on functional groups to work together more harmoniously. The rush to get products into the marketplace is greater than ever before; at the same time, customers are much more demanding about what they want in these products. The result is that we can expect customers to want customised products delivered immediately. The key to developing a truly marketing-oriented organisation that achieves high levels of customer satisfaction is cross-functional integration.

A major challenge for marketers has been the development of mechanisms for reducing conflict between the marketing department and other business functions. Working closely with human resources and information technology professionals, two major facilitating mechanisms have emerged that have assisted in this area: cross-functional teams and an information technology infrastructure. To illustrate this functional integration, we can look at Hewlett-Packard's team approach to all of its product development. From concept to market entry, teams of engineers, marketers, manufacturers, financiers and accountants bring together traditionally functional-level information into a cohesive program for product introduction. All information is shared across functional groups, and reports are prepared regularly that include details of interactions among functions.

The retailing industry has also made great strides via the electronic highway in that the reduction in the need for human intervention speeds up the transaction process and reduces the chances of error and conflict occurring across functional groups. Consequently, teamwork and shared information result in better communication between marketing and other business functions, which ultimately results in a more satisfied customer.

business strategy
The second level of the strategic hierarchy that deals with the overall direction of strategic business units.

functional strategy
The third level of the strategic hierarchy that deals with implementation of the strategic direction at an operational level.

Goodman Fielder on-line

Visit the Goodman Fielder site and see how many different SBUs you can identify. Were you aware of all the different products and brand names that Goodman Fielder owns? Why do you think it continues to trade with this large range of different brand names, instead of rebadging them all as GF brands?
www.goodmanfielder.com.au

Marketing orientations

2 Explain the four competing business orientations that impact marketing strategy

As noted in Chapter 1, four competing orientations strongly influence the marketing activities within an organisation. These orientations are commonly referred to as production, sales, marketing and relational marketing orientations. Each will now be discussed.

Production orientation (focusing on manufacturing efficiency)

A **production orientation** is an organisational philosophy that focuses on the internal capabilities of the firm rather than on the desires and needs of the marketplace. A production orientation means that management assesses its resources and asks these questions: 'What can we do best?' 'What can our engineers design?' and 'What is easy to produce, given our equipment?' In the case of a service organisation, managers ask: 'What services are most convenient for the firm to offer?' and 'Where do our talents lie?' Some have referred to this orientation as a *Field of Dreams* orientation, referring to the line in the Kevin Costner movie, 'If we build it, they will come.'

There is nothing wrong with assessing an organisation's capabilities; in fact, such assessments are major considerations in strategic marketing planning (as discussed later in this chapter). The only downfall of the production orientation is that it doesn't consider whether the products the organisation efficiently produces also meet the needs of the marketplace.

In the 1980s, PPG Industries scientists spent considerable time, effort and money developing a windshield that would let in filtered sunlight but block out the heat. They were convinced that this new product was significantly better than existing windshields. However, when the new windshield was introduced in 1991, car manufacturers refused to buy it. They didn't like the bluish colour or the price of the windscreen.[4] This is a classic example of a production orientation that failed to consider the needs and wants of the marketplace. Often consumers, be they other organisations (as in the case of car manufacturers) or individuals, don't want what is best for them. This windshield may have had many features that were superior to existing windshields, but the customers didn't see these as important enough attributes for them to change their existing purchasing patterns. Price was obviously a more important attribute than heat transference.

In addition, a production orientation doesn't necessarily doom a company to failure, particularly not in the short run. Sometimes what a firm can best produce is exactly what the market wants. The organisation 3M's commercial tape division developed and patented the adhesive component of Post-it™ Notes a year before a commercial application was identified. In other situations, such as where weak competition exists or where demand exceeds supply, a production-oriented organisation can be very successful.

Sales orientation (focusing on selling existing products)

A **sales orientation** addresses the belief that people will buy more products if aggressive sales techniques are used and that high sales result in high profits. Not only are sales to the final buyer emphasised, but also intermediaries are encouraged to push manufacturers' products more aggressively. To sales-oriented organisations, marketing means selling things and collecting money.

---

production orientation
A philosophy that focuses on the internal capabilities of the firm, rather than on the desires and needs of the marketplace.

sales orientation
The idea that people will buy more goods and services if aggressive sales techniques are used and that high sales result in high profits.

As with the production orientation, the fundamental issue before a sales-oriented organisation is a lack of understanding of the needs and wants of the marketplace. Often these organisations find that despite the quality of their sales team, they cannot convince people to buy products they don't need or want.

Marketing orientation (focusing on customer needs and wants)

The **marketing orientation** proposes that the social and economic justification for an organisation's existence is the satisfaction of customer wants and needs while meeting organisational objectives. It understands that a sale doesn't depend on an aggressive sales team, but rather on a customer's decision to purchase a product. What is of primary importance is that a business is defined not by what the business thinks it produces, but by what the customers think they are buying – the perceived value. The **marketing concept** includes the following:

- focusing on customer wants and needs so that the organisation can distinguish its product(s) from competitors' offerings;
- integrating all the organisation's activities, including production, to satisfy these wants; and
- achieving long-term goals for the organisation by satisfying customer wants and needs legally and responsibly.

The marketing concept recognises that there is no reason why customers should buy one organisation's offerings rather than those of another unless they are receiving a perceived better value from the exchange.

Understanding your competitive arena and competitors' strengths and weaknesses is a critical component of the marketing orientation. This includes assessing existing or potential competitors' actions and strategies.

Another dimension of the marketing orientation is societal orientation. Organisations adopting this orientation or philosophy believe that an organisation exists not only to satisfy customer wants and needs and to meet organisational objectives, but also to preserve or enhance individuals' and society's long-term best interests. You will have read about ethically oriented organisations in a number of other chapters in this text that have adopted this approach as the focus for their businesses. These organisations aim to ensure poor and underprivileged communities receive fair and equitable payment for their goods and labour and they only deal with other like minded organisations. The Body Shop is a classic example of an organisation with a well publicised social conscience. McDonald's is another classic example of a company that has embraced the societal orientation. Ronald McDonald House Charities supports Ronald McDonald Houses™ throughout Australia, as well as other programs that directly help seriously ill children to live happier, healthier lives. McDonald's Australia Limited pays all administration, management and other non-income-generating costs for Ronald McDonald House Charities. One hundred cents in every dollar raised goes directly to programs which help to give seriously ill children a better tomorrow. It is also involved in fundraising activities for the Starlight Foundation and other large charities that focus on terminally ill children. This is one way that McDonald's can demonstrate a commitment to children and a societal conscience.[5]

marketing orientation
A philosophy that assumes that a sale depends on a customer's decision to purchase a product.

marketing concept
Idea that the social and economic justification for an organisation's existence is the satisfaction of customer wants and needs while meeting organisational objectives.

Ronald McDonald House on-line

Visit the site to find out how the organisation is involved in various charities and activities to aid ill children. Did you know how involved this charity was before you visited the site?
www.rmhc.org.au/home

Relationship marketing orientation (focusing on relationships with existing suppliers and customers)

relationship marketing orientation
The marketing orientation philosophy which focuses on the value of the repeat sale rather than on making a sale that meets the needs and wants of the marketplace.

The philosophical approach used in the **relationship marketing orientation** is to expand the marketing orientation focus from one where making a sale meets the needs and wants of the marketplace, to a focus on the value of the repeat sale, thus establishing a relationship with the customer rather than a one-time exchange. Equally, this orientation recognises the other parties that complement or aid in facilitating the exchange as being essential to the success of the organisation. As such, the focus is on the development of long-term, mutually satisfying exchanges between the organisation and its customers (both organisational and individual). Some of this approach was covered in Chapter 6 earlier when we discussed services.

Having identified the impact and importance of the characteristics of an organisation's marketing orientation, it is now appropriate to discuss the process that organisations use to achieve their established purpose – in particular, their strategic objectives – and the role of marketing in strategic planning.

The nature of strategic planning

3 Understand the importance of strategic planning

Marketing is one of a number of important organisational functions. (Finance, human resource management and information technology are others, as mentioned early in the chapter.) Thus, the development of successful marketing strategies and plans must reflect the organisation's overall intent. If marketing goals and objectives differ from those of the organisation as a whole, then confusion and wastage will occur within the organisation. In addition, confusing messages will be sent to the organisation's customers and stakeholders, which will result in poorer overall performance and loss of confidence. Well-prepared and organisationally aligned planning ensures that all the functional areas of the organisation are striving to meet the same goals.

planning
The process of anticipating future events and determining strategies to achieve organisational objectives in the future.

strategic planning
The managerial process of creating and maintaining a fit between the organisation's objectives and resources and evolving market opportunities.

Planning is the process of anticipating future events and determining strategies to achieve organisational objectives in the future. **Strategic planning** is the managerial process of creating and maintaining a fit between the organisation's objectives, resources and the evolving market opportunities. The goal of strategic planning is to achieve the organisation's objective in the most cost-beneficial manner.* Thus, strategic planning requires long-term commitments of resources.[6]

The implication of this process is that errors in judgement can threaten the organisation's survival, but on the other hand, a good strategic plan can help to protect an organisation's resources against competitive onslaughts.[7] For example, if video hire companies had considered that they were only in the business of hiring out videos and hadn't adopted a broader perspective of hiring out entertainment products, they wouldn't have seen the opportunity to take up games and DVDs and, consequently, most of them would now be out of business.

> *Personal communication with Professor S. Mehta (11 February 2002): '... with the generic use of marketing these days, it is unrealistic to consider all organisations, including non-profit and government bodies, as striving for long-term growth and profit maximisation.'

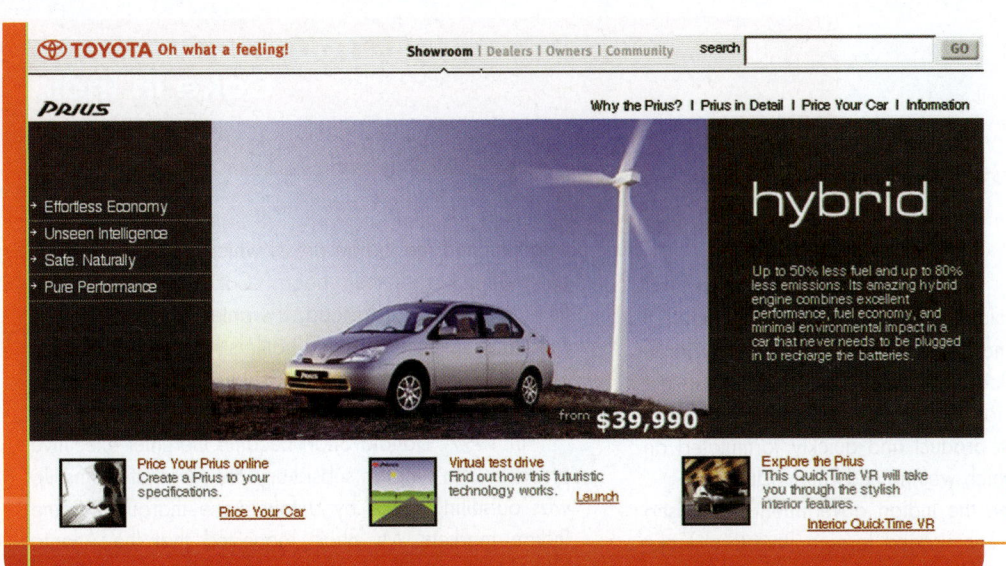

This hybrid car recognises future demand for a car with less emissions.

An organisation's strategic plan is normally based around the four steps of:

1. defining the company mission;
2. setting company objectives and goals;
3. designing the business portfolio; and
4. planning the marketing and other functional activities.

Hence, strategic planning covers the entire activities of the organisation, including all of the **strategic business units (SBUs)** and each functional area. Developing functional strategies and plans is the fourth step in the strategic planning process. One technique for identifying opportunities is to seek strategic windows. A **strategic window** is the identification of an opportunity for a limited period in the future and managing the organisation's resources so that there is a fit between the key market needs and the ability of the organisation to meet those needs at an optimum level.

In the next section, we will focus on the development of marketing strategies and plans that are in line with the company's overall strategic plan.

strategic business unit (SBU)
A subgroup of a single business or collection of related businesses within the larger organisation.

strategic window
The limited period during which the 'fit' between the key requirements of a market and the particular competencies of a firm are at an optimum.

Marketing strategy and plans

It should now be apparent that the marketing strategies and plans must be drawn from the organisational strategy. In the same way, financial, information technology, human resource management and any other key element of an organisation must be aligned to the organisational strategy. This section will look specifically at marketing strategy and the subsequent marketing plan. Marketing strategy is the longer-term view of the marketing effort for an organisation. The marketing plan provides the application planning tools and responsibilities necessary to ensure that marketing activities are conducted at the appropriate time by the appropriate person in order to achieve the marketing strategy.

Global Perspectives

Thumbs down for Coke in India

For years, Coca-Cola was India's leading soft drink, but in 1977 Coke left India when a new government ordered the company to reduce its stake in the Indian unit and turn over its secret formula. Coke's bottlers in India were suddenly without a product and quickly formulated an alternative cola, which was named Thums Up.

In 1993, when the Indian government liberalised the economy and encouraged foreign investors, Coke returned. Coke decided that the easiest way to gain a commanding lead in the Indian marketplace was to purchase Thums Up, along with other soft drinks such as Limca, a cloudy lemon drink. Coke's plan was simple: take out its biggest competitor and gain access to the more than 50 bottlers that distributed Thums Up throughout India. The rest, Coke thought, would be easy, because, after all, India already knew Coke well, and consumers were surely ready to welcome back their old favourite.

Wrong. Much had changed in the 16 years between 1977 and 1993. A new generation had grown up without Coca-Cola and was therefore not clamouring for its return. Additionally, Pepsi had entered the Indian market before Coke, and was turning the new generation into the 'Pepsi generation'. Pepsi had already made quick strides in the Indian market by staffing operations with Indians and signing up cricket stars idolised by millions of Indians as endorsers.

To make matters worse, Coke battled with its Indian bottlers, who became less cooperative. Coke also shunned the Indian press, which splashed bottlers' complaints across their pages. Coke also didn't want to push Thums Up; instead, it wanted to focus on 'The real thing'. Consumers and bottlers loyal to the popular Thums Up brand believed that Coke was trying to kill the brand, which caused further problems.

In 1997, Donald Short became the chief executive of Coca-Cola's Indian subsidiary. He saw that Thums Up was outselling Coke by a four-to-one margin in some Indian markets. Mr Short requested that the Atlanta office reprint his Bombay business cards to read CEO of Thums Up, rather than CEO of the Coca-Cola Company. He hired Indian professionals and pushed Coke brands heavily with tie-ins to cricket and the movies. He improved relations with bottlers and hoped to double the number of sales outlets to one million by the year 2000. At the same time, Mr Short had no qualms about giving Thums Up top billing and the highest level of expenditures, because the brand remains the company's biggest seller and is the fastest-growing brand in India.

Coke expected its overall sales in India to grow by 20 per cent in 1998, compared to a disappointing 5 per cent in 1997. Pepsi still outsells the Coca-Cola brand, but Coke is ahead of Pepsi in sales if Thums Up is included. In the longer term, Coke may find it hard to push both Coca-Cola and Thums Up. Coke only promotes two sugar colas in India, but Mr Short plans to export Thums Up out of India.[8]

Should Coke pursue the growth option of exporting Thums Up into international markets where Coke already competes?

---

marketing strategy
The activities of selecting and describing one or more target markets and developing and maintaining a marketing mix that will produce mutually satisfying exchanges with target markets.

Specifically, it can be said that **marketing strategy** management addresses several long-term decisions that will affect the organisation's long-term performance, its allocation of resources and, ultimately, its success. These issues include:

1. What is the organisation's main marketing activity at a particular time?
2. How will it reach its goals?
3. What are the appropriate target market(s)?
4. What are the most appropriate marketing objectives for the organisation for each of the target market(s)?
5. What is the appropriate marketing mix for each product in each market such that satisfactory exchanges of value occur for the organisation and the customer?

In contrast, operating decisions, such as those made in the development and implementation of the marketing plans, probably won't have a big impact on the long-run profitability of the company. For example, deciding to change the supplier of cardboard boxes for packaging cornflakes, or to alter the delivery schedules for products, or to use more television advertising and less print advertising won't impact directly on the long-term goals of the organisation and are the sorts of decisions that corporate management doesn't need to be involved in.

Marketing planning involves designing activities relating to marketing objectives and the changing marketing environment. Marketing planning is the basis for all marketing strategies and decisions. Issues such as product lines, distribution channels, marketing communications and pricing are described in the **marketing plan**.

The marketing plan is a written document that acts as a guidebook of marketing activities for the marketing manager and all persons in the organisation who are involved in the marketing effort. In this chapter, you will learn about the importance of writing a marketing plan and the types of information contained in a marketing plan. The chapter opening vignette helps to illustrate the importance of both marketing strategy and planning.

marketing planning
Designing activities relating to marketing objectives and the changing marketing environment.

marketing plan
A written document that acts as a guidebook of marketing activities for the marketing manager.

Developing and implementing a marketing plan

Why write a marketing plan?

Marketing can be one of the most expensive and complicated business components, but it is also one of the most important business activities. The written marketing plan lists clearly stated activities that help employees to understand and work towards common goals. By specifying objectives and defining the actions required to attain them, the marketing plan provides the basis for comparison between actual and expected performances. Additionally, writing a marketing plan also allows the marketing environment to be examined (external analysis) in conjunction with the inner workings of the organisation (internal analysis). Once written, the marketing plan provides a reference point between where the organisation hopes to be and where it is, and allows the opportunity to modify the plan in light of changing and unforeseen circumstances. Finally, the marketing plan allows the marketing manager to enter the marketplace with an awareness of opportunities and possibilities.

What is a marketing plan?

A marketing plan outlines the needs of the organisation, and therefore it can be written in many different ways. Most organisations need a written marketing plan because the scope of a marketing plan is large and complex, and detail is usually lost if communicated orally. Regardless of the way a marketing plan is presented, there are elements common to all marketing plans (see Exhibit 13.1). These include defining the organisational mission and objectives, performing a situation analysis, describing target markets, establishing the components of the marketing mix for each target market, and stating the implementation and control processes. Based on this structure, other elements that may be included in a plan are budgets, implementation timetables and required marketing research efforts.

4 Discuss the importance of writing a marketing plan and define its elements

B&T Marketing and Media on-line

This on-line magazine often provides interesting case studies of marketing activities and plans for a range of companies. If you visit the site and type 'Objectives', in the search option, you will get a list of case studies that you can study. They are interesting and useful for ideas and examples of marketing objectives and plans.
www.bandt.com.au

Exhibit 13.1
Elements of a marketing plan

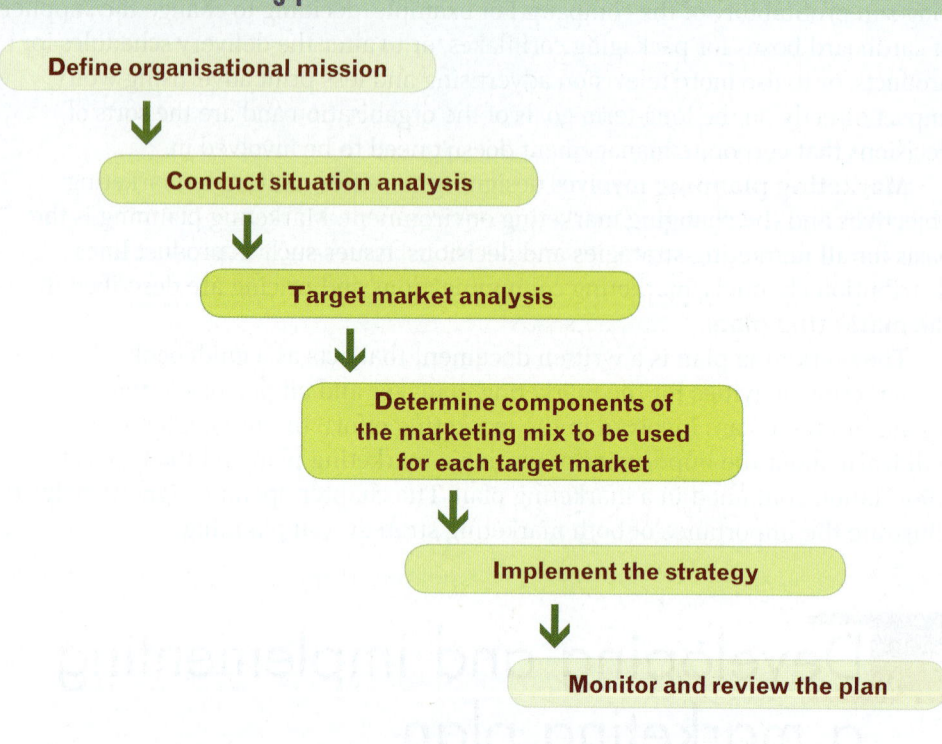

```
Define organisational mission
          ↓
Conduct situation analysis
          ↓
Target market analysis
          ↓
Determine components of
the marketing mix to be used
for each target market
          ↓
Implement the strategy
          ↓
Monitor and review the plan
```

Let's now consider the common elements of the marketing plan in a little more detail, beginning with defining the marketing objectives.

Defining the organisational mission and objectives

The foundation of any marketing plan is first answering the question, 'What business are we in and where are we going?' The answer is the firm's **mission statement**. A mission statement should focus on the market or markets the organisation is attempting to serve, rather than on the good or service offered. Otherwise, a new technology may quickly make the good or service obsolete and the mission statement irrelevant to company functions.

Mission statements that are stated too narrowly suffer from marketing myopia. (**Marketing myopia** means that the business is defined in terms of goods and services, rather than in terms of the benefits that customers seek.[9]) By correctly stating the organisational mission in terms of the benefits that customers seek, the foundation for the marketing plan is set. Many organisations are now focusing on redesigning their mission statements, as they are often reproduced on their home page. As the mission statement is thus exposed to the world, it needs to be free of jargon, simple to read and yet expansive in its content in order to explain where the organisation is going and what orientations it is adopting.

A **marketing objective** is a statement of what needs to be accomplished through marketing activities. To be useful, these stated objectives should be realistic, measurable, time-specific and allocated to a responsible person. In order to achieve marketing objectives, a number of specific tasks or tactics are usually outlined that state in detail how things need to be done. The most important part of setting objectives is that they are measurable; otherwise, it is impossible to determine success or failure.

---

mission statement
The firm's long-term vision based on a careful analysis of benefits sought by present and potential customers and analysis of existing and anticipated environmental conditions.

marketing myopia
Business defined in terms that are too focused on one aspect of the organisation's markets (its goods and services), rather than seeing the whole picture (the benefits that customers seek).

5 Describe the criteria for stating good marketing objectives

marketing objective
A statement of what is to be accomplished through marketing activities.

The marketing objective for the launch of the Yowie ice-cream product by Cadbury early in 2002 was to launch the product to the five- to 12-years demographic, with fun, energetic, exciting and entertaining brand qualities.[10] This objective is reasonably broad and doesn't really contain any measurable benchmarks for use in determining if the launch was successful. The measurement of this objective is found in the tactics detailing how the objective is to be achieved. Still, the objective could be more detailed, as in the case of a recent NRMA marketing campaign which had the following objective: 'To increase the client's home loans brand awareness by 10 per cent and loan applications by 15 per cent on a budget of about $200 000 in a fiercely contested category where millions of dollars are spent each month.'[11] This objective has more measurable outcomes and states clearly what is to be achieved.

Performing a situation analysis

The first stage in performing a situation analysis to identify market opportunities is conducting an environmental analysis.

The external marketing environment

6 Discuss the external environment of marketing and explain how it affects an organisation

If you have worked through Chapters 6 to 11, you will understand that managers create a marketing mix by uniquely combining product, distribution, promotion and pricing strategies. The marketing mix is, of course, under the organisation's control and is designed to appeal to a specific group of potential buyers, more commonly known as the **target market**.

Over time, managers must alter the marketing mix because of changes in the environment. Also, as markets mature, new consumers become part of the target market while others drop out. Those who remain may change their tastes, needs, incomes, lifestyles and buying habits from the original target consumers.

Although managers can control the marketing mix, they cannot control elements in the external environment. Exhibit 13.2 shows the controllable and uncontrollable variables that affect the target market, whether the market is other businesses or final consumers. The uncontrollable elements on the outer edges of the diagram continually evolve and create changes and influences to the target market. In contrast, managers can shape and reshape the marketing mix, depicted by the yellow circle in the exhibit, to influence the target market.

target market
A group of people or organisations for which an organisation designs, implements and maintains a marketing mix intended to meet the needs of that group, resulting in mutually satisfying exchanges.

Understanding the external environment

Unless marketing managers understand the external environment, the organisation cannot intelligently plan for the future. Thus, many larger organisations assemble a team of specialists to continually collect and evaluate environmental information, a process called **environmental scanning**. The goal

environmental scanning
Collection and interpretation of information about forces, events and relationships in the external environment that may affect the future of the organisation or the implementation of the marketing plan.

Exhibit 13.2
Effect of controllable and uncontrollable variables that affect the target market

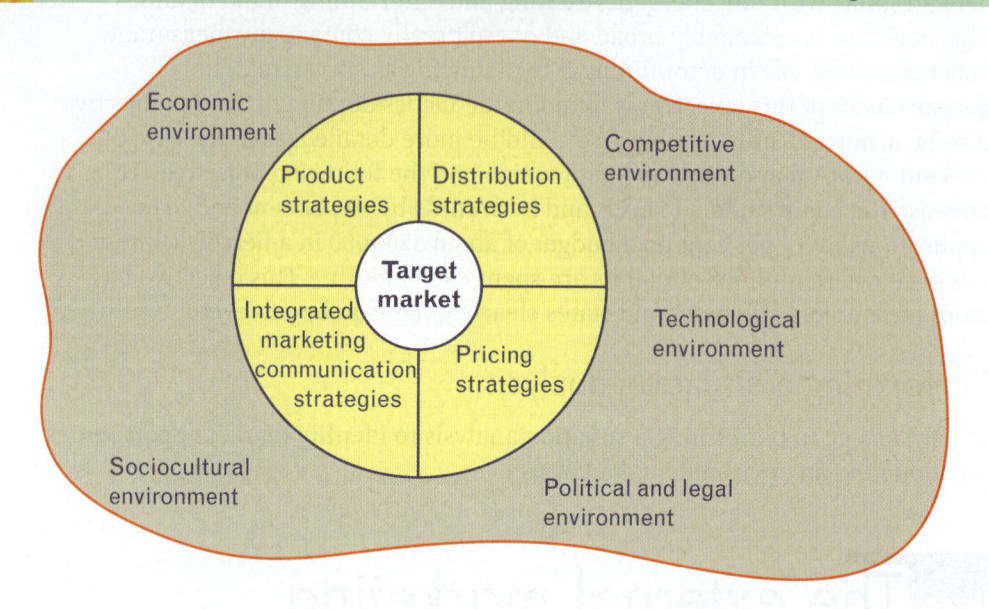

[Diagram: Target market at the centre surrounded by controllable variables — Product strategies, Distribution strategies, Pricing strategies, Integrated marketing communication strategies — all enclosed within the uncontrollable variables: Economic environment, Competitive environment, Technological environment, Political and legal environment, Sociocultural environment.]

in gathering the environmental data is to identify future market opportunities and threats. For example, as technology continues to blur the line between personal computers, digital television, the Internet and other entertainment technologies, a company such as Sony may find itself competing against companies such as Hewlett-Packard and Compaq. Recent trends by Microsoft, Nintendo and Sony to develop game machines that access DVDs and the Internet show the diversity of providers and the merging of technologies to offer more, faster and better options for the entertainment market. Is this information an opportunity or a threat to Hewlett-Packard and Compaq marketing managers?

Environmental management

No one organisation is large or powerful enough to create major change in the external environment. Thus, marketing managers are basically adapters to, rather than agents of, change. For example, News Corporation is one of the world's largest vertically integrated media companies. Its global operations include newspaper and magazine publishing on three continents, significant book publishing interests, major motion picture and television production and distribution operations, as well as television, satellite and cable broadcast operations in the United States, Europe, Asia, Australia and Latin America. In addition to his role as chairman and chief executive of News Corporation, Rupert Murdoch serves as chairman and chief executive of Fox Entertainment Group. But even with all this influence on the way the world sees itself, News Corporation is still unable to control the environmental aspects of its markets.

However, an organisation is not always completely at the mercy of all external environmental elements and it can sometimes influence an external event. The environments that are more readily to be influenced by an organisation or section of the community are the elements in the political environmental. This is seen clearly in government election periods, where government and opposition policies change rapidly in response to community sentiment. When a company implements strategies that attempt to shape the external environment within which it operates, it is engaging in **environmental management**.

Tools such as **SWOT analysis**, IFE (internal factor evaluations) and EFE (external factor evaluations) matrices and other techniques can be used here to consider the organisation's strengths and weaknesses (internal to the organisation), and opportunities and threats (external to the organisation).

When examining external opportunities and threats, marketing managers must analyse aspects of the marketing environment. Internal scanning usually reviews issues such as the financial considerations, managerial style, corporate culture and geographic dispersion of the organisation. To help with these reviews and to understand the internal environment, some organisations use techniques such as business portfolio analysis and market attractiveness analysis.

While you need to be aware that these market analysis techniques exist, you don't, at this stage, need to be able to implement them. They are, after all, only some of the multitude of tools available to help the market analyst define and describe the market.

The factors within the external environment that are important to marketing managers can be classified as sociocultural, demographic, economic, technological, political and legal, and competitive.

> **environmental management**
> When a company implements strategies that attempt to shape the external environment within which it operates.

> **SWOT analysis**
> Identifying internal strengths (S) and weaknesses (W) and also examining external opportunities (O) and threats (T).

Sociocultural environment

Social change is perhaps the most difficult external variable for marketing managers to forecast, influence or integrate into marketing plans. Social factors include our attitudes, values and lifestyles. Social factors influence the products people buy, the value they determine a product to have, the effectiveness of specific promotions, and how, where and when people expect to purchase products.

To begin the review of sociocultural components we will look at the common age group classifications used by marketers. These groups are identified as they tend to have the same behaviour if they are born within a group, and that behaviour is different from the behaviour of persons born in other years. We will consider four groups in detail:

- Baby boomers (1946–64)
- Generation Xers (1961–80)
- Generation Ys (1979–94)
- Generation Z (1994 to present)

7 Describe the sociocultural factors that affect marketing

Baby boomers: demanding change

Baby boomers are identified as a group of people who were born after the Second World War and before the mid-1960s. This group, or cohort, created a blip in the age group pattern of the population, as more people were born during this period than in any other prior period or subsequently (as can be seen in Exhibit 13.3). A second blip, about one-fifth the size, can be seen in the following years representing Generation Y, which will be discussed later.

> **baby boomers**
> People born between 1946 and 1964.

Exhibit 13.3
Components of Australian natural population increase

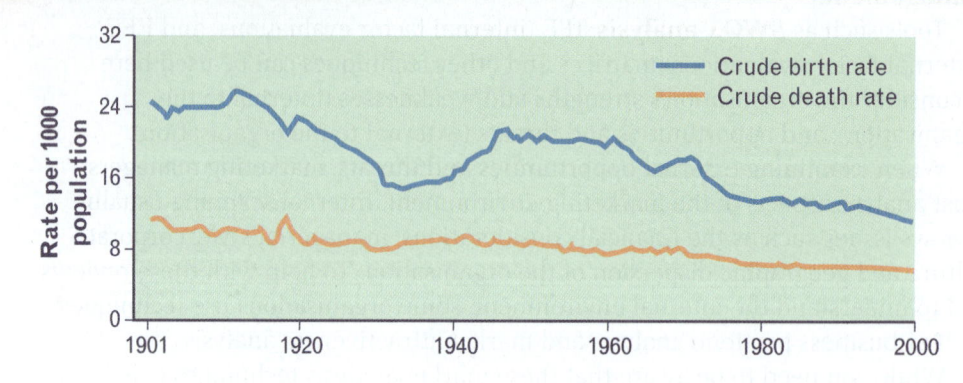

Source: ABS, Australian Historical Population Statistics, Cat. No. 3105.0.65.001; Australian Demographic Statistics, Cat. No. 3101.0.

The impact of the baby boomers over the years has been quite substantial in Australia and New Zealand. In the 1960s, the hippie and civil-rights movements were the foundation of the baby boomers in their young adult years. In the 1970s, the baby boomers moved into the young family life cycle and their need for better family care and facilities for young children became a cry to the politicians. In the 1980s, the baby boomers were the capital of industry and rode the wave of greed and self-indulgence. Their families were older, and with dual family incomes the norm, families became less important than careers. By the 1990s, the baby boomers had seen that material things were not as important as they had made them in the 1980s, and they once again made an effort to develop family and community as the focus of their efforts. Now, in the noughties, the baby boomers are looking at retirement and the meaning of life.

As this discussion shows, as the baby boomers have aged they have changed their values and attitudes, resulting in shifts in cultural norms. These changes have affected the marketing strategies adopted by organisations. For example, the oldest baby boomers are now over 60, but still clinging to their youth. This group cherishes convenience, which has resulted in a growing demand for home delivery of items such

Baby boomers are a more demanding cohort of people than any other group in history.

as large appliances, furniture and groceries. In addition, the spreading culture of convenience explains the tremendous appeal of prepared take-away foods and the necessity of VCRs and mobile telephones. Businesses offer the individualistic baby boomers a growing array of customised products, services, houses and retirement villages, cars, furniture, appliances, clothes, holidays, jobs, leisure time and even beliefs.

The importance of individualism among baby boomers led to a **personalised economy**, which requires successful organisations to deliver goods and services at a good value on demand. To do this, organisations must understand their customers extremely well. In fact, the intimacy between producer and consumer is exactly what makes an economy personalised. Characteristics of the personalised economy include:

- *Customisation*: Products are custom designed and marketed to ever-smaller target markets.
- *Immediacy*: Goods and services are delivered at the convenience of the consumer rather than that of the provider.
- *Value*: Organisations need to be value competitive or to create innovative products that can command premium prices.

personalised economy
Delivering goods and services at a good value on demand.

Because middle-aged and older consumers buy more reading materials than any other age group, the market for books and magazines should remain strong throughout the early 2000s. However, it has been noted that people who buy magazines on the newsstand tend to be younger, so newsstand sales may falter, whereas subscription sales may take off.

In review, the baby boomers are concerned with their children, their jobs and their retirement. Nevertheless, some things will never change: they are a little selfish about their leisure time, a little careless about the way they spend their money, remain suspicious of the status quo, and they will always love rock'n'roll.

Generation X: savvy and cynical

The second age cohort marketing managers have defined is the **Generation Xers**. These are the first generation latchkey children – products of dual-career or single-parent households. This group entered the workforce in the era of downsizing and downturns, so its members are likelier than the previous generation to be unemployed and underemployed. On the other hand, many have higher education, and because they have been bombarded by multiple media since the cradle, they are perceptive and cynical consumers.

Generation X
People born between 1961 and 1980.

Generation Xers are savvy and cynical consumers who are more materialistic but less hopeful than previous generations. This combination of high aspirations and low expectations makes Generation X a challenge for marketers.

The members of Generation X don't mind indulging themselves – in fact, they devote a larger-than-average share of their spending dollars to restaurant meals, alcoholic beverages, clothing, and electronic items such as televisions and stereos.[12] They are more materialistic than past generations, but have less expectation of achieving their goals. Perhaps it is this combination of high aspirations and low expectations that makes Generation X such a challenge for marketers. Due to their high education level and low expectation, they are a group that don't like to be marketed to.[13]

For example, marketers at Ford had presented its 4WDs by showing qualities of roughness and toughness, with advertisements featuring 4WDs climbing rugged mountains or going through mud. However, they quickly realised that this was not going to work with Generation Xers. The company created a new version of its popular 4WDs, with flared fenders, jazzy graphics and youthful names. The promotion campaign attempted to infuse the vehicle with personality by combining adventuresome sports with the truck. For example, one ad featured a young surfer shooting the curl in the bed of a 4WD parked in the middle of a paddock. There is minimal copy – just one line listing five features and a new logo.[14]

Generation Y: born to shop

The next cohort we will look at is **Generation Y**. Although Generation Y is much smaller than the baby boomer cohort, its members are plentiful enough to put their own footprints on society. Generation Y was born into a world so different from the one their parents entered that they could be on different planets. The changes in families, the workforce, technology and demographics in recent decades have affected their attitudes, but in ways unpredictable to marketers. Generation Y is also driving the educational software industry, whose products are designed to help infants as young as six months learn to identify numbers, shapes, colours, words and body parts.

In response to this unique set of needs we can see apparel manufacturers are also targeting the Generation Y crowd, which prefers jeans, baggy shorts and baseball caps to dress-up clothes. Carmakers are courting their parents with minivans and sports recreational vehicles, many with built-in child seats and

Generation Y
People born between 1979 and 1994.

Although smaller in number than the baby boom generation, Generation Y has already had a significant impact on how companies market to families and to children and teens. Changes in demographics, workforce and technology pose particular challenges as marketers attempt to identify the needs and wants of this group.

audiovisual equipment. Hotels and cruise lines are also targeting these families by offering kids' programs, and some shopping centres, furniture stores and even supermarkets provide on-site babysitting. Restaurants are setting out crayons, putting changing tables in rest rooms and offering more take-away services, all to serve families with children.

Generation Z: the silent generation

The final generational group, **Generation Z**, will be one that will have children and grandchildren in the 22nd and 23rd centuries. Not much is yet known about the demography of this generation, except that much of technological changes that have occurred over the lives of the baby boomers will be irrelevant to this group. MP3 players will be the norm, on-demand TV movies will be the expectation and environmental concerns will be normal everyday issues for them. These kids are optimistic, well informed and without many of the political and social stigmas that affected the thinking and value systems of their parents (generation Xers and Ys) and grandparents (baby boomers). As yet marketers have not quite worked out what makes this group tick commercially, but as the oldest are only 11 then there is still time to reflect on this.

Generation Z
People born between 1994 and present

While it is good to appreciate the unique characteristics of the various age cohorts, it would be unrealistic to consider that all baby boomers, for example, will react in the same way in all circumstances. If this were the case, nationality, religion and culture would have no impact or influence on the decision-making process for an individual. Hence, a good marketer needs to consider other sociocultural aspects of the environmental scan and these will now be considered.

Marketing-oriented values

There are major changes in the values, world views and ways of life of people compared to 20 years ago. The first of these changes reflects the type and quantity of goods and services people select, and why customers respond to marketing activities in unexpected ways if the same process is continually rolled out. These current and potential customers are good at efficiently sourcing information, seizing on something they are interested in, synthesising information into a 'big picture' and exploring that topic in depth. The second change is in the world view. Since the events of 11 September 2001, we have seen an inordinate growth or resurgence in traditionalism, ethnicism and patriotism. The world view is modernism, in that high value is attributed to personal success, consumerism, materialism and technological rationality. This can be seen, for example, in the rate of take-up and upgrading of mobile phones in New Zealand and Australia.

Growth of component lifestyles

A lifestyle is a mode of living; it is the way people decide to live their lives. **Component lifestyle** is the recognition of the various components in people's lives that meet their diverse needs and wants. These components in turn influence the goods and services people select to meet their specific needs and wants. This is quite different from the rather traditional view of stereotyping people. For example, one may have considered an accountant to be typically boring and dull. However, this is a stereotype and nowadays we could have an accountant who is into extreme sports, has a full and active social life, is a gourmet cook and a dedicated single parent. Each of these lifestyles is associated

component lifestyle
The practice of choosing goods and services that meet one's diverse needs and interests rather than conforming to a single, traditional lifestyle.

with different goods and services and represents different target markets. For example, for the gourmet, marketers offer cooking utensils, wines and exotic foods through magazines such as *Gourmet Traveller*. The fitness enthusiast buys Nike equipment and special jogging outfits and reads *Women's Fitness & Sport* magazine. Component lifestyles increase the complexity of consumers' buying habits. The accountant may own a BMW but change the oil himself or herself. He or she may buy fast food for lunch but French wine for dinner, own sophisticated photographic equipment and a low-priced home stereo, and shop for socks at Kmart or Big W and for suits or dresses at Hugo Boss.

The unique lifestyle of every consumer can require a different marketing mix. Sometimes blending products for a single target market can result in failure. To the bright young founders of WebTV, it looked like they were on a winner when they offered the market television that could be hooked up to the Internet. The goal was to capture the couch potatoes who would be intrigued by the World Wide Web. After burning through an estimated US$50 million to advertise the new service, WebTV and partners Sony and Philips Electronics counted a disappointing 50 000 subscribers.

The problem that the founders of WebTV now acknowledge was the wrong marketing message. Couch potatoes want to be better entertained, whereas computer users are content to explore the Internet using PC screens.[15]

Component lifestyles have evolved because consumers can choose from a growing number of goods and services, and most have the money to exercise more options. Rising purchasing power has resulted from the growth of dual-income families, providing more disposable income, in addition to society's overall increased wealth. The phenomenon of working women has probably had a greater effect on marketing than has any other social change. Following from this last comment on component lifestyle is the consequential change in the character of families.

The changing character of families

8 Explain the importance to marketing managers of multiculturalism and growing ethnic markets

multiculturalism
When a society has more than one ethnic culture, the society receives benefits as a result of this diversity.

The traditional family structure of mother, father and two children represents less than a quarter of Australian families today. The growth in the number of working women has meant an increase in dual-career families, which in turn has allowed for greater household incomes. However, it has also meant that families are time poor. There is greater reliance on home entertainment, and family members' roles, responsibilities and purchasing patterns are changing. Consequently, the marketplace is also changing, so the marketer must adapt to this new environment.

Multiculturalism recognises and celebrates cultural diversity, in that it provides more opportunities than challenges within a community. It also recognises the social and economic responses to the rights, obligations and needs of the country's culturally diverse population; the promotion of social harmony among the different cultural groups in our society; and the benefits our cultural diversity has offered in terms of market diversity and expansion.

The changing face of Australia's and New Zealand's population has seen a marked change in how we behave, what we eat, what we purchase, what we believe and how we conduct our lives (our life philosophies). This, in turn, requires the marketer to be aware of cultural changes and to make necessary adaptation to the goods and services offered and to the communication processes adopted in presenting those products to the market. Examples of these changes include the rejection of super-slim models and the cry for advertising to use more realistic models, and the introduction of a wider range of food items and the acceptance of Asian and other cuisines into mainstream diets.

Economic environment

In addition to sociocultural factors, marketing managers must understand and react to the economic environment. The three economic areas of greatest concern to most marketers are the distribution of consumer income, inflation and recession.

9 Identify consumer and marketer reactions to the state of the economy

Rising incomes

As disposable (or after-tax) incomes rise, more families and individuals have more money to spend on non-essential items. This new level of affluence isn't limited to professionals or even to individuals within specific age or education brackets. Rather, it cuts across all households, well beyond what businesses traditionally consider to be markets for high-priced goods and services. This rising affluence in Australia and New Zealand stems primarily from the increasing number of dual-income families.

Inflation

Inflation is a general rise in prices without a corresponding increase in wages, which results in decreased purchasing power. In times of low inflation, businesses seeking to increase their profit margins can do so only by increasing their efficiency. If they significantly increase prices, no one will purchase their goods or services.

In higher inflationary times, marketers use a number of pricing strategies to cope, and must be aware that inflation causes consumers either to build up or diminish their brand loyalty. Inflation pressures consumers to make more economical purchases, while still attempting to maintain their standard of living.

In creating marketing strategies to cope with inflation, managers must realise that, despite what happens to the seller's cost, the buyer isn't going to pay more for a product than the subjective value he or she places on it. No matter how compelling the justification might be for a 10 per cent price increase, marketers must always examine the perceived value and not just the price.

inflation
A general rise in prices without a corresponding increase in wages, which results in decreased purchasing power.

Recession

A **recession** is a period of economic activity when income, production and employment tend to fall – all of which reduce demand for goods and services. The problems of inflation and recession go hand in hand, yet recession requires different marketing strategies:

- *Improve existing products and introduce new ones*: The goal is to reduce production hours, waste and the cost of materials. Recessions increase the demand for goods and services that are economical and efficient, offer value, help organisations to streamline practices and procedures, and improve customer service.
- *Maintain and expand customer services*: Many organisations postpone the purchase of new equipment and materials. Sales of replacement parts and other services may become an important source of income.
- *Emphasise top-of-the-line products and promote product value*: Customers with less to spend will seek demonstrated quality, durability, satisfaction, and capacity to save time and money. High-priced, high-value items consistently fare well during recessions.

recession
A period of economic activity when income, production and employment tend to fall – all of which reduce demand for goods and services.

Having looked at the first two external environmental forces, it is now appropriate to look at the influences technology has on the environment.

Technological environment

10 Identify the impact of technology on an organisation

Sometimes new technology is an effective weapon against inflation and recession. New machines that reduce production costs can be one of an organisation's most valuable assets. The power of a personal computer microchip doubles about every 18 months. Any nation's ability to maintain and build wealth depends, in large part, on the speed and effectiveness with which machines that lift productivity can be invented and adopted.

The Japanese are masters at translating the results of R&D into goods and services. For example, VCRs, flat-panel displays and compact disc players are based on American research that wasn't exploited commercially in the United States. Japanese companies took the results of this **primary research** and, through **applied research**, developed these new products for sale to consumers. Similarly, many Australian and New Zealand researchers conducting primary research have had to turn to companies overseas to convert their primary research to applied research and then into marketable products. The development of new or improved products through innovation and adaptation can create vast new challenges for marketing managers.

primary research
Pure research that aims to confirm an existing theory or to learn more about a concept or phenomenon.

applied research
Attempts to develop new or improved products.

One of the greatest opportunities of this decade is the tremendous growth of the Internet. The Internet has also helped marketing to operate more efficiently through better communications. The use of email has exploded in the past several years. Email enables companies such as Ford Motor Company and Nestlé to communicate quickly with employees in far-flung operations throughout the world. The convenience of email results in many of us using it for personal messages as well as business matters.

As has been discussed throughout the text, technology is also being influenced by many other means of electronic data management and communication. These advances require the marketing manager to investigate these new media for use in and integration into the traditional marketing mix for an organisation, its products and its various target markets.

Political and legal environment

11 Discuss the political and legal environment of marketing

Business needs government regulation to protect innovators of new technology, the interests of society in general, one business from another, and consumers. In turn, government needs business, because private enterprise provides employment and generates taxes that support public efforts to educate our youth, protect our shores, and so on. The private sector also serves as a counterweight to government. The decentralisation of power inherent in a private-enterprise system supplies the limitation on government essential for the survival of a democracy.

Every aspect of the marketing mix is subject to laws and restrictions. It is the duty of marketing managers or their legal advisers to understand these laws and conform to them, because failure to comply with regulations can have major consequences for an organisation. Sometimes just sensing trends and taking corrective action before a government agency acts can

Chapter 13 Marketing strategy

The growth of the Internet has created new challenges and great opportunities for marketing managers in nearly all industries. Amazon.com has leveraged the technology of the Internet and created the most successful Web-based retail operation to date.

Australian Competition and Consumer Commission
on-line

What does the ACCC do? Does it serve consumers or businesses?
www.accc.gov.au/docs/summary/sumnov97.htm#12

www.executive.govt.nz/96-99/minister/mcdonald/mca/annex2.htm

help to avoid regulation. This didn't happen in the case of the tobacco industry. As a result, Joe Camel and the Marlboro Man are fading into the sunset along with other sponsorship strategies used to promote tobacco products.

However, the challenge isn't simply to keep the marketing department out of trouble, but to help it implement creative new programs to accomplish marketing objectives. It is all too easy for a marketing manager or sometimes a lawyer to say no to a marketing innovation that actually entails little risk. For example, an overly cautious lawyer could hold up sales of a desirable new product by warning that the package design could prompt a copyright infringement suit. Thus, it is important to understand thoroughly the laws established by the federal government, state governments and regulatory agencies to control marketing-related issues.

Ethics in Marketing

The myth of email privacy

Michael Smyth, a regional manager at Pillsbury in Pennsylvania, fired an email to his supervisor, blasting company managers and threatening to 'kill the backstabbing'. Backstabbing may have been the right word. Though Pillsbury had assured employees that email was private, it intercepted the message and fired Smyth. When he sued for wrongful discharge, the court threw out the case. He learned the hard way: never expect privacy for email sent through a company system.

Typically the company asserts ownership of email messages. To boost morale and encourage communication among employees, the company may also promise a degree of privacy. But as the Pillsbury episode shows, such promises aren't binding. It will take time for practices to become more coherent.

Employees who are adept with computers occasionally take privacy into their own hands. Using software they buy or download from the Internet, they encrypt, or scramble, mail they don't want the boss to see. Before you try this, beware. Encryption is still somewhat cumbersome – penpals must have the same software, for one thing. And if you're working for a paranoid boss, scrambling may afford less protection than you think. Says a computer designer in an office where the boss's email snooping preceded a savage firing spree: 'I was afraid that if I merely sent an encrypted letter, they'd think I was up to something bad.'

Bottom line: if you write love notes on a company PC, you're wearing your heart on your screen. The only true safe ways to send? Be subtle when you flirt or lampoon the boss. Or pay for your own Internet account and use it at night on your home machine.[16]

Unless it is a customer service call, companies rarely monitor employees' telephone calls. Should they monitor an employee's email? Did Michael Smyth deserve to be fired? What would you do if you were told to monitor another employee's email and report your findings to your boss?

Australian state laws
on-line

How do governments explain consumer laws to consumers? Does this site help the consumer with legal issues on consumption of products?
www.consumer.gov.au/html/legislation.htm

Federal legislation

Commonwealth laws that affect marketing fall into several categories. Product fitness and integrated marketing communications accuracy are covered by the *Trade Practices Act 1974*, while privacy issues are addressed by the *Privacy Act 1998* (enacted December 2001) and the *Prices Surveillance Act 1983*. New Zealand's *Fair Trade Act 1986* also has similar goals and objectives.

Regulatory agencies

Although some state regulatory bodies more actively pursue violations of their marketing statutes, Commonwealth government regulators generally have the greatest clout. The Australian Competition and Consumer Commission (ACCC) and the Australia New Zealand Food Authority (www.ausfoodnews.com.au/flapa) are the agencies most directly and actively involved in marketing activities.

The ACCC is a statutory authority responsible for ensuring compliance with Parts IV, IVA, V and VA of the *Trade Practices Act* and the provisions of the Conduct Code, and for administering the *Prices Surveillance Act*.

Competitive environment

The final environment to be considered is the competitive environment. The competitive environment operates within a given industry category – that is, the number of competitors an organisation must face, the relative size of the competitors and the degree of interdependence within the industry. Management usually has little control over the competitive environment confronting an organisation. However, even when faced with a highly competitive environment, innovative smaller organisations can survive and even prosper.

12 Explain the basics of foreign and domestic competition

Industry

Industry analysis involves the review of the industry size, trends, stage of evolution, demand characteristics, and the structure of any existing or emerging segments that could influence the organisation's ability to survive, prosper and/or perish. In terms of the competitive environment, the industry analysis sets the foundation for the subsequent stages of analysis, which include consideration of the competition and the competitors.

The banking hole in the wall

Entrepreneurial Insights

Many years ago an organisation was on the cutting edge of banking technology. The company had developed a new banking service that provided banks with the hardware and software to provide an electronic money teller after hours and which could be installed into a bank wall, thereby providing 24/7 access. The organisation was very successful and was able to capture the market for the automatic teller machines (ATMs) that we know today.

After a few years the organisation, like all good organisations, conducted a strategic marketing audit and defined the industry it was in as automatic teller machines. It developed its long-term and medium-term plans based on this analysis. Unfortunately for the organisation, a new competitor was looming on the horizon and this second organisation analysed the market as being electronic banking. Accordingly, it developed a new product that allowed the traditional tellers to be electronically managed and, as a by-product, the software could also manage the ATM. Overnight, the original supplier of the ATMs was out of business due to its failure to conduct a proper audit of the environment.

When did the original ATM provider make its first mistake? How could this have been overcome?

Competition

Competition is influenced dramatically by the scope and dimensions of the marketplace in which the organisation operates. For example, two organisations could both be delivering accounting services to their markets. However, one may be serving a very local market, while the other may be serving an international market. Accordingly, even though these two organisations are in the same industry, the competitive forces within the marketplaces they serve are quite different.

Global competition is the strategy an organisation adopts to provide the same product in all markets around the world. In the cola market, Coca-Cola and Pepsi are in intense competition throughout the world. Both of these organisations are savvy international competitors. They each conduct business in scores of different countries with very similar products. They must consider the competition the other provides in the global arena, as well as competition in the domestic markets within which they operate. That is, in some countries, in addition to the competition from the other international brand, there will also be competition from domestic or local brands.

International competition is the strategy an organisation adopts to provide to different countries products that are usually different or modified in some way. The different strategies adopted – global or international – can influence the way the marketer views the environmental forces that can, in turn, influence the strategic analysis an organisation adopts in terms of the environmental scan being undertaken.

global competition
The strategy an organisation adopts to provide the same product in all markets around the world.

international competition
The strategy an organisation adopts to provide products that are usually different or modified in some way to different countries.

Competitors

Scanning the competitors is also an activity that the marketing officer should undertake. In particular, the marketing person is looking for traits that will allow them to project how these organisations will behave when the environmental conditions of the marketplace change. For example, in the domestic airline industry in Australia it is clear that if an airline strives to gain market share by reducing its ticket prices, its competitors will react swiftly either to match or improve on the reduced price so as to retain its market share. Accordingly, if you were aware that this was the expected behaviour of your competitors, it is unlikely that you would adopt a pricing war strategy.

Thus, when considering the competitive environment, it is important to consider the three dimensions of industry, the competition and the competitors.

Having looked at the various elements of the environmental scan that an organisation should consider before developing organisational strategies, it is appropriate to consider the issue of ethics and morals. Ethics and morals play an important part in the strategic development of an organisation and determine how it behaves within its original culture and on the world stage. These issues will be considered later in this chapter.

Describing target markets

Once the internal and external environments have been examined, the next step in creating a marketing plan is to identify and describe the target market for the good or service. Target marketing (described in detail in Chapter 4) essentially

Global Perspectives

The French government steps into the Coke versus Pepsi turf wars

The French government rejected Coca-Cola Co.'s proposed US$880 million purchase of Orangina from Pernod Ricard, SA, on antitrust grounds. The move shows how Coke is coming under greater scrutiny as rival PepsiCo, Inc. is drawing attention to Coke's dominance in the global soft-drink business. When Coke reached its agreement to buy Orangina, Pepsi cried foul; it relies on Orangina to distribute Pepsi products in cafes, hotels and other 'on-premises' locations. Furthermore, Pepsi argued that Coke's purchase of Orangina would give its archrival a near monopoly in France, because Coke already controls about 50 per cent of the French carbonated soft-drink market.

Despite those complaints, Coke officials and industry analysts seemed confident that the French government would approve the deal, although only after Coke agreed to certain conditions to satisfy competition and labour concerns. Coke, based in Atlanta, in the United States, addressed the latter concern by signing an accord with Orangina employees, guaranteeing jobs and salaries until the year 2000 and maintaining a 35-hour week.

But the government, in its decision, said the French antitrust authorities' recommendation 'substantiated the serious risks' to competition being impeded in the on-premises market. 'Intensive discussion with the Coca-Cola Co. did not result in sufficient commitments to prevent the risks' to competition, the French government said.

Pepsi wouldn't speculate on whether it would make an offer for Orangina. 'We're obviously pleased' by the government's decision, the spokesperson said. 'This sends an important signal that France has solid and well-defined rules regarding open competition and is prepared to enforce those rules.'[17]

Do you think that the French government should get involved in the Coke versus Pepsi battle for market share? If you were Pepsi management, what factors should you consider before making an offer to buy Orangina? Do you think Pepsi could market Orangina, which is a lightly carbonated drink that contains orange juice and pulp, in Australia and New Zealand?

---

involves the identification of large enough groups of potential customers who can be reached with your communication efforts and who have the desire to purchase your product. The discussion in Chapter 4 also details the various bases that can be used to describe or segment target groups, and it may be useful here to revise that material so as to refresh your memory. Your consumers are very important to your organisation's marketing strategy, and their needs and wants should determine the type of marketing orientation, as well as the most appropriate **marketing mix** strategy, to be used.

It is unrealistic to think that your product will appeal to all people everywhere. For the majority of organisations, target marketing allows them to differentiate their product, which in turn allows them to have a stronger appeal to a smaller group of customers, rather than having a very weak appeal to the whole market.

Establishing components of the marketing mix for each target market

This is where all the fun begins! Here is where marketers become like artists. Just like a painter mixes and uses colour to form visually attractive images, a marketer uses the **four Ps** to create something that appeals to the consumer.

marketing mix
A unique blend of product, distribution, promotion and pricing strategies designed to produce mutually satisfying exchanges with a target market.

13 Describe the elements of the marketing mix

four Ps
Product, place, promotion and price, which together make up the marketing mix.

Tradeoffs are made between the price and the product features, the place where it is made available and the promotion it receives. The whole marketing mix is a jigsaw puzzle and you need to work out where to put all the pieces.

We have looked at each of the marketing mix elements in detail in Chapters 6 to 11. Here we will review the four areas of the marketing mix that must be considered when developing a marketing plan:

- *Product*: The product needs to be defined in terms of core, actual and augmented product attributes. This means that you need to realise that your product may be more than just its tangible components. For example, if you own a video rental store, you do more than rent videos – you are in the home entertainment business. If you manage a sporting team, the product is more than just the athletes themselves or the matches played – you are providing an entertaining and emotional experience for your customers as well. Product decisions involve decisions about the characteristics of various kinds of products, the depth and breadth of the product range, and so on. (Refer to Chapter 6 to refresh your memory of these concepts.)

- *Promotion*: Promotion involves telling the target market about the product (or service or idea). Promotion is all about communicating with your customers and other interested stakeholders and includes advertising, public relations, personal selling and sales promotion (see Chapter 10).

- *Place*: Place, or distribution, refers to where a product is made available to the target market, when it will be made available, and through what channel of distribution. Decisions need to be made here about how widely distributed the product will be, and about what intermediaries will be involved in the process of getting the product to the end consumer and what their roles will be (see Chapter 8).

- *Price*: Setting a price isn't just about using a formula, as you have already read in Chapter 11. Marketing managers must consider the kind of competition in the target markets, as well as possible customer reactions to different price levels. They don't just work out the cost of production and add x per cent. Price is about value and customer perceptions as well.

Once marketers understand their internal and external environments, know who their customers are, and where their organisation, and therefore their marketing effort, should be heading, they can then manipulate these marketing elements in an attempt to achieve success. For most organisations, there are a number of different marketing mixes for each different target group, even for the same or similar products.

In the Yowie launch example outlined earlier, Cadbury had a slightly different marketing mix for parents and for children. While the price and product decisions remained the same for each group, the promotion and distribution decisions differed. Essentially, the promotional campaign for children focused on integrated advertisements on Nickelodeon cartoons between 2 p.m. and 5 p.m. on weekdays. There was also a virtual game room and a website that allowed children to play games, win prizes and chat to each other. The parents were targeted through the website (with different areas explaining various aspects of the Yowie's environmental alliances), newsletters and emails, as well as point-of-purchase displays designed to appeal to adults and to children. Thus, while the product was the same, slightly different marketing mix applications were used to achieve the result of an increase in sales of the product by 27 per cent.[18]

Chocolate Boutique Café on-line

How does this home page communicate its products? Does the organisation offer more than chocolate products? www.chocolateboutique.co.nz

Chocolate Boutique Cafe
Passionate about Chocolate

Our Shop
Chocolates
Gifts
Hampers
Order

just imagine...

The smell of chocolate & coffee...the sight of 100's of handmade chocolates
in a cabinet...rows of jars of candy and chocolate lining the wall...
luxurious gift wrapping, ceramic, candles, toiletries and soft toys.
Gifts include international range of chocolates.
70% + Bittersweet chocolate our speciality.

...that's the Chocolate Boutique Cafe - passionate about chocolate

Read about the history of chocolate here.

Find out out why we are The President's Choice !

WINNER AUCKLAND TOP SHOP 2000 "speciality and gifts"
1/323 Parnell Road, Parnell, Auckland, New Zealand I Tel : 0064 9 377 8550
Fax : 0064 9 377 8760
or 5 Mokoia Road, Birkenhead, North Shore, Auckland, New Zealand I Tel : 0064 9 418 2450
contact : barbara@chocolateboutique.co.nz

another WOW! project by iroom

The Chocolate Boutique Cafe presents its products in a way that entices its target markets and highlights their needs.

You can see that the exact mix of marketing variables will depend on the characteristics of the target group and on the objectives of the organisation. Once the marketing plan has been designed, it then needs to be implemented and measured for success. This stage will be discussed next.

Implementation and control processes

Implementation is the process that turns marketing plans into action assignments and ensures that these assignments are executed in a way that accomplishes the plans' objectives. Implementation activities may involve detailed job assignments, activity descriptions, time lines, budgets and lots of communication. Although implementation is essentially 'doing what you said you were going to do', many organisations repeatedly experience failures in strategy implementation. Brilliant marketing plans are doomed to fail if they are not properly implemented. The key to successful implementation is to detail who is responsible for doing what tasks, by when, how, and with what resources. This ensures that all involved know their responsibilities and that there has been adequate thought given to the allocation of appropriate resources to achieve the desired results. It is not enough to give everyone a job; if insufficient money, people or time is allocated to doing the job, then all the planning will have been in vain. These detailed communications should be part of the written marketing plan.

14 Explain why implementation, evaluation and control of the marketing plan are necessary

implementation
The process that turns marketing plans into action assignments and ensures that these assignments are executed in a way that accomplishes the plans' objectives.

Other reasons for the failure of many good marketing plans, in addition to poor implementation plans, are:

- Planning in isolation – not considering all functional areas in the organisation and/or not adequately considering the external environment
- Tradeoffs between short-term and long-term objectives – for example, a desire to increase sales revenue in the short term through price discounting may erode brand equity and customer loyalty to the product in the long term
- Resistance to change by those internal to the organisation and a desire to cling to the way it has always been done.

Once implemented, the marketing plan needs to be monitored to ensure that all the activities are on target and to detect any external factors that might impinge on the plan's success, such as competitor activity, economic changes or, perhaps, technological issues. **Marketing control** involves measuring and evaluating performance and taking corrective action if required. This control is achieved by conducting a **marketing audit**, which provides a foundation for a comprehensive and systematic method of evaluating performance. During the marketing control process, there may also be a need to alter marketing plans to ensure that marketing goals are achieved within the set guidelines. You should remember that planning is *not* an annual process but an *ongoing* process. This means that the planning and control processes should be ongoing within the organisation, with plans constantly being updated, modified or changed as a result of objectives being achieved or in response to internal and external forces. Sound planning involves creativity and the ability to challenge existing assumptions.

While gauging the extent to which marketing objectives have been achieved during the specified period is part of the **evaluation** stage, there are four common reasons for failing to achieve a marketing objective. These are: unrealistic marketing objectives, inappropriate marketing strategies in the plan, poor implementation, and changes in the environment after the objective was specified and the strategy was implemented.

marketing control
The measuring and evaluating of performance and taking corrective action if required.

marketing audit
A thorough, systematic, periodic evaluation of the goals, strategies, structure and performance of the marketing organisation.

evaluation
Gauging the extent to which the marketing objectives have been achieved during the specified period.

Social and ethical behaviour

15 Describe the role of ethics and ethical decisions in business

Regardless of the intensity of the competition, organisations must also compete in an ethical manner. **Ethics** refers to the moral principles or values that generally govern the conduct of an individual or group. Ethics also can be viewed as the standard of behaviour by which conduct is judged. Standards that are legal may not always be ethical, and vice versa. Laws are the values and standards enforceable by the courts. Ethics consists of personal moral principles and values rather than societal prescriptions.

Defining the boundaries of ethicality and legality can be difficult. Often, judgement is needed to determine whether an action that may be legal is indeed ethical. For example, the selling of alcohol, tobacco and X-rated movies to 17-year-olds is illegal, while certain groups of the community would suggest that all of these activities are unethical.

Morals, on the other hand, are the rules people develop as a result of cultural values and norms. Culture is a socialising force that dictates what is deemed right and wrong. Moral standards can also reflect the laws and regulations that affect social and economic behaviour. Thus, morals can be considered a foundation of ethical

ethics
The moral principles or values that generally govern the conduct of an individual or group; the standard of behaviour by which conduct is judged.

morals
The rules people develop as a result of cultural values and norms.

behaviour, but it must be understood that morals are based on a person's culture. Thus morals, which are usually characterised as good or bad, may have different connotations and meanings within and between cultures. This good and bad – or effective and ineffective – view of morals can have several different perspectives. The following are some examples of different views of good and bad morals:

1. If a salesperson sells a new stereo or television set to a disadvantaged consumer knowing full well that the person can't keep up the monthly payments, is the salesperson still a good one? What if the sale enables the salesperson to exceed her quota? Here the person can be identified as a good salesperson who makes or exceeds the assigned quota, but also as a bad one in that she sold something she knew the person couldn't afford.
2. A doctor who runs large ads for discounts on open-heart surgery would be considered bad, or unprofessional, in the sense of not conforming to the norms of the medical profession, but good in terms of offering surgery at a price people can afford. Here, good and bad morals can be considered in terms of conforming and deviant behaviours.
3. 'Bad' and 'good' are also used to express the distinction between criminal and law-abiding behaviour.
4. A Muslim who eats pork would be considered bad, as would a fundamentalist Christian who drinks whisky. Here the terms 'good' and 'bad' are defined by a person's religion, and these religions can look on the same activity in markedly different ways.

Morality, ethics and legality are not clear cut and depend on a person's culture, experiences and understanding of societal norms.

Morality and business ethics

Today's business ethics consist of a sub-set of major life values learned since birth. The values businesspeople use to make decisions have been acquired through family, educational and religious institutions, and society's acceptable norms.

Ethical values are situation-specific and time-oriented. Nevertheless, everyone must have an ethical base that applies to their conduct in the business world and in their personal life. One approach to developing a personal set of ethics is to examine the consequences of a particular act.

- Who is helped or hurt?
- How long-lasting are the consequences?
- What actions produce the greatest good for the greatest number of people?

A second approach stresses the importance of rules. Rules come in the form of customs, laws, professional standards and common sense. Consider these examples of rules:

- Always treat others as you would like to be treated.
- Copying copyrighted computer software is against the law.
- It is wrong to lie, bribe or exploit.

The third approach emphasises the development of moral character within individuals. Ethical development can be thought of as having three levels:[19]

- *Preconventional morality*, the most basic level, is childlike. It is calculating, self-centred and even selfish, based on what will be immediately punished or rewarded.

- *Conventional morality* moves from an egocentric viewpoint towards the expectations of society. Loyalty and obedience to the organisation (or society) become paramount. At the level of conventional morality, an ethical marketing decision would be concerned only with whether or not it is legal and how it will be viewed by others.
- *Postconventional morality* represents the morality of the mature adult. At this level, people are less concerned about how others might see them and more concerned about how they see and judge themselves over the long run. A marketing decision-maker who has attained a postconventional level of morality might ask, even though it is legal and will increase company profits, is it right?

Ethical business decision-making

How do businesspeople make ethical decisions? There is no cut-and-dried answer. Studies show that the following factors tend to influence ethical decision-making and judgements:[20]

- *Extent of ethical problems within the organisation*: The healthier the ethical environment, the greater is the likelihood that marketers will take a strong stand against questionable practices.
- *Top-management actions on ethics*: Top managers can influence the behaviour of marketing professionals by encouraging ethical behaviour and discouraging unethical behaviour.
- *Potential magnitude of the consequences*: The greater the harm done to victims, the more likely it is that marketers will recognise a problem as unethical.
- *Social consensus*: The greater the degree of agreement among managerial peers that an action is harmful, the more likely it is that marketers will recognise a problem as unethical.
- *Probability of a harmful outcome*: The greater the likelihood that an action will result in a harmful outcome, the more likely it is that marketers will recognise a problem as unethical.
- *Length of time between the decision and the onset of consequences*: The shorter the length of time between the action and the onset of negative consequences, the more likely it is that marketers will perceive a problem as unethical.
- *Number of people to be affected:* The greater the number of persons affected by a negative outcome, the more likely it is that marketers will recognise a problem as unethical.

Ethical guidelines

Many organisations have become more interested in ethical issues. One sign of this interest is the increase in the number of large companies that appoint ethics officers. In addition, many organisations have developed a **code of ethics** as a guideline to help marketing managers and other employees make better decisions.

Creating ethics guidelines has several advantages:

- It helps employees to identify what their organisation recognises as acceptable business practices.
- It can be an effective internal control on behaviour, which is more desirable than external controls such as government regulation.

Clean Up Australia on-line

The annual national clean-up day started as a community effort. What organisations are now part of this program? Does this make them socially responsible organisations?
www.cleanup.com.au

code of ethics
A guideline to help marketing managers and other employees make better decisions.

- It helps employees to avoid confusion when determining whether their decisions are ethical.
- It facilitates discussion among employees about what is right and wrong and ultimately creates better decisions.

However, organisations must be careful not to make their code of ethics either too vague or too detailed. Codes that are too vague give little or no guidance to employees in their day-to-day activities, and codes that are too detailed encourage employees to substitute rules for judgement.

Although many organisations have issued policies on ethical behaviour, marketing managers must still put the policies into effect. They must address the classic 'matter of degree' issue. One of the most recent changes in the ethical debate for organisations in Australia is the development and enactment of the *Privacy Act*. This piece of legislation was put in place because organisation failed in their ethical

Corporate social responsibility

responsibilities to keep individuals' personal data out of the public domain. Ethics and social responsibility are closely intertwined. Besides questioning tobacco companies' ethics, one might ask whether they are acting in a socially responsible manner when they promote tobacco. **Corporate social responsibility** is an organisation's concern for society's welfare. This concern is demonstrated by managers who consider both the long-range best interests of the organisation and its relationship to the society within which it operates. In particular, there are four corporate social responsibilities:

1. To pursue financial goals (economic responsibility)
2. To obey the law (legal responsibility)
3. To do what is right, just and fair (ethical responsibility)
4. To be a good corporate citizen (philanthropic responsibility).

16 Discuss corporate social responsibility

corporate social responsibility
Business's concern for society's welfare.

Connect it

Looking back at the story at the start of the chapter, you should now understand that the external environment affects all organisations and their marketing mixes. The opening vignette illustrated how changing perceptions of the use of a product and changing demographics can present marketing opportunities. In this case, we see that sports shoes are not really designed to help an athlete and can, in some cases, do more harm than good. However, the producers of these shoes are willing to spend large sums on promoting the image that is associated with the sports shoe and an active lifestyle. Further, we see that some organisations such as New Balance have identified a trend in the market and have exploited it to the point of capturing a large portion of the middle-aged target market.

Scanning the marketing environments for change, and identifying when to make product variations to take advantage of that change, is an important element of successful marketing. Equally, other uncontrollable variables could affect New Balance adversely. Changing cultural values could shift away from exercise and fitness for middle-aged consumers, thereby reducing demand for New Balance products. New shoe technology could render New Balance shoes obsolete. Or a general economic downturn might substantially decrease demand for all types of athletic goods.

Summary

1 Discuss the three levels of strategy.
There are three levels of strategy that together form a 'heirarchy of strategy' within a firm. The most over-arching strategic level is that of corporate strategy which deals with the decisions about the types of business in which the firm will operate. The next level is the business strategy level which deals with strategic decisions at the SBU area of responsibility. The final level of strategy deals with the operational level of the firm and is called functional strategy.

2 Explain the four competing business orientations that impact marketing strategy.
The four business orientations are:

a Production orientation which focuses on the internal capabilities of the firm
b Sales orientation which focuses on agressive sales techniques
c Marketing orientation which focuses on consumer decision-making
d Relationship marketing orientation which focuses on the value of the repeat sale rather than on making a sale that meets the needs and wants of the marketplace.

3 Understand the importance of strategic planning.
Planning is the process of anticipating future wants and determining strategies to acheive organisational objectives. Strategic planning is the managerial process of creating and maintaining a fit between the organisation's objectives, resources and evolving market opportunities.

4 Discuss the importance of writing a marketing plan and define its elements.
Strategic marketing planning is the basis for all marketing strategies and decisions. The marketing plan is a written document that acts as a guidebook of marketing activities for the marketing manager. By specifying objectives and defining the actions required to attain them, a marketing plan provides the basis on which actual and expected performance can be compared. Although there is no set formula for a marketing plan or a single correct outline, basic factors that should be covered include stating the business mission, setting objectives, performing a situation analysis of internal and external environmental forces, selecting the target market(s), delineating a marketing mix (product, place, promotion and price), and establishing ways to implement, evaluate and control the plan.

5 Describe the criteria for stating good marketing objectives.
Objectives should be realistic, measurable and time-specific. Objectives also must be consistent and indicate the priorities of the organisation.

6 Discuss the external environment of marketing and explain how it affects an organisation.
The external marketing environment consists of sociocultural, economic, technological, political and legal, and competitive variables. Marketers generally cannot control the elements of the external environment. Instead, they must understand how the external environment is changing and the impact of change on the target market. Then marketing managers can create a marketing mix to effectively meet the needs of target customers.

7 Describe the sociocultural factors that affect marketing.
Within the external environment, social factors are perhaps the most difficult for marketers to anticipate. Several major social trends are currently shaping marketing strategies. First, people of all ages have a broader range of interests, defying traditional consumer profiles. Second, changing gender roles are bringing more women into the workforce and increasing the number of men who shop. Third, the greater number of dual-career families has led to a poverty of time, creating a demand for time-saving goods and services.

8 Explain the importance to marketing managers of multiculturalism and growing ethnic markets.
Multiculturalism is the recognition and celebration of ethnic groups that add diversity to society. Growing multiculturalism makes the marketer's task more challenging, as niches within ethnic markets may require micromarketing strategies. A third strategy is to seek common interests, motivations or needs across ethnic groups.

9 Identify consumer and marketer reactions to the state of the economy.
Marketers are currently targeting the increasing number of consumers with higher discretionary income by offering higher-quality, higher-priced goods and services. During a time of inflation, marketers generally attempt to maintain level pricing in order to avoid losing customer brand loyalty. During times of recession, many marketers maintain or reduce prices to counter the effects of decreased demand; they also concentrate on increasing production efficiency and improving customer service.

10 Identify the impact of technology on an organisation.
Monitoring new technology is essential to keeping up with competitors in today's marketing environment. Often an organisation can be led to a myopic view of the world because it is constantly dealing with the day-to-day activities and not considering how things can change.

11 Discuss the political and legal environment of marketing.
All marketing activities are subject to state and federal laws and the rulings of regulatory agencies. Marketers are responsible for remaining aware of and abiding by such regulations. Some key laws that affect marketing are the federal *Trade Practices Act*, the *Privacy Act*, the *Prices Surveillance Act* and other state legislation. Refer to the Web addresses in this section for current details.

12 Explain the basics of foreign and domestic competition.
The competitive environment encompasses the number of competitors an organisation must face, the relative size of the competitors and the degree of interdependence within the industry. Declining population growth, rising costs and shortages of resources have heightened domestic competition. Yet with an effective marketing mix, small organisations continue to be able to compete with the giants. Meanwhile, dwindling international barriers are bringing in more foreign competitors and offering expanding opportunities for Australian and New Zealand companies abroad.

13 Describe the elements of the marketing mix.
The marketing mix (or four Ps) is a blend of product, distribution (place), promotion and pricing strategies designed to produce mutually satisfying

exchanges with a target market (as discussed in Parts 3 and 4). The starting point of the marketing mix is the product offering. Products can be tangible goods, ideas or services. Distribution strategies are concerned with making products available when and where customers want them. Promotion includes personal selling, advertising, sales promotion and public relations. Price is what a buyer must give up to obtain a product and is often the easiest of the four marketing mix elements to change.

14 Explain why implementation, evaluation and control of the marketing plan are necessary.

Before a marketing plan can work, it must be implemented – that is, people must perform the actions in the plan. The plan should also be evaluated to see if it has achieved its objectives. Poor implementation can be a major factor in a plan's failure. Control provides the mechanisms for evaluating marketing results in light of the plan's goals and for correcting actions that don't help the organisation reach those goals within budget guidelines.

15 Describe the role of ethics and ethical decisions in business.

Business ethics may be viewed as a sub-set of the values of society as a whole. The ethical conduct of businesspeople is shaped by societal elements, including family, education, religion and social movements. As members of society, businesspeople are morally obliged to consider the ethical implications of their decisions.

Ethical decision-making is approached in three basic ways. The first approach examines the consequences of decisions. The second approach relies on rules and laws to guide decision-making. The third approach is based on a theory of moral development that places individuals or groups in one of three developmental stages: preconventional morality, conventional morality or postconventional morality.

Many companies develop a code of ethics to help their employees make ethical decisions. A code of ethics can help employees to identify acceptable business practices, can be an effective internal control on behaviour, can help employees avoid confusion when determining the ethicality of decisions, and can facilitate discussion about what is right and wrong.

16 Discuss corporate social responsibility.

Responsibility in business refers to an organisation's concern for the way its decisions affect society. There are several arguments in support of social responsibility. First, many consumers feel business should take responsibility for the social costs of economic growth. A second argument contends that organisations act in their own best interest when they help to improve the environment within which they operate. Third, organisations can avoid restrictive government regulation by responding willingly to societal concerns. Finally, some people argue that because organisations have the resources to solve social problems, they are morally obliged to do so.

In contrast, there are critics who argue against corporate social responsibility. According to one argument, the free enterprise system has no way to decide which social programs should have priority. A second argument contends that organisations involved in social programs don't generate the profits needed to support the business's activities and earn a fair return for shareholders.

In spite of the arguments against corporate social responsibility, most businesspeople believe they should do more than pursue only profits. Although a company must consider its economic needs first, it must also operate within the law, do what is ethical and fair, and be a good corporate citizen.

Review it

1. Which of the following is *not* one of the uncontrollable factors for marketing managers?
   a Social change
   b Economic conditions
   c The marketing mix
   d Political and legal factors

2. The fact that many consumers are choosing products that meet diverse needs and interests rather than conforming to traditional stereotypes means they are likely piecing together
   a The management of their environment
   b Component lifestyles
   c Changing roles
   d The poverty of time

3. A viewpoint in New Zealand culture that places high value on personal success and technological rationality is known as
   a Cultural creativity
   b Traditionalism
   c Heartlandering
   d Modernism

4. This group of consumers is often known as Australia's mass market and yet today it has the earning power to prefer many customised products and services.
   a The baby boomers
   b The seniors
   c Generation X
   d Generation Y

5. _____ occur(s) when all different ethnic groups in an area are embraced.
   a Poverty of time
   b Modernist values
   c Multiculturalism
   d Stitching niches

6. Which of the following pieces of federal legislation was designed to control false advertising?
   a Trade Practices Act
   b Privacy Act
   c Goods and Services Act
   d Advertising Federation Act

7. Marketers that have attained a(n) _____ level of morality might ask, even though it is legal, is it right to do this in the long run?
   a Unconventional
   b Preconventional
   c Conventional
   d Postconventional

8. When considering corporate social responsibility, organisations that focus mainly on persuing financial goals are operating within which sphere of corporate social responsibility?

Define it

applied research 490
baby boomers 483
business strategy 473
code of ethics 500
component lifestyle 487
corporate social responsibility 501
corporate strategy 472
environmental management 483
environmental scanning 481
ethics 498
evaluation 498
four Ps 495
functional strategy 473
Generation X 485
Generation Y 486
Generation Z 487
global competition 494
implementation 497
inflation 489
international competition 494
marketing audit 498
marketing concept 475
marketing control 498
marketing mix 495
marketing myopia 480
marketing objective 480
marketing orientation 475
marketing plan 479
marketing planning 479
marketing statement 478
marketing strategy 478
mission statement 480
morals 498
multiculturalism 488
personalised economy 485
planning 476
primary research 490
product orientation 474
recession 489
relationship marketing orientation 476
sales orientation 474
strategic business unit (SBU) 477
strategic planning 476
strategic window 477
SWOT analysis 483
target market 481

    a   Philanthropic responsibility
    b   Ethical responsibility
    c   Legal responsibility
    d   Economic responsibility

9   Oragnisations that attempt to be good corporate citizens are operating with philanthropic responsibility.
    a   True
    b   False

Check the Answer Key to see how well you understood the material. More detailed discussion and writing questions and a video case related to this chapter are found in the Student Resources CD-ROM.

Click it

Online reading

INFOTRAC® COLLEGE EDITION
For additional readings and review on marketing strategy, explore InfoTrac® College Edition, your online library. Go to: www.infotrac-college.com and search for any of the InfoTrac key terms listed below:
- organisational marketing strategy
- strategic window
- marketing planning
- baby boomers
- marketing myopia

Answer key

1   *Answer*: c, p. 481 *Rationale*: The marketing mix represents the group of factors in marketing planning that is under the control of the organisation and its managers.

2   *Answer*: b, p. 487 *Rationale*: In the past, lifestyles were often associated only with one's profession. Today, many consumers have component lifestyles – that is, they have many different lifestyles based on their personal preferences. Thus, they require many goods and services to meet their widely diverse lifestyles.

3   *Answer*: d, p. 487 *Rationale*: Modernism is a value set that places high value on consumerism and materialism.

4   *Answer*: a, p. 483-5 *Rationale*: Baby boomers represent the largest subcultural group in Australia. They have a sense of individualism that has led to preferences for customised products. The term personalised economy has been used to describe how products succeed by offering customisation, immediacy and value.

5   *Answer*: c, p. 488 *Rationale*: Multiculturalism is the combining of many cultures and rejoicing in the diversity and market expansions it offers the community.

6 *Answer*: a, p. 492 *Rationale*: The *Trade Practices Act*, passed in 1974 and subsequently amended to meet the changing needs of the community, was created to broaden the power of the ACCC to outlaw false and deceptive advertising practices.

7 *Answer*: d, p. 500 *Rationale*: At the level of postconventional morality, marketing managers are less concerned about how some others might see them and are more concerned about how they judge themselves over the long run.

8 *Answer*: d, p. 501 *Rationale*: Unless the organisation can make a profit and maintain good economic performance, the other three responsibilities are moot.

9 *Answer*: a, p. 501 *Rationale*: Companies who consider the impact of their operations on others and the environment are being philanthropic in their approach to corporate responsibility.

Cross-functional connections
SOLUTIONS

Questions

1 **If you were the partners of Johnasen, Browne and Cooper-Smith, what market segments would you focus on? Why?**

This case shows the life-cycle progression for the practice and how the markets it serves vary as the practice matures. To address this question, you need to understand that the market the practice can serve is any activity that requires an architect. It is through the process of segmentation that the various market segments are identified. Further, evaluating each segment and comparing them to the practice's strengths will help to identify the best segments that will offer Johnasen, Browne and Cooper-Smith a strategic competitive advantage.

From the case, you need to identify the following strengths of the practice: heritage and conservation (interior and exterior); interior design for heritage projects; 'sympathetic infill'; high-quality heritage replication of residential and commercial projects; and international opportunities. Once these are identified, you need to consider the viability of each segment and then make your recommendation.

2 **Why are costs so important to Johnasen, Browne and Cooper-Smith in developing a pricing strategy?**

Determining a pricing strategy for an organisation is a difficult task and one that is often overlooked. As the practice grows, the partners tend to focus on winning the next job and on the revenue it will bring to the practice, rather than on the costs associated with running the practice. Like all businesses, Johnasen, Browne and Cooper-Smith must look at the fixed costs of being in business, the variable costs of getting the next job, and the return on investment that could be earned if the money were used or invested in other areas.

It is only once all these financial demands are taken into consideration that Johnasen, Browne and Cooper-Smith can truly estimate the cost of winning the next job and the revenue it must earn to make the practice successful.

However, this isn't the end of the pricing strategy; it's just the beginning. A pricing strategy considers where the organisation is positioned in the marketplace and how stable the industry is with respect to the organisation's competitors. In a volatile market, the organisation may choose to take on a loss-leader strategy if it believes it can outlast the competition in the longer term, but in a stable environment where there are many similar competitors it may be best to position the organisation at the premium end of the market where it can charge higher-than-market rates. Thus, to answer this question, you must consider the cost aspects of Johnasen, Browne and Cooper-Smith, the environments within which they must operate, and the position of the practice in the minds of the market's consumers.

3 **Why is the implementation of a marketing plan so important for Johnasen, Browne and Cooper-Smith?**

A marketing plan begins with a review of the environmental conditions and capabilities of the organisation. It then looks at the strategic direction and intent of the organisation and instigates a plan of action to reach its goals. From this

PART FIVE CLOSING
QUESTIONS

base, the organisation can then project its resource needs and the timeliness of the various actions required to deliver services to the market and its customers in an efficient manner.

The success of the marketing plan lies in its ability to be flexible enough to adjust to changing market conditions, with the activities of the plan being delegated to specific persons within set timeframes. It is only through auditing the plan that the partners can understand how Johnasen, Browne and Cooper-Smith is performing and instigate modifications of the plan (resources) and the practice's strategic direction so that the practice can adapt to and improve its position in a changing environment.

4 How should Johnasen, Browne and Cooper-Smith communicate and promote the services that they offer?

Communication and promotion are the lifeblood of a service industry. In this case, although Johnasen, Browne and Cooper-Smith can develop a mass-market promotional strategy to develop recognition, it will only be through referrals and word of mouth that the practice will truly succeed. In considering a strategy for the future, Johnasen, Browne and Cooper-Smith need to adopt the concept of integrated marketing communication (IMC). This concept holds that all communications of the firm need to be consistent and aligned with its marketing objectives. Accordingly, to respond to this question, you must:

(a) Infer the strategic direction of the practice
(b) Establish the best communication strategy for the selected market segments. These strategies can range from business-to-business communications such as word of mouth and referrals, to Web pages for the international market.

5 If the activities in Southeast Asia become a reality, how would this affect the service offering provided by Johnasen, Browne and Cooper-Smith?

For Johnasen, Browne and Cooper-Smith to move from a domestic service provider to an international service provider, there are a number of considerations that need to be addressed. The first and most important issue is how the practice will conduct business in a new culture and business environment. This step is critical, as it determines the future acceptance of the practice, its ability to operate efficiently in a new country, and its ability to work within the legal and governmental restrictions of the new country. Other considerations are the legal standing between the two countries and an understanding of business cultural differences by the practice. Once this is recognised and understood, Johnasen, Browne and Cooper-Smith must then decide whether to operate from Australia, operate as a new company in the new country, or develop a strategic alliance with an existing organisation.

The second aspect relates to the marketing strategy of the practice and to whether this is the stepping stone to other international work or a one-off venture. This decision will have a major impact on the resources of the practice. Concurrent with this step is the need to consider the service offering provided in the new country. Does it remain an architectural practice firm, or does it move into other areas, such as project management, to ensure the integrity of the project?

PART FIVE CLOSING
MARKETING PLANNING ACTIVITES

Putting it all together

Developing a marketing plan is one of the key tools used by marketers to ensure that their marketing strategy for a particular product has a greater chance of success. A marketing plan has many sections. At the end of each of the last four parts, you have been asked to complete portions of the marketing plan according to the sections or topics that have been covered in that part. In this final part of the book, you will now see the plan come together.

By now, you should have completed the activities for the marketing plan at the end of Parts 1, 2, 3 and 4. If you are progressing through the text in this manner, you will already have addressed the idea of the consumer decision-making process, and investigated how organisations conduct research on the marketplace and how they segment the market such that specific markets can be targeted to make effective use of the organisation's resources while maximising its principal objectives. Additionally, you will have considered the marketing mix elements and their impact on the organisational objectives.

This part has considered the final elements that can influence both the customer and organisational marketing efforts. In particular, it addressed the issues of the marketing environments, ethics, and the marketing process and strategy.

As noted earlier, the marketing planning process isn't easy and does take time. In addressing the questions below, you will build up a marketing plan for the organisation for your selected product. It is at this stage that we can combine all the answers to the questions from the previous parts to develop the marketing plan.

Activities

Before we start combining the answers for the marketing plan, let's first address some final questions from the topics covered in Part 5. You should be able to address the following:

- Describe the organisation in terms of length of business, key players, strengths and weaknesses, organisational culture and orientation.
- Define the organisational structure in terms of divisions, strategic business units, and customer interfaces such as storefront, Internet, and so on.
- Define the organisation's mission statement.
- Scan the environment for external forces and describe their impact on the opportunities for and threats to the organisation.
- Consider developing appropriate market and industry models to identify trends and possibilities for the organisation.
- Identify the organisation's competitive advantage.
- Identify the ethical and legal issues the organisation must respond to or interact with in order to remain an ethical and legal organisation.
- Identify the resources needed to achieve the organisation's future goals.
- Identify the tasks needed to be completed, by whom and when.

Drafting the marketing plan

Collate all the answers to the questions you have completed throughout the parts in this text for the selected organisation and product. Consider the structure of a marketing plan as presented at the commencement of this section on marketing planning activities. Using this structure, fill in the plan with the information you have gathered during the course of studying this text.

Refer to the worksheets you have compiled on your Student Resources CD-ROM and to the outline of a marketing plan provided at the end of Part 1.

PART FIVE CLOSING
Marketing plan

Marketing plan

I Business mission

II Objectives

III Situation analysis (SWOT analysis)

A. Internal strengths and weaknesses

B. External opportunities and threats
- Social
- Demographic
- Economic
- Political, legal and financial
- Competition
- Technological
- Ecological

IV Marketing strategy

A. Target market strategy

B. Marketing mix
1. Product
2. Place/distribution
3. Promotion
   a. Advertising
   b. Public relations
   c. Personal selling
   d. Sales promotion
4. Price

V Implementation, evaluation and control

Now review the plan, looking for gaps in the information, inconsistencies between your findings, and alignment with the organisation's mission and objectives. Modify the plan and then congratulate yourself for successfully drafting a marketing plan.

Suggested reading

The marketing planning activities have been developed by Peter Reed in relation to his book *Strategic Marketing Planning* (Melbourne: Thomson Learning).

A

accessory equipment Goods, such as portable tools and office equipment, that are less expensive and shorter lived than major equipment.

active website A website that permits two-way communication between an organisation and its customers.

actual product A product's parts, styling, brand name and packaging that combine to deliver the core product benefits.

adaptive channel An alternative channel initiated when a firm identifies critical but rare customer requirements that they don't have the capability to fulfil.

adopter A consumer who was happy enough with his or her trial experience with a product to use it again.

advertising Impersonal, one-way mass communication about a product or organisation that is paid for by a marketer.

advertising appeal Reason for a person to buy a product.

advertising campaign Series of related advertisements focusing on a common theme, slogan and set of advertising appeals.

advertising objective Specific communication task a campaign should accomplish for a specified target audience during a specified period.

advertising response function Phenomenon in which spending for advertising and sales promotion increases sales or market share up to a certain level but then produces diminishing returns.

advocacy advertising Form of advertising in which an organisation expresses its views on controversial issues or responds to media attacks.

agents and brokers Wholesaling intermediaries who facilitate the sale of a product from producer to end user by representing retailers, wholesalers or manufacturers and don't take title to the product.

AIDA concept Model that outlines the process for achieving promotional goals in terms of stages of consumer involvement with the message; the acronym stands for Attention, Interest, Desire and Action.

applied research Attempts to develop new or improved products.

atmosphere The overall impression conveyed by a store's physical layout, decor and surroundings.

attitude Learned tendency to respond consistently towards a given object.

audience selectivity Ability of an advertising medium to reach a precisely defined market.

audit Form of observation research that features people examining and verifying the sale of a product.

augmented product Additional customer services and benefits that are built around the core and actual products and support these offerings.

Australian and New Zealand Standard Industrial Classification (ANZSIC) codes A detailed numbering system developed to classify businesses by their main production processes.

automatic vending The use of machines to offer goods for sale.

average fixed cost (AFC) Total fixed cost divided by the quantity of output.

average total cost (ATC) Total costs divided by quantity of output.

average variable cost (AVC) Total variable costs divided by quantity of output.

B

baby boomers People born between 1946 and 1964.

bait pricing Price tactic that tries to get consumers into a store through false or misleading price advertising and then uses high-pressure selling to persuade consumers to buy more expensive merchandise.

banner advertising A prominent region on a Web page that is used to display a paid advertisement.

base price The general price level at which the company expects to sell the good or service.

basing-point pricing Price tactic that charges freight from a given (basing) point, regardless of the city from which the goods are shipped.

BehaviorScan Scanner-based research program that tracks the purchases of 3000 households through store scanners.

belief Organised pattern of knowledge that an individual holds as true about his or her world.

benefit segmentation The process of grouping customers into market segments according to the benefits they seek from the product.

brainstorming Getting a group to think of unlimited ways to vary a product or solve a problem.

brand A name, term, symbol, design or combination thereof that identifies a seller's products and differentiates them from competitors' products.

brand equity The value of company and brand names.

brand loyalty A consistent preference for one brand over all others.

brand mark The elements of a brand that cannot be spoken.

brand name That part of a brand that can be spoken, including letters, words and numbers.

brand personality The type of person or personality traits that the brand represents.

break-even analysis Method of determining what sales volume must be reached before total revenue equals total costs.

business analysis The second stage of the screening process where preliminary figures for demand, cost, sales and profitability are calculated.

business product (industrial product) Product used to manufacture other goods or services, to facilitate an organisation's operations or to resell to other customers.

business services Expense items that don't become part of a final product.

business-to-business electronic commerce (B2B) Using the Internet to conduct business between two or more organisations.

business strategy The second level of the strategic heirarchy that deals with the overall direction of strategic business units.

business-to-business marketing The marketing of goods and services to individuals and organisations for purposes other than personal consumption.

business-to-consumer electronic commerce (B2C) Using the Internet to conduct business between an organisation and individual consumers.

buyer Department head who selects the merchandise for his or her department and may also be responsible for promotion and personnel.

buying centre A group including all those persons who become involved in the purchase decision.

C

cannibalisation Situation that occurs when sales of a new product cut into sales of a firm's existing products.

cash discount A price reduction offered to a consumer, an industrial user or a marketing intermediary in return for prompt payment of a bill.

category killers Term often used to describe speciality discount stores because they so heavily dominate their narrow merchandise segment.

central-location telephone (CLT) facility A specially designed phone room used to conduct telephone interviewing.

chain stores Stores owned and operated as a group by a single organisation.

channel Medium of communication – such as a voice, radio or newspaper – for transmitting a message.

channel conflict A clash of goals and methods between distribution channel members.

channel control A situation that occurs when one marketing channel member intentionally affects another member's behaviour.

channel leader (channel captain) Member of a marketing channel that exercises authority and power over the activities of other channel members.

channel members All parties in the marketing channel that negotiate with one another, buy and sell products, and facilitate the change of ownership between buyer and seller in the course of moving the product from the manufacturer into the hands of the final consumer.

channel partnering (channel cooperation) The joint effort of all channel members to create a supply chain that serves customers and creates a competitive advantage.

channel power The capacity of a particular marketing channel member to control or influence the behaviour of other channel members.

chemist A retail store that stocks pharmacy-related products and services as its main draw.

clickstream The sequence in which a person visited Web pages in a website.

closed-ended question Interview question that asks the respondent to make a selection from a limited list of responses.

co-branding Placing two or more brand names on a product or its package.

code of ethics A guideline to help marketing managers and other employees make better decisions.

cognitive dissonance Inner tension that a consumer experiences after recognising an inconsistency between behaviour and values or opinions.

commercialisation The decision to market a product.

communication Process by which we exchange or share meanings through a common set of symbols.

comparative advertising Form of advertising that compares two or more specifically named or shown competing brands on one or more specific attributes.

competitive advantage The idea that a product can solve a set of customer problems better than any competitor's product.

competitive advertising Form of advertising designed to influence demand for a specific brand.

component lifestyle The practice of choosing goods and services that meet one's diverse needs and interests rather than conforming to a single, traditional lifestyle.

component parts Either finished items ready for assembly or products that need very little processing before becoming part of some other product.

computer-assisted personal interviewing Interviewing method in which the interviewer reads the questions from a computer screen and enters the respondent's data directly into the computer.

computer-assisted self-interviewing Interviewing method in which a mall interviewer intercepts and directs willing respondents to nearby computers where the respondent reads questions on the computer screen and directly keys his or her answers into the computer.

computer disk by mail survey Like a typical mail survey, only the respondents receive and answer questions on a disk.

concentrated targeting strategy A strategy used to select one segment of a market or targeting marketing efforts.

concept test Test to evaluate a new-product idea, usually before any prototype has been created.

consumer behaviour Processes a consumer uses to make purchase decisions, as well as to use and dispose of purchased goods and services; also includes factors that influence purchase decisions and the use of products.

consumer decision-making process Step-by-step process used by consumers when buying goods or services.

consumer product Product bought to satisfy an individual's personal wants.

consumer sales promotion Sales promotion activities to the ultimate consumer.

continuous media schedule Media scheduling strategy, used for products in the latter stages of the product life cycle, in which advertising is run steadily throughout the advertising period.

convenience product A relatively inexpensive item that merits little shopping effort.

convenience sample A form of non-probability sample using respondents who are convenient or readily accessible to the researcher – for example, employees, friends or relatives.

convenience store A miniature supermarket, carrying only a limited line of high-turnover convenience goods.

cooperative advertising Arrangement in which the manufacturer and the retailer split the costs of advertising the manufacturer's brand.

core product The problem-solving core benefits that customers are really buying when they obtain a product.

corporate social responsibility Business's concern for society's welfare.

corporate strategy The highest level of the strategic heirarchy that deals with the overall direction of the organisation.

cost per contact Cost of reaching one member of the target market.

coupon Certificate that entitles consumers to an immediate price reduction when they buy the product.

credence quality A characteristic that consumers may have difficulty assessing even after purchase because they don't have the necessary knowledge or experience.

crisis management Coordinated effort to handle the effects of unfavourable publicity or of another unexpected, unfavourable event.

cross-tabulation A method of analysing data that lets the analyst look at the responses to one question in relation to the responses to one or more other questions.

culture Set of values, norms, attitudes and other meaningful symbols that shape human behaviour and the artefacts, or products, of that behaviour as they are transmitted from one generation to the next.

cumulative quantity discount A deduction from list price that applies to the buyer's total purchases made during a specific period.

customer satisfaction The feeling that a product has met or exceeded the customer's expectations.

customer value The ratio of benefits to the sacrifice necessary to obtain those benefits.

D

database marketing The creation of a large computerised file of customers' and potential customers' profiles and purchase patterns.

decision support system (DSS) An interactive, flexible, computerised information system that enables managers to obtain and manipulate information as they are making decisions.

decline stage A long-run drop in sales.

decoding Interpretation of the language and symbols sent by the source through a channel.

demand The quantity of a product that will be sold in the market at various prices for a specified period.

demographic segmentation Segmenting markets by age, gender, income, ethnic background and family life cycle.

department store A store housing several departments under one roof.

derived demand The demand for business products.

development Stage in the product development process in which a prototype is developed and a marketing strategy is outlined.

differential advantage One or more unique aspects of an organisation that cause target consumers to patronise that firm rather than competitors.

diffusion The process by which the adoption of an innovation spreads.

direct channel Distribution channel in which producers sell directly to consumers.

direct marketing (direct-response marketing) Techniques used to get consumers to make a purchase from their home, office or other non-retail setting.

discount store A retailer that competes on the basis of low prices, high turnover and high volume.

discrepancy of assortment Lack of all the items a customer needs to receive full satisfaction from a product or products.

discrepancy of quantity Difference between the amount of product produced and the amount a customer wants to buy.

discussion list Anyone on a particular mailing list can participate in an exchange of ideas, where participants can contribute their comments to an ongoing dialogue. This electronic conversation is treated like a threaded discussion, in which any reply to a previous message is linked to the original message.

distribution resource planning (DRP) Stock control system that manages the replenishment of goods from the manufacturer to the final consumer.

dual distribution (multiple distribution) Use of two or more channels to distribute the same product to target markets.

dynamic website A website that provides consumers with information but does not permit them to communicate with an organisation.

E

e-business Includes all communications and transactions with an organisation's stakeholders, such as customers, suppliers, government regulators, financial institutions, employees and the public at large.

e-commerce The conduct of business transactions electronically – and hence has a slightly narrower focus than e-business.

80/20 principle Principle that holds that 20 per cent of all customers generate 80 per cent of the demand.

elastic demand Situation in which consumer demand is sensitive to changes in price.

elasticity of demand Consumers' responsiveness or sensitivity to changes in price.

electronic data interchange (EDI) Information technology that replaces the paper documents that usually accompany business transactions, such as purchase orders and invoices, with electronic transmission of the needed information to reduce stock levels, improve cash flow, streamline operations, and increase the speed and accuracy of information transmission.

electronic distribution Distribution technique that includes any kind of product or service that can be distributed electronically, whether over traditional forms such as fibre-optic cable or through satellite transmission of electronic signals.

e-marketing Traditional marketing using electronic methods.

empowerment Delegation of authority to solve customers' problems quickly – usually by the first person the customer notifies regarding a problem.

encoding Conversion of the sender's ideas and thoughts into a message, usually in the form of words or signs.

environmental management When a company implements strategies that attempt to shape the external environment within which it operates.

environmental scanning Collection and interpretation of information about forces, events and relationships in the external environment that may affect the future of the organisation or the implementation of the marketing plan.

e-tailing Using the Internet to sell retail products and services.

ethics The moral principles or values that generally govern the conduct of an individual or group; the standard of behaviour by which conduct is judged.

evaluation Gauging the extent to which the marketing objectives have been achieved during the specified period.

everyday low pricing (EDLP) Price tactic of permanently reducing prices 10 to 25 per cent below the traditional

levels while eliminating trade discounts that create trade loading.
evoked set (consideration set) Group of brands, resulting from an information search, from which a buyer can choose.
exchange The idea that people give up something to receive something they would rather have.
exclusive distribution Form of distribution that establishes one or a few dealers within a given area.
experience quality A characteristic that can be assessed only after use.
experiment Method a researcher uses to gather primary data.
express warranty A written guarantee.
extensive decision-making Most complex type of consumer decision-making, used when buying an unfamiliar, expensive product or an infrequently bought item; requires use of several criteria for evaluating options and much time for seeking information.
external information search Process of seeking information in the outside environment.
extranet A private electronic network that links a company with its suppliers and customers.
e-zine Abbreviation for electronic magazine – an on-line publication similar in concept to a printed magazine.

F

factory outlet An off-price retailer that is owned and operated by a manufacturer.
family brand Marketing several different products under the same brand name.
family life cycle (FLC) A series of stages determined by a combination of age, marital status, and the presence or absence of children.
feedback Receiver's response to a message.
field service organisation Organisation that specialises in interviewing respondents on a sub-contracted basis.
fixed cost Cost that does not change as output is increased or decreased.
flexible pricing (variable pricing) Price tactic in which different customers pay different prices for essentially the same merchandise bought in equal quantities.
flighted media schedule Media scheduling strategy in which ads are run heavily every other month or every two weeks, to achieve a greater impact with an increased frequency and reach at those times.
FOB origin pricing Price tactic that requires the buyer to absorb the freight costs from the shipping point (free on board).
focus group Seven to 10 people who participate in a group discussion led by a moderator.
four Ps Product, place, promotion and price, which together make up the marketing mix.
frame error Error that occurs when a sample drawn from a population differs from the target population.
franchise The right to operate a business or to sell a product.
franchisee Individual or business that is granted the right to sell another party's product.
franchiser Originator of a trade name, product, methods of operation, and so on, that grants operating rights to another party to sell its product.
freight absorption pricing Price tactic in which the seller pays all or part of the actual freight charges and does not pass them on to the buyer.
frequency Number of times an individual is exposed to a given message during a specific period.
frequent buyer program Loyalty program in which loyal consumers are rewarded for making multiple purchases of a particular good or service.
full-line discount store A retailer that offers consumers very limited service and carries a broad assortment of well-known, nationally branded 'hard goods'.
functional discount (trade discount) Discount to wholesalers and retailers for performing channel functions.
functional strategy The third level of the strategic heirarchy that deals with implementation of the strategic direction at an operational level.

G

Generation X People born between 1961 and 1980.
Generation Y People born between 1979 and 1994.
Generation Z People born between 1994 and the present.
generic product A no-frills, no-brand-name, low-cost product that is simply identified by its product category.
generic product name Identifies a product by class or type and cannot be trademarked.
geodemographic segmentation Segmenting potential customers into neighbourhood lifestyle categories.
geographic segmentation Segmenting markets by region of the country or world, market size, market density or climate.
global competition The strategy an organisation adopts to provide the same product in all markets around the world.
global marketing Marketing that targets markets throughout the world.
global vision Recognising and reacting to international marketing opportunities, being aware of threats from foreign competitors in all markets, and effectively using international distribution networks.
gross margin Amount of money the retailer makes as a percentage of sales after the cost of goods sold is subtracted.
group dynamics Group interaction essential to the success of focus group research. Through the use of focus groups, manufacturers can discover many new uses for their products.
growth stage The second stage of the product life cycle when sales typically grow at an increasing rate, many competitors enter the market, large companies may start acquiring small pioneering firms and profits are healthy.

H

heterogeneity Characteristic of services that makes them less standardised and uniform than goods.
hit Each occurrence of a Web page being visited by a Web surfer.
horizontal conflict Channel conflict that occurs among channel members on the same level.
hypermarket Retail store that combines a supermarket and full-line discount store in a space ranging from 200 000 to 300 000 square feet.

I

ideal self-image The way an individual would like to be.

implementation The process that turns marketing plans into action assignments and ensures that these assignments are executed in a way that accomplishes the plans' objectives.

implied warranty An unwritten guarantee that the good or service is fit for the purpose for which it was sold.

independent retailers Retailers owned by a single person or partnership and not operated as part of a larger retail institution.

individual branding Using different brand names for different products.

inelastic demand Situation in which an increase or a decrease in price won't significantly affect demand for the product.

inflation A general rise in prices without a corresponding increase in wages, which results in decreased purchasing power.

infomercial Thirty-minute or longer advertisement that looks more like a TV talk show than a sales pitch.

informational labelling Designed to help consumers make proper product selections and lower their cognitive dissonance after the purchase.

InfoScan A scanner-based sales-tracking service for the consumer packaged-goods industry.

innovation A product perceived as new by a potential adopter.

inseparability Characteristic of services that allows them to be produced and consumed simultaneously.

institutional advertising Form of advertising designed to enhance a company's image rather than promote a particular product.

intangibility Characteristic of services that cannot be touched, seen, tasted, heard or felt in the same manner in which goods can be sensed.

integrated interviewing A new interviewing method in which a respondent is interviewed on the Internet.

integrated marketing communications (IMC) The method of carefully coordinating all promotional activities to produce a consistent, unified message that is customer-focused.

intensive distribution Form of distribution aimed at having a product available in every outlet at which target customers might want to buy it.

internal information search Process of recalling information stored in the memory.

international competition The strategy an organisation adopts to provide products that are usually different or modified in some way to different countries.

Internet Worldwide telecommunications network allowing access to data, pictures, sound and files throughout the world.

Internet marketing One form of e-marketing utilising the Internet.

interpersonal communication Direct, face-to-face communication between two or more people.

interstitial advertisement An advertisement that appears in a separate browser window – also referred to as a 'pop-up' ad.

introductory stage The full-scale launch of a new product into the marketplace.

involvement Amount of time and effort a buyer invests in the search, evaluation and decision processes of consumer behaviour.

J

joint demand The demand for two or more items used together in a final product.

just-in-time production (JIT) Redefining and simplifying manufacturing by reducing stock levels and delivering raw materials just when they are needed on the production line.

K

keystoning Practice of marking up prices by 100 per cent, or doubling the cost.

L

leader pricing (loss-leader pricing) Price tactic in which a product is sold near or even below cost in the hope that shoppers will buy other items once they are in the store.

learning Process that creates changes in behaviour, immediate or expected, through experience and practice.

lifestyle Mode of living as identified by a person's activities, interests and opinions.

limited decision-making Type of decision-making that requires a moderate amount of time for gathering information and deliberating about an unfamiliar brand in a familiar product category.

logistics The process of strategically managing the efficient flow and storage of raw materials, in-process stock and finished goods from point of origin to point of consumption.

logistics information system Information technology that integrates and links all the logistics functions of the supply chain.

logistics service Interrelated activities performed by a member of the supply chain to ensure that the right product is in the right place at the right time.

loyalty marketing program Promotional program designed to build long-term, mutually beneficial relationships between a company and its key customers.

M

macrosegmentation Method of dividing business markets into segments based on general characteristics such as geographic location, customer type, customer size and product use.

major equipment Capital goods such as large or expensive machines, mainframe computers, blast furnaces, generators, aeroplanes and buildings.

mall intercept interview Survey research method that involves interviewing people in the common areas of shopping malls.

management decision problem Broad-based problem that requires marketing research in order for managers to take proper action.

manufacturer's brand The brand name of a manufacturer.

marginal cost (MC) Change in total costs associated with a one-unit change in output.

marginal revenue (MR) The extra revenue associated with selling an extra unit of output or the change in total revenue with a one-unit change in output.

market People or organisations with needs or wants and the ability and willingness to buy.

marketing The process of planning and executing the conception, pricing, promotion and distribution of ideas, goods and services to create exchanges that satisfy individual and organisational goals.

marketing audit A thorough, systematic, periodic evaluation of the goals, strategies, structure and performance of the marketing organisation.

marketing channel (channel of distribution) Set of interdependent organisations that facilitate the transfer of ownership as products move from producer to business user or consumer.

marketing communication Information passed on from marketers to the public, including consumers, via a range of promotional activities.

marketing concept Idea that the social and economic justification for an organisation's existence is the satisfaction of customer wants and needs while meeting organisational objectives.

marketing control The measuring and evaluating of performance and taking corrective action if required.

marketing-controlled information source Product information source that originates with marketers promoting the product.

marketing intelligence Everyday information about developments in the marketing environment that managers use to prepare and adjust marketing plans.

marketing mix A unique blend of product, distribution, promotion and pricing strategies designed to produce mutually satisfying exchanges with a target market.

marketing myopia Business defined in terms that are too focused on one aspect of the organisation's markets (its goods and services), rather than seeing the whole picture (the benefits that customers seek).

marketing objective A statement of what is to be accomplished through marketing activities.

marketing orientation A philosophy that assumes that a sale depends on a customer's decision to purchase a product.

marketing plan A written document that acts as a guidebook of marketing activities for the marketing manager.

marketing planning Designing activities relating to marketing objectives and the changing marketing environment.

marketing research The process of planning, collecting and analysing data relevant to a marketing decision.

marketing research objective Specific information needed to solve a marketing research problem; the objective should provide insightful decision-making information.

marketing research problem Determining what information is needed and how that information can be obtained efficiently and effectively.

marketing strategy The activities of selecting and describing one or more target markets and developing and maintaining a marketing mix that will produce mutually satisfying exchanges with target markets.

market segment A subgroup of people or organisations sharing one or more characteristics that cause them to have similar product needs.

market segmentation The process of dividing a market into meaningful, relatively similar and identifiable segments or groups.

market share A company's product sales as a percentage of total sales for that industry.

mark-up pricing Cost of buying the product from the producer plus amounts for profit and for expenses not otherwise accounted for.

Maslow's hierarchy of needs Method of classifying human needs and motivations into five categories in ascending order of importance: physiological, safety, social, esteem and self-actualisation.

mass communication Communication to large audiences.

mass customisation (build-to-order) Production method whereby products are not made until an order is placed by the customer; products are made according to customer specifications.

mass merchandising Retailing strategy using moderate to low prices on large quantities of merchandise and lower service to stimulate high turnover of products.

master brand A brand so dominant in consumers' minds that they think of it immediately when a product category, use situation, product attribute or customer benefit is mentioned.

materials-handling system Method of moving stock into, within and out of the warehouse.

materials requirement planning (MRP) Stock control system that manages the replenishment of raw materials, supplies and components from the supplier to the manufacturer.

maturity stage A period during which sales increase at a decreasing rate.

measurement error Error that occurs when there is a difference between the information desired by the researcher and the information provided by the measurement process.

media mix Combination of media to be used for a promotional campaign.

media schedule Designation of the media, the specific publications or programs, and the insertion dates of advertising.

medium Channel used to convey a message to a target market.

merchant wholesaler Institution that buys goods from manufacturers and resells them to businesses, government agencies, and other wholesalers or retailers and that receives and takes title to goods, stores them in its own warehouses and later ships them.

microsegmentation The process of dividing business markets into segments based on the characteristics of decision-making units within a macrosegment.

mission statement The firm's long-term vision based on a careful analysis of benefits sought by present and potential customers and analysis of existing and anticipated environmental conditions.

modified rebuy Situation where the purchaser wants some change in the original good or service.

morals The rules people develop as a result of cultural values and norms.

motive Driving force that causes a person to take action to satisfy specific needs.

multiculturalism When a society has more than one ethnic culture, the society receives benefits as a result of this diversity.

multiplier effect (accelerator principle) Phenomenon in which a small increase or decrease in consumer demand can produce a much larger change in demand for the facilities and equipment needed to make the consumer product.

multi-segment targeting strategy A strategy that chooses two or more well-defined market segments and develops a distinct marketing mix for each.

N

need recognition Occurs when a consumer is faced with an imbalance between actual and desired states.

new buy A situation requiring the purchase of a product for the first time.

new product Product new to the world, the market, the producer, the seller or some combination of these.

new-product strategy Linking the new-product development process with the objectives of the marketing department, the business unit and the corporation.

niche One segment of a market.

noise Anything that interferes with, distorts or slows down the transmission of information.

non-cumulative quantity discount A deduction from list price that applies to a single order rather than to the total volume of orders placed during a certain period.

non-marketing-controlled information source Product information source that is not associated with advertising or promotion.

non-probability sample Any sample in which little or no attempt is made to get a representative cross-section of the population.

non-store retailing Shopping without visiting a store.

O

observation research Research method that relies on three types of observation: people watching people, people watching activity, and machines watching people.

odd–even pricing (psychological pricing) Price tactic that uses odd-numbered prices to connote bargains and even-numbered prices to imply quality.

off-price retailer Retailer that sells at prices 25 per cent or more below traditional department store prices because it pays cash for its stock and usually doesn't ask for return privileges.

open-ended question Interview question that encourages an answer phrased in the respondent's own words.

opinion leader Individual who influences the opinions of others.

optimisers Type of business customer that considers numerous suppliers, both familiar and unfamiliar, solicits bids and studies all proposals carefully before selecting one.

order processing system System whereby orders are entered into the supply chain and filled.

outsourcing (contract logistics) Manufacturer's or supplier's use of an independent third party to manage an entire function of the logistics system, such as transportation, warehousing or order processing.

P

penetration pricing Pricing policy whereby a firm charges a relatively low price for a product initially as a way to reach the mass market.

perception Process by which people select, organise and interpret stimuli into a meaningful and coherent picture.

perceptual mapping A means of displaying or graphing, in two or more dimensions, the location of products, brands or groups of products in customers' minds.

perishability Characteristic of services that prevents them from being stored, warehoused or inventoried.

personalised economy Delivering goods and services at a good value on demand.

personality Way of organising and grouping the consistencies of an individual's reactions to situations.

personal retailing Representatives selling products door-to-door, office-to-office or through party plans.

personal selling Planned presentation to one or more prospective buyers for the purpose of making a sale.

persuasive labelling Focuses on a promotional theme or logo and consumer information is secondary.

pioneering advertising Form of advertising designed to stimulate primary demand for a new product or product category.

planned obsolescence The practice of modifying products so those that have already been sold become obsolete before they actually need replacement.

planning The process of anticipating future events and determining strategies to achieve organisational objectives in the future.

point-of-purchase display Promotional display set up at the retailer's location to build traffic, advertise the product or induce impulse buying.

position The place a product, brand or group of products occupies in consumers' minds relative to competing offerings.

positioning Developing a specific marketing mix to influence potential customers' overall perception of a brand, product line or organisation in general.

predatory pricing The practice of charging a very low price for a product with the intent of driving competitors out of business or out of a market.

premium Extra item offered to the consumer, usually in exchange for some proof of purchase of the promoted product.

prestige pricing Charging a high price to help promote a high-quality image.

price What is given up in an exchange to acquire a good or service.

price bundling Marketing two or more products in a single package for a special price.

price fixing An agreement between two or more firms on the price they will charge for a product.

price skimming Pricing policy whereby a firm charges a high introductory price, often coupled with heavy promotion.

price strategy Basic, long-term pricing framework, which establishes the initial price for a product and the intended direction for price movements over the product life cycle.

primary data Information collected for the first time. Can be used for solving the particular problem under investigation.

primary research Pure research that aims to confirm an existing theory or to learn more about a concept or phenomenon.

private brand A brand name owned by a wholesaler or a retailer.

private-label brands Brands that are designed and developed using the retailer's name.

probability sample A sample in which every element in the population has a known statistical likelihood of being selected.

processed materials Products used directly in manufacturing other products.

product Everything, both favourable and unfavourable, that a person receives in an exchange.

product advertising Form of advertising that promotes the benefits of a specific good or service.
product category All brands that satisfy a particular type of need.
product development Marketing strategy that entails the creation of marketable new products; process of converting applications for new technologies into marketable products.
product differentiation A positioning strategy that some firms use to distinguish their products from those of competitors.
product item A specific version of a product that can be designated as a distinct offering among an organisation's products.
product life cycle A concept that provides a way to trace the stages of a product's acceptance, from its introduction (birth) to its decline (death).
product line A group of closely related product items.
product line depth The number of product items in a product line.
product line extension Adding additional products to an existing product line in order to compete more broadly in the industry.
product mix All the products an organisation sells.
product mix width The number of product lines an organisation offers.
product modification Changing one or more of a product's characteristics.
product offering The mix of products offered to the consumer by the retailer; also called the product assortment or merchandise mix.
production orientation A philosophy that focuses on the internal capabilities of the firm rather than on the desires and needs of the marketplace.
profit Revenue minus expenses.
profit maximisation When marginal revenue equals marginal cost.
promotion Communication by marketers that informs, persuades and reminds potential buyers of a product in order to influence an opinion or elicit a response.
promotional allowance (trade allowance) Payment to a dealer for promoting the manufacturer's products.
promotional mix Combination of promotion tools – including advertising, public relations, personal selling and sales promotion – used to reach the target market and fulfil the organisation's overall goals.
promotional strategy Plan for the optimal use of the elements of promotion: advertising, public relations, personal selling and sales promotion.
psychographic segmentation Market segmentation on the basis of personality, motives, lifestyles and geodemographics.
publicity Public information about a company, good or service appearing in the mass media as a news item.
public relations (PR) Marketing function that evaluates public attitudes, identifies areas within the organisation that the public may be interested in, and executes a program of action to earn public understanding and acceptance.
pull strategy Marketing strategy that stimulates consumer demand to obtain product distribution.
pulsing media schedule Media scheduling strategy that uses continuous scheduling throughout the year coupled with a flighted schedule during the best sales periods.
push money Money offered to channel intermediaries to encourage them to 'push' products – that is, to encourage other members of the channel to sell the products.
push strategy Marketing strategy that uses aggressive personal selling and trade advertising to convince a wholesaler or a retailer to carry and sell particular merchandise.

Q

quantity discount Price reduction offered to buyers buying in multiple units or above a specified dollar amount.

R

random error Error that occurs because the selected sample is an imperfect representation of the overall population.
random sample Sample arranged in such a way that every element of the population has an equal chance of being selected as part of the sample.
raw materials Unprocessed extractive or agricultural products such as mineral ore, timber, wheat, corn, fruits, vegetables or fish.
reach Number of target consumers exposed to a commercial at least once during a specific period, usually four weeks.
real self-image The way an individual actually perceives himself or herself.
rebate Cash refund given for the purchase of a product during a specific period.
receiver Person who decodes a message.
recession A period of economic activity when income, production and employment tend to fall – all of which reduce demand for goods and services.
reciprocity A practice where business purchasers choose to buy from their own customers.
recruited Internet sample Respondents are pre-recruited. After qualifying to participate, they are sent a questionnaire by email or directed to a secure website to fill out a questionnaire.
reference group Group in society that influences an individual's purchasing behaviour.
relationship marketing A strategy that entails forging long-term partnerships with customers and is based on the marketing orientation.
relationship marketing orientation The focus of marketing activities on keeping existing customers and suppliers.
relationship selling (consultative selling) Sales practice of building, maintaining and enhancing interactions with customers in order to develop long-term satisfaction through mutually beneficial partnerships.
repositioning Changing consumers' perceptions of a brand in relation to competing brands.
research design Specifies which research questions must be answered, how and when the data will be gathered, and how the data will be analysed.
retailer Channel intermediary that sells mainly to consumers.
retailing All the activities directly related to the sale of goods and services to the ultimate consumer for personal, non-business use.
retailing mix Combination of the six Ps – product, place, promotion, price, personnel and presentation – to sell goods and services to the ultimate consumer.

Glossary

return on investment (ROI) Net profit after taxes divided by total assets.
revenue The price charged to customers multiplied by the number of units sold.
routine response behaviour (habitual buying behaviour) Type of decision-making exhibited by consumers buying frequently purchased, low-cost goods and services; requires little search and decision time.

S

sales orientation The idea that people will buy more goods and services if aggressive sales techniques are used and that high sales result in high profits.
sales process (sales cycle) The set of steps a salesperson goes through in a particular organisation to sell a particular product or service.
sales promotion Marketing activities – other than personal selling, advertising and public relations – that stimulate consumer buying and dealer effectiveness.
sample A sub-set of a population.
sampling Promotional program that allows the consumer the opportunity to try the product or service for free.
sampling error Error that occurs when a sample somehow does not represent the target population.
satisficers Contact familiar suppliers and place the order with the first to satisfy product and delivery requirements.
scaled-response question A closed-ended question designed to measure the intensity of a respondent's answer.
scanner-based research A system for gathering information from a single group of respondents by continuously monitoring the advertising, promotion and pricing they are exposed to and the things they buy.
screened Internet sample Internet sample with quotas based on desired sample characteristics.
screening The first filter in the product development process, which eliminates ideas that are inconsistent with the organisation's new-product strategy or are obviously inappropriate for some other reason.
search quality A characteristic that can be easily assessed before purchase.
seasonal discount A price reduction for buying merchandise out of season.

seasonal media schedule Media scheduling strategy that runs advertising only during times of the year when the product is most likely to be used.
secondary data Data previously collected for any purpose other than the one at hand.
segmentation bases (variables) Characteristics of individuals, groups or organisations.
selective distortion Process whereby a consumer changes or distorts information that conflicts with his or her feelings or beliefs.
selective distribution Form of distribution achieved by screening dealers to eliminate all but a few in any single area.
selective exposure Process whereby a consumer notices certain stimuli and ignores other stimuli.
selective retention Process whereby a consumer remembers only that information that supports his or her personal beliefs.
self-concept How a consumer perceives himself, or herself, in terms of attitudes, perceptions, beliefs and self- evaluations.
self-esteem The opinion one holds of oneself.
sender Originator of the message in the communication process.
service The result of applying human or mechanical efforts to people or objects.
service mark Trademark for a service.
shopping product Product that requires comparison shopping, because it is usually more expensive than a convenience product and found in fewer stores.
simulated (laboratory) market testing Presentation of advertising and other promotional materials for several products, including a test product, to members of the product's target market.
social class Group of people in a society who are considered nearly equal in status or community esteem, who regularly socialise among themselves, both formally and informally, and who share behavioural norms.
socialisation process How cultural values and norms are passed down to children.
societal marketing orientation The idea that an organisation exists to satisfy customer needs and wants, and organisational objectives, but also to preserve or enhance an individual's and society's long-term best interest.
spatial (place) discrepancy Difference between the location of the producer and the location of widely scattered markets.
speciality discount store Retail store that offers a nearly complete selection of single-line merchandise and uses self-service, discount prices, high volume and high turnover.
speciality product A particular item that consumers search extensively for and are very reluctant to accept substitutes for.
speciality store Retail store specialising in a given type of merchandise.
sponsored website A non-commercial website that presents content targeted at a special interest.
status quo pricing Pricing objective that maintains existing prices or meets the competition's prices.
stimulus Any unit of input affecting one or more of the five senses: sight, smell, taste, touch or hearing.
stimulus discrimination Learned ability to differentiate among stimuli.
stock control system Method of developing and maintaining an adequate assortment of products to meet customer demand.
straight rebuy Buying situation in which the purchaser reorders the same goods or services without looking for new information or investigating other suppliers.
strategic alliance (strategic partnership) A cooperative agreement between business firms.
strategic business unit (SBU) A subgroup of a single business or collection of related businesses within the larger organisation.
strategic channel alliance Cooperative agreement between business firms to use the other's already established distribution channel.
strategic planning The managerial process of creating and maintaining a fit between the organisation's objectives and resources and evolving market opportunities.
strategic window The limited period during which the 'fit' between the key requirements of a market and the particular competencies of a firm are at an optimum.

subculture Homogeneous group of people who share elements of the overall culture as well as unique elements of their own group.

supermarket A large, departmentalised, self-service retailer that specialises in food and some non-food items.

supplies Consumable items that don't become part of the final product.

supply The quantity of a product that will be offered to the market by a supplier at various prices for a specified period.

supply chain The connected chain of all the business entities, both internal and external to the company, that perform or support the logistics function.

supply chain management (integrated logistics) Management system that coordinates and integrates all of the activities performed by supply chain members from source to the point of consumption that results in enhanced customer and economic value.

supply chain team Entire group of individuals who orchestrate the movement of goods, services and information from the source to the consumer.

survey research The most popular technique for gathering primary data in which a researcher interacts with people to obtain facts, opinions and attitudes.

SWOT analysis Identifying internal strengths (S) and weaknesses (W) and also examining external opportunities (O) and threats (T).

T

target market A group of people or organisations for which an organisation designs, implements and maintains a marketing mix intended to meet the needs of that group, resulting in mutually satisfying exchanges.

teamwork Collaborative efforts of people to accomplish common objectives.

telemarketing The use of the telephone to sell directly to consumers.

temporal (time) discrepancy Difference between when a product is produced and when a customer is ready to buy it.

test marketing The limited introduction of a product and a marketing program to determine the reactions of potential customers in a market situation.

trade allowance Price reduction offered by manufacturers to intermediaries, such as wholesalers and retailers.

Trade Practices Act Law that prohibits wholesalers and retailers from selling below cost.

trademark The exclusive right to use a brand or part of a brand.

trade sales promotion Sales promotion activities targeted at a channel member, such as a wholesaler or retailer.

two-part pricing Price tactic that charges two separate amounts to consume a single good or service.

U

unbundling Reducing the bundle of services that comes with the basic product.

undifferentiated targeting strategy Marketing approach that views the market as one big market with no individual segments and thus requires a single marketing mix.

uniform delivered pricing Price tactic in which the seller pays the actual freight charges and bills every purchaser an identical, flat freight charge.

unique selling proposition Desirable, exclusive and believable advertising appeal selected as the theme for a campaign.

unitary elasticity Situation in which total revenue remains the same when prices change.

universal product codes (UPCs) Series of thick and thin vertical lines (bar codes), readable by computerised optical scanners, that represent numbers used to track products.

universe The population from which a sample will be drawn.

unrestricted Internet sample Anyone with a computer and modem can fill out the questionnaire.

unsought product A product unknown to the potential buyer or a known product that the buyer does not actively seek.

usage-rate segmentation Dividing a market by the amount of product bought or consumed.

V

value Enduring belief that a specific mode of conduct is personally or socially preferable to another mode of conduct.

value-based pricing The price is set at a level that seems to the customer to be a good price compared to the prices of other options.

variable costs Costs that vary with changes in the level of output.

vertical conflict Channel conflict that occurs between different levels in a marketing channel, most typically between manufacturer and wholesaler and between manufacturer and retailer.

virtual community People with a common interest who interact on and contribute content to a communal website.

W

want Recognition of an unfulfilled need and a product that will satisfy it.

warranty Confirms the quality or performance of a good or service.

wireless link A radio or infra-red link between two or more electronic devices.

World Wide Web (Web) Component of the Internet designed to simplify text and images.

Z

zone pricing Modification of uniform delivered pricing that divides the total market into segments or zones and charges a flat freight rate to all customers in a given zone.

Chapter 1

1. Story of the bionic ear: Graeme Clark, *Sounds from Silence* (Sydney: Allen & Unwin, 2000); www.cochlear.com/rcs/cochlear/publisher/web/candidates/choosing_nucleus/BEI/bionicstory/index.jsp, History of the cochlear implant; G.M. Clark, Y.C. Tong and J.F. Patrick, *Cochlear Prostheses* (Melbourne: Churchill Livingstone, 1990); The Royal Victorian Eye & Ear Hospital, Department of Otolaryngology (home of the Cochlear Implant Program): www.rveeh.vic.gov.au/services/entservices.htm; G.M. Clark, Preface, 'Supply – Candidature for Cochlear Implants – New Directions', *Australian Journal of Audiology*, in press; G.M. Clark, 'Research Advances for Cochlear Implants', *Auris Nasus Larynx*, vol. 25, 1998, pp. 73–87; G.M. Clark, 'Speech Processing for Cochlear Implants', in S. Greenberg and W. Ainsworth (eds), *Springer Handbook of Auditory Research: Speech Processing in the Auditory System* (Springer Verlag, in press); G.M. Clark and P.A. Busby, 'Perceptual Studies on Cochlear Implant Patients with Early Onset of Profound Hearing Impairment', in *Textbook of Perceptual Hearing* (Cambridge, Mass.: MIT Press, in press); www.btfunds.co.nz/wnew/wnew_health.html; Glenda Price, 'World All Ears for Hearing Implant Growth', *Australian*, 5 November 2001.
2. www.mambo.com.au.
3. Peter D. Bennett, *Dictionary of Marketing Terms*, 2nd edn. (Chicago: American Marketing Association, 1995), p. 115.
4. Philip Kotler, *Marketing Management*, 9th edn. (Englewood Cliffs, NJ: Prentice-Hall, 1997), p. 11.
5. Cravens, Lamb and Crittenden, *Strategic Marketing Management Cases* (New York: McGraw-Hill, 1999), p. 79.
6. www.virginblue.com.au/questions/main.html.
7. Kevin J. Clancy and Robert S. Shulman, 'Marketing – Ten Fatal Flaws', *The Retailing Issues Letter*, November 1995, p. 4.
8. Jonathan B. Levine, 'Customer, Sell Thyself', *Fast Company*, June–July 1996, p. 148.
9. Rolan T. Rust, Anthony J. Zahorik and Timothy L. Keiningham, *Service Marketing* (New York: HarperCollins, 1996), p. 375.
10. Leonard L. Berry, 'Relationship Marketing of Services', *Journal of the Academy of Marketing Science*, Fall 1995, pp. 236–45.
11. www.cancercouncil.com.au/cncrinfo/schools/tobacco_bulletinfinal2311.pdf.
12. Becky Ebenkamp, 'Main Street Revisited', *Brandweek*, 7 April 1997. © 1997/98 VNU Business Media Inc. Used with permission from Brandweek ®.
13. Kotler, op. cit., p. 22.

Chapter 2

1. Hannen, 'Wine: Makers Get Even Bolder', *Business Review Weekly*, 25 January 2001.
2. T. Readgold, 'Strategy: Wine for the World', *Business Review Weekly*, 13 October 2000.
3. Nancy Ten Kate, 'The Marketplace for Medicine', *American Demographics*, February 1998, p. 34.
4. Eric D. Bruce and Sam Fullerton, 'Discount Pricing as a Mediator of the Consumer's Evoked Set', in Donald L. Thompson and Cathy Owens Swift (eds), *1995 Atlantic Marketing Association Proceedings* (Orlando: Atlantic Marketing Association, 1995), pp. 32–6.
5. F. Kelly Shruptrine, 'Warranty Coverage: How Important in Purchasing an Automobile?', in Brian T. Engelland and Dennis T. Smart (eds), *1995 Southern Marketing Association Proceedings* (Houston: Southern Marketing Association, 1995), pp. 300–3.
6. S. Lloyd, 'The Brand Thing', *Business Review Weekly*, 21 July 2000: www.brw.com.au/newsadmin/stories/brw/20000721/6467.htm (accessed 1 February 2001).
7. Don Umphery, 'Consumer Costs: A Detriment of Upgrading or Downgrading of Cable Service', *Journalism Quarterly*, Winter 1991, pp. 698–708.
8. Robert L. Simison, 'Infiniti Adopts New Sales Strategy to Polish its Brand', *Wall Street Journal*, 10 June 1996, pp. B1, B7.
9. Adapted from *The Daily Telegraph*, 'Profit is not super cheap', February 19 2005; www.supercheapauto.com.
10. Bill Stoneman, 'Beyond Rocking the Ages: An Interview with J. Walker Smith', *American Demographics*, May 1998, pp. 44–9.
11. Diane Crispell, 'Core Values', *American Demographics*, November 1996.
12. Robert Levine, 'The Pace of Life in 31 Countries', *American Demographics*, November 1997, pp. 20–9; John Robinson, Bart Landry and Ronica Rooks, 'Time and the Melting Pot', *American Demographics*, June 1998, pp. 18–24; John P. Robinson, Toon Van Der Horn and Ryichi Kitamura, 'Less Work, More Play: Life's Good in Holland', *American Demographics*, September 1993; Robert Levine, 'Re-learning to Tell Time', *American Demographics*, January 1998, pp. 20–5.
13. Elia Kacapyr, 'Are You Middle Class?', *American Demographics*, October 1996.
14. Grahame R. Dowling and Richard Staelin, 'A Model of Perceived Risk and Intended Risk-handling Activity', *Journal of Consumer Research*, June 1994, pp. 119–34.
15. Chip Walker, 'Word of Mouth', *American Demographics*, July 1995, pp. 38–44.
16. Norihiko Shirouzu, 'Japan's High-school Girls Excel in Art of Setting Trends', *Wall Street Journal*, 24 April 1998, pp. B1, B6.
17. Stephen E. Frank, 'Tiger Woods Plugs American Express', *Wall Street Journal*, 20 May 1997, pp. B1, B14.
18. James U. McNeal, 'Tapping the Three Kids' Markets', *American Demographics*, April 1998, pp. 37–41.
19. Matthew Klein, 'He Shops, She Shops', *American Demographics*, March 1998, pp. 34–5.
20. Marcia Mogelonsky, 'The Breakfast of Everyone', *American Demographics*, February 1998, p. 36.
21. Nancy Ten Kate, 'Two Careers, One Marriage', *American Demographics*, April 1998, p. 28.
22. Dana Milbank, 'More Dads Raise Families without Mom', *Wall Street Journal*, 3 October 1997, pp. B1, B2.
23. Maxine Wilkie, 'Names that Smell', *American Demographics*, August 1995, pp. 48–9.
24. Nora J. Rifon and Molly Catherine Ziske, 'Using Weight Loss Products: The Roles of Involvement, Self-efficacy and Body Image', in Barbara B. Stern and George M. Zinkhan (eds), *1995 AMA Educators' Proceedings* (Chicago: American Marketing Association, 1995), pp. 90–8.
25. William D. Wells and David Prensky, *Consumer Behavior* (New York: John Wiley & Sons, Inc., 1996), p. 46.
26. Maria Mallory and Kevin Whitelaw, 'The Power of Brands', *US News & World Report*, 13 May 1996, p. 58.
27. 'Asian Culture and the Global Consumer', *Financial Times*, 21 September 1998, p. 1.
28. Yumiko Ono, 'Tiffany Glitters, Even

in Gloomy Japan', *Wall Street Journal*, 21 July 1998, pp. B1, B18.
29 Gene Del Vecchio, 'Keeping it Timeless, Trendy: From Barbie to Pez, "Ever-Cool" Kids Brands Meet Both Needs', *Advertising Age*, 23 March 1998, p. 24.
30 Steven Lipin, Brian Coleman and Jeremy Mark, 'Pick a Card: Visa, American Express and MasterCard Vie in Overseas Strategies', *Wall Street Journal*, 15 February 1994, pp. A1, A5.

Chapter 3
1 Justin Martin, 'Are You As Good As You Think You Are?' *Fortune*, 30 September 1996, p. 143.
2 Jonah Gitilitz, 'Direct Marketing in the B-to-B Future', *Business Marketing*, July/August 1996, pp. A2, A5.
3 Sager, op. cit., pp. 154–62.
4 Robert W. Haas, *Business Marketing*, 6th ed. (Cincinnati, OH: South-Western College Publishing, 1995), p. 190.
5 Amy Cortese, 'Here Comes the Intranet', *Business Week*, 26 February 1996, p. 76.
6 Alan M. Patterson, 'Customers Can Be Partners', *Marketing News*, 9 September 1996, p. 10.
7 Ira Sager, 'How IBM Became a Growth Company Again', *Business Week*, 9 December 1996, pp. 155–6.
8 www.bhpbilliton.com/bb/home/home.jsp (accessed 21 November 2001).
9 'The Science of Alliance', *The Economist*, 4 April 1998, p. 69.
10 D. James, 'If You Can't Beat Them … a Strategic Alliance?' *Business Review Weekly*, 18 May 1998.
11 David Woodruff, 'VW's Factory of the Future', *Business Week*, 7 October 1996, p. 52.
12 Michael D. Hutt and Thomas W. Speh, *Business Marketing*, 5th ed. (Fort Worth, TX: Dryden, 1998), p. 121.
13 Frank G. Bingham, Jr, and Barney T. Raffield, III, *Business Marketing Management* (Cincinnati, OH: South-Western College Publishing, 1995), pp. 18–19.

Chapter 4
1 Emily Ross, 'Retail: Juice Bars Extract Growth From a Fruity Fashion', *Business Review Weekly*, 16 February 2001. Reproduced with permission.
2 *Marketing*, October 1997.
3 From Ernest Beck and Rehka Balu, 'Europe is Dead to Snap! Crackle! Pop!', *Wall Street Journal*, 22 June 1998. Reprinted by permission of the *Wall Street Journal*. © 1998 Dow Jones & Company, Inc. All rights reserved worldwide.
4 David Leonhardt, 'Hey Kid, Buy This', *Business Week*, 30 June 1997, pp. 86–8.
5 Emily Nelson, 'Kodak Focuses on Putting Kids Behind Instead of Just in Front of a Camera', *Wall Street Journal*, 6 May 1997, p. B8.
6 Mark Spiegler, 'Betting on Web Sports', *American Demographics*, May 1996, p. 24.
7 Mark Maremont, 'Gillette's New Strategy is to Sharpen Pitch to Women', *Wall Street Journal*, 11 May 1998, p. B1; Tara Parker-Pope, 'Minoxidil Tries to Grow Women's Market', *Wall Street Journal*, 27 January 1997, p. B1.
8 Alex Taylor, III, 'Porsche Slices up its Buyers', *Fortune*, 16 January 1995, p. 24.
9 Karen Benezra, 'The Fragging of the American Mind', *Superbrands*, 15 June 1998, pp. S12–S19.
10 Much of the material in this section is based on Michael D. Hurt and Thomas W. Speh, *Business Marketing Management*, 6th edn. (Hinsdale, IL: Dryden Press, 1998), pp. 176–81.
11 Australian Bureau of Statistics, 1996 Census, Table B03, Cat. No. 2020.0.
12 From Jared Sandberg, 'Ply and Pry: How Business Pumps Kids on Web', *Wall Street Journal*, 9 June 1997. Reprinted by permission of the *Wall Street Journal*, © 1997 Dow Jones & Company, Inc. All rights reserved worldwide.
13 'How Spending Changes During Middle Age', *Wall Street Journal*, 14 January 1992, p. B1.
14 'Marketers Reveal Industry Dos and Don'ts; Say Capitalize on Relationship Building', *Selling to Seniors*, November 1997, pp. 1–2.
15 Lyn Drummond, 'Single Mingle', *Sunday Age*, 17 February 2002.
16 www.halledit.com.au/bizops; www.halledit.com.au/bizops/from/fd037.html; www.dymocks.com.au/asp/about.asp; Jeff Rubin, 'Businesses Gain a Foothold Through Niche Marketing', *Wall Street Journal*, 25 June 1998. Reprinted by permission of the *Wall Street Journal*, © 1997 Dow Jones & Company, Inc. All rights reserved worldwide.
17 Susan Chandler, 'Kids' Wear is Not Child's Play', *Business Week*, 19 June 1995, p. 188.
18 These examples were provided by David W. Cravens, Texas Christian University.
19 Elaine Underwood, 'Sea Change', *Brandweek*, 22 April 1996, pp. 32–6.
20 Kathryn Hopper, 'Polished and Profitable', *Forth Worth Star-Telegram*, 22 March 1996, pp. B1, B3.

Chapter 5
1 From Bernadette Tracy, 'What Makes Women Click?', *IAB Online Advertising Guide*, Spring 1998. Reprinted by permission of Bernadette Tracy, President, Netsmart-Research.com.
2 Adapted from 'Keebler Learns to Pay Attention to Research Right from the Start', *Marketing News*, 11 March 1996, p. 10.
3 'Why Some Customers Are More Equal Than Others', *Fortune*, 19 September 1994, pp. 215–24.
4 Ibid.
5 'Major US Companies Expand Efforts to Sell to Consumers Abroad', *Wall Street Journal*, 13 June 1996, pp. A1, A6.
6 Andrew Bean and Michael Roszkowski, 'The Long and Short of It', *Marketing Research*, Winter 1995, pp. 21–6.
7 This section is adapted from James Watt, 'Using the Internet for Quantitative Survey Research', *Quirk's Marketing Research Review*, June–July 1997, pp. 67–71.
8 From Douglas A. Blackmon, 'Familiar Refrain: Consultant's Advice on Diversity Was Anything But Diverse', *Wall Street Journal*, 11 March 1997. Reprinted by permission of the *Wall Street Journal*. © 1997 Dow Jones & Company, Inc. All rights reserved worldwide.

Chapter 6
1 Matt Murray, 'Kodak Considers Selling Discount Film to Compete with Private-label Brands', *Wall Street Journal*, 4 June 1997, p. B3.
2 www.petersonhouse.com.au (accessed 30 April 2001).
3 *The Age*, 'Get set for a food fight', February 27, 2005.
4 Noreen O'Leary, 'The Old Bunny Trick', *Brandweek*, 18 March 1996, pp. 26–30.
5 Brandon Mitchener, 'Mercedes Adds Down-market Niche Cars', *Wall Street Journal*, 21 February 1996, p. A10.
6 'Make it Simple', *Business Week*, 9 September 1996, p. 96.
7 Ibid.
8 Simon Lloyd, 'Brand values surge', Interbrand, www.interbrand.com (accessed 29 March 2005), November 2004.

9 *Business Week* July 22 2004, Interbrands annual ranking of the "best Global Brands" In August 2nd Issue.
10 Simon Lloyd, 'Brand values surge', Interbrand, www.interbrand.com (accessed 29 March 2005), November 2004.
11 Peter H. Farquhar et al., 'Strategies for Leveraging Master Brands', *Marketing Research*, September 1992, pp. 32–43.
12 Kiley, D, 2005, 'Brands abroad under fire', *Business Week*, January 5 (accessed 29 March 2005), www.businessweek.com/the_thread/brandnewday/archives/00000008.htm.
13 GMI Poll, 2005, 'Global backlash against US brands: Can Tsunami Relief efforts stem the Anti-American tide?' February 2 (accessed 29 march 2005), WWW.gmipoll.com/press_room_wppk_pr_02022005.phtml.
14 Diane Crispell and Kathleen Brandenburg, 'What's in a Brand?' *American Demographics*, May 1993, pp. 26–32.
15 Building strong brands, 2005, http://groups.haas.berkeley.edu/marketing/PAPERS/AAKER/BOOKS/BUILDING/brand_personality.html (accessed 29 March 2005).
16 Aaker, J, 2004, "Brand personality dimensions of Jennifer Aaker", www.valuebasedmanagement.net/methods_aaker_brand_personality_framework.html (accessed 29 March 2005).
17 Van Den Bergh, 2005, 'Air NZ a leader in fatigue data', Fairfax New Zealand, Monday 28 March, accessed 29 March 2005.
18 Sandra Baker, 'Savvy Shoppers', *Fort Worth Star-Telegram*, 31 March 1996, p. D1.
19 Chad Rubel, 'Price, Quality Important for Private Label Goods', *Marketing News*, 2 January 1995, p. 24.
20 L. Kaye, 'Mars Bars 'n' Cars', *B&T Weekly*, 1 May 2001.
21 'Cobranding Just Starting in Europe', *Marketing News*, 13 February 1995, p. 5.
22 David D. Kirkpatrick, 'No T-shirts! Landmark Buildings Trademark Images', *Wall Street Journal*, 10 June 1998, pp. B1, B12.
23 Maxine Lans Retsky, 'You Can Make Your Mark with Your Signature', *Marketing News*, 23 September 1996, p. 13.
24 From Michelle Wirth Fellman, '"Ti-Gear": Owning Up to a Name', *Marketing News*, 26 October 1998, p. 2. Reprinted by permission of the American Marketing Association.
25 Michael Rapoport, 'Clash of Symbols: DKNY Sues DNKY Over Trademark', *Wall Street Journal*, 26 August 1996, p. A7B.
26 Lisa Brownlee, '*Polo* Magazine Angers Polo Ralph Lauren', *Wall Street Journal*, 21 October 1997, p. B10.
27 Maxine Lans Retsky, 'Who Needs the New Community Trademark?' *Marketing News*, 3 June 1996, p. 11.
28 Shannon Dortch, 'Metros at Your Service', *American Demographics*, May 1996, pp. 4–5.
29 'The Manufacturing Myth', *The Economist*, 19 March 1994.
30 David Kirkpatrick, 'Old PC Dogs Try New Tricks', *Fortune*, 6 July 1998, pp. 186–8.
31 Betsy Spethman, 'Getting Fresh', *Brandweek*, 20 May 1996, pp. 44–7.
32 M. Ligerakis, 'Drawing a Strongbow', *B&T Weekly*, 6 October 2000.
33 Tammy Reiss, 'Hey, It's Green – It Must Be Healthy', *Business Week*, 13 July 1998, p. 6.
34 A.C. Nielsen, *Top 100 Brands, 2000*.
35 'Packaging to Tempt Every Man (and His Dog)', *B&T Weekly*, 2 March 2001.
36 'Just Enough Packaging', *Wall Street Journal*, 7 September 1995, p. A1.
37 'A Biodegradable Plastic Gains Notice', *Wall Street Journal*, 4 February 1993, p. A1; Robert McMath, 'It's All in the Trigger', *Adweek's Marketing Week*, 6 January 1992, pp. 25–8.

Chapter 7

1 Brian O'Reilly, 'The Secrets of America's Most Admired Corporations: New Ideas, New Products', *Fortune*, 3 March 1997, p. 60.
2 P. McIntyre, 'Slow Death in the Grocery Aisles', *Business Review Weekly*, 7 February 2002.
3 www.brw.com.au/newsadmin/stories/brw/20000324/5147.htm (accessed 29 January 2001).
4 Sam Bradley, 'Hallmark Enters $20B Pet Category', *Brandweek*, 1 January 1996, p. 4.
5 'New But Not Necessarily Improved', *Wall Street Journal*, 15 January 1997, p. A1.
6 www.brw.com.au/newsadmin/stories/brw/19991112/4090.htm (accessed 29 January 2001).
7 *New Product Management in the 1980s* (New York: Booz, Allen & Hamilton, 1982), p. 3.
8 Norhiko Shirouzu, 'For Coca-Cola in Japan, Things Go Better with Milk', *Wall Street Journal*, 20 January 1997, p. B1.
9 Ibid.
10 'New Products', *Fort Worth Star-Telegram*, 11 May 1997, p. E1.
11 Mark Maremont, 'How Gillette Brought its MACH3 to Market', *Wall Street Journal*, 15 April 1998, p. B1.
12 Ibid.
13 Tom Lynch, 'Internet: A Strategic Product Introduction Tool', *Marketing News*, 22 April 1996, p. 15.
14 Linda Grant, 'Gillette Knows Shaving – and How to Turn Out', *Fortune*, 14 October 1996, on-line.
15 Roy Rivenburg, 'A Close Shave is Good News in the Gillette Laboratory', *Fort Worth Star-Telegram*, 29 June 1996, p. E6.
16 'Procter & Gamble Co. to Test a New Spray for Removing Odors', *Wall Street Journal*, 8 May 1996, p. A5.
17 Croft, op. cit.
18 Lynch, op. cit.
19 R.M. McMath, 'Copycat Cupcakes Don't Cut it', *American Demographics*, January 1997, p. 60.
20 R. Kiermaier and S. Butscher, 'Develop Only What Customers Want, at Their Price', *Marketing News*, 17 March 1997, p. 6.
21 J. Baumwall, 'Why Didn't You Think of That?', *Marketing News*, 22 April 1996, p. 10.
22 D. Cravens, *Strategic Marketing*, 5th edn. (New York: McGraw-Hill, 1997), pp. 244–5.
23 Paul Best, 'DVD Eclipses the Video Star', *The Age*, 21 February 2002.
24 www.ipodlounge.com.

Chapter 8

1 Mandy Bryan, 'Gateway Retreats as PC Sales Dive', *Australian Financial Review*, 30 August 2001, pp. 1, 18.
2 Daniel Lyons, 'Games Dealers Play', *Forbes*, 19 October 1998, pp. 132–4; Andrew Serwer, 'Michael Dell Rocks', *Fortune*, 11 May 1998, p. 58; David E. Kalish, 'Dell Computer Outsmarts IBM, Compaq', *AP Online*, 19 August 1998; Raju Narisetti, 'IBM Plans to Sell Some Gear Directly to Fight Its Rivals', *Wall Street Journal*, 5 June 1998, p. B6; Evan Ramstad, 'PC Playing Field Tilts in Favor of Dell', *Wall Street Journal*, 21 May 1998, p. B8; 'Dell Selling PCs in China Through Its Internet Store', *New Straits Times*, 25 August 1998, p. 22.
3 Richard Gibson, 'Attention, Wal-Mart Shoppers: You Want Fries With That?', *Wall Street Journal*, 25 July 1997, p. B6.
4 www.ptm.com.au/ptm-irp/profile.
5 'Fujitsu, Oracle Form Strategic Alliance in Asia', *Reuters*, 21 August 1997.

6   David Frederick Ross, *Competing Through Supply Chain Management: Creating Market-winning Strategies Through Supply Chain Partnerships* (New York: Chapman & Hall, 1998), pp. 60–1.
7   Francis J. Quinn, 'Supply-chain Management Report: What's the Buzz?', *Logistics* Management, February 1997.
8   Ross, op. cit, pp. 9–12.
9   Quinn, op. cit.
10 Ross, op. cit.
11 Ibid.
12 This section is based on John L. Kent, Jr and Daniel J. Flint, 'Perspectives on the Evolution of Logistics Thought', *Journal of Business Logistics*, vol. 18, no. 2, 1997, p. 15; and Francis J. Quinn, 'What's the Buzz?', *Logistics Management & Distribution Report*, 1 February 1997.
13 Benefits based on Francis J. Quinn, 'The Payoff! Benefits of Improving Supply Chain Management', *Logistics Management*, December 1997, p. 37.
14 Theodore P. Stank, Patricia J. Daugherty and Alexander E. Ellinger, 'Pulling Customers Closer Through Logistics Service', *Business Horizons*, September 1998, p. 74.
15 Ibid.
16 James Aaron Cooke, 'Warehousing: Great Expectations', 1998 Annual Report, *Logistics Management & Distribution Report*, July 1998.
17 'KPMG: Customer Service Increasingly Important in Supply Chain Management', M2 *PRESSWIRE*, 28 September 1998.
18 Quinn, 'Supply-chain Management Report: What's the Buzz?', op. cit.
19 Francis Quinn, 'Team Up for Supply-chain Success', *Logistics Management*, October 1997, p. 39.
20 Toby B. Gooley, 'On the Front Lines', *Logistics Management*, June 1997, p. 39.
21 Ibid.
22 Susan Avery, 'Purchasing Forges New Supplier Relationships', *Purchasing*, 5 June 1998.
23 Erick Schonfeld, 'The Customized, Digitized, Have-it-your-way Economy', *Fortune*, 28 September 1998, pp. 114–24.
24 Evan Ramstad, 'PC Playing Field Tilts in Favor of Dell', *Wall Street Journal*, 21 May 1998, p. B8; Andrew Serwer, 'Michael Dell Turns the PC World Inside Out', *Fortune*, 8 September 1997; Evan Ramstad, 'Dell Takes Another Shot at Booming Home-PC Market', *Wall Street Journal*, 16 December 1997, p. B4.
25 Robert Keehn, 'Transforming the Grocery Industry', *Meeting the Challenge of Global Logistics*, Report Number 1207-98-CR (New York: The Conference Board, Inc., 1998), pp. 25–7.
26 William Pesek, Jr, 'Inventory Control Stabilizes Economy: Better Management Helps Companies Avoid Missteps', *Wall Street Journal*, 29 August 1997, p. B8.
27 Anna Wilde Mathews, 'Cargo in Ships Offers Clues to What Will Go Under Tree', *Wall Street Journal*, 6 August 1997, p. B1.
28 Ramstad, 'Dell Takes Another Shot at Booming Home-PC Market', op. cit.
29 Douglas A. Blackmon, 'Shippers Pitch Power of Gizmos, Gadgets', *Wall Street Journal*, 2 June 1997, pp. B1, B4.
30 Eryn Brown, 'Costs Too High? Bring in the Logistics Experts', *Fortune*, 10 November 1997.
31 Ibid.
32 Raju Narisetti, 'How IBM Turned Around Its Ailing PC Division', *Wall Street Journal*, 12 March 1998, pp. B1, B6.
33 Anna Wilde Mathews, 'Logistics Firms Flourish Amid Trend in Outsourcing', *Wall Street Journal*, 2 June 1998, p. B4.
34 www.budget.com.au/partnersandprogrammes/fastbreak/fastbreak.html.
35 www.qantas.com.au/club/unwind.html.
36 'Sticking to the Web', *Chain Store Age*, June 1998, pp. 153–5.
37 M. Lawley, A. Koronios, J. Summers, M. Gardiner and N. Brown, *Report of the Exploratory Investigation of the Maranoa On-line Community Portal*, May 2001 (commissioned by the Maranoa On-line Community Portal Action Group).
38 www.cdnow.com/cgi-bin/mserver/SID=75072187/pagename=/MN/PROMO/promo_in_the_media.html/promoid=1686.

Chapter 9

1   Frank G Bingham, Jr, Charles J. Quigley, Jr, and Elaine M. Notarantonio, 'The Use of Communication Style in a Buyer–Seller Dyad: Improving Buyer–Seller Relationships', *Proceedings: Association of Marketing Theory and Practice*, 1996 Annual Meeting, Hilton Head, South Carolina, March 1996, pp. 188–95.
2   M. Ligerakis, 'Renault's Back in Australia with a New Campaign', *B&T Marketing and Media*, 4 June 2001.
3   www.masterfoods.com.au/features/bbq/woolworths.asp (accessed 7 April 2005).
4   H. Bawden, 'Marketers Join the Big Brother Rush', *B&T Marketing and Media*, 17 April 2001.
5   Ibid.
6   L. Kaye, 'Branson Pulls Virgin Mobile Stunt', *B&T Marketing and Media*, 1 November 2000.
7   See Don E. Schultz, Stanley I. Tannenbaum and Robert F. Lauterborn, *Integrated Marketing Communications* (Lincolnwood, IL: NTC Business Books, 1993).
8   Jeff Jensen, '"Godzilla" Effort Looms Over '98 Movie Marketing', *Advertising Age*, 4 May 1998, p 12; Jeff Jensen, 'Monster-size Outdoor Ads Presage Arrival of "Godzilla"', *Advertising Age*, 6 April 1998, p. 3.
9   www.creatablemedia.com.au (accessed 7 April 2005).
10 Moore N, 2005, 'Capturing the food court', *B & T Marketing and Media*, 3 February.
11 Shea, F, 2005, 'The Shopping Centre becomes an integrated medium', *B & T Marketing and Media* 3 February.
12 Philip J. Kitchen, 'Marketing Communications Renaissance', *International Journal of Advertising*, vol. 12, 1993, pp. 367–86.
13 Ibid, p. 372.
14 AIDA concept based on the classic research of E. K. Strong, Jr, as theorised in *The Psychology of Selling and Advertising* (New York: McGraw-Hill, 1925) and 'Theories of Selling', *Journal of Applied Psychology*, vol. 9, 1925, pp. 75–86.
15 Thomas E. Barry and Daniel J. Howard, 'A Review and Critique of the Hierarchy of Effects in Advertising', *International Journal of Advertising*, vol. 9, 1990, pp. 121–35.
16 Kim Cleland, 'The Marketing 100: Colgate Total, Jack Haber', *Advertising Age*, 29 June 1998, p. s44.
17 Elyse Tanouye, 'Drug Ads Spur Patients to Demand More Prescriptions', *Wall Street Journal*, 22 December 1997, p. B1; Patricia Braus, 'Selling Drugs', *American Demographics*, January 1998, pp. 26–9; Michael Wilke, 'Prescription for Profit', *Advertising Age*, 16 March 1998, pp. s1, s26; Robert Langreth and Andrea Petersen, 'A Stampede is on for Impotence Pill', *Wall Street Journal*, 20 April 1998, pp. B1, B6; Ira Teinowitz, 'New TV Guidelines Bring Wishes for Further Changes', *Advertising Age*, 16 March 1998, p. s10; also see David Stipp and Robert Whitaker, 'The Selling of Impotence', *Fortune*, 16 March 1998, pp. 115–24.

18 Marvin A. Jolson, 'Broadening the Scope of Relationship Selling', *Journal of Personal Selling & Sales Management*, Fall 1997, p. 75; also see Donald W. Jackson, Jr, 'Relationship Selling: The Personalization of Relationship Marketing', *Asia–Australia Marketing Journal*, August 1994, pp. 45–54.
19 Bingham, Quigley and Notarantonio, op. cit., pp. 188–95.
20 Geoffrey Brewer, 'The Customer Stops Here', *Sales & Marketing Management*, March 1998, pp. 30–6.
21 www.sanitarium.com.au.
22 'Can Your Reps Sell Overseas?', *Sales & Marketing Management*, February 1998, p. 110.
23 Andy Cohen, 'Global Dos and Don'ts', *Sales & Marketing Management*, June 1996, p. 72; Esmond D. Smith, Jr and Cuong Pham, 'Doing Business in Vietnam: A Cultural Guide', *Business Horizons*, May–June 1996, pp. 47–51; 'Five Tips for International Handshaking', *Sales & Marketing Management*, July 1997, p. 90, from Dorothea Johnson, director of the Protocol School of Washington; Tricia Campbell, 'What to Give Overseas', *Sales & Marketing Management*, September 1997, p. 85; 'Negotiating: Getting to Yes, Chinese-style', *Sales & Marketing Management*, July 1996, pp. 44–5; Michelle Marchetti, 'Selling in China? Go Slowly', *Sales & Marketing Management*, January 1997, pp. 35–6; Sergey Frank, 'Global Negotiating: Vive Les Différences!', *Sales & Marketing Management*, May 1992, pp. 64–9.
24 'It's No Secret: Why Dell Gives Customers Insider Access to Prices and Products', *Sales & Marketing Management*, May 1998, p. 93.
25 www.amway.com/infocenter/i-didY.asp, accessed 9 August 2001.
26 'Sticking to the Web', *Chain Store Age*, June 1998, pp. 153–5.
27 M. Lawley, A. Koronios, J. Summers, M. Gardiner and N. Brown, *Report of the Exploratory Investigation of the Maranoa On-line Community Portal*, May 2001 (commissioned by the Maranoa On-line Community Portal Action Group).
28 www.cdnow.com/cgi-bin/mserver/SID=75072187/ pagename=/MN/PROMO/promo_in_ the_media.html/promoid=1686.

Chapter 10

1 www.fipp.com/printer_firendly/1530 (accessed & April 2005).
2 www.amsrs.com.au/index.cfm?a=detail&id=1712&eid=110 (accessed 8 April 2005).
3 www.itfacts.biz/index.php?id=P462 (accessed 7 April 2005).
4 Advertising Federation of Australia: www.afa.org.au/index2.asp?pid=22; Advertising Federation of Australia: www.afa.org.au/WebStreamere?page_id=3067 (accessed 8 April 2005).
5 'Big increase in ad spend', special report, 26 March 2004, *B&T Marketing and Media*.
6 Ibid.
7 '1998 Advertising-to-sales Ratios for the 200 Largest Ad Spending Industries', *Advertising Age*, 29 June 1998, p. 22.
8 'Time Spent with Media', *Standard & Poor's Industry Surveys*, 14 March 1996, p. M1; 'Radio & TV Broadcasting: Commercials Clog the Airways', *Standard & Poor's Industry Surveys*, 12 May 1994, p. M35.
9 G. Belch and M. Belch, *Advertising and Promotion: An Integrated Marketing Communications Perspective* (New York: McGraw-Hill, 2001).
10 Amitava Chattaopadhyay and Kunal Basu, 'Humor in Advertising: The Moderating Role of Prior Brand Evaluation', *Journal of Marketing Research*, November 1990, pp. 466–76.
11 Rajiv Grover and V. Srinivasan, 'Evaluating the Multiple Effects of Retail Promotions on Brand Loyalty and Brand Switching Segments', *Journal of Marketing Research*, February 1992, pp. 76–89; see also S.P. Raj, 'The Effects of Advertising on High and Low Loyalty Consumer Segments', *Journal of Consumer Research*, June 1982, pp. 77–89.
12 Jean Halliday, 'Ford Corporate Ads Push "A Relationship of Trust"', *Advertising Age*, 4 May 1998, p. 3.
13 Michael Burgoon, Michael Pfau and Thomas S. Birk, 'An Inoculation Theory Explanation for the Effects of Corporate Issue/Advocacy Advertising Campaigns', *Communication Research*, August 1995, p. 485(21).
14 H. Bawden, 'McDonald's in Sponsorship Row', *B&T Marketing and Media*, 6 August 2001.
15 Mark Maremont, 'How Gillette Brought Its MACH3 to Market', *Wall Street Journal*, 15 April 1998, pp. B1, B10; Sharon T. Klahr, 'Gillette Puts $300 Mil Behind Its MACH3 Shaver', *Advertising Age*, 20 April 1998, p. 6.
16 E. Scacco and J. Hawke, 'Comparative Ads Make Your Claim', *B&T Marketing and Media*, 10 November 2000.
17 M. Ligerakis, 'Panadol Seeks Cure for Herron Sales Jump', *B&T Marketing and Media*, 9 April 2001.
18 Martin DuBois and Tara Parker-Pope, 'Philip Morris Campaign Stirs Uproar in Europe', *Wall Street Journal*, 1 July 1996, pp. B1, B5; 'French Block Philip Morris Ad', *New York Times*, 26 June 1996, p. C5.
19 Maremont, 'How Gillette Brought Its MACH3 to Market', op. cit.; Klahr, 'Gillette Puts $300 Mil Behind Its MACH3 Shaver', op. cit.
20 Mark Maremont, 'Close vs Safe: Rivals Prepare to Market New Razors', *Wall Street Journal*, 29 September 1997, pp. B1, B6.
21 Klahr, 'Gillette Puts $300 Mil Behind Its Mach3 Shaver', op. cit.
22 Anon, 'Hunch Sparks Weet-Bix Strategy', *Adnews*, 8 October 1999.
23 M. Ligerakis, 'The Arnott's Parrot Comes Alive', *B&T Marketing and Media*, 27 October 2000.
24 Marc G. Weinberger, Harlan Spotts, Leland Campbell and Amy L. Parsons, 'The Use and Effect of Humor in Different Advertising Media', *Journal of Advertising Research*, May–June 1995, pp. 44–56.
25 Noreen O'Leary, 'New Life on Mars', *Brandweek*, 6 May 1996, p. 44(3).
26 Roger Thurow, 'Shtick Ball: In Global Drive, Nike Finds Its Brash Ways Don't Always Pay Off', *Wall Street Journal*, 5 May 1997, pp. A1, A10.
27 Johnny K. Johansson, '"The Sense of Nonsense": Japanese TV Advertising', *Journal of Advertising*, March 1994, pp. 17–26.
28 Audrey Snee, 'Kodak Divides Up China in Order to Conquer It', *Ad Age International*, January 1998, p. 20; Juliana Koranteng, 'Reebok Finds Its Second Wind as It Pursues Global Presence', *Ad Age International*, January 1998, p. 18; James Caporimo, 'Worldwide Advertising Has Benefits, But One Size Doesn't Always Fit All', *Brandweek*, 17 July 1995, p. 16; Ali Kanso, 'International Advertising Strategies: Global Commitment to Local Vision', *Journal of Advertising Research*, January–February 1992, pp. 10–14; Wayne M. McCullough, 'Global Advertising Which Acts Locally: The IBM Subtitles Campaign', *Journal of Advertising Research*, May–June 1996, pp. 11–15; Martin S. Roth, 'Effects of Global Market Conditions on Brand Image Customization and Brand Performance', *Journal of Advertising*,

Winter 1995, p. 55(21). Also see Carolyn A. Lin, 'Cultural Differences in Message Strategies: A Comparison Between American and Japanese Television Commercials', *Journal of Advertising Research*, July–August 1993, pp. 40–7; Fred Zandpour et al., 'Global Reach and Local Touch: Achieving Cultural Fitness in TV Advertising', *Journal of Advertising Research*, September–October 1994, pp. 35–63.

29 'Radio: No Longer an Advertising Afterthought', *Standard & Poor's Industry Surveys*, 20 July 1995, p. M36; Rebecca Piirto, 'Why Radio Thrives', *American Demographics*, May 1994, pp. 40–6.

30 H. Bawden, 'Bid Up to $45K for Big Brother Spot', *B&T Marketing and Media*, 10 July 2001.

31 Kim Cleland, 'Arthritis Foundation Turns to Infomercial', *Advertising Age*, 9 June 1997, p. 14.

32 'Outdoor's Reincarnation: Cool Urban Art', *B&T Marketing and Media*, 30 March 2001.

33 Ibid.

34 Rhonda L Rundle, 'Outdoor Plans Billboard-sized Purchase', *Wall Street Journal*, 11 July 1996, p. B6; Cyndee Miller, 'Outdoor Gets a Makeover', *Marketing News*, 10 April 1995, pp. 1, 26.

35 S. van Wyk, 'How Long Can the Banner Ad Survive?', *B&T Marketing and Media*, 10 November 2000.

36 C. Rumble, 'Ad Agencies Hold Back the New Economy', *B&T Marketing and Media*, 15 November 2000.

37 Kate Maddox, 'ANA Study Finds Marketers Triple Net Ad Budgets', *Advertising Age*, 11 May 1998, p. 63.

38 'Year in Review: Interactive/Web Becomes a Viable Channel', *Advertising Age*, 22 December 1997, pp. 21–2.

39 Sally Goll Beatty, 'Internet Ad Proponents Try a New Tack', *Wall Street Journal*, 25 September 1997, p. B8.

40 Jupiter Communications, 2000, August 16, www. Retailindustry. about.com/library/bl/bl_jup0816.htm (accessed April 2005).

41 Pierre Berthon, Leyland F. Pitt and Richard T. Watson, 'The World Wide Web as an Advertising Medium: Toward an Understanding of Conversion Efficiency', *Journal of Advertising Research*, January–February 1996, pp. 43–54.

42 Cybergold website at www.cyber-gold.com.

43 Laurie Freeman, 'Internet Visitors' Traffic Jam Makes Buyers Web Wary', *Advertising Age*, 22 July 1996, pp. S14–15.

44 Jeff Jensen, 'Disney, Gillette Sign for Adsticks', *Advertising Age*, 8 June 1998, p. 48.

45 Adapted from pres releases from the Land Transport safety Authority Website, www.landtransport.govt.nz (accessed 8 April 2005) and Veldre, D, 2003, 'Drink driving campaign sends message', *B & T Marketing and Media*, 16 May.

46 Anon, 'Promo Marketing Now at $6 Billion a Year', *B&T Marketing and Media*, 24 July 2001.

47 Raju Narisetti, 'Many Companies Are Starting to Wean Shoppers off Coupons', *Wall Street Journal*, 22 January 1997, p. B1.

48 Laura Reina, 'Manufacturers Still Believe in Coupons', *Editor & Publisher*, 28 October 1995, p. 24; Betsy Spethmann, 'Coupons Shed Low-Tech Image; Sophisticated Tracking Yields Valuable Consumer Profile', *Brandweek*, 24 October 1994, p. 30(2); and Scott Hume, 'Coupons: Are They Too Popular?', *Advertising Age*, 15 February 1993, p. 32.

49 M. Ligerakis, 'Kellogg Brings Rock 'n' Roll to Brekky', *B&T Marketing and Media*, 2 July 2001.

50 Kate Fitzgerald, 'Instant-reward Coupons Show Rebound', *Advertising Age*, 12 May 1997, p. 20.

51 William M. Bulkeley, 'Rebates' Secret Appeal to Manufacturers: Few Consumers Actually Redeem Them', *Wall Street Journal*, 10 February 1998, pp. B1, B2.

52 Judann Pollack, 'Pop Tarts Packs More Pastry for Same Price', *Advertising Age*, 5 August 1996, p. 6.

53 Richard Gibson, 'At McDonald's, a Case of Mass Beaniemania', *Wall Street Journal*, 5 June 1998, pp. B1, B8.

54 Mark Lacek, 'Loyalty Marketing No Ad Budget Threat', *Advertising Age*, 23 October 1995, p. 20.

55 Ginger Conlon, 'True Romance', *Sales & Marketing Management*, May 1996, pp. 85–90.

56 Keith L Alexander, 'Net Surfers Rack Up Travel Miles', *USA Today*, 29 September 1997, p. 1B.

57 Kate Fitzgerald, 'Guinness Looks to Its Past to Freshen 5th Pub Giveaway', *Advertising Age*, 30 March 1998, p. 46.

58 'Samples Have Ample Impact', *Sales & Marketing Management*, September 1997, p. 108.

59 News, 'Sampling in the Salon', *B&T Marketing and Media*, 2 July 2001.

60 M. Ligarkis, 'Lindt Strategy Wins Hands and Hearts', *B&T Marketing and Media*, 30 March 2001.

61 Kate Fitzgerald, 'Venue Sampling Hot', *Advertising Age*, 12 August 1996, p. 19.

62 Matthew Martinez and Mercedes M. Cardona, 'Study Shows POP Gaining Ground as Medium', *Advertising Age*, 24 November 1997, p. 43.

63 Rebecca Piirto Heath, 'Pop Art', *Marketing Tools*, April 1997.

64 Yumiko Ono, 'For Philip Morris, Every Store Is a Battlefield', *Wall Street Journal*, 29 June 1998, pp. B1, B6.

65 Dean Takahashi and Evan Ramstad, 'Quake Sequel Beefs Up Blood and Guts', *Wall Street Journal*, 9 December 1997, pp. B1, B16.

66 News, 'Reaching the Abs – But Who are They Today?', *B&T Marketing and Media*, 23 July 2001.

67 L. Kaye, 'I'll Have What She's Having', *B&T Marketing and Media*, 14 June 2001.

68 Robert Berner, 'Thanks to the Gap, Stock Exchange Lets Suits Cut Loose for One Day Only', *Wall Street Journal*, 26 September 1997, p. B10A.

69 Berwyn, B, 2005, 'Backed by Action', *The Vail Trail*, Thursday April 7, www.Vailtrail.com/newsdetail.cfm?NewsID=2986 (accessed 8 April 2005).

70 Jean Halliday, 'BMW Driver Tour Hypes New 3-Series', *Advertising Age*, 8 June 1998, p. 8.

71 News, 'Reaching the Abs – But Who are They Today?', *B&T Marketing and Media*, 23 July 2001.

72 Bart Ziegler, 'Checkmate! Deep Blue is IBM Publicity Coup', *Wall Street Journal*, 9 May 1997, pp. B1, B4.

73 James A. Roberts, 'Green Consumers in the 1990s: Profile and Implications for Advertising', *Journal of Business Research*, vol. 36, 1996, pp. 217–31.

74 G. A. Marken, 'Getting the Most from Your Presence in Cyberspace', *Public Relations Quarterly*, Fall 1995, p. 36(2).

75 Lisa Bransten, 'Companies Are Talking Up Chat Rooms; More Companies See Them as Way to Improve Service', *Wall Street Journal*, 15 December 1997, p. B5B.

76 News, 'The Campaign that Saved George Patts', *B&T Marketing and Media*, 14 June 2001.

Chapter 11

1 Media release, 18 November 2004, Hutchinson 3G Australia Ltd.

2 'How IBM Turned Around Its Ailing PC Division', *Wall Street Journal*, 12 March 1998, pp. B1, B4.

3   Gordon Fairclough, 'Governments Can Be Addicted to Cigarettes,' Wall Street Journal, October 2 2000, A1. Used with permission.
4   From Anne Swardson, 'In France, It's On Sale When the State Says So', International Herald Tribune, 6 January 1998. © The Washington Post. Reprinted with permission.
5   Praveen Kopalle and Donald Lehmann, 'The Effects of Advertised and Observed Quality on Expectations About New Product Quality', Journal of Marketing Research, August 1995, pp. 280–90; Akshay Rao and Kent Monroe, 'The Effect of Price, Brand Name, and Store Name on Buyers' Perceptions of Product Quality: An Integrative Review', Journal of Marketing Research, August 1989, pp. 351–7; Gerard Tellis and Gary Gaeth, 'Best Value, Price-seeking, and Price Aversion: The Impact of Information and Learning on Consumer Choices', Journal of Marketing, April 1990, pp. 34–5.
6   William Dodds, Kent Monroe and Dhruv Grewel, 'Effects of Price, Brand, and Store Information on Buyers' Product Evaluations', Journal of Marketing Research, August 1991, pp. 307–19; see also Akshay Rao and Wanda Sieben, 'The Effect of Prior Knowledge on Price Acceptability and the Type of Information Examined', Journal of Consumer Research, September 1992, pp. 256–70; Ajay Kalra and Ronald Goldman, 'The Impact of Advertising Positioning Strategies on Consumer Price Sensitivity', Journal of Marketing Research, May 1998, pp. 210–24.
7   Donald Lichtenstein and Scott Burton, 'The Relationship between Perceived and Objective Price–Quality', Journal of Marketing Research, November 1989, pp. 429–43.
8   'Store-brand Pricing Has to be Just Right', Wall Street Journal, 14 February 1992, p. B1; see also George Cressman, Jr, 'Snatching Defeat from the Jaws of Victory', Marketing Management, Summer 1997, pp. 9–19.
9   Dawar Niraj and Phillip Parker, 'Marketing Universals: Consumers' Use of Brand Name, Price, Physical Appearance, and Retailer Reputation as Signals of Product Quality', Journal of Marketing, April 1994, pp. 81–95.
10 Charles Quigley and Elaine Notarantonio, 'An Exploratory Investigation of Perceptions of Odd and Even Pricing', in Victoria Crittenden (ed.), Developments in Marketing Science (Miami: Academy of Marketing Science, 1992), pp. 306–9.

Chapter 12

1   The names used in this case study are fictitious and the circumstances are adaptations of circumstances the author is aware of and which relate to several architectural practices. Acknowledgement is also made of assistance from Michael Gardiner, Department of Marketing, University of Southern Queensland, in formulating the questions and model answers that accompany this case study.
2   J. Kirby, 'Metal Storm to Test US Market', Business Review Weekly, 3 December 2001.
3   Statistics New Zealand, 2000; Australian Bureau of Statistics, 2000.
4   ABS, International Merchandise Trade, Australia, Cat. No. 5422.0, 19 February 2002.
5   'For Peruvians, Fizzy Yellow Drink is the Real Thing', International Herald Tribune, 27 December 1995, p. 3.
6   D. Rocks, Blunders in International Business (Cambridge, CT: Blackwell Publishers, 1993).
7   'Global Products Require Name-Finders', Wall Street Journal, 11 April 1996, p. B5.
8   'Don't Be an Ugly-American Manager', Fortune, 16 October 1995, p. 225.
9   'Portrait of the World', Marketing News, 28 August 1995, pp. 20–1.
10 'Kenya Set to be the World's Largest Tea Exporter', African Business, November 1997, p. 46.
11 Zulia Hu and Mohsin Kahn, 'Why is China Growing So Fast?', International Monetary Fund Staff Papers, March 1997, pp. 103–31.
12 'Profiting from India's Strong Middle Class', Marketing News, 7 October 1996, p. 6.
13 'Pop Radio in France Goes French', International Herald Tribune, 2 January 1996, p. 2.
14 Ibid.
15 'Ultimatum for the Avon Lady', Business Week, 11 May 1998, p. 33.
16 Craig Smith, 'CD Piracy Flourishes in China, and West Supplies the Equipment', Wall Street Journal, 24 April 1997, pp. A1, A12.
17 'This is One the White House Can't Duck', Business Week, 8 April 1996, p. 52; see also Moshe Givon, Vijay Mahajan and Eitan Muller, 'Software Piracy: Estimation of Lost Sales and the Impact on Software Diffusion', Journal of Marketing, January 1995, pp. 29–37; Smith, op. cit.; 'Beijing's Backyard Industry', International Herald Tribune, 19 March 1998, p. 12.
18 'Can China Avert Crisis?', Business Week, 16 March 1998, pp. 44–9.
19 Rahul Jacob, 'The Big Rise', Fortune, 30 May 1994, pp. 74–90.
20 'Kodak Divides up China in Order to Conquer It', Ad Age International, January 1998, pp. 20–3.
21 'Can TV Save the Planet?', American Demographics, May 1996, pp. 43–7.
22 'Marketing Board Games is No Trivial Pursuit', Dallas Morning News, 14 January 1996, pp. 1EF, 4F.
23 'Kiddi Just Fine in the UK, But Here It's Binky', Marketing News, 28 August 1995, p. 8.
24 'To All US Managers Upset by Regulations: Try Germany or Japan', Wall Street Journal, 14 December 1995, p. A1.
25 From James Aaron Cooke, 'Global Supply Chain: How Rich Products Went Global', September 1998. Reproduced with permission from Logistics Management &Distribution Report. © 1998 Cahners Business Information. Logistics Management & Distribution Report is a trademark of Cahners Business Information. All rights reserved.
26 G. Bruce Knecht, 'Pedaling Success: Bertelsmann Breaks Through a Great Wall with its Book Clubs', Wall Street Journal, 18 September 1998, pp. A1, A6.
27 Greg Steinmetz and Tara Parker-Pope, 'All Over the Map', Wall Street Journal, 26 September 1996, pp. R4, R6.
28 'Global Retailing 97', Ernst & Young special report for Chain Store Age, December 1997, p. 4.

Chapter 13

1   Danny Kingsley, ABC Science Online, 31 October 2001: www.abc.net.au/science/news/stories/s404220.htm (accessed 25 November 2001). © 2001 ABC.
2   'Sports Shoes: The Shocking Truth', News in Science, ABC, 31 October 2001.
3   www.goodmanfielder.com.au/dir065/gfsite/gflimited.nsf/content/About+Us++Operating+Divisions.
4   Stephen Baker, 'A New Paint Job at PPG', Business Week, 13 November 1995, pp. 74, 78.
5   www.mcdonalds.com.au/home (accessed 5 April 2002).

6 David Cravens, *Strategic Marketing* (Chicago: Irwin, 1987).
7 Tary Knight, 'The Relationship between Entrepreneurial Orientation, Strategy, and Performance: An Empirical Investigation', in Barbara Stern, George Zinkhan, Peter Gordon and Bert Kellerman (eds), *AMA Marketing Educators' Conference Proceedings* (Chicago: American Marketing Association, 1995), pp. 272–3.
8 Nikhil Deogun and Jonathan Karp, 'For Coke in India, Thums Up is the Real Thing', *Wall Street Journal*, 29 April 1998, pp. B1–B2.
9 Theodore Levitt, 'Marketing Myopia', *Harvard Business Review*, 1 September 1975, pp. 1–14.
10 'Yowie's Virtual Holiday with Nick's Kids', *B&T Marketing and Media*, 15 March 2002.
11 'NRMA Targets Switchers in a New Campaign', *B&T Marketing and Media*, 14 March 2002.
12 Susan Mitchell, 'How to Talk to Young Adults', *American Demographics*, April 1993, pp. 50–4.
13 'Xers Know They're a Target Market, and They Hate That', *Marketing News*, 6 December 1993, pp. 2, 15.
14 'Easy Pickup Line? Try Gen Xers', *Advertising Age*, 3 April 1995, pp. 5–22.
15 'Are Tech Buyers Different?' *Business Week*, 26 January 1998, pp. 64–8.
16 Eryn Brown, 'The Myth of Email Privacy', *Fortune*, 3 February 1997. © 1997 Time Inc. Reprinted by special permission.
17 From Nikhil Deogun and Amy Barrett, 'France Rejects Coca-Cola's Purchase of Orangina', *Wall Street Journal*, 18 September 1998. Reprinted by permission of the *Wall Street Journal*. © 1998 Dow Jones & Company, Inc. All rights reserved worldwide.
18 'Yowie's Virtual Holiday with Nick's Kids', op. cit.
19 Based on Edward Stevens, *Business Ethics* (New York: Paulist Press, 1979).
20 Anusorn Singhapakdi, Skott Vitell and Kenneth Kraft, 'Moral Intensity and Ethical Decisionmaking of Marketing Professionals', *Journal of Business Research*, vol. 36, March 1996, pp. 245–55; Ishmael Akaah and Edward Riordan, 'Judgments of Marketing Professionals about Ethical Issues in Marketing Research: A Replication and Extension', *Journal of Marketing Research*, February 1989, pp. 112–20; see also Shelby Hunt, Lawrence Chonko and James Wilcox, 'Ethical Problems of Marketing Researchers', *Journal of Marketing Research*, August 1984, pp. 309–24; and Kenneth Andrews, 'Ethics in Practice', *Harvard Business Review*, September–October 1989, pp. 99–104.

accelerator principle 71
accessory equipment 83
actual product 186, 187
adaptive channels 257
adopter 236
adoption
   process 239
   rate of 237–8
advertising
   advocacy 351
   alternative media 363
   appeal 355–6
   and brand loyalty 348
   campaign 353–7, 367
   comparative 352–3
   competitive 351
   and the consumer 348
   cooperative 359
   creative decisions 354
   definition 310–11, 346
   effects of 346–9
   executing the message 356–7
   executional styles 357
   global challenges 358
   institutional 350–1
   Internet 362–3
   magazine 360
   and market share 347–8
   media decisions 359–67
   media scheduling 366–7
   newspaper 359–60
   objective 354
   outdoor media 361–2
   pioneering 351
   product 351–3
   product benefits 354–5
   and product attributes 348–9
   radio 360–1
   response function 347
   television 361
   types of 349–53
   World Wide Web 362–3
advocacy advertising 351
age
   and consumer buying decisions 49–50
   segmentation 115
agents 252
AIDA concept 320–3
applied research 490
attitudes and consumer buying decisions 56–7
Amazon.com 491

audience selectivity 366
audit 161
   marketing 498
augmented product 187
Australian Broadcasting Authority Act 352
automatic teller machines (ATMs) 493
automatic vending 286
automation 280
average fixed cost (AFC) 397
average total cost (ATC) 397
average variable cost (AVC) 397

baby boomers 483–6
bait pricing 417
base price 414–19
basing-point pricing 416
behaviour
   post-purchase 33–4
   routine response 35
   social and ethical 498–501
   see also ethics
BehaviourScan 165
beliefs and consumer buying decisions 56–7
benefit segmentation 119—20
BHP 79
bionic ear 2–3
brainstorming 226
brand
   definition 195
   equity 196
   individual versus family 201
   loyalty 197, 248
   manufacturer's 200, 201
   mark 195
   master 196, 197
   names 195
   national 201
   personality 198, 199
   private 200, 201
   switchers 368
branded products versus generic products 199–201
branding 195–204
   benefits 195–9
   co-branding 201–2
   complementary 201
   cooperative 201
   decisions, major 200
   individual 201
   ingredient 201
   strategies 199
break-even analysis 400

brokers 252
build-to-order 274
Burke, Inc. 89–90
business analysis, new product 237
business buying behaviour 73–7
    buying centres 73–4
    buying situations 76–7
    customer service 77
    evaluative criteria 75–6
    purchasing ethics 77
business customers, major categories 81–2
    governments 81–2
    institutions 82
    producers 81
    resellers 81
business ethics 499–500
business marketing, Internet 144
business products
    accessory equipment 83
    business services 85
    component parts 84
    definition 82, 187
    major equipment 82
    processed materials 84
    raw materials 83
    supplies 84–5
    types 82–5
business-to-business
    alliances 89–90
    channel structures 256
    marketing 68
business servives 85
business strategy 472–3
business versus consumer markets 69–73
businesses and marketing 14–15
buying
    behaviour, habitual 35
    centres 73–6
    decision and marketing mix 325
    nature of 72
    situations 76–7
    see also consumer buying decisions

cannibalisation 129
CarsDirect.com 259
cash discounts 414
catalogues 334
category killers 285
CD-ROM 152
central-location telephone (CLT) facility 154
chain stores 283
channel 316

channel conflict 263
channel control 262
channel leader (channel captain) 263
channel members 249
channel of distribution 249
channel power 262
channels *see* marketing channels
chemists
co-branding 201–2
Coca-Cola Company 224, 225, 478, 495
Cochlear implant 2–3
cognitive dissonance 34
collusion 413
Colombia Sportswear 458–61
commercialisation, new product 231
communication
    definition 314
    feedback 317–18
    integrated marketing communications (IMC) 312–13
    interpersonal 315
    marketing 239, 314
    mass 315
    message transmission 316
    process 315
    process and promotional mix 318–19
    receiver and decoding 316–17
    sender and encoding 315–16
comparative advertising 352
competition
    global 494
    international 494
    and price 402–3
competitive advantage 9
competitive advertising 351
competitive environment 493–4
complementary branding 201
component lifestyles 487–8
component parts 84
concentrated targeting strategy 127
concept test 226
conflict, channel 263–5
consideration set 32
consultative selling 330
consumer
    and advertising 348
    behaviour 26–7
    business versus consumer markets 69–73
    contests and sweepstakes 371–2
    coupons and rebates 369–70
    decision-making process 27–34, 35, 39
    education 377

evaluation of alternatives 32–3
and involvement 34, 36
loyalty marketing programs 371
markets, segmenting 113–16
point-of-purchase promotion 373
post-purchase behaviour 33–4
premiums 371
product 188, 255–6
and purchase 32–3
sales promotion 367, 368
sampling 162, 372–3
consumer buying decisions
age and family life-cycle stage 49–50
attitudes 56–7
beliefs 56–7
culture and values 39–42
culture differences, understanding 42
external influences 38
factors influencing 38–57
families 48, 49–50
gender 49
internal influences 48–51
learning 54–5
life-style 50–1
motivation 53–4
opinion leaders 46
perception 52–3
personality 50–1
psychological influences 52–5
reference groups 45–6
self-concept 50–1
social class 44
social influences 45–8
subculture 44
types of 34–8
contact efficiency 250
convenience products 188–9
convenience sample 162
convenience stores 283, 285
cooperative advertising 359
cooperative branding 201
core product 186, 187
corporate social responsibility 501
corporate strategy 572
cost(s)
average fixed cost (AFC) 397
average total cost (ATC) 397
average variable cost (AVC) 397
determinant of price 397–401
estimation 410
fixed 397
marginal cost (MC) 397

per contact (media advertising) 364
variable 397
coupons and rebates 369–70
creative decisions 354–7
Creatable Media 314
credence quality 205
crisis management 379–80
critical thinking 94
cross-tabulation of data 164
culture
components of Australian 40
and consumer buying decisions 39–42
differences, understanding 42
and global marketing 442–5
and notion of time 444
see also subculture
cumulative quantity discounts 414
customer(s)
competitor's 368
demands of large 407
loyalty 368
needs and wants 28–9, 475
satisfaction 11–13
service 77
value 9, 10

data
collection and analysis 163–4
primary 152
secondary 150–2
database marketing 145
databases on CD-ROM 152
decision support system (DSS) 144
decision-making
ethical business 500
extensive 35
limited 35
process, consumer 27–34, 35, 39
decoding 316–17
Dell Computer 247–8
demand 69–71
defined 69, 394
derived 69
determinant of price 394–7
elasticity of 394–7
estimation 410
fluctuating 71
inelastic 69, 394
joint 70
nature of 394
demographic makeup 450–1
demographic segmentation 115

department stores 283, 285
derived demand 69
development, new product 227–9
differential advantage 308
diffusion 236
direct channel 255
direct mail 334
direct marketing 310, 332–5
discount stores 283, 285
discounts 414–15
discrepancy
　of assortment 250
　of quantity 249
　spatial (place) 250
　temporal (time) 250
discussion boards 151
distribution
　decisions 282, 286–9, 457–62
　dual (multiple) 257
　electronic 288–9
　exclusive 262
　and global markets 456–7
　intensity levels 261–2
　intensive 261
　selective 261–2
　for services 286–8
　strategy 403
distribution resource planning (DRP) 276

80/20 principle 120
economic development and global marketing 445–6
economic environment 489–90
economy, personalised 485
elasticity, unitary 395
elasticity of demand 394–7
electronic data interchange (EDI) 276
electronic environment
　and global marketing 462–3
　and price 404–7
electronic retailing 288–9, 335
encoding 315–16
Enforcement Technology, Inc. (ETEC) 243–4
environment
　competitive 493–4
　economic 489–90
　political and legal 446–9, 490–3
　sociocultural 483–8
　technological 490
environmental damage 209
environmental management 482–3
environmental scanning 481

error
　measurement 162
　sampling 163
　types of 162–3
ethical
　behaviour 498–501
　business decision-making 500
　guidelines 500–1
ethics
　business 499–500
　code of 500
　definition 498
　in marketing 55, 78, 123, 166, 222, 264, 328, 377, 399, 492, 498–501
　price strategy 413–14
　purchasing 77
evaluation of alternatives 32–3
evaluative criteria 75–6
event sponsorship 377
evoked set 32
exchange, marketing 7
Exco 79
experience quality 205
experiments (causal design) 161
extensive decision-making 35
external information, search 30
external marketing environment 481–3
extranet 404

family
　brands 201
　changing character of 488
　and consumer buying decisions 48, 49–50
family life cycle (FLC) 115–16
feedback 317–18
fixed cost 397
field service organisation 163
flexible pricing 416
fluctuating demand 71
FOB origin pricing 415
focus group 157
franchising 283
freight absorption pricing 416
frequency (media advertising) 365
frequent buyer programs 371
Frito-Lay company 148
functional discounts 414
functional strategy 473

gender
　and consumer buying decisions 49
　segmentation 115

Generation X 485–6
Generation Y 486–7
Generation Z 487
generic product name 203
generic products
   defined 199
   versus branded products 199–201
geodemographic segmentation 117
geographic, segmentation 113–14
global
   competition 494
   logistics and supply chain management 458–61
   retailing 461–2
   vision 440
global marketing
   benefits 440–2
   channels 457–62
   and culture 442–5
   definition 133, 439
   demographic makeup 450–1
   distribution 456–7
   and economic development 445–6
   electronic environment, impact of 462
   external environments 442–51
   importance of 441
   and Internet 462
   mix 451–62
   and political structure 446–9
   and pricing 456
   product and promotion 451–6
   and technological development 445–6
Goodman Fielder 472, 473
goods, difference between services 205–6
gross margin 284
group dynamics 157

habitual buying behaviour 35
heterogeneity 206
horizontal conflict 263

idea generation 223–6
idea screening 226
ideal self-image 51
implementation and marketing plans 497–8
income segmentation 115
incomes, disposable 489
independent retailers 282
individual brand 201
industrial product 187
   channel structures 256
industry analysis 493

inelastic demand 69
inflation 489
infomercial 361
information search 30–2
informational labelling 210
InfoScan 165
ingredient branding 201
innovation 236
inseparability 205–6
installations 82
institutional advertising 350–1
intangibility 205
integrated interviewing 155
integrated logistics 267
integrated marketing communications (IMC) 304–5, 312–13
internal influences on consumer buying decisions 48–51
internal information 30
international competition 494
Internet
   advertising 362–3
   business marketing 144
   definition 151, 404
   and global marketing 462
   marketing strategy 491
   and pricing 404
   samples, screened and recruited 156–7
   secondary data 151
   surveys 155
   websites 379
   see also retailing, on-line
interpersonal communication 315
interviews
   computer-assisted personal 154
   computer-assisted self-interviewing 154
   in-home personal 153–4
   mall intercept 154
   telephone 154
invention, product 452–3
involvement, consumer 34, 36
   interest 36
   marketing implications 37
   perceived risk of negative consequences 36
   previous experience 36
   situation 36
   social visibility 36
issue sponsorship 378–9

Johansen, Browne & Cooper-Smith 434–7
joint demand 70

just-in-time manufacturing 275

Kellogg 114
keystoning 398

Labelle Management 138–9
labelling 210
leader pricing 417
learning and consumer behaviour 54–5
leasing 73
legal considerations and political structure 447–9
legal environment 447, 490–3
lifestyle(s)
   component 487–8
   and consumer buying decisions 50–1
   psychographics 117
   segmentation 117
   segmentation of snack-food market 120
   see also family life cycle (FLC)
Lifestyles magazine 341–2
limited decision-making 35
logistics
   contract 280
   decisions 266–70
   information system 272
   Integrated 267
   service and cost 271–2
   trends 280–2
loyalty
   brand 197, 248
   customer 248, 371
   marketing programs 371

macrosegmentation 121
magazine advertising 360
mail order 334
major equipment 82
Mambo 5–6
management
   crisis 379–80
   decision problem 150
   environmental 482–3
   uses of marketing research 146–7
   supply chain 266–70, 458–61
manufacturer's brands 201
manufacturing and services marketing 206–7
manufacturing efficiency 474
marginal cost (MC) 397
marginal revenue (MR) 399
marked-up pricing 398–9
market
   definition 110, 111
   segment 111
   share 393
   share and advertising 347–8
market segmentation *see* segmentation, market
marketing
   audit 498
   and businesses 14–15
   career opportunities 15
   communication 239, 314
   communications, integrated 304–5, 312–13
   concept 475
   control 498
   database 145
   decision support systems 144–5
   definition 6–7
   direct 310, 332–5
   environment, external
   ethics 55, 77, 123, 166, 222, 264, 328, 377, 399, 492, 498–501
   exchange 7
   implications of the adoption process 239
   implications of involvement 37
   implications of perception 53
   importance of 14–15
   intelligence 144
   management, Implications 235
   miscues 89–90, 429
   myopia 480
   niche 128
   objective 480
   orientations 8–9, 474–6
   overview 17
   planning 479
   process 16–17
   and society 14, 445–6
   strategy 97–8, 236, 477–9
   studying 13–15
   test 229–31
   see also global marketing
marketing channels
   adaptive 257
   alternative arrangements 256–8
   business-to-business 256
   choice, factors affecting 258
   conflict 263–5
   consumer products 255–6
   contact efficiency 250–1
   definition 249
   and distribution decisions 282, 286–9
   distribution intensity 261–2

global 457–8
industrial products 256
intermediaries and their functions 251–4
market factors 259–60
members 249
multiple 257
non-traditional 257
overcoming discrepancies 249–50
partnering 265–6
power, control and leadership 262–3
producer factors 260
product factors 260
relationships 262–6
specialisation and division of labour 249
strategic alliances 258
strategy decisions 258–62
structures 254–8
marketing mix
and buying decision 325
definition 495
designing, implementing and maintaining 129–33, 497–8
four Ps 98–100, 129–33, 495–7
global 451–61
and product life cycle 236
and product types 190
and promotion 308–9
marketing plan 96–100, 477–9
audit 498
control processes 498
definition 479
developing and implementing 479–81
elements 480
evaluation 498
implementation 479–81
integrating price and IMC
organisational mission and objectives 480–1
and target markets 480
writing 479
marketing research
conducting 167
definition 145
management uses 146–7
objective 149
problem 149
project steps 148–65
recommendations 164–5
role of 145–8
marketing-controlled information source 31
marketing-oriented values 487
mark-up pricing 398–9

Mars Inc. 191
Maslow's hierarchy of needs 54
mass customisation 274
mass communication 315
mass merchandising 285
materials handling 278–9
materials requirement planning (MRP) 276
measurement error 162
media and advertising
budgets 364
mix 364
scheduling 366–7
selection considerations 364–6
types 359–63
medium and advertising 354
merchant wholesalers 251
message adaptation 453–5
message transmission 316
microsegmentation 121–2
mission statement 480
modified rebuy 77
morality and business ethics 499–500
morals 498
motivation and consumer buying decisions 53–4
multiculturalism 488
multiple distribution 257
multiplier effect 71
multi-segment targeting strategy 128–9

national brand 201
natural resources 450–1
need recognition 28–30
needs and wants, customer 475
new buy 76
new products
business analysis 227
categories 221–2
commercialisation 231–2
definition 221
development process 222–7
idea generation 223–6
idea screening 226
publicity 376
spread of 236–9
strategy 223
test marketing 229–31
newsgroups 151
newspaper advertising 359, 360
niche marketing 128
noise 316
non-cumulative quantity discounts 414

non-marketing-controlled information source 30
non-probability sample 162, 163
non-store retailing 286
non-traditional channels 257

observation research 160
odd–even pricing 418
on-line retailing 335
opinion leaders 46–7
optimisers 122
order processing system 275–6
outdoor media 360, 361–2
outsourcing (contract logistics) 280
ownership (retail operations) 282–3

packaging 207–10
    functions 208–9
    recycling and environment 209
    storage, use and convenience 209
penetration pricing 411–12
Pepsi-Cola 495
perception and consumer buying decisions 52
perceptual mapping 131
perishability 206
personal retailing 332–4
personal selling 309, 328–32
personalised economy 485
personality and consumer buying decisions 50–1
persauding 320
persuasive labelling 210
pioneering advertising 351
planned obsolescence 194
planning 476
point-of-purchase promotion 373
political environment 490–3
political structure and global marketing 446–9
population profiles 123–4
Porsche buyers, taxonomy 117
positioning 129, 132
post-purchase behaviour 33–4
predatory pricing 414
premiums 371
prestige pricing 408
price
    base, fine-tuning 414–19
    bundling 418
    buyers 368
    and competition 402–3
    cost determinant of 397–401
    defined 284–5, 390
    demand, cost and profits 410
    demand determinant of 394–7
    discrimination 413
    and distribution strategy 403
    electronic environment 404–7
    and evaluative criteria 75–6
    fixing 413
    importance of 390–2
    and large customers 407
    and marketing plan 391–2, 428, 496
    predatory 414
    product 409–13
    product life cycle 401–2
    and promotion strategy 407
    relationship to quality 408–9
    skimming 411
    strategy 410–13
    strategy, legality and ethics 413–14
pricing
    bait 417
    basing-point 416
    break-even 400–1
    flexible 416
    FOB origin 415
    freight absorption 416
    geographic 415–16
    and global marketing 456
    goals 409–10
    leader 417
    mark-up 398–9
    odd–even 418
    penetration 411–12
    prestige 408
    proactive 430
    professional services 416–17
    profit maximisation 399
    psychological 418
    status quo 394, 413
    tactics, special 416–19
    two-part 418–19
    uniform delivered 415
    value-based 415
    variable 416
    zone 416
pricing objectives
    profit-oriented 392–3
    sales-oriented 393–4
    status quo 394
primary data 152
primary research 490

private brand 201
private-label brands
probability sample 162, 163
proactive pricing 430
processed materials 84
producers and marketing channel 260
product(s)
    actual 186, 187
    adaptation 455–6
    advertising 351–3
    attributes and advertising 348–9
    augmented 187
    business 187
    category 232
    characteristics and rate of adoption 237–8
    consumer 188
    containing and protecting 208
    convenience 188–9
    core 186, 187
    definition 186
    development 224
    differentiation 129
    and global marketing 451–6
    identification 195
    industrial 187
    invention 452–3
    item 191
    line 191
    line contraction 194–5
    line depth 193
    line extensions 194
    mix 191
    mix width 193
    modification 193–4
    name, generic 203
    nature of 323–4
    placement 376
    promoting 208–9
    selling existing 474–5
    shopping 189
    speciality 190
    types of consumer 187–91
    types and marketing mix 190
    unsought 190–1
    see also new products
product life cycles (PLC) 232–6
    decline stage 235
    definition 232
    and diffusion process 239
    growth stage 234
    implications for marketing management 235
    introductory stage 233
    and marketing mix strategy 236
    maturity stage 234
    stages 232, 233–5, 324–5, 401–2
production orientation 8, 474
production scheduling 274
professional services pricing 416–17
profit
    definition 391
    estimation 410
    maximisation 392, 399
    satisfactory 392–3
profit maximisation pricing 399
promotion
    definition 308
    and global marketing 451–6
    goals and AIDA concept 320–3
    goals and tasks of 319–20
    and marketing mix 308–9
    point-of-purchase 373
    and price 407
    sales 311, 367–74
    trade sales 373–4
promotional allowances 415
promotional goals and marketing mix 320–3
promotional mix 309, 310–19
    advantages 318
    and AIDA 322–3
    and available funds 326
    and buying decision 325
    and communication process 318–19
    definition 310
    disadvantages 318
    factors affecting 323–7
    and product life cycle 324
    push and pull strategies 326–7
promotional strategy 308
    push and pull 326–7
psychographic segmentation 117–19
psychological influences on consumer buying decisions 52–7
psychological pricing 418
public relations (PR) 312, 375–80
publicity 312, 376
    managing unfavourable 379–80
purchase and consumers 32–3
purchase volume 71
purchasing ethics 77
push money 373

quality
    credence 205

discount 414
experience 205
evaluative criteria 75
relationship to price 408–9
search 205
questionnaire design 158–61
questions
closed-ended 158
open-ended 158
scale-response 158

radio advertising 360–1
random sample 162
raw materials 83
ideal self-image 51
reach (media advertising) 364
rebates 369–70, 412
recession 489–90
reciprocity 73
recruited Internet sample 156
recycling and environment 209
Red Bull 345–6
reference groups 45
relationship marketing 11–13
and strategic alliances 78–80
relationship marketing orientation 8, 476
relationship selling 329–32
reminding 320
repositioning 133, 194
research
applied 490
and development 224
observation 160
primary 490
research design 150
retail operations
automatic vending 286
catalogues and mail order 334
category killers 285
chain stores 283
chemists 283
classification of 282–5
convenience stores 283, 285
department stores 283, 285
direct mail 334
discount speciality stores 283, 285
discount stores 283, 285
franchising 283
full-line discount stores 283, 285
level of service 283
main types of 285–6
mass merchandising 285

off-price 283
on-line retailing 335
price 284–5
product assortment 283–4
restaurants 283
shop-at-home networks 288, 335
speciality stores 283, 285
supermarkets 283, 285
telemarketing 334–5
types of stores 283
retailers 251
independent 282
retailing
electronic 288–9, 335
global 461–2
non-store 286
on-line 288–9
personal 332–4
role of 282
return on investment (ROI) 393
revenue 391
routine response behaviour 35
Roy Morgan mind-set 118
Roy Morgan Value Segments 119
Ryanair 412

sales
maximisation 394
orientation 8, 9, 474–5
promotion 311, 367–74
see also selling
sales-oriented pricing objectives 393–4
sampling
consumer 162, 372–3
convenience 162
definition 162
errors 163
non-probability 162
probability 162
random 162
types 163
satisfaction, measuring 147
satisficers 122
scanner-based research 165
screened Internet sample 156
screening, idea 226
search quality 205
seasonal discount 145
secondary data 150–2
segmentation, market 110–11
bases (variables) 113
definition 110, 111

global issues 133
importance of 112
profiling and analysing 124
selecting descriptors 122–4
steps 113–33
segmentation descriptors 122–4
segmenting business markets 121–2
segmenting consumer markets 113–16
selective exposure 52
self-concept and consumer buying decisions 50–1
self-esteem 55
self-image, consumer 50–1
selling
consultative 330
global dos and dont's 331–2
personal 328–32
relationship 329–32
see also sales
sender 315–16
service(s)
business 85
channels and distribution decisions 286–8
definition 204
difference between goods 205–6
evaluative criteria 75
importance of 204
mark 202
services marketing in manufacturing 206–7
shop-at-hime networks 288, 335
shopping products 189
simulated (laboratory) market testing 230
social
behaviour 498–501
class 44–5
influences on consumer buying decisions 45–8
responsibility, corporate 501
socialisation process 48
societal marketing orientation 8
society
fully industrialising 446
industrialising 446
and marketing 14, 445–6
pre-industrial 445
traditional 445
sociocultural environment 483–8
special pricing tactics 416–19
speciality products 190
speciality store 283, 285
sponsorship 377–9
status quo pricing 394, 413

stimulus 28
straight rebuy 77
strategic alliance
definition 78
and relationship marketing 78–80
strategic business units (SBUs) 472–3, 477
strategic channel alliances 258
strategic partnership 78
strategic planning 476–7
strategic window 477
strategy, organisational overview 472–3
subculture 44
supermarkets 283, 285
suppies 84–5
supply 396
supply chain
integrated functions 268–9, 270
management 266–70, 458–61
process 267
sourcing and procurement 273–4
team 273
survey research 153–8
surveys
computer disk by mail 155
Internet 155
mail 154–5
sweepstakes 371–2
SWOT analysis 96–7, 483

target market strategy 97–8
target markets 494–8
advantages and disadvantages 125
characteristics 325
concentrated targeting 127
controllable variables 482
definition 481
multi-segment targeting 128–9
selecting 125–9
uncontrollable variables 482
undifferentiated targeting 125–6
technological development and global marketing 445–6
technological environment 490
telemarketing 334–5
television advertising 360, 361
test marketing
alternatives to 230–1
definition 229
high cost of 230
trade allowance 373, 415
trade discounts 414
Trade Practices Act 352, 413

trade sales promotion 367
trademarks 202
transaction- versus partnership-based firms 265
transportation and supply chain 279–80
two-part pricing 418–19

undifferentiated targeting strategy 125–6
unfair trade 413
uniform delivered pricing 415
unique selling proposition 356
unitary elasticity 395
universal product codes (UPCs) 210
universe 162
unrestricted Internet sample 155
unsought products 190–1
usage-rate segmentation 120

value-based pricing 415
values and consumer buying decisions 39–42
variable pricing 416
vertical conflict 263

wants, customer 28–9, 475
warehousing 279–80
wholesalers, merchant 251
wireless links 404
World Wide Web (Web) 151, 362–3

Yakult 92–3

zone pricing 416